From MANCHURIAN PRINCESS to the AMERICAN DREAM

An Anecdotal Memoir of Two Immigrant Lives

ANNA CHAO PAI

This book is dedicated to the memory of a remarkable man, my husband of fifty-seven years, David Hsien Chung Pai (1936–2016), whose enthusiasm for this book was a major force in inspiring me to write it and finish the project. I have done it, my love. Rest in peace.

And to our family and our friends, whose great love and support have taught me that life is still worth living despite the enormous emptiness left by a loved one's loss.

PREFACE

The inception of this book occurred following the passing of my mother, when I realized that my husband, David, and I were the only ones in our family with any real experience in China and Chinese culture. I needed to create a source that my children and their children could use to learn about their Chinese heritage. The histories of our two families really began with David's and my grandparents' generation.

The tumult of the twentieth century in China began with the end of the last dynasty, the Qing Dynasty, and its empress dowager, Se Xi Tai Ho, as a result of the Chinese Revolution led by Sun Yat Sen in 1911. This was followed by a period of warlords, including my grandfather, gaining control of large areas of the country. Then, in 1931, the invasion of Manchuria by the Japanese led to their advance into China and formal war in 1937. Finally, the civil war between the Nationalists of Chiang Kai-Shek and the Communists led by Mao Tse-Tung ended in victory for the Communists and escape to Taiwan by the Nationalists in 1949.

In all of this, members of David's and my families not only were actively involved but also, in some cases, played leading roles. It was important to us that our two sons, their American wives, and their four American children be aware of the role our predecessors played in modern Chinese history and become familiar with some aspects of Chinese culture.

As I started to write a memoir of my life, I recognized that a major factor in my life was the impact of immigration on my parents, especially on my mother. While most immigrants to the United States seek better lives than what they had, my parents came seeking safety from the Japanese and left a life of luxury and power to become ordinary American citizens. In the end, the transition to ordinary was traumatic for my mother, who became mentally unbalanced. This autobiography is as much about Mommy as it is about me.

In 2009, my husband, David, and I moved to a retirement community in Davidson, North Carolina, called the Pines of Davidson. I believe it was karma or some kind of fate that brought us here, for we became close neighbors with two retired professors of English, Drs. Liz Evans and Gill Holland. The latter spent three sabbatical leaves in China from his teaching post at Davidson College. He is so expert in the Chinese language that at one point, he could translate classical Chinese poetry.

When Gill heard about my family and David's, he became another force of encouragement for me to write and finish this book. Both he and Liz volunteered to read my manuscript and have corrected the English and given constructive suggestions to improve the telling of our stories.

Besides my two writing gurus, several others have read the manuscript as it has evolved over the years. I am eternally grateful to my late husband, Dr. David H. C. Pai, whose knowledge and love of Chinese history added substance to the facts in this book. Also, I am indebted to Gill's wife, Siri; Cary Johnston and her husband, Edwin Townsend; and Dr. Adrienne and Ken Pedersen for their comments and interests, and especially for their invaluable help in correct placement of the photo collages. Also, I thank my "big sister", Ellen Eller, for her unfailing and vital support and encouragement throughout the process of preparing the manuscript and figure collages for publication. These friends and so many others, and our family, made this eight year project possible. Without their help, I, trained in stiff scientific writing, would not have been able to produce a book that hopefully will be able to entertain as well as offer some knowledge of Chinese history and culture.

I need to add a special thanks to my daughter-in-law Susan Scott Pai, wife of Ben. During the terrible last days of David's life and after his death, Susan was with me multiple times a week to help with whatever I needed. I was fortunate that she had the time to help since the Montessori high school where she taught biology and chemistry had closed after the spring semester of 2016. My friends at the Pines who saw her here selflessly and cheerfully giving of her time said, "Everyone needs a Susan in their life!"

Her husband, Ben, my older son; my younger son, Mike; and his wife, Katherine, were all working jobs, but they too contributed what they could to help me get through the turmoil of being first a caretaker of an ill husband and then a widow having to take over finances for the first time. I am blessed to have caring children and daughters-in-law; I don't think I could have survived the traumas without their love and intelligent help.

To return to this book—I hope my family's experiences will also provide some insight into the impact of immigration on people who are ripped from their homes and then find themselves beginning life in a foreign country where they have to learn a foreign language and eventually lose all that they left behind. It required great courage on the part of my parents to survive, and this book is a testament to them and all of my family.

I need to add here the names of a number of people who have contributed to this book and played a major role in my ability to narrate about something that caused thousands of people angst, disappointment, and disbelief. Sweet Briar College has been educating women for 114 years. I am a graduate of the college, class of 1957. It was, in fact, my first real home in the United States. On March 3, 2015, the temporary president of a small but well-respected liberal arts college for women, Sweet Briar College, made a public announcement.

The president announced that he, the board of directors of the college, and the chair of the board had unanimously voted to close the college in August because of insurmountable financial challenges. In the next four months, this decision, arrived at in secret, elicited an outpouring of anger and frustration from the tens of thousands of the college's alumnae, its faculty and staff, and the students and parents of students. When the legal maneuverings ended four months later, numerous people asked me to include in this book a narrative of the fight to keep the college open, a fight that—because of the secrecy and timing of the announcement—was one we would wage against all odds.

I have tried to recount the work of many alumnae and friends of the college in chapter 31 in a historic sequence of events. I received help from many people in writing about this fascinating and historic episode, especially Tracy Stuart, who overnight responded to the school's decision to close by organizing a nonprofit corporation called Saving Sweet Briar Inc., and Sarah Clement, who became chair of the board of directors of the corporation. In addition to Tracy and Sarah, I owe gratitude to Ellen Bowyer, former Amherst County Attorney, who carried our fight to court. All three sent me their perspectives on what happened, and I hope I have done justice to them and others.

I must mention the Honorable Teresa Pike Tomlinson, Sweet Briar class of 1987 and mayor of Columbus, Georgia, for delivering an electrifying commencement address at Sweet Briar in May 2015 that fueled a resurgence of effort on the part of supporters of the college. I also would like to express my appreciation to Elizabeth Frenzle Casalini, a 1987 alumna and daughter of my classmate Cynthia Ottaway. Lele, as Elizabeth is known, kept many of us updated as events developed, and she helped me, a dinosaur in the age of social media, get my message across on Facebook. The use of social media allowed alumnae to immediately organize and begin legal actions, showing the country and the world the power of social media. The effectiveness of immediate mass communication and the passion of Sweet Briar's alumnae for their alma mater were unprecedented.

This story must be told, will no doubt be told more than once, and will serve in future campaigns of small liberal arts colleges and single-sex colleges in their fight for survival.

David encouraged me to include what transpired in 2015 and the successful fight we alumnae and others waged against terrible odds. He was more than proud of the passionate loyalty of Sweet Briar alumnae and wanted desperately to see this book published, but ironically, his terminal illness of congestive heart failure, which required my constant attention, prevented me from being able to finish it in time for him to read it. But there was no question in my mind that I would finish it—for him.

INTRODUCTION

In telling this story of my family and our experiences as immigrants to the United States, I have included references to a number of my relatives and other people involved in our lives. Few of them had English names. To help those who find remembering Chinese names difficult, I include in this introduction a list of the individuals' names and their positions in my family's and my life.

Remembering names is even more difficult because the English spellings of Chinese words have changed over the years. The Wade-Giles system of transcription of Mandarin Chinese was developed in the late nineteenth century and used for most of the twentieth century. Under Communist rule, a different system, Pinyin, has been used. The latter is closer to the way the names are pronounced in Mandarin Chinese, the national dialect. For example, David's family's name is traditionally spelled Pai, while it is spelled in the People's Republic of China as Bai, which is closer to its pronunciation of "Bye."

One other aspect of Chinese names is that the family name is written and pronounced first. Secondly, there often is a generation name given to all children of the same generation. Finally, the given name is last. David's Chinese name is Bai Xien Chung. Bai is the family name, Xien (*X* is now used in China for the Chinese *sh* sound, so David's generation name is pronounced Shien) is the generation name, and Chung is his given name. Also, the Communists combine the middle generation name with the given name in writing.

When David's name is written in English, it is David Hsien Chung Pai based on the classic Wade-Giles system. One of his ancestors of twenty generations ago wrote a list of generation names for the subsequent thirty-six generations. Hsien is the twentieth generation name, and all nine of David's brothers and sisters have it as part of their names. Our children, Ben and Mike, have Fa as a generation name, and their children have Ke as the twenty-second generation name.

I will give both names below, first the traditional way of spelling and then the most recent spelling of the names. In the Chinese language and the Chinese culture, we call our relatives by specific titles depending on their relationship to our parents. For example, I call my father's father Yeh Yeh, and I call his wife Nai Nai. I call my mother's father Lo Yeh, and her mother is Lo Lo. Our aunts and uncles on both sides are also given different titles, but I need not go any further in this book.

I also include a family tree of my two grandfathers and their descendants to help clarify our family situation (figure 1).

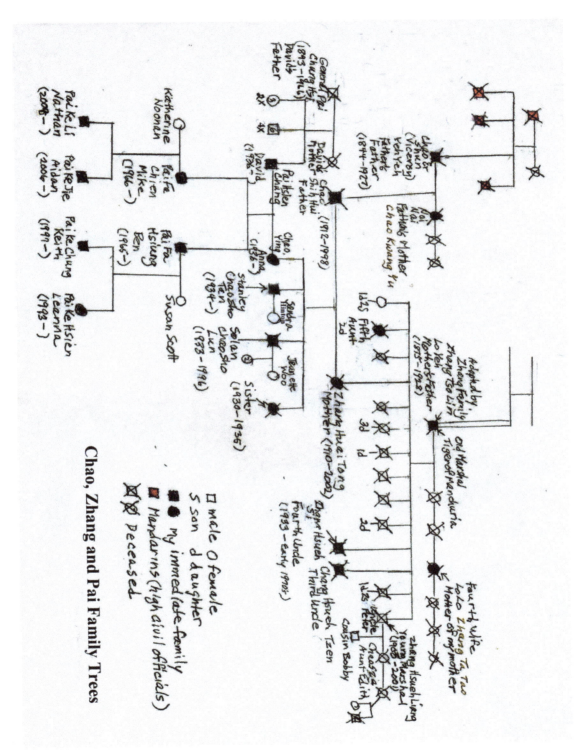

Fig 1 A family tree showing the Zhao, Zhang, and Pai families.

NAMES AND RELATIONSHIPS

Chao Er Shun (Zhao Ershun), Yeh Yeh: My father's father and Viceroy of Manchuria during the last decades of the Qing Dynasty, the highest civil official of Manchuria

Chang Tso Lin (Zhang Zuolin), the Old Marshal, Lo Yeh: My mother's father, military aide to Yeh Yeh, warlord in control of Manchuria after the revolution in 1911

Chang Huai Tung (Zhang Huaitung): My mother

Chao Shih Hui (Zhao Xirhue): My father

Chang Hsueh Liang (Zhang Xueliang), Uncle Peter, the Young Marshal: My mother's oldest sibling, a half brother, coinstigator of the Xian Incident in 1936

Yang Hucheng: General of the Northwestern Army, coinstigator of the Xian Incident in 1936

Chiang Kai Shek: Generalissimo and leader of the Nationalist Army, who lost

China to the Communists in a civil war

Soong Mai Ling (Madame Chiang Kai Shek): Wife of the generalissimo

General Pai Chung Hsi (Bai Chongxi): David's father, noted military strategist and administrator

Mao Tse Tung (Mao Zedong): Leader of the Communist movement that defeated Chiang Kai Shek

Chou En Lai (Zhou Enlai): Leader under Mao in the Communist movement

Chao Sze (Chao Yi Ti, Zhao Yiti), Aunt Edith: The Young Marshal's second wife

Chao Sho Lun (Zhao Xolun, Solan Chao): My oldest brother

Chao Sho Tan (Zhao Xotan, Stanley Chao): My older brother

Nai Nai: My father's mother

Lo Lo: My mother's mother

I include a map of China showing Manchuria and some information about the country where I was born in Beijing so long ago (figure 2).

All figures are presented as collages (if there are multiple figures for the chapter) at the end of each chapter. If only one figure is in a chapter, it will be included also at the end of the chapter. Some chapters have no figures available. Figure numbers and legends will identify them to the reader

- Outline of Mainland China
- Outline of Manchuria

Area: 9.6 million square kilometers (2% smaller than the United States)

Population: over one billion four hundred million. Fifty six different ethnic groups; 90% Han

Geographic Location: Northernmost (lat. 48N) in line with Quebec. Southernmost (Hainan Island lat.18N) in line with Jamaica. Distance north to south, 2100 miles, east to west, over 3,000 miles

Shanghai: Commercial center on the East Coast

Xian: Ancient capital of China, site of Xian Incident where my uncle captured Chiang Kai Shek

Shenyang: Also known as Mukden, capital of Manchuria, large area once controlled by my grandfathers

Beijing: Capital of China, noted for Forbidden City, Tien An Men Square

Major rivers: Yellow River in the north; Yangtze River in mid China

Fig 2 China including Manchuria

Chapter 1

NEAR THE END OF ORDINARY

Her hands fluttered in the air like falling autumn leaves. The skin was papery and thin to the point of being translucent, and the veins stood out in the absence of any fleshy tissue. The finger joints were knobby from arthritis. She often had looked at her swollen joints and sadly shaken her head at how the years had robbed her hands of their beauty. Her skin was pale, and because there was so little tissue, the fingers looked long, and the hands were skeletal in appearance.

They were beautiful to me in a grotesque way.

My mother used both hands to beckon to me; for the most part, she was no longer communicating vocally. She pointed her fluttering hands at the pillow behind her. She wanted the pillow placed lower to help her sit more erect. The uncontrolled movement of her hands was due to senile Parkinson's. She was ninety-two, and, unknown to us, had only days left in her life.

I did as she asked, trying to move her to a more comfortable position. I found it difficult to move her, as she was now a dead weight, albeit a slight weight. I'd been horrified when the nursing home nurse told me she weighed less than ninety pounds. Still, moving nearly ninety pounds that could not help at all by shifting was hard, and she glared at me for moving her so little.

"*Mahmee*," I said in Mandarin, "I can't move you higher. Help me by trying to push with your feet."

She moved her feet but ineffectually, from side to side. She looked at me in disgust and waved me away. Once again, I felt as if Mommy blamed me for something that displeased her, though I could not defend myself and certainly could not tell her that she was at fault. In Chinese culture, children were not supposed to contradict their parents, something children often do in American culture. As soon as I sat down, she beckoned to me again, as she had at least twenty times, it seemed, on that visit.

"*Bu yao*," she said in a voice that had turned guttural months earlier. "I don't want it." She pointed to the pillow.

In exasperation, I took the pillow out from under her, knowing that in minutes, she would motion for me to replace it. *You're doing it to me even now*, I thought. *You are intentionally making me angry so that I react and then feel guilty for reacting.* When relatives wanted to visit her, giving me a day off, I warned them of what she would do. Yet when I asked if she'd behaved, they said there'd been no repeated demands for anything. I could only shake my head.

Was she really doing it on purpose, or was she just oblivious to the fact that she was harassing her daughter and no one else? Was it something she had done for so long it had become habit? Or was she so uncomfortable that she was at a loss as to what to do? Was the request for a pillow followed by a request to take it away again and again just a reflection of the level of her discomfort and desperation to find something to make her feel better?

Late in her life, it had become difficult to discern what was real and what was Mommy taking out her frustrations and anger on whomever was near—and that was usually me.

I had made her some *shee fan*, a thick rice porridge with minced chicken meat, which I fed her in small amounts with a teaspoon. She was so thin. I'd been alarmed a few months before when, while helping her move, I realized I felt only bone in her arms and shoulders. Toward the end of her stay at the assisted-living facility, no amount of coaxing would induce her to eat even things we knew she used to love, such as chocolate ice cream.

We didn't realize until it was too late that either she had forgotten how to swallow, or she was no longer able to swallow normally. She choked on everything she ingested.

One morning, I received a phone call from the facility telling me she had to be hospitalized because she could not breathe. We rushed to the hospital. She had a small blood clot in her lung. She had been stabilized, but they would keep her for observation and medication.

Mommy motioned to her mouth and said, "*Wo yow shray*" (I want water).

I found the nurse assigned to her, a small Asian woman who was probably Filipino. I thought, *Good. Mommy will listen better if she's Asian.* I asked her if I could have some water, since I'd noticed with some annoyance there was no pitcher on Mommy's table, as there usually was in a hospital room.

"You'll have to feed it to her very slowly. She doesn't swallow properly and will choke if she's allowed to drink normally. We have thickened water for her, but she doesn't like it," the nurse told me.

I was stunned. That was the first I had heard about the issue. It became apparent to me why she had stopped eating at the assisted-living facility. She had complained to me that the aides there were forcing her to eat, and she didn't like it. I had ignored her complaint since she was losing weight and had to eat. If she wasn't eating on her own, someone there had to pressure her. In fact, I was grateful they cared enough to do that.

The nurse gave me a plastic teaspoon and a small paper cup of water. *If she's thirsty*, I thought to myself, *how is this little bit going to be enough?* I started giving her a half teaspoon at a time. She asked for the cup.

When I told her the nurse had said she had to take it slowly, she put her hands together and shook them up and down, the Chinese way of beseeching, begging me to give her more.

The gesture tugged at my heart. I thought, *If I hold the cup*—which I had to because of the tremors of her hand—*I can control the amount she takes in*. The first sip was fine. The second was not. Suddenly, as she swallowed the water, she flung her hands out and opened her mouth wide. She was choking and not breathing. I panicked and hit her on the back.

"Call the nurse!" I screamed at David.

Oh God, did I kill her? He rushed out, and before the nurse came back, I heard a strangled breath, and she began to cough. The nurse did not need to remonstrate with me. She could tell by my face that I was frightened by the incident.

"Are you okay, Mrs. Chao?" she asked.

My mother nodded and reached for the water again.

"No, Mrs. Chao," the nurse said, "You can't drink the water from a cup."

My mother sighed and shook her hand despairingly. When the nurse left, she tried again to reach for the cup. This time, I refused to let her have it. With a sigh, she sank back onto her pillow, accepting the sips from the spoon with resignation.

When she was transferred from the hospital to the nursing home, I spoke to those in charge and warned them about the swallowing problem. They said they would give her only thickened water and would take care in feeding her. Every day I would ask about her intake of food. Whether or not they were only telling me what I wanted to hear, they said she was eating pretty well.

Still, I knew she would like some Chinese food, so I brought her shee fan every time I went to visit her. On some days, she would eat almost a cup of it, which would ease my mind for that day. How we see only what we want to see. Thinking back, I realize that cup of porridge probably supplied only a hundred calories of nourishment.

We never stayed long, as there was nothing much we could do other than feed her. Always a garrulous woman in her younger years, she had stopped talking about the same time she began walking with the aid of a walker. When she did talk, it was in a different, guttural voice and in short, choppy phrases. I wondered if she had had some small strokes that resulted in the change. She would sleep much of the visit.

Yet she seemed to understand what I said to her. She seemed interested only in what her grandchildren and great-grandchildren were doing. She would ask if Mike, our younger son, had found a girlfriend yet. When I said possibly, she brightened.

"*Jung guo ren?*" she asked. "Chinese?"

"No, *may guo ren*" (American), I answered.

She shrugged as if to say, "Oh well."

Periodically, nurses would come in to change her diaper. She'd had to be put in disposable diapers since she lost the ability to walk on her own. She was a proud woman. Being kept in diapers must have been an affront and loss of face. I could imagine how she must have suffered—*cher koo* ("eat bitterness")—in having to put up with those indignities.

When she asked me to take her to the bathroom, it was another request to which I could not respond. She was too heavy for me to carry, and I was afraid I would injure her while trying to carry her.

I'm so sorry, Mommy, I thought to myself. To her, I simply said, "I can't do it, Mahmee. You have to use the diaper."

She would react with anger and disgust that I was showing so little filial piety.

I have more than once wondered why I could not show more love to my mother. At most, I would give her a peck on the cheek when I greeted her or when I left her. The hugs I give so freely to my family and friends were something I could not give to Mommy.

One day, when I was around nine years old, I was practicing the piano, and Mommy was vacuuming in the same room. I suddenly realized she was crying while vacuuming. If it had been anyone else, I would have turned to ask what was wrong, but I continued to play, pretending I did not know she was crying.

Why?

I have thought of that incident often with not a small feeling of guilt. It was just one of the signs she was unhappy. About what I never knew, as she and my father never talked to us about their problems. I yearned deeply for the closeness I had seen between other mothers and daughters, and I must acknowledge that I was part of the problem. I never made enough of an effort to overcome my reluctance to express some sympathy to my mother.

Yet there was something that I now understand acted as a barrier between us: language. In thinking about the piano-playing episode, I now recognize that one basic problem was my lack of vocabulary in Chinese to appropriately express sympathy to Mommy. I could not use English, with which I would have had no trouble finding the right words, as then she would not have understood me. Our cultural divide was wide in communication between us. It was not either one's fault. We just didn't realize we had that barrier.

Later in life, I did not like the fact that I could apparently harbor resentment for the things she did—not only to me but also to others in my family—to the point where my feelings were paralyzed against my own mother. Yet clearly my feelings were paralyzed much earlier.

I am no psychologist, but one guess is that as children, my siblings and I were nurtured really by our wet nurses, young women who had given birth and were lactating. They gave us the warm bodies and hugs that made babies feel secure and loved. As we children grew, we came to understand that they were not our parents.

Our parents were beautiful people who would ask us to be brought to them for a moment of attention and then taken away again to be cared for by the wet nurse. Our parents were to be obeyed without question. I have to believe we youngsters viewed them with awe rather than love.

As the years passed, my father belittled my mother frequently, sometimes implying and sometimes actually saying that she was incapable of understanding something we were discussing. While it might have been true, it was cruel, I thought. His thoughtlessness hammered into her that she was, in comparison to him, uneducated and intellectually deficient.

Some of his biting behavior stemmed from some problem that happened in the early 1940s that my parents never disclosed to their children. I could feel the estrangement between my parents and Mommy's mother and brother and between my parents also. In addition, I am sure Daddy was brought up by his elderly father to be a classical scholar or official, as was my grandfather's own experience. However, after the Chinese Revolution of 1911, that way of life disappeared along with dynasties and emperors. Daddy was probably ill prepared for life in twentieth-century America. It is to his credit that he nevertheless managed to find a career that met the needs of his family. I have often wondered what he could have been if his life circumstances had been different—probably anything he wanted to be.

When I was able to succeed in graduate schools, receiving a master's degree and later a PhD, it must have made my mother both proud and jealous. More than once, when my father acquiesced to a request from me, Mommy said with envy, "He'll do whatever you want him to do." It must have been a source of great annoyance to her.

After immigration to the United States, my mother found herself in a situation in which there was only one way to excel over Daddy: in her cooking. She taught herself to cook, and she cooked well. One of her dishes frequently acclaimed by dinner guests was a tofu dish. Friends would ask her for the recipe. Like most Chinese cooks, Mommy never cooked by recipe but arrived at dishes by trial and error with imprecise measurements.

Having been brought up to never lie, I was astonished as a teenager when she told me of a secret she used when asked about her cooking. "Never give the complete ingredients if friends ask how you cook something they cannot," she said. "That way, they will never produce a dish that is quite as good." Thinking back on it, I find this idea a poignant ploy on her part just to be better in something and be recognized as someone to be respected. It was sad there was little else that could bring her the notoriety she missed having.

It was true that Mommy was relatively uneducated, but that was due entirely to the classical Chinese discrimination against women. It was not her fault. My father was educated not only by his father, a classical scholar, but also by private tutors. Later, he attended classes at Fu Ren University, from which he graduated. As a woman, Mommy had tutors who taught her to read and write, but that was the end of her education.

When I went to college, Mommy said to me more than once that I needed to acquire knowledge and skills.

"You don't want to have to depend completely on a man. You must be able to live independently!" she would say earnestly.

I understood what she was trying to tell me. She was completely dependent on Daddy, and that awareness was a bitter pill for her to swallow. Her advice was almost a plea, and that no doubt played a role in my seeking graduate education.

Women in Mommy's China were only meant to add heirs to the family and manage the servants. In the culture of those days, women were believed to be the determiners of the sex of the child. Their worth as a wife depended on whether they gave birth to a boy or a girl. That erroneous idea persisted in many countries in the Far East and Middle East and probably still is the bane of women in some parts of the world today.

One day after he had again dismissed Mommy by saying she couldn't understand and should just forget about something, I got up enough courage to admonish Daddy. The way he spoke was so harsh—akin to telling her how stupid he thought she was—that I couldn't accept it. I strongly doubt that my admonishment made any impression on him, however.

At times, when she lapsed into sleep at the nursing home, I looked at my mother's small figure in bed. She had lived a tumultuous life for ninety-two years, and her life had changed from being a true princess, the pampered, beautiful daughter of a Manchurian warlord, to being an immigrant who had to raise three small children and do her own cleaning and cooking and then, at the end of life, a helpless and sick woman in a nursing home. Her working children could only visit sporadically rather than tending to her full-time, as we would have if we'd been home early in twentieth-century China.

Her experience as an immigrant to the United States was different from the experiences of most immigrants. Rather than a rags-to-riches experience, hers was a progression from riches to ordinary—something she'd never expected—and to be ordinary was intolerable for her. I hoped her brain had degenerated at the end so she could no longer remember the hard times.

I would wonder while looking at her if I could expect to become like her as I grew older. I thought, *I should be able to take my old age better because I am a part of this society, of this world in which she never felt completely comfortable.* In thinking about this book, I came to realize that to understand my mother's reactions to life in the United States and therefore understand some of the factors that contributed to her never reaching what she considered her American dream, one would need to know of her life in China as a Manchurian princess.

It is my hope that in writing about my mother, I will better understand our agitated relationship, and perhaps I will also understand myself better.

CHAPTER 2

THE ARRANGED MARRIAGE OF MY PARENTS

Both of my parents came from families with historically important backgrounds. My mother, Zhang Huai Tung (figure 3), was the third and, by her own account, favorite daughter of a warlord, the Tiger of Manchuria, Marshal Zhang Tso Lin (figure 4). My father, Chao Shih Hui (figure 5), was the only child of the Viceroy of Manchuria, Chao Er Shun, the highest-ranking civil servant in that region during the last of the dynasties, the Qing Dynasty (figure 6). I write the names of people as the Chinese write them: family name first, generation name second, and given name last.

Manchuria is comprised of three large provinces, Liaoning, Jilin, and Heilongjiang, from south to north, respectively (please see the map accompanying the introduction). It is an enormous region comparable in area and climate to the combined states of North and South Dakota, Montana, Wyoming, Iowa, and Nebraska. To be named viceroy was therefore a great honor, as the person in that position was to govern the entire region. Manchuria is also called simply the Northeast (Dong Bei) by Chinese. My parents always referred to it as Dong Bei. Its position in China would be comparable to New England in the United States.

My paternal grandfather (Yeh Yeh in Chinese), Chao Er Shun, was sixty-nine when Daddy was born. One of the few Mandarins who did not have multiple wives at the same time, Yeh Yeh had lost his first two wives to illness. They did not bear him any children. His third wife (whom I call Nai Nai, mother of my father), Zhao Kwang Yu, was perhaps thirty or forty years younger than Yeh Yeh (figure 7). She gave him his son in 1912. The child was a true treasure for the old man, someone to carry on the Chao family name, something important to Chinese (figure 8).

My mother's father, Zhang Tso Lin, had been a young military aide to Yeh Yeh (figure 9).

He later gained control of resources-rich Manchuria in the 1920s after the Chinese Revolution overthrew the Qing Dynasty in 1911. He was considered a warlord and eventually was given the nicknames Old Marshal and the Tiger of Manchuria. My maternal grandfather, the Old Marshal, was to me Lo Yeh.

Although Lo Yeh and Yeh Yeh were at least one generation different in age, because of Yeh Yeh's unusually advanced years when he first became a father, their children were similar in age (in fact, Mommy was two years older than Daddy). Given the close relationship between my two grandfathers and the great changes that occurred in China with the revolution and the downfall of the dynasty system, it seemed natural for them to make a match of their children. (For Chinese parents, matching children for marriage was a custom followed widely into the early twentieth century. It is rarely done today in Chinese cities, but some matches are made in rural areas.)

However, Lo Yeh was not in favor of the match because of the generational difference between the two. For example, people in the Zhang family who were nephews of Daddy's might be decades older than he. Adults would then be in the position of giving obeisance to a child, as demanded by Chinese culture. This would be contrary to another Chinese custom of the young respecting older people.

After Lo Yeh died in 1928, his oldest son, the Young Marshal, succeeded him and approved of the match. The two families then arranged a marriage between my father and mother, which took place later in 1928.

It was enormously interesting to me when I took my parents to see the movie *The Last Emperor,* and my mother told me her mother, Lo Lo, Zhang Ta Tao, the fourth wife of the Old Marshal (figure 10), had been approached by representatives of Pu Yi, the last emperor. They had requested a picture of my mother to include in the group from which Pu Yi was to choose his wife. My grandmother had refused. *Thank you, Lo Lo*, I thought.

Interestingly, her reason for refusing to allow Pu Yi to consider Mommy was because Lo Lo did not want her daughter to be what she was: a fourth wife. She had been forced to marry Lo Yeh by her parents. She was protecting her daughter from becoming a lesser wife, as she herself was, a position she always resented.

My mother was a beautiful woman, with large brown eyes, double eyelids (important to Chinese for beauty), and an engaging personality (figure 11). She had a sense of style that I admired and wished I had, but all her life, she fought with contradictions and struggles of her own making.

My father was handsome (figure 12) and bright and was doted on and spoiled as the only child of an elderly father (figure 13).

The photograph in figure 13 includes a poem written by Yeh Yeh that speaks of the importance of teaching his young son to learn the classics and of the level of behavior befitting a scholar and high official. His vision for Daddy was no doubt that Daddy would have a career similar to his own career as a scholar and viceroy. In the photograph, Daddy was nine years old, and Yeh Yeh was seventy-eight. Daddy's nickname, Tien Tse, as the poem refers to him, means "Gift from Heaven."

I realized when I saw the photo that Daddy's upbringing was classic, and therefore, he was not prepared for life in the twentieth century, much less as an immigrant in America. It is a wonder to me that he was able to adjust to life in the United States as well as he did. I have no doubt his two years spent in graduate studies at Cornell and Duke laid the basis for his adjustment. Mommy was never under pressure to learn English, so she suffered from her immigrant life more than anyone in the family. Still, when I look at the photograph of the nine-year-old boy with his seventy-eight-year-old father, and I see him so serious and stiffly formal, I feel some sadness and wonder about his childhood.

My paternal grandmother, Nai Nai, was, as I mentioned, much younger than my grandfather. One day, when my mother was angry with my father, as she was constantly later in their lives, Mommy pulled me aside and said, "Don't tell your father I told you, but his mother was actually a *ya toh* (servant)! He married her, and then she had your father."

She was clearly trying to disparage Nai Nai and, thus, Daddy also. Having been raised in the United States, I only blinked at that piece of information, but to her, it was clearly something shameful, akin to British royalty marrying a commoner in past years. I guess when I did not act shocked, my lack of reaction was no doubt an annoyance to Mommy.

Yet I had been told from early childhood that Daddy's mother was treated with the deference that a matriarch was due, so to me, it was not anything scandalous. In fact, I felt even more respect for Yeh Yeh, who was obviously someone with a democratic outlook beyond his era. He not only took a servant for his wife but also saw to it that she received the respect she deserved for bearing him a son. Unquestionably, she was the head of the family after his death, and Mommy, despite her attempt to disparage Nai Nai in my eyes, always showed proper respect and filial piety for Daddy's mother to others.

It was due to Nai Nai's unquestioned authority, however, that I never knew my sister, who died of dysentery before I was born. The oldest of my siblings, she was around five years old when she became ill. A Chinese physician who attended her wanted to inject fluid into her, as dysentery dehydrated the patient. It was a time when IV techniques were not available. When my grandmother saw the size of the needle, she gave orders that it could not be used because it would be too painful. My sister died of dehydration. My parents grieved her loss but accepted my grandmother's decision with resignation.

Yet one fact told me that their acceptance must have been painful. While looking through a number of photograph albums Daddy made and kept, which were the sources of the family photographs for this book, there were numerous shots of my two brothers and me as babies and toddlers in China. Knowing Daddy, there must have been many photos taken of his first child. But there was not a single image of my sister in any album.

My sister was beautiful and bright, my parents always told me. I don't know what they did with her pictures. I was particularly welcomed to the family, Daddy once told me, because I was born the year after my sister died. I know that among my two brothers and me, I was our father's favored child. Perhaps having my sister's photos was too painful for my parents, and they ordered servants to remove them.

I have no other knowledge of Nai Nai's family or background. I remember Nai Nai only vaguely. I remember cracking watermelon seeds for her—the roasted, salted ones that Chinese like to munch on—when her own teeth were no longer good enough to do so.

I was told that Yeh Yeh was a humanitarian who opened his home to the common folk at Chinese New Year, providing them with food and dispensing money. In a country whose officials often profited greatly by graft and corruption, he had a reputation for being honest and was held as a model of the Confucian ideal of an honorable leader. The consequence of his generosity, according to Mommy, was that he never accumulated the great wealth that was available to him. With the money problems my parents had in the last half of their lives, I know that was something she regretted.

By the time the Young Marshal approved the match following the assassination of the Old Marshal in 1928, an event I will discuss later, Yeh Yeh had passed away also, in 1927. But both grandfathers could rest in peace about this: from the point of view that it was always of great importance for a match to be made between appropriate families, the Zhang and Chao families could not have done better. My mother told me she was allowed to look at the young man to whom she was betrothed not long before they were to marry. She hid behind some curtains to get a peek at him when he came to visit her home. She thought he was handsome. She didn't voice those thoughts but only demurely nodded when her mother asked her if she thought him acceptable.

The wedding itself was a civil wedding. She was woken up early in the morning. The maids in attendance spent hours getting the complex and bejeweled hairpins in her hair just right and dressed her in the elegant hand-embroidered red silk robes traditional in Chinese weddings among children of highly ranked families of that time (figure 14). She was transported to the Chao household in a sedan chair carried by four men.

It was an uncomfortable time in her life, she told me. She had to hold an apple in her mouth, though she could not explain to me the reason behind that tradition. She said the sedan chair swung as the men half walked and half trotted through the roads. Musicians accompanied the entourage, their music loudly announcing an important wedding.

She was enclosed by the satin and silk embroidered curtains, all in red, the color of celebration. She got such motion sickness from the swaying of the sedan chair that she nearly fainted while trying to keep from vomiting. At last, she arrived. The rest of the ceremony was a blur to her because of nausea and nervousness. Figure 15 is an old photo taken after the wedding with all who were in attendance. I can only guess at the identity of a handful of people in the photograph.

Decades later, on the occasion of their twenty-fifth wedding anniversary, Daddy wrote a poem that can be seen in its entirety in figure 16. Later, he divided the poem into four sections, with each section focusing on an important phase of their life together, and placed a photograph that represented each phase above the poem. We needed the help of David's brother, Bai Xienyung, a renowned modern Chinese scholar and writer, to translate the poem, as it was written in classical Chinese. The poem in figure 14 tells of Daddy's anxiety as the Young Marshal was deliberating whether the match should be made.

> To wait for consent I walked in anxious circles,
>
> One hundred circles, one thousand circles.

Having survived so much doubt,

We finally are married—even though there was no great fanfare.

But were I a peacock, my tail would be opened

With pride and joy at having you!

At first, you were very shy, hiding your face behind a fan

Which only inflamed my ardor for you!

An old god in art blessed us and wished us to produce offspring.

Fig. 3 My mother: third of six daughters and third from the right, Zhang Huai Tung.

Fig. 4 Marshal Zhang Tso Lin, the "Tiger of Manchuria".

Fig. 5 My father Zhao Shih Hui, an only child.

Fig. 6 My father's father, the Viceroy of Manchuria, Zhao Er Shun

Fig. 7 My father (around age 3) and his mother, Zhao Kwang Yu.

Fig. 8 My father (18 months old) and his delighted father (71 years old).

Fig. 9 My two grandfathers:

Zhao Er Shun (my Yeh Yeh) on the front row, fourth from the right.

Zhang Tso Lin (my Lo Yeh) directly behind him.

Fig. 10 Left to right: Third Uncle's wife, my Lo Lo, and Mommy.

Fig. 11 Mommy.

Fig. 12 Daddy.

Fig. 13 Daddy with Yeh Yeh

Fig 14 Mommy (18 years old) and Daddy (16 years old on their wedding day in 1928)

為永金諾義遷延
萬轉千迴秦晉聯
未譜霓裳迎鳳輦
初吟卻扇羞雲軿
屏開孔雀下雲軿
卜近柔鄉愛更憐
南極仙翁善頻禱
萁堂瓜瓞總緜之

Fig 15 After the wedding with all who attended.

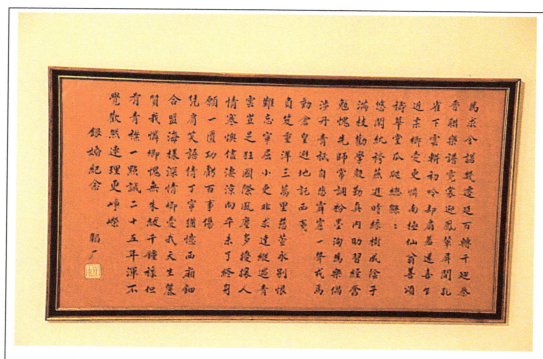

Fig 16 My father's calligraphy of a poem he wrote on their 25th anniversary.

CHAPTER 3

THE VICEROY, MY PATERNAL GRANDFATHER, YEH YEH

Yeh Yeh, my father's father, Chao Er Shun, was the second son in his family. His success came through the system of civil examinations that determined the careers of young men in China in those days. It was extremely democratic, a true meritocracy. If a young man tested well, he was given a higher, more desirable position than others who tested less well, regardless of his background and wealth.

Obviously, men from wealthier families had the advantage of more education and tutoring. Yeh Yeh's father was himself a mandarin, or high civil servant. He fathered four sons, all of whom tested well and became mandarins (please refer to the family tree in the introduction).

Chao Er Shun became an official in 1867, and his breakthrough occurred in 1874, when he became a *chin-shih* official, which was the highest rank one could reach in civil service, with his election to the Hanlin Academy (see again figure 6). Membership in the academy, which was founded in the eighth century, was limited to the most elite scholars in China. Yeh Yeh's two other brothers, also chin-shih, were themselves accomplished officials, although they were less famous. A third brother who died in his early forties was also chin-shih and was considered the brightest of the four brothers.

Yeh Yeh continued to ascend through official positions, becoming viceroy of Shansi, which was then Hunan. He was instrumental in reforming the mining industry to become self-sufficient and free of foreign control. Later, he became a court minister and viceroy of a series of provinces, beginning with Guandong and Hunan, and lastly, he became viceroy of Manchuria, the highest position of civil service.

He was credited with educational reform, and some of the early revolutionaries received financial help from him, which probably saved his life when the dynasty was overthrown. Among those to whom he became a patron was my maternal grandfather, Zhang Tso Lin (Lo Yeh). As the revolutionaries rose up against the Qing Dynasty, Yeh Yeh was able to maintain control of Manchuria with the help of military units, such as the troops of Lo Yeh.

However, when the Chinese Revolution overthrew the Qing Dynasty in 1911, Yeh Yeh was in immediate jeopardy. It had been customary in Chinese history that when a dynasty was overthrown, all high officials of that dynasty would either commit suicide or be executed. Even their families would be eliminated so that descendants could not seek retribution. My mother told the story of how Lo Yeh saved Yeh Yeh, to whom he was an aide, and Yeh Yeh's family.

At a meeting of the high-ranking military men of the revolution to discuss the fate of the Qing Dynasty officials, Lo Yeh, Zhang Tso Lin, reportedly took his revolver out of its holster and, placing it firmly on the table, said, "No one touches the viceroy and his family."

Thus, the lives of Yeh Yeh and my family were spared. As a respected elder, Yeh Yeh was given the assignment to write and edit a history of the Qing Dynasty, which was published in 1928, the year after his death.

I cannot imagine Yeh Yeh's joy when he was presented with a son in his sixty-ninth year (see again figure 8). I have often wished I had the opportunity to meet both my grandfathers. Mommy often proudly expressed her admiration of Daddy's scholarship, which was due to training by Yeh Yeh. By the time of my parents' wedding, Yeh Yeh had died in September 1927. Lo Yeh was assassinated shortly before they were married in June 1928.

Daddy was sixteen when Yeh Yeh died. Many officials and common people paid their respects, beating their chests and wailing in sorrow. Daddy knelt in front of the coffin, paying obeisance and kowtowing in the Chinese tradition. When the coffin was closed, he cried out, as tradition demanded, "*Baba, xiao xin ding tze*!" (Father, be careful of the nails!), referring to the nails used to secure the coffin top. I've always thought this a poignant tradition showing love and filial piety to the end.

Daddy's erudition was attributed to Yeh Yeh, who was a classical Chinese scholar. Daddy told me that when he was a child, Yeh Yeh would wake him early in the morning. Then Yeh Yeh would ask him to recite a passage in a book. In those days, people actually memorized books. I cannot even memorize a page now!

Daddy also remembered having to learn calligraphy with brushes. The position of his hand and the firmness of his grip on the brush were lessons taught with the help of a ruler swung across the knuckles. His calligraphy was wonderful. I have saved as art a poem he wrote in commemoration of my parents' twenty-fifth anniversary (see again figure 16).

The form of each ideogram is lovely. Every stroke is in proportion to the entire word, and where each stroke thickens or thins adds to the art of the calligraphy. When a student is taught to write a word, he must write the strokes in a designated sequence. In traditional Chinese writing, as in this figure, the poem or essay is read from right to left, starting on top of the line farthest right and following the words to the bottom of the line. Then one proceeds to the next vertical line.

At the end, the calligrapher, or the owner of the piece of art, uses his seal to imprint onto the paper. Note that each word of the poem is the same size, as if a machine produced the writing. I might be biased, but I have seen few samples of calligraphy that I like better than my father's. Yeh Yeh, you taught him well! Later,

I will include four photographs that illustrate the four paragraphs of the poetry and explain the sentiments of the four paragraphs. Figure 14 is the first of the four photographs.

To Chinese, calligraphy is a true art. There are different styles of calligraphy just as there are different styles of painting. I enjoy good handwriting in both English and Chinese, and I wish that in the United States today, instructors placed as much emphasis on cursive handwriting as they did in the schools of my childhood.

Chapter 4

THE OLD MARSHAL, MY MATERNAL GRANDFATHER, LO YEH

Marshal Zhang Tso Lin, the Tiger of Manchuria, was a self-made man of determination and leadership. Born to poor country folk in Fengtien Province in Manchuria, Lo Yeh actually was not born into the Zhang family. There was an old Chinese practice that helped a family to carry on the family name even if they had no sons. If there was a family with many sons who were related or close friends, they could give up one of their boys to be adopted by the family needing a son. This practice was known as *guo jee,* and Lo Yeh became a Zhang through guo jee. My niece once commented that the Zhang family really knew how to pick a prize boy to join their family. How true!

I know nothing else about the Li family, who gave Lo Yeh to the Zhang family. I have been told both families were poor. Guo jee was practiced at all levels of society in those days. Lo Yeh's adoptive mother was married to the village veterinarian. As a young man, he acquired veterinary knowledge of how to treat large domestic animals, such as horses, from his adoptive father.

Barbara Tuchman, in her book *Stillwell and the American Experience in China*, described Lo Yeh as an ex-bandit. The charge infuriated my brother and me because we heard a very different story from Mommy about the incident that marked him as a bandit in some records.

Lo Yeh had treated a rich landlord's horse at the landlord's request. Instead of being paid for his services, he was thrown out by the landlord. Determined to get justice for himself, one night, he returned to the home of the landlord to take a horse as payment. He encountered a servant, and a fight ensued, in which the servant was killed. Grandfather took a horse, which he felt was owed him. While the act branded him as a bandit to some, his reputation as a Robin Hood spread among the poor.

Lo Yeh enlisted in the military as a young man and fought in the Sino-Japanese War of 1894–1895. After the war, he returned to Manchuria and organized a militia to defend his home district and other villages that requested protection. His leadership abilities emerged, and his army increased quickly in size and power. At the time, he was also called a bandit by some because he and his forces were not part of the Imperial Army. He was truly a Robin Hood.

I suspect, knowing the personalities of my mother, her brothers, and her famous half brother, Zhang Xueliang, Lo Yeh was a charismatic person. It is not hard for me to understand why men wanted to follow him. Lo Yeh's children all shared a wonderful sense of humor, a warmth that was irresistible. When Mommy and Daddy were with friends, she and Daddy both seemed always to be at the center of conversation. They had a way with words and acted out their stories with comical facial expressions that made their listeners smile and laugh out loud. Lo Lo, Mommy's mother, was not like that. She was quiet and reticent, perhaps because of her life, so I have to attribute these traits to Lo Yeh.

All Lo Yeh's children whom I knew also possessed a fierce patriotism that must have come from their upbringing. They must have idolized their father. My mother often said her father would not allow or ignore injustices. She said proudly that he would have executed men he felt were guilty of wrongdoings. She told us they once discovered that the meat they were having for dinner was bad and wormy. Incensed, Lo Yeh banged the table and ordered the butcher to be executed. It would have been done too, she said, if it had not been for the intervention of Lo Lo, who calmed him down.

During his early years, Lo Yeh became an ally to Yeh Yeh, who was then the military governor and viceroy of Manchuria (see again figure 9). Through a series of military and political moves, with the support of his patron and future in-law, Lo Yeh gained more divisions of troops and control over territories, and by 1920, he had control over all of Manchuria and, later, Inner Mongolia. That the Old Marshal had total control over the troops and territory of Manchuria was unquestioned. His authority in Manchuria was absolute. During his rule, Manchuria enjoyed a period of peace and stability.

Mommy did not disguise her pride that her father had such power. One of her constant themes as she struggled through life in America was that she was the daughter of Marshal Zhang Tso Lin and thus, without question, should have been admired and respected. My brothers and I could not understand and were embarrassed by her attitude. We thought, *Who cares? The Old Marshal can be admired, but we're only relatives.* The reality, though, lay between those disparate attitudes.

The respect in which my grandfathers and uncle are held is underscored time and time again as Chinese friends and acquaintances find out who they are. I inevitably see raised eyebrows and hear awe in their voices, followed by words of praise and esteem for my grandfathers and uncle.

It is an attitude that is truly different for Americans, for whom being relatives of prominent people is interesting but not a source of awe. For example, I attended a memorial event in New York City's Chinatown for my uncle the Young Marshal, who died in 2001. Just because I was a relative of his, people I did not know grabbed me to have their photograph taken with me. I was someone to be honored simply because I was a relative.

This is a reflection of the importance of family relations in Chinese culture. Because my relatives are well known and respected, I am also to be honored. The flip side of the coin is that if someone in the family were to act in a disgraceful manner, the onus also falls on the entire family. Therefore, youngsters know that their actions define not only themselves but also their parents, siblings, and family members.

If one person in the family loses face, everyone loses face. It is a powerful pressure that does not affect Western families as much. Given my mother's somewhat exaggerated sense of her importance, she was strongly inclined to see her children's imperfections as a negative reflection of her worth as a wife and mother.

I understand that now, but her fury about my older brother Stanley, who sustained brain-damaging problems during birth and as a toddler during our childhood, was a source of resentment not only for Stanley but also for my oldest brother, Solan, and me as well. I will discuss this problem more fully later.

Chapter 5

ASSASSINATION: THE YOUNG MARSHAL ASCENDS

Even before the 1920s, the Japanese already had designs on Manchuria. They coveted the resources and the land of the area and sent many diplomatic forays to Yeh Yeh as well as the Old Marshal, seeking to advance their interests in Manchuria. There were Japanese diplomats and military men everywhere, Lo Yeh's daughter, my oldest aunt, told me. The historic photograph in figure 9 certainly proves the presence of countless Japanese officials.

To some, it appeared that when Lo Yeh first gained control of Manchuria, he was cooperating with the Japanese, but in retrospect, historians have credited him with compromising with the Japanese on minor issues and resisting on major ones. In part, this might have been due to his recognition that the Japanese could support his resistance to increasing Russian interests in Manchuria.

Lo Yeh had fought against the Japanese in the Sino-Japanese War in the 1890s and against the Russians in the Russo-Japanese War in 1905. The Chinese were what one history book refers to as irregular allies of the Japanese in the war against the Russians. War was not declared between Russia and Manchuria, but Lo Yeh deemed the Russians more of a threat than the Japanese.

The Japanese had attempted to convince the Old Marshal that they could build a railroad in Manchuria that would improve transportation in such a large area, but they wanted to be given control of the railroad. The Old Marshal refused to agree to the proposal because it was further evidence to him that they wanted to increase their own control over Manchuria through the rail system.

In 1926, the Nationalist armies under Generalissimo Chiang Kai Shek started moving to the north in a campaign known as the Northern Expedition. The campaign, which lasted from 1926 to 1928, was an effort to have the northern warlords join the Nationalist movement and unite China. The Japanese in Manchuria who had been negotiating for the railroad unsuccessfully were worried about the possible unification of the Old Marshal with the Nationalists. Such a move would present a great obstacle to their ambitions.

In 1928, without consulting with Tokyo, the Japanese in Manchuria acted on inside information about a train trip Lo Yeh was planning to take to travel to Manchuria from Beijing. They decided to assassinate the Old Marshal, hoping they might achieve their goals with a less determined successor. There is evidence that the Shenyang Japanese decided to take things into their own hands and, without consulting or receiving approval from Japan, decided Lo Yeh had to be eliminated.

The Old Marshal had been warned that his trip might be too public and would expose him to possible harm, but Lo Yeh said he would not consider moving around secretively or hiding his itinerary, as it would show the Japanese that he feared them. That bravado, alas, cost him his life.

Apparently, the Japanese had acquired inside information about which car he was riding in and the train's itinerary. Terrorism is not something just recently invented by religious fanatics in the Middle East. As the train passed a certain point on a railroad trestle in Huang Gu Ton, near Shenyang (figure 17), the Japanese detonated a bomb that tore through his car.

My third uncle, my mother's younger brother, who was in a different car from Lo Yeh, ran to the decimated car that carried his father and found him with severe head and throat injuries that ultimately proved to be fatal. Lo Yeh was covered with blood but gave orders that nobody be allowed to see him. Over and over, he said, *"May sher"* (No problem). He did not want the Japanese or anyone who'd collaborated in the assassination attempt to know how badly he was injured.

Zhang Xueliang, the Old Marshal's oldest son, who had already commanded some of the Manchurian troops, succeeded the Old Marshal at the age of twenty-nine. He was thereafter known as the Young Marshal of Manchuria. He too played a significant role in determining the course of modern Chinese history. However, at the time of the bombing, the Young Marshal, who was in Beijing, needed a few days to stabilize his control. In fact, he had to travel incognito, dressed as a woman, to return safely to Shenyang, as his life was in danger also.

Word was sent out to all, including the Japanese, that the Old Marshal was only wounded and was recuperating at home in Shenyang. He had been carried to the house of his fifth wife, where he died shortly after arriving (figure 18).

The Japanese hypocritically sent officials to the home to wish him a speedy recovery but also no doubt to verify that he was still alive and recovering. They were told only that the Old Marshal was not ready to receive visitors. The pretense went as far as to have a soldier imitate his voice to call out orders so that the Japanese were convinced he was still alive.

By the time the death of the Old Marshal was announced, Uncle, the Young Marshal, had consolidated his control of the Manchurian troops. The Japanese were prevented from taking any immediate military action. They did try right away, however, to convince the Young Marshal to collaborate with them, but they wanted control over the government of Manchuria in return for Japanese support politically and militarily.

Uncle listened to their arguments and cajolery. No doubt they felt they could easily sway the Young Marshal because of his reputation in his younger days as a womanizer and opium addict, but they gravely misjudged him. According to my cousin Pauline Tao, the oldest of the Young Marshal's children, Uncle told the Japanese, "All that you offer is very interesting, but you have forgotten one important thing: I am Chinese!"

With that, the Young Marshal convinced the Japanese officials that he would never agree to be their puppet in Manchuria. What the Japanese feared did materialize when the Young Marshal, believing that Chiang Kai Shek was the best hope to unify China, shifted his allegiance to the Nationalists, the Kuomingtang (Nationalist) Party.

When funeral services were held for the Old Marshal, Daddy told us that the Japanese, in continuing hypocritical fashion, sent representatives to the funeral and expressed their condolences. Daddy knelt before his soon-to-be father-in-law's coffin and swore to him he would care for Mommy as long as he lived. Daddy was to fulfill that promise until his death in 1998.

The Japanese no doubt were deeply disappointed by the resolve of the Young Marshal. Uncle Zhang Xueliang might have been a spoiled, handsome playboy with no interest in the governance of Manchuria when he was in his teens and early twenties; however, when his father was assassinated, he took control over the Manchurian forces and showed his ability to lead his forces and his people.

The young man, however, was still under the influence of his addiction to opium. When he decided to join the Nationalists under Chiang Kai Shek, Chiang ordered him to rid himself of the addiction. We have heard that Uncle went onto a boat and isolated himself in the middle of a harbor to kick the addiction cold turkey. He succeeded and was never an addict again.

That was one of the few instances in which Chiang could be said to have benefitted the Young Marshal. In many other important ways, Chiang's future actions were to prove bitter disappointments to Uncle.

Fig 17 Site of the bombing of Lo Yeh's train in Shen Yang.

Fig 18 Fifth Wife's House in the Zhang Family Compound in Shenyang.

Chapter 6

THE XIAN INCIDENT, 1936

With the death of the Old Marshal and the Young Marshal's rejection of their advances, the Japanese opted for direct action and invaded Manchuria in 1931. The invasion marked the real beginning of World War II in the Pacific, ten years before the attack on Pearl Harbor.

The Manchurian troops were known to be fearsome in battle, but to my uncle's consternation, Chiang ordered the Young Marshal to withdraw his troops from Manchuria, essentially ceding the area to the Japanese. Chiang wanted the Manchurian troops to fight the Chinese Communists instead of the Japanese while he conserved his own troops. During the Japanese occupation, Manchuria was given the name Manchukuo, and the Japanese installed Pu Yi as the last emperor.

For the next five years, the Japanese brutalized the people of Manchuria. Though they never admitted that atrocities were perpetrated on the Manchurian population, later records showed that the Japanese invaders not only raped, killed, and tortured people but also carried out experiments similar to what Hitler did to Jews in Germany. It is not known how many Chinese people died at the hands of the Japanese, but the number had to be enormous.

During that time, the people of Manchuria pleaded with my uncle, asking him to return with his troops to fight the Japanese. Uncle more than once in turn pleaded with Generalissimo Chiang to allow him to return to Manchuria to fight and free the people from the Japanese. He was repeatedly denied. Furthermore, even though Chiang promised he would send in reinforcements for the troops and arms when they were needed in Uncle's battles against the Communists, Chiang never sent anything.

Pauline, the Young Marshal's oldest child, whom I interviewed at the Young Marshal's funeral service in 2001, said her father was deeply touched by one particular Chinese student who had submitted a moving written plea to him to help the people of Manchuria. It was the last straw for the Young Marshal. He knew he had to act on behalf of the people of his homeland.

In December 1936, unable to tolerate Chiang's orders anymore, Marshal Zhang Xueliang and General Yang Hucheng of the Northwestern Army of China (figure 19) took matters into their own hands and carried out a coup now known as the Xian Incident. In twentieth-century Chinese history, it remains a famous and important event.

Chiang visited the Young Marshal's headquarters in Xian in December 1936 to plan a final assault on the Communist forces. Chiang was staying at Hua Qing Tse, a lovely resort (figure 20).

On the night of December 12, the Young Marshal's troops attempted to capture Chiang Kai Shek. Chiang had brought only a small number of troops, who tried to protect the generalissimo, but Uncle's forces overcame them. Hearing the gunfire, Chiang, thinking it was the Communists, jumped out the window of his bedroom on the ground floor (figure 21) and, with help from soldiers, climbed a wall surrounding the compound. When he jumped down from the wall, he hurt his back. However, he was able to clamber onto a nearby hill to hide in a cave. See again figure 20, which shows a plaque at the site of the cave about two-thirds of the way up the hill. Uncle's troops found him and captured him in the morning. He was shivering and needed help to make his way down the hill, having injured his back.

Uncle and General Yang demanded that Chiang agree to stop the war against the Chinese Communists. They also urged Chiang to agree that the Kuomintang troops would join with the Communists to fight the Japanese. Madame Chiang and Zhou Enlai of the Communists flew to Xian to take part in the deliberations with Chiang.

For two tense weeks, there was much discussion and debate, some of which was likely heated. Finally, Chiang Kai Shek acquiesced and gave his word that there would be a united front against the Japanese. That one action saved the Chinese people, especially Manchurians, and it created an unintended result: diverting Nationalist troops away from battling the Communists and toward the Japanese eventually, in 1949, allowed the Communist movement to gain strength and defeat Chiang Kai Shek in the civil war that followed the end of World War II.

Having obtained Chiang's word to fight the Japanese rather than the Communists, Uncle told Chiang he would be released and allowed to fly back to his headquarters in Nanking. Further, since there were elements under General Yang who wanted Chiang dead, Uncle told Chiang he would fly back with him because his presence on the plane would prevent it from being shot down by those not wanting Chiang released. It was still Uncle's belief that only Chiang could eventually unite China.

Uncle's decision to accompany Chiang required great courage because he knew he would be court-martialed. Indeed, he professed to us during a visit many years later that he deserved a court-martial, and accordingly, he was arrested as soon as he stepped off the plane. Since the Xian Incident had become big news all over the world, Chiang knew that how he handled the Young Marshal's case would be the center of international attention.

After a short trial, Uncle was found guilty and was sentenced to ten years in prison at hard labor. Chiang then announced that he was granting amnesty to the Young Marshal in a move meant to cast himself as a merciful and magnanimous leader. However, Uncle was actually placed under house arrest. He remained incarcerated in that manner for the next fifty years. Wherever Chiang found himself during World War II and in the failing civil war afterward, he would have Uncle moved to be with him under arrest.

Mommy and Daddy told us they were deeply worried that Chiang would execute Uncle. While Chiang allowed Uncle to live under house arrest, probably because Uncle had saved his life, Chiang acted in a brutal manner toward General Yang. After Chiang flew back to his headquarters following the Xian Incident, General Yang left China, no doubt expecting that he too would face arrest and incarceration. However, in 1937, when China and Japan formally declared war, General Yang returned home to join the war effort and was immediately captured by Chiang Kai Shek.

He was held captive for more than a decade until the Nationalists lost a mishandled civil war to the Communists, and Chiang had to flee to Taiwan. Before he left China, he gave orders to his henchmen to execute General Yang and kill Yang's wife and children. General Yang's secretary received a similar fate, as did the secretary's wife and children. No doubt in fear of retribution and harm to his family, Uncle's first wife and their two sons and a daughter moved to the United States to live in California.

One of the most heart-wrenching moments for my parents in the aftermath of the Xian Incident was the decision of Uncle's concubine, who was to later become his second wife, to give up their son and join Uncle in captivity. She was a lovely young woman known as Zhao Sze, or the fourth daughter in the Zhao family. Her real name was Zhao Yi Ti (figure 22). Younger than Uncle by more than ten years, she had the same surname as Daddy but was not related. She had met my uncle when she was fourteen, and the two fell deeply in love (figure 23). In the early years of their relationship, Zhao Sze was not allowed to live in the Zhang compound in Shenyang, Manchuria, where my grandfather lived. Instead, Uncle built an apartment building outside the compound, and Zhao Sze lived in one of the apartments so Uncle could visit her frequently.

When Uncle was arrested by Chiang in 1936, Zhao Sze was the mother of a five-year-old boy fathered by Uncle. She decided to join the Young Marshal in captivity and share whatever was to be his fate. She turned the boy over to an American friend, who raised him as part of his own family. Bobby, their young son, my cousin, was brought to the United States for his safety. Uncle's first wife was so moved to hear of Zhao Sze's devotion to Uncle that she released Uncle from their marriage vows.

My mother told me that the day Zhao Sze decided to join the Young Marshal, she said goodbye to her son, who was crying and clinging to her, as he was old enough to be aware that she was leaving him. She carried him to a bathroom, locked him in from the outside, and left. They were all in tears. My parents unlocked the boy after her departure and turned him over to the American friend. Bobby lived most of his life in California. I last saw him at Uncle's funeral service in Hawaii in 2001 (figure 24).

My brother Solan and I felt that not only the action of the Young Marshal but also the love and commitment of Zhao Sze should be honored. We talked about collaborating on a book about their love story, but unfortunately, Solan ran out of time, as I will discuss later. At the time Zhao Sze made her decision, it was not clear that they would not be executed. She did not want to live without the man she deeply loved.

Our feeling is that Chiang spared both of them because of Uncle's bravery in flying with him back to his headquarters, which thwarted those, including General Yang, who wanted Chiang dead. Their story has so touched the public that it has been retold in many books and movies made both on the mainland and in Taiwan and Hong Kong.

Chiang made sure that Uncle and Auntie would be moved along with him as the civil war progressed. They lived in Taipei, Taiwan, after the Nationalists lost the civil war. The loss to the Communists was due to the ineptness of Chiang as a military leader. He refused to listen to the noted, widely respected military strategist General Pai Chung Xi (figure 25), whose popularity among the Chinese people made the paranoid Chiang worry about the general possibly usurping power. Chiang took the advice of others—yes-men who were less able to strategize.

Because of the overwhelming advantages Chiang had in troops, arms, resources, and air force over the Communists, the widespread belief of analysts is that the Nationalists should never have lost to the Communists. Chiang and his remaining forces were forced to leave the mainland and occupied the island of Taiwan in 1949.

Uncle and Zhao Sze lived in several locations in Taiwan. As time went on, Chiang treated him less restrictively. Figure 26 shows the couple enjoying a visit to the governor of Taiwan at the governor's invitation. Of course, they were always accompanied by Chiang's secret service. Eventually, Uncle was able to move to a large, comfortable house in Beitou, a suburb of Taipei, the capital city of Taiwan. The house was built and paid for by Uncle because the house that Chiang assigned to them was of poor quality. We visited them there in 1985.

There was a painting by Madame Chiang prominently displayed on a wall. They were not uncomfortable there, and in 1961, Pauline, his oldest child and only daughter, was told she could visit her father and stepmother as often as she wished. The servants and cook who served them were probably also part of the Nationalist secret service. All visitors had to be recorded by name, and information about their activities had to be on record.

In 1964, when my parents were in Taiwan visiting the Young Marshal, my uncle called them one day at their hotel and urgently requested they come to his home. Anxiously, they hurried there, wondering what was wrong. With a big smile, Uncle informed them he was about to marry Zhao Sze, whom I will refer to as my aunt hereafter. Uncle had obtained a divorce from his first wife, and having been converted to Christianity by Madame Chiang Kai Shek, he was married by an official of the church to the woman who was to spend fifty years of house arrest with him. They also took on the names Peter and Edith.

I must say this of the Young Marshal: to me, his was the purest form of patriotism. He proved he had no agenda for himself and put the welfare of the people of Manchuria and China first and foremost. After he released Chiang Kai Shek, he told him he deserved to be arrested and charged with treason and kidnapping. In 1985, we heard this from him directly when we had the opportunity to visit him while he was still under house arrest. I discuss our visit in 1985 in chapter 51. People in all aspects of China's politics recognize his selfless love of country and the Manchurian people, and he is held in the highest honor in the minds of Chinese people everywhere.

Uncle, eighty-five at the time of our visit (figure 27), was still able to walk vigorously. He refused any help from us. Figure 28 shows Uncle with his visitors in 1985. Uncle and Aunt Edith became quite close to my brother Solan and his wife, Jeannette.

Uncle was attended to by a servant who was a former soldier and no doubt one of Chiang's spies. When Chiang was on his death bed, he ordered his son to continue to keep Uncle under house arrest. After his son, Chiang Jing Kuo, died in 1986, the people who came to power in Taiwan held no desire to keep the Young Marshal under arrest. Uncle's release finally occurred in 1986, when he was eighty-six years of age.

When Uncle Peter and Aunt Edith were finally released from house arrest in 1986, they moved to a comfortable apartment in Honolulu. My fifth uncle's wife and daughters lived nearby. They were involved almost daily with overseeing the care of the elderly couple (figure 29). Uncle Peter and Aunt Edith were obviously still well off, as they had round-the-clock servants who provided all the services they needed.

In 1990, Uncle and Auntie accepted the invitation of a number of Chinese American organizations to celebrate his ninetieth birthday in the United States. In New York City, we attended a dinner given in his honor at a large Chinese restaurant that the celebration took over entirely. The behavior of the crowd of people who were invited to the celebration was an eye-opener for me. It gave me a glimpse of what celebrities had to endure with the paparazzi and their fans.

We seated Uncle and Auntie at a central table. They were immediately surrounded by adoring people, all of whom wanted to take pictures of and with the couple. They wanted photos of themselves standing behind the national hero and heroine. There were endless flashes of light as people with anything from point-and-shoot cameras to fancy single-lens reflex cameras shot away.

My reaction to the behavior of the admirers ranged from understanding their excitement to awe at the depth of their intensity to concern for Uncle's well-being. Behind Uncle Peter, people jostled each other, trying to find room to stand. At one point, I placed chairs behind him to try to give him some space between him and the people wanting to be close, but of course, they just picked the chairs up and moved them away.

Finally, Uncle asked for some relief, as the flashing of camera lights was blinding him. A loudspeaker then announced that the photo session was through, and people responded to entreaties to return to their tables and give the old couple some respite. It was apparent to everyone that they were suffering from the pushing and shoving around them.

Their trip included Uncle Peter's visits with several of the Chinese ladies who had known him well in China. I understand that the reunions did not always include Auntie, who was in ill health and remained in their hotel room at times. I am sure that for Uncle at least, the reunions were among the most enjoyable moments of the trip.

They of course visited with their son, Bobby, and his family in California. We heard from my brother Solan and his wife, Jeannie, that Bobby and his family had visited his parents in Taiwan also. Despite the long separation because of their incarceration by Chiang Kai Shek and the painful parting from Bobby when he was a young boy, the family enjoyed time together in freedom. If Bobby harbored any resentment toward his parents for being given to others to care for him, understanding the circumstances and their bravery must have helped him adjust to his life in the United States.

I am sure Uncle Peter and Aunt Edith welcomed their return to Hawaii. They must have been gratified, though, to see on their trip how widely the Young Marshal was respected and how much their incarceration increased the level of respect. Chiang Kai Shek no doubt damaged his own reputation by being so insistent on controlling their lives and refusing them freedom, when their so-called crime had been to save the people of Manchuria from the atrocities committed by the Japanese.

Aunt Edith died in 2000, and there can be no doubt Uncle Peter keenly felt her absence. Mommy said the Chinese believe if one of a longtime couple dies, the danger point for survival of the other partner would be two years. If the partner survived for two years, he or she could survive countless more. At the time of Auntie's passing, Uncle was losing his hearing and also his eyesight. Relatives living in Hawaii near him visited daily, and he had around-the-clock caretakers. The Young Marshal passed away in 2001 at the age of 101, one year after becoming a widower.

We attended his funeral in Hawaii and were deeply moved to see that not only were official representatives of both Communist and Nationalist governments sent to honor Uncle, but also, hordes of young Chinese attended. Students who had studied the Xian Incident came to pay their respects to a Chinese national hero. Uncle and Auntie are entombed side by side on a lovely hillside in Honolulu (figure 30). A large group of relatives were at the funeral, most of whom I did not know (figure 31). I will identify only those sitting in the front row and a few who are standing. I will not give their Chinese names but only their relationships in the family. In the front row, second from the left, is Cousin Bobby, Uncle Peter's and Auntie Edith's son, whom they gave to an American to raise when they were incarcerated; his wife, Nora, is seated to Bobby's right. To Bobby's left, in order, are my sixth aunt (the only child of the Old Marshal still alive at the time of this writing), seventh uncle's widow, second uncle's widow, fifth uncle's widow, and fourth uncle's widow. Bobby's half sister, Uncle Peter's daughter, Pauline, is farthest right in the front row. My fifth uncle's daughters, Linda and Gloria, are dressed in white behind my fifth uncle's widow. David and I are in the back row, farthest right. Linda has been a wonderful help in identifying members of the family.

The reunion with her brother in New York City for his ninetieth birthday, however, was not entirely something that gave my mother pleasure. Shortly after Uncle Peter and Aunt Edith returned to Hawaii, Mommy told me that Uncle had given her younger sister, my fifth aunt, $5,000. With hurt in her voice, she lamented that he had not given her a penny.

Not knowing how close they were as siblings, I could not understand why Uncle had acted as he did. I tried to assuage Mommy's feelings by saying that he might have felt my fifth aunt and uncle needed monetary help more than Mommy and Daddy. But while I was trying to help her feel better, Mommy only shrugged, as she usually did when I appeared to disagree, and dismissed me as not understanding anything. I wasn't disagreeing, yet I could not even voice that protest.

Once again, I felt my limitations in the Chinese language keenly because I could not communicate as I knew I could in English. Yet Mommy would not be able to understand me or my thoughts because of her limitations in English. I have no doubt that the language barrier, as much as anything, as I mentioned earlier, was the reason for our dysfunctional relationship: we had no way to communicate.

I knew she was deeply hurt and felt left out. I am certain she considered this a slap in the face and would not forget the pain. I wish I could have made her feel better.

Fig. 19 General Yang Hucheng (left), Young Marshal (center), Chiang Kai Shek (right)

Fig. 20 Hua Qing Tse, Site of the Xian incident, now a museum

Fig 21 Chiang Kai Shek's bedroom at the resort

Fig. 22 A young Zhao Yi Ti

Fig. 23 A young Zhang Xueliang

Fig. 24. My cousin, Bobby Zhang and I at the funeral service for his father, the Young Marshal

Fig. 25 General Bai Chongxi, my father-in-law

Fig 26 The Young Marshal and Zhao Sze enjoying a visit on Taiwan

Fig 27 Uncle at 85 with David

Fig 28 Uncle Peter and Aunt Edith with Jeannie and Solan

Fig 29 Behind Uncle Peter and Aunt Edith are Fifth Uncle's wife (center) flanked by three daughters and a son-in-law

Fig 30 The flower bedecked tombs of Uncle Peter and Aunt Edith in Hawaii

Fig 31 The Zhang family at the funeral of the Young Marshal

Chapter 7

LIFE AS A MANCHURIAN PRINCESS

In Loh Yeh's turbulent and exciting household, Mommy grew up as the eldest of four children by the Old Marshal's fourth wife. Among all the daughters of the Old Marshal, she was number three (see again figure 3).

The opulence that surrounded her is difficult for me to relate to. On a family *Roots*-like trip to China in 2005, our guide in Shenyang told us there was said to be one hundred cooks during the Old Marshal's rule. That figure is difficult for me to accept. Perhaps there were different cooks assigned to the different wives and their families. When I asked the guide about it, he only shrugged. At that time, we were told there were also quite a few soldiers living in and around the compound. That too would have increased the need for cooks.

At any time of the day or night, Mommy recounted, she could call the kitchen for any dish she wished to eat. They had two kitchens: one for Chinese food and one for Western cuisine. The latter was considered a special treat for them. She always enjoyed eating Western food, something for which we were grateful by the time she had to be moved to assisted-living facilities in the United States.

Each wife and her children lived in a separate house on the family compound. They did not always get along. Mommy remembered ostracizing the children of a stepmother she did not like. In fact, she boasted with little sign of embarrassment or remorse that she once had driven a young concubine from the compound.

Everyone had a personal servant along with the general servants. Indeed, Mommy said, some of the servants had their own servants. She couldn't remember how many servants in all there were. The children of her generation usually were not allowed knowledge of political or military goings-on, especially the girls. How can we ordinary people relate to such an opulent life style?

One famous incident occurred right in their house in Manchuria shortly after the death of the Old Marshal. The Young Marshal was certain there had been inside information given to the Japanese so they knew which car the Old Marshal would be in on that last fateful train ride, one reason being that Japanese officials who were on the train that was bombed left the train at the station before the bombing took place.

According to Pauline Tao, Uncle's oldest child, Uncle believed the evidence pointed to two men. One was an officer in the Manchurian military command. His name was Yang Yuting. He attended the Japanese Military Academy as a young man at the behest of the Old Marshal. Apparently gifted, he became chief of staff for the Old Marshal and then governor of Jiangsu Province.

The second man was Tsong Minkuai, who was governor of Heilongjiang Province in Manchuria and also worked under my grandfather, the Old Marshal. In 1929, the year following the assassination, the two men established the Manchurian Railroad Administration with Tsong in charge. The railroad was built by the Japanese. The project was a continuation of close ties that both men had with the Japanese during the Old Marshal's control of Manchuria. Pauline mentioned that Japanese so-called advisers were everywhere.

Further, after Uncle resumed control of the Manchurian forces following the death of his father, he was openly disrespected by both Yang and Tsong. They were known to disobey orders and were open in their feelings about him. Uncle believed the two were interested in usurping power from him but would need Japanese help to be successful.

Pauline said there was talk about what to do about the two men. Uncle wanted to arrest them and jail them, but Uncle's first wife, Pauline's mother, persuaded him that left alive, they would be unending sources of trouble. Further, if they had been involved in the assassination, they deserved to be executed. Her words helped Uncle come to the decision to have them eliminated. He invited both men to dinner at home and used that occasion to put an end to their lives.

Mommy said the Young Marshal told his younger siblings to stay away from the room in which he was to entertain the traitors. Yang's favorite fruit was a Chinese melon usually grown in the western provinces, *ha mi gua*. When that was served, it was the signal for one of Uncle's aides to shoot both men. So the executions took place right in the home. Pauline said she heard the gunshots.

We saw the room when we visited the mansion in Shenyang on a trip in 2005. It was called the Tiger Room because there were two stuffed tigers in it (figure 32). I assume they were hunted and shot by Uncle. If this sounds to our modern American ears like unusually barbaric behavior, it occurs to me that similar frontier justice was also practiced early in the twentieth century in the Wild West of America.

Mommy and her sisters spent their days learning to be good wives and being tutored. Mommy never attended school, though her younger sister was allowed to attend school in England for a time. Lo Lo was pretty progressive, from what Mommy said. For example, she would not allow her daughters to experience the agony of bound feet. Her own feet had been bound, but they were not as badly disabled as the feet of some—she could walk. I always found it unbelievable that her toes were curled under her feet.

According to Mommy, Lo Yeh loved Lo Lo, but she could not easily accept his taking on other concubines, although she herself was the fourth wife, nor did she want to be his concubine, but her parents forced her to accept him. He was, after all, the Tiger of Manchuria. Mommy believed her spirit was what Lo Yeh admired in Lo Lo.

Mommy remembered that Lo Lo frequently railed against being a concubine and the restrictions that were placed on women in those days, such as the lack of an equal amount of education as the men. That Lo Lo allowed her youngest daughter, my fifth aunt, to attend school overseas in England was almost unheard of and another indication of her strong will. No doubt her discontent was what led to her refusal to give Mommy's picture to the last emperor.

In those days of multiple wives, the children were numbered chronologically and not just within their own family group. The boys were numbered separately from the girls. Thus, Mommy was daughter number three, her younger sister was my fifth aunt (another girl had been born between the two to a different wife), and Mommy's two full brothers were my third and fourth uncles. By his six wives, the Old Marshal had eight sons, who are shown in chronological order in an indistinct photograph (figure 33), and six daughters (see again figure 3). All but the youngest daughter have passed on as of this writing.

Fig 32 The Tiger Room

Fig 33 Eight sons of my LoYeh

Chapter 8

HALCYON DAYS IN BEIJING

As I mentioned earlier, we children never really saw our parents much while we were living in China, only when they were in the mood to play with us. We each had our own nursemaid. Rich people in those days hired women who were lactating to nurse their infants. I don't remember the name of my nursemaid anymore, but I do remember I felt comfortable with her—more comfortable than with my own mother.

She was a kind-looking, attractive young woman. I'm sure I felt a bond with her that was similar to the bond most infants have with their mothers in America. I just hope she did not suffer much in her life. My leaving her when I was three to immigrate to America must have been difficult for both of us. I wish I knew her name. I would have looked her up on our trips in the 1980s to China. Figure 34 is the only photograph I have of my nursemaid. In it, she is holding me, and I am fat and happy.

Daddy once drew a diagram of our house at Bei Ping Ma Se (figure 35). Our living quarters were surrounded by a garden on the right side of the large, square property as one entered the front door. On the left side were two stables, a tennis court, some servants' quarters, a garage, and a jai alai court.

Daddy, who was a good athlete, and friends used to play jai alai, a fast-paced sport in which the players have curved baskets tied onto their wrists, and they hurl a hard rubber ball against the wall of the arena. There are two men to a team, and points are won depending on where the ball is thrown against the walls and bounces and how the ball is retrieved by the other team.

I have never played the sport and have only seen it played once, in Florida, where there was much betting going on about the players and who would win. Daddy told us the sport could be dangerous because the ball was hard, and the ball could be thrown to travel at high speeds, well in excess of one hundred miles an hour.

There was also a tennis court. Tennis had just gotten the attention of the rich in China at that time, in the mid-1930s. Uncle, the Young Marshal, had a tennis court at his elegant home. He told us a story about having asked an older man who had never seen tennis played to come watch him play a set. At the end of play, Uncle asked his friend, "Well, what do you think of tennis?"

His friend replied, "It was very interesting but seemed to require so much energy. Why don't you tell someone to play for you?" Spoken like a true Chinese aristocrat of the times—who obviously missed the point of the sport!

At the front of our house, a sentry house stood guard and led to a long walk to the entrance. A small temple for worshipping ancestors was on the outside, as well as a house for one of our uncles. At the front door, the entrance led to an all-purpose room to receive guests. Then came a courtyard with another parlor on the right, next to the garden, and a house on the left, which was initially for Mommy but later changed to a study.

One of my fondest memories of the Beijing house from the trip I took with Mommy and Lo Lo in 1950 (which I will discuss further in chapter 14) was an apricot tree in one of the courtyards. It produced abundant fruit. When the fruit was ripe, we picked those on lower branches by hand. A couple of the servants and I used long sticks to hit the branches with fruit too high for us to reach. We easily knocked the ripe apricots off the branches, and the fruit fell down onto a few layers of sheets on the ground. It was so much fun, and the fruit could not have been sweeter.

There were a number of rooms that were the residence of Nai Nai, Daddy's mother. As one left Nai Nai's house, there was another courtyard. To the left of the courtyard was the house in which we children lived with our maids. To the right was Daddy's study. Then was a house for our parents, which stretched the width of the courtyard adjacent to more servants' quarters. The kitchen was probably in the area of the servants' quarters. The diagram was probably not drawn to scale, as it was done purely by memory.

The compound was typical of Chinese residences of the rich, with tiled roofs and elegant wood carvings of gates and windows, such as in figure 36. See also figure 37 behind my parents.

There was no central heating, of course; there was no electricity. I remember shivering while we took sponge baths in the winter. On cold nights, in addition to thick blankets and quilts, servants placed heated bricks—wrapped with towels to prevent burns—under the top sheets of our beds to warm the beds before we got in for the night. We had a well dug near the entrance to our property that supplied us with cool water useful to cool watermelons that we placed in the well bucket in the summertime. The water had to be boiled to be potable. There was always a supply of boiled water, both hot and cold, in the house. Even today, visitors to China are given boiled water to drink.

There were outhouses on the property that were emptied by so-called night-soil collectors, who then sold the night soil to farmers to be used as fertilizer. After the Communists won the civil war, estates such as ours were to be given to as many families as there was room for. Many were torn down to be replaced by multistory buildings.

One aspect of the design of the houses caused me considerable pain as a toddler. Each doorway into the compound, for some reason, had a piece of wood at ground level that jutted upward several inches and covered the entire entrance so that one had to step over the piece of wood to gain entrance. Perhaps it was to keep evil spirits out or to hinder people whose presence was not welcome. One day we were returning from an outing, and I was told we had visitors. Delighted and excited, I ran to enter the compound to see them.

Being around two years old, I did not negotiate the step over the wood well, and I tripped, falling headfirst and gashing the tip of my chin when I fell. They called a doctor, and with the help of several people to hold me still, I received stitches to the wound—without anesthesia. I don't remember much more than screaming bloody murder the whole time. I still have a small scar on my chin, but it's not noticeable unless you look closely. It was a well-executed but painful treatment!

For my parents, those six years or so of living in Beijing were the most comfortable of their married life in China. The second of Daddy's twenty-fifth-anniversary poems focused on happy memories for them. They and their marriage had matured (figure 37), and they were parents of three young children. Solan was three years older than I. He was born in 1932, and Stanley was about a year and a half older than I (figure 38). They were born at home with the help of midwives. I was the only one born in a hospital. I have wondered if the difficulties Stanley had at his birth caused our parents to depend on a hospital when I was due. The poem Daddy wrote with the photograph of them at home in Beijing (figure 37) spoke of the years we were in Beijing before war against Japan was declared formally in 1937. Recall that we were in Beijing because the Japanese had invaded Manchuria in 1931. The poem ended with the need for us to immigrate immediately to a country they thought was populated, in his words, by "barbarians" but one that promised safety from Japan. It was the end of their Shangri-La:

> These were good days after our marriage, in Beijing.
>
> We had a wonderful life, the life of aristocrats!
>
> We produced children; they were the fruit of our tree.
>
> You advised me to continue my education, to learn more.
>
> I tried, but I did not feel I lived up to expectations.
>
> I frequently practiced writing and art.
>
> All of a sudden like a thunderbolt—war broke out!
>
> We had to leave home and join barbarians!

The last word in the poem was what they thought of Americans—not very different from what Americans thought of Chinese in those days. Ignorance existed on both parts.

We left China to come to the United States in 1938. The third of Daddy's twenty-fifty-anniversary poems dealt with the crushing development of immigration. The photograph was of my parents on the boat taking them away from their home and a lifestyle they did not know they would never again enjoy (figure 39).

> We make a journey of 30,000 li away from Mother.
>
> My lasting regret is that I never saw her alive again.

I became a minor official; though I never pushed for myself.

I accepted a place in life as someone unimportant …

If I could climb on clouds, so what of it?

I see conflict in this world through my work in the United Nations.

I am saddened by the lack of peace.

I fear so small a chance of peace, perhaps in 10,000 years?

Can you feel in this poem his disappointment in himself for not having reached a position of renown, as he had been brought up to achieve? In his mind, it did not matter how well he performed as a simultaneous interpreter—he had failed his parents. This unrealistic expectation of young Asian men placed an extreme pressure on their lives.

We had to return to China a year later because Nai Nai had become sick. She was a heavy smoker. She was not that old, probably only in her late fifties or early sixties. By the end of her life, she was quite gaunt (figure 40).

Alas, in those days, travel by boat from California to China took weeks, and by the time we reached Beijing, Nai Nai had already passed away. We children were not told what illness she had. Her weight loss might have resulted from heart problems, cancer, or maybe emphysema, to which Daddy himself would eventually succumb. He had started smoking at the age of twelve. The cigarettes available to them in China were probably coarsely made compared to those in the United States.

As people came to the house to pay their respects, I watched the funeral from afar since children were not allowed to take part. Embedded in my mind is the sight of a man with a shaved head kneeling in front of the coffin and crying so hard he drooled. To a toddler, that was an amazing sight, to know that grown men could cry like that.

Her death made a deep impression on me. It was the first time I realized we humans are all mortal. One night in bed, I suddenly thought of myself as an old woman about to die. I cried and cried in fear, but I could not explain my feelings to anyone. It occurs to me now that I was so young, as were my brothers, that no one had ever spoken to us about death. I did not know the words related to death. The maids were all concerned and could not understand my discomfort.

Fig 34 My nursemaid and me

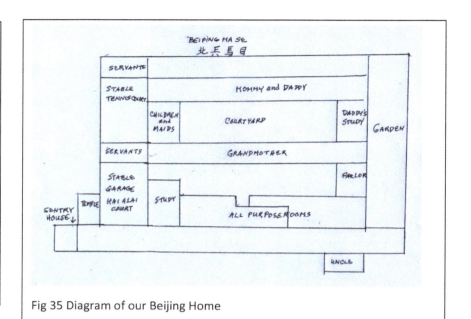
Fig 35 Diagram of our Beijing Home

Fig 36 Elegant carvings and window treatments

Fig 37 Mommy and Daddy circa 1937

Fig 38 My brothers and I circa 1938

負笈重洋三萬里
慈萱永別恨難忘
寧屈小夾孤永逵
縱過書玄賞足狂
國際風塵多擾攘
人情冷暖德妻涂
向平未了終為願
一匱功虧萬年傷

Fig 39 On the boat carrying them to a new life

Fig 40 Nai Nai circa 1939

Chapter 9

MY EARLY YEARS IN THE UNITED STATES

When we first came to the United States in 1938, Daddy enrolled at Cornell University in Ithaca, New York, to study sociology. I began my schooling in Ithaca, where I was enrolled in nursery school. I was actually a year younger than my passport indicated, so I began school a full year younger than the other children in my class. Without any ability to speak English at the time, I could not communicate with my teachers when I needed to go to the bathroom the first day. I was in tears until they realized what was wrong. It was a scary time for me, but if my parents said I was to go to school, I went, no matter how unhappy I was. Figure 41 shows the house we lived in while Daddy studied at Cornell University. Figure 42 shows Mommy in her first role as an American housewife. She does not look happy. I do not remember ever having a Boston terrier in the family, but I would not be surprised if the dog in the picture was ours. Mommy loved dogs. I have a distinct memory of many garter snakes in our backyard. There were so many that we lost our fear of the wriggly black things.

I now find it remarkable how quickly Mommy was able to adjust to the life of a housewife, whether or not she was happy to be one. As I mentioned before, she had never seen the inside of a kitchen, but she became a good cook of Chinese dishes. Figure 43 shows Mommy sitting at a sewing machine, making clothes. She was capable of making the Chinese dresses that were uncomfortable but complementary when worn with the side slits up to the level of the knees or higher. I am certain she was taught sewing by a Chinese person, and it was a skill for which she should have gotten credit from Daddy. We children did not think anything of her ability to cook and sew. Wasn't that what mothers were supposed to do?

While life was difficult early in our transition to life in the United State and I struggled to learn English, I did make some friends in the year we spent in Ithaca. Figure 44 shows me with a child with whom I was obviously a close friend. Thank goodness young children pick up language easily and quickly!

It is typical of a child that one of my few memories of that time of life was a call from the police that a crazy man was on the loose and might be in our region. I believe there was what we called an insane asylum not far from our house. The call ordered that all children should stay indoors and not play outdoors until we were notified it was safe. We stayed in the house and peeked through the curtains in both excitement and apprehension. We never saw him, and we were all terribly disappointed when the all-clear call came.

For reasons that are not clear to me, perhaps because of the winters in Ithaca, when we returned to the United States in 1940 after his mother died, Daddy decided to transfer to Duke University to finish his master's degree in sociology. We moved frequently—every year after that—in the 1940s. My brothers and I never knew why we were moving at any time. Since we had been essentially brainwashed that we were not to question anything our parents said or did, we simply followed orders. It was the Chinese way.

I first really learned to speak English in Durham, North Carolina (figure 45). It must have been comical to hear a little Chinese kid speaking English with a Chinese *and* a southern American accent. When we moved north later, I remember being laughed at for pronouncing *crayons* as "cree-ons," with the accent on the last syllable, but that was the way I'd learned the word.

While we were in Durham, World War II started for the United States. Daddy was listening to the broadcast of a Duke football game, when an announcement came over the loudspeakers at the field that all military personnel had to report to their headquarters. It was, of course, a result of the bombing of Pearl Harbor by the Japanese on December 7, 1941. My parents were not unhappy that the bombing had happened, because we knew the United States would now join the Chinese fight against the Japanese. While war against the Japanese had been officially declared in 1937 in China, it was a fight that China had been waging, without much success, since the invasion of Manchuria in 1931. Our country desperately needed the help of the United States.

We had a victory garden in Durham, and I remember helping—or so I thought—Mommy plant the garden and water the seeds she let me put in the ground. Knowing how poor the soil is now, with much clay, I wonder if our efforts ever yielded more than a small harvest. I do remember picking cucumbers and being told to take a bite because it would be delicious. I didn't think it was delicious, though—but it did mean that we got things to grow.

Growing vegetables must have seemed to Lo Lo and Mommy (Daddy was never a participant, as he was studying in graduate school) like the same kind of hardship a peasant in China would have experienced, but they seemed to enjoy their work. As a child, I could not put in perspective the fact that the Old Marshal's daughter now had to plant seeds for food. I admired their ability to have plants grow, as the seeds I put in the ground myself never seemed to germinate.

I shared a bedroom with Lo Lo when she lived with us. She used to make me laugh when she bent her legs, because her knees made such a clicking noise. My knees also clicked but only as I squatted or did exercises in gym class in school. Hers made multiple clicks as she bent her legs. In Durham, I saw Lo Lo moving slowly on the front walk, bent over, feeding the ants with crumbs of bread. As I said earlier, I guess I know from whom my mother's and my love of animals came, though I do know that Lo Yeh, the Old Marshal, was a veterinarian in his younger adult years.

While Lo Lo was my roommate, I saw the result of a Chinese tradition I mentioned earlier, the binding of women's feet, which I believe is one of the most barbaric traditions ever perpetrated against women. Lo Lo's feet had been bound but not to the extent that was thought to be the ultimate form, the ideal known as golden lotus, which was as small as three inches. Women with golden-lotus feet had to be carried, as they could not balance on such small feet or tolerate the pain. Lo Lo could at least walk, though not fast and never far.

To keep the feet so small, binding began when the child was young, around age four to seven years. Many bones in the growing foot had to break, and Lo Lo's toes were severely bent under the soles of the feet. Sometimes the toenails were also removed to prevent the nails from growing into the soles (figure 46). Fortunately for my mother and her sisters, this torture was not practiced on them.

Lo Lo never complained about having to have her feet bound. No matter how cruel the tradition, if it is something one grows up with, it is usually accepted, until enough members of society realize its cruelty and rebel. None of the girls in the family of the Old Marshal had her feet bound, and the tradition was abandoned for the most part in the early twentieth century.

One day, while living in Durham, for reasons I don't recall but most likely due to racism, my brothers and I got into an argument with some local black children. The argument concluded with their telling us to go back to China and our telling them to go back to Africa. We went home to get our cocker spaniel, a sweet dog named Ping ("Peace" in Chinese), as our ally. When they saw him, the black children ran away, and we were proud and petted Ping on the head for, we thought, having run them off. Then they returned with a German shepherd, and I think Ping, our erstwhile warrior, beat all of us back to our house!

The argument might also have had something to do with the war. Although the Chinese were eventually glorified in movies as allies and brave fighters against the Japanese, people in the United States could not distinguish between Chinese and Japanese by appearance alone. To avoid being castigated, Chinese children sometimes had notes pinned on them saying they were Chinese.

In those days, there were far fewer Chinese in America overall because of the immigration quotas that existed as law in the United States for many decades. It should be remembered that the Chinese Exclusion Act of 1882 was still in place at that time.

The law had been enacted when Chinese immigrants were considered a job threat to American workers, even though some of the Chinese workers had been kidnapped and brought to the United States in the manner in which African men were brought to the United States: in chains as slaves. Chinese women were similarly kidnapped to become prostitutes. Other Chinese came on their own in search of the riches purported to be everywhere. One name the Chinese gave to San Francisco, for example, was Jiu Jin Shan, or "Old Gold Mountain."

When competition between the Chinese immigrants and American workers and European immigrants escalated, it led to a period in which there was an attempt at ethnic cleansing of Chinese. Because there were greater concentrations of Chinese in the western states of America, actions taken against them were more numerous and more severe there than in the East.

Chinatowns across the West were burned to the ground, and lynching was not uncommon. A book authored by Jean Pfaelzer, *Driven Out,* documents (remove the underscore) this period in the second half of the nineteenth century. This was the disturbing history behind the Chinese Exclusion Act of 1882. It is something that many—probably most—Americans have never heard of. The Chinese culture, however, has not caused Chinese immigrants to have a widespread feeling of deserving or expecting entitlements because of past atrocities. Instead, we just feel we have to do better than anyone, including Americans, in every field so that people will want us to work with them. It was another pressure on young Chinese to succeed in academia.

Only when the United States and China were resisting the Japanese aggression together as allies during World War II did President Franklin Delano Roosevelt finally feel compelled to ask Congress to repeal the Chinese Exclusion Act. The repeal did not occur until December 1943, two years after the United States declared war against the Japanese. Finally, China was then deemed a critical ally for tying down a large Japanese force on its mainland.

Fig 41 Our first house in America

Fig 42 Mommy experiences life as a house wife

Fig 43 Mommy at a sewing machine making clothes

Fig 44 Me and probably my first friend in the United States

Fig 45 Daddy and me in Durham, NC in 1940

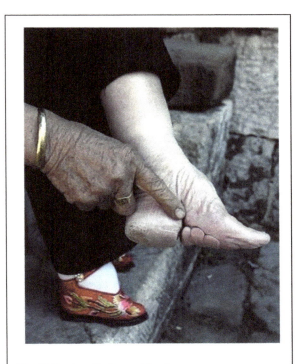
Fig 46 Photo of a bound foot

Chapter 10

ACADEMIA AND SELF-WORTH

When I was in second grade, I was told one day to go to the auditorium of my school and then ushered onto the stage. Bewildered, I was given some piece of paper with a few other children. The audience applauded us, though I wasn't sure for what, and we were sent back to our classrooms. The award, my father later explained, was for scholarship of distinction. I had no idea what the words meant, but I knew the award was something good because it pleased my parents. Daddy took me to a five-and-dime store and told me I could buy anything I wanted. I bought a bag of marbles for about twenty cents. I was a tomboy to the hilt!

Most readers will not remember the life Americans had during the war, when everyone was encouraged to support the war effort by understanding why everyday items would be difficult to obtain. I also remember that I won a spelling contest in my class, perhaps in the third grade. The prize was a small box of safety pins, which my mother and grandmother were happy to receive from me when I got home from school.

Those were the first two of a number of academic honors and awards I have received in my life, all the way through to the end of my career as an academician. I can honestly say I never felt myself the equal of fellow students or colleagues of whom I thought highly. When my major professor in college, Miss Belcher, called me to say that I would be inducted as an alumna into Sweet Briar College's Theta chapter of Phi Beta Kappa, that otherwise august organization took an immediate hit in my estimation. If I could get in, I thought, then they must have accepted very ordinary minds!

One of the things in my life that I would change if I could was declining to attend the induction ceremony at Sweet Briar College. My family was living in New Jersey at the time. We didn't have much money, but we had enough for me to buy a plane ticket. I chose not to go because I thought it was wasteful to spend the money to allow me to be honored in person. I know Miss Belcher was disappointed that I was not there, and it bothered me that she was. Maybe she had made a strong argument in my favor.

I attribute my feeling of being unworthy of honors to Chinese culture, in which children are urged to excel and not told how wonderful they are at every turn, as we now treat our grandchildren. "Good job!" is a constant in our conversations with our grandchildren. My parents rarely gave my brothers and me praise. To excel was simply what was expected. But we knew they were pleased when we received some kind of recognition for our work, as in the event for which I was allowed to buy marbles. Poor Stanley was constantly being scolded for not excelling. I believe Chinese culture is too extreme in its pressure on youngsters to excel, and American culture is too extreme in the other direction; it is not demanding enough.

Our parents seemed to be freer with praise as we entered adulthood, but I remember more instances of being chewed out than praised as a child. That type of upbringing no doubt leaves one with the feeling that one can never be good enough. My big brother Solan received the brunt of their criticism, as he was the number-one son and, in the classical system of Chinese families, was expected to be the one to take over the family when he matured.

Sometimes when I run across a forgotten paper of mine, written years earlier, I find myself thinking, *Hey, this is pretty good!* As I got older, I realized that due to waiting tables for four years in college, playing and starting on varsity teams every semester, holding student government office every year, and majoring in the toughest major in the school (biology), it is somewhat understandable that I did not graduate even cum laude, though I thought my average was good enough (I remember seeing once that I was seventh in my class in grade point average). I simply felt I was not smart enough and was disappointed that my parents could not revel in an honor for me at graduation.

Is it in my genes, or did my parents instill in me this feeling of never being good enough despite some evidence to the contrary? I found myself often being asked to be chair or an officer no matter where I went or what organization I joined, and time and again, colleagues asked me to represent the biology department I taught in at Montclair State University in New Jersey in important matters. Yet my feeling was that the requests came because the others were less able than ordinary, and I was only ordinary, not because I was extraordinary.

If there is anything I can say for myself, it is that the fear of failure—and believe me, it was there—never stopped me from trying to do something, whether in sports or academia. Did I think I was PhD material? I never even thought I would be able to finish a master's degree program. I never thought I was capable of anything out of the ordinary. Thank goodness there were others to show me the way.

The help I received as a student in believing I was capable of more than I thought I could do was something I kept in mind during my own career as an educator. My favorite letter from a student was from a biology major known to be a C student. She worked hard in my class and came to see me often during my office hours, and she ended up with a well-earned B grade. The letter thanked me for showing her that she had the ability to be a better student than she'd thought she could be. You are welcome, young lady, and you need not thank me, but thank my teachers.

Chapter 11

WE MOVE TO WASHINGTON, DC

After Daddy got his MA in sociology at Duke, which was pretty useless as a career base for a Chinese in America at that time, in keeping with the classical Chinese tradition of civil service, we moved to Washington, DC. A big problem developed: Daddy received a draft notice. It had to be a mistake, I thought. There we were, Mommy without any ability to take care of us because she could hardly speak English and three young children—eleven, not quite ten, and seven. Fortunately, he was able to get a job at the Chinese embassy, which protected him from the draft.

We stayed in and around Washington for a few years, for the duration of the war. Although I was only around eight, I remember hearing about the death of Franklin Roosevelt while I was at a playground, on a swing. I didn't understand why people were so sad since, in those days, there was no television to provide instant news. I did not listen to news on the radio either because I preferred *Jack Armstrong*, *The Shadow*, and all those good programs. Do you remember the decoding rings that came in cereal boxes? I was always disappointed in the messages I decoded. They were all kind of silly, I thought.

One milestone in my maturation occurred while we lived in Washington. A game my brothers and I liked to play was cowboys and Indians. Of course, cowboys were the good guys and always chased the bad Indians. We didn't have any toy guns, so we used our forefingers and shouted, "Bam! Bam! You're dead!" One day, while playing that game, I happened to look at a passerby who was smiling patronizingly at me. Suddenly, my extended arm and pointed forefinger seemed to me to be embarrassing. I never played that game again. I was ten.

At that point, our family finances were apparently falling apart, because there was talk about having to go back to China. As an adult, I can now understand why my parents were in such a bad mood so often. Money difficulties cause many relationships to develop resentments. Add to that the fact that my parents were immigrants in a country they never fully understood or adjusted to. It is not surprising to me that they ran out of the money (probably gold) they had brought with them from China.

Times were tough. Someone stole our amah, a term we used for an all-purpose maid. My family had brought her with us when we immigrated, but she left us for better pay elsewhere. That didn't help my mother either. Not having domestic help was an entirely new experience for my parents, and things happened as a result of their never having had to be the sole adults to care for their children.

My oldest brother, Solan, became ill with the mumps while we were living in DC. He was around thirteen, and I was ten. One night, my parents went out, and Solan developed a high fever. I woke up when I heard some noise. It was my big brother walking around. He either was walking in his sleep or was delirious. Stanley was up too, and the two of us didn't know what to do since Solan was bigger than both of us. I followed him fearfully and watched him bump hard into a wall and moan as he fell backward. The impact kind of woke him up, and he went back to bed.

Stanley and I went back to bed too, but I stayed awake and was glad to hear Mommy and Daddy come home. I have to believe they were willing to leave us alone because they didn't know how sick Solan was. It scared the two of us younger siblings badly. I was afraid Solan was going to get violent, and then what would we do? Remember that cell phones were not in existence at that time. As a parent now, I know I would not have left three children alone with the eldest sick. It just is another example of how impractical and ignorant my parents were regarding parenting, but remember that they never had to do any parenting in China.

I have some good memories of the years we spent in Washington too: the movies cost us children eleven cents during the day on weekends, and we got to see part of a serial, maybe a cartoon, and a main feature. My brothers would urge me to ask for the money for the movies. I guess I was the favorite or at least the child least likely to get yelled at. Ice cream sodas cost ten cents, and we could go to High's Ice Cream Parlor and get a five-cent cone that contained not just a scoop but a slab of ice cream. On a hot, humid Washington, DC, summer day, nothing tasted better. We would walk to the shop after dinner as a family, and we children would be in a high state of excitement.

Around that time, I got my first inkling that I had athletic potential. I ran down to the corner drugstore one beautiful day. For some reason, I was full of myself and wanted to run as fast as I could, and I had to dodge pedestrians at full speed. *Wow,* I thought, *they probably think I'm really fast and admire me for moving so well.* Looking back on that moment, I guess the truth was probably that they were annoyed with the Chinese kid who was running through, in front of, and around them. Ah, the innocence of youth!

When I realized that perhaps I was able to do things athletically better than most people, I began to play sports in earnest—not with other girls, however, as I found that my big brother Solan, a good athlete himself and one often chosen to be a captain (an amazing fact given that we were usually the new kids on the block), and his buddies accepted me as someone who could play ball with them. I played baseball and flag football with them. In fact, when Solan and another boy were choosing players for their teams, I was chosen before some boys. I cannot remember playing sports with any other girls in those days.

One difference between my mother and me was that she always enjoyed having dolls, even to her last days. She never could understand why I would choose sports over playing with dolls. I always felt dolls were boring. If we were to have a conversation, I'd have to supply both sides of it for the doll. I would have much preferred to have a baby sister.

My interest and participation in sports became another source of conflict between my mother and me. In her mind, for girls to engage in activities that normally were for boys was something she found unacceptable. For one thing, she was worried that acting like a boy eventually would cause me difficulty socially.

"Boys will not think about you as a date," she warned, "and you will have trouble getting married."

Since I was a preteen, her warning did not fill my head with dread. Besides, I was having too much fun. Another problem in Mommy's mind was that my exposure to the sun day in and day out was giving me a deep tan. Part of the Chinese ideal for beauty in women in my mother's day was to be as lily white in skin color as possible.

She admonished me to wear hats to protect my face. However, this tomboy found wearing hats was not helpful when searching the sky for a pop-up or running hard and trying to keep a hat on my head. Most of the time, I simply abandoned the hat shortly after a game began.

In those days, we did not have sunscreen, and there was no knowledge that the sun could give people skin cancer. We did not know, as we do now, that tanning was the skin's only way of protecting itself from damage from UV light.

Mommy, you were right to nag me about protecting myself from the sun. Now that I am eighty, I have liver spots everywhere on my face and on my arms and legs, where I was exposed to the sun while wearing sleeveless tops and shorts. I wish I could have told her this.

CHAPTER 12

OUR LIVES AS IMMIGRANTS

We had immigrated to America to escape certain death at the hands of the Japanese. Lo Lo and her children, with the exception of my fourth uncle, who stayed to fight the Japanese, all came to the United States. Mommy only briefly described the chaos that we fled as the Japanese advanced from Manchuria to the south. Daddy was always sent to safety first, while Mommy stayed behind to shepherd us children to safety.

I always accepted Mommy's professed courage during those difficult days. After Daddy found safety in Hong Kong, she had to take a trip to rejoin us children in Beijing that required she be on a train going through Japanese lines. She told me she dressed as a Buddhist and pretended to be saying prayers with prayer beads the whole time. She said the Japanese, being Buddhist themselves, left her alone.

I thought of her situation and how courageous she had to be to expose herself to possible detection and subsequent fatal consequences.

It confused me later when she would become irrational with fear at what, to my mind, were small physical pains, such as the thought of having to go to the dentist. She bit her dentist one time! I guess one does what one has to do, especially when children are involved.

When we lived in Durham while Daddy was studying at Duke University, Lo Lo made a pet of a squirrel that would come running when he heard her crack walnuts and pecans outside during the day. I remember trying to pet the squirrel and getting a bite on the finger for my troubles. Did you know that squirrel teeth are as sharp as needles and easily penetrate flesh? In those days, we were blissfully ignorant of rabies and other problems plaguing animals that we know of today.

As much as I loved her, Lo Lo was the source of perhaps my most traumatic experience as a child, when I was around ten years old. We were living in Washington, DC, and Lo Lo was renting an apartment in the house next to ours. I was playing in the driveway and heard a bloodcurdling yell from normally quiet and dignified Lo Lo. Startled, I looked up. She was leaning out of her second-floor window. She was crying and screaming at me to get Mommy.

Always meticulous, usually with hair put up in a bun, her long hair that day was loose and blowing around and over her face with the wind. She was having a nervous breakdown and looked it. For years afterward, I had nightmares of her suddenly appearing in my bedroom doorway at night and coming toward me in that state. I would wake up terrified.

I ran to get Mommy, who ran into Lo Lo's apartment. Mommy told me later she pinned Lo Lo to the bed and screamed at her to cry it out. I have no idea what a medical professional would have done, but what Mommy did worked, as Lo Lo calmed down eventually and was normal again in a couple of days. I had a real respect for what my mother did in the crisis because I was so frightened by my grandmother's appearance. That she even was willing to confront Lo Lo at the time was something I greatly admired. I wish I had told Mommy that at some point.

In our entire lives in the United States, Mommy rarely did anything that would elicit respect on our part. In hindsight and now that I am much older than she was when Lo Lo had her breakdown, I realize part of the reason was that Mommy never had command of English, nor was she exposed to life in America to any extent since her friends were all Chinese immigrants and socialized only with one another. Linguistically and culturally, we could not communicate with our mother as we would have liked.

In those days, Chinese never spoke about seeing a psychologist or a psychiatrist when someone in family had a mental or behavioral problem. To suggest going to such a specialist would have implied that the person was crazy. Later in our lives, when Mommy became more and more irrational, we never pursued the need for psychoanalysis. For one thing, someone would have had to translate the questions for Mommy and then translate her answers back to the practitioner. However, it was our opinion that our parents would have felt insulted at such a suggestion that inhibited Solan and me from bringing up the possibility. I believe Daddy's life would have been much easier if we had been able to give her some professional help.

Also, a lot of Mommy's separation from American culture and society was due to Daddy handling much of what their lives required, even the mundane things, such as going to the grocery store or making phone calls. I don't know if he intentionally kept her cloistered or was so impatient with her that he preferred carrying out chores himself. She did not drive, so transportation was something for which she also was dependent on Daddy.

I never fully understood the problem and never got the straight story from my parents, but I did know that great tension had built up between Mommy and Daddy and Lo Lo, which contributed to Lo Lo's breakdown.

Chapter 13

HARD TIMES

It should not be surprising that my parents ran out of money. Neither had ever had to worry about finances, and they knew nothing about how to manage their resources in their new country. My parents never learned to handle money or plan for the future while we were in the United States. They kept money in the bank and knew little about investing. They depended on the thought that they could always write home for money. However, when the Japanese controlled so much of China eventually, it must have been traumatic for them to face a situation wherein they were in danger of being paupers.

A lot of their cavalier attitude and ignorance of money management rubbed off on Solan, my oldest brother, and on me. We received no advice from Daddy about finances because he did not understand how the American system of finances worked. Fortunately for our families, Solan and I both were able to carry on successful careers and married spouses who were more able than we to handle our finances for the future. Solan became a well-known, world-class ob-gyn in New York, and I, in true keeping with my lack of interest in money, became an academician. Solan and I ended up supporting our parents partially for thirty years after Daddy retired from the United Nations.

I also knew that while we were living in Washington in the mid-1940s, because Daddy had to avoid being drafted for World War II by working for the Chinese embassy, money was tight for us. Solan and I have wondered how a noncitizen immigrant with small children was sent the draft notice Daddy told us he had received. I wonder if he misunderstood whatever notice he got. We were fortunate indeed that he found a job with the Chinese embassy that protected him from the draft and protected Mommy, who could not speak English well, from facing her life alone in the United States with young children. They must have been panicked.

We were almost forced to return to China because there was not enough to live on. I remember losing a dime once and being devastated that I had done so. I expected to be excoriated for my indiscretion, but when I tearfully confessed to my parents that I had lost the dime, they instead comforted me and just said to be more careful in the future. I thought, *I don't understand adults!*

My impression was that they were involved in some kind of bad investment, but they would never tell us what the problems were. I think now that this was the reason we were in such desperate straits. When we lost our amah, Mommy found herself the sole caregiver to her children and the only cook for the family. Remember, this was someone who had never seen the inside of a kitchen in China. It must have been a traumatic time for her. But because we were never told what happened, we children never understood how traumatic it was.

The war ended, and when the United Nations was formed in 1945, Daddy applied for a job. After testing, he was hired as the first simultaneous interpreter for Chinese to English and English to Chinese. His scholarly training and aptitude for languages held him in good stead and saved us from having to return to China. He stayed with the United Nations, becoming the chief Chinese–English interpreter.

We learned that scholarship and knowledge of languages were not the only requirements to be a simultaneous interpreter. There had to be some extra ability in those who passed the test. Daddy often mentioned testing people who knew both languages well but failed to be able to interpret from one language to another while listening to a speech. My third uncle eventually joined Daddy in simultaneous interpretation.

We moved from our house in Washington to a house in Silver Springs, Maryland, in a rural neighborhood. The best thing about being there was that it was within walking distance of three stables that housed horses. I love horses and asked to be allowed to go riding. Daddy and Mommy refused my request, saying that Daddy, when he was a child, had suffered a broken arm by falling off a horse. It was also probably too expensive for me to ride.

I used to walk down to the nearest stable and bring an apple or carrot to give to a gentle horse that became my buddy. He had an outside stall, and when he saw me walking toward him, he would move his head up and down as if he were nodding a greeting. I remember helping the stable hands to curry him. Visiting the stables was great fun for me, and I did it as often as I could.

While we lived there, a notorious crime was committed that was similar to the crime perpetrated on Charles Lindbergh's child decades earlier. A kidnapper used a ladder to get into a second-floor bedroom through a window and took a child.

I do not remember the resolution of the crime, but it made my parents nervous about the safety of my brothers and me at night. Their solution was to buy three Chihuahua puppies. We were each given a puppy to sleep with us at night. The thought was that the dogs would at least bark a warning if they saw anyone trying to enter our rooms. Mine was a white Chihuahua that my parents named Queenie. She was a sweet dog, and I didn't mind her company. Our old cocker spaniel, Ping, had passed away before we moved to Silver Springs, so it was a happy thing for us to have dogs in the family again.

All the moves we made from one city to another were upsetting to my brothers and me because they meant going to a new school and leaving friends we had just made. Maybe that's one reason I never belonged to cliques in any of the schools I attended. Maybe another reason was my being an Asian during World War II, when Asians were not commonly seen in the United States. I wasn't exactly welcomed in the beginning by new classmates. By the time I entered college, I had attended twelve different schools, including the change from grade school to middle school and then to high school.

I can look back on this today and say the moving was good for me, though, to learn to cope with each new and possibly unfriendly environment. I'm sure it built character and strengthened my backbone to have to enter so many different schools so many times. However, as a kid, each first day at each school was terrifying! I knew that as I walked down the halls, every head would turn to stare at me. If I was lucky, that was all they would do. If I wasn't lucky, I would hear insults spoken low but loudly enough for me to hear.

I think now that my lifelong problem of not remembering people's names was in part due to my habit of not really looking at people when I first met them. I did not look them in the eyes because I was shy as a child, and I feared trouble if I, an immigrant, were thought to be too forward. Looking away or down at the floor was a form of submission and something safer to do.

Occasionally, good memories resulted from the moves too. After Maryland, we lived in Long Beach, Long Island, for about six months after Daddy got his job at the UN. Our rented house was right across the street from an old resort hotel called the Lido. The hotel was right on Long Island Sound; however, as it was winter, few clientele were at the hotel. There were large rocks instead of beach areas leading to the sound. We enjoyed climbing and playing among the large rocks. Given that none of us knew how to swim, I wonder, thinking back, whether my parents even recognized the possibility that we could have tripped and fallen into the ocean.

I was still in grade school, in seventh grade, when we lived in Long Beach. I don't remember my teacher's name, just that she had black hair. When I told her my family had to move before the school year was half over, she gave me a surprise farewell party with a cake. I was astonished that she cared for me that much after such a short period of time. Or was she just being nice to a minority kid who worked hard in school?

Thus, early on in my academic career, I learned that teachers truly cared about their students. In junior high school, there was a new teacher of mathematics. He was a tough guy who looked and sounded like a marine, and all the students were scared of him, including me. One day he asked two classmates to write their solutions to a homework problem on the board. They were both wrong.

Then he called on me, and nervously, I put my solution on the board. As I was finishing, the bell rang to end the class. I was the last one to leave because I was at the board, writing. As I was picking up my books to leave and passed him, we made eye contact. He looked tired and frustrated.

He said quietly, "God bless you, Anna."

I was so surprised that I don't remember if I even said thank you to him. I remember feeling sorry that he was so sad.

I knew I had to grit my teeth and get through the first few days at a new school because as soon as the teachers got to know me, they liked me well enough, as did my teacher at Long Beach. As soon as I was discovered to be a good athlete, I would be put on school teams, and my teammates would become my best friends. When I contributed either in the classroom or on a playing field, I was accepted. I have always been grateful for athletic talent that gave me a path to friendship and acceptance.

About that time, Mommy had to undergo a goiter operation. We moved to Princeton, New Jersey, so she could recuperate at my third uncle's house. I was sent to board at a school in the countryside. I don't remember much about that time, but I do remember enjoying being close to my third uncle's children, my first cousins Leona, Clarence, and Humphrey.

My third uncle had married a woman known for her beauty from Canton in the south of China (see again figure 10). She was a quiet, unassuming person whom I respected and cared a lot about. When my third uncle and my mother were competitive about their children and bragged to each other about our achievements, she never participated. She made us feel comfortable and at home.

I was a year younger than my cousin Leona, whose personality was like her mother's. Both she and my older cousin Clarence were terrific students and musically gifted. Clarence could play the piano by ear. I always envied his ability to sit and play without music any song he wished. He was cast as the modern major general in a performance of *The Pirates of Penzance* at his high school. To this day, I remember some of the lyrics of different roles that Clarence, my siblings, Leona and I sang over and over in rehearsing, such as "I am the very model of a modern major general / I've information vegetable, animal, and mineral," and "Beautiful Mabel, I would if I could, but I am not able!" We all came to know that entire operetta well since Clarence asked us to play different roles while he rehearsed his.

Leona, or Lee, had a lovely soprano voice, something else I envied. I was an alto and always sang the harmony in choral works. I wanted to sing the major tunes of songs. As I have aged, my alto voice has slid down to tenor range, and I might end up a baritone. In my next life, I have groused, I will be a coloratura soprano who can play the piano without music!

My brothers and I never were close to their youngest brother, Humphrey, who was several years younger than we and so never played with us much. I always felt, though, that our two sets of parents were constantly comparing us and making us feel as if Solan and I needed to compete with Clarence and Lee, but we enjoyed being with them. Figure 47 shows my third uncle's family with Lo Lo. She is flanked by my third uncle and auntie. Clarence is in the back, Humphrey is in the front, and Leona is next to her mother.

One of our favorite games was ghost, when we children would go into the ground floor's large study, turn off all the lights, and hide. The person who came into the dark room to find someone was the ghost. It was a thrilling game because just being in the dark was thrilling. We were mean to Stanley one night when we all jumped out the ground-floor window while he was the ghost. The poor guy was in there for a long time before we called him out. I must feel guilty to remember that incident.

When Lee became engaged to an American boy after graduating from college, she caused great upheaval in her family. There was shouting and tears because he was not Chinese, but the couple persisted and were eventually married. He turned out to be a wonderful husband to Lee and a wonderful son-in-law to my aunt and uncle. Later, Clarence also married an American girl—without a word from his parents. The difference was that Leona was leaving her family, and Clarence was bringing a woman into the family. The difference in their parents' reaction was due to a Chinese outlook.

That we were never to forget our Chinese origins was impressed on us in many ways. When I was around six, I was not allowed to eat meat because I was not pronouncing the word in Mandarin for meat, *ro*, correctly. I was thus persuaded not only to speak Chinese but also to enunciate the words without an American accent.

To this day, I can speak Mandarin pretty well, though my vocabulary is woefully limited. Without my parents, our need to speak Chinese has disappeared. With the lack of practice, my spoken Chinese has degenerated as I forget a language that is essentially dependent on memory alone. When Chinese who do not know me hear me say a few sentences, they assume I am as fluent as anyone brought up in China. Sometimes that puts me in embarrassing situations when I don't understand what they're saying or when they ask me to interpret for Americans.

On the other hand, I'm grateful for having the ability to speak conversationally. It makes socializing with Chinese much easier. My countrymen and countrywomen sometimes, though, are linguistic snobs. When they ask if my children speak Chinese and I say no, they greet the information with a tsk-tsk attitude.

It wasn't that David and I didn't try to get some knowledge of the Chinese language into our sons. Mrs. Qien, a friend in Livingston, New Jersey, where David and I lived for more than four decades, was known to be a Chinese scholar. We signed Ben and Mike up for Chinese class with her. However, because David and I speak English to each other, our children suffer from a lack of need to use the Chinese they learn. Also, there is no alphabet and no formal grammar, although my sons and granddaughter, while in college, took Chinese language courses and had textbooks that contained some discussion of grammar.

Tenses are indicated by the words used. For example, *Jin tien ta lai* means "Today he or she comes." *Tsuo tien ta lai la* means "Yesterday he or she came." In both cases, the word *come* (*lai*) is used, but the words *today* (*jin tien*) and *yesterday* (*tsuo tien*) indicate present or past tense.

The national dialect is Mandarin. Another source of difficulty for anyone, such as an American, in learning to speak it properly is to have an ear to recognize how one word spoken with four different inflections can mean different things. For example, *tong* can mean "candy," "soup," "lie down," or "burn," depending on the inflection with which the word is spoken.

Therefore, to master the language, whether spoken or written, requires constant exposure and use. Trying to get my own boys to practice their Chinese, when David and I only spoke English with them and each other, became such a tedious job that we finally decided all the arguments and tears weren't worth it, and we stopped the Chinese lessons.

To return to our earlier wanderings, the United Nations building in New York City had not yet been built, and the UN met at Lake Success on Long Island. My first home with my parents on Long Island was in

New Hyde Park when I was in eighth grade. Figure 48 shows that by that time, having lived in several places in the United States, the family was familiar with the American domestic lifestyle. We stayed in New Hyde Park for probably less than a year before we moved to Mineola, also on Long Island. That was in my freshman year of high school, and again, through sports and classes, I made a number of close friendships. Alas, I lost them when an unusual circumstance took me out of school for a year after I finished my freshman year.

Fig. 47 Third Uncle's family in Princeton, NJ

Fig. 48 Mommy and I are cooking. Daddy and Stanley are doing yard work.

Chapter 14

MY TRIP BACK TO REVOLUTIONARY CHINA

After her nervous breakdown, my family eventually decided that Lo Lo should return to China to live with my fourth uncle, who was her favorite son, or perhaps she requested it. My fourth uncle, despite his upbringing as the son of a warlord, chose to join the Communist movement after World War II and rose to be head of the Chinese navy for the Communists. The civil war in China was drawing to a close with the defeat of Chiang Kai Shek and the Nationalists' retreat to Taiwan, and it was deemed a relatively safe time to travel to and live in China. It was 1950.

I was chosen to accompany Mommy and Lo Lo because neither could speak English well, and they needed an interpreter on the train trip across the United States. We were to board one of the President ocean liners in California to sail the Pacific to Hong Kong. In those days, that line of ships was considered the premier way to reach Asia from the west coast of the United States. From Hong Kong, we would board a smaller boat to travel north to Beijing.

Daddy was needed at work; Solan was in his senior year of high school, so he could not go with them while preparing for precollege exams; and they didn't think Stanley could handle the job, so by process of elimination, I was the designated escort. I was not happy about the prospect of losing an entire year of schooling and again losing good friends I had met at Mineola High.

Unexpectedly, that train trip we took is one of my fondest memories. I was fifteen, and it was a great adventure. The cross-continent train trip took three days. We passed the time by playing cards and looking out the window at the passing scenery. The beds on the train were comfortable, and the food in the dining room was good.

Mommy and Lo Lo enjoyed the trip—Lo Lo because she was going home and Mommy because Lo Lo was happy. It was the closest I had ever felt to my mother and Lo Lo. I remember laughing and chatting with them, something that did not happen often in our lives and was never to happen again.

While we took one of the largest ocean liners that existed in those days, I became terribly seasick as we went to sea. Dinner was brought to me the first day because I couldn't get out of bed. It was fancy—pheasant under glass—because Mommy and I were going first class. To this day, the thought of pheasant under glass evokes sensations of nausea.

The trip, which lasted three weeks, felt like three years. I stayed on deck as much as possible because my motion sickness was greatly diminished there. One young Chinese student who stayed on deck even more than I wore sunglasses and looked like a raccoon in reverse, with white all around his eyes and the rest of his face deeply suntanned, by the time we arrived in Hong Kong.

Lo Lo traveled third class at her request, where most of the Chinese passengers on the ship were, and the food they received was Chinese. Mommy and I often went to third class for dinner because of the food. I remember watching Lo Lo play bridge with some of the young students, who were openly patronizing. On the first hand she played, she bid and made a slam. I think the patronization stopped right there. Come to think of it, I wonder where she learned to play bridge. My parents never played.

When we arrived in Hong Kong, it was the middle of the night. Lo Lo was so eager to taste *sho bing yo tiao*, a favorite Chinese breakfast combination of an unleavened sesame bread and fried dough strips, that she asked the hotel people to get her some right then. They apologized and said that nothing was available at four o'clock in the morning but promised to get us some as soon as day broke.

We were to travel to Beijing from Hong Kong by a smallish boat that carried cargo north to Nanjing. If I remember right, we were then to meet my fourth uncle, who would drive us to Beijing. The small boat was a different experience from the large President Lines ship we had just spent weeks on. One day I was on deck, standing at the railing of the boat, when I saw something that to this day is a mystery to me. It looked like a big snake, but it was so far away I could only see something black, long, and flexible without any details. It jumped into the air from the ocean and splashed down immediately. It never surfaced again. I was all alone, so no one could confirm what I saw, but I did see it, and I knew it was there because of the splash it made when falling back into the water.

At that time, the Chinese Communists had already taken control of Northern China, including Beijing. We eventually arrived in Beijing. My fourth uncle came in a limousine to pick us up (yes, even in Communist countries, some animals are more equal than others). After having bounced around for several days in rickshaws in Hong Kong, we felt the limousine ride was a marvel of comfort. Americans are spoiled by aspects of life that most people in the world consider luxuries.

My fourth uncle, Lo Lo's youngest child, was handsome, I thought, and bright (figure 49). I wished I could have gotten to know him better. He was unable to stay long with us and left after just a couple of days. We were never to see him again.

I have always admired my fourth uncle, Zhang Xuesi, as he had come from the same luxury and power as my mother yet decided to abandon all that to join the Communist movement. I wish I had been mature enough to recognize how unusual that was and ask him to explain why. To fight for China against Japan no doubt was a decision that stemmed from the same patriotic fervor that his oldest half brother, the Young Marshal, showed when he captured Chiang Kai Shek and forced him to fight the Japanese. But what motivated my fourth uncle to join the Communists? My guess is that he was not disowning his own family—he was happy to see his mother and sister—but recognized and wanted to help eliminate the enormous inequality between the haves and the have-nots that existed in Chinese society at the time.

I was surprised that he not only was accepted into the Communist movement but also made progress in promotions until he was named head of the Chinese Communist Navy. He had fought well in the civil war for the Communist movement. However, later, his crime was Mao Tse Tung's perception of Uncle's loyalty to Lin Biao, one of the Communist generals who helped defeat Chiang Kai Shek but who fell into disfavor with Mao.

Toward the end of his life, Mao Tse Tung seemed to become paranoid. When Lin Biao realized Mao suspected him of betrayal, he attempted to flee by plane. Mao had his plane shot down, and whomever Mao suspected of being an ally of Lin Biao was jailed. My fourth uncle was imprisoned by Mao Tse Tung and the Gang of Four in the 1960s. He died in prison, and Mommy understandably never forgave the Communists.

In 2005, David and I took our family to China and visited Xian, Guilin, Beijing, and Shenyang, among other places, in hopes of educating our American daughters-in-law and our grandchildren about David's and my families' places in twentieth-century Chinese history. I will discuss the trip in detail later. We asked some officials we met why my fourth uncle had been imprisoned. They could not explain it. We can only assume it was due to the irrational, insane actions of the Cultural Revolution era (1966–1976) and to Mao's degenerating ability to think clearly.

To me, my fourth uncle's story is a poignant one—a young man gave up his life of luxury out of love of country and joined a rebellion by people who wanted to eliminate the corruption of the system. Hoping to lead China into a position of power in the world, he joined the Communist movement. He was bright, worked hard, and climbed the ladder to become the head of the navy. Then, for no reason other than the degeneration of the mental capacity of Mao, he was thrown into prison, was tortured, and died. It is a story that deserves to be told.

When the Chinese Communists were accepted into the United Nations as the People's Republic of China (PRC) in the 1950s, Mommy insisted Daddy leave his job, not wanting him to have any contact with the people who'd killed her youngest brother. She screamed at and harassed Daddy until he could no longer resist and retired. Part of the reason Solan and I had to support our parents for so long was because Daddy simply had not worked long enough to build up a sufficient pension. He was only in his forties when she made him retire.

It was the first sign of a serious degree of irrational behavior by Mommy, something that spread to other aspects of their lives and increased as the years went by.

Mommy blamed my fourth uncle's wife for helping to jail him, and Mommy accused her of being a

Communist Party member for not helping him be released. Mommy ranted and railed about this to us with no evidence other than what she seemed to have fabricated in her own mind. When she railed against my fourth aunt, there appeared to be little basis for her charges. All we could do was keep silent during her tantrums. The tragedy added to her hatred of the Chinese Communists. It seemed to me at the time that Mommy seemed to need to hate more than to love. It made me feel even more estranged and almost fearful of my mother's future.

Lo Lo stayed in Beijing for the rest of her life and died there in the 1960s. When she was in her last days, Mommy wanted to go see her. To Mommy's deep humiliation and shock, Lo Lo refused to see her and asked for my fifth aunt instead. She died without any of her children by her side. The photographs sent to Mommy showed only my fifth aunt's husband at the memorial service for Lo Lo (figure 50). Lo Lo's cruel refusal to see Mommy reflected to me a lingering deep resentment against my parents because of the mystery behind what happened to their relationship in the United States.

It was a terrible loss of face for Mommy and for us in her family to know. It must have cut Mommy deeply and probably haunted her to the end of her days. I felt bad for her. I am sure that trauma and humiliation and perhaps some emotional instability that might have been transmitted from Lo Lo to Mommy led to the irrational state of mind in my mother's later life.

Fig 49 Fourth Uncle

Fig 50 Fifth Uncle (Fifth aunt's husband) in Western suit at funeral service for Lo Lo

Chapter 15

LIFE IN REVOLUTIONARY CHINA ATTRACTS ME

The strongest impression I have of that visit to China in 1950 is the pervasive sense of excitement and pride expressed by the people. The Communists had already taken control of China, and Beijing was still the capital. Every day, it seemed, I would hear the sound of cymbals and drums in the street, and there would be a group of young people, usually young women, dancing in a conga-like line a revolutionary dance they called *niu yong ger*. They would sway in tempo with the drumbeat, swinging their arms from side to side, wearing padded Mao uniforms, and ever smiling. I wish I had photographs of my days in China that year. Daddy was the family photographer, and he was not with us. I did not even have a camera then.

I was curious to learn whether being in a country where everyone looked like me and my family would give me a feeling of belonging. That feeling was something I truly wanted because all the time we were in the United States, our parents were looking to return home to China. However, the fact that the Communists won the civil war changed my parents' minds about returning. We were living in the only house we owned in Beijing that had not yet been taken over by the government. It was out in the country, and the property was large. There was a big chicken farm on the back part of it. We had a wall all around the property to give us privacy from the neighbors, and the source of water was a well with cold, clear water that we still had to boil to make it potable. We kept watermelons in the well bucket to keep them cold since there were no refrigerators.

There were no electrical appliances because there was no electricity, and there was no running water. We took mostly sponge baths with water heated by fire. I can still feel the chill of being wet during the cold weather. I did not look forward to getting in bed because I thought the sheets would feel uncomfortably icy. It was a pleasant surprise that hot water bottles and a heated brick had been put into the beds to make the sheets cozy and warm, and it was wonderful to have the warm rubber bottles to put my feet against.

As China was a third-world country in the 1950s, few Chinese had modern bathrooms. Our toilets were in outhouses that were cleaned frequently by collectors of night soil, as solid waste was called, who then sold the night soil to farmers for fertilizer, as I noted before. Whatever produce we bought had to be carefully cleaned, and rarely did we eat uncooked vegetables. Salad was not part of the Chinese meal at that point.

One of my favorite memories is hearing the people who came around in the mornings selling *sho bing yu tiao,* a favorite breakfast of the Northern Chinese of a sesame bread and a cruller type of fried dough. It was the combination Lo Lo asked for as soon as our ship docked in Hong Kong. The cruller was the filling for the sesame bread sandwich. Low carb it wasn't! The salesmen would shout out about their wares, and the sound would bounce all through the neighborhood. Our longtime estate keeper, Woo Jing, faithful to the Chao family all through World War II and the civil war, would run out to buy the food and bring it in piping hot and fresh. Delicious!

We had two big black dogs that seemed to have some mastiff in them. They helped guard the house from burglars and other intruders. I remember feeding them a type of steamed corn bread we called *wowotao*. It was supposed to be peasant food and good only for the dogs, but I liked the taste of the corn bread. I guess I'm a peasant at heart!

Later, when we had returned to the United States, the Communists decreed that nobody should have dogs or any pets since the animals were fed food that people could eat. They went around to all the homes, removed all the pets, and killed them. My mother never forgave the Communists for that either—nor did I—and it only added to her hatred. I read that during that time someone risked his life to smuggle four shar-pei dogs out of China into Hong Kong. All the shar-peis that exist today are descendants of those four dogs.

It must have been a painful disappointment to both my parents to realize they would never return to their home. Indeed, what they remembered as their home and lifestyle no longer existed. I do not know what happened to Woo Jing. He has surely passed away.

During our stay in Beijing in 1950, we observed the anniversary of the death of my father's father, Yeh Yeh. To do so, we burned paper money to symbolize giving him riches in heaven. Later, when the Communists confiscated our home and built apartments on the property, I heard that his grave had been moved, but to this day, I do not know to where it was moved. In 2005, we took the family to China on a wonderful *Roots* trip. I asked a number of people to look into where his grave might be, but no information was available.

I was surprised and taken aback during the visit in 1950 in Beijing to learn how archaic the attitude toward sex was in China. One day a male cousin came to visit. They began to talk about someone I knew. I asked if she was pregnant yet, as she had mentioned during our last visit together that she was hoping to start a family. My mother immediately apologized for me for mentioning pregnancy and said, "She's going to be a doctor," as if that explained why I was so forward. I wonder if she would have felt the need to apologize if the cousin had been a woman.

At the chicken farm to whom we had rented the back part of our property, a virus had killed many of the chickens the year before. We had some chickens of our own kept near our house too, and those that belonged to us were also attacked by the virus. One old female remained. When Mommy saw that she was sitting on a brood of eggs, she brought the hen and her eggs into the house and put the nest in her bedroom.

Every day the old hen would leave the eggs; walk through the house to the outside to do her business, eat, and drink; and then cluck her way back to the eggs. After the eggs hatched, there was a parade of chicks following their mother to the outside. Some of the babies, as they grew, became tame. I remember sitting on the porch and having one or another hop onto my lap.

One day I watched the old hen defend her babies. A chicken hawk hovered and was about to swoop down to pick up one of the chicks. The old mother hen saw this and flew up to meet the hawk with all kinds of squawking. The baby chicks scattered. She scared off the hawk, which recognized a furious adversary.

A favorite memory of that trip to China involves an old lady whose relation to us I no longer remember who had been allowed to live at our house during the war. I was sitting on the front porch, playing with the chickens. Suddenly, she turned to me and said in all seriousness, "In my next life, I will come back as a hen and lay an egg for you every day."

I knew she was expressing her gratitude to my parents for allowing her to stay at our home in safety during the war years. She was a Buddhist, and Buddhists believe in reincarnation. I thanked her and thought with some internal amusement, *How many people have had the privilege of being told by someone that he or she will come back as a hen and lay an egg every day for them?* I know I will never starve!

Another of my favorite memories of that stay in Beijing is the day the apricots on the tree that grew in our courtyard were ripe enough to pick. We spread a sheet on the ground under the tree, and I was given a long bamboo pole. I swung the pole against the higher branches, and the fruit fell to the ground onto the sheet. That was how we harvested our apricots. They were as sweet as sugar.

Did I feel that I belonged in China after spending some three months in Beijing with Mommy and Lo Lo? Not completely. Because of my clothing and hair, I was identified as a visiting overseas Chinese. Not long after we had settled in Beijing, I went with my mother to a shopping area. As we walked, a young woman suddenly grabbed at the blue jeans I was wearing and asked, "Where did you get these?"

Startled, I simply answered, "In the United States." She nodded and walked away.

Everyone wore the Mao uniform at that time: a simple cotton top with a Mandarin collar and cotton pants (see again figure 50). I realized the high quality of American blue jeans were the envy of the people there. However, despite not feeling completely comfortable in Beijing, I enjoyed being there. I wondered if I could possibly feel I belonged, given time.

My visit to my homeland was a wonderful eye-opener to this American. The excitement of the people for the victory of the Communists made me feel their pride that China would no longer be the doormat for the Western world. I enjoyed the people I was with, and being in a different environment was energizing too. Thus, when Daddy came to escort Mommy and me to return to the United States, I told him I had to talk to him about returning.

I told him, "Daddy, I want to stay in China to help restore the country."

Momentarily, Daddy looked stunned. He realized from his work at the UN that things were not going well between China and the United States. Shaking his head at my declaration, he told me he would not allow me to stay. "If you do not go back with me, you will never be able to leave China," he said.

Indeed, not long after we returned to the United States, the Bamboo Curtain, as it was called, dropped to isolate China from the rest of the non-Communist nations.

Had I stayed, I would not have been allowed to leave. No doubt during the Red Guard days in the 1960s and early '70s, I would have been one of the first to be picked out for abuse or death with my bourgeois family history and my upbringing in the United States. I certainly would not have tolerated the forced admissions of guilt by the victims of the Cultural Revolution. For being outspoken, I would have been subject to unthinkable treatment or the more merciful fate of execution. Thanks, Daddy!

Chapter 16

STANLEY'S CROSS TO BEAR

Acceptance by our peers was easy for me and my oldest brother, Solan. He too was a good athlete and a good student, and his peers looked up to him. But it was not the same for my older brother Stanley. I learned that when Stanley was born, he did not breathe right away. His brain had thus been damaged at birth, and a childhood blow to his head from a swing had further injured it. The damage made it difficult for him to learn, and he was also not very coordinated. Daddy liked to take pictures of our family and even had a movie camera. One film I saw showed my brothers and me as young children playing. I guess I was about three years old, and Stanley was about four and a half. We were told to run toward the camera, and though we started out at the same place, I easily outran my bigger brother. Figure 51 is a photograph of Stanley with Nai Nai when he was four. He was a cute youngster.

As we grew, Stanley was not able to make friends as easily as Solan and I did. As I mentioned earlier, Solan and I were good athletes, and we had our teammates as our first friends. Stanley did not have that avenue to acceptance because he was not athletic. I would see him at lunchtimes in middle school and high school, sitting alone. I think changing schools as often as we did was hardest on Stanley. Occasionally, I would sit with him, but most of the time, he was alone. It bothered me, but friendship is not something that can be forced on people. I could only shut my mind to the discomfort he must have faced everywhere we went. I hoped the reputations Solan and I developed helped him in an indirect way.

My older brother didn't have it any easier at home. Mommy was constantly berating him for his grades and his looks—for everything. Rather than recognizing and accepting his limitations, she refused to acknowledge that his problems were physical. She accused him of being lazy and shiftless. Their estrangement began in earnest when he became a teenager and occasionally rebelled.

She would moan aloud that she didn't know why she'd been given the terrible fate of having Stanley for a son. She constantly held Solan and me up to him. It made us feel terrible, but being Chinese, we accepted whatever our parents said as being the law—until we were grown enough to recognize the injustice of that treatment.

When Solan and I were old enough to work at paying jobs, we worked every summer at jobs we ourselves found, but Stanley could not. One summer, I worked as a receptionist at the Cloisters, a Gregorian monastery at Fort Tryon Park in New York City. It was peaceful, with recorded Gregorian chants played all day every day. There I learned that if I had to do a lot of dialing on the phone, it was better to use the eraser end of a pencil rather than my finger. Remember, in those days, we didn't have buttons to push on the phone; rather, there was a circular dial with holes over the numbers that we moved in a clockwise direction.

Another summer, I worked in a ten-cent store, as they were called then. I was assigned to the candy counter sometimes and to the cosmetics counter at other times. The neighborhood was not the best, and I saw men, transsexuals, come to the counter to buy lipstick and other cosmetics. At first, they startled me. One day a man with a five o'clock shadow came to the counter. When I asked if I could help him, he asked me about lipstick and hair rollers—for himself! I thought he was dressed a bit strangely, in what looked like a dress. It was an education for me to work there.

I tried to find work for Stanley, but it was hard to find something he could do. I did find him a job at the ticket window of a movie theater, but he had to leave the job because he could not figure out change fast enough. In those days, cash registers didn't give the amount of change a customer should get, as the registers of today do. (I suspect a fair number of present-day cashiers would be out of jobs if they didn't have machines that told them how much they needed to give to customers.) That he couldn't find work for himself or keep a job meant more resentment on my mother's part.

To Stan's credit, the treatment he received from our mother never really caused him to question himself. He was angry and no doubt saddened by the lack of maternal nurturing and love, but he continued to believe in himself. Figure 52 shows my brothers and me with Mommy.

Stan was around thirteen. He would volunteer to do things, such as singing at school events. He has a nice baritone voice, and he sought approval from friends by singing. Sometimes that effort was not successful, yet he would volunteer again. I admit I felt bad for him when things did not go as he wished. He lived through more than I believe I could have tolerated. I came to respect him greatly for that. His fortitude eventually led him to better days, as you shall see.

How I wish my relationship with Mommy had been one that would have allowed me to earnestly discuss Stanley's problems with her in a way that might have changed her way of thinking and made her feel better as well as improved her relationship with her son. In today's world, with all the programs for children with learning problems, I think about how much easier life would have been for Stanley. There might have been such programs back then in the 1940s, but Mommy and Daddy would not have known to ask about them.

I wish today that I had not been so compliant with my parents' actions. I could have been more of a positive factor in helping to make our dysfunctional family more functional. I developed even more resentment against Mommy because of the constant cruel comments she made to Stan. It never occurred to me that she could not help herself. I continue to wonder how I could have been better as a voice of reason. But when Mommy became so imbalanced, would it have made a difference in our lives?

Fig 51 Nai Nai and Stanley

Fig 52 Stanley smiling and standing next to Mommy

Chapter 17

YEARNING AND DISCRIMINATION

At about that time in my life, during my high school years, I had sudden periods when I felt a deep sadness. It was a yearning for something, but I never knew what it was. My belief today is that it was a sadness for the way I felt about Mommy and also sadness at not belonging anywhere. Mommy and Daddy always told Solan, Stanley, and me that we were not Americans and would be returning to China one day. In Chinese, we always referred to Americans as *wye guo ren* (foreigners), even though we were the foreigners in America. That feeling eventually left me when I went to college and met my husband, but until then, I suppose I felt lost.

I never was part of any clique in the many schools I attended. A clique was simply a group of close friends who did not socialize as much with other students. I never felt I was in a clique because our parents drummed into us that we were not one of *them*. Also, I was never at any school for more than a year. Moving a lot didn't help matters.

As I matured, I was brainwashed into believing that American men were not possible mates. I never was asked out when I was in high school because I never stayed in one school long enough to form relationships, and I was too shy.

My first date came on an occasion when I had to ask someone to escort me to a dance when I was a sophomore at Great Neck High School. We had moved to Great Neck after Mineola. I asked a Chinese boy I had met in one of my classes, and he agreed. He was a gentleman, but I did not enjoy the date because a girl having to ask a boy out at that time was humiliating.

The only time I dated an American boy was in my first year in college. A boy who knew a girl in my class saw me and asked her to set us up on a blind date. She would not take no for an answer. Finally, I relented. It was a miserable time because I felt so guilty that I couldn't relax. He noticed my tenseness, and I felt I had to explain the situation to him. We left the picnic early. He was a nice guy and good looking, and I felt bad and really angry. I was practicing reverse discrimination.

Intellectually, I knew there was no reason I should not see American boys socially, but the brainwashing was so effective that I knew I couldn't date them and be fair to them. I was angry at myself for not being able to overcome my sense of guilt of discriminating against American boys, and I disliked that I was put in that position as a woman.

Yet at the same time, I also felt uncomfortable with Chinese men who had come to the United States as grownups. To me, they were stiff and difficult to converse with. We had little in common. *Too Chinese*, I would say to myself.

At that time, there were few eligible Chinese girls, so the young men were all anxious to impress, but their overzealousness turned me off. They also were clearly agitated, shall we say, and often had sweaty palms that I hated to have to touch while dancing. I felt sorry for them. I think that in all, I received eight proposals of marriage before David asked me and I said yes.

My big brother Solan was allowed to date American girls, however, because he was a boy and would be bringing a wife into our family. Contrarily, if I were to marry an American boy, I would be leaving the family and going into his, the same problem faced by my cousins Leona and Clarence. It is the Chinese way of thinking, to be sure. On the other hand, it can also be an American way of thinking too, as evidenced by an episode in Solan's life.

Solan fell in love with a classmate at Cornell, a lovely, nice young woman from West Virginia. I will call her Julia—that's not really her name. Her family was in steel production and wealthy. I liked her a lot, and she and Solan were clearly head over heels in love with each other and seemed to be a wonderful couple. But tragically, their romantic dreams were never to come true.

Julia's parents sent one of her brothers to visit with us in our apartment in New York, where we had moved to be near the United Nations building. His mission was clearly to evaluate us. I dressed in a Chinese dress that I knew by looks and whistles made me attractive to men. I wanted Julia's brother to be impressed with us enough to bring his parents a positive evaluation. In retrospect, dressing like a Chinese was probably the wrong thing to do, but at the time, I thought it was the best thing to do.

I hated having to parade myself in front of the young man while feeling as if I were begging for his approval, but I did it for my brother and Julia; they did not deserve that situation. Remember that the Korean War had just ended, and China had sent in hordes of soldiers to support the North Koreans. That probably was another negative in the minds of Julia's family.

There no doubt also was suspicion on the part of Julia's parents that part of the reason we approved of their relationship was that we knew of their wealth. As we were immigrants, they might have thought marriage was our way to some of their fortune. It would have been understandable. Little did they know of our family history and wealth. But how could they have known without bothering to know us? The inevitable end result was that they decided not to approve of or accept Solan and Julia's relationship.

They told Julia not to see Solan again. She would be disowned if she married him, and she would not be allowed to see her family again. They would cut her off immediately. As much as she loved Solan, she could not bring herself to accept isolation from her family. Her heartbreaking choice was to tell Solan not to see her again. Her parents forced Julia to withdraw from Cornell immediately.

I ached for my big brother and was furious to think that anyone had the right to judge him as a person and forbid him to see a girl he loved. He was so upset that Mommy and Daddy drove to Cornell to prevent him from hurting himself. I can imagine how insulted they must have felt to have their son rejected from a relationship with a so-called barbarian as being not good enough. In my mind, I sent a message to Julia's parents: *You will be sorry!*

In my heart, I knew my big brother was an outstanding human being; however, we never expressed our love for each other growing up. I have to believe it was due to our parents' reticence in expressing affection to us and vice versa. (That applies more to Mommy than to Daddy). When he left home to go to Cornell, though, Solan wrote me a long letter saying that he did not know why our upbringing had stifled our ability to say how much we loved each other as siblings and that he wanted me to know how proud he was of me. I responded in kind and deeply believed he would be capable of accomplishing great things, which happened.

Solan was devastated about Julia. Although we never saw her again, I know she was also deeply affected. More than four decades later, in 1995, Solan heard from her, and she wanted to see him. They met for lunch. She told him she had married an American, but the marriage eventually had broken up, and she was divorced. She had let herself go in appearance, Solan said, and was smoking heavily, even though she had already had breast cancer. There is no question in my mind that Julia's parents destroyed her life. What a poignant meeting that lunch must have been! But I'm sure it gave both of them closure from a traumatic incident.

Solan pulled himself together well enough to graduate from Cornell. He then was drafted into the army and served for two years. During that time, he decided he would try to enter medical school when he was discharged. After his discharge from the army, he met the woman he was to marry. Fortunately, Solan married well. He married a lovely, petite Chinese woman, Jeannette Woo (figure 53), from Shanghai who supported him as he prepared to enter the field of medicine. Figure 54 shows Jeannie in her wedding dress, and figure 55 is a photograph of their two daughters, whom I love as my own.

Mommy and Daddy had given Solan three choices of areas to major in: medicine, agriculture, or engineering. He majored in political science. The irony of that to me was that with his talents and engaging personality, which always resulted in him as a leader among friends, he would have been successful as a politician. He would have been ethical and trustworthy as a leader. But because he needed to take required courses to qualify for medical school that he had not taken as a poli-sci major, Solan had a lot of catching up to do.

Jeannie worked while he studied, and the GI Bill helped a great deal in paying for school. He entered Columbia Medical School in New York City, and he interned and did his residency at Columbia Presbyterian Hospital, eventually becoming the chief resident in obstetrics and gynecology. He told me the first time he put on the white physician's jacket, he was so excited that he got a headache. He stayed on as a staff physician at Columbia Presbyterian for decades. Later, he moved to Long Island to North Shore Hospital and ended up chair of the OB-GYN department at St. Luke's Hospital in New York City. My big brother, not surprisingly, became a world-class physician in the field of obstetrics and gynecology.

As his practice matured, he became known for developing programs to help indigent women in Harlem and Chinatown in New York City. He testified in Albany about the medical needs of indigent women and also practiced for a time at both Chinatown and Harlem hospitals. He was credited with significantly reducing the number of perinatal deaths of infants in the two neighborhoods. He was able to convince a number of young Chinese American medical doctors to follow him into Chinatown to tend to the needs of people there.

Both neighborhoods have honored him, and young doctors he encouraged to follow in his footsteps carried on his work after he was too ill with colorectal cancer to continue. My beloved big brother died in 1996. A meeting room at Columbia Presbyterian Hospital, now New York Presbyterian Hospital, is named after him in his honor.

During that time, Solan harbored some resentment against our parents. When he and Jeannie were struggling to make ends meet during his medical school days, my father was spending lavishly, using his savings on his Chinese opera hobby. Solan was bitter that they never gave him any financial help. He told me, "I even had to earn money by giving my blood."

Later, when he and Jeannette had only daughters and I had given birth to two sons, I could not convince Mommy—even though I had a PhD in genetics—that it was not Jeannie's fault but Solan's that they had only girls and that it was not something attributable to me that I had given birth to two boys.

Mommy's clear preference toward my sons as grandchildren hurt Solan deeply. I wish I could have that period of time available to us again, because I could have tried to soften the hurt by pointing out what I now believe: that Mommy could not help herself because of her upbringing to favor boys rather than girls. But perhaps too she was a mother-in-law who would always feel her own daughter and son were superior to any daughter-in-law.

Our experience with overt discrimination when Julia's parents punished Solan for being Chinese taught me a sense of the anger and frustration that all people feel when they are judged to be unworthy simply on the basis of their ethnicity or color. At the time, the American dream for us seemed to depend on the color of our skin. We vowed to be so good in whatever we did that those who otherwise might have looked down on us because of our ethnicity would eventually beg us to work with them.

The recent success of many Chinese Americans in science, industry, and commerce in the United States, including my husband and some of our Chinese American friends, is our redemption.

Fig 53 Solan and Jeannie after their engagement

Fig 54 Mrs Solan Chao

Fig 55 Patty Ann (Mei) on the left and Carolyn (Shrong) on the right.

Chapter 18

OUT OF SCHOOL AGAIN—IN PARIS

I spent my freshman year in high school, the year before I went to China, at Mineola High School on Long Island, and I again had to bid my friends there goodbye when we returned from China. We were to move to Great Neck. I spent my sophomore year at Great Neck High School. It was a good school, and there were a number of foreign students because the UN met at nearby Lake Success on Long Island.

We lived in a rented house within walking distance of a park. There were public tennis courts there, and I had my first introduction to that sport. I can still see Solan and Daddy playing. Solan would be frustrated by Daddy, who would chip and slice his shots, while Solan wanted to blast the ball.

At that time, I took a step in my social maturity: I learned to dance the fox-trot. Clarence, my third uncle's son, taught me the fox-trot when his family was visiting us. I can remember some of the songs we danced to, including "Harbor Lights" and "Tennessee Waltz." To this day, when I hear those two songs, I think of my dance lessons and high school in Great Neck.

As I mentioned earlier, I also had my first date around that time. I had to attend a dance at the school. I can't remember why I had to, but I remember having to ask someone to go with me. I felt awkward when I called a Chinese boy in one of my classes (Victor or Vincent?) who had been friendly with me. I apologized and told him he was not obligated to say yes, but he was nice and agreed, and he escorted me to the dance.

I was uncomfortable the whole night because I had been the one to ask him and not vice versa. Today girls probably ask boys out all the time, but they did not in that time. I felt humiliated that I had done the inviting. Mommy was thrilled, though, and made me put on makeup and curl my hair—something else I felt was embarrassing. I thought I looked awful (I still do), but I tolerated it because she was so excited (figure 56). I avoided the boy for the rest of the year. I am sure I was the worst date of the year!

I gave Mommy some trouble again when I objected to putting on lipstick and any other cosmetics in my teenage years. If I put on lipstick a little crooked, it was again a reason for Mommy to chastise me. Eventually, I gave in and agreed to use lipstick, but I would not use any other cosmetics, to my mother's exasperation.

Then my academic life was interrupted again. This time, the UN was meeting at the Palais de Versailles in France. Solan could not go because he was in his senior year of high school, and I don't remember what arrangements they made for him and Stanley, but I was the only one dragged out of school again to go with Mommy and Daddy to live in Paris for three months. I didn't realize it then, but travel is one of the most educational things one can do. I was sixteen.

For three months, we lived in a small apartment not far from the Arc de Triomphe de l'Étoile in Paris. My high school French had to provide us some means of getting on in Paris. I was old enough at the time to be curious about that foreign country and the lives of people there. We discovered that even the smallest restaurants, which might have been described as holes in the wall, offered delicious food.

We also learned it was difficult to get steaks cooked beyond rare. At one restaurant, Mommy ordered steak well done. When the cook brought it out, it was rare, almost bloody. She showed Daddy, who called the waiter over and handed him the steak, saying something like "*Bien cuille sy'l vous plait*" (Well done, please). The waiter shrugged a little, nodded, and went off. When he came back, the steak was still rare. Though it was not quite as bloody, it was still too rare for Mommy. Three times, they sent the steak back, and finally, they simply gave up. Daddy ate what he could of the steak and gave Mommy what he'd ordered.

I was also introduced to steak tartar in Paris. We were eating in a fairly fancy restaurant one day. I saw a waiter with a gleaming aluminum cart walk past our table. There was a pile of ground raw meat on a plate and various other things on the cart. I recognized scallions and other spices. *Oh, wow*, I thought, *he's going to cook a special dish!* He stopped at the next table and began spooning the meat onto a plate. *Hmm*, I thought, *where's the source of fire for cooking?* To my astonishment, after adding various things to the meat, he presented the plate of raw meat to the man at the table. I was then told that one ate steak tartar raw. Live and learn!

My favorite lunch was a baguette—a long, narrow loaf of French bread—and pâté *fois gras*. It was a common sight to see the French walking with loaves of bread under their arms. I also enjoyed marrons *glacée*, or caramelized chestnuts. Needless to say, I gained weight because of those delicious treats!

Some of my favorite memories from Paris are of Daddy reading from a classic Chinese love story called "The Dream of the Red Chamber." He read the passages out loud to me since I could not read Chinese. I did not, however, enjoy the mah-jongg parties they had with friends. The parties seemed to last forever, when I wanted to sleep.

I took French lessons at Berlitz in Paris. One day while I was there, I felt something creeping up my leg. I didn't know what it was, but I didn't like it. I knew my instructor was too far on the other side of the table to be touching me, but what else could it be? I thought maybe a bug was crawling up my leg. I used my other leg to try to brush it off. It kept going up my leg.

Later, I looked and realized it was my stocking, which had a run in it. The run was advancing up my leg. I had not ever experienced a run in my stocking before. With the pantyhose we have now, there are few such runs. I was abashed to have even wondered about my Berlitz instructor!

My French improved greatly. Daddy had a good ear for language, and he told me the French, for example, pronounced words beginning with *p*, such as *petite*, almost as if the *p* were a *b*. He must have hammered that into Mommy, because thereafter, she would say while shopping for petite sizes that she was shopping in the "bahteete" section for clothes.

But Daddy really didn't know French, and it was left up to me to buy groceries and run errands. My French was better than my parents', but it wasn't good. Once, I went to a butcher store with the intent to buy fresh bacon for my mother but had all kinds of problems communicating that. I ended up with pork loin, something totally different.

While in Paris, I also tried smoking for the first time. One day when Mommy and Daddy were both out, I snuck a cigarette from a pack lying around. I went into the bathroom, opened the window, took a puff and then another, and then inhaled. I got so sick immediately that the nausea ended my experiment right then and there. I threw up, flushed the cigarette down the toilet, and waved the smoke out the window. I did not try again until I was in college.

Upon returning from Paris, I enrolled in the Rhodes School in New York City, which offered courses during the spring and summer that would allow me to make up yet another year of lost schooling. I had already lost one year on the trip to China with my mother. I can't remember how I commuted to the city—probably on the train. I was taking courses that would have been those of a junior in high school.

I joined the glee club at Rhodes School since there was no gym or physical education at Rhodes. One of the members of the glee club was a Chinese boy whose name I no longer know. I do remember, though, that everyone in glee club teased the two of us as the only Chinese students and tried to get us involved with each other. He was fairly good looking too. Although I denied having any interest in him, I did hope he would ask me out. But he never made a move, and neither did I. I believe his name was Edward.

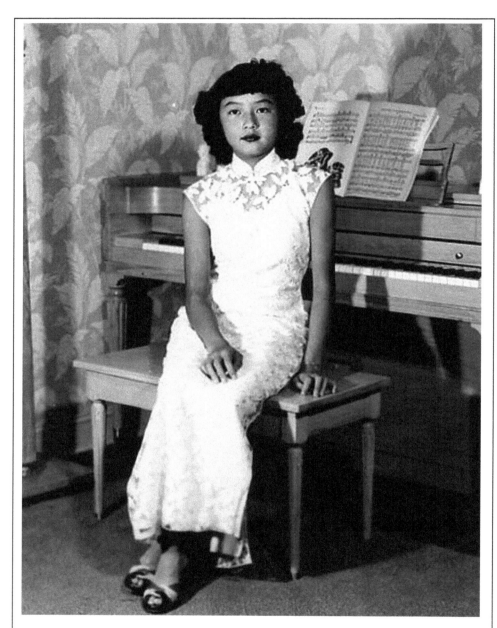
Fig 56 My first formal dance.

Chapter 19

THE SOCIAL GRAPEVINE

For my senior year of high school, I returned to Great Neck High, where there were a number of Chinese and other nationalities in the student body because of the nearby presence of the United Nations at Lake Success. A distant cousin of mine was a student there, Betty Chen. Because I had not been at GNH for two consecutive years, I was not eligible for National Honor Society, and I watched with some envy as Betty and others were inducted into NHS. As it was my second year at Great Neck, though, I was comfortable in attending classes, since I had many friends there already. I continued to play on varsity sports teams and worked hard at my studies. GNH was a large school, and my graduating class was around a thousand, if I remember correctly.

At the graduation ceremony, when it was announced that I had won the American History Award for the highest average, Daddy hurtled over people to get a photograph of my getting the award, I was told. I was not thrilled by the honor, however, because I had taken American history at Rhodes and for some reason had to repeat it as a senior at Great Neck High. I felt a little unworthy since my classmates who took American history had probably not taken it twice. I was glad the award was so exciting for my parents; however, I was prouder of Stanley for being able to graduate that same year.

Men were becoming part of my life. I dated a young man who was a scion of the family of a rich textile-industry tycoon out of Shanghai. He was quite a bit older than I, in his early twenties. Barry (I will not use any real names of former dates) was one of the sons of my mother's many friends whom my mother insisted I date. Mommy mentioned more than once how well off his family was. We would go out to dinner and sometimes dance. John, his younger brother, was interested in my first cousin Leona, and we double-dated sometimes. While the boys were perfect gentlemen and treated us well, I found that we had little in the way of common interests.

To show you how backward I was then, I never even let Barry hold hands with me. Barry loved to sing, and he had a mildly good voice. His favorite song he would sing to me was "In the Still of the Night."

One day he said to me, "Someday, Anna, you will be great."

I didn't know what he meant and still don't, and the comment surprised me, but I must have been flattered and not a little curious, because I still remember that statement. I was inexperienced and socially dumb. I guess Mommy expected me to marry as young as she had, at the age of eighteen, but I knew I was not ready.

One positive thing that came out of knowing Barry and John was that one day John invited me to drive to Virginia with him to visit Cousin Leona at Sweet Briar College. Lee, a year older than I, was a freshman at the college. I had never heard of the small women's college before. When we arrived, I fell in love with the place. It was in the Virginia countryside and had its own farm.

The campus was lovely, with woods and rolling fields as part of its 3,200 acres (figure 57).

It used to be a plantation, and when Daisy Williams, the daughter and only child of the owners, passed away at a young age, her parents decreed in their will that their home should be used as an institution of higher learning for young women and should be called Sweet Briar College. The plantation house became the president's house (figure 58).

What attracted me during our visit was that the student body was small, around five hundred all told. It seemed most of the students knew each other, and the classes were small, which resulted in close student–faculty relationships. I liked the intimacy of it all. I had never lived in such an environment before and decided I would apply to Sweet Briar as well as Bryn Mawr, Wellesley, and Cornell.

Even though Barry and I had gotten to know each other well, I told Barry I did not want to see him anymore soon after my trip to see Lee. I think by that time, Barry had had enough of me too.

Even though I was naturally shy and for a time felt awkward in social circumstances, I soon was dating quite a bit, all with boys outside of school. In the next few years, I was the lucky recipient of a number of such dates. I dated college friends of Solan's or sons of my parents' friends. Eventually, my shyness and awkwardness faded away, and I found myself enjoying many dates and, if truth be told, a total of eight proposals of marriage.

Remember, this was in the early 1950s. There was only a fraction of the number of Chinese in the United States that there are today. I sympathized with the young men in their seemingly desperate attempts to persuade me to accept them as more than just friends. I wonder if the eventual relative paucity of women in China because of the one-child policy will create the same competitiveness among young men there.

Now I know how young men hate the idea of women to whom they are attracted wanting to be just friends. I know this from having had two sons who have denounced such an experience with a girl. Fortunately, they both eventually were married well to smart and lovely women. I, however, hated having to reject young men I enjoyed seeing and with whom I was having fun, because once they proposed and I declined, I never saw them again.

The memory of one young man lingers. One of Solan's friends from Cornell who was already a graduate student asked me out. Gordon was a good student getting a doctorate in engineering. He was in his upper twenties and was ready to marry and settle down. He was a full ten years older than I.

I enjoyed going out with him because he was a good dancer, enjoyed dancing, and taught me how to dance the tango. I have always loved music and was excited by the rhythm of music. During that time, a song called "Blue Tango" was popular. Anyway, we became so good at dancing the tango (though I never moved my head the way the professional dancers do, which I thought—and still think—looks silly) that people would stop their own dancing to watch us.

I really enjoy dancing, so I saw him often (though I eventually married someone who liked dancing just a little better than having a root canal!). Had I continued to see Gordon, I'm sure we would have done a lot of dancing. I understand from friends who know him that he and his wife put a dance floor in their own home, so he must still be dancing but perhaps a slower tango.

At the time, Gordon became serious with me and wanted to get married. He would steal kisses from me and be obviously excited to be with me. But his ardor worried me, and I told Solan, who in turn became concerned and told him I wasn't ready to settle down and said he should not see me anymore. I felt bad about that, as I knew how much Gordon cared about me.

Because there were so few Chinese in the metropolitan New York City area, I discovered that a grapevine existed, and people spread rumors around without basis. I had dated one young man two or three times, and a friend called me one day to ask if I were engaged to him. I had no intention of getting engaged to anyone and was annoyed that people did not have better things to do than talk about me and the social scene. I have never cared to pry into other people's affairs, and I was annoyed there were people interested in mine.

The summer after graduation from high school, I found a job waiting tables at the Great Neck Country Club, along with some Chinese American friends and also, if I remember correctly, cousin Clarence and cousin Betty. That summer, I learned what alcohol drinks were named because I was assigned at times to the men-only lounge, where alcoholic beverages were served. I had no idea what names drinks had other than terms like *whiskey* and *bourbon*.

I will never forget my first drink-order experience. A man ordered Chivas Regal on the rocks. I thought he was speaking a foreign language. Reluctant to expose my ignorance, I asked him to repeat his order, remembered it, and repeated it verbatim to the bartender. I thought, *Why would anyone want his liquor poured onto rocks?*

Fascinated, I watched as the bartender poured the liquid out of a bottle marked Chivas Regal onto ice cubes. *Aha!* Chivas Regal was the brand name of a scotch, and rocks were not rocks but ice cubes. By the end of the summer, I could pretty well identify what went into the making of many drinks. Since Daddy occasionally drank by himself and not where his children could watch and Mommy didn't drink at all, the culture of cocktails was totally foreign to my brothers and me.

One unforgettable teenage stunt we decided to attempt was to see how many of us could jam ourselves into a tiny two-seater car owned by one of our buddies who also worked at the country club. I believe we managed somehow to stuff eight of us into the car, with some hanging out of the open doors, and drove a few feet to the front door of the club. Thinking back on it now, I realize we risked our lives, but we all enjoyed the fun tremendously, laughing until we could hardly breathe. Ah, youth!

Fig 57 Partial view of Sweet Briar College, photograph courtesy of Aaron Mahler.

Fig 58 The President's House at Sweet Briar College, photograph courtesy of Aaron Miller.

Chapter 20

WARM, DRY HANDS

After I graduated from high school, I enrolled in Sweet Briar College. I had been accepted into the other schools I'd applied to, but they offered me either no scholarship (Cornell) or only small scholarships (Bryn Mawr and Wellesley). Sweet Briar offered me almost a full scholarship and the prospect of working on campus, waiting tables, from my freshman year on through all four years, which would provide spending money. Daddy, who never knew how to handle money or say no to any expense for Mommy, was always broke, and with Solan not yet graduated from Cornell, I needed the financial help.

Being in college did not slow my socializing since it was now known to the Chinese community that I was single and had come of age. There were so many young men who wanted to date me that when I returned for Christmas vacations, I would have a date every night I was home. I had a great time, except that almost without exception, the boys would get too serious, and I would have to tell them not to call me anymore. The poor guys never knew how unsophisticated I was about marriage and sex. Mommy was always disappointed each time I rejected a suitor. She had been married at the age of eighteen, and she never considered that I was too young to do the same.

One of the things I did not enjoy at that time was going to dances put on by some Chinese fraternities, which were social groups for Chinese men. My dates were not always members of the fraternities, as the parties were open to the public, but two or three times, I was among the women chosen as candidates to be queen of the dance that year. I was always uncomfortable in those beauty contests. The other girls seemed to be excited to be called to the front of the crowd. I wanted to disappear into a hole! Figure 59 shows me during one of those times. I am the only one in Chinese dress, looking around for an escape. The other girls always seemed much more sophisticated to me than I was. I think most of them were older than I was. I did not win any of those contests, thank goodness, but my mother was delighted I had been chosen as a candidate. She would hear from either my date or his mother about the dance and contest.

One time, in my freshman year, Tom, another friend of Solan's, gave me his fraternity pin. I had no idea that if a girl was pinned, it meant she was serious with the boy and was going steady with him. I didn't understand why my Sweet Briar friends were so excited that I had a pin, until they explained the American tradition to me. I gave the pin back to Tom the next time I saw him.

Another young man who became serious with me was Jim. I don't remember how I met him. He was probably the most sophisticated of the young men I dated. He was from Hong Kong, and he was attentive and did romantic things, such as sending me a cake and flowers for Valentine's Day. He was the most attentive of my serious beaus.

He also was the best dresser of the men I dated—my husband and sons would probably describe him as a greaseball. He wore jewelry, such as cuff links and bracelets. He was generally different from the others, but for some reason, I was not drawn to him. I don't remember chatting with him about anything of importance. He was good looking and was disappointed and not a little insulted that he could not sweep me away.

Life was good at that time because of my social life as well as life at Sweet Briar, where, for the first time, I stayed in one place for four years with many of the same friends. They became the sisters I wanted so much. I loved them, and they returned my love. We acted like the teenagers we were. Figure 60 shows me with two of my classmates: Helen Smith and Elaine Newton. The years 1953 to 1957 were among the happiest of my life. I worked hard and played hard (figure 61). I could not have chosen a more suitable school. I did not know it, but I needed the intimacy of a small college. I have been fortunate in my life to have made choices, through no fault of my own, that could not have been better.

In my junior year, my roommate, Peggy Liebert, then president of the YWCA on campus (figure 62), decided to hold a mixer for foreign students at nearby schools Washington and Lee, University of Virginia, and Virginia Military Institute. I told her that was a nice idea, but I had no intention of going.

I hated mixers because they were, to me, just an opportunity for young men to look over young women like shoppers in a meat market. I felt sorry for the girls who were not asked by anyone to dance and felt embarrassed. While I did not have trouble being asked to dance, I hated the sight of some of my friends, terrific people who were less attractive at first sight, twisting their hands and staring at the floor as boys passed them by.

However, Peggy told me I had to go.

"Peggy," I said, "I grew up in the United States—I'm as American as apple pie and you!"

"You might not be a foreign student, but you look like one, and you're my roommate, so please go!" she said.

So I did. A number of Asian boys attended, including several Keydets (a term to distinguish themselves from the cadets of West Point) from Virginia Military Institute. One of them asked me to dance, and I immediately thought he was different from the usual boys. The boys who asked me to dance at mixers, especially if they were Asians, were usually so tense and nervous that their hands would be clammy and awful to hold. This one had warm, dry hands. His name was David Pai, and he seemed very much in control of himself. I was impressed, but I was also dating Jim at the time.

David introduced himself to me, and during the following months after the mixer, he called me several times for dates. I declined, feeling it would be unfair to Jim. Finally, in the spring, David called again. He later told me that had I declined to see him once more, he would not have called me thereafter. The Louie

Armstrong Orchestra was to play at the dance at VMI, and I loved Satchmo, so I said yes—and the rest, as they say, is history.

Jim and I parted ways. I began to see David more often. We became engaged in 1958, and we married in 1959. I'm not sure who was happier when I met a man I fell in love with—Mommy or me. Mommy had lost hope that her tomboy daughter would ever settle down with a nice Chinese man, and I loved being in love and also was no longer a target for lonely young men. Looking back on it, I believe my sweet roommate probably knew I was restricted in dating American boys and gave me a chance to meet men I could date. It worked, Peggy, and I thank you for my life!

Two things attracted me to David besides his warm, dry hands and good looks (figure 63).

One was his passionate dislike of Chiang Kai Shek, which stemmed from how Chiang had treated his father, once the top military man in the Chinese Nationalist Army. My mother's family was not in the Chiang camp either because he'd incarcerated Uncle Peter and Aunt Edith.

David's father, Pai Chung Xi, general of the army, was at various times chief of staff of the Revolutionary Army (1926–1928); deputy chief of the general staff, Republic of China (1937–1945); and minister of national defense, Republic of China (1946–1948) (see again figure 25). He had also established himself as an able administrator in his home province of Guangshi, where he had improved education and in general the lives of his people.

He was a man whose military strategies were legendary, and his administration as the leader of the province of Guangxi was equally highly touted. He was the only Nationalist general whom Barbara Tuchman wrote positively about in her book *Stilwell and the American Experience in China*. Nonetheless, General Pai found himself ignored by Chiang Kai Shek during the civil war against the Communists.

Chiang was paranoid and worried that General Pai, who was popular and respected, was interested in taking over the Nationalist government. Like most despots, Chiang surrounded himself with sycophants who would prove themselves incompetent militarily. Had Chiang listened to the general's advice on how to carry out the military strategy to defeat the Communist army in the civil war, many believe the Nationalists would never have lost the civil war to the Communists. When David spoke of this, his sincere respect for his father impressed me. David idolized his father, and the general chose David and his older sister, Diana, to be with him and keep him company when the headquarters were in Chungking during World War II while the rest of the siblings stayed with their mother in Guangxi, their home province.

General Pai was the lay head of the Muslim community in China. David's family kept a (male-only) record of their family tracing back twenty-one generations to a Persian merchant who traveled by boat to China and settled in China in the thirteenth century (figures 64 and 65). His descendants became sinicized but maintained Muslim beliefs. Mommy knew about their religion and cautioned me when David first invited me out to dinner. "Don't order pork!" she said. So I ordered a vegetable dish. David ordered Chinese pork meatballs! While General Pai practiced various aspects of Muslim tradition, I learned quickly his children did not.

The second thing that attracted me was David's willingness to speak to me bluntly and chastise me. That might sound strange, but the reason was that all the other young men would do anything to please me and gain my favor, almost to the point of being obsequious. It is a quirk of my personality that such fawning was uncomfortable.

One day I was annoyed with David because he had not been careful in making plans to meet my parents at an outing, and we could not find them. It was a hot day, and we wandered through a large park, searching, and I nagged at him. After a short time, he replied angrily for me to leave him alone. I was stunned into silence but realized I respected him more because of his willingness to express his annoyance with me.

As I mentioned earlier, I met David at a mixer for foreign students that my roommate Peggy had organized at Sweet Briar. She also invited me to visit her parents on their farm near the Potomac River one Thanksgiving holiday. There I was taken on an early morning goose hunt. I was happy the hunters I was with did not succeed in bringing down a goose, but another group did. We had the goose for dinner. I found it to be too rich and did not eat much of it. One pleasant memory I still have of that visit is Peggy's mother insisting we eat a full bowl of ice cream every night before bed. Yummy. Alas, my friend Peggy passed away suddenly in 2010. However, she knew that David and I had married; in fact, she had attended our wedding. I hope that gave her some gratification.

The same year I entered Sweet Briar College, my parents celebrated their twenty-fifth wedding anniversary. The fourth and last photo was taken in their apartment in New York City, and the last poem was written there (figure 66).

The poem is as follows:

> We are still intimate; we remember always the wedding,
>
> Then the good life, and then, immigration.
>
> My love for her is ever deep as the ocean;
>
> Her natural beauty stirs my mind and I love her more!
>
> I regrettably am not a high official nor am I rich,
>
> Nonetheless my love is sincere and I am faithful.
>
> These 25 years have passed too quickly!
>
> May the future bring us more love.

They look like a loving couple in the photograph. I believe they both came to truly love each other.

However, for reasons that my brothers and I never understood, their relationship began to break down shortly after their twenty-fifth anniversary. They began to argue frequently. Whether that had anything to do with money, Lo Lo, or the Chinese Communists entering the United Nations, I can only guess. Perhaps all of those reasons, the onset of Mommy's menopause, and a further decline in her mental state were factors.

As immigrants, they had no older relatives or peers they could depend on for sage advice. Did they even know about menopause and its consequences? That is something I have never considered until now. All I know is that the fourth photo and poem were the last of Daddy's proclamations of love for Mommy, though they were married until his death in 1998, seventy years after their wedding as teenagers. I am convinced they still loved each other but could not overcome a real wedge between them.

Fig 59 An uncomfortable candidate for Queen of the dance.

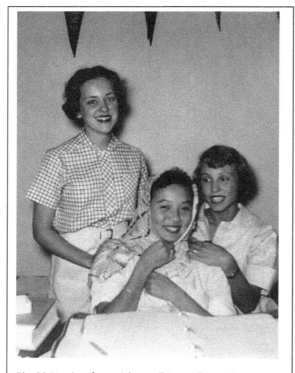
Fig 60 Having fun with my "sisters" at college.

Fig. 61 The Sweet Briar Lacrosse Team

Fig 62 My roommate for three years at Sweet Briar College, Peggy Liebert

Fig 63 VMI Keydet David Pai '58

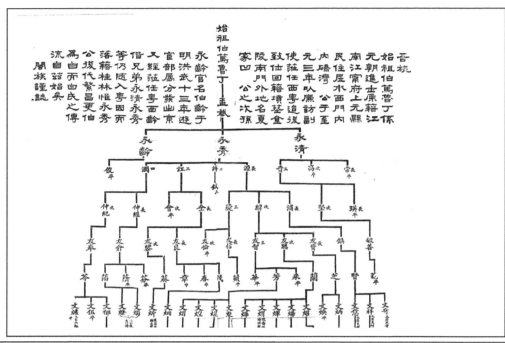

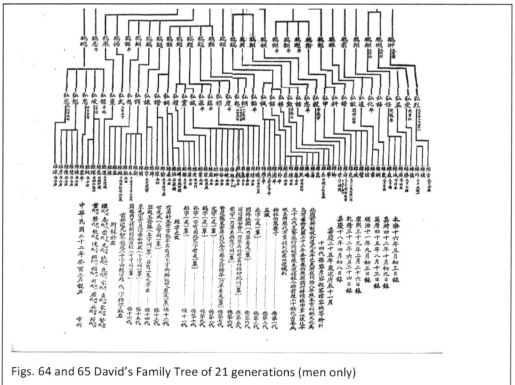

Figs. 64 and 65 David's Family Tree of 21 generations (men only)

From Manchurian Princess to the American Dream

憑肩笑語情叮嚀
猶憶西窗細合監
海樣深情卿愛我
天生麗質哀憐卿
怡喜朱履手鍾祿
但忍青襟一點誠
二十五年渾不覺
歡然連理交崢嶸

Fig 66 Daddy and Mommy in NYC on their 25th wedding anniversary

Chapter 21

STANLEY MAKES A LIFE

I quickly found a home at Sweet Briar, but at the time, my brother Stanley was having a hard time with my mother. Neither Solan nor I was at home to serve as a buffer between him and Mommy. He could not go to college. That was clear to all of us. What made the situation more difficult was that he also was not qualified for any kind of meaningful job. My mother was furious.

She considered herself a victim of bad luck or poor fortune. How could she, the daughter of the Old Marshal, have an inadequate child? I can never forget the look on my brother's face as our mother berated him. It was a combination of fear and embarrassment but also rebellion and anger since he rightly did not feel he had done anything wrong. To me, her behavior was psychological child abuse.

I mentioned earlier that when Stanley was born, he did not breathe for about a minute, perhaps more. Then, as a toddler, he walked too close to children on wooden swings and was hit hard on his head by one of them. To this day, he has a dent in his head that indicates perhaps his skull was fractured.

In those days, there was little regard for youngsters with learning disabilities compared to today. I don't know if there were any technical schools to teach him a craft. Even if there were, I doubt my parents would have cared to enroll him because they would have felt manual labor was below our station in life.

My mother scolded him for his shortcomings and let him know in no uncertain terms that he was a burden to her. She felt his lack of success academically and in every other way was due to recalcitrance and could not understand it was because of neurological damage. I resented that she could not and wondered why. It would be many more years before I realized Mommy was beginning to be incapable of logic and rational thinking.

I was frustrated that I could not even argue with her because we had been brought up to never contradict or oppose our parents. Daddy often repeated the Chinese saying "There is nothing under the sun that parents can do wrong."

Stanley was all along a victim. He could be stubborn, yes, but basically, he is a gentle and kind human being. He had enough moxie to realize he was being treated unfairly and could only resent his treatment by our mother. He knew he was unable to do sports, and after trying, he stopped. Solan and I were not complete angels either in how we treated Stanley. He angered us sometimes when out of sheer stubbornness he would refuse to do something we suggested, even when it was in his best interest. If anyone outside the family showed him some interest and concern, he would light up and do anything for that person. His obvious joy in such a person made my heart heavy because I knew the relationship would not be a long one, and eventually, Stanley would be on his own again.

He enjoyed singing and, like Solan, had a nice baritone voice, but even when he tried to find a place for himself in school by singing, he failed. As I mentioned earlier, there was a student recital of some sort while we were in high school, and Stanley signed up to sing. I was tingling with excitement and apprehension when it was his turn at the microphone. He started well enough, singing strongly, but then disaster struck: he forgot the words to the song and had to stop in the middle of the song and leave the stage.

But through all his tribulations, Stanley never gave up on himself. Had something like the singing fiasco happened to me, I would have had trouble facing students afterward and tried to hide. I was impressed that Stanley's attitude never changed. He was his usual self, as if nothing had happened. Could it be that somehow, for the sake of survival, his brain refused to acknowledge his standing in life at school, even at a young age? Or was he endowed with extraordinary courage? I think maybe a bit of both.

After graduating just barely from high school, Stanley was drafted into the US Army. He served for two years, and I felt some relief that at least he was being cared for and had food and shelter. I never heard him describe his experiences as a soldier or how his fellow soldiers treated him. When he was discharged, he tried to re-up but was rejected. He had to return home, and I was relieved I was at Sweet Briar and did not have to bear the cross of being home.

I believe it was in my sophomore year at college that the tortuous relationship between my mother and brother came to a head, and she threw him out of the apartment. My parents did not give him any money but did allow him to pack his things. I do not know what triggered the event. All I know is that I received a phone call from Stanley saying he was no longer allowed to live at home. They had simply turned him out.

My parents never mentioned him when I was home during holidays that year. I could not understand how they could just abandon their child, but I still could not broach the subject and tell them what I really thought about their decision. I cannot remember Solan talking to them about it either. I was grateful to be away at school but felt guilty about being grateful.

I could not accept Mommy's constant moaning about her terrible fate and life. She had a faithful husband who provided for the family, and Solan and I had excelled in school from grade school to college. Why were Stanley's shortcomings such a terrible burden for her to bear? I could not admire my mother because of that, and I think she knew how I felt.

Stanley first stayed a few days with Solan and Jeannie but then decided to strike out on his own and left New York City. He called me at Sweet Briar a while later and asked for money to go home, hoping he'd be accepted again there. I sent him what I could, and it should have been enough to get him home. He was to call me when he arrived home. I hoped to hear after a week or so that he had arrived and that Mommy had relented and let him stay, but I didn't hear from him, and he never showed up at home.

I was worried that something had happened, and since he hadn't told me where he was, I wondered if I would see him again. In my imagination, I feared for his well-being. Could he wisely use the money I'd sent without having the money stolen or taken from him? Was he forced to stay in slums? Where was he sleeping? Was he starving? What could I do to find him? I knew my parents would never let me leave school to look for him.

His indomitable will to survive caused his wanderings to end in Buffalo, New York, where he resides to this day. A month or more later, I received a letter from Stanley stating that he had used up the money I'd sent him and had wandered into a Baptist mission that helped indigent people. He wrote he had changed his mind about going home and had nowhere else to go.

They had given him a bed and food to eat and accepted him as one of theirs. In return, he had run errands for them and carried out chores in the mission. In fact, they told him he could stay there and work for them. Even more, he had been studying Christianity with them and had become a born-again Christian. He signed his letters "Yours in Christ, your brother, Stanley Chao." He stayed with the mission for thirty years. I told Mommy about this development, and she seemed to accept the information with some relief. Eventually, she allowed him to return to their apartment for a visit.

I could not have been happier that he was safe, though always in the back of my mind I wondered if anyone was taking advantage of him. As always, whenever he felt accepted, he would do anything for anybody and be happy. But my fears were unnecessary because those at the mission really did take care of him, and they in turn were gratified by his acceptance of the Baptist church's teachings. In fact, he became a lay preacher for them.

Then an unexpected development occurred that softened Mommy's feelings even more about Stanley: Stanley found love and a life companion. He met Sandy Hinton in a young people's gathering sponsored by the mission. Sandy, some ten years younger than Stanley, also had some developmental handicaps. Though she did not go to college either, she is more capable than Stanley in dealing with money, and to this day, she works as a home health-care aide and manages their finances.

Solan and Jeannie, Mommy and Daddy, and I attended their wedding. I do not remember why David was not there, probably because of work. I was relieved my parents wanted to attend, as they'd expressed astonishment that Stanley could be so fortunate as to find a life companion. My brother could not have been more fortunate. We have all said that Sandy could not be more devoted and compassionate. It seemed to me that some in her family were not happy she was marrying Stanley. A relative sitting in front of us was crying during the ceremony, and it did not appear to be out of joy. But Stan and Sandy were happy beyond words (figure 67). He sang to her during the ceremony, and she looked thrilled. They shared, and still share, a deep faith in the Bible, and he has continued to preach even after retiring from the mission.

I was proud of my parents for acting like parents during the wedding. I have to believe Mommy must have felt some regret for having sent her son away without any support from them. For him to have a wife and a job with people who were fond of them both was no doubt a huge relief for my parents. It certainly was for Solan, Jeannie, and me.

At times, Stan also held other jobs, such as loading cartons onto trucks for a department store. At one point, he injured his leg on the job and received worker's compensation for his injury. His eyesight, which was never perfect, continued to be a handicap for him, and he often had to become a house husband while Sandy continued her work as a home health-care aide. She told me he was able to make good dumplings that they both liked to eat.

Solan, along with David and I, helped them buy the house where they still live. It is not a fancy neighborhood, but because of that, the house cost $11,000 in the late 1960s. They rent out their upstairs rooms and have continued to live without problems in the same house. Solan and I were always amused that they paid off their mortgage before either of us did.

Figure 68 shows the house they have lived in for more than forty years. They have clearly taken good care of it. Once, when I asked Sandy if she would consider moving down to much warmer North Carolina, where David and I moved when we decided we needed a retirement community, her answer was a quick: "Oh no! I'd miss the cold and snow!"

Solan, David, and I traveled to Buffalo when Stanley was ordained as a lay minister for the mission in 1970. We all were proud of that ceremony. I was thrilled to see how genuinely affectionate the people of the mission were toward Stanley and Sandy and how comfortable the couple were in their midst.

I was also touched when Stanley introduced Solan and me to his friends. He showed us he was proud of our accomplishments and made sure everyone knew that Solan was a medical doctor and I was a PhD. Solan and I had never talked with Stanley about what we were doing academically because we didn't want to rub it in that we'd succeeded, but Stanley showed us that day in Buffalo that he was proud of us.

His marriage to Sandy, along with his newfound religion, seemed to further soften my parents' feelings about Stanley. While Mommy did not formally belong to a religion, she leaned toward Buddhist teachings and respected those who were religious. Also, Stan was working at the mission and had kept the job for years. The fact that he could keep a job was a revelation to her, and that someone was willing to marry him and was caring for him was another source of wonder for her.

In 1980, I decided we needed to have a professional take a picture of the whole family, including Sandy and Stan. David and I had started going to a professional photographer when Ben was five years old, and we decided to have a photo portrait of the family every five years. In 1980, Ben was fifteen, so it was time again for family portraits to be shot. I invited Stanley and Sandy down to stay with us in Livingston.

Figure 69 is the photograph that resulted. You can see on their faces that there is not a shred of evidence that either my brother or sister-in-law held any resentment against my parents. On the contrary, Sandy more than once said she was happy she could call my parents Daddy and Mommy.

As relieved as I was over how well Mommy had accepted Sandy and Stanley back into our family, Mommy said something to me the day of our family portrait that caused my concern over her mental well-being to deepen. That afternoon, after we returned home from the photography studio, Mommy called me in an agitated state and said, "The photographer stole fifty dollars from my purse! I had a fifty-dollar bill in my purse, and now it's gone. You have to get it back for me!" I was stunned.

"But, Mommy, how do we prove you had it, and if they do have a fifty-dollar bill, how do we prove it's yours?"

She fussed about the matter for several days and then ended by again accusing me of being uncooperative and disrespectful. It was to be the beginning of many years of paranoia developing in my mother. Should I have given her a fifty-dollar bill anyway? I had no one to ask.

I admire Sandy and Stanley for their courage, love of life, and deep faith. Even more than that, they continue to believe in themselves. There is no bitterness in them. They are doing well, and David and I are managing a trust fund for them from sales of Mommy's jewelry. She left her things to me alone when she passed away. I decided that Stanley was overdue for some help from her for the life he had to endure at home. I also decided that the proceeds from the sale of her jewelry will be divided between Stanley and Solan's two daughters.

In 2015, Stan and Sandy accepted an invitation to come visit us at our retirement home. Figure 70 shows a good time was had by all. Our neighbor, Gill Holland, a retired English professor at Davidson College, drove the three of us around the college campus and other properties the college owned.

Stanley and Sandy never had children, something I think was for the best. It would have been difficult for them because of the expenses and problems that parenthood would have incurred. That they have been able to make a comfortable life for themselves is an achievement that I feel exceeds anything Solan and I might have managed to achieve in our careers and family lives.

Fig 67 Photo of our family and the happy newly weds

Fig 68 Stanley and Sandy's house

Fig 69 A formal portrait of the family in 1980

Fig 70 Stanley, Sandy and myself in 2015 photo courtesy of Dr. Gill Holland

Chapter 22

MY FIRST REAL HOME, SWEET BRIAR COLLEGE

I will now return to my college years. Because the tension at home was high, Sweet Briar and its lovely rural campus were a haven for me. My parents were quarreling with each other almost as much as Mommy was verbally abusing Stanley. One evening, when I was home for a holiday, after a particularly unpleasant day, I broke down in tears in my bedroom. Solan saw me crying and asked why I was upset.

I told him I thought we had a really dysfunctional family. I said, "Not one part of the family is close to another. Daddy and Mommy aren't getting along. Stanley is fighting with everyone, and you and I are so competitive with each other that we don't really talk."

Solan calmed me down by saying, "It does look that way, doesn't it? But we'll work our way through all this. For whatever reason, you and I have always been competitive with each other because Mommy and Daddy are so intense that we do well in school. But I don't feel that you're my adversary—competitor, yes, but not adversary. There's a difference."

Remember that when he entered college, Solan wrote me a long letter about how proud he was of me, even though for some reason we could never talk about our feelings about each other. I was happy to receive the letter. It made me love my big brother to the point of idolizing him. When I first heard the song "Wind Beneath my Wings," I immediately thought of him.

In addition to our new sibling relationship, instrumental for my growth as a person at that time was my entry to college and a different environment.

During orientation week at Sweet Briar College, I and other entering freshmen were asked if we had nicknames. The only one I ever had was Chips, which a basketball teammate at Great Neck High gave me because I loved potato chips and frequently had them as a snack. However, it was not generally used in high school. However, when I said that was my nickname, I was then called only Chips at Sweet Briar, and to this day, Sweet Briar people still use that name for me.

To my great relief and gratitude, my fellow students quickly accepted me, in part because I established myself as varsity material for a number of sports. I had played basketball and softball for both Mineola and Great Neck High Schools and was chosen for Sweet Briar teams in those sports. It was yet another example of how athletics played an important role in my life.

I played field hockey for the first time at Sweet Briar and became proficient enough to be added to the varsity team in my freshman year. Actually, I found it was safer to be on the varsity rather than playing field hockey in gym class because the worse the players were, the more likely they were to swing the stick too high and cause injury. The better players could control their sticks.

A classmate, Nancy Godwin, who was to become my suite mate in our junior and senior years (figure 71), was one of the students I had to be careful of. While Nancy was a terrific actress, a good student, beautiful and sophisticated, one thing she was not was coordinated. I remember her charging toward me with her stick about eye level while I was goalie one day, and her body was totally out of control. We laughed about it throughout our sixty years of friendship, though at the time, I found it rather threatening. She reminded me that the first words I spoke to her were "If you hold your stick that high, you'll hurt someone!" and of course, I meant me.

Thinking back on those years, I realize we knew nothing about training, warming up, or any of the techniques used today to develop athletes. We simply put on our little skirts, went out onto the field or court, and started running. I remember my lungs burning when the temperature was low. The college did not offer a physical education major, nor does it now. If we'd had a physical education major, I probably would have seriously considered it as a major for myself.

On the other hand, the attitude toward women's sports, even at a women's college, was that women were incapable of much athletic performance because of our allegedly inferior physical makeup. I agree we cannot compete with men in most sports, but in those days, we were told, for example, that women were not built to make jump shots in basketball and that we should not even try.

It wasn't until my senior year, when we played James Madison University, that we saw they had a black team member who had a jump shot. We watched her with our mouths open as she scored some thirty points against us—which was nearly the total number of points we usually scored as a team. Our guards had no idea how to guard a jump shooter and could only helplessly watch her go up and down.

Women's stamina was in question also. As basketball players, we were not allowed to dribble more than twice. When I played with my sons years later, they could dribble circles around me. I never played against people who dribbled continuously. We played half-court hoops, and we were either guards or forwards. Only forwards could shoot; guards were only allowed to guard. I was a forward, and the most points I ever got in a game was sixteen. Since our scores were usually only in the thirties, sixteen was a high number.

Some of my buddies came to watch our hoops games—not often because we were a bad team until my senior year. It wasn't until then that we even won a game. What a celebration we had then! In fact, we were good enough to win several games that year. My buddies raised a cheer for me spontaneously: *"Akalacka Ching, Akalacka Chow, Akalacka Ching Ching Chow Chow Chow!"* My maiden name, Chao, was pronounced as "Chow." Today I doubt anyone would make up such a cheer for fear of being politically incorrect, but I knew they were truly cheering for me, and it felt good to me.

My parents always told us America was not our home—China was—and we were not Americans but would always be Chinese. I believe now that one result of that brainwashing was the feeling that we belonged nowhere. The deep feelings of sadness I mentioned earlier stopped after I had attended Sweet Briar for a couple of years. I felt I had found my first real home. I belonged, and I realized it was okay to be an American.

People accepted me for who I was, not for what I was. I could be myself and discovered with joy that I was liked. My studies were interesting and stimulating, and it was the only place where I had lived for more than a year. I felt I was part of an extended family at college.

I understand that my parents wanted us to feel Chinese because of their dream of returning to their homeland. They did not want us to feel American because their backgrounds instilled into their brains that we were better than the commoners of the United States. My parents must have felt more acutely than my brothers and I did that they did not belong. The awareness eventually that they would never return to China to live must have been a cause for deep sadness on their part. Still, they did not apply for American citizenship until they were in their eighties.

I learned quickly at Sweet Briar that the South was different culturally from the North, where I had lived most of my life. Early in my freshman year, I took the bus with some friends to the nearest town, Lynchburg. There I got my first taste of discrimination against blacks. The discrimination wasn't directed against me, but it showed me how things were.

The bus was fairly crowded in front, so I began to walk to the rear, where there were seats available. The next thing I knew, my classmate grabbed me and pulled me back to the front. "No," she whispered. "You don't want to sit back there—that's for the colored people." I was so surprised that I meekly obeyed her and returned to the front. It never occurred to my friend that I too was a person of color, just not black.

There were still so few foreign faces, especially in a town like Lynchburg, that I felt myself something of a curiosity there. While walking with a classmate down the street that day, I met two boys around eight years of age walking in the opposite direction. When they saw me, they stopped in their tracks, and their mouths dropped open. As we passed them, they whispered to each other. Then I heard them running after us. They passed us and pretended to be looking in a store window down the street so they could get another look at me as we walked by again.

Remember that the civil rights movement was only beginning in the early 1950s. I also learned that race relations were not a subject to bring up at Sweet Briar. After we returned from Lynchburg that day, I mentioned at the dinner table my experience on the bus and while walking in Lynchburg. The next thing I knew, there was a more-than-lively debate about discrimination.

It turned into a heated argument, not so much with me but between some of my southern and northern friends. After that, I would say what I thought only if asked about civil rights, and I was hardly ever asked. I personally never felt any discrimination at school, and my election to student government office every year was testament to my acceptance by schoolmates.

In the fall of my freshman year, Daddy and Mommy came to visit me during parents' weekend for the first time. I was surprised and touched by something Mommy asked. We were sitting on campus after they had settled into their hotel room near the campus.

We were chatting, when Mommy turned to me and said, "You don't like it here, do you? You can come home."

It seemed as though she really missed me. I suppressed a smile at the ingenuous way she was probing for a way to persuade me to leave.

"No, Mommy. I love it here. Everyone is so friendly, including the professors. I will graduate in four years, and I will be home during the summers." She shrugged.

As a freshman, I was elected vice president of my class, which surprised me and gave me confidence that I would have no trouble finding friends. Recently, I found a handwritten note from my father congratulating me for having been elected VP. He wrote, "We are so proud of you. You have brought honor not just to yourself but to the entire family."

The letter surprised me, as they had said little to me when I was deciding which college to go to. I didn't think they were that interested in my academic future. They never took me or Solan to see any colleges. They probably never knew that was something to do, so I simply applied to the two I had heard about from relatives who'd attended them (Cornell and Sweet Briar) and the ones I had read good things about (Bryn Mawr and Wellesley).

Sweet Briar also provided me with some lifelong friends. One of the happiest moments in my life occurred in the beginning of school in the fall of 1954. A dear friend, Virginia "Gina" Marks, a gentle, sweet Texan, had told me before the spring semester of 1954 ended that she had decided to transfer back to a Texas school. More than one student from Texas had done so, and I was sad she was not returning. It was like losing a member of my family.

As I had been elected house president for my sophomore year, I was at Sweet Briar before classes started in the fall to greet students who were returning early to help with freshman orientation. I was sitting in the basement of Manson dormitory, which was a student lounge where one could relax and chat with friends. Suddenly, the door opened, and Gina poked her head in, smiling, and said, "I'm back!" I shrieked with joy. We graduated together and have kept in touch through all the years afterward. Figure 72 shows me with two of my best friends from college at a reunion. My guess is that this was around 1987, our thirtieth reunion.

Gina was one of the Sweet Briar College graduates I had the privilege to know who was able to persevere despite enormous pressures of life. After many years of marriage, her marriage disintegrated through no fault of her own, and she was left to support her four young children. To do so, Gina entered graduate programs and received a PhD in education policymaking and administration from Washington University in St. Louis. I believe Gina and I both profited from our undergraduate education at a women's liberal arts college. Both of us ended up with advanced degrees that I, for one, never had thought I was capable of attaining.

As a junior, I was elected to the Judicial Board, which adjudicated violations of the honor system, and as a senior, I was again elected to the board. While it was flattering to be put up for those elections and to be elected, looking back on it, I know I overextended myself. Those positions took up much time. At the same time, I was on varsity squads of different sports, and about a month after school began, I was allowed to wait tables.

That was the best-paying job on campus, and I was the first student Sweet Briar ever had allowed to wait tables in freshman year. We student waitresses became good friends with the kitchen people, who would occasionally save us choice pieces of food to eat after we served. They were kind people. I hoped the college paid them enough to be comfortable.

The cooks and help in the kitchen were all local folks. Some had deep accents. Some were not only southern but also lived in the hills of Appalachia and had their own dialect. It took me a few weeks to get used to their drawl and understand their language.

A doctor in the military whom I met at a symposium once told me he had the same problem in understanding their dialect. He had done some pro bono work for the local people. One lady had told him that at one time, she had been ill with "Smilin' Mighty Jesus." Only when he heard her description of symptoms had he realized she meant spinal meningitis.

Looking back on my life, I sometimes wonder if I would do everything the same way again. While it looked like a terribly difficult life, at the time, it didn't seem so hard to me, or at least not intolerably hard. But I'm old today, and I was a youngster then, with limitless energy.

The student waitresses had a small room on the second floor, above the dining room, where we could get green uniforms to put over our clothes. After waiting tables, we threw the uniforms into a big pile in the room. If we didn't have a class, we sometimes sat at a small table or sprawled on a cot in the room and just hung out. We talked about everything. Some of my best friends came from waiting tables. I was proud when a professor one day said to me that her most thoughtful students were student waitresses.

One day June Berguido, a freshman, and I, a junior, were chatting in the student waitress room. She was mature and already a leader in her class. She was an athlete, and we were teammates on the basketball team. I hated to play against her in practice—she was a guard, and I a forward—because she had long arms and was strong. She came from a fairly wealthy family, and she and her five sisters all had attended a private school, Shipley, which was across the street from Bryn Mawr in Pennsylvania. She told me when the seventh child in the family had been born a boy, her whole school had celebrated.

She became one of my best friends and one of the students at Sweet Briar whom I respected the most. She was a brilliant student who made straight As and was sensitive to social injustices. The fact that she was elected president of student government in her senior year proved that her classmates and others felt the same about June as I did.

One day in the student waitress room, I told her about my worries about Stanley and my mother. To my astonishment, when I looked up, I saw tears streaming down her face. She felt such compassion for Stanley and for people in general. Unsurprisingly, when she started a career after graduation from Sweet Briar, it was as a social worker in Buffalo, New York, working with drug and alcohol addicts.

June was an example of a friendship that people let lapse to great regret later. As the years flew by, we corresponded less and less with each other, until we really only exchanged letters at Christmas to catch up. She married and had two girls, but then the marriage fell apart, and she got divorced. Figure 73 shows June and me when we last visited each other. Then she had a companion for many years, a man several years older than she, and he died in his sixties. Her world then centered on her daughters again and, as they matured and married, her grandchildren. Focused on my own family and career, I didn't do much to stop us from drifting apart. Our friendship was always in the back of my mind, but I never felt I had the time to call or write long letters.

Then, in 2003, I received a long letter from June saying she wanted us to be close again and see each other. In it, she had written, "I have regretted that we have been so busy with family and jobs that we have neglected our own friendship."

I wrote her back a long letter. I told her how much she meant to me: "June, my admiration and affection for you has never waned. I admire you for not just your remarkable intelligence but your equally high moral standards."

I suggested a time when we could visit with each other and told her to let me know if the timing was good for her also. To my surprise, I did not get the quick response from her that I expected. When thinking about her, I wondered if I had offended her by not being more communicative over the years.

Two months later, in August, I received a letter from her daughter explaining why I had not received a reply from June. That athletic, lean, vibrant, compassionate, brilliant person had had a massive heart attack and died in her early sixties. I was heartbroken.

June was visiting her daughter and playing with her two-year-old grandson. That morning, she told her daughter she was not feeling well and thought she might be coming down with the flu or something. She complained of pain in her mouth and asked her daughter to take the baby to day care in case she had something the baby could catch.

When her daughter went home to check on June at lunchtime, she found June in bed, dead. I had not heard of mouth pain as a symptom of impending heart attack, but I certainly know of it now. It is a symptom that women especially commonly get when a heart attack is pending. Even in death, June had left her friends a piece of information that might save their lives.

The daughter found my letter on her desk. June had read it but hadn't had time to respond. I was glad she had read it and knew how much I cared for her. I went to visit one of her daughters a few months later. She showed me and another close friend and classmate of June's a video of June's funeral services. I don't remember why I could not make the funeral, but I had sent a eulogy that was read by her daughter.

In part of the eulogy I sent, I wrote, "Having been an immigrant and bumping around in this country during World War II when being Asian was not a good thing, I found my first real home in America at Sweet Briar. And because of friends like June, I found myself. I am eternally grateful to have had her in my life."

I wonder if June had a sense of her life being cut short that prompted her to write the letter to me. Had she been diagnosed with heart problems? Recently, I found some letters she wrote after I graduated, in which she told me of her activities as student government president at Sweet Briar. Some of the letters were ten pages long. It saddened me that we had drifted apart and not seen each other for years. Dear reader, life can be stunningly short. Do not let those you love drift away.

During mealtimes at Sweet Briar, I learned that how people treated service people, such as waitresses, reflected their true self and worth. One girl whose name I have forgotten but whose face is etched in my mind was always gushingly friendly toward me—except when I had the waitress uniform on. Then she would look away when she entered the dining room and never greet me. I have since made it a point to treat all service people with great respect, and I made sure my sons did too.

In fact, I have proof that I succeeded all too well in that endeavor. One day when the boys were around nine and ten, we went to a movie. We stopped in an ice cream parlor before entering the movie house, and the boys ordered ice cream for about a dollar each. I left thirty cents for a tip, and they thought it was too little. I pointed out that it was way more than 10 percent, but they kept badgering me when we were seated in the theater. Finally, I had to get up and leave the movie house to put down another quarter before they would let me alone. I pretended to complain about them but was pleased that my sons were so caring.

Fig 71 My suitemate of two years and dear friend for life, Nancy Godwin Baldwin

Fig 72 Myself with Nancy Baldwin standing, and Gina Paget seated to my left.

Fig 73 June and I visiting in the 1970's

Chapter 23

I BECOME A ZOOLOGIST

When it came time to choose a major at Sweet Briar, I decided to major in zoology. I had always been interested in nature and how living things became the way they were. I loved languages too, especially the Romance languages and English too, and did well in those courses. Actually, I found the course work at SBC overall fairly easy the first year, thanks to good advanced courses and preparation for college at Rhodes School in New York City and at Great Neck High School.

There were only two members of the faculty available in the biology department at Sweet Briar, Miss Jane Belcher and Miss Miriam Bennett, who was a brand-new PhD. They all had doctorates, but tradition at Sweet Briar at that time said to address professors as Miss, Mrs., or Mr. The botanist, Miss Elizabeth Sprague, was on sabbatical leave the two years I was a biology major, so I was perforce a zoology major. I believe there were only six in my graduating class who majored in biology, which Miss Belcher told me was the hardest major in the college in which to get A grades. Happily, things are different now. Biology at times is the most popular major at Sweet Briar College.

I have always thought I had a streak of sadomasochism in me. I majored in the toughest major as an undergraduate. The course I found most difficult in the biology curriculum was genetics. Guess what I went on to study in graduate school? First, I studied embryology for my master's degree at Bryn Mawr College, and then I studied genetics for my PhD at the Albert Einstein College of Medicine.

My main interest was in developmental genetics, probably the blackest of the black boxes in biomedical sciences. Developmental genetics deals with how genetically identical cells of the early embryo begin to differ from each other to eventually become the myriad tissue and cell types found in the fully developed individual. It is the result of gene regulation, at that time a complex and incompletely understood topic.

To be honest, I think my struggles with genetics as an undergraduate began with the wonderful retired University of Virginia professor (whose name escapes me now) who took Miss Sprague's place in teaching genetics. He had been part of the genetic revolution in the United States in the early years of the twentieth century, when a number of scientists realized that Gregor Mendel's studies of the patterns of inheritance in peas had merit.

Mendel, a Bavarian monk who had a background in mathematics and horticulture, recognized some patterns of inheritance of traits in pea plants by controlling the pollination of plants. From his studies in 1865, he realized that making assumptions could explain the patterns, namely that genetic traits were determined by pairs of units, one from each parent. Also, some traits were dominant over others, which were recessive, and when combinations of traits were studied, there was a random assortment of how the different pairs of units were transmitted. We, of course, now refer to the units of heredity as genes.

In the 1930s, many studies revealed the basic knowledge about heredity that led to studies on the biochemical and molecular level in the 1940s and, beyond that, resulted in our awareness of DNA and the brave new world of genetic engineering and cloning.

I don't remember the gentleman's name who taught us genetics at Sweet Briar, but he was rotund and spoke loudly. I think he was hard of hearing, which was why he spoke so loudly. He also couldn't control his spittle when he lectured, and we all learned to sit at least a row of seats back from him. He was an adventurer and showed us pictures of himself dressed in leaves in the midst of tribes in the Amazon. He was quite a character!

During the semesters that he taught, he brought his wife with him to live on campus. One lasting image is of him trudging through the campus with his head up, shoulders back, and stomach leading as she followed behind with her head down, much shorter than he, struggling to keep up. As much as I respected him as one of the pioneers of genetics, I'm afraid he was not very clear as a lecturer, and I was often befuddled. As usual, I thought I just wasn't smart enough to catch on.

The professors at Sweet Briar had no time or facilities to carry on research of their own, but because of the small size of the student body, they came to know their students well. It was not uncommon for us to be invited to our professors' homes since most lived right on campus in houses built fairly close to the academic buildings. This too has changed. Today all professors are involved in research and frequently sponsor students to do independent research.

In those days, students and faculty developed friendships in other ways. I remember once spending the night at Miss Belcher's house because her dog was about to give birth to puppies, and of course, her majors wanted to witness the amazing process. On another occasion, she took some of us to hunt for morels, the edible cone-shaped mushrooms, which she then sautéed in butter. They were delicious. But she also served canned, fried grasshoppers, which I politely declined!

I learned early on that I was more suited to be a researcher in the laboratory than a naturalist in the great outdoors, although I loved the outdoors. On one field trip, I thought I found something interesting, some small, oval-shaped black entities on the ground. I thought since they were the shape of eggs, they must have been eggs. With excitement, this city girl scooped them up and took them to Miss Belcher. With a chuckle, my professor informed me that I had found rabbit poop.

For entomology class, I went on a field trip by myself one day. I was armed with a net and a glass jar, and my assignment was to capture some bumblebees. I found some buzzing near wildflowers on the road to the dairy. Not having used nets ever to capture flying insects, I discovered it was much harder than I'd imagined. I ended up sparring with the bee I tried to net, and the bee flew at me in its irritation.

I did eventually capture it, sweating profusely and unhappy about the whole experience. At that point, I decided I should stay in the lab. I think Miss Belcher had reached the same conclusion.

Chapter 24

REAL SCIENTIFIC RESEARCH

After I'd taken a number of biology courses, Miss Belcher told me about a research training program at the Jackson Memorial Laboratory in Bar Harbor, Maine, for the summer after my junior year in 1956. A center for cancer research, it offered a summer research training program for college students as well as a research training program for high school students. Miss Belcher suggested I look into the program for college students and volunteered to write me a letter of recommendation.

I had no other plans since I usually worked during the summers to earn money. I was not sure I was smart enough to participate in such a program, but I convinced myself there was little to lose and much to gain. In those days, as I mentioned before, there was no opportunity for any student to do any independent research at Sweet Briar College. Today the students have ample opportunity and the facilities and equipment to carry out high-quality research on the campus.

To apply for the Jackson Lab Research Training Program, applicants had to write a letter describing their interest in some aspect of biomedical research. Miss Belcher added her letter of recommendation for me. The staff scientists then read through the applicants' letters and choose one to work with him or her on a one-to-one basis for the summer. For students at small schools, such as Sweet Briar, the opportunity to experience real scientific activity was and still is life-changing.

To my great surprise, I received a letter from a Dr. LeRoy Stevens (figure 74), who invited me to spend the eight-week course in his laboratory, helping in his research on embryonal carcinoma, a cancer of germ cells in mice. I could not have been happier to respond immediately that I would be coming. I took a long bus trip from New York City to Portland, Maine. Dr. Stevens had said he would drive me from Portland to Bar Harbor, and he met me at the bus terminal in Portland in the afternoon.

When we arrived at the bridge to Bar Harbor, which was located on Mount Desert Island (also called Acadia National Park), it was twilight. The Blue Nose Ferry that carried people from Bar Harbor to Nova Scotia was on its way. The row of lights in portholes gleamed against the darkening side of the boat. The entire scene—several islands surrounded by blue waters, all reflecting the red of the setting sun, and the Blue Nose moving serenely through the calm waters—was one of the most beautiful sights I had ever seen.

Since Bar Harbor is on Mount Desert Island, the scenery is beautiful everywhere. One day I was sitting on some rocks right by the ocean, when I saw another unforgettable sight: a sailboat was moving from my left to my right, and right behind it was the edge of a mass of dark rain clouds, with a bright silver edge from the sun that the clouds were hiding. The boat was trying to avoid the impending storm by outracing the clouds, but gradually, inexorably, the clouds overtook the boat, and it was enveloped in a curtain of rain.

The worst part of that summer was learning to handle mice. Dr. Stevens's research was on mice, as was most of the research done by the scientists at Jackson Laboratory. But the strain of mice (129) Dr. Stevens worked on were fairly docile, and after my initial discomfort, I was able to work with them easily.

Dr. Stevens's research interest was on a type of testicular tumor that was derived from abnormal sperm cells. The malignant ones were called embryonal carcinoma cells, or EC cells for short, and the benign ones were called teratomas. EC cells were undifferentiated cells that spread like all cancers and killed the mice. When EC cells underwent changes to become a cell type (thus acting like stem cells), they lost their malignancy and became teratomas.

Teratoma tumors were found to have muscle cells, teeth cells, and almost all kinds of tissue types—even, on occasion, the beginning of an embryo. That was not surprising since germ cells, of course, had the potential to develop into all cell types in the embryos. The question of interest was the following: What were the factors that caused sperm cells to become ECs or teratomas?

My project was to feed ground sweet pea seeds to pregnant mice to see how they affected the development of the aorta of the fetuses and, if defects in the aorta resulted, how the defects might affect the incidence of tumors in the testes. To do this, I had to grind the seeds with a mortar and pestle and mix the powder into the mouse food. I ground so many that I ended up with bursitis in my right shoulder at the end of the summer.

We found that there were indeed aortic abnormalities in the fetuses. There were kinks and twists of that major artery in the body. That alone was of interest because people in some parts of Africa suffering from drought and starvation were known to have eaten seeds of the sweet pea plant. They were found to have died of circulatory problems, and my project showed why. I was hoping there was a link to testicular tumors, but there was no increase in the frequency of tumors in fetuses that had aortic defects.

Our results were worthy of publication, but unfortunately, Dr. Stevens never found the time to write a paper about the topic. Years later, when I returned to Jackson Lab for a workshop and he was a scheduled speaker, he publicly pointed me out and apologized for never having written that paper.

Decades later, when research in stem cells became a hot topic, some recognized that Dr. Stevens's work on EC cells was the beginning of the recognition that there were cells capable of being transformed into different cell types. While my project made not one iota of contribution to stem cell research since it never was published, I found it gratifying that Dr. Stevens got his due and that, for a short time, I had contributed to his work.

I loved that summer at Bar Harbor. Dr. Stevens could not have been nicer or more concerned with my progress. I had a nice person as a roommate, Charlotte Bidwell, and became close friends with a young man—Paul, I believe his name was. It was a thrill to be among those exceptionally bright young people, all of whom were dedicated to the biomedical sciences. David Baltimore, a Nobel Prize–winning scientist (for the discovery of the viral enzyme reverse transcriptase), was an alumnus of the program.

Some of those in my year eventually became prominent as researchers or medical doctors. We all were inspired by our mentors and the talks that other staff scientists gave us. Some of us were invited to their homes as guests, and we sometimes babysat for them also.

The exposure to real research was so exciting that it propelled me into wanting to further my biology education after college. There is the logic of looking at previous research related to the phenomenon of interest. Then there is the challenge of designing experiments, hopefully to result in data that will further the understanding of how the phenomenon occurs and the factors that influence its development.

No matter how small the discovery, finding something new and interesting can cause hair to stand on end. After all, it is information no one else in the world has seen.

That summer of 1956, our counselor was Dr. Jim Miller, and he and his wife and toddler daughter became my good friends. I used to take his daughter into the wild blueberry fields behind our dorm to pick the fruit for our cook to make into muffins and pancakes. The toddler, of course, ate more than she saved, but she was just as cute as she could be. I stayed in touch with them for years afterward but eventually lost contact, as I did with everyone I knew there.

Fig 74 Dr. Leroy Stevens

Chapter 25

SUMMER FUN IN BAR HARBOR, MAINE

I will never forget July Fourth that summer—it was straight out of a Norman Rockwell painting. First, we walked to the town of Bar Harbor, which was only two miles from the lab. In those days, it was not nearly as beset by tourists as it is today. At the town green, a square, we watched as little fireworks were set off, and everyone clapped as if we were watching the Macy's July Fourth fireworks display.

There was a three-piece band that played waltzes afterward for everyone to dance on the square. At the time, the musicians looked to me to be past middle-aged. I got tired of dancing waltzes and went up to the leader of the band to ask if they could play some other music. "Nope" was his brief answer, and they went on to oompah-pah some more.

With a group of friends, we bought some live lobsters, salad, corn, and melted butter and took them back to the lab, where we clambered onto the rocks next to the ocean at Highseas, a seaside mansion that had been donated to Jackson Lab and was used for the precollegiate research training program. There we built a fire and boiled the lobsters and corn. That was one of the most delicious picnics I've ever had. What a wonderful day we had, and what a memorable day and summer. I think back on the opportunities I have had and marvel at my good luck.

That summer too, I had my first experience on a sailboat. One of the guys, Tom, who later became the head of a department in a major midwestern medical center, said he wanted to show me and another of the students what it was like to go sailing. I told him I didn't even swim, and he said that was no problem as long as I wore a life jacket. So off we went on a small sailboat, and I still don't know enough to say what kind it was. But it was simple enough that Tom could handle the sails by himself.

It was a beautiful, sunny day, and the sailing was wonderfully relaxing. Then the wind died down, and we were totally becalmed. Eventually, somebody came by in a motorboat and towed us back. Poor Tom was frustrated by the experience. I've never been on a sailboat since.

Bar Harbor used to be the summer playground for the rich, including the Astors and the Vanderbilts.

There were mansions all over. But at that time, in the 1950s, most of the original owners had become too old to travel or had died, and their heirs were not as devoted to Bar Harbor. The younger generations also did not want to have to pay property taxes, and the mansions were left unoccupied.

Thus, there were sales of the great big houses for what seemed to me to be little money. One beautiful, enormous mansion was on sale for $23,000. I enjoyed being able to go into the large houses and trying to envision the grand parties they used to have and the grand ladies in their ball gowns coming down the elegant winding staircases. What we got out of the sales of the houses was the chance to purchase books for little money from their libraries, which the heirs did not want.

We also found a dusty old bookstore in downtown Bar Harbor that sold books for ten cents each. I bought a whole set of Charles Dickens and some other classics. Ten cents apiece was a price I could handle. We also found some really old books, including one on etiquette in the nineteenth century. We sat around and read to each other aspects of Victorian etiquette and howled with laughter. We compared what was acceptable then to what was acceptable for us. For example, the Victorians required women to cover up from neck to toes in clothing, and we sat there in shorts and T-shirts.

One night in August, Paul told me he knew there would be a shower of meteorites in the sky, so we sat on the lawn on a beautifully clear night and watched shooting stars flash across the sky, sometimes multiple ones and sometimes single ones. We sat and talked about our hopes for the future and what we had learned that summer. That meteorite shower, the Perseus shower, happens every year, but never have I seen it as well as that night. We had little light and air pollution, and I'm sure we saw every meteorite. It was magical.

Finally, it was time to leave one of the most satisfying summers I'd ever spent. Everyone wanted to go up Cadillac Mountain, the highest peak in Maine, to watch the sunrise. Our cars could not accommodate everyone, so a friend and I stayed behind. I was not used to staying up all night and was already too tired to go. I slept most of the way home on the bus.

I have no photographs of those wonderful weeks in Bar Harbor. My interest in photography did not develop until much later, after I had finished my studies and was established in teaching at the collegiate level. It caused me regret when I realized in writing this book that I also really have no photos of my graduate days at Bryn Mawr and then at the Sue Golding Graduate Division of the Albert Einstein College of Medicine. I was working so hard at my studies and research that there was no time to think of doing anything else.

Chapter 26

SOLAN MARRIES; CHINESE OPERA

When I returned home from my first summer as a student at Jackson Lab, to my delight and surprise, Solan had met a young woman whom he had been dating that summer, and he was already engaged to her. See again figure 53. He hadn't even known her when I left for Maine, and by the time I returned, they were betrothed.

I was happy for him because he had been so hurt by Julia's family's rejection of him.

After they were married, Solan decided he would become a physician after all. Remember that he had rejected my parents' order to major in premed, engineering, or agriculture and instead had majored in political science. After serving his requisite two years in the US Army and meeting and marrying Jeannie, he realized his interests—and the practicality of earning a decent wage—were in medicine.

Those were hard times for the young couple. Jeannie had to work, and they scraped, saved, and borrowed so he could attend school at Columbia University. Also, at that time, remember that the GI Bill was a source of money that made it possible for people who had served in the armed forces to return to school.

Solan and Jeannie have two daughters: Carolyn, nicknamed Shrong ("A Pair" in Chinese, indicating a desire for another child), and Patricia Ann, nicknamed Mei ("Little Sister" in Chinese). They are two beautiful girls (see again figure 55). Jeannie's mother was half Irish, so Shrong and Mei are one-eighth Irish. For some reason, Amer-Asian and Euro-Asian children seem always to be unusually good looking. They seem to express the best traits of both groups.

I would like to now give a brief introduction to an important aspect of Chinese culture and one that was especially important for my parents: Beijing opera. There are many forms of Chinese operas—for example, Cantonese opera. My parents taught me that the aristocrat of Chinese operas was Beijing opera. Their involvement in bringing it to the Chinese community in the New York metropolitan areas coincided with Solan's struggles to finish the prerequisite courses for medical school. Unfortunately, that meant little financial help for my brother from our parents.

During the time I was in high school, my parents revealed to us their depth of training in Beijing opera.

While in Beijing, Mommy and Daddy were trained in that popular aspect of Chinese art and culture. Because of their family background, they received training from some of the top performers of their day. It would be like being trained in New York City by the likes of Luciano Pavarotti and Renee Fleming at their peak of popularity. For those wishing to have a career in Chinese opera, the training begins at a young age and includes not only voice and acting lessons but also acrobatics.

I know Daddy possessed the talent to become proficient enough to perform with stars on stage in Beijing because I have found photographs taken of him when he performed in Beijing (figure 75). I found that photo placed side by side with figure 76, a photo of an American Indian chief. Like Daddy, I too noticed the similarities of the two headdresses. Daddy was playing the role of a warrior.

Mommy was deeply involved also, but curiously, I have found no photographs showing her on a professional stage among the many photographs of Daddy onstage. However, I know she performed, perhaps only once, and it was another source of acclamation for them both. It was likely she mainly worked backstage rather than performing, as Daddy did.

That experience and training allowed them to successfully organize a troupe in New York City and obtain instruments and costumes appropriate for a number of different operas. The art started in the eighteenth century, blossomed in the nineteenth century, and became an important part of Chinese culture. Stories are often based on historical events and Chinese legends. The costumes are obviously of a different era and often of the Song Dynasties (AD 960–1279).

My parents began to put on performances in New York City while I was in high school and into my college years. I attended the first performance of their opera group, which was known as Yeh Yu. The excitement among the Chinese in the audience was palpable. They could barely contain themselves as the actors appeared onstage. Tradition allowed the audience to shout "*Hao*!" (Good!) loudly whenever something occurred onstage they liked, even in the middle of singing, acrobatics, or acting. There were shouts of "Hao!" as soon as the curtain rose. During the first arias, I saw people wiping tears of joy from their faces. For many, it had been decades since they had attended such a performance, and it reminded them of home.

It was fun too for me to watch the performers putting on makeup, some with the help of others but some by themselves. Mommy said that in China, professional cosmeticians would draw the magnificent faces representing different roles. She always put makeup on Daddy. Painted faces represented warriors and kings. If I remember right, white painted faces represented the bad guys, and red faces represented the good guys. Those acting as clowns received less-impressive painted faces.

The roles of young men were indicated by actors with shaved faces who sang part of the time in falsetto voices and part of the time in natural men's voices to indicate the change in voices as men reached puberty. Daddy made a handsome young man even when he was middle-aged (figure 77).

Young leaders and warriors were sung in natural voice. Older men's roles would be depicted by the wearing of beards and sung in natural voice. Old men were designated with white beards and sang in natural voice, and old women had their hair wrapped in hats and bands and sang in natural voice. Mommy would always act as a mature man and thus would wear a beard (figure 78). All, including David and I, were impressed with the quality of her singing and acting. She also made a good-looking male character, albeit a rather short one—Mommy was barely five feet tall.

Women often were played by men. Initially, only men were performers of Chinese opera. Women began to take part in the late nineteenth century. In fact, the biggest "female" stars in Beijing opera in the 1930s, when my parents became active in Beijing opera, were men. They sang in falsetto voice, as did women who sang as women. The men were often quite beautiful when made up like women. During the years my parents were learning Beijing opera, the most famous opera star in all of China was Mei Lanfang, a woman impersonator.

My parents knew him well. I do not know for sure, but I would not be surprised if Daddy performed opposite Mr. Mei more than once. The falsetto voice that women impersonators used was equal to the range in which women sing, while the range of falsetto voice for the roles of young men was closer to that of countertenors in Western opera and song.

On one trip we took to Hong Kong, a well-known opera star who was a woman impersonator and knew my parents invited us to his apartment. I can't remember his name, though I believe his family name was Chen, and I don't remember the apartment well, but I was fascinated by the opera star. He was slim, as he had to be to take on his female roles, and his whole being, including the way he moved and spoke, was almost overly feminine—not surprising since he had been trained since he was a child. However, later, my parents told me he had fathered some seven or eight children in his marriage. He certainly must have been masculine in other ways!

What talent Daddy had. There is no doubt in my mind he could have been a professional opera star. Mommy only once performed onstage with Yeh Yu and did well. I could certainly understand the delight my parents derived from being able to once again exhibit their beloved art. The other times Daddy performed, Mommy acted as the cosmetician, and she was quite professional at it. Some people tried to put on their own cosmetics and overpainted their faces.

I was impressed that my father could play such different roles—a young man (most frequently), a mature man, or a warrior—and be very good in each. He was often acclaimed aloud by the audience after a particular scene or aria. Furthermore, when he was not singing, Daddy also acted as conductor of the small orchestra that provided background rhythm and music. The conductor of Beijing opera held a castanet-like instrument in one hand and a small drumstick with the other, which he used on a small solid drum. Other members of the orchestra included the players of at least two upright string instruments called *hoo chin* and *ar hoo*, a small cymbal, a gong, and sometimes a banjo-like instrument called a pi-pa. The Yeh Yu orchestras usually had no more than six members due to the small number of people trained as Chinese opera musicians in New York City. Professional orchestras were larger.

To my everlasting surprise and awe, none of the performers and orchestra members, including Daddy and a second man who conducted when Daddy was singing, had any music sheets or libretto. They did everything by memory; nobody had any written music. In fact, I wonder if the operas were ever written down on paper. They all just remembered what needed to be done for the music and the staging from the days in China when they were trained and performed. Most of them were talented amateurs and, like my parents, highly trained ones.

I want to say a word about the music. The music was altogether different from Western music. I was born into a family in which my parents were constantly humming arias from the operas. Daddy often drummed chopsticks on the table as if he were conducting an opera. Whether because of exposure or because I inherited the right genes, I enjoyed listening to Beijing opera. David, on the other hand, was not fond of the music. The falsetto singing was grating to him.

I was proud that my parents were able to organize and find talent so that the performances were of high quality, and I was proud they could bring such joy to so many people who loved being able to hear—live—their beloved operas again. There were, of course, mistakes made by people who were not as well trained. For example, there were untrained men who were to march around as soldiers, but every so often, one would wander in the wrong direction. However, people understood that they were not professional actors. Sometimes someone would accidentally knock over a chair or small table. That elicited chuckles, but the audience was so delighted to have the operas to watch and listen to that they quickly overlooked such mistakes.

Even I, this tomboy, was drafted to participate in one opera. When I returned home one year from college, I was given the unhappy news that I was to be one of several women who were to act as part of the entourage of a star. It required no spoken lines, thank goodness, but I found difficult the manner in which I was to walk. All movements in Beijing opera are stylized and often exaggerated. For example, I had to walk in an exaggerated feminine way, swaying and being soft, with one foot in front of another. My protests reached deaf ears, as my parents did not have enough players for the opera. I survived but told them no more. I was happy to escape back to Sweet Briar.

The more important the role, the more elegant the robes they wore, and the colors also indicated their positions. Yellow robes were worn by kings and emperors, with embroidery of wavy lines on the bottom of the robes. Somehow, they were able to find and buy appropriate robes and costumes. Solan and I always believed Daddy used his savings to purchase many of the costumes, and they could not have been inexpensive.

I doubt Daddy even thought of foregoing his hobby to make life easier for Solan and Jeannie. Late in his life, I remember my father apologizing for not having supported us the way he was supported as a young man and instead having to have us support him. Indeed, Solan and I chipped in monthly amounts to give to my father for probably the last thirty years of his life.

At the same time, performing successfully gave both Mommy and Daddy a thrill of celebrity they had never experienced in life in America, and I was sorry when they no longer had the thrill to look forward to. Mommy had an alto voice, and I'm sure that's where I got my alto voice. Hers was not a strong voice because she was already in her midforties, but she reached back in memory to sing beautifully whatever role she had volunteered for. I enjoyed going backstage after the opera was over and seeing her face flushed with excitement, relief, and pleasure as people gathered around her with compliments and flattery. I was happy she was happy about something.

However, at about the time I was a junior in college, things were not going well for my parents in their opera group. Apparently, there was a triangle of romance among three of the members of the group. My parents had assumed roles of leadership and tried to help resolve the difficulties. Not surprisingly, the three members involved rejected their help and resigned from the group. One of them was the best of the female stars. My parents were embarrassed and could not understand why their friends reacted the way they did.

I know Mommy and Daddy acted because they thought they could help and even should help. It was the Chinese way; it was their Chinese way. I believe that mistake was again a reflection of their experience as respected offspring of powerful fathers. It never occurred to them that they were treading in sensitive areas where their intervention might not be welcome. It must have been a difficult situation for them. I remember my mother bemoaning aloud about the lack of gratitude of their former friends.

Eventually, the three joined some other singers of Beijing opera and started a group competitive with my parents' Yeh Yu group. Eventually, Yeh Yu disbanded, and my parents did not perform again. I was actually happy that happened, because they were getting older, and I always feared they might falter onstage (which they never did). When Yeh Yu disbanded, I'm sure my parents were not happy that what had given them so much enjoyment was no longer available. They also felt they had lost face when their attempt to help failed.

It was the beginning of a reduction in socializing for my parents, which culminated in some two decades of virtual isolation at the end of their long lives. Their friends were too old to travel from Manhattan to New Jersey, and apparently, they did not want to drive in the opposite direction to meet their friends in Manhattan, as they never asked us to drive them to be with any former friends. I believe their experience with the three former friends made them hesitant to socialize.

They also moved from their house in Allendale to a small house at Lake Hopatcong, almost an hour farther west in New Jersey, which made it even harder for them to reach their friends or for their friends to reach them. Daddy had a long commute then to the United Nations building on First Avenue in Manhattan. He had to take a bus and then the subway to reach work. However, by that time, their relationship was so difficult that he was not unhappy to be apart from Mommy. Seeing my parents' relationship deteriorate in the last decades of their lives together taught David and me that social isolation is injurious and should be avoided to whatever extent possible as a couple ages.

Fig 75, 76 Photographs showing similarities of headdress in Chinese Opera and formal American Indian headdress

Fig 77 Daddy in costume as a young man

Fig 78 Mommy in costume as a mature man

Chapter 27

THE STUDY OF LIFE

My freshman year at college began with some academic success. Students who qualified for freshmen honors at Sweet Briar College were paraded into an assembly at the beginning of the second semester. As I walked into the room, I saw Diane "Duffy" Duffield, a teammate and someone who was friendly with me, break into a big, beautiful smile and applaud (figure 79). I was touched that she was so happy. For the first time, I realized my achievements were important to my friends as well as my family.

Many of the most loyal members of the class of 1957 are shown in figure 79. They remain sisters even as we reach past our sixtieth reunion. I must say that the nurturing quality of life at Sweet Briar rendered relationships of classmates to the status of real sisterhood. It is a unique aspect of being an alumna of Sweet Briar College, as the next chapter will show.

There were only six of us majoring in biology in my class. I enjoyed modern languages, and if I hadn't been so masochistic, I might have majored in French or modern languages. Getting A grades in the nonscience courses was not too difficult, but I was more challenged by biology. I was intrigued by how life is what it is, especially how our cells, which are genetically identical in early development, when the fertilized egg cell divides, become so different in later development.

A course I didn't care for much was anatomy—too much memorization. It was boring to me, and my memory has never been good, just like Mommy's. Later in life, as I struggled to keep up with developments in genetics while teaching, the thought crossed my mind that while I needed to amend my notes every semester because of the speed with which geneticists were gathering new facts and insights, the anatomy professor could use almost the same lecture notes for millions of years.

My major professor seemed to take an interest in me from the beginning. She was merciless when I turned in my first biology paper, however. I write well, but I was writing like an English major, not using scientific objectivity and specificity. She crossed out about a third of what I had written, and that was the beginning of my training to write like a scientist: brief, to the point, factual, and, to me, dry and boring, albeit necessary. The training in scientific writing was a big help to me in graduate school.

One of the benefits of being at a small institution, such as Sweet Briar, was that the faculty–student relationship could be close. As I said previously, biology majors were invited on more than one occasion to Miss Belcher's house: to have dinner, to sample wild morels that she taught us to gather, and to witness her beagle whelping a litter of puppies. She had a shock of white hair cut short, and she dressed informally at all times. She smiled a lot and laughed heartily. We became good friends. The only photo I have of her is in one of my wedding album shots (see figure 96) after my wedding ceremony.

Jane Belcher cared very much for her students and was ready to help their careers in any way she could. She was the one who recommended I go to Jackson Laboratory the summer after my junior year and wrote a letter of recommendation for me that got me into that competitive program. I have been told that the Greek word for enthusiasm stems from a root that means "the fire within." That program was really what lit the fire in me to take graduate work seriously after college. Miss Belcher definitely opened the first door to my career.

But what really gave me a jolt and launched me into science was a course I took with a young woman who had just joined the faculty at SBC, Miriam Bennett. She taught embryology, and as a junior, I took the course and was stunned by looking at a live eighteen-hour chick embryo whose tubular heart had not yet folded into the chambers we're familiar with and had not yet even been enclosed within the body of the embryo. But the little tube was pulsating and contracting already—wow!

I could feel goose bumps rising in my excitement. I had to find out how that happened. Although I could learn of the process of how the tube folded to become a heart with four chambers, I also learned that development was all about gene regulation, the most complex and least understood phenomenon in gene expression.

We were all afraid of Miss Bennett. She was all business. Perhaps being a professor for the first time caused her some anxiety as well. None of us were able to get close to her in a friendly way, as we were with Miss Belcher, but she knew her science, and I found myself well prepared for graduate work when I was accepted to Bryn Mawr College for an MA degree in embryology with world-class embryologist Jane Oppenheimer. I had read some of Miss Oppenheimer's papers and was inspired by them. I could hardly believe I was accepted into Bryn Mawr's MA program and wondered if I could succeed in finishing a difficult degree program that was actually like a mini-PhD.

While it was a great disappointment to me that I did not graduate even cum laude from Sweet Briar, years later, the faculty of Sweet Briar elected me to be an alumna member of Phi Beta Kappa's Theta chapter of Virginia. When Miss Belcher called me to tell me about the induction ceremony, I declined to go down to Sweet Briar for it. I felt that an honor for myself wasn't worth the trip. I know Miss Belcher was disappointed, and as I said previously, I wish I had gone. It was a dumb decision.

One tradition at Sweet Briar College was for each senior to choose an entering freshman as a little sister who would receive advice and information about college life from her big sister. In turn, the little sister would alter and iron the senior robe given to the big sister to wear in her senior year and do other small favors to help make senior year a little easier. Winnie Ward was my little sister, and I love her as a real sister (figure

80). She asked me to be a bridesmaid in her wedding. We have stayed friends for sixty years. We continue to write to each other, she still addresses me as Big Sis, and I still address her as Little Sis.

Yet another of my lifelong Sweet Briar College friends was Dotsie Woods (figure 81). She was a year behind me, and we became close friends quickly. She had a sweet smile and was quick to laugh. She was an athlete, one of our best tennis players. Dotsie invited me to her home at one point, and it was there that I learned to use fruit instead of sugar in my breakfast cereals. It seems obvious now, but at that time, I thought her father, who started the use of fruit instead of sugar, was smart to do so. The other students at the college thought highly of Dotsie and elected her to be head of the Judicial Board, which adjudicated violations of the honor system at Sweet Briar. At the end of my senior year, June Berguido was elected president of student government that same year. I couldn't have been prouder of the two.

I no longer remember the year I was invited to return to Sweet Briar to be on a panel discussing the attributes of the college, but I recall that Dotsie was there in the audience. I guess I moved my friend because I received from her a small needlepoint pillow. On one side, she had placed her initials and mine, and on the other side was a needlepoint of a Sweet Briar rose. I still have that pillow and display it. One of my deep debts to my college is the kind of long-lasting friendships we were privileged to have established with terrific people.

Many years later, when my grandson Keith enrolled as a music major at Belmont University in Nashville, Tennessee, Dotsie and her husband, Dr. Alex McLeod, and David and I had a minireunion in Nashville, where the McLeods live. It was fun to see my friend again. Whenever I have met my college buddies at reunions or elsewhere, we feel quickly about each other as we did at college. That was something I learned at the first Sweet Briar reunion I ever attended: that which drew us together as schoolmates was integral in true friends and would remain unshakeable even if life paths resulted in our being far apart for many years.

Fig 79 Class of '57 at our 20th (?) reunion. Diane is fourth from the left second row at the reunion. I am in the front row.

Fig 80 My little sister Winnie Ward and her husband

Fig 81 Dotsie Woods McLeod

Chapter 28

DAVID AND HOLLYWOOD

By my senior year, I had become seriously interested in the VMI Keydet with warm, dry hands whom I had met at Peggy's mixer. (Thank you again, my sweet roommate!) He invited me to dinner several times in New York City during our vacations from school.

One interesting experience I had occurred when David invited me to a simulation of the VMI Keydets' Ring Dance for the movie *Mardi Gras*, which was being filmed at VMI in his senior year. The Ring Dance, a major event for the Keydets, was usually held for juniors at VMI in celebration of their getting their class rings. The movie starred Pat Boone, and it was interesting to see how movies came into being.

The movie people were clearly interested in filming the big dance, and it was a visually stunning affair. All the dates were dressed in big white bouffant gowns. I borrowed one from Diane Duffield, my buddy. I did not own such a gown and had no money to buy one. I think Diane had one for being elected to the May Queen's court, a tradition at Sweet Briar. Her willingness to let me use her gown was one of several favors Diane did for me while we were classmates.

The dance was held in the spacious VMI gym. We were lined up on the stairs leading from the ground floor up to the running oval on the second level. Then we were to walk down the stairs into the gym. Each of us held a large bouquet of red roses. The Keydets were dressed in their formal uniforms: bluish-gray jackets and white pants. They looked handsome.

Unfortunately, they lined us up alphabetically by our date's last name, so I ended up on the top level since David's last name, Pai, began with *P*. The physics of being at the end of a long moving line is that those toward the end of the line find themselves practically running, even though those at the front start out walking slowly. Thank goodness they stationed Keydets all along the stairs to catch us as we stumbled in our high heels and bouffant gowns while holding large bouquets of red roses and running to keep up with those in front.

Three times, I had to endure that trip, and three times, as I reached the gym floor, the director yelled, "Cut!" I never did get into the movie—rats! The filmmakers also made the rest of the weekend somewhat not enjoyable, as occasionally they confined the Keydets to quarters to prepare them for some other scene. When they did so, we dates wandered aimlessly around, waiting for the boys to be released.

I did get a cashmere sweater out of it. The opening scene of the movie had the Keydets lined up in formation to march to breakfast. Each officer of the different companies saluted the camera and announced that his company was ready and present.

David spoke into the camera: "C Company all present and accounted for!"

Because he had a speaking part in the movie, union rules required that David be paid a minimum weekly wage of ninety dollars. In 1958, ninety dollars was a lot of money. He bought me a cashmere sweater with the money. Nice! Years later, when our boys were around seven and eight years old, we saw that *Mardi Gras* was being shown on TV. We excitedly told the boys what to expect, and they were excited that their daddy was in a movie and would be on TV. When the time came, we all sat expectantly in front of our set. Guess what? They had cut David's scene from the TV version of the movie! We were all disappointed.

I first was impressed with David when he invited me to dinner when we were both in New York City on vacation and talked about his father, a legendary general in the Chinese Nationalist Army. David told me about a conflict between Chiang Kai Shek and his father. Chiang feared anyone who was competent and popular, and General Pai was clearly both. The general and his family were kept under surveillance by Chiang's secret service men after the Nationalists retreated to Taiwan. When they drove to shops, for example, a car would follow them. David's parents both died while in Taiwan. His mother died when only in her fifties in 1962 of high blood pressure while on the operating table. His father died of a stroke in 1966. Their unexpected deaths meant that I never met them, to my everlasting regret.

I continued to enjoy my days at Sweet Briar. I made many lifelong friends, and they returned my friendship. Duffy invited me to visit her home one vacation, and she and her gracious parents took me to see my first Broadway musical, *Kismet*. It was magical! To this day, after countless exposures to Broadway offerings, when I hear the music from *Kismet*, it brings back memories of excitement. In fact, I loved all the parents of my friends. My roommate's parents treated me as though I were their daughter too. I still remember the soup bowls filled with ice cream that Mrs. Liebert insisted we eat before going to bed. It was an obligation I enjoyed thoroughly.

Duffy and I were teammates on the field hockey and basketball teams, and both of us were chosen for the varsity squad. I reveled in playing sports, and the exhilaration of competition, whether we won or lost, was fuel for my soul. I rejoiced in being able to do what I needed to do in competition. As I said, I wonder sometimes whether I would have majored in physical education if there had been such a major at Sweet Briar. How different my life would have been! I believe karma leads us down different pathways in life, and we will never know how our lives could have differed. I don't believe my life could ever have been better than it was and is.

I was fairly sure I would be chosen my senior year for the Blazer Award, an award given to the top athlete in the senior class. I was happy when Miss MacDonald called me and told me I had been chosen for the honor. When all varsity athletes were called together in the gym for the announcement, I was sitting with my friend June. I pretended not to know who the award winner was, and when they called my name, I leaped up and felt my face flush as the applause and whistles told me my teammates approved.

I received a green blazer with the Sweet Briar seal on one of the breast pockets. It was one of my favorite jackets for years, but I lost it in one of my moves from home. I don't believe the school has that award anymore, but they do have an Athletic Hall of Fame, which was started in 1997. That year, I was inducted as one of the charter members. The two other inductees whom I knew were Bee Thayer (second from the left in figure 82), with whom I worked on the Sweet Briar Board in the 1980s, and Cannie Chrysler Shafer (next to me on my left). Cannie is the niece of my senior year suite mate, Nancy Baldwin. I asked Nancy to introduce me at the 1997 induction ceremony.

There were three other inductees whom I thought had much better credentials than I did. One had represented the United States in equestrian sports in the Olympics. Another was named All-American in field hockey. A third was a top amateur golfer. I wondered why I was chosen, as I'd only played varsity at Sweet Briar. When I asked the president, I was told that loyalty and serving Sweet Briar's interests after graduation were also considered in making the choices.

Fig 82 The Charter Inductees of Sweet Briar College Athletic Hall of Fame

CHAPTER 29

I LEAVE MY FIRST REAL HOME

Before I knew it, my idyllic four years at Sweet Briar came to an end. Leaving my first and only home, where I felt secure and knew I was loved and respected, was a traumatic event for me. I wrote an essay expressing my feelings at having to leave college. It was the rambling of an overly tired senior facing the last of the final load of exams and already grieving at the prospect of not being with my dear friends again at Sweet Briar as a student. I include it here:

> I sit in this room very tired and trying to study. It is 2:30 a.m. now, and only three of us are left in the smoker. My eyes are beginning to ache, so I must stop. I am going to sleep for a little while, but it looks like I'll have to get up at five. It's the last exam I'll take here—I must do well.
>
> I must because I owe it to my professors, who care so much about us; I must because of my friends, who have such confidence in me, confidence that I fear I will fail. I must because these four years have been so good I must not do less than a decent job of ending them.
>
> I look around the room and see the old desk and the candy machines and watch the tired vapor of smoke gliding about the light of the lamps. I see two students with weary, sloping shoulders trying to remember that last equation or that last date of a historic event. A familiar sight, but then all has been familiar …
>
> All that has happened this year, every day that was lived, every friend I have seen, every place I have gone, every breath of air has been familiar, has been something I've tried to hold; are things that I am losing.
>
> How many times this year, how many times a day, have I stopped and looked very hard, trying to impress in my mind the dear, close, familiar sights? The balcony outside the lab, where I can gaze upon the first place I have ever belonged, where I've been given a chance to learn and to give of myself what there is to offer. And the campus as I leave the gym after a practice and the delicious cold air hits me and

makes me feel alive and good, and the countryside is misty with the dusk or red with the sunset—that glorious sunset!

I need to remember the faces of people young and old, some more beloved than others but everyone familiar. Remember the refectory where hundreds gather every day, and there is a constant hum of companionship broken now and then by laughing while I and others rush or saunter around, conspicuous in green uniforms, laughingly full of mischief or in muttering resentment against the system or illogical thinking.

And the student waitresses' room, with paint peeling from the walls, at times filled with kids sprawled over the bed and under piles of uniforms or gathered in intense groups, mulling over anything from paychecks to the universe and swapping ignorance after dinner coffee. As one writer put it, "God, how they talked," and so we did; we talked and talked and talked—and I shall never forget. Take it in, my eyes; hold it, my heart—hold, hold, hold.

And now no more. Even as I sit in this smoker, they are all memories—can it be possible? I look again around the room, and suddenly, I do not understand, yet I do not know what I do not understand. The room is a little world with no time. It is here; I am here, but outside, time is rushing by, yet I know time is really in the room too. I know that as I sit, I come closer and closer to the memory of my sitting here. What a weird feeling—to know that I am living a memory ...

It is now later in the day, and I have finished my exam. It was terribly difficult, and I tried my best. I am in the dell now, and the breeze is refreshing, but the feeling of earlier this morning is still with me, bothering me. My mind wanders unhappily to my friends. Each one of them has shared a special part of me; each one has a different meaning, and now they are all breaking up.

I just found another graduation present left on my desk with a simple note. It joins a bewildering number of others in a gesture that about opens the floodgates each time. Each one reminds me of the giver, of some characteristic I have delighted in, and of the moments of friendship we have shared. It's so hard to leave them. I've only gotten to know them, it seems, and have had only a couple of short years to be with them, to learn from them, and, in some cases, to be comforted even by their presence.

Some I have known but a few months—thank goodness friendship takes only a few moments to establish. What will I do without them? New friends that I make will never replace these, only join them in my affection, for I refuse to acknowledge that true relationship is transient. If it is, then the most meaningful aspect of life for me is transient, and it cannot—must not—be!

We have just received our diplomas; the great ceremony that our parents have endured the weekend for is nearer completion. I look at the leather-bound sheepskin in my hand and wonder at it. As a symbol of my college days, it will always be precious, but as a climax—which it is to many people—it is to me a letdown. It shall be a symbol always.

The hood has been placed around my shoulders, and my tassel is on the left side of the mortarboard. We stand now, and they are playing the recessional. The back row of seniors—now graduates—begins to file out. I see it is almost time for us to leave. I turn to June to tell her I will not say goodbye yet knowing it is goodbye to one of my best-loved friends. I must leave abruptly, for the sadness comes …

And now the time has come, the very hard time that we have shuddered at and put off in our minds for months, saying, "Won't it be terrible?" And it is. I shall long remember my well-loved friends as my companions at work and play, revolutionizing all philosophy and religion, or dancing like idiots in the refec before we served the dinner dance of a big weekend, sharing sad and happy news and moods.

But I shall remember them as I see them now too, on the day of our departure for different worlds. I shall remember them returning and sharing my unhappiness. We are unable to say anything—we could not even if we were not choking and crying, as we resolved not to do.

We can only look hard at each other, silently asking that we not be forgotten, putting everything we feel in this look. Look, my eyes; hold them, my heart—hold, hold, hold.

As rambling as this essay is, it reflects my feelings at leaving the first home I had ever known and the first family that, unlike my own family, was not dysfunctional, in which my sisters loved me as I loved them and my professors showed their confidence in me by recommending me to advanced programs.

It also reflects my uncertainty about the years directly ahead of me. Would I succeed? If I did not, what would I do? However, there was comfort in my relationship with David. Marriage and a family were comforting and even exciting thoughts. But the most important aspects of what my years in college gave me were along the lines of who I was as a person, what I could do as a person, and how people reacted to me.

My college experience also gave me an assuring sense that it was all right to be American; there were aspects of both Chinese and American cultures that were worth abiding by, and some aspects of both were not.

For example, I prefer the openness of Americans in their relationships with others to the sometimes impenetrable shell around Chinese. On the other hand, I have always thought it strange that American strangers are willing to pour out their life stories to me, as some of the people I have sat next to on airplane flights to meetings have. It would not surprise me if I sat next to another Chinese passenger and we did not exchange a word during the whole trip.

When I applied to Sweet Briar, little did I realize how much I needed a small college and close friendships with my professors. It was pure luck that while I was accepted into all the colleges I applied to, only one college offered almost a free ride through scholarships and a job on campus, which made deciding where to go easy.

My parents never had a hand in my choice of colleges. They could not have been helpful because they themselves had never gone through the American process of choosing an undergraduate experience. I doubt they even understood what *liberal arts* meant, and because I am a woman, while what I did at the college level was not insignificant to them, it certainly was not as important to them as Solan's studies. In some ways, it was an advantage over Solan's experience, wherein they even gave him the choice of majors they wanted him to take. Somebody, though, was watching over me.

Later, when I was asked to serve on the board of directors at my alma mater, I accepted immediately, and I served from 1984 to 1992. During my tenure as chair of the Academic Committee, I pushed hard for Sweet Briar to offer a more rigorous degree program in the sciences that would result in a bachelor of science degree. Also, I helped install a college honors program that would begin in freshman year and offer interdisciplinary seminars and require research on the part of participating students, with a presentation of their work that would be open to the general student body.

CHAPTER 30

MY FIRST TEACHING EXPERIENCE

The summer after my graduation from Sweet Briar, I was fortunate enough to be asked to serve as a counselor for the precollegiate research training program at the Jackson Laboratory in Bar Harbor, Maine. I was delighted to accept the job. We were housed in Highseas, a mansion that had been donated to Jackson Lab for the purpose of providing a place for high school summer students. It was on a beautiful site overlooking the Atlantic Ocean.

The program was set up so that college students like myself were in direct control of the high school kids. We in turn were supervised by the staff scientist, who gave a research project for the students to carry out. I was disappointed my group would not be doing anything related to development or cancer. The only thing I remember about the project my charges carried out was that a psychology staff member had us study what mice would do under different conditions.

It was interesting to see how the group of bright youngsters interacted with each other. The first couple evenings, after dinner, we gathered together to chat and get to know one another. Initially, the competitive, outstanding students would let it be known how smart they were, casually dropping information as to their class standings or SAT scores.

One would say he or she had gotten the maximum score on the SAT, and another would respond, "Me too!" Then they realized they were all equally good and all had outstanding records in school. After the first two nights, nobody mentioned academic achievements or grades again.

I enjoyed the teaching part of being a counselor that summer. The kids were fun as well as smart. One morning, we woke to find an ugly fish that someone had found on the beach. It was a fish that could blow itself into a balloon. It was still alive, and the mouth was opening and closing. They had put it on a platter in the middle of the dining room table as if it were being served. I told them in no uncertain terms to end its suffering.

Another time, some boys came back to Highseas with wonderful blackberries. They were huge and sweet. I asked if the berries were really wild. Where had they found them? One answered that they'd found them in a field. With tongue in cheek, he added that oddly, they seemed to be growing in rows. I was glad nobody had seen them and run them off.

I wrote my reaction to having had a wonderful summer with those talented, interesting youngsters. In reading it, I realize that the summer had much to do with my later decision to become a career educator. Following is an excerpt from that diary entry:

> In front of me is the glowing, beautiful, comforting fire … Tonight it is the center of a half circle of sleepy and sad but happy people, young people who are holding on to the last moments of a beautiful summer and the last precious hours of newfound friendships … I feel the nearness of my young companions and know this has been a good, really good, part of my life … And at this moment, I am content …
>
> We did many wonderful things this summer: picnics, exploring bookstores, singing folk songs with Ellie (a student) and her guitar … I have watched them change over the summer and have been proud as they did change. They learned many things, among them that though gifted, they have their equals and even betters and that what they will do with their abilities and opportunities is the important thing, not what they have done. And I have been proud to see them accept each other's weaknesses and take strangers into their friendship immediately and willingly.
>
> The room resounds still with their voices calling to each other and arguing vehemently about a controversial theory … I see their faces too so vividly, and funny, I only see them as they are laughing and shall remember them always this way.
>
> And I have been proud to see them meet new opinions and ideas wonderingly and eagerly but critically. I have seen them accept criticism with appreciation and the little I could do to excite them about their work, and they made me feel I did something worthwhile at least—and perhaps, perhaps, this type of work is worth a lifetime's worthwhile …
>
> Now I too am dressed to leave. As I walk toward the front door, I see with a strange gladness that my fire is not cold but alive—a new log has been placed there to revive it, just as new situations give life new meaning.
>
> The plane takes off. Beside me, Ellie says, "Gee, I can still hear their voices."

Even after I had earned my doctorate, I returned three times more to the Jackson Lab during my career as an academician for workshops and to be brought up to date on developmental genetics research. I saw Dr. Stevens only briefly each time, and we never really resumed our friendship. He passed away in the 1990s.

I often think back to those summers at Bar Harbor and wonder about the friends I knew there but never followed up on. I wonder how many became career scientists. I know Tom, the fellow who took us sailing, became a well-known medical doctor and was head of a department at one of the large midwestern universities.

One of the young men who was also a counselor in the high school program in the summer of 1957, Harold, also became a medical doctor and a well-known epidemiologist. He became a staff physician at Columbia Presbyterian Hospital, the same hospital in which my brother Solan became a staff physician. I heard in 2006 that Harold had also passed away.

Chapter 31

THE ATTEMPT TO CLOSE SWEET BRIAR COLLEGE IN 2015

On March 3, 2015, fifty-eight years after I left my first home as a graduate of Sweet Briar College, I was curious about an email I received from the college. When I opened the email, it included a video of the interim president of the college, James "Jimmy" F. Jones Jr., addressing the Sweet Briar community. What he said floored me. With a somber face, he announced that because of insurmountable financial difficulties, he and the board of directors had voted to close Sweet Briar College in August of that year. *What!*

I ran from my study and blurted out to David, "They're closing Sweet Briar!"

He could not believe his ears. "What?" he said. "You're kidding!"

He joined me as I replayed the announcement. We both sat there shaking our heads.

The college had hired financial consultants, Jones said. Their analysis of Sweet Briar's endowment, finances and history, and the declining numbers of enrollment of freshmen in recent years had resulted in their conclusion that the 114-year-old college was financially unsustainable. He said they had "turned over every stone," having hired financial consultants and interviewed two hundred alumnae about future giving. They felt the decision was a courageous one made while they still had enough resources to close the college and help students, faculty, and staff find other schools and positions. I wish I could repeat what he said exactly, but somehow, the video I saved has disappeared from my computer.

My mind was numb. Just a few months before, a member of the college's Development Office had visited us and persuaded us to donate what, to us, was a significant amount to endow the biology department at Sweet Briar with a donation in the form of an annuity. David and I were happy to do so because we had heard biology students talk about their research done under the supervision of their faculty. In fact, I believe all the sciences were offering training in research with faculty during the school year and in the summertime.

We were impressed with the quality of the research and education being offered to students. As a former student from a time when there was no research done at the college at all, I found the cutting-edge research going on exciting. Faculty in my time did not have the equipment or the lab facilities that exist now. Even so, my professors tried to help me in other ways. Recall that my biology professor, Miss Jane Belcher, helped me gain acceptance into the summer research training program at Jackson Laboratory in Bar Harbor, Maine. She knew it would benefit me if I were to look for a career in science after graduation, and she was right. Without that taste of real research, I doubt I would have decided to go on to a PhD program.

We'd made our decision to donate an annuity to the Sweet Briar College biology department just less than a year before the closure announcement, sometime in the summer of 2014. They had come to us, and now they were closing the college? I emailed the Development Office person who had persuaded us to donate and asked her if she had known about the plan to close the college when she had come to us. She told me she had not, and we discovered shortly that the decision to close had been arrived at in total secrecy and that the board members had signed nondisclosure agreements and could not and would not be able to discuss anything about the deliberations with anyone.

Nobody knew that the question of closing was on the agenda of the 2014–2015 annual board of directors meeting—not the faculty, not the staff, not the students, and not the alumnae, including former board members like myself. They fraudulently continued to press alumnae to donate to the college as if nothing had changed. They had even accepted students who applied to attend as freshmen in the fall of 2015 to maintain the impression that all was well. Remember too that freshmen accepted to colleges often have to pay deposits to reserve places at the schools. The administration planned to use the money from those accepted and all unrestricted donations, including all alumnae donations to the 2015 annual fund of the college, to close Sweet Briar—a move 180 degrees opposite of the purpose of the donations, which were to help support the education of young women at Sweet Briar.

As I mentioned before, I was on the board for eight years from 1984 to 1992. We never conducted secret discussions. What we discussed and what we decided was information open and accessible to all. Secrecy in such a responsible position was never a consideration on the part of our administration then. We knew our charge was to serve the college, its faculty, and its students the best way we knew how. I knew there were always many alumnae on the board, and in fact, the majority of the members in 2015 were alumnae. How could they have allowed things to transpire in what appeared to be such a secretive way?

My former classmate and suite mate Nancy Baldwin passed away in 2014. Not only did she have a degree from Sweet Briar, but she returned after graduation to be the director of admissions for decades and then to edit the alumnae magazine. She lived on campus. No alumna loved the college more. Her niece, Sophia Hart, established a scholarship in Nancy's memory, and numerous friends, including me, contributed to it. It appeared to be in jeopardy of also being used by the administration to close the school.

Therefore, beyond the question of whether small liberal arts colleges could be sustained in that day and age, there was a further question that would affect many more institutions than schools, such as Sweet Briar College: whether nonprofit organizations in general could accept donations for a specific cause and then use the money for other purposes.

The closing of my alma mater therefore represented two important principles of American society, and it garnered widespread interest, as reflected in articles written about the closing in mass media, including in the *New York Times*, the *Washington Post*, the *Roanoke Times*, and numerous newspapers in many cities in Virginia and elsewhere; in journals involved with higher education; and on radio and TV news programs.

So much publicity was generated about Sweet Briar closing that I thought when the situation was over—and I assumed it would be decided in our favor—we should write to the president and the board a thank-you note for having created so much attention and publicity not just for Sweet Briar College but also, to some extent, for all small women's liberal arts colleges.

The first lawsuit was filed by the Amherst County attorney acting on behalf of the Commonwealth of Virginia, naming as defendants Sweet Briar Institute; Paul G. Rice, chair of the board of directors; and the president, James F. Jones Jr. The introduction to that suit by Amherst County attorney Ellen Bowyer stated the following:

1. This case arises from the Defendants' recent announcement that they are closing Sweet Briar College, a highly successful institution of higher education that has served young women from Virginia, from across the nation and, indeed, from around the world for over a century. The closure attempt is not only precipitous and unwarranted, it is also unlawful.

2. The Commonwealth seeks injunctive relief against the Defendants, pursuant to Title 57, Chapter 5 ("Solicitation of Contributions Act") of the Code of Virginia, and pursuant to Title 64.2, Chapter 7 ("Uniform Trust Code ") of the Code of Virginia.

3. Among other relief, the Commonwealth seeks to enjoin the Defendants from (i) taking steps to close the College; and (ii) using funds raised by charitable solicitations for purposes other than the solicited purposes or the general purposes of the College.

4. The Commonwealth also seeks to have Interim President and Board removed from their positions, and a special fiduciary appointed to take possession of the College's assets and administer those assets, and to appoint a new President and Board to continue operations of the College.

We were all aware that time was of the essence in the case because of faculty needing to seek positions elsewhere and also because of students committing to attending other schools. Further, the defendants were found to have already begun actions to close the college in 2014. The county attorney pointed out the following:

> The College began "teach out" agreements with other schools a few months prior to the College's announcement, and the College retained legal counsel specifically to assist with closure actions in November or December of 2014.

Having so acted, they waited until March 3, 2015, to announce their plans to use any and all assets of the college to close it.

The faculty of Sweet Briar were hit particularly hard by the decision arrived at in secrecy. Since the planned closure was announced late in academic year 2014–2015, most vacancies in academia had been filled by that time, and it would be difficult for them to find other positions. Further, those faculty members who had built their own houses on campus faced economic disaster since they owned their houses but not the land the houses were on. (Faculty rented the land they lived on for one dollar a year.) A faculty friend in that situation pointed out that they nonetheless received orders from the administration to begin packing up immediately.

The unbelievable turn of events caused the outraged alumnae well versed in social media (i.e., the younger alums) to begin immediately contacting other alumnae to organize in opposition to the announcement of closure. I too began to receive dozens of emails every day, all asking the same questions and looking for ways to help prevent the closure.

The earliest heroine among the alumnae was Tracy Stuart of the class of 1993 (figure 83), now a real estate agent working in Connecticut and Martha's Vineyard. Tracy sprang to action and stopped work to focus full-time on doing what she could to save the college. She realized the fight would require suing the college and contacted friends who were lawyers in the South to find out the names of Virginia lawyers who could fight the decision. Ashley Taylor Jr. and William Hurd, partners at a prestigious Richmond law firm, Troutman Sanders LLP, were the last two lawyers whose names Tracy uncovered that day.

After speaking with Ashley and Bill, Tracy felt they were the right ones to fight the case, so she retained Troutman and Sanders. Then she immediately hired a PR firm, Rhode Island–based CK Communications to help inform the community that a legal fight was underway. Tracy then began contacting multiple alumnae by phone and through social media. Ashley Taylor recommended she set up a nonprofit corporation, which Tracy called Saving Sweet Briar Inc. (SSBI), and form a board of directors for the company.

Tracy then began to interview alumnae to create the alumnae board for SSBI, working as the founder and director of Saving Sweet Briar Inc. with Troutman; Eric Cote from CK Communications, who sent press releases about the legal involvement; and her own personal advisers. At that point, a group of seven alumnae became the board of SSBI with bylaws in place and convened their first board meeting on March 17.

Figure 84 shows the alumnae of the board of SSBI in the spring of 2016, following their designation, along with Tracy Stuart as distinguished alumnae. From left to right, they are Christine Boulware, Sarah Clement, Jo Ann Soderquist Kramer, Sally Scott Freeman, Brooke Linville, and Ellen Ober Pitera. Sarah Clement (SBC '75) was nominated to be board chair, and Christine Boulware (SBC '77) was nominated as the secretary of the 501c3 organization.

Sarah received an MA in English from Columbia University in 1977 and a JD degree from University of Virginia Law School in 1984. She was in private practice for nine years in Washington, DC, in the areas of civil and administrative litigation. She then entered government service with a federal agency in the field of employment law. She has been an administrative judge with that agency for more than twenty years.

Also on the board of SSBI were two alumnae who had been members of the Sweet Briar board of directors but resigned in protest over the manner in which President Jo Ellen Parker and Board Chair Paul F. Rice governed. They were Jo Ann Soderquist Kramer (SBC '64), a retired senior director of air and naval defense systems for General Dynamics Corporation, and Christine Boulware (SBC '77) of Chicago, director of her own executive search firm. I was more than impressed with the résumé of each board member.

The first board member Tracy picked was her class president, Ellen Ober Pitera. Two alumnae, Sally Mott Freeman and Brooke Linville (SBC '04), also were asked to join the board. Brooke, who had attended Sweet Briar for only two years, met Tracy on the phone in the early days of the fight. When Tracy asked Brooke if she would like to have her website operate under SSBI, Brooke quickly agreed.

The board of SSBI gave the thousands of motivated alumnae a focal point for how to participate in response and in opposition to the sudden announcement of imminent closure. They gave us directions on how to contribute to a legal battle to save our college.

I was fascinated by the speed and efficiency of the initiation of protests against the closing and against the manner in which the closure decision had been made. I asked Sarah if she could describe the sequence of events leading up to the establishment of SSBI in the early days of that nightmare. I include here, with her permission, her gracious willingness to do so in an email:

> Shortly after the closure announcement on March 3, Tracy Stuart, SBC '93, started thinking about what she could do to oppose the closure of the college. Like hundreds of other alumnae, she emailed or called SBC friends and classmates and began talking. By that night she had decided she needed to sue the college to stop the closure. She began calling lawyer friends from W&L (Washington and Lee University) and other people she knew from Virginia to find out whether there were any lawyers they would recommend who could handle such a case. The names Ashley Taylor Jr., and William (Bill) Hurd of Troutman Sanders LLP in Richmond kept coming up. By March 4, Tracy had contacted Ashley and begun discussing the possibility of legal action to stop the announced closure of Sweet Briar College.
>
> Meanwhile, Nancyellen Keane, SBC '78, posted on Facebook on March 4 that she was hosting a call that night at 5 pm for "all alumnae lawyers" to discuss the closure announcement. She happens to be an attorney who works at Troutman Sanders LLP in Richmond! I saw her Facebook post and dialed in to the conference call she hosted the evening of March 4. There were about twenty-five people on the call, some of them were alumnae lawyers and some were just alumnae who were interested in discussing ideas about opposing the closure. Tracy Stuart also joined the conference

call to hear what others were saying about legal avenues, since she had been pursuing this avenue on her own all that day as well. I met Nancyellen and Tracy for the first time on that call and my name and number were shared since I was an alumna lawyer who lived in Virginia and could serve as a local point of contact.

At the same time, Brooke Linville, living in Boise, Idaho, with her husband and two young toddler sons, who attended Sweet Briar for her freshman and sophomore years but transferred and graduated from George Washington University in 2004, created a website called SavingSweetBriar.com. Brooke and her husband have a web development business in Boise. Tracy and Brooke got in contact and started talking about how to raise money to oppose the decision to close the college.

Over the next few days, Nancyellen Keane and I, and other lawyers at her firm (Troutman Sanders in Richmond) had a couple of conference calls. Separately, Tracy paid a retainer to hire Ashley Taylor of Troutman Sanders to explore legal action to oppose the closure of SBC. Ashley formed a legal team that included Nancyellen and other Troutman lawyers, and they advised Tracy to form a nonprofit, incorporated in the state of Virginia, so that she could have a proper vehicle to raise money to sponsor and finance any litigation undertaken to stop the closure. Saving Sweet Briar, Inc., (SSB, Inc.) was formed and incorporated on March 9.

Tracy was advised to form a Board of Directors for this nonprofit, and she began calling various alumnae she had met via email, or Facebook, or telephone, or others recommended for the Board of the nonprofit she had just formed ... Tracy interviewed me and others by telephone, and came up with the six people she asked to serve on the Board of SSB, Inc.: me (we had never met, just talked on the phone and texted for a week or so); Jo Ann Kramer (Tracy had never met her either, but she was recommended as a former member of the college Board of Directors); Christine Boulware (ditto); Sally Mott Freeman (Tracy had never met her, but she was recommended); Brooke Linville (Tracy Had never met her but was aware that Brooke had already created a website that could be the vehicle for the fundraising needed to undertake any litigation); and Ellen Pitera (Tracy's classmate from SBC '93—this is the only person on the Board that Tracy knew!).

We six joined Tracy as the Board of Directors of Saving Sweet Briar, Inc. At the first meeting of that Board, the members voted me as Chair and Christine Boulware as Secretary. There are no other officers on SSB Inc. and we did not have any committees or subcommittees. Instead we each chose an area to focus on to help in the effort to reverse the decision to close the college.

Tracy and I were the legal points of contact; JoAnn and Sally worked on major donors and large gifts; Ellen focused on current students and their needs; Christine works as an executive search professional, and she focused on finding good people for a possible new Board of Directors for the college if we were successful; Brooke of course took on the website and fundraising via social media.

Our roles were pretty fluid and we all helped out in whatever way necessary for as long as necessary. Sally described our work on the SSB Board as "building the bicycle as we're riding it" which was absolutely true. Troutman developed a brilliant legal strategy involving a lawsuit brought by the Amherst County Attorney in the name of the Commonwealth of Virginia, and our case was off and running at a very fast pace.

The Amherst County Attorney filed the first lawsuit. That case was based on two Virginia statutes, the Charitable Solicitations Act and the Virginia Uniforrn Trust Code. Subsequently, the faculty also filed a lawsuit against the college on a breach of contract theory, and a group of students, parents, and alumnae filed a separate lawsuit also on a breach of contract theory. By April, the college thus faced three lawsuits.

The faculty had basis for claiming breach of contract because they were hired to teach continuously if they had tenure; the students could claim breach of contract because when they were accepted as freshmen, that acceptance was presumably for four years of education at the college. In fact, the faculty unanimously voted no confidence in the college president, the board of directors, and the chair of the board following the announcement.

In frustration and anger over the announced closing, I posted a letter on Facebook to Sandra Taylor (SBC '74), the president of Sweet Briar College's Alumnae Association, and Missy Witherow (SBC '80), who was in charge of alumnae affairs at the college. It was the first posting I, a dinosaur in the world of social media, had ever attempted other than comments on others' postings now and then. I include a draft of the letter below. The date was March 11, 2015.

Dear Sandra Taylor and Missy Witherow,

I don't know if you two will ever read this, but I must still express my disappointment in alumnae who are actively involved in closing our Alma Mater. The decision if it stands is a blow to women's colleges and what they offer to young women. We received excellent education due to great faculty, small classes and the personal relationships between students and mentors. But just as important, Sweet Briar has always been known for unique nurturing of young women, giving them the self-confidence to meet challenges and set goals. You and other members of the Board must love the college for all it has to offer to be in the positions you hold. How then were you persuaded to reach this decision?

The argument that President Jones gave about finances rings very hollow. You all only interviewed 200 alumnae, of which I was one. But never was it mentioned to me that Sweet Briar was on the verge of closing, NEVER! Had it been truthfully presented, even 200 alums would no doubt have vowed support and increased their dollar support of the college. And do explain why you did not contact every alumna alive? I have seen estimates ranging from 10,000 to 20,000 of us are still living. How do you know that one of us isn't in contact with some charity foundations that could have provided deep pockets to solve our endowment problems?

President Jones gave as an answer on the phone during the conference calls he held after the announcement, that making this situation public would have required years to arrive at the same decision. Is Sweet Briar not worth a couple of years of the Board's time? I was on the Board for eight years in the 80's when the same questions came up, and we survived because of the support of the alumnae. We have always been a rock in support of the college, not just a stone like the alternatives he and Rice said you all turned over.

President Jones has been at Sweet Briar for less than a year. This fact and making the decision in secret is one of the reasons we and others in public are stunned and outraged by the decision, and the manner in which it was achieved. We are not unaware that making the announcement late in the academic year puts opposition to closing at a huge disadvantage as far as time available to act is concerned.

I cannot believe you are still asking people (including my husband and me) to donate to help you close the college. I can only say that if we do not get our donations back in case the college is actually closed, I plan to go to court. I hope so much this will not be necessary. I promise you the money is not the important thing here, the principle is. I will not allow my donations to help close the college, something I adamantly oppose! My donations were for specific causes that you are in fact eliminating if the college is closed.

In the worst case, if we do not succeed in reversing the decision to close, another question that has been asked and not answered is, why the endowment cannot be used to pay off our 26 million dollar debt? Arithmetic says that surely 84 million dollars is more than enough to pay off our debts even if we must close. In such an unthinkable situation, what happens to whatever remains of the endowment and the money that the sale of the college would bring?

When asked this question on the conference calls, again there was no real answer. If it is as unclear as Jones said it was on the conference phone call, then why in the world did you all feel you could even make a decision? The alumnae of Sweet Briar are too smart and well educated not to see the weaknesses of the arguments given in support of the decision. It only makes sense if a deal has already been struck—which would make the secretive decision even more unacceptable.

President Jones seems to think that the decision was "courageous." Do you fully understand what closing is doing to the present students and those accepted for the fall as freshmen, the faculty, and staff? Their lives are being totally messed up. Why is that courageous?

Are you aware that in less than a week, the web site set up to Save Sweet Briar has accumulated more than two million dollars? We now have lawyers to help us. What makes anyone think we couldn't have done more for the endowment? We have so many brilliant and accomplished alumnae who I am convinced can also help in creating new programs and directions for Sweet Briar that will attract enrollment.

Instead of doing what you can to close the college, I implore you to do what you can to save it. Until and unless you, the other alumnae on the Board, the other administrators, the "President," and the Board Chair come to alumnae and the public finally in a forthright manner and answer our questions openly, I and many others will forever question the ethics of what you all did and how you made the decision in secret, regardless of the legal outcome of our fight.

In enormous sadness and anger, Anna Chao Pai ('57)

Unknown to me until later, when responses to my post came in enthusiastic and complimentary replies, the younger alums had worried that they saw little in the way of posting from us older alumnae. One alumna later commented that she was concerned by the lack of communications from members of older classes. It made her wonder if older sister alums were supporting the closing and if there was a bloc of Sweet Briar graduates on the college's side in the matter. They need not have worried. I believe many of the alumnae of my age would have spoken up had they been more comfortable with social media.

My post apparently gave the younger alums some relief from that concern and, in doing so, helped increase their hopes for success. I was also told that my letter generated more than four hundred likes, more than any other posting during the course of our opposition. I was flabbergasted! It showed me the power of social media. I believe that perhaps Rice and Jones underestimated the power of social media in their plans to close the college—and the depth of the passion of its alumnae.

Many caring friends said to me initially that they believed the odds against our opposition to closing might be too great to overcome and advised me not to be overly optimistic about our chances. Sweet Briar, throughout its 114-year history, has been beset by doubts that such a small school, particularly such a small single-sex school located in rural Virginia, could attract enough students to stay open. But it has prevailed because of its excellence in education, its nurturing of its students, and, of course, its setting: more than 3,200 acres of prime Virginia land in the foothills of the Blue Ridge Mountains. It has frequently been lauded in polls as among the best programs and campuses in the country. However, in light of the secrecy and timing of the announcement of closing, the odds against us were great.

I want to share some history pertinent to the legal fight that ensued: Our college was established through the will of Indiana Fletcher Williams, who owned the 3,200-plus acres. The land had been a plantation. She and her husband had only one child, a girl, Daisy Williams, who tragically died when she was only sixteen years old. The grieving mother wrote a will stipulating that after she and her husband passed away, the land should be used to establish an institution for the education of young women in perpetuity in the memory of her daughter.

Following is a quote from the will:

> I give and devise ... all my real and personal property ... unto (four trustees and their survivors) as Trustees upon the trusts ... I direct the said trustees forthwith after my decease to procure the incorporation in the State of Virginia of a corporation to be called the "Sweet Briar Institute," ... formed for the object and with the power of establishing and maintaining within the state of Virginia, a school or seminary for the education of girls and young women.

Those directions were followed, and Sweet Briar College was formed as a testamentary trustee. As stated in the suit brought against the college and its administrators by Amherst County attorney Ellen Bowyer (in figure 85, she is in a beige suit, facing the camera) on March 30, the college was incorporated as a nonstock nonprofit corporation under the name Sweet Briar Institute in 1901. Ms. Bowyer was the first to file a suit on behalf of the Commonwealth of Virginia. The case was filed in Amherst County Circuit Court, but due to the recent retirement of the Amherst County Circuit Court judge, it was heard by Judge James F. Updike Jr. of Bedford County Circuit Court.

Bowyer's suit referenced a suit brought to a federal district court in 1967 to overturn an aspect of the will that limited enrollment to white girls and young women. In ruling in favor of Sweet Briar College at that time to allow students of color to attend, to quote Bowyer's suit, the federal district court made several rulings now directly pertinent to the case at hand, including the following:

a. "The will of Indiana Fletcher Williams ... created the trust whereby the institution was established and has been operated since 1901."

b. "The college is now chartered by Virginia as a non-stock, non-profit corporation and as such a testamentary trustee ..."

c. "The college's or board's administration of the trust is always subject to the supervision of the State court."

d. "The point is that doubt of the legal and moral right of Sweet Briar to deviate from terms of the will can plague the college until an answer is procured from the State courts.

The question of the college being a trust because of the will of Indiana Fletcher Williams was a key legal point in our opposition to the closing decision. As trustees of a trust, the administration of the college could not make a decision that violated the terms of the trust, such as closing the college without seeking permission from the state courts. In other words, the administration could not independently decide to close the college but could only request that the Amherst County Circuit Court consider whether the college should close. The lawyers for the college's administration argued that the college was simply a corporation, and therefore, they, like the officers of any commercial corporation, had the right to make a decision about closure or any other matter pursuant to their own business judgment.

Interestingly, the Attorney General of Virginia, Mark Herring, filed an amicus brief with the circuit court that claimed Ellen Bowyer had no jurisdiction to sue since she was the County Attorney for Amherst County and not the Attorney General. That action raised concerns immediately among alumnae that the Attorney General was in favor of the closing. On April 10, the Attorney General's press secretary was quoted in media reports as saying that in her meeting with the Attorney General's office, Bowyer was asked to coordinate her efforts, "but that did not happen."

The County Attorney then responded to that mischaracterization. "There was never any request that I coordinate my actions with the Attorney General's office," Bowyer said. "I would have been delighted to have coordinated action with the Attorney General's office, and I would have confirmed my response in writing. But there was no such request. Instead, I offered to copy the office on all legal filings and to generally keep the office apprised of what I was doing. I have done that, and I will continue to do that."

Fairly early after the announcement of closure, the County Attorney was informed that a good deal of document shredding was occurring in the offices at Sweet Briar College. She wrote to the lawyers for Rice and Jones and made clear the shredding must stop. She never learned what was shredded or how much information was destroyed.

Some of the alumnae active on Facebook asked alumnae to write to the Attorney General to try to persuade him to change his mind. Friends on Facebook reported that groups of alumnae then attended public talks by the attorney general, many dressed in pink and green—the school colors—and some carrying signs about saving the college. They followed him to public events, declaring their opposition to closing SBC. We sent letters to Attorney General Herring and in various ways made clear to him we possessed extraordinary passion for and loyalty to our Alma Mater.

The Attorney General, who is elected to office in Virginia, could not miss our message and realized the widespread nature of the interest in our struggle. He then made it known that he would attempt to initiate mediation between all parties to the various lawsuits against the college. That sounded hopeful to David and me. An agreement to settle out of court would be one way to quickly stop the defendants from continuing to act to close the college rather than having the suit draw out over a long period of time. The latter path could have led to a situation in which we might have won, but it would have been a Pyrrhic victory, as we no longer would have had any students or faculty left. One might wonder if the school considered that possibility when they decided to announce the closing so secretively and so late in the academic year.

While Jimmy Jones, in his announcement, had avowed that they had turned over every stone in searching for ways to keep the college operating, the County Attorney's suit pointed out that in 2006, Sweet Briar had conducted a successful $110 million capital campaign under President Elizabeth Muhlenfeld, who had retired in 2008. Yet since then, the college had not attempted any capital campaigns that could have been used to pay bond interest and principal, thus further reducing the current debt load.

The County Attorney's suit further pointed out the following:

> Consultants were hired to "study" the College's condition by surveying 200 of 20,000 alumnae. The consultants and College staff members interviewed alumnae in person, in their homes, all over the country during February 2015, yet upon information and belief, made no mention of the severe need for funds during the interviews. It is not clear that any final consultant report or survey results have even been completed …
>
> The Board cited a lack of students interested in matriculating to the College, yet, upon information and belief, the Board never seriously considered recruiting additional students through obvious channels. For example, the Board never seriously considered recruiting international students, even though there is a large base of interested students seeking to attend the College from abroad. Additionally, the Board apparently never seriously considered recruiting from preparatory schools focused on equine sports, as had been advocated by the ousted Board members, even though Sweet Briar is renowned for its equine program.

An interesting fact about enrollment is that in academic year 2007–2008, the last year of Betsy Muhlenfeld's presidency, Sweet Briar College had record enrollment. How did the college fall back so quickly in Jo Ellen Parker's and Jimmy Jones's years?

A member of the board of directors, alumna Maggie Patrick, wrote a mea culpa article after listening to the rousing, brilliant commencement speech delivered in May 2015 by alumna Teresa Pike Tomlinson (class of '87), the twice-elected mayor of Columbus, Georgia, encouraging the graduating seniors and alumnae not to lose heart and to continue our efforts to save the college. The speech was posted in the *Roanoke Times* on May 24. Ms. Patrick wrote that she had been a young member of the board of directors and had noticed a disturbing change in how the college was administered. With her permission, I'm including the following excerpt:

> I experienced a strong shift in Sweet Briar's governing culture that concerned me … but I allowed myself to be convinced by Sweet Briar's leadership that this new order was necessary—that dissent or meddling would further endanger our stability.
>
> These changes are primarily linked to the hiring of Dr. Jo Ellen Parker and the

subsequent, drastic reshuffling of Sweet Briar's leadership both in the senior staff and on the Board's executive committee. While turnover can be a natural effect of a new presidency, the changes we witnessed were startling, especially as we first lost the Dean (Dean Jonathan Green) who had been one of the college's most trusted leaders, creative thinkers, and advocates for women's education on the national stage. His departure was followed by several others, including the VP of Finance, the Dean of Enrollment Management, the VP of Development, and the Campus Chaplain, in addition to several staff members in administrative positions across campus ...

The school is facing closure because key people in positions of power poorly governed the school. They froze out the broader board membership and even fired members who disagreed with their policies. They ignored strong enrollment management strategies urged by the board just a few years ago and instead drastically raised the discount rate. (This refers to the action of taking money from the endowment to reduce tuition for students as a way to attract students to enroll; however, that practice reduced the amount of incoming money for the college from students' tuition). They did not pursue a capital campaign despite completing a successful campaign on time and over goal only seven years ago. *They fired or pushed out leaders in several key positions across campus, including the Dean of Enrollment Management, the Vice President of Development, the Director of Marketing, the Director of Alumnae Relations, and the Director of the Annual Fund. None of these five critical, revenue-increasing positions was replaced* (emphasis mine).

During Jo Ellen Parker's years at Sweet Briar, there was a veritable exodus of many staff members and members of the faculty. At least ninety people left for one reason or another. Some senior staff members, as mentioned above, were not replaced. Some two dozen faculty retired. Not only were the senior staff members of admissions and development forced out, but also, many young employees left.

I am sure that anyone who learned about these facts shared with me enormous outrage that Rice and Jones would still blatantly point to a lack of student interest in matriculating at Sweet Briar to justify their decision to close the college. If there were acceptable reasons for their actions, why were they not brought out in litigation? None ever were.

One explanation for why the full board, which was composed of mostly alumnae, voted to close a school they loved might be found in human history. There are many inexplicable examples of decent people tolerating governments and leaders that carried out questionable activities. The first that comes to my mind is what occurred in Nazi Germany in the 1930s. The attempted closing of Sweet Briar might be another example. We will never know for sure.

Despite the negative effects of Sweet Briar's leadership of Rice, Parker, and Jones, a closer look at real numbers also belies their claims of unsustainable finances. In the county attorney's suit, the section "The

Decision to Close the College Is Not Warranted" gave reasons to keep the college operating and allow it to continue offering a unique educational opportunity to young women. The county attorney's suit included the following:

> 33. A review of the College's annual financial statements from 2010 to 2014, show that annual operating deficits were more than offset by the endowment's investment gains, grants, gift and alumnae giving. This pattern resulted in an *increase* of the College's net assets (total assets minus total liabilities) over the last five years from $126 million to $134 million. During the same period, the College's *debt load decreased* from approximately $42 million to $25 million while its *endowment increased* from $85 million to $95 million (emphasis mine).
>
> 34. In March 2015, two officials from Birmingham Southern and Wilson College with experience turning around struggling institutions of higher education opined that Sweet Briar is not in an unsustainable or dire financial position, and that there is no immediate need to close the College. These experts believe Sweet Briar College can be operated successfully and have offered their assistance. Letters attached …
>
> 35. Recent statistics have indicated that applications to the College have significantly increased over the past three years.

This was a conclusion also presented by others, such as Professor Dan Gottlieb, associate professor and chair of the psychology department. He carefully analyzed the available statistics pertaining to the college and showed that despite a smaller-than-normal entering class in fall of 2014—which, in part, could have been due to the lack of leadership and expertise in admissions and enrollment—the financial picture was not what the defendants claimed. On May 29, the *Washington Post* published Professor Gottlieb's analysis and conclusions, part of which I quote here with his permission:

> As of Summer of 2014 Sweet Briar College was above average on all measures of institutional financial health. Despite short-term problems, a business person would have been delighted by the opportunities available with Sweet Briar's history, $164 million in assets, $30 million in liabilities, and $60 million per decade donated by alumnae …
>
> *Enrollment:* There is no evidence that enrollment is declining, either at Sweet Briar or at women's or liberal arts colleges. This claim is simply false. Numbers people please check for yourself: the data are publicly available.
>
> *Tuition revenue and discount rate:* Across women's and liberal arts colleges, tuition revenue per student has shown no decline, and inflated-adjusted tuition revenue has been increasing for at least 20 years …

A five-year 40 percent drop in tuition revenue from degree-seeking students is an outlying, sector-defying change that has nothing to do with decreased student interest and everything to do with poor strategy and a lack of appropriate personnel.

Liabilities (bonds and deferred maintenance): Sweet Briar has $26 million in bond debt. Liquid assets might be less than that amount but far greater than the annual payments. Is it unusual that I have a mortgage that far exceeds my savings? There are real (though solvable) bond issues, but the claim that they might have led Sweet Briar to close in the middle of a school year is not credible.

A consultant report listed $29 million in deferred maintenance costs, but the VP of Finance is on record as saying that over a decade only $6.9 million is absolutely essential. Per-square-foot maintenance costs in the report are consistent with those of other colleges.

Endowment Spending: Over the last 20 years, Sweet Briar has spent more out of its relatively large endowment than is considered sustainable by an average of around $3 million/year. When President Jo Ellen Parker took over in 2009, the deficit was declining. She needed to close an 8–10 percent gap between expenses and revenue. She cut staff, faculty, and benefits, but also instituted ideologically driven changes in recruiting and financial aid that dropped total revenue by 15–20 percent, obscuring the fact that Sweet Briar had already found a blueprint for sustainable endowment spending.

Retention and Yield: Sweet Briar's retention rates—the measure of how many freshmen continue on to sophomore year there—are typical for a sector that is not crumbling. The claim that four-year graduation rates dropped from 70 percent to 54 percent in the span of around 15 years is misleading. Those numbers are 20-year high and low points, respectively. If we look at numbers just one year removed, we see a drop from 61 percent to 57 percent.

Sweet Briar leaders have made misleading through numbers an art form.

Has another college or business in as strong financial shape as Sweet Briar ever chosen to close?

The above information shows how I think the entire board of director members were misled and voted for closure. The hearing on Ellen Bowyer's complaint and motion for preliminary injunction was held on April 14 in Bedford County Circuit Court with the Honorable James W. Updike Jr. presiding. His rulings included his decision that Troutman Sanders could serve as special counsel to the county attorney, who did have standing to prosecute. However, he sided with the college that Sweet Briar was a charitable nonstock corporation rather than a trustee.

The Amherst County attorney, with the assistance of special counsel from Troutman Sanders LLP, who had joined the case on April 15, immediately took the case on an expedited appeal to the Supreme Court of Virginia on the trust issue. Judge Updike also issued a sixty-day injunction ordering that the defendants could not use funds raised by charitable solicitations to operate the college to close the college. The term of the injunction began on April 15, 2015.

Later in April, a group of students, parents of students, and some alumnae who had earlier filed suit against the same defendants for breach of contract appeared in court before Judge Updike. The judge set aside the parents and alumnae and focused on the students' case. Judge Updike then ruled that acceptance of students to the college constituted a legal, binding contract. Therefore, deciding to close the college the way they had, without warning, in his words, "creates a legal basis for finding, not in legal terms, that ain't right." He then extended to six months the temporary injunction against selling the college's assets for the purpose of closing the college.

Saving Sweet Briar Inc. noted in a summary of legal proceedings that on April 29, the county attorney filed a petition with the Supreme Court of Virginia, arguing that a permanent injunction under the Virginia Uniform Trust Code was warranted because "Sweet Briar Institute is both a charitable corporation and a trustee." In support of the appeal, three well-known and highly respected Virginia professors of trust law filed amici curiae briefs. They were J. Rodney Johnson, professor emeritus at the T. C. Williams School of Law, University of Richmond; John E. Donaldson, professor emeritus at Marshall-Wythe School of Law, College of William and Mary; and Robert T. Danforth, professor at Washington and Lee University School of Law.

An alumna who was there told me there were so many alumnae at the first hearing before Judge Updike in Bedford that another courtroom had to be made available to handle the overflow. Similarly, when the case reached the Virginia Supreme Court on June 4, 2015, there was also an overflow crowd, wearing pink and green and holding Sweet Briar College banners, at the hearing. All seven of the supreme court justices were present to hear the oral arguments, which reflected an awareness on the part of the supreme court justices of the widespread interest in the case and the need for rapid adjudication.

> In the 32-minute hearing, the justices reserved their toughest questions for Woody Fowler, the lawyer representing the (Sweet Briar BOD) Board.
>
> "Why," asked a justice, "are you contesting this so strongly?" Denying that his side was fighting to close the school, Fowler said this was a battle for the right of the board to make its own decisions.
>
> "I'm sorry," replied a justice, "but that sounds like an overstatement. This is just a preliminary injunction."
>
> "You're being asked," said Fowler, "to allow for an orderly wind-down, or you're being asked to allow a crash-and-burn."

Another justice quickly responded that Fowler omitted a third option: adhering to the 1901 will by the late Indiana Fletcher Williams and keeping a women's college alive in perpetuity.

On June 9, the supreme court issued a ruling that held that Judge Updike had erred in finding that the law of trusts could not apply to a corporation and sent the case back to Judge Updike to determine a final ruling on the closing of the college. The ruling of the Supreme Court of Virginia played a big role in the announcement on June 20, 2015, that the parties participating in mediation had reached an agreement. That same day, Ellen Bowyer announced the following:

> She had joined with Attorney General Mark Herring, Sweet Briar College, and Saving Sweet Briar, Inc. in a Memorandum of Understanding that will provide for the College's continued operation under new leadership …
>
> The agreement will result in the appointment of a new Board of Directors—including a directorship for an Amherst County representative—and the new Board is expected to appoint Phillip Stone, the former President of Bridgewater College and a prominent Virginia attorney, as College President. All litigation challenging the College's closure will be dismissed, and the 2015–2016 school year is expected to continue as originally planned prior to the March 3, 2015, announcement.

On June 22, 2015, the historic legal fight to keep Sweet Briar College open for the academic year 2015–2016 reached its end point in Bedford County Circuit Court, where it had begun in April. As County Attorney Bowyer described it, Judge Updike was to rule on whether the agreement was acceptable to him.

> In a generous and gracious statement, Judge Updike announced that the amicus curiae briefs of the three trust professors—the central tenet of which is that Sweet Briar College is a testamentary trustee subject to the Uniform Trust Code, which the County Attorney has standing to enforce—expresses the correct statement of law in the case. Thereafter, upon his affirmation of the settlement order—including his quoting William Faulkner's Nobel Prize acceptance speech for the proposition that Sweet Briar College "will not merely endure, it will prevail"—Judge Updike received a standing ovation and a rousing Sweet Briar cheer.

Later, at a late-June reunion dinner with alumnae and husbands of the class of '57, we learned from Ellen Bowyer that the judge had watched the ovation and cheering and listened to the school songs they sang with a big grin on his face. Since usually courtrooms were somber places with little outburst from observers in the room tolerated by judges, that was, to say the least, an unusual spectacle. The agreement set off celebrations by students, alumnae, faculty, staff, and their families everywhere and was reported widely in media. David and I felt tremendous relief.

As part of the agreement, Attorney General Mark Herring agreed to release restrictions on $16 million of the college's endowment "to help fund the College's ongoing operation" (which, by the way, was not used or needed by the new administration). Saving Sweet Briar Inc. was to convert pledges and forward cash donations of $12 million to be delivered in installments, with the first installment to be delivered on July 2. SSB not only delivered the money on time but also delivered more money than was agreed to and did so earlier than was required. While the agreement allowed ten members of the previous board of directors to remain, all members of the board who'd voted for closure resigned, as did Rice and Jones.

The memorandum of understanding that was to be approved by Judge Updike stated that Rice and Jones would resign, and a newly formed board was expected to appoint Phillip C. Stone Sr. as president of Sweet Briar College. Of the twenty-three previous board members, thirteen were asked to resign and replaced. In actuality, as mentioned above, all twenty-three members who had voted for closure resigned and were replaced. The new president, Phillip C. Stone Sr. (figure 86), had been president of Bridgewater College for sixteen years and guided it through some financially difficult times to put it on solid footing. He also had served as president of the Virginia Bar Association.

A lawyer for alumnae in opposition to closing, Ashley L. Taylor Jr., said of Mr. Stone, "He is well situated to both turn a school around, interact with the legal issues relating to the school that may remain, and to address any accreditation concerns the accrediting body may have." Sweet Briar College could not have been more fortunate to have Dr. Stone available and willing to take over as president.

Philip Stone is a brave man who is true to his own convictions. As an educator, he firmly believes in the value of liberal arts education. In an email to me, he said he was called by a friend who asked if he was surprised by the announcement because

> Since I had earlier chaired the accrediting commission for the south I might have learned of problems at SBC that were not known to the public. I assured him that SB was "gold." That its last 10-year re-accreditation in 2011 had revealed no problems. When he asked if I thought it could be saved, I said of course it can be saved. Its endowment is still larger than that of most small colleges.

When Troutman Sanders called to ask if he would be willing to be president of Sweet Briar College, Dr. Stone agreed. He wrote:

> When I was called the next day, there was no discussion of salary or a contract (it was not mentioned until I had been in office a couple of weeks). I simply was not willing to stand by and see this great liberal arts college go under if I could do anything to help … Ten days before I was to start I had no college documents—by laws, audits, faculty rosters, etc—and I did not know a soul on campus. I had a conference call with the outgoing board chair and the vice chair; I met a few minutes on campus with Jimmy Jones and also met with the senior staff.

President Stone described graphically what he faced when the keys were turned over to him:

On June 30th, two days before I was to start, and notwithstanding the highly publicized settlement agreement that was to keep the college open, the outgoing administration sent a notice to the faculty and staff that everyone was terminated as of that date. (A few staff needed for the "closing" had later termination dates). As a result, at the time of my election, July 2, the college had no faculty, almost no staff, no students, no riding program, no food service and no Junior Year Abroad program. The college was closed except for turning out the lights! My first act as President, taken 15 minutes after my election and before I actually arrived on campus, was to rehire everyone—with a web site posting!

President Stone came to speak to the Charlotte Area Sweet Briar Alumnae Club in July, and he began his talk by saying, "Let's be blunt: the alumnae saved Sweet Briar College!" He went on to remind us that because the freshman class was small due to understandable concern for the future of the college on the part of applicants, for the next four academic years, we would have a deficit in revenue because of the small class. It was his opinion that by December 2016, we would have a better idea about the ability of Sweet Briar College not only to survive but also to endure and prevail. (In the fall of 2016, some 150 new students entered Sweet Briar.)

I approached him before his talk and introduced myself as Anna Pai. He shook my hand and said with a twinkle in his eye, "Chips!" After his straightforward and practical talk, a classmate of mine, Dot Duncan Hodges, came up with the fine idea of presenting President Stone with a large stein she had bought while a student at Sweet Briar with our class year embolden on it. We then invited him to become an honorary classmate of '57. He exclaimed with thanks that we were an extraordinary class that once set a record for a reunion donation. The man had obviously done his homework.

The members of the new Board of Directors are impressive also. The Board consists of eleven alumnae who graduated from 1963 to 2015, and all are capable, effective women. The chair of the BOD is Teresa Pike Tomlinson, who gave an inspiring commencement speech in June at Sweet Briar (figure 87). Teresa is a twice-elected Mayor of Columbus, Georgia. A graduate of Sweet Briar in 1987 and of Emory University School of Law in 1991, she was the first female partner of the law firm of Pope, McGlamry, Kilpatrick, Morrison, and Norwood LLC in Columbus, where she specialized in complex litigation. She is married to Wade H. Tomlinson. I would like to see her run for POTUS one day!

The Vice Chair of the BOD at the outset was General Charles C. Krulak of Birmingham, Alabama (figure 88), who has since had to retire from the board due to health problems. I read blogs he wrote that encouraged Sweet Briar alumnae to continue to oppose the closing of our Alma Mater, something he did not believe was warranted. General Krulak had spent thirty-five years in the military, ending with four years as commandant of the US Marine Corps.

He also served for two years as deputy director of the White House Military Office under Ronald Reagan and George H. W. Bush. While he served for four years (2011–2015) as president of Birmingham-Southern College, he refused to take a salary or benefits and lived in student housing. Under his leadership, the college significantly increased new student enrollment every year, among other improvements. He and his wife still live in Birmingham.

With leaders like President Stone, BOD Chair Tomlinson, BOD Vice Chair General Krulak, and all members of the board—who are not only capable but also specialists in various fields, such as fund-raising, enrollment management and accreditation consulting, technology, engineering and service networking, business ownership, financial management, and banking—the future of Sweet Briar certainly looks bright. They and all of us who are part of the Sweet Briar community remain aware of the difficult problems we face, but the need to make available a Sweet Briar experience for young women is important enough for us all to continue to pledge our support and fight for the college's existence.

We will never know the answers to many questions that still confound because of the agreement to dismiss all litigation. For example, to repeat the question that one of the Supreme Court of Virginia justices asked of the defendants' lawyer, "Why are you contesting this so strongly?" Indeed, one wonders why after alumnae responded so strongly and donated $21 million in pledges and cash. Further, one suit was filed by the Amherst County attorney with help from a well-known law firm, Troutman Sanders, on the basis that the college was a trustee, and faculty voted unanimously no confidence in the president and board and filed suit for breach of contract, and a third suit was filed by students, parents, and alumnae also for breach of contract. Why was there a continuing attempt to close the college? Why didn't they just walk away?

Where was the money to go, and what were they planning to do with it? Never did they respond with specifics to those questions. The answer was always vague and said to be something to be determined yet. Their determination to close the college has been estimated to have cost the college and its supporters millions of dollars.

Another thought came to mind after I learned that for two years, the college did not have a full-time Director of Admissions, full-time Director of Development, full-time Director of Public relations, or full-time Director of Enrollment Management. For them to point to a decline in the number of new students in the fall of 2014 as evidence of a lack of interest in a small private liberal arts institution boggled my mind. Yet Board Chair Rice has been successful as an engineer and owned his own technical company. He is a multimillionaire. Could a person with that much business acumen really not see what missing the above administrators would do to enrollment of students?

Rumors flew, but we will never know the truth, as Board Chair Rice was never put in the position of testifying under oath. After his taking part in announcing the closure on March 3, 2015, I never saw Rice again. Neither he nor Jones attended commencement, in part because the graduating seniors requested they stay away to preserve the dignity and peace of their graduation.

Why was there such a period of document shredding even before the first lawsuit was filed? What were the documents? We will never know. All the questions and queries about motivation have been generated by the secrecy with which the closing was attempted. At a meeting with college administrators some three years later in 2018, I was told that no real evidence had been found to indicate the attempted closure was to benefit any of the fired former presidents or the chair of the board of directors. Still, can we find reasonable that the actions of the three were solely due to incompetence?

What we do know is that our victory was a historic event. A new plaque has been placed at the foot of the monument on Monument Hill to commemorate the fight to save Sweet Briar. Rarely has there been such a situation that energized alumnae to the extent that so many donated in support of the legal fight even before knowing that SSBI would be given a tax-deductible status.

After Judge Updike ruled that the closing must stop and that Sweet Briar "will not only endure, but prevail," dozens of alumnae volunteers showed up for days at the college (figure 89). They were willing to carry out maintenance cleaning, paint classrooms and Sweet Briar House after the Joneses left, and do whatever they could all over campus to ensure a beautiful campus and buildings for the new president and his family and for the 320 new students and upper-class students who returned. What extraordinary love and loyalty my sister alumnae demonstrated! Their volunteerism saved the college an estimated $15,000 that workmen would have had to be paid. Such volunteer work has continued the last two years as well and has become a tradition.

In a classy move, several colleges that had welcomed Sweet Briar transfer students after the announced closing, such as Agnes Scott College, Hollins College, Mary Baldwin College, and Lynchburg College, offered to return their money if the students wanted to return to Sweet Briar. Many students who had already transferred joyously accepted the refunds to return to their alma mater. When the doors opened for the fall semester, Sweet Briar received some 320 students—280 on campus and the rest in Junior Year Abroad programs.

I was told 75 percent of the faculty returned and were welcomed with open arms by President Stone. Because of the lateness of the March 3 announcement, many had thought the college would have lost so many students and faculty that there would be no chance for classes even if we could get an injunction to stop the closing. It was probably a conclusion for practical people who had not had the Sweet Briar experience. Those of us who had experienced Sweet Briar knew better!

There is no question in my mind that Rice and Jones made two serious mistakes. They underestimated the power of social media for organizing opposition quickly—really just overnight—and they underestimated the courage, passion, love, and intense loyalty of the alumnae.

I hope the manner in which alumnae took things into our own hands and used social media to overcome the enormous odds against us will serve as a beacon of light for other institutions beset by similar problems—if their graduates feel about their college as we feel about Sweet Briar. At the very least, the announced closure by Sweet Briar College administrators has induced administrations of other small liberal arts institutions to look at their own situations carefully.

They could join Sweet Briar in sending our erstwhile administrators thanks for doing such a poor job for a well-respected college and waking other institutions to the potential end result. What do present students feel about the college staying open? *Forbes Magazine* has an annual article on which colleges, small, medium, and large, show the most school spirit through submissions by their students. In 2015, the clear winner for the small colleges was Sweet Briar College.

We are aware that while we've saved Sweet Briar, we must continue to work hard for her because we want to extend her life so that generations of young women can benefit from her extraordinary ability to nurture as well as educate. After experiencing the extraordinary efforts needed to reopen the college, President Stone has been the source of a new rallying cry for Sweet Briar College: "At Sweet Briar, the impossible is just another problem to solve!" Here's to the next 114 years!

Fig 83 Tracy Stuart, '93 courtesy of Tracy Stuart

Fig 84 The alumnae Board of SSB, Inc, photo courtesy of Sweet Briar College

Fig 85 Amherst County Attorney Ellen Bowyer after a court hearing

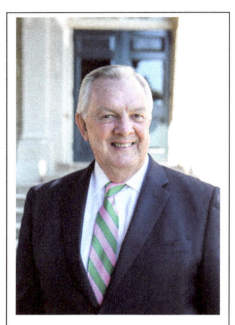

Fig 86 President Phillip C Stone, Sr, photo courtesy of Sweet Briar College

Fig 87 The Hon. Teresa Pike Tomlinson, '87

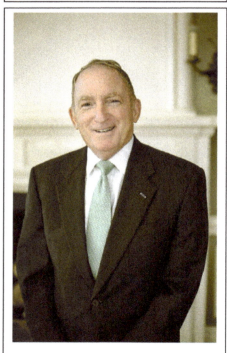

Fig 88 General Charles C Krulak, photo courtesy of Sweet Briar College

Fig 89 A volunteer alumna cleaning a hallway with a close companion, photo courtesy of Sweet Briar College

Chapter 32

BRYN MAWR AND JANE OPPENHEIMER

I will now go back to life for me in 1957. Approaching graduation from Sweet Briar, I had to decide what to do. I knew what I did not want—I felt I needed more education, and I did not want to live at home. I seriously thought of medical school, but there were at least two big obstacles. One was that in those days, there was almost no funding for scholarships or grants to medical school, and I knew my parents could not afford to send me. Going into debt was not an option.

Another was that medical training was a minimum of seven or more years, and I wanted to be married and have a family without waiting that long. Ironically, graduate school turned out to be just as long, and I ended up waiting until I was thirty to have my first child. But there were more training grants and assistantships for graduate students.

Sometimes I wonder how I would have done as a physician. My favorite article in a science magazine is one that describes the manner in which a doctor confronts a patient with confusing symptoms and then figures out the problem and its solution. I think I would have liked being a diagnostician. I'm not sure, though, how I would have handled losing patients to one illness or another. However, my big brother Solan, who had the biggest heart of anyone I know, was able to deal with the sad aspects of losing patients, so perhaps I could have also. It's a moot point.

I chose to apply to graduate programs. Having read the papers on fish embryology of Dr. Jane Oppenheimer, a professor at Bryn Mawr College, I wanted to study with her. I was accepted into Bryn Mawr's MA program, and she became my major professor. Later, the chair of the biology department, whose name has left my mind, told me I had been accepted because I not only had trained in the Jackson Lab's summer research training program but also had been invited to return as a counselor for the precollegiate group the next summer. What an example of one door opening other doors!

Miss Oppenheimer (as at Sweet Briar, professors were called Miss rather than Dr.) was one of the most brilliant persons, if not the most brilliant, I'd ever met in my life (figure 90). She was, at the time I entered

Bryn Mawr, teaching herself Russian. She loved languages and felt compelled to learn on her own a different language every five years.

Her studies on zebra fish embryology made her a world-class scientist recognized by all for her astute interpretation and ingenious experiments on development in those vertebrates. Having taught in a state institution where research facilities and equipment were limited, I realize now how impressive Miss Oppenheimer's achievements were since she accomplished them in a small private school, not in a large research university. One thing that helped her was that Bryn Mawr did have doctoral students, so she could rely on them for assistance in research.

My interests were all in mammalian systems after my two wonderful summers at Jackson Lab in Maine. I asked Miss Oppenheimer if I could do research on mammalian systems. She agreed, and while she had nothing to give me in mammalian development, one of her good friends was a female faculty member at the Albert Einstein College of Medicine in New York City. She told me she would talk to Dr. Salome Waelsch about my possibly doing some research with mice. I was given a master's thesis project by Dr. Waelsch, who later became my PhD supervisor. Another door had opened.

With the wisdom of hindsight, looking back at my two years at Bryn Mawr, I realize I should have joined Miss Oppenheimer in her own research. First of all, as I mentioned, she was a brilliant scientist. Secondly, doing research with zebra fish required far less money and time than doing research with mice because her fish had much shorter generation times than mammals. In developmental studies, the shorter the generation time of the animals one studies the better to gather as much data in as short a time as possible.

Working with a genius, however, had its trials and tribulations. Miss Oppenheimer had a quirky personality. When I first started at Bryn Mawr, I was used to saying, "Yes, ma'am," and "No, ma'am," since I had gone to college in Virginia. When I first answered her as the southerners had taught me to do at Sweet Briar, she leaned back and asked me in an annoyed voice why I was saying *ma'am* to her. She seemed to think I was being fresh to her.

"Why are you saying *ma'am* to me?" she asked one day out of the blue. Flustered, I hastened to tell her that was how we'd spoken to our professors at Sweet Briar.

"Well," she said, "don't do that with me." I almost answered, "Yes, ma'am!"

She had health problems too, especially with her back. One day she came into the lab limping. I asked if she was okay. She told me she had turned over in bed and sprained her ankle. Now that I'm older than she was at that time, I understand the frustration she felt. I could never be sure of her mood when she came to work. On good days, she was as sweet as she could be; on bad days, I stayed out of her way as much as possible.

She was funny too. She had a dog—if I remember right, a beagle. She brought him to work with her and into her classes. Usually, he was well behaved and just lay there while she lectured. One day while she was lecturing, he needed to go out. Without breaking off her lecture, she got up, went through the classroom door, and opened the building door for him. Of course, nobody could hear what she was saying as she left the room and went into the hall. She came back still lecturing.

There was a nice young man, industrious and polite, who was in charge of keeping the animal room clean, but he nearly ruined my research. The mice Dr. Waelsch had given me to study were kept in cages on moveable racks, with many cages per rack. One day as I was teaching a baby zoology course (as a graduate assistant, I taught a lab every semester and carried out other chores, which exempted me from paying tuition), a fellow graduate student came to the door and motioned frantically to me. When I found out what was wrong, I nearly had a heart attack.

The animal room had a drain in the center so the animal room cleaner could hose his sweepings into the drain. While hosing down the animal room, he had carelessly pushed the rack on which I had my entire mouse colony. That day, one of the legs of the rack he'd pushed went into the drain, and the whole thing tipped over, scattering cages and mice all over. When I saw him, he was obviously upset, and I didn't have the heart to yell at him—which would have made me feel better.

Although I lost a few mice that were fatally injured by the fall, I was able to restore the colony using the methods of identification Dr. Waelsch had taught me. Every mouse was given a series of nicks in its ears when it was incorporated into the research, and the nicks and coat color of the mice were then recorded in a book and as backup on cards also. Every cage was also numbered. With the elaborate system, I could put every mouse back into its own cage. It took me two days, but at least most of my colony was still there, though the mice were all pretty badly shaken up.

Miss Oppenheimer was also upset by what had happened. To calm me down, she invited me to dinner at her house. I don't remember much of what she served, but I do remember that she served me turtle soup. It was the first time I'd had it, and I'm not sure that given my druthers, I would have eaten it. Clearly, she thought it was a delicacy, and she was doing me a great favor by serving it, so I ate it. I was surprised at how good it tasted.

In the summer of 1958, after a year at Bryn Mawr, I was accepted as a summer research assistant at the Carnegie Institute Genetics Laboratory at Cold Spring Harbor on Long Island. I cannot remember who suggested I apply for a position there or how I knew about their summer program. At any rate, I was told that if I waited tables there, I would not have to pay for my room and board for the summer. Students would be assigned to a staff scientist and given a research project to carry out.

My supervisor was Dr. Phillip Hartmann, who was working on the histidine locus (gene) in salmonella bacteria. I was to expose bacteria cultures to ultraviolet light to produce mutations. Dr. Hartmann was interested in genes controlling the expression of the gene coding for histidine, an amino acid.

I was not comfortable working with bacteria, as I had never had time yet to take microbiology in college—in fact, I'm not even sure microbiology was offered at Sweet Briar at that time—so I had to learn the most basic techniques at the beginning. I remember the first time I had to draw up some culture of salmonella using a one-milliliter pipette. The bore of the pipette was so narrow and small I thought I had to suck hard to get the bacteria into the glass pipette. When I felt salty fluid in my mouth almost immediately, I realized I had sucked way too hard. I was lucky the pipette mouth end was stuffed with some kind of material so that idiot students like me would not get salmonella in the mouth along with the culture medium.

Eventually, after the first few days, I had learned enough to carry out the routine of radiating the bacteria with ultraviolet light. Dr. Hartmann analyzed the results. I never learned what his conclusions were based on the experiments we did, but I learned some techniques of microbiology.

I enjoyed the atmosphere at Cold Spring Harbor. It was exciting to see some of the most famous molecular biologists of the time, people whose papers I had read or tried to read and understand, and it was an exciting time in genetics and molecular biology. Even James Watson of Watson and Crick fame was there. At the time, he was still quite young, having just five years previously published the paper he coauthored with Francis Crick on the molecular structure of DNA. (He'd entered the University of Chicago on a tuition scholarship at the age of fifteen.)

Dr. Watson, who had received a PhD by the time he was only around twenty-three years old, gave a talk eagerly anticipated by both students and staff scientists. I was bemused by the fact that he gave the talk in a wrinkled shirt, sandals with no socks, and a pair of shorts he had made by cutting the legs off a pair of pants. I no longer remember what he spoke about, but I knew I was privileged to hear him.

One day while walking on the campus of Carnegie Laboratory, I saw a small gray-haired woman in overalls working in a small cornfield behind the laboratory building. I asked a staff scientist who she was, though I knew. I had at one time read some papers written by a famous geneticist who had published a revolutionary analysis of genes in maize (corn). I knew she worked at Cold Spring Harbor. I was told the person I saw was indeed Barbara McClintock (figure 91).

As the foremost cytogeneticist of her time, Dr. McClintock gave visual proof that chromosomes can exchange pieces of themselves with other chromosomes in the process we call crossing over. She did that work with Harriet Creighton. She also focused on genetic regulation in maize. She discovered there were genetic elements that seemed able to move about in the chromosomes of maize that could control the expression of other genes. The idea that genes could move around from one site on a chromosome to another, or from one chromosome to another, was revolutionary at the time.

She moved a cot into her laboratory, I was told, as she often slept in the laboratory in order to continue working at odd hours. Like many of her generation, she—and her work—received little recognition because of her gender. She had been given a position at the University of Missouri in 1936 but soon realized she would probably not receive tenure no matter what she achieved in her research. Finally, she'd accepted an invitation to join the Carnegie Institute Genetics Laboratory at Cold Spring Harbor in 1941, and she continued to work there until the end of her career.

My generation and those younger can thank the brave, brilliant women of Dr. Waelsch and Dr.

McClintock's generation for paving the way for us. I believe there is still discrimination against women in some areas, as I will mention later, but there are cracks now appearing in the glass ceiling thanks to their pioneering work.

However, there was so much criticism of the concept of controlling elements and moving genes that Dr. McClintock stopped publishing papers on them in 1953, the year Jim Watson and Francis Crick published their paper on the molecular structure of DNA. It was too anti-intuitive for most scientists to think that the genome of a living organism was not stable. Given my own struggles in reading and understanding her research papers, I was reassured when I heard a Nobelist say he could not understand her work at the time either.

However, in the 1960s, studies of bacteria and viruses showed they had genetic elements that could move to different sites in their chromosomes and control the expression of genes, turning them on or off. Scientists then remembered Dr. McClintock's work on maize genetics, and her work was rediscovered in the 1970s.

In 1983, she was awarded the Nobel Prize in Physiology or Medicine. When she was interviewed by a journalist and asked what she planned to do with the money, she had no idea the Nobel Prize carried money and, thus, had no plans whatever. The unassuming, brilliant woman died in 1992, and I felt privileged I had seen her and many others in the flesh at Cold Spring Harbor.

After a summer of being together, the student research assistants at Carnegie Institute decided to celebrate and have a party at the end of the program. Although I worried about it, I took part in cooking the lobsters and corn on the cob in the lab's steamers, which were used to sterilize research glassware. Watermelons were injected with alcoholic drinks and placed in the lab's cold rooms to be cooled. I hoped the smell of lobsters in the steamers would not be a problem afterward. I have a feeling our celebration was not an event that Carnegie Lab allowed to develop into a tradition!

We enjoyed our picnic greatly, though I could not eat the watermelon since I am allergic to alcohol. After dinner, some dove into the water of the harbor that was right next to our campus. When they emerged, fluorescent plankton moved in bright streaks down their bodies. It is an image I will not forget. Nature is so impressive!

It was a lovely end to a remarkable summer for me. I saw many famous geneticists and had the opportunity to hear them speak. One evening, I was in the lab, finishing something, when a leader in the study of human chromosomes came in. He was a friendly Chinese man. I am not sure of his name (Dr. Hsu?) or the question I asked, but I remember that he was so enthusiastic about the new knowledge of human chromosomes that I got an hour-long lecture, along with his drawings of the human karyotype on the blackboard.

As I look back on my experiences, I am increasingly amazed at how fortunate I was to have had the opportunities to meet some of my scientific idols and at the fun I had during my training as a scientist. Along with my experiences at the Jackson Lab in Bar Harbor and with Drs. Waelsch and Oppenheimer at a developmental biology seminar in Oak Ridge, Tennessee, being in the company of such talented and enthusiastic scientists made a possible career in research attractive to me.

At Bryn Mawr, we were to take courses and do an independent research project. There would be an oral examination, a thesis to write and defend, and two foreign-language examinations. The setup was to give students an experience akin to studying for a PhD. In actuality, Bryn Mawr's master's degree program was truly a minidoctorate.

I had gone to Bryn Mawr without any confidence that I could handle graduate work. The rigor of their MA program was daunting. French was a snap for the language exams because I had taken four years of French courses at Sweet Briar, but I didn't have another language. My Chinese was not nearly good enough to read and write. I decided to try to learn German on my own. I chose German because some of the best work in embryology had been done in Germany. It was not a smart choice for the exam, however. I should have chosen either Spanish or Italian, which are closer to French. A number of the graduate students and I met with a German professor once a week. She was nice and donated her time to try to teach us enough to pass the required test, which was to be done without a dictionary.

In June, we all took the exam. I failed, as I'd thought I would. The complexity of the German language was by no means intuitive. In the fall, the German professor met with graduate students again, and every one of us was there again. We greeted each other with somewhat embarrassed smiles, as most of us had never failed anything in our lives. The second time around, most of us passed. The exams consisted of reading scientific papers in our own fields and translating them into English.

I'm sure today that exam is no longer a requirement, as the computer allows for instant translation of papers in many languages. At any rate, I never had any need in my career to translate a paper in a different language, and I quickly forgot what little I knew in German.

In my second year at Bryn Mawr, I had to decide what to do after I finished my MA program. As I said, I was not certain I was graduate school material when I started, but clearly, as I fulfilled one requirement after another, that uncertainty was alleviated. I broached the subject one day with Miss Oppenheimer and told her I didn't know if I could be successful in getting a PhD. Her unequivocal response was "Absolutely—you must go on!" I respected her so much that if she believed I could do it, then I could, and I also began to plan life with David.

Fig 90 Jane M. Oppenheimer 1911-1996; Professor of Biology, Bryn Mawr College. Photograph Courtesy of Bryn Mawr College.

Fig 91 Dr. Barbara McClintock. Photo courtesy of Carnegie Institute Genetics Laboratory at Cold Springs Harbor

Chapter 33

LIFE AT BRYN MAWR AND LIFE WITH DAVID

By that point, my relationship with David had become serious. Since David's parents were in Taiwan and not allowed to leave, David introduced me to his oldest sister, Patsy Loo, and her husband, David. It was an important meeting for us because Patsy (figure 92) was the oldest sibling in the United States. As the oldest, she acted as the titular head of the family, and we needed her approval. They invited me to dinner at their home in New Rochelle, New York. I knew she would report back to their parents. In effect, the meeting would determine if the family would approve of me as a wife to one of their favorite sons.

Patsy made us a home-cooked meal. The province in which they grew up was Guangxi, in the south of China, not far from Szechuan Province. Food in both provinces leaned heavily toward hot and spicy, while I had grown up with Northern Chinese food, which was not at all spicy.

The first dish she presented was hot and spicy sautéed seafood and vegetables. David served me some and put it on my plate. I was prepared to eat it and declare it delicious, except when I put some in my mouth, it was so hot and spicy I could hardly talk. I knew I could not spit it out, or else I would insult the chef, whose approval I was seeking, so I tried to ignore the pain of the fire in my mouth and chewed it and swallowed it. It hurt all the way down!

Patsy saw the tears building in my eyes and asked, "Is it too hot for you?"

I apologized and said, "It is delicious, but my reaction is simply due to being a northerner. I am not used to this cuisine."

Patsy laughed and said she had prepared some nonspicy dishes. "Please eat those instead of the spicy ones."

Patsy quickly became one of my favorites among David's siblings. A lovely woman with a quick smile and warm heart, she was always kind and a lot of fun. I expected I would get a gracious report from her to her parents. Patsy was one of David's favorite siblings too. She was never arrogant and laughed easily at herself.

She was a wonderful human being and a loving person. It was easy to respect her as a big sister and the head of the family in the United States.

I was no longer dating anyone else but David, and following the approval of my becoming a member of their family, we became engaged in 1958 during my first year at Bryn Mawr. He presented me with an old diamond ring his mother had sent to him to give to me. The sizable diamond was mounted on a setting that made the diamond protrude in the air close to an inch. Quickly, we changed the setting to a simple, plain one, but the diamond was beautiful and eye-catching nonetheless. Figure 93 shows my family the day Mommy and Daddy had a party to celebrate our engagement in New York City.

When David graduated from VMI in 1958, I attended his graduation. To my consternation, I had a fender-bender accident while driving his car on campus. Someone had parked with the rear of his car sticking out, and as I was looking for a space, I bumped into it. VMI Keydets were not allowed to have cars or drive on campus, so they generally rented parking from residents of Lexington, the lovely college town where both VMI and Washington and Lee College are located. When dates visited, the girls could go retrieve the cars to drive. Needless to say, I was embarrassed by the accident, especially since I'm a good driver and had not ever had an accident. But David shrugged it off. The graduation was a lot of fun. It was a happy occasion. We joined his buddies at parties and enjoyed private moments with each other.

While I was in my second year at Bryn Mawr, David was in his first year of a master's degree program at Lehigh University, which is not far from Bryn Mawr. We were able to visit each other fairly easily because of the proximity of the two schools. It was a welcome change from the all-day bus trips we'd taken while he was still at VMI and I was at Bryn Mawr in Pennsylvania.

His being near came in handy one time because a Chinese man I had met at a party for Chinese students in the area became interested in me and continued to call. I kept telling him I was engaged and was not going to date anyone else. Then, one day, he insisted he was coming to Bryn Mawr to see me. I was somewhat alarmed and called David, who came over to confront the man. When he saw David, the man backed down and apologized. I never saw him again, thank goodness. It was an example to me of the benefits of having a serious beau—besides the fun aspects.

My years at Bryn Mawr were intense because of the academics, but there were good times as well that made life fun. One memory I have of Bryn Mawr that makes me smile is a train trip that a Sweet Briar classmate and I took together to New York City.

Elaine Kimball was teaching at Shipley Preparatory School, which was across the street from Bryn Mawr. We went to the dining car to get something to eat, when two boys in their teens, obviously high school students, came into the car, saw us, and asked if they could join us. Elaine and I made eye contact and were at once of a mind to play along with the boys. We both were young looking, and I suspect they thought we were in high school.

The boys put on all the charm they could. One started talking to me and the other to Elaine. The whole time, I was laughing on the inside. It was typical of boys to think they could snow girls. After a while, my young man asked what I was studying, and I told him I was studying embryology. He asked what year I was in, and I couldn't lie and said I was in graduate school.

He did a double take and asked, "What year is Elaine at Shipley?"

I confess I hesitated in answering, wondering if I could carry on the pretense. Finally, I said, "She's on the faculty there."

His buddy was still busy trying to charm Elaine, when my guy leaned over and, in a loud voice, asked Elaine, "And what do you teach at Shipley?"

That was the end of our little tryst. The boys excused themselves politely and left, blushing, to sit at another table by themselves. Elaine and I had a great laugh later. The boys actually were kind of cute. We probably taught them something they could use in future attempts to develop quick friendships with women.

Another memory is from teaching a lab when my students in beginning biology were dissecting preserved crayfish. One called me over to help identify something. She said in a perplexed voice that it was black. When I looked closer, I saw that she had completely cut through the crayfish and was looking at the black wax of the dissecting tray. I hoped she did not have aspirations to be a surgeon one day.

Another time, during the same lab, a fellow teaching assistant and I couldn't figure out what a structure was. We told the student it was part of the digestive system. Only later did we realize we'd been seeing the remains of what the crayfish had last eaten. Oh well. Hopefully that student wasn't damaged as a biologist because of our teaching!

David and I also had the best pizza we'd ever eaten while I was at Bryn Mawr. A number of people had told me there was a mom-and-pop pizza restaurant not far from school that was really good. One day when David came to visit for the weekend, we decided to try the pizza. The restaurant was actually a house with the living room converted into a dining room. From our table, we could look into the kitchen, where a gray-haired lady was making the pizza. My friends were correct. The pizza was the best we had ever eaten, and the topping was just the right combination of tomato sauce, cheese, and meats.

I lived in a big old building with cedar shingles on the periphery of the Bryn Mawr campus. It housed a group of graduate students. I had a small bedroom and a small sitting room, where I had my desk. There was room for a table, on which I ate my meals. The residents of the house shared a kitchen, where we prepared our meals and shared a community refrigerator.

Food, at that time, was not a priority for me because of my workload, so I would make a quantity of something, such as a stew, and eat it for a whole week. By the fourth day, the food no longer attracted me or induced an appetite. I lost a good ten pounds that first year, which was just as well, as I had gained ten pounds at Sweet Briar.

One of the graduate students had a family in the big house, including a young son named Bartholomew. The boy, around four years old, was always running around in the house, looking for cookies and candy handouts. I can still hear his mother's shrill voice calling, "Bartholomew!" every day. One day I saw him on my floor and did a double take. There, written on his forehead in lipstick, was a message from his mom to us: "No food!"

I became friends with the maintenance man who did chores at our big house. I believe I called him Big John. He loved fried rice. In return for favors, such as driving me to the grocery store, I would make him fried rice. One day Big John called me to join him in the back of the house. "Here. I want to show you something," he said. He had one of the house shingles and held a match to it. It practically exploded into flames.

I was appalled and looked at him with alarm.

"Just wanted you to know that if there's ever a fire in the house," he said, "you hafta get outa there just as quick as you can!"

John was also a reason for me to feel ashamed of myself one night. I was returning from the biology building that was just up a small hill from our big house. I was tired because I had worked hard, and it was late. Suddenly, I saw the shadow of a black man coming up the hill toward me. Immediately, I felt apprehensive and thought about turning back to the biology building, but with relief, I saw that it was John. My apprehension turned to sheepishness as I realized my fear had been in part because I saw a black man.

I decided to take the train home for Thanksgiving vacation in 1957. I called a taxi to take me to the train station. A white-haired senior citizen was driving the taxi, and as we drove out of the Bryn Mawr campus, he asked if I was Chinese. I, of course, answered in the affirmative.

He told me, "I taught English for several years at St. John's in Shanghai."

"Really?" I replied. "How did you like teaching in China?"

"I liked it," he answered. "The students worked hard."

"Why did you leave?" I asked.

"There was a warlord up north in Manchuria who was coming south in the 1920s and wanted all foreigners to leave. They called him the Tiger of Manchuria."

Oh my gosh, I thought, *he's talking about the Old Marshal, my grandfather!* I debated with myself about whether I should tell him. Would he still be holding a grudge and turn around to take me back to Bryn Mawr? Or would he be so angry he'd tell me to get out of his taxi? Before I could come to a decision, we arrived at the train station, and I never told him of the coincidence.

A distant cousin lived not far from Bryn Mawr, and I saw him and his German wife frequently. Jeffrey Chu, whom I called Chu Biao Guh in Chinese, which means "Older Male Cousin Chu," had attended my parents' wedding as a child in China. He had always had a warm big-brother feeling toward me. One day David and I borrowed his car so we could go out, since David sometimes took a bus or train to Bryn Mawr from Lehigh.

That day, it began to snow heavily. It didn't bother us, as we could stay indoors. Suddenly, I heard some scraping noises. I looked out my window, and there was Chu Biao Guh, putting chains on the tires of his car. I'm sure part of the reason was because he was afraid we'd wreck his car if we went out, but also, he had a family feeling toward us and wanted to keep us safe.

Chu Biao Guh was another brilliant person in my life (figure 94). He was a pioneer in the computer industry, a core member of the team that designed the first American electronic computer, the ENIAC. He served as chairman and CEO of Santec Corporation, chief engineer at Univac Division of Sperry and Rand, and director of BTU, among other positions.

In the 1970s, he began to travel to China and served as adviser to the chairman of the Science and Technology Commission. It surprised me initially that he would consider helping the Communist government in developing their computer capabilities. When I asked him why, he responded simply, "I'm not just helping them with computers; I want to teach them free enterprise." It must have been gratifying to him when Deng Shiao Ping turned China's economic policy toward free enterprise and launched that country into a position of economic power in the world in the 1990s.

Jeffrey held a special place in my family's heart because, as I mentioned, as a child of about ten, he had attended my parents' wedding. He always said my parents were the last connection he had to China, and I always felt the same way about Jeffrey. When he passed away in early 2011, I felt my last real connection to China was gone.

It was an exciting time for me because of David Pai. One day, knowing David was planning to visit me, I decided to try to make dinner for us. I had a Chinese cookbook. I knew David liked lobster, so my menu for us was fried rice and Cantonese lobster. I bought a lobster at the grocery store where we all shopped and had everything I needed.

Now, as a scientist, I needed to follow many protocols, so I assumed following cooking instructions would be no problem. To my dismay, however, when we sat down to eat, the lobster was terribly overcooked. The lobster tail was so rubbery that we could have used it as a basketball!

To add to my embarrassment, when I was making the dessert, Sara Lee pound cake with ice cream and whipped cream, I had never used canned whipped cream before. I bought the canned whipped cream because I had no electric mixer I could use to whip the cream. I ended up getting whipped cream on David's face instead of on his cake. When he just laughed and did not leave in a rage, I figured he really must love me. Fortunately, as time passed, I became a reasonably good cook with his suggestions about how to improve my dishes.

Fig 92 David's oldest sister Patsy Loo, photo courtesy of the Loo family

Fig 94 Jeffrey Chu (right), my Chu Biao Guh, Yung and Nancy Wong, two close Tiger friends to his right

Fig 93 Solan, Stanley and David are on the floor, and Jeannie is behind Solan

Chapter 34

MARRIAGE AND A FULL-TIME TEACHING JOB

David and I had determined we would get married after I graduated from Bryn Mawr. He had one more year left for his MS degree in engineering from Lehigh. The date we chose for the big event was August 29, 1959. Mommy was happy with my choice of husband. David was Chinese, a good student, and a respectful young man, and not least, his father was a well-known and highly respected celebrity, so I was marrying well.

However, in her attempt to be a good mother to me, she astonished me again with how out of touch she was with life in general. At the time I was engaged and planning the wedding, I had my BA degree in zoology and my MA degree in embryology, so I knew something about biology. One day Mommy said to me in a whisper, "The day before the wedding, I will tell you about what you will be doing with David as your husband in bed."

All I could manage in reply was "Okay, thank you."

I don't know if she forgot what she promised because of the excitement and presence of so many family members and friends, but that conversation never took place. Her comment told me that she herself had been totally ignorant of sex when she married Daddy, and she had no comprehension about my studies and what biology was about. It reminded me of the incident when I had accompanied Mommy and Lo Lo to Beijing in 1950 and asked a cousin about someone being pregnant. Mommy immediately had apologized for my forwardness and said I planned to be a medical doctor one day. Clearly, she grew up at a time when anything having to do with sex was verboten to girls in polite company.

We decided with our families to have a church wedding. It was something my parents wanted as a ritual, although we were not brought up to be members of a particular religion. David's family, on the other hand, was known to have derived from a Persian merchant whose Chinese version of his name was Baiderludin. David has a family tree that shows only the males (of course) in a family of more than twenty-one generations (see again figures 64 and 65). His father, General Pai Chung Xi, was the lay head of the Muslim community in China.

His family did keep some Muslim traditions, such as not eating pork at home. David and his brothers and sisters, however, did not adhere to Muslim dietary restrictions when they were away from home, as I learned when he first took me to dinner and ordered pork meatballs. *He's my kind of Muslim*, I thought. When I asked him about it, David said, "I'm on the reform side of Muslims."

Formal religion in my own family was nonexistent when we were growing up. Mommy was probably more Buddhist than Daddy, sometimes referring to Lao Tien Yeh, a godlike figure in the sky in her mind, but I knew she wanted me to be married in church in a wedding gown, which, in her mind, was the proper thing to do in the United States. David and I contacted a small church in Riverdale, New York, where David's sister Patsy had been married. We interviewed the pastor, who said he would be happy to marry us, so the stage was set for August 29, 1959.

Our wedding-day weather was one of the worst summer days I had ever experienced anywhere. It was ninety-five degrees and 95 percent humidity. Figure 95 shows David and me walking up the aisle after we became man and wife. I believe we were just as happy about thinking about changing into cooler clothes as we were about being married! David's eyeglasses kept fogging up on him, but the excitement of having so many friends and family together to celebrate with us compensated somewhat for our misery. Figure 96 shows my Sweet Briar professor and three close lifelong college friends at the reception line. I changed into a red lace Chinese dress after the ceremony for our reception in a Chinese restaurant (figure 97). Thank goodness our cars and the restaurant were well air-conditioned.

Since neither David nor I tolerate alcohol well, we pretended to drink pink champagne by squashing maraschino cherries into ginger ale to toast our friends at all the tables (figure 98). Daddy later said our wedding was the second time he had ever gotten drunk (you can see his hand next to David's in the figure as he joined us to toast every table). The first time was the night before my aunt Chao Sze was to join my uncle the Young Marshal in captivity and an uncertain future, as I described earlier.

David and I spent our wedding night at the Plaza Hotel. I was nervous, and so was he, but we survived the night. The next day, we drove to Lake George. The bad weather followed us there, and it began to rain. It was so hot and humid that we had to leave our honeymoon cottage, as mold was starting to build on our shoes. We drove north to find cooler temperatures and ended up for a couple of days in Stowe, Vermont. The trip was lovely but short, and we had to return to our house in Bethlehem to start our lives together.

We had spent some time before the wedding looking for a place to live while David finished his master's degree at Lehigh. Two funny incidents stick in my mind that happened while we were searching. At one place, a woman was showing a part of her house that had been renovated into an apartment for rent.

In chatting with us about what we were doing, she found out I had a master's degree and was thinking about getting a PhD at Einstein College of Medicine. The lady then did something that always annoyed me.

In those days, many ladies responded to my being in graduate school by using big words or talking about something they did that they thought would make them sound intelligent to me. It was as if they thought I would look down on them if they were just themselves, something I would never do. It used to make me angry. Anyway, the lady suddenly began talking about her six-year-old daughter and how clever the child was. "Everyone says how promiscuous she is!" she proudly exclaimed.

The other incident involved the landlady of the bottom half of a house we ended up renting. We set about looking for a place to live in Bethlehem since David had another year before graduation. One place we saw and liked was the bottom half of a house for rent. It had a living room, a dining area, a small kitchen, and one bedroom. The kitchen had a tiny gas refrigerator with a freezer that was just big enough for one small package of Birds Eye frozen veggie or one small tray of ice cubes—but not both. Still, the price was right, and it was clean and close to Lehigh.

Mrs. Goldberg (not her real name), the owner of the house, was showing us around. She had a heavy Jewish accent. Having lived in New York City for years, I could identify Jewish accents easily. I told her I had worked one summer at the Albert Einstein College of Medicine. Einstein had been established by contributions from Jews to accommodate Jewish students, who were often discriminated against when applying to medical schools. It was a division of Yeshiva University, which was affiliated with the Jewish religion.

When I added that Einstein was a part of Yeshiva University, the rotund, pleasant lady threw her hands out to me and, with a beaming smile, said, "The moment I saw you, I knew you was one of us!" To this day, when we see someone we can identify as Jewish, we say he or she is "one of us."

That story and a fifty-year-long (so far) friendship with our best Caucasian (and Jewish) friends, Marty and Ellie Gruber, convinced us that much is shared by the Chinese and Jewish cultures, including the strength of family and an emphasis on education and productivity. In addition, as Ellie once told me, the Jewish calendar is some 250 years older than the Chinese calendar.

"Do you know what the significance of that is?" she asked me, and I shook my head. "The real significance," she said, "is that Jews had to do without Chinese food for two hundred fifty years!"

We all roared with laughter because the Grubers were fans of Chinese cuisine, and so were the many Jews who were residents of Livingston, New Jersey, where we lived for forty-two years. Livingston had something like five temples, and about one-third of the population were Jewish.

Fig 95 Mr. and Mrs. David Pai

Fig 96 Jane Belcher, Winnie Ward, Dotsie Woods and Nancy Godwin

Fig 97 David and me; August 29, 1959

Fig 98 Immediately to my left is Dr. Henrich Waelsch, next to him is my Ph.D professor Dr Salome Wealsch, my cousin Jeffery Chu and his first wife Elsa and Soo Ling Li, a friend.

Chapter 35

MORAVIAN SEMINARY FOR GIRLS

In his last year at Lehigh, David was earning around $1,500 for the year. I had gotten a teaching position at a small girls' prep school, Moravian Seminary for Girls, in Green Pond, Pennsylvania, for the princely sum of $3,000 for the school year—remember, this was with a master's degree! And you know what? We even saved money because our lives were so simple, and the cost of living in Bethlehem, Pennsylvania, was so low.

One of our favorite meals was a steak, pepper, and onion sub we bought at an Italian restaurant for around three dollars. The restaurant was a hole in the wall, and one had to walk down some steps to enter it, but they really knew how to make that sub. We have never found a restaurant or fast food place that could equal their Philadelphia steak sandwich.

I also did some cooking, though not always successfully. Still, I made a couple of dishes that were good enough that David would occasionally invite his fellow Chinese engineering graduate students over for a meal. In the absence of any Chinese restaurants, the young men were happy to eat any approximation of Chinese cooking. We were happy there and adjusted to married life well.

That year was my first experience in being a full-time faculty member. I had to learn how to order and organize labs for biology, and I also taught beginning algebra. My mentor there was Nancy Stableford. A biologist with a doctorate from Yale, she taught me how to organize my lectures and labs. Her interest in Moravian was especially keen since her daughter, Kitty, was a student there.

Having gone through the public education system wherever we lived, I had no clue of the environment of a prep school. I liked it. The student body was small enough that teachers could get to know our students well since class sizes were small. I realized quickly that some of the students who boarded at the school were girls from families that could not care for them and sent them away to school. We young teachers became their big sisters or mother figures (figure 99). My heart went out to those students. I did what I could to give them what they needed: friendship and compassion. Two other faculty members at Moravian were also in their twenties and became close friends of David and me, especially Joanie Miller, who taught English. For nearly sixty years, Joanie and I have stayed in touch. The other was the physical education teacher, Sissy

MacHenry. We three formed a fun group and occasionally acted as young as our students. The head mistress of the school was Lily Thurman, and she had to chastise us for our shenanigans at times.

I wasn't much older than some of the students; about ten years separated me and the sophomores I was teaching. I ended up becoming close to some of my students, especially Rebel Teeple and Mimi Humbert (figure 100). Mimi was a good student from a good family and eventually went on to become a good research biologist. Rebel was not a strong student, but she was a compelling youngster beset with family problems. Rebel was also one of the most fun students I've ever had, very natural and naive.

One day Mimi told Rebel she had signed the two of them up as partners for the three-legged race at a festival the school was putting on.

"Great," said Rebel. "Who's the third leg?"

Another time, I had read an article that said there was some evidence that peanut butter could help people with anemia. When I mentioned that in class, Rebel raised her hand and asked, "Where do they smear it? On the knees?"

She was naturally funny and had the courage to be herself. She became an airline flight attendant, which was a perfect job for her, as she had developed into an attractive woman, and she ended up marrying an attorney she met on one of her flights. Their Christmas cards show a huge family, including some adopted children. We visited them once and found her husband, Sal, to be a nice guy.

Mimi, after graduation from college, became the head research assistant in a lab at Johns Hopkins, where they worked on fragile X syndrome, which results in mental retardation. She married an educator, Bill Mules, who became head of a private school in Maryland and then one in New Jersey. He then accepted a position at the American School in London, where he served as head master for ten years. With her credentials, she was able to accept a job in London in a lab, doing more research. Both Rebel and Mimi turned out to have good lives. I couldn't be more pleased.

There were other students too who looked at me as more of a big-sister figure than a teacher, but those two were the most affectionate. Students do not always understand how fond and proud educators can be of their students. They allow us to give back to society what we have been privileged to receive in the way of education and a way of life. Nothing is more thrilling than seeing the fog of confusion lift in the mind of a youngster who suddenly, finally, sees the clear light of understanding.

The second semester for David was not an easy one. One day we drove down to Washington, DC, for David to play a basketball game in a tournament for Chinese graduate students. I wondered what kind of basketball we would see. David was to be the point guard for his team from Lehigh. He played the first game in earnest and with exuberance. Halfway through the game, however, David turned to pass the ball and twisted his ankle, untouched by human hands.

He could not continue. We assumed he had a bad sprain. I drove us to his VMI classmate's home, where we were to spend the night. Fortunately, his classmate's mother was a registered nurse. When she looked at David's ankle, which was beginning to turn all kinds of colors, she knew it was worse than a sprain and told us to go to the nearby hospital's ER. An x-ray confirmed her suspicion that David had fractured a bone in his ankle.

We were befuddled by how just pivoting on a basketball court could end up fracturing an ankle bone, but the x-ray was undeniable, and David was put into a cast up to his knee. It would be many weeks before he could walk without crutches again.

My time at Moravian continued to bring unexpected adventures. One day one of my students brought me tiny raccoon babies. Their eyes were still not open, and they were dripping wet. She had seen a raccoon with a litter of babies in a nest in a drain pipe. When a storm had broken, she'd remembered the raccoons and run to see if they were all right. The mother had left with one of her babies, but four others had remained there and been in danger of drowning.

So whom did they go to? The biology teacher, of course (figure 101). With the help of the students who had retrieved the babies from the drain pipe, I cleaned them and warmed them under the light of a lamp. I called a veterinarian to ask what kind of milk to feed them, and I bought doll baby bottles that actually worked. The raccoons held on to the bottles as human babies would have. I was concerned they might chew the nipples and swallow the pieces, but they knew to just suck.

As our landlady had specified that no pets were allowed, I had to smuggle the raccoons in and out of the house in a paper carton that served as their nest. Transporting them was a little tense if she was around, as I hoped the babies would not start chattering and squealing while we were within earshot of Mrs. Goldberg. They were wonderful little animals who used their front paws like hands. When I held them to my chest, they put their front legs around my neck. They were beguiling, and the students loved them (figure 102).

One day, though, the biggest of the litter, whom I called Big Stuff, nearly caused me to have a car accident. I was driving to school, and as usual, I had put the cardboard box of raccoon babies on the passenger-side floor. Big Stuff crawled out of the box, unknown to me. Suddenly, I spotted him under the brake pedal! I couldn't shoo him out and realized that if I needed to brake, I would squash him. Finally, the tip of his tail was visible, and I stepped on it. Big Stuff yelled in protest, but he left his hiding place, and I could pull over and put him back in the box.

Although we enjoyed our life in Bethlehem, at the end of the academic year, David finished his master's degree in civil engineering, and we moved to New York, where we both had been accepted to graduate schools. David was to enter the engineering PhD program at NYU's the Heights campus in the Bronx, and I had accepted Dr. Waelsch's invitation to get a PhD in genetics at Albert Einstein College of Medicine, Sue Golding Graduate Division, which was in the northeastern Bronx.

By that time, the raccoons were fairly independent and eating solid foods. I gave them to students and others at Moravian, hoping they would live long, happy lives. I hated to give them up, but I knew I could not take them with us.

I was gratified that my students were so upset at the news I would be leaving, especially Rebel, who cried on the phone when she called to ask me to stay and say she would miss me. I guess I was the big-sister figure for a kid who needed someone to care for her as much as I did. Rebel and Mimi came to our apartment after we had settled into one in the Bronx and stayed overnight. They truly felt like my kid sisters. I always had wanted a sister and wished mine had not died. I was happy to respond to their affection.

Fig 99 Joan Miller who taught English is to my left, and to her left was Sissy MacHenry, the physical education teacher

Fig 100 Mimi is on the left, and Rebel on the right

Fig 101 David and me with baby raccoons

Fig 102 Students playing with baby raccoons

Chapter 36

STUDYING FOR A PHD; I MEET THE TIGERS

Our move to New York was aided considerably because Robert, David's brother, had found us a ground-floor apartment in the Fordham Hills complex where he lived with his wife, Kathy, and baby son, Eric. The apartment was reasonably priced, and with one bedroom and a combination living and dining room, it had all the room we needed.

We signed the lease for the small apartment and then hunted for furniture. Since David was still on crutches, we kept shopping to a minimum. On one trip from Bethlehem to the Bronx, where the apartment was located, we stopped at a highway store on Route 22 that sold cheap bedroom furniture and bought a bed, two end tables, and a chest of drawers.

Leaving the store, we noticed a furniture store across the highway that was advertising sales on living room furniture. Our visit there resulted in our paying for a set of a plastic-covered sofa and chairs for the living room and a table and four chairs for the dining room. If I remember right, we paid less than $500 for all the furniture we bought.

In a matter of about an hour, we had furnished our whole apartment. The cheap plastic furniture would present some problems, depending on the climate. When it was cold, the cushions would be slippery, and one had to take care not to slide onto the floor when sitting down. When the temperature was high in the apartment, one had to take care not to stick to the warm plastic covers. But we were young and knew we couldn't afford anything better, so we tolerated our less-than-perfect furnishings.

I had spent that first summer as lab assistant for Dr. Salome Glueckcsohn-Waelsch at the Albert Einstein College of Medicine, who had given me mice for my master's degree thesis. When I decided to get a PhD, it was a natural thing to speak with Dr. Waelsch (see again figure 98), who immediately accepted me as a student. Einstein was in the northeast corner of the Bronx. It took me at least a half hour to commute because I had to go by way of Fordham Road, a heavily trafficked road.

Dr. Waelsch had immigrated to the United States in the 1930s to escape the Nazis in her native Germany.

Her first husband had committed suicide, and she was married to a brain cancer specialist, Dr. Heinrich Waelsch, when I became her graduate student. They had two children, a boy and a girl, who were teenagers when I first started my studies with Dr. Waelsch.

An article in the *New York Times* about Dr. Waelsch's election to the National Academy of Science many decades later told of her struggles with discrimination against women in science in the 1940s. She had gotten her terminal degree in the 1930s with the foremost embryologist in the world at that time, Hans Spemann. Yet when she was living in New York City, she could not find a job regardless of her résumé. Finally, Columbia University offered her lab space—but no salary. She worked for a couple of years before they finally offered her a paying job. In reading that article, I finally understood some of her attitudes that I had found disturbing.

Dr. Waelsch has been referred to as the founder of mammalian developmental genetics because of her interest in and study of mutations that affect some aspect in the development of mice. She was acknowledged for her science by election in 1973 to the National Academy of Sciences, a prestigious honor. In 1993, she received the National Medal of Science from President Bill Clinton. Those were only two of the awards she received toward the end of her career.

Because she did not forget her struggle to be recognized in her early years in the United States, Dr. Waelsch was protective of me when I became her graduate student. Once, she warned me to be careful of the men I might work with or for. "They will stab you in the back because you are a woman," she said.

However, the stamina required for the strong women of her generation to compete in a man's world came with a price. Dr. Waelsch—and, I expect, others like her—could be difficult. Whenever people who knew her or worked with or under her got together, the subject of the conversation invariably focused on Salome stories. Certainly she had faced extreme hardship and losses that affected her attitudes.

One evening in my first year of study with her, I invited Dr. Waelsch and her husband, Heinrich, to dinner in our apartment. I cooked some Chinese dishes served buffet style. To my surprise, Salome made a plate of food for her husband and then helped herself. I would never have thought of making a plate for David, and he would not have wanted me to. I guess it was the European custom for the wife to serve her husband first.

Because I had studied with Jane Oppenheimer, a close friend of Dr. Waelsch, I think Dr. Waelsch immediately believed I was a pretty good student since she had as much respect for Miss Oppenheimer as I did. That association served as an advantage for me in being accepted as one of her graduate students, but it might also have led Dr. Waelsch to have higher expectations of my career development, especially in her lab, than were warranted.

Einstein, in those days, was in its infancy as a graduate institution. There really were no courses designed for graduate students, only for medical students. Again, that was both a disadvantage and an advantage for me. The disadvantage was that I had to travel within the city a lot to go to classes in other institutions. The advantage was that I was allowed to take courses from any university in the city. I took an advanced genetics class at Fordham University; a genetics course at Columbia University with one of the foremost geneticists of the time, Theodosius Dobzhansky; and a microbiology class at Columbia with a well-known microbiologist whose name I have forgotten. Dr. Waelsch also allowed me to accompany her to various meetings. It was a treat for me, a student, to meet many of the scientists whose papers I had read.

I wanted to have a keepsake of one meeting attended by a large number of the most well-known scientists. I decided to draw caricatures of several of them. Figure 103 shows my amateurish attempts. The last names identify each scientist. I taped each to a card or sheet of paper, and the tape, over the decades since I made the drawings, has turned brown.

As I had only worked with mice and never had a course in microbiology either at Sweet Briar or Bryn Mawr, the subject matter fascinated me, and I signed up for a course in microbiology at Columbia University. I made an appointment with the Columbia University professor once in the middle of the semester, and one of my questions was how scientists could be so precise about single-celled organisms that they could not see without a strong microscope. I'm sure he was amused by my naïveté and ignorance. He never gave a test or assigned a paper to write. At the end of the semester, he posted grades on the classroom door. I got an A and wondered how in the world he had ever come up with that grade.

I understood the material of another Columbia professor, Dr. Theodosius Dobzhansky, much better because he was a human geneticist working with populations and phenomena I could relate to. As he lectured, his appearance struck me. His gray hair was in a crew cut, and he had a habit of walking back and forth in front of the class with his hands clasped behind his back. He had a potbelly. One day I felt compelled to draw a caricature of him in the margin of a page.

I then completely forgot I had done so. Later in the semester, I went to Dr. Dobzhansky for help on a subject he had lectured on. When I turned my notes to the page with notes on the subject, there was the caricature.

"Oh-ho, Mr. Genetic Drift himself!" the good professor said with a chortle.

I turned all shades of purple in embarrassment, but he was more amused than annoyed, thank goodness. I never drew another caricature again. Unfortunately, I cannot find the notes that had the drawing of Dr. Dobzhansky.

When I had finished my courses, I had to go through the oral preliminary exam for the doctorate. In those days, the process began with Dr. Waelsch inviting six faculty members from Einstein and other institutes of higher learning. Dr. Bob Auerbach, a former student of Salome's who was teaching at the University of Wisconsin at Madison, was one of the committee members. He had invited me to go to him for my doctorate when I was working at Einstein with Dr. Waelsch in the summer following my graduation from Bryn Mawr. I declined with thanks, thinking not only of my debt to Dr. Waelsch but also of the winters in Wisconsin. Dr. Ernst Scharrer of Einstein was another on my committee for the oral exam. I no longer remember the others.

My committee sat around a table, and each in turn could ask anything he or she wanted of me. I counted that there were about 250 years of brilliant biological research experience of every kind on that committee. To say they were daunting would be an understatement.

The night before, I was so nervous I couldn't sleep, and I woke David up to tell him so. What could he do but just tell me to relax? Well, I didn't, and I was a nervous wreck when the time came for me to meet my committee. Later, one of them told me there had been a brilliant student at Columbia University who froze at his prelims. He could not answer any of their questions, though they all knew he was brilliant and would be a good scientist. Finally, the last questioner asked him what his name was. The student mumbled his name, and they passed him. I wasn't as lucky. My committee took turns probing my mind.

I cannot remember a single question, but for whatever they asked, whatever I answered was apparently sufficient, and they passed and congratulated me. Dr. Waelsch was beaming. I did not know at that moment that she was planning to have me be her heir apparent and assumed I would stay on to work with her. Perhaps that was the system she knew from Germany. But for me, David's career had priority over mine, and wherever he needed to go, I would follow.

Since David was working full-time at Foster Wheeler Corporation in energy research, I was a year ahead of him in taking and passing my prelim exam. When time came for him to take his oral exam, the thought crossed my mind that while I was certain David would pass his preliminary oral exam, it was possible he might not. Maybe he'd run into a professor who would give him trouble.

I decided then that if he could not continue, I would drop out of my PhD program. I wanted him, the man of the family, to be the doctor. It was archaic thinking and no doubt due to my growing up in a Chinese culture at home that was male-oriented. I needed not to worry, however, as David slept well the night before his exam and passed easily.

In 1963, David took a summer off from his work and study to spend time with his father in Taipei, Taiwan. David's mother had died the previous year. I could not join him, as my research for my thesis was at a critical stage, which I shall discuss in the next chapter. I missed him very much that summer, but one great benefit we both received occurred when a family friend, Victor Li, knowing that David was away, invited me to join a group of his Chinese American friends for the day. They were all going to a friend's apartment for a softball game and dinner afterward.

Victor knew I was an athlete and had played quite a bit of softball in school and in the Livingston Recreation Department's women's softball league. We drove to the apartment of Ann and Albert Yu, where I met a group of young (we were all in our twenties) Chinese American friends. We divided into two teams, and I played shortstop for one.

The only thing I remember about the game was that my team was on the field, and a fellow was on second base, when a single was hit into the outfield. The runner on second tried to run home, but I caught a perfect relay throw from the outfielder, turned, and threw it to our catcher. Unfortunately, the catcher was in the wrong position—behind home plate rather than in front of it—and as my throw to him arrived at the plate, so did the runner. The runner ran into the ball. The catcher was too far back and should have been in front of the plate to give me a clear target. The ball glanced off the runner's head, knocking his glasses off. Victor was impressed with my throw, but I was mortified. Fortunately, the runner's glasses did not break, and he suffered no real injury.

After the game, we all piled into the Yu apartment. Ann, a terrific cook, had made a huge pot of fried rice that we ate for dinner. Although I never connected with any of the other participants, Ann and Albert became our good friends, and through them, when David returned, we were introduced to a group of their college friends whom they had met while attending Barnard College and Columbia University.

Because they were classmates, the group, for the most part, were of the same age, most born in the year of the tiger (a Chinese astrological symbol), about two years younger than David and I were. Once they discovered that David and I were pretty good tennis players and bridge players also, they eagerly accepted us into what our children eventually referred to as the Tiger Group. David and I, though, were honorary Tigers since we were born the year of the rat.

We got together fairly frequently through the years, although we were all busy with graduate school or establishing careers. Eventually, the core of the Tigers were us, the Yus, Yung and Nancy Wong, P. Y. (Yung's cousin) and Mimi Chia, Oscar and Frankie Tang, and Victor and Lily Chang. Another couple, Tony and Emily Limpe (figure 104) were also part of the Tiger Group, and like us, they were honorary Tigers because they were three years older than the real Tigers.

Most of the time, we would play tennis during the day and then bridge or games in the evening (figure 105). The photo of us playing a game was girls against the boys. I can tell that David had done something that caused Lily and Nancy, two of our more competitive tigresses, to object to whatever he did. We had such wonderful, fun times together. Occasionally, we went bowling too. We enjoyed each other's company and knew we would have good tennis matches. Lily, perhaps because of her upbringing in Communist China, was the most politically liberal of the Tigers. She often found herself in raging debates about political and financial events in the United States with the more fiscally conservative Tigers, P. Y., Yung, and David. Their discussions were always on friendly terms, and we usually ended up laughing with each other. I think the basis of our strong bond was sincere respect for each other and our common experiences growing up as immigrants in the United States.

Besides our common recreational interests, I have always been proud of each of the Tigers as we matured. Through hard work and intelligence, each Tiger succeeded in his or her career. Frankie taught Chinese cooking. Oscar switched from engineering to finance and formed Reich and Tang investment group, which they sold at great profit eventually. Yung, with a PhD, worked successfully in venture capital investments. Nancy was a noted marketing executive for General Foods. P. Y. was the banker in the group and was vice chairman of Citibank before retirement. Victor worked for Goldman Sachs and then worked for Paul Volcker at the Federal Reserve. David and Tony stayed in engineering. Tony eventually owned his own engineering firm, and Emily was involved in office affairs for the company. David would become CEO and president of Foster Wheeler Development Corporation, a subsidiary company of Foster Wheeler Corporation, a leading international engineering, construction, and manufacturing company in the oil, gas, and power industries. I became a professor at Montclair State University.

Remember that all the Tigers' achievements took place during a time when Chinese men and women had to struggle against discrimination in industry and commerce. Our closeness was based not only on reciprocal respect for each other but also on common experiences as young Asian immigrants, common interests in sports and bridge, and likeable personalities. All were strong forces that have forged friendships that have lasted for a lifetime.

Albert became an architect, though his career and life were tragically cut short by cancer. He died in his early thirties and was the first loss of a friend we experienced. Ann worked many years as a computer consultant for IBM. Years after Albert died, Ann married Jim Rigby, an IBM coworker. We also lost to cancer too soon, in the 1990's, Frankie Tang and Mimi Chia. Both Oscar and P. Y. have remarried.

Frankie and Oscar were the first to have a home with a tennis court. Every year, Frankie would organize a weekend-long tennis tournament with rankings for every person, including non-Tiger guests as well. There were prizes for the winners. Eventually, Yung and Nancy, Tony and Emily, P. Y. and Mimi, and David and I all had houses with tennis courts, where we held our own tournaments or just informal matches we made with each other. Only once in several decades did I ever win a tournament, and I believe David won once also.

There was a period of several years when one or more of the Tiger Group women were pregnant, since we were all of childbearing age. It was an advantage to the pregnant ones when they played. The rest of us would be nervous about possibly hitting them when they played net at doubles. We would consequently hit the ball too gently and have it swatted back for a point or try to avoid them and hit too wide. We did not do well against pregnant opponents!

Our group of friends had a total of sixteen children, only two of whom married: the Limpes' son, Stephen, and the Tang's eldest daughter, Tracy. The rest of us could only hope there would be more couples from our many offspring, but it was not to be.

As one might expect, our tournaments dwindled down with our increasing age. Some of our children, as they grew, were generally good athletes and replaced us in the tournaments. From their earliest years, they were exposed to a lot of tennis, and some became excellent players, too good for the parents to compete against. Most Tigers have now converted to golf.

We traveled as much as we could with our friends, though David and I had to skip some of the trips due to my teaching commitments. We did visit Egypt, Spain, Portugal, and Hawaii with them on different occasions. The trips were not only enormously interesting, but traveling with dear friends enhanced the enjoyment we got from sharing experiences.

Having these close friends and others has made our lives much more fulfilling and joyful. I would wish for my sons and their families to have similar good luck in developing friends who are almost as close as family.

Fig 103 Caricatures of well-known scientists at a scientific meeting

Fig 104 Left to right: Mimi Chia, me, Emily Limpe, Yung and Nancy Wong, Victor and Lily Chang, Frankie and Oscar Tang, Second Row: David, Tony Limpe, and P.Y. Chia at the wedding of the Wong's son, Michael

Fig 105 Tigers playing games

Chapter 37

MUSCULAR DYSGENESIS (MDG)

One of the banes of graduate students studying any aspect of modern genetics, especially in the molecular areas, in the 1960s was the competition that existed from several labs working on the same phenomena. I spoke to one student at a meeting who was on his third thesis research project. By the time he was halfway through the first two, some other lab had published papers on the same problem.

I was fortunate in that regard. I studied a spontaneous (natural and not induced) mutation that Dr. Waelsch had found in her mouse colony. Because it was a natural mutation, it was highly likely we were the only lab to have it, and therefore, there would be no competition. The mutant newborn mice never lived more than a few minutes after birth. They were half-moon-shaped, and the skin seemed loose and bluish in color in contrast to normal newborn mice, which were pink since mice were born without hair.

Dr. Waelsch taught me a complex system she used to identify each mouse in her enormous colony, using a clip to punch holes in both ears. In the left ear, the holes represented tens of numbers (ten, twenty, etc.), and in the right ear, there were nicks along the edge of the ear to represent single numbers, one through nine. Each cage was numbered, and the occupants of each cage were described and recorded in record books and also on five-by-three-inch cards. It was the system that had allowed me to restore my colony of mice at Bryn Mawr after the cleaning fellow tipped the entire rack of cages over, releasing all the mice.

The first step in my research was to determine whether the mutation was due to a single gene change, what kind of gene change occurred, whether the mutant gene was dominant or recessive, and whether the gene was X-linked (on the X chromosome) or autosomal (on a chromosome that was not one of the two sex chromosomes). Tracing the pattern and ratios of normal and mutant offspring would give me the answer.

Fortunately, it was a simple autosomal recessive gene. Carriers (mice with just one copy of the mutation) were perfectly normal. Only animals that inherited two copies of the gene from parents that were both carriers showed the mutant phenotype (appearance). That was fortunate, as a genetically complex trait could have delayed my research for a significant amount of time.

Upon dissecting the newborn mice after they had died, I was astonished to find no visible signs of skeletal musculature. The heart was of normal size and shape, so cardiac musculature was not affected. Later studies

I carried out showed that smooth musculature, such as in the digestive tract, was also normal. The lack of skeletal muscles also explained why the skin of the mutants was so loose—there was nothing for the skin to be attached to by the connective tissue.

It also explained why the newborn mutants looked bluish. Without musculature, they could not breathe, and lack of oxygen turned them bluish instead of the healthy pink color of normal newborns. With the absence of normal musculature during development, I saw a number of abnormalities of bone structure, probably due to the absence of musculature attachment, which accounted for the strange moon shape of the newborn mutants.

I also studied the various anatomical aspects of the abnormal musculature. My research on mdg was eventually published as two papers in the journal *Developmental Biology*. Those were exciting days, as I could work without the pressure of having to compete with other labs. Nobody else had those mice.

One day, when I was working on some newborn mutant mice, Dr. Waelsch came into the lab to see what I was doing. She asked, "May I try dissecting one?"

I quickly got up so she could sit at the lab counter.

After a while, she looked up, smiled, and said, "This is so much fun! I wish I had more time to work on research."

It was to me a sad testimony that she now had to spend most of her time writing for grants to fund her work and that of her students. It is the price paid by the primary researcher of a lab today. It made me doubt I would want to become the head of a lab.

We decided to call the mutation muscular dysgenesis (*dysgenesis* means "abnormal development"), and the gene symbol would be mdg. In the process of getting a PhD, the easiest part was supposedly the dissertation defense, but for me, that step again was terrifying. I could not sleep the night before, just as I had not slept before taking my qualifying exam to get into the PhD program. When I walked into the conference room where the defense was to take place, I again saw sitting before me the same seven established scientists, including Dr. Waelsch, who had been involved in my oral prelims. The difference there was that I knew more about my thesis than they did.

The year was 1964, and I no longer remember the questions they asked or how long it took me to answer them all. I only remember feeling tremendous relief when it was over, and they shook my hand in congratulations. I cannot tell you how well I did, but obviously, I did well enough to pass. The only grades given for oral exams or dissertation defenses were pass and fail.

Other laboratories have since continued studies on muscular dysgenesis. The mdg gene apparently is responsible for a subunit of a protein involved in excitation and contraction of skeletal musculature. Without the normal protein, the critical function of excitation and contraction is not possible, and the musculature is essentially paralyzed and degrades.

I think I was only the third graduate student at Einstein to have succeeded in getting the PhD under Dr. Waelsch up to that point. The school was only in its tenth year. Among the many memories of those years at Einstein is the day in 1963 when a lab assistant burst into the lab where I and another graduate student were working and said, "President Kennedy's been shot in the stomach!" We quickly turned on the radio and listened disbelievingly to the news, which got worse and worse until it was announced that he had been shot in the head and had died. Will any who remember that day ever forget where they were and what they were doing? I don't think so.

I stopped working on my research and drove home, greatly saddened. David came home, and we spent the rest of the day watching the events of that historical day unfold. We also watched the funeral procession with Jackie Kennedy and her children. Will any of us forget the toddler John John saluting his father's casket?

Life eventually returned to normal, though the shock of events caused us all to be more somber than usual. I finished the research and wrote my thesis. Under Dr. Waelsch's guidance, I adapted the thesis for publication.

It took two years at Bryn Mawr and four at Einstein to complete my MA and PhD degrees. David and I had postponed trying for a baby for all those years. Once I'd completed my PhD studies, we could now turn to trying to start a family.

Graduation day was a happy one for my parents, David, and me (figure 106). My master's degree and a PhD were something Mommy and Daddy could be proud of, especially since I don't think they expected I would go in that direction. Possibly, they were somewhat surprised by the fact that I actually had achieved what they always had considered a high level of academia, something they could brag about, and no doubt it gave my mother relief to know that her daughter would not have to depend totally on her husband.

The Chinese culture focuses heavily on academic achievement, so obtaining a doctorate was something to celebrate, even though my parents' focus was more on what Solan was doing in higher education. For those of a Chinese background, pressure was intense on the firstborn son, who was expected to take the leadership of the family.

David had to work on his thesis research for another year after I had finished. I was able to type his thesis for him. He had little trouble in defending his work and received his doctorate in 1965. I know his degree meant a great deal to his parents, especially his father, with whom David was close. As I mentioned earlier, during the war years in China, when the family was separated, General Pai chose David and his second sister, Diana, to stay with him, while David's mother kept the other eight children with her. The general always made sure David and Diana received the best possible education growing up. Figure 107 shows a young David with his proud father during the commemoration of a victorious battle against the Communists. Figure 108 is a portrait of his parents.

Figure 109 shows a photo taken when David was ten years old. It was the last time a photograph of his entire family was taken, due to the Chinese civil war and the movement of the older group of siblings to the United States.

It is a testament to the military brilliance of General Pai that the Chinese people gave him the nickname of Xiao Zhugo (Little Zhugo Liang) after a legendary military strategist of the Three Kingdoms era in Chinese history. Yet near the end of the civil war, Chiang Kai Shek refused to consult General Pai and would not allow him to take part in strategy sessions with Chiang's less capable military people. David said Chiang always feared that anyone who was talented and popular with the people, such as the Young Marshal and General Pai, might try to usurp his power. Rather than use their talent, he would ignore them as a way to control them.

I have always regretted that I never met either General or Mrs. Pai. David and I were immersed in our graduate studies after our marriage in 1959 and could not take the time to travel to Taiwan. As I mentioned earlier, his parents were not allowed to leave Taiwan, as Chiang had their every movement spied upon by his secret service. Just as he was worried about the Young Marshal, the generalissimo (Chiang) always feared that the general might defect to the mainland, where their popularity clearly continued.

In truth, he did not need to worry about those two men, who were more interested in defending their country than they were in personal power—something Chiang apparently could not believe or understand.

David's mother died unexpectedly in 1962 before either of us had finished our studies for our doctorate degrees. David managed to spend a wonderful summer with his father in 1963, which I could not share, as I was in the last stages of my research and the writing of my dissertation. Then the arrival in 1965 and 1966 of our two baby boys made traveling impossible. In 1966, the general unexpectedly died of a stroke, so we never met face-to-face.

Despite his conflicts with Chiang Kai Shek and the latter's treatment of him and his family, David's father died respected by Chinese in general for his military brilliance. Even the Communists respected him for his fight against the Japanese after the Xian Incident. Chiang recognized the general's popularity, and to honor General Pai's defense of China against the Japanese, he ordered a state funeral in Taipei, Taiwan, that included the army band and honor guards at the funeral. Chiang (figure 110) was the first person to bow to the casket, followed by dozens of officials of the Nationalist government of Taiwan. David and the rest of his family are dressed in white robes and bowing with Chiang in figure 110.

I wonder, in looking at the photo of an aged Chiang, whether he might have thought at that moment about his mistake in not trusting General Pai. Had he done so, he surely would not have suffered such an abject defeat at the hands of the Communists despite the Nationalists' advantage of having an overwhelming number of soldiers, arms, and airplanes. He and his military aides simply did not conduct the war well enough to win. The Communist movement also won the support of the people of China, especially in the countryside.

General Pai was interred according to Muslim customs in a cemetery reserved for Muslims outside of Taipei, Taiwan. David's brother Richard had been given the responsibility of constructing a grand memorial for his parents. Figure 111 shows the family at the cemetery, removing the coffin from the hearse. In 2013, the tombs of David's parents were declared to be the basis for a Muslim cultural center in Taiwan (figure 112).

Fig 106 Dr. Waelsch and "Dr." Anna Pai

Fig 108 General and Mrs. Pai Chung Xi

Fig 107 David and the General

Fig 109 A photograph of David's entire family of ten children, 1946

Fig 110 Chiang Kai Shek about to bow to General Pai's casket

Fig 111 At the cemetery

Fig 112 The tombs of David's parents

Chapter 38

WORK AND MOTHERHOOD

During the five years that David and I were getting our PhD degrees, we were able to do little for my parents because of the intensity of our studies and research. My mother also bemoaned the fact that she had no grandchildren. Solan and Jeannie were busy with his medical studies, and none of us could afford either the expense or time to have children.

Stanley was well established and involved in the Baptist mission in Buffalo, New York, that had rescued him years before and was proud of what they asked him to do. He had found religion, and it gave him and Sandy, his wife, great meaning in their lives. Sandy also had been trained as a home health aide and had obtained a position with a company that assigned her various clients. Stanley and Sandy seemed satisfied with their lives, and I could not have been more relieved or proud.

The year after I received my PhD degree, I stayed on to work with Dr. Waelsch, and David continued with his work and studies. I had always wanted a family, and I tried to get pregnant for more than a year with no success. The thought that I might be barren began to weigh on my mind. I wanted children very much, and I felt that not being able to conceive was no doubt a failing on my part. I had heard that women who waited for years before trying for a baby often had problems. I was twenty-nine and had been married since I was twenty-four. Had I waited too long? I finally went to my gynecologist, a close friend of Solan's on the staff of Columbia Presbyterian Hospital, who made the right diagnosis and chose the right treatment.

Meanwhile, Solan and Jeannie were the first to present a grandchild to my parents. In 1964, they had a beautiful baby girl they named Carolyn, whom we call by a Chinese nickname, Shrong, which means "Double," as a wish for a pair of children. Then, in the winter of 1964, I tested positive for pregnancy. Mommy and Daddy were in Taiwan, visiting General Pai, and we sent them a telegram bearing the good news. They were all as thrilled as we were.

For someone who wanted children as badly as I did, the discomforts of pregnancy were nothing to me, and the joys of pregnancy far outweighed its well-known discomforts. When the baby began to move in utero, we were ecstatic. At work, however, Dr. Waelsch did not share my joy and instead seemed to resent my pregnant state.

In retrospect, I believe my starting a family, along with our plans to move to New Jersey to be nearer David's work, made her realize that whatever plans she had for me in her lab in the future were no longer possible. I felt some guilt about that, even though I had never told her I would stay at Einstein after graduation. Yet she had been totally supportive of me during the course of my graduate work, and I owed her much.

She then ordered me to take over the mundane maintenance of the mouse colony from Lucy, a prospective graduate student. Lucy would be taking over my research project, which was an extension of my studies on mdg. I was stunned and saddened. I spent the last months of my time with Dr. Waelsch marking mice, dipping them in antiseptic baths, and doing all the various routine duties for a lab assistant rather than a research associate.

Needless to say, I felt embarrassed and hurt. On the other hand, she probably felt that I had not lived up to her expectations. I regretted that. I resigned my position in Dr. Waelsch's lab two months before the baby was due. Not only did she have Lucy there as a prospective graduate student, but also, a second young woman had started to work with the mice as a prospective graduate student. I wished them both well and sincerely hoped they could give Dr. Waelsch the quality of work she demanded and deserved. I thanked Salome Waelsch for all she had done for me, but our parting was not exactly affectionate.

In retrospect, I never actually considered staying on with her after I got my PhD, just as I left Miss Oppenheimer after I finished my master's degree. Perhaps since the PhD was a terminal degree, there was more reason for Dr. Waelsch to expect me to stay on as a research colleague. I had met two of her previous students who'd completed their PhDs with Dr. Waelsch. Both were well established in their careers elsewhere, which was another reason I did not consider my leaving Dr. Waelsch to be something to which she would react negatively.

We did not correspond much after I left Einstein. However, a well-known female scientist of Dr. Waelsch's generation who was doing research in Philadelphia called me to say Dr. Waelsch had told her I moved to New Jersey. She asked if I would be able to accept a position in her lab. I gratefully thanked her for the offer but declined, as I had two babies and lived a full hour away from Philadelphia. I was glad to know that Dr. Waelsch still thought enough of me to recommend me for a job. I hoped she was able to continue her mouse colony and had graduate students who were able to do for her what I could not—namely, continue to work with her on mutations she found in her colony. I often thought of my mutant mice and was pleased years later to see that she had sent carriers of the mdg gene to former students for further analysis.

I was able to get some information about Salome because in the 1990s, a former student of mine at Montclair State University, Greg Prelich, who had gone on for a doctorate in genetics, was hired to be on the faculty at Einstein in the genetics department. I also heard from Dr. Harold Klinger, whom I had met when I was Dr. Waelsch's graduate student. He joined the department the last year I was there. Harold and I occasionally reconnected at the home of a mutual friend, Mike Sherman, who, you might remember, had invited me into his lab for a sabbatical leave.

Harold told me Dr. Waelsch had stayed on at Einstein following her retirement. The school had allowed her to have an office and space to maintain her mouse colony. When she was in her nineties, they decided they could no longer accommodate her, and she had to leave and enter retirement.

When I became pregnant, I was determined to push out of my mind all the birth abnormalities I knew about from my courses and research in embryology. My baby was going to be perfect, I told myself. I carefully followed my doctor's orders for a healthy diet and a restriction on weight gain.

No one was happier than I at our prospective parenthood. As the pregnancy proceeded, each stage was a reason to celebrate. When I was sitting in a lecture at Einstein around the fifth month, the baby moved so much that I looked around to see if anyone was aware of my lab coat moving. I was quite pregnant with Benjy while I was typing David's thesis in 1965, and I remember having to reach for the typewriter over my bloated abdomen, which was not at all an inconvenience for me.

Only those who have gone through the disappointment of failing to become pregnant for some time and then the happiness of succeeding can understand the joy I felt at those routine experiences. I can sympathize with those who have never been able to conceive. It is one of the most profound tragedies of a woman's life.

In March 1965, I was ready to pop. On the night of March 9, David and I went out to dinner with Solan and Jeannie. We went to a Chinese restaurant that served spicy, hot dishes. I don't know if that was what precipitated my labor, but around midnight, I woke up and felt a contraction.

Having taken a course for first-time mothers at Columbia Presbyterian Hospital, I waited for the contractions to increase in frequency, which they did not long after I woke up. After three hours, they started coming five minutes apart, but then some would take ten or twenty minutes. Still, I decided I had better wake David.

When I did, the ensuing events were unexpected and confusing. I expected David to jump up and run around to get things ready and call the doctor. He did call the doctor but then calmly went to the bathroom to brush his teeth. Then he made himself a cup of tea and had the tea with some cookies. *Wow*, I thought, *this man is something else! His first child, and he's having a cup of tea?*

While that was going on, my contractions became more consistent and closer together. After David finished his snack, he came into the bedroom, where I was sitting on the edge of the bed in great discomfort. He took one look at me; did a double take; and, realizing we had to hurry to the hospital, started to rush around.

Later, he told me he was taking his time because he thought my contractions had only started at three o'clock rather than midnight, and he expected we would have a lot more time before having to go to the hospital. That was an example of how a little knowledge about something, such as our information from our course for first-time parents, can lead to erroneous ideas. I obviously had not explained the situation well when I woke him up.

The hospital, at that time of night, was no more than twenty minutes away. I was admitted and examined by a young resident who asked me why I had waited so long, as the dilation and other signs indicated I was on the verge of delivery. Dr. Todd, my ob-gyn, then arrived, and we went into the delivery room.

I had been given some anesthesia, which made me nauseous. After a few minutes of straining, I threw up, and that forced the baby out. My firstborn, Benjamin Fa Hsiung Pai, was a healthy baby boy nineteen inches long and seven pounds, born at around six thirty in the morning. He was perfect. Because baby Benjy had taken so little time to arrive, Dr. Todd said the next time, he would induce the baby so I wouldn't give birth in the car on the way to the hospital. I decided not to tell him the story of David and his snack.

Not long after we returned home with the baby, David finished his degree, and his graduation loomed. David was loath to go to his ceremony since NYU graduated thousands every year. There were so many graduates at every level that the event took place on their football field. Each department announced the degree to be given, and students receiving the degree would stand and be acknowledged as a group. There were so many graduates that I never even saw where David was sitting.

I knew General Pai would like to have photos of him in his doctoral cap and gown, so I had insisted he go to the graduation. We took photos following the graduation ceremony. One of my favorite pictures of all time is one I took of David in cap and gown, holding and looking down at his two-month-old son, a chubby, perfect, beautiful baby (figure 113).

After David received his PhD, we moved from our first home in the Fordham Hills apartments to Metuchen, New Jersey. Our five-year stay in the Bronx was five times longer than I had lived anywhere before, excluding Sweet Briar, but David had to carpool more than an hour each way from the Bronx to Carteret, New Jersey. That he was able to do so while taking night classes was testament to his determination and stamina. When I became pregnant again, we decided that it was only fair for us to move close to his job. It did not enter my mind at the time that I could work and give my baby to day care.

After nearly twenty-four years of classes and research, I was prepared to stay at home. Ben favored the Chao family features and looked more like me than he did David. He had the double eyelids that Chinese coveted and big earlobes, which my mother said signified a noble son and good fortune. He had the Pai upper lip, which protruded enough to be cute and noticeable.

At every stage of his infancy, the progression of changes as he grew bigger and more aware of his surroundings was a source of great interest and delight. To my surprise, David, a doting father, was even willing to change diapers. I'd never thought the son of a great general, brought up in part by soldiers and neurotic, as was the whole family, about cleanliness, would ever deign to change diapers. It said something about the man I married.

Benjy was a good sleeper. When he was asleep, little would wake him. A frightening thing happened one day when he was sleeping in his crib, which was next to the wall in our dining area. That wall separated our apartment from our neighbor next door. Suddenly, I heard a loud noise, and some plaster fell from the wall above into Benjy's crib.

When I saw a drill's head had come through the wall, I ran next door and pounded on the door. The worker, who had miscalculated how thick the wall was, apologized profusely and said he would repair the hole. I could only be grateful that he had not drilled lower and near my baby's head! We moved Benjy's crib next to a wall that separated our bedroom from the living room area.

In 1966, David was devastated by his father's death and flew to Taiwan to participate in the funeral services. As I mentioned earlier, the general had chosen David to keep him company during World War II. The father and son had enjoyed various activities together, and David frequently had accompanied his father at an early age to various events (see again figure 107). They were very close.

Although we never met face-to-face, I did speak with David's parents over the phone when he and I had just become engaged. I was uncomfortable in doing so because my Chinese was so basic. There is a tradition of formal speech in Chinese when circumstances dictate that it should be used. Had I known how, I would have done so with my mother-in-law, but I could only haltingly use conversational Chinese.

I did my duty, though, and provided them with a grandson as our first child, and I am sure they were happy that both David and I were studying for our doctorate degrees. Mommy was of course delighted with her second grandchild, a boy. She and Daddy doted on our baby son (figure 114). In a way, I wished Jeannie could have had a son and we a daughter, which would have caused my mother's affection to be stronger for Solan's children.

As luck would have it, Solan had two daughters, and I had two sons. After waiting about five years for grandchildren, my mother had four in four years. My second son, Mike, was born fifteen months after his big brother, on June 14, 1966. In 1967, Solan's younger daughter, Patricia Ann, whom we call Mei (Little Sister), was born. Those two girls, beautiful and sweet, are as close to me as the daughters I always wanted but never had (figure 115).

As I mentioned earlier, I tried to convince my mother that the sex of any child was determined by the father, not the mother. I had a PhD in genetics, and my mother simply refused to believe it was true. Her attitude was still that it was Jeannie's fault that Solan only had daughters, and it was to my credit that I had sons. I could see conflict in the future about that matter between Mommy and Solan and knew there would be no convincing my mother otherwise. That was what she had been brought up to believe, and fair or unfair, that was what she believed.

Fig 113 David with his firstborn son, Benjy

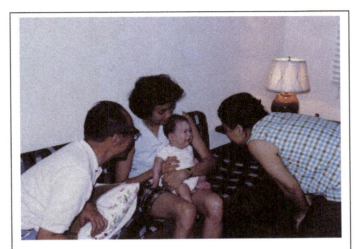

Fig 114 Mommy and Daddy playing with an amused Benjy

Fig 115 Solan holding Shrong and Jeannie holding Mei

Chapter 39

WE BECOME PARENTS AGAIN

Having had so much difficulty in becoming pregnant with our first child, we thought we could take some liberties with regard to contraception after Ben was born. However, before the year was up, I realized I was pregnant again. Child number two surprised us, but we were not unhappy with the prospect since we wanted more than one child anyway, and I was no longer working after our move to New Jersey.

We remembered that Dr. Todd had told us he would induce birth for the next child because of how quickly Ben had been born. When the time came, we had prepared a suitcase. We stayed with my parents in New York City, as we needed my mother to care for Ben while I was hospitalized after the birth. In those days, women stayed in the hospital for a week after giving birth, during which time we rested and got acquainted with our new family member.

We had parked the car right in front of the apartment building on 104th Street and West End Avenue, feeling lucky to have found such a convenient spot. To our consternation, the next morning, when we were scheduled to have the baby induced, we walked out to find our car had been double-parked in. Since we were surrounded by high-rise apartment buildings, there was no way to track down the owner of the other car.

Before we had a chance to panic, however, my father drove up to us on his way to work at the United Nations building. When he saw us flag him down, he laughed, pulled over, and drove us uptown to Columbia Presbyterian Hospital. No doubt that made him late for work, but I think he was excused given the circumstances.

Solan greeted us and accompanied us to the room where I received an injection to induce the onset of the birthing process. Dr. Todd was there, and a nurse injected me with a hormone that would begin the contractions. It was not a pleasant injection, as it was into the back. The nurse told me to relax.

"If you squirm," she said, "I'll just follow you!"

It did not take long for the hormone to do its job. At one point, a loud noise startled me as the baby flipped in the uterus. It was so loud that the nurse who was monitoring my progress heard the slapping sound and was startled too.

"What was that?" she cried as she jumped to my side.

"It wasn't me," I replied. "This is one impatient kid!"

Putting the stethoscope on my abdomen, she assured me the baby was fine. Less than an hour after the injection, Michael Fa Hsiung Pai (figure 116) entered the world, another healthy seven-pound boy.

Solan had taken David to the cafeteria for lunch, but before they could finish eating, Solan was paged and told of his new nephew. They ate hurriedly and rushed up to the maternity ward. My second son was the image of his father (figure 117). He looked so much like his old man that when Mike was around eight years old, we showed him an old photo of his father around the same age. "I don't remember that picture being taken," he said, thinking it was an image of himself. On the other hand, Ben looked like his old lady's side of the family.

Dr. Todd had been worried that I had become pregnant again fairly soon after Ben's birth and advised me to get some help in case I had to have bed rest during the latter stages of the pregnancy. As I said, we had moved after David's graduation to a small house in Metuchen, New Jersey, which was a lot closer to his work in Carteret, New Jersey.

I consulted the landlady who owned the small house—a cottage, really—about where I could go to get some domestic help. She suggested getting an au pair from Spain for a year. She herself was Spanish, and she knew of a young woman in her early twenties who wanted to come to the United States as an au pair for a year. She spoke English and was educated with a college degree. Into our lives marched Isabel Julbe (figure 118). She was a bright, self-confident young woman who liked working with young children. Her grasp of the English language was enough for us to communicate with each other. Ben accepted her without trouble, and she proved to be good with the baby. Because of her presence, and with my parents' help, David and I decided we could consider finally taking a vacation. We had been married for seven years and had never taken a vacation. We decided to go to Bermuda.

Bermuda was as beautiful as I had thought. We spent most of our days there (one week) playing golf. One day I was looking at the scenery on one of the tees. It was a beautiful day; the sky was blue, and the ocean looked calm. The houses nearby were painted in pastel colors. I turned and said to my caddy, "What a wonderful place!" I meant it as a compliment, of course.

He was an African Bermudan and startled me with his reply: "That depends on where you stand and what you see."

It abashed me, the tourist, to think everyone felt the same way.

It reminded me of the Bob Dylan song "Blowin' in the Wind" and the last of the lyrics: "How many times must a man look up before he sees the sky / an' how many ears must a man have before he can hear people cry? / The answer, my friend, is blowin' in the wind. / The answer is blowin' in the wind."

Mommy and Daddy volunteered to stay in our home to supervise Isa and the children. I happily accepted their wish to supervise while we were gone. In retrospect, I should have foreseen that there would be a problem between Isa and Mommy. Both of them felt they were the primary care for our children. By the time we returned, I was beset with complaints from Mommy about Isa being disrespectful and from Isa about Mommy ordering her around. I took great pains to smooth things over and succeeded in explaining that some of their problems were no doubt due to language difficulties.

Isa stayed with us for a year, and it was good to have a second pair of hands to manage life with two babies who were almost like twins. She was bright and responsible, and I hope she has had a good life. She should be close to seventy by now. I hope she married a good man and had her own children and grandchildren to care for.

I could not have been happier with my two boys. We now had a foursome for golf, tennis, and bridge—we thought. Alas, that dream never came true because aside from Mike becoming a golfer, the boys never became interested in any of the three activities: Mike became an excellent golfer and played for Cornell; neither of them liked tennis enough to play it seriously; and neither was a bridge player. Ben's card game of choice is poker, and he was good at team sports, such as basketball and baseball. We did not force them to play with us if they didn't care to.

Because David had had such a long commute to work while we both were in graduate school in the Bronx, he was determined to find a house when we finished that would be so close to wherever Foster Wheeler decided to move that he could walk to work. The town turned out to be Livingston, in what was considered northern New Jersey. The house we found was one we saw the first day our real estate agent took us to available properties.

It was a four-bedroom colonial that was close to an elementary school, even closer to a junior high school, and only a mile from Foster Wheeler, where David would work. We thought it was too expensive at first ($45,000) and looked further. However, after looking at numerous houses slightly farther away from Foster Wheeler, 12 Wingate Drive, in a new development, seemed to be the best deal for us, and in 1968, we moved to the first home we would live in as a family. Mike was two and a half, and Ben was four.

They were good boys. Both would grow up as good students, and both were good athletes, though Ben was a little more of a natural athlete. Mike was the grinder of the two and became a scratch golfer as he grew. Sports continued to play a big role in our lives. We loved watching the boys playing T-ball, an introduction to baseball for youngsters too young to play in Little League. The ball was placed on a tee instead of being thrown to batters. Both boys showed good hand-eye coordination. Their games were hilarious at times, and unlike in Little League, parents were not as intense and had fun watching the little ones, who had no clue about baseball strategy.

One day one of Ben's teammates fielded a ground ball nicely—and turned around to throw it to one of the outfielders instead of to the first baseman.

"Billy, what did you do that for?" his startled father cried.

"He's my fwiend!" was the explanation. The game went on.

We started both boys on golf when they were around ten and eleven. Interestingly, when it was apparent Mike was more likely to progress in golf faster than Ben, the latter stopped playing golf and continued with team sports. Mike was determined to become a good golfer, although he realized by the time he was in high school that he probably could not be a professional golfer. Still, he was good enough to be on the high school golf team and also played for Cornell in college. Later, he would find that he needed to be as good as he was to qualify for jobs in the golf industry.

It is incredible how good golfers must be to have aspirations to be a professional. Mike was a scratch golfer in his teens, meaning he played well enough to be able to equal par on a course. We asked him if he had any aspirations to be a pro. He told us that to be a pro in the sport, a golfer had to have at least a plus-four or plus-five handicap, meaning he had to be able to not only par eighteen holes but be four or five strokes under par. "I can't touch those guys" was his realistic answer. He then set his sights on eventually working in some way in the golf industry.

Ben starred in baseball and basketball in high school. He was on the New Jersey All Prep School baseball team. He played center field and was a leadoff batter. His idol was Yankees center fielder Mickey Rivers. Ben would trot out to his position shuffling like Mickey. While he did not play in college, he has played in recreational leagues into his forties and has always been the best player on his teams, even though he has had teammates who played for their college teams.

Both sons were enrolled in the public school system in Livingston through elementary school. The first weekend after we moved into our first house, we received a phone call inviting us to join a new Chinese organization called the West Essex Chinese Association, which was started by a group of Chinese friends who wanted a means of socializing with members of the Chinese community.

We were interested and agreed to attend the first meeting in the basement of one of the organizers' homes. There were some two dozen families who had agreed to join. We all took turns standing and introducing ourselves to the others, explaining our decisions to live in Livingston. The reputation of Livingston's school system was a big reason for every family to decide to live there.

Mommy and Daddy had also decided to move out of New York City, to Lake Hopatcong in western New Jersey, while we were in Metuchen. I can only guess at the reason that prompted them to leave a comfortable, large apartment and an easy commute for Daddy to the United Nations. In retrospect, I realize the embarrassing episode with their former friends in the Chinese opera group Yeh Yu might have caused Mommy to want to be far enough away for them to isolate themselves.

Also, they had earlier found a small house not too far from the lake in a fairly rural and wooded area that they used for a summer house. Typical of my father's lack of experience and sense about finances, they found it too expensive to continue to pay rent for the New York City apartment as well as a mortgage for the summer house. Loath to forsake the area in Lake Hopatcong, they decided to give up the apartment and move to New Jersey.

The place was quiet and lovely, but it was also nearly a two-hour commute for Daddy to the United Nations. He drove the car to where he could catch a bus that would take him to New York City and then the subway. They lived in Lake Hopatcong for a few years until the commute to New York City was too wearing and also too expensive to continue. They wanted to move closer to New York City, which would bring them closer to Solan, who was then living in Allendale, New Jersey, while we were in Livingston.

Solan found a house for sale on the street where he and his growing family lived and helped our parents move there. It was a lovely neighborhood, and the house was a ranch house, which was good for my parents, as they would not need to climb stairs. What I thought was an ideal situation, however, turned into a conflict of major proportions between my parents and my brother and sister-in-law.

Mommy befriended a stray cat that began to visit them daily. The more food she put out, of course, the more regularly the cat would visit. Further, other stray cats were also drawn to their house by the abundant food Mommy supplied.

The neighbors began to complain to Jeannie because the number of cats had grown to the point where they were messing up the lawns of their neighbors, who also were worried that some of the cats were feral and might be carrying diseases that their own cats could contract.

When Jeannie and Solan relayed their complaints to Mommy, she refused to believe there was a problem and would not stop feeding the cats. Her stubbornness resulted in an intolerable problem for Jeannie with her friends and neighbors, and it put Solan in a distressing and exasperating position between his mother and his wife.

I began receiving frequent phone calls from Mommy, who complained about the situation. It made her more willing to pick on what she perceived as Jeannie's faults.

"She is inventing complaints by the neighbors," Mommy said, "to give me trouble." It became clear to all of us that having them continue to live there would only escalate the problem, so only a short couple years after they had moved to Allendale, Mommy and Daddy decided to move away.

We all realized that Mommy's emotional well-being was deteriorating. Not only was she constantly angry with Jeannie, but also, she and Daddy were constantly quarreling. If we had been an American family, I know we would have taken steps to bring her to a psychologist or psychiatrist. However, even the suggestion that she might need one would have been taken as disrespect for our parent. In addition, with her limited ability to speak English, could she even have responded to questions? The concept of taking Mommy to a psychiatrist was something that Daddy could not accept either. It was just too foreign to Chinese culture.

There were other seemingly practical American things that my parents viewed differently. When David and I approached them one day about a living will, they told us (in partial jest) we must want them to die. In China, they said, one did not talk about such things with one's parents. In retrospect, I wish I had bitten the bullet and looked for a Chinese psychiatrist. It might have made Daddy's life with Mommy from that time on less of the nightmare it became.

The logical place for them to move to from Allendale was someplace near David and me. We found a house in Livingston that had three bedrooms and a finished attic Daddy could use for an office. It turned out to be his man cave, somewhere he could go to get away from Mommy's rage. There was a sizable fenced-in backyard with a chain-link fence, which was good for Daddy's dog, Blue. The fenced-in yard made Mommy feel more secure than a yard open to the street. For Daddy, there was a bus that traveled from Livingston to the Port Authority Bus Terminal in New York City.

Being near us initially brought some happiness to them because they were able to see Ben and Mike frequently. I had accepted a part-time teaching position at Montclair State College in 1969, and I welcomed the help Daddy could give me eventually in picking the children up from school when meetings and other reasons prevented me from doing so.

Equally important was the presence of a good Chinese restaurant, North Sea Village, only a long block away from their house. As the years went on and we all got older, Mommy did less and less cooking for herself and Daddy. Whereas they formerly would join us when we ate out, they also became more reluctant to leave their house. Social isolation became their norm. Phone calls kept them in touch with their friends, but even those phone calls dwindled and were infrequent.

Because we patronized North Sea Village often ourselves, we came to know the owner well. Although the restaurant did not do routine delivery of orders to houses, Mr. Chen agreed one day to deliver food to my parents. That was a huge contribution to my peace of mind. I knew that at least my parents would have enough to eat. However, their self-imposed exile from the outside world was unhealthy for both of them and led to more arguments.

During the years when Mommy's behavior became more difficult, Solan and Jeannie and David and I tried to keep our own relationship and that of our children close. It was gratifying to me that Ben, Mike, Shrong, and Mei grew up close to each other (figure 119).

Mike and Ben were also fortunate to have cousins from some of David's siblings who lived fairly close, all in the metropolitan northeast. Robert, David's older brother, had one son: Eric. David's oldest sister, Patsy, had two sons: Mark and Carl. The families visited each other often, and the Pai cousins also have remained close friends (figure 120). That closeness made David and me happy, for if anything were to happen to either or both of us, we knew the boys would have strong support from members of both families.

Fig 116 Proud me and number two son, Mike, circa four months

Fig 117 Our family when Ben was 4 and Mike 3

Fig 118 Isabel and Mike around 2 years old

Fig 119 The four cousins in horseplay

Fig 120 Left to right: First cousins: Mike, Carl, Ben, Mark, and Eric.

Chapter 40

LIVINGSTON, CONCENTRATION, AND HOUSEKEEPERS

I was elated beyond words to have my children, even more so than my parents were. They did not know we had tried for such a long time before succeeding in getting pregnant. I loved nursing the babies, feeling their warmth, and having them grasp my finger. Every new development was a source of excitement and pride. At an early time, when they were about a month old, they responded to us with smiles, which required much camera activity. It was then that I began to enjoy photography. Photography always had been my favorite form of art, but I had never indulged before in that activity.

David had finished his engineering PhD degree from NYU in 1965. Shortly afterward, we moved to Metuchen, New Jersey, in 1965 to be closer to David's work. We rented a small cottage with probably less than 1,200 square feet of space and low ceilings. Our good friends Marty and Ellie Gruber (figure 121) came to visit one day, and Ellie too had a beautiful baby boy about seven months old.

As we chatted, she exuberantly tossed the baby up into the air and actually threw him into the low ceiling of our living room. He wasn't injured, but thereafter, she was known to my mother, who was also visiting, as the Lady Who Threw Her Baby into the Ceiling. Mommy could never remember the American names of our friends, so their identities were established by anything they did that was memorable for her.

Ellie was a stay-at-home mom when she wasn't substitute teaching. She is active in civic affairs and volunteers in many aspects of life in Ridgewood, New Jersey. Marty and Ellie also have two girls, Stacey and Joelle, who are wonderful in their own right and work for nonprofit organizations. I respect Ellie for her humanitarian outlook, and she is one of the naturally funniest people, and one of the most caring people I know.

As the years passed and we and the Grubers increased the depth of our friendship, we were proud to hear of Marty's progress as an educator in New York University's department of finance. He eventually became a chair professor. His son, the baby who made contact with our ceiling, was Jon Gruber, and he too became a professor, at the Massachusetts Institute of Technology, after studying for his PhD at Harvard. His expertise is in health-care economics, and he was greatly involved in Mitt Romney's health-care policy in Massachusetts, aspects of which were incorporated into Obamacare. Jon and his wife have two boys and a girl. I have told them all that Jon is as brilliant as he is only because his mother threw him into our ceiling—it must have rearranged the neurons in his brain!

Marty and David met one summer in a French course when they and I were in PhD programs. They both were taking the course in an attempt to pass the requirement for a second foreign language for their PhDs from Columbia University and New York University, respectively. On the first day of class, when the instructor asked all the students to read French, the two were the only ones who requested to be passed over—and for good reason: their hilarious mispronunciation of French. That bond cemented their friendship and was unbreakable. Despite their deficiency in pronunciation, both passed their French exam with little trouble.

We discovered that we all enjoyed playing tennis and bridge and over the years have enjoyed each other's company and those two activities. We have seen Marty and Ellie more frequently and more consistently than any other friends. When I am in need of a chuckle, I ask either honored gentleman to count for me in French. Mutual respect is probably the main reason for our enduring friendship.

One of the TV programs I used to watch when I was nursing baby Mike was a game show called *Concentration*. There was a board with about two dozen rotating blocks, each with a number on one side and a prize written on the backside. Two contestants vied for prizes by trying to find matching blocks that had the same prize written on them when rotated.

One contestant began by calling two numbers. If the gift on the back side of both blocks was the same, that gift was given to the contestant. For example, if I called numbers two and fourteen and both had "Fur coat" written on the back, "Fur coat" would be written on a board behind me, and I could call out two more numbers. If the gifts written on the back of the blocks did not match, the blocks were turned back to their numbers. The opponent then had a turn to try to find a match. As the game proceeded, the contestants had to commit to memory which unclaimed prize was on which numbered block.

When two blocks had matching gifts, they were removed from the group, revealing part of a puzzle board underneath the blocks. The puzzle could be drawings or letters that formed a phrase or the name of something or someone. There were also wild-card blocks and punitive blocks, such as "Forfeit a gift," which meant the one who matched it had to give up one of his or her gifts. A contestant won when he or she figured out the puzzle, and the winner received whatever gifts were listed on his or her side as prizes for winning. I had little trouble in figuring out the phrases, but my memory had always been weaker than I would have liked, so I assumed I would not be good at *Concentration*.

I liked nursing Mike while the program was on because young Benjy, then less than two years old, was mesmerized by the turning blocks and would watch quietly. Isa would watch with us, and we would try to match the blocks and guess the puzzle. She did not do as well as I because of the language difficulty she had with English.

One day she said to me, "Why you don't go on this program? You guess well."

I was somewhat taken aback by her question because I didn't think of myself in the role of a contestant on a TV game show. But the more I thought about it, the more reasons I thought of for trying out for the program. I did not hold a job. I had Isa to care for the children, even if I had to spend three or four hours traveling to New York City to be on the show. I could bottle breast milk for the baby. I had nothing to lose and possibly something to gain.

I decided to call the number the program instructed viewers to call if they had interest in playing the game. I was told to go to NBC Studios to take a test to establish whether I could play well enough to be considered. I did well enough, because they called one day shortly after the test to say I had been chosen to be a contestant. I thought, *Uh-oh*, since I'd applied with tongue in cheek, not expecting to be accepted. Maybe they needed a minority contestant.

I was told to show up in the audience for a couple of days before I would be called to participate. At that time, game shows had become popular on TV, and there were known to be people who started to appear on different game shows to walk off with prizes, as if playing games were their source of income. Professional players, they were called. I had to sign a form agreeing not to go on another game show for five years after I finished with *Concentration*.

Before each show, both when I was a member of the audience and when I was a contestant, professional cosmeticians put facial makeup on me, which was a new experience, as I had no patience for makeup. If I ever was involved in something that Mommy felt required makeup, she would insist on putting it on me. It was not something I appreciated, as I felt makeup was like a mask—not real. But I knew it was something the program insisted on, and I didn't mind the way they did it.

Not knowing anything about makeup, I asked the artists what they were using and watched how they used it. While I did not use any cosmetics for many decades afterward, now that I am old, that knowledge helps in my attempts to hide the presence of ubiquitous age spots brought on by many years of exposure to sunlight while playing sports without the benefit of sunblock.

I have no idea how I managed to get by. The idea of going on national television right now would create panic in my mind. I believe my experience in graduate school was what helped me be so calm in the games, and that was perhaps the edge I had over nine of my opponents. I said to myself that if I could twice face scientists with 250 years of experience questioning me on anything they wanted during my oral preliminary exam and my thesis defense, I should surely be able to handle something in which I had nothing to lose.

I do not remember any of the games I won—I won nine contests. Every program had two puzzles to solve, so I was on TV for five days. The host was Hugh Downs. He seemed to be a nice man, but we contestants never saw him until the program was on the air, so we never got to know him at all. I guess that's a privilege stars can claim as celebrities.

The first time I played, I won both contests. I gleefully called David, who was at work, and said, "Guess what? I won!" As I continued to win, I would call and list the prizes I had won that day. David would respond with laughter.

I won many prizes, including a trip to Puerto Rico for two, a TV set, a beaver fur coat, pots and pans, and cash. I wanted badly to win a car, which occasionally was on the board for a game, but in the ten games I played, there was never a car for a prize. However, we had to pay taxes on all that I won, so we would have needed help had I won a car.

The only game I still remember—and I will until my dying day—was the game I lost. My opponent in that game was introduced to me as an engineer on a nuclear sub. My immediate reaction was that he must be smart, and I needed to solve the puzzle as soon as possible. Wrong on both counts!

When we played, I realized the puzzle began with "Aren't you a sweet" fairly early. As soon as I saw the word *sweet*, I jumped at the answer. I had seen a program on TV the day before in which the term *sweetie pie* was used, and that was what I guessed for the puzzle. Wrong again! My opponent, who I know now had no clue about the puzzle, was able to make a match and said, "Aren't you a sweetheart?" and that was right.

What made the loss so memorable to me was that if I had won a tenth game, I would have been recalled to play in *Concentration*'s Tournament of Champions at the end of the year. Also, the nuclear engineer turned out to be a real dud at solving puzzles. In his next game, which was against an equally inept opponent, the two matched all the blocks, revealing the entire puzzle, and neither one could solve it. I was screaming the answer in my head for them—*Country sausages!*—and kicking myself for underrating myself against the engineer.

Just remembering the incident brings back a strong tendency for more self-flagellation. But I must force myself to remember that had someone guaranteed I would win nine games, much less one, I would have jumped at the chance. Still....

We had Isa with us for a year. We lost connection with her shortly after she returned to Spain, and I hope she has had a good life. She was a good person and deserved a good life. After she left, we decided to leave Metuchen and move to Livingston, New Jersey. Foster Wheeler Corporation, David's place of work, had relocated their main headquarters to Livingston after having had offices in New York City and lab spaces in Carteret, New Jersey.

David was so tired of commuting to New Jersey and going to school at night to get his doctorate that he said we would look at houses to buy right in Livingston, and we would start in neighborhoods close enough for him to walk to work. It was a young neighborhood. I once counted that Wingate Drive, just our portion of it, boasted dozens of children, most of them boys. There was no end of playmates for Ben and Mike. That was the best aspect of Wingate Drive.

The house was a colonial (figure 122). Our backyard was next to a small wooded area that separated our property from Heritage Junior High School's playing fields. There would be no houses built behind us, and the proximity to the junior high eventually would be good for the boys.

I liked the layout of the house, with the TV room and den next to the garage and a mudroom and laundry area between the den and the kitchen, where there was a door to the backyard. In those days, 1968, most houses did not have the open concept that characterizes houses today. Before we moved our furniture in, Benjie and Mike ran from room to room on the first floor as if they were in an indoor playground. Our new home had perhaps three times the amount of space we'd had in our rented home in Metuchen, and our boys were delighted.

We were to live at 12 Wingate Drive for the next sixteen years. David was happy to be less than two miles from work. He never walked the distance, though, because there were busy streets to cross and a shopping mall before he could reach Foster Wheeler's campus. The mall's proximity pleased our housekeepers, who could walk there on their days off.

We decided after having a year with an au pair that we would try having a live-in housekeeper. I was toying with the idea of going back to work. I felt uncomfortable with the thought of not passing on the knowledge from my twenty-plus years of education. It seemed such a waste. If I could find something I wanted to try, we would need a caretaker in our home for the children.

We found a good housekeeper by going to a company that specialized in providing people with green cards that allowed them to work legitimately in the United States. Our first housekeeper from the company was Chita Campos, a young woman in her twenties from El Salvador. She was smart and carried out instructions accurately. Chita worked with us for two years and then met and fell in love with a man who lived in New York City. Chita wanted to move to live with Peter in the city and said she knew someone who could take her place and already had her green card.

We were happy to accept her friend, whom I will call Carmen. Carmen was a delight when she came to us. She was an energetic, attractive young woman, and best of all, like Chita, she spoke English. She had a pleasant personality, and we could not have been happier to welcome her into the family. Our boys, at the time, were three and four years old. I trusted Carmen and saw how she responded warmly to my children. Carmen once described her brother to me as a glass of Coca-Cola—everyone liked him. I felt the same way about Carmen.

Life with Carmen in our home was wonderful. It took her little time to understand our daily schedule of activities. She was wonderful with the boys, and they responded well to her. I had complete confidence that she would always have their well-being in mind. To me, the primary role of my housekeepers was to care for the boys when I was not home. Their duties in housework were to give me the time to be with my children and my husband.

We never kept track of any of our housekeepers on their days off, feeling it would be an intrusion to do so. If they were leaving to go somewhere overnight, they only needed to tell us they would not be home. If something delayed their return, they were to call and tell us. However, things began to change about six months after Carmen came to us.

My ideal housekeeper, whom I had begun to call my friend, continued to do her work, but she began to change in her appearance, looking tired and distracted. She looked as if she were losing weight.

I mentioned the weight loss one day, and she laughed and said, "I'm trying to lose. Thank you for seeing it."

I thought she might have been experiencing a spell of homesickness, and I didn't think much of it. How we block out of our minds that which we don't want to see!

One day I returned from grocery shopping, and she called me from upstairs.

"Mrs. Pai, come upstairs, please," she said in a voice that was somehow a little strange.

I did as she asked and found her ironing some laundry. She had circles under her eyes, and I was alarmed. How did I not know something was terribly wrong? With my heart in my throat, I asked her, "What's wrong, Carmen?"

"Nothing," she said. Then she made me freeze by saying, "I would like you to send a telegram to President Nixon for me."

"What? Why do you want me to send President Nixon a telegram?"

"Tell him I am ready to help him in any way I can—for the United States!"

Carmen was clearly out of her mind. I told her I would send the telegram and excused myself. I ran downstairs and called David to come home immediately. I was happy he was so close by. He rushed home, and I explained what had happened. I also called a friend who was a practicing psychiatrist. He said she needed help and to get her some right away. We agreed we should take Carmen to the local hospital emergency room. I called my parents to pick up the children and keep them for the rest of the day.

The children! My skin developed goose bumps when I realized that if I was gone, my little ones would be alone in the house with someone losing her mind. But they were fine and did not know anything was wrong. Still, the realization made me shake for the rest of the day.

Carmen did not resist our order to get in the car. I drove, and David sat next to her in the back seat. Carmen was a bigger woman than I, and in case she began to struggle, David would be more capable of controlling her than I. In any case, I sped to the Saint Barnabas Hospital's emergency room, which was only five minutes away from our house by car.

When we got there, the receptionist looked at Carmen and said, "She was here in the middle of the night but refused treatment and left. We had no right to detain her."

Carmen had walked the two-plus miles to and two-plus miles from the hospital in the middle of the night alone! She obviously knew that something was wrong and that she needed help, but perhaps she had become fearful of a place she was unfamiliar with and decided to go home. Again, she told us she wanted to go home.

We did not know what to do, and when we got home, we told her to go to bed and take a nap, as obviously she had not slept all night. I called my psychiatrist friend, and he said in no uncertain terms that we had to get her committed, and he said to tell the hospital that if they did not take her, we would call the police to take her to be treated at the hospital, something they then could not deny.

She was a threat to herself and possibly to others, my friend said. I did not believe she would harm the children, but I could not take a chance with her in that state, and I worried she might do something to herself if desperate enough.

We did as he urged us to do. We saw that she was not asleep. We told her we had to go back to the hospital. Thank goodness Carmen did not put up much resistance, although she insisted she was okay. The good woman, even with a befuddled mind, knew she needed help. She had, after all, sought help on her own. The second time we brought her to the emergency room, we related what the psychiatrist had said, and the hospital took her in and kept her for two weeks.

The doctors found in her pocketbook several vials of prescription drugs—amphetamines, or speed. Carmen was a speed addict. She had apparently gone to different doctors, asking for prescriptions to lose weight. Remember, in those days, there were few computer networks. Today I doubt she could have succeeded in hiding the fact that she had so many prescriptions for the same kind of drugs.

I called Chita, and she immediately came back to our home and said she would stay until I had another housekeeper. Chita had not known Carmen had a drug problem. Chita told us about a cousin in El Salvador who wanted to come to the United States to work. She knew Dina Campos well and was convinced she would work well with us. We agreed and immediately filed papers to allow Dina to immigrate.

We called Carmen's brother, who lived in California, while she was in the hospital. We asked him to come take Carmen to live with him, as we could not continue to use her with two toddlers in the house and uncertainty about her addiction in the future. We bought her brother a round-trip ticket and Carmen a one-way ticket to California. My heart was broken when her brother admitted to me that she had been found to be a drug addict recently in El Salvador. She had tried on her own to cure herself. Her family had all thought she was cured. Obviously, however, her addiction was too strong to overcome.

We wished her well when she packed up and left with her brother.

I told her, "If you can leave drugs alone, Carmen, and a doctor tells us you are cured, if we don't have someone else already working here, you will always be welcome. We will always be your friends."

"I'll try," she replied in a small voice.

About two months later, Chita received a phone call from Carmen's brother, who relayed the stunning news that Carmen was dead. In California, she apparently had continued to get prescriptions for amphetamines. Continued heavy usage of the medicines had resulted in internal bleeding that caused her death. I broke down in angry tears. What a waste of a wonderful person! Later, I read that people addicted to amphetamines commonly suffered cerebral hemorrhages and bleeding in the liver.

Fig 121 Marty and Ellie Gruber, lifelong friends

Fig 122 Our first home: 12 Wingate Dr., Livingston, NJ

Chapter 41

DINA, CORGIS, AND A RETURN TO WORK

Chita was duly apologetic about having recommended Carmen as our housekeeper, but of course, she'd done so in total ignorance of Carmen's problem. She said Dina, her cousin, knew little English but could learn. It took us a few months to get approval for the papers that would allow her cousin to immigrate to the United States and work for us. Chita also stayed on for a week after Dina arrived to train her cousin. I tried to learn some Spanish so I could communicate with Dina, and Chita assured me I could always call her for interpretation help.

Dina was two years older than I and a sturdy and energetic woman in her thirties. Her mother had brought up Dina and her brother by working as a seamstress. Her father had left the family, as she said many El Salvadoran men did. She assured us we need not worry that she might find a man to settle down with, as had Chita. I discovered that despite her childhood in poverty, Dina was, ironically, pickier about food than I, who had never had to worry about hunger. One day, when David was to meet some businesspeople for dinner, I said to Dina, "Let's just make ourselves sandwiches. I don't feel like cooking, and David won't be home."

In no uncertain tones, Dina replied, "I don't eat sandwiches for dinner."

I was astonished. I asked her how she'd developed such an attitude, since my brothers and I were used to eating whatever my mother served. Dina responded that if her mother had cooked something she didn't like—and her mother had done all the cooking for her—she simply hadn't eaten anything that day. *Willful* is a word that I found fit Dina Campos to a T as our relationship continued for more than forty years. Another adjective might be *spoiled*.

Her resentment toward her father for abandoning the family was deep and constant. It was the reason she said she would never marry. She had no respect for the men of El Salvador at all. In addition, I think Dina was affected by growing up in poverty. It meant she had to do what was necessary to survive. That in turn meant focusing on her own needs as priority.

Thus, she said, "Even though a man may be faithful, marriage still means a woman has to cater to the man's desires. No." She shook her head with a down-turned mouth. "I don't want to have to cater to anyone!" I was to find out that her attitude also extended to her employer.

I came to admire that independent woman who had maintained her self-respect despite poverty. However, at the same time, egocentricity meant she could be obstinate as an employee. I probably told her at least ten times over the forty-two years she worked for us that if she had worked for most people, she would have been fired many times over for things she did, such as disobeying orders. She would laugh and shake off my chastisement, which made me chafe even more. David was reluctant to chastise her when I felt she should have been, because he feared she would leave us. Dealing with Dina Campos became an exercise in teeth grinding.

She would say with a laugh after being chastised, "In my country, we say when two people argue, it is because they love each other," and off she would go, unfazed by my words.

But Dina was loath to leave us too. She loved taking care of the boys and was protective of them. That was my priority for any housekeeper, so I was confident they would be cared for if I had to leave for any reason. It made retaining her to work for us easier in spite of her obstinacy. Dina also loved Chinese food, and after I reentered the world of academia, I told her that if she wanted me to cook Chinese, she would have to be cook number two and do the cutting that almost every dish required, because I would not have the time.

I taught her how to cut meat for each dish, whether in small chunks, shreds, or slices, and always across the grain of the meat. The vegetables also needed to be cut in a specific way for each dish. She was happy to learn if it meant she would get authentic Chinese food. She frequently criticized food we ate at restaurants as being not as good as what we had at home. It was important to that picky eater that she eat quality cooking—that was, someone else's quality cooking since she did not enjoy cooking for anyone.

One responsibility Dina accepted and was trustworthy in carrying out was watering my bonsai collection. For most people who attempt to create the miniaturization of trees but find them not surviving, the reason is the watering of the trees. There is little soil, and it must have good drainage. To my pleasure, I found that Dina had a green thumb and could take on the watering chore for me, which, in hot weather, could require watering every day and perhaps even twice a day (figure 123).

I discovered that her green thumb, while productive, was undisciplined, which reflected Dina's personality. She would take the equivalent of cuttings from plants she knew and liked while walking past neighbors' plantings, breaking the tips of branches, and put them in the ground to root, and they invariably rooted. The next thing I knew, there would be small seedlings of something sprouting in the middle of roses, for example.

Two other great pleasures Dina shared with us were sports and dogs. Sports were favorite hobbies that everyone in our family shared. Both my sons, Ben and Mike, proved they were good athletes. Baseball was one sport Dina had known in El Salvador. As the boys grew and entered the T-ball league, Little League, and Babe Ruth League, Dina was their most ardent and certainly most obstreperous fan.

When she watched the New York Mets playing on television at home, we frequently heard loud denunciations of errors ("*Estupide!*") and equally loud squealing of joy when they won ("*Ha-ha, si!*"). When the boys were old enough, she took them to Shea Stadium for Mets games. Eventually, she joined us in supporting the New York Giants football team and the New York Knicks basketball team. She became more than a housekeeper and more a part of the family. The children, to this day, now in their middle ages, consider her a second mother.

When she joined us, Mike was four, Ben was five, and we already had a dog, a Pembroke Welsh corgi. Corgis are known to most people as the dogs of England's Queen Elizabeth. The queen has had that breed of corgi ever since she was a young girl. We now have our sixth corgi and love him as much now and possibly more than ever.

We came to have corgis because in those early years, David was traveling a lot for Foster Wheeler, and since he was away from home so much, I told him I wanted a dog. The boys were babies, and I argued that a dog would provide some protection. At least it would bark if it heard something or someone. To be honest, though, since I'd grown up with dogs, I just missed having one.

Now, David denied this, but I am telling the truth. I knew David was not keen on having a dog in the house. In China, he had dogs, but they were not pets, as they are in the United States. They had a function—hunting—and were not allowed in the house.

When I broached the subject again, he established some criteria that a house dog had to meet to be acceptable to him: it could not be too big like my brother Solan's golden retrievers; it could not be too small like the Chihuahuas we'd had when he and I first started dating (they had not liked David); it could not have long hair; and it could not smell like the golden retrievers. I felt as if a dog had to be able to write its name before it could qualify to be a Pai dog!

I bought a thick book, *An Encyclopedia of Dog Breeds*, which contained pictures and text about each breed. One day, while scanning through the book for a medium-sized dog with short hair that hopefully did not smell, I happened to watch the Westminster Dog Show going on at Madison Square Garden on TV. It just happened that a Pembroke Welsh corgi was in the final judging group for the championship that year. It seemed to fit all the David Pai criteria to be a Pai dog, though, of course, I had no idea if it smelled. I'm happy to say PW corgis do not smell!

The beautiful corgi did not win that year, and since that year, I believe only once or twice in the past forty-plus years has another corgi been in the final judging group. Corgis are in the herding group of dogs and must compete against graceful dogs with long legs. With the corgis' short legs, they waddle when they walk and usually don't have a chance to be chosen for the final championship judging. However, lucky for me, while I was looking for the right breed, I saw a corgi in the final judging group. That had to be karma.

Our first corgi was a male whom we named Rusty because of the red-and-white coat he had. Rusty was what the breeder eventually said was a tough dog. Had I known better, I would have sent him back to her. By the time he was a year old, he indicated a fairly aggressive personality. He would growl at the children if they walked too close to him while he was eating. He was unwilling to stay inside our backyard and jumped onto a boulder near the fence to jump over and run to the junior high fields. Every so often, we would see his white rump trotting toward the school.

Still, he developed a fondness for our family and Dina. When the boys were in elementary school, Rusty—and all the corgis thereafter—would know when it was time for the boys to return home. Rusty would lie down on the small landing where the stairs turned a right angle to go up to the next landing (figure 124), where he could look through the small window next to the front door, which was too high for him to see through when he was standing on the ground floor. When he saw the boys approaching, he would tremble with excitement and bark a greeting.

All our corgis seemed to have an internal clock. If we lost track of time for some reason and forgot to feed one, a short-legged dog was soon by our side, staring a hole through us with an expression that told us he was hungry. Dogs might not speak, but they can certainly communicate!

Our next-door neighbors had a miniature poodle named Tiger. They would let Tiger out unleashed. If Rusty was in our backyard, Tiger would tease Rusty by running up and down by our fence, believing Rusty could not jump the fence from the ground with his short legs. We requested more than once that our neighbors stop letting Tiger out without a leash—a request they obviously disregarded. One day, while Tiger was teasing him, Rusty got out of the yard by going up the boulder and then jumping over the fence. Instead of going straight ahead to the junior high, he turned at the corner of the yard and charged at Tiger.

I describe my corgis as torpedo-like. They are long compared to their height (4:1), and they are quick and strong for their size. Tiger never knew what hit him and was bowled over and over. We heard the ruckus and managed to control Rusty before he could really hurt Tiger. After getting him in the house, we petted him and said, "Good boy, Rusty!" Tiger did not tease Rusty after that.

Dina's presence in our family freed me of many of the chores I normally would have had to take care of and allowed me time to focus on my career as a scientist and an educator. I received a couple of job offers after I graduated from Einstein, one from Rutgers University and one from a research laboratory in Philadelphia with Dr. Bea Minz, who was a friend of Dr. Waelsch's. I assumed Dr. Waelsch had probably given my name to Dr. Minz, but because both places were too far from our new home, I had to decline both offers.

I remained at home for three years following graduation and leaving work from Einstein. I enjoyed watching my boys grow, but I found that being home was something I did not entirely enjoy. Having been in school for some twenty-four years, I felt that my education was being wasted. I felt a great sense of obligation to those who'd taught me and to those who did not have the opportunities I'd had. Also, being in genetics meant great changes were taking place fast in my field of expertise, and I was falling further behind on developments. When Mike was three and able to communicate fairly easily, I decided the time had come to look for positions.

I wanted to start teaching part-time, as I felt my boys were too young for me to teach full-time. I was able to find such a position at Montclair State College, which some years later became Montclair State University, the largest of the public state schools in New Jersey, and now has more than eighteen thousand students. It was only twelve miles from home, and they were willing to give me half a teaching load.

The biology department, which had just lost an embryologist to retirement, found my degree in genetics an excellent fit for their curriculum. I was surprised to hear that the only genetics course the biology department offered was a two-credit nonlab course. I knew that had to change because the immediate future would see a meteoric rise in importance for genetics. Most geneticists knew their field was on the brink of an era of great progress toward the understanding of gene structure and function. In science, what we can understand we inevitably look to control. Genetic research and literature were rife with discussions of gene manipulation and genetic engineering, for example.

Since my education had been in private institutions of higher learning, the faculty at Montclair all asked in my interviews if I could tolerate teaching at a public institution. I didn't think I would have any problems, but I did find a huge range of capabilities and preparedness in the student body for college-level courses due to almost open admissions. Indeed, having many poorly prepared students required some adjustment on my part. Those who taught in private colleges and universities had a much more uniformly prepared student body, and for them, there was far less difficulty in finding a level of rigor that would both educate students and be fair.

In the fall semester of 1969, I began what would be a nearly three-decade career in teaching at Montclair State. I quickly came to develop great respect for most of my students. Almost all of them held jobs—in some cases multiple jobs—in order to afford college. I empathized with them, having been the first student Sweet Briar allowed to wait tables all four years.

A few students told me their families did not even want them to go to college but wanted them to find jobs to help the families' finances. They were paying their own way through Montclair State, as did many others. Most of our students took more than four years to graduate. I realized if a college education meant that much to them, they surely deserved the best instruction I could give them.

Graduation was my favorite event of the academic year. Many students were the first in their family to graduate from college, and the pride and euphoria of the seniors and their families were wonderful to behold and to hear. As each graduate was announced, his or her relatives would loudly celebrate with an intensity I had never witnessed in my own graduations. It was pure joy. Like my own children, my students were my academic children, and I rejoiced with them. I always removed my cap when I passed the biology graduates on the recessional. To this day, hearing some of the music that was played during the graduation ceremonies, such as "Pomp and Circumstance," evokes a feeling of nostalgia and joy.

Fig 123 Dina Campos watering my bonsai collection

Fig 124 Rusty greeting the boys home from school.

Chapter 42

THE END OF REASON AND THE END OF A DREAM

When we found a house in Livingston that met with Mommy's approval, my parents moved in, happy to move away from Allendale. Their house was about a seven-minute drive from our house, as it was on the opposite side of Livingston from Wingate Drive. There was plenty of room in the backyard for Mommy to have a small vegetable garden, which she liked to work in. The house was essentially a Cape Cod house. There was an attic that Daddy used as an office (and for refuge from Mommy), and there was a basement through which one could enter the garage.

At that point, we began to witness the beginning of a serious deterioration of Mommy's emotions and mental capacity in several ways. One involved Daddy's job at the United Nations. Upon news that Communist China would be admitted to the United Nations in 1971, Daddy had to work hard to learn the changes that the Communists made in the written Chinese language.

Their goal was to simplify the ideograms, which sometimes could contain twenty or more strokes, into ones requiring fewer strokes. That made some words unrecognizable, so those trained in classical Chinese, like my father, needed to essentially learn what the changes were so they could read memos sent by the Communist Chinese delegation as well as newspapers and magazines coming out of China.

Mommy objected deeply to the presence of the Communists because of what they had done to her brother, my fourth uncle, who had been jailed during the Cultural Revolution and died there. She also abhorred the Communists because the government had annexed the family's property in China when they won the civil war, and of course, the destruction of all pets in the 1950s and 1960s was anathema.

She wanted Daddy to have nothing to do with the Communists when they were accepted into the UN, which, of course, was impossible since Daddy had to meet them and be able to discuss what he was expected to do for them as a member of the Secretariat.

Mommy harangued Daddy constantly, demanding that he resign from the United Nations. Her arguments were sometimes close to being hysterical rants.

"You know what they did to my younger brother—they are all murderers! Why do you want to work with them? Are you a Communist sympathizer?"

Daddy would try to explain his actions and the effect that leaving so quickly would have on his retirement pension and usually ended up finding refuge in his attic office with his faithful dog, Blue.

Finally, perhaps a year or two after the Communists had gained membership in the United Nations, Daddy, against his better judgment, capitulated and resigned from his job as a simultaneous interpreter.

"I can't live with her like this anymore," he said, shaking his head.

He had worked so short a time that his pension would not be enough for them to live on comfortably. Fortunately, by that time, Solan, David, and I were earning salaries and could chip in each month to help my parents' finances. They both knew, however, that we could only replace a fraction of his salary. We had our children and their college careers to consider.

When I returned to part-time teaching at first and then, three years later, a full-time position, I encountered problems that working mothers have always had to deal with. Early in my teaching career, I was concerned about leaving my young children as much as I had to, despite knowing that Dina was devoted to their care. I told my department secretary to be sure to call me whenever the children or Dina called. One day I was lecturing and saw the secretary appear at the window of my lecture room's door, gesturing that I had a phone call from home.

It was Mike, who was then about four years old.

"Hi, Mike. What's up?" I asked.

"Hi, Mommy. Can I have some water?" he responded.

"Ask Dina to give you some water if you're thirsty. Mommy has to go back to work," I said, a little annoyed that he'd called for something he clearly could have gotten from our housekeeper.

After I returned to my classroom, in about five minutes, the secretary was back, signaling that I had another phone call. I apologized to my class and ran to the phone. It was my younger son again.

"Hi, honey. What do you need now?" I asked.

"Can I have some apple?" he asked.

"Please ask Dina, Mikey. These are all things she can help you with. Please don't call unless you have a problem, okay? Mommy's working."

I returned to my patient students and explained that Mike had just learned how to use the phone to get in touch with me and seemingly just wanted to talk to his mother. In about five more minutes, the secretary was there, beckoning to me again and laughing. My class laughed as well.

I picked up the phone and, in an irritated voice, said, "What is it, Mike?"

"Mommy," he said in a small voice, "what's a problem?"

Needless to say, I was taken aback, somewhat nonplussed that I had not had more patience with my little boy and obviously had not explained to him clearly enough about the use of the phone. After work, when I returned home, we had a long session about what a problem might be. My son did not interrupt me at work thereafter unless he had a real problem.

My children were not the only generation I was concerned about. At about that time, my parents showed they needed more of my attention also. The term for a generation required to care for parents and also their own children, *sandwich generation*, could not be more apropos.

Whenever I had time, I would take my mother shopping, and it would bother me deeply if she would not purchase something she liked because she thought it was too expensive.

"Ooh," she would say in a startled tone, "that dress is so expensive! It's forty dollars!"

"Mommy," I said, "you haven't shopped in a long time. Everything is more expensive now. It really is a reasonable price."

She would shake her head and sigh. Given her background, for her to be reduced to thinking a forty-dollar dress at Sears was too expensive tugged at my heart. I would insist she buy it, and I paid for it.

While her children's American dream continued, Mommy seemed less and less able to enjoy life in the United States. Looking back at the situation, I wish we had done more to decrease the social isolation my parents found themselves in. I'm not sure what we could have done because Mommy did not want to see their old friends, but we should have tried harder.

Another indication of Mommy's state of mind had to do with my attempts to find household help for her. Since they now lived in Livingston, I thought the perfect solution would be to have Dina go to their house once or twice a week to help out. Wrong! After about a month, Mommy told me she did not want Dina to work in her house anymore.

"I don't trust her," she said.

I was stunned. "But what has she done for you to not trust her?" I asked.

"She's stealing money, and she's too affectionate with your father," Mommy answered.

I couldn't believe my ears. No matter how difficult it was to have Dina as a live-in housekeeper, she had shown me total honesty when it came to our having money around the house, and Dina was the last person in the world who would have tried to steal any man's affection. But I knew that Mommy was already giving Daddy such a hard time about working with Chinese Communists that he didn't need to have her suspicions about Dina added on as another sore point between the two, so I told Dina, "Mommy said she doesn't need help for a while." Dina just shrugged and asked no questions. She understood that Mommy was generally unhappy about her life. In the ensuing months and years, I found a number of other housekeepers to help out. None of them lasted more than a month before Mommy wanted them gone. One, she said, had stolen her wedding photograph.

"Mommy, why would she want your wedding photograph?" I said.

"Because it is so beautiful," she said.

The poignant answer touched my heart. She was back in her youth in China. In her mind, she was so outstandingly beautiful that of course the servant (as she thought of the housekeepers) would want her picture as a bride, and the servant no doubt knew whose daughter she was too.

I looked at my mother, and she looked defiant, as if she expected an argument with me. She had developed the first symptoms of senile Parkinson's, and her head was moving up and down a little, but her mouth was set in a way that told me it would be useless to argue. I looked away, signaling that I would not contradict her.

Another time, Mommy accused a housekeeper of stealing a pot of stew she had cooked, because Mommy, in her mind, was such a wonderful cook that the servant could not resist having some of her food. By that time, I knew that protesting would only increase her animosity toward me. I could do nothing to convince her of the irrationality of her complaints. My last resort was to be present whenever Dina went to clean my parents' house. My presence allowed her to work, and Mommy could not complain because I was there and could watch her behavior.

At about that time, Mommy brought home a cat she had seen in Chinatown in New York City that seemed to be homeless. That signaled the beginning of a period in which she collected numerous homeless cats. Whether they were truly homeless or not, we will never know. She kept the cats in the garage, where she stored several steamer trunks of things she had brought from China and never used. She placed area rugs over the trunks, and the cats had room to move and climb as they wished. At least she was not feeding feral cats and bothering the neighbors.

I believe at the height of her collection, there were more than twenty cats in the garage. Some of the ones she brought home were pregnant. When the weather was warm enough, she had a large cage built in the backyard, and one by one, she would carry the cats into the cage to enjoy the outdoor air. At first, I worried she might hurt her back in doing that, but my mother was a tough old lady, and I accepted that the activity was providing her with considerable exercise. But again, it also was an activity that reflected excess, something most people would have found impractical.

Years later, when the cats had all died, Mommy told me once that she never had liked cats. In total disbelief, I asked her why she'd had more than a dozen cats. She'd been taught once when young, she said, that Buddha said the surest way people could go to heaven when they died was to be good to animals. She was preparing her way to heaven!

In 1971, David and I were able to persuade Mommy and Daddy to join us and our sons for a week's vacation at Disney World in Orlando, Florida. It was the first and last time we were to travel for fun with my parents. They agreed, knowing we liked to play golf and, while playing, needed supervision for the children. I think Mommy was pleased we trusted her to watch the boys for a few hours all by herself. We had a wonderful time, and I hoped Mommy would enjoy the trip.

One day David and I played golf with Daddy on one of Disney World's great courses. One moment stands out in my mind. Daddy hit his drive under some palm trees. He took out a fairway wood and pounded the ball from the rough toward the green. Delighted with his shot, he followed the ball intently—and walked smack into a tree! Somewhere in Orlando, there remains a palm tree with a dent in it. Nothing was hurt but his feelings, and he laughed in embarrassment at having walked into a tree. I wish we could have had more such times together.

In 1972, we were all excited by President Richard Nixon's plans to visit China. It was the first time any American president had visited China. From the point of view of the Chinese, the trip represented respect on the part of the Western power. It was something that gave the people great pride and joy. It also represented a significant change in the balance of power, as the United States and China were now allied against Russia.

Most exciting for our family, especially my parents, was the promise that images of Beijing were to be shown on television. When the time came, we gathered about the television set in high anticipation. As the program continued and followed the president on his tour, Mommy and Daddy sat in stunned silence. I wondered what they were thinking. It was our first exposure to my birthplace since we'd immigrated in 1940 following my grandmother's death.

After about a half hour of a tour of Beijing as it was then, my mother quietly said, "I don't recognize anything."

That was the moment both my parents realized that even if we were to have an opportunity to return to China, it would be to a foreign land, not the China they had known and not the life they remembered and coveted. While they did not say anything else, unspoken was the sad understanding that they could not return to their home. For them, there was no more home as they knew it. This had been my mother's dream—not my brothers' or my American dream, but her dream to return to the prosperity and celebrity she had as a Manchurian princess.

She did not cry then. Perhaps when we left them, she—or both—did. Thereafter, there was no more talk about returning to China. Indeed, my parents never traveled outside the United States from then on.

When the boys were five and four, I decided we needed to have professional family portraits every five years. We found a good portrait photographer only fifteen minutes from our house, and every five years, we had him shoot a portrait of our sons and our family.

In 1980, I arranged for my entire family to be photographed by the same professional, whom we had used twice by then. Solan, Jeannie, and their daughters joined Mommy, Daddy, and our family. We also sent Sandy and Stanley tickets to come to Livingston to join us in the photograph. See again figure 70. The rare reunion was enjoyed by all the young cousins, who always had delighted in each other's company. Daddy was clearly happy we were all together. More than once, he had bemoaned the fact that we were not living in a family compound like the one we'd had in Beijing. Mommy was not as happy because of Jeannie's and Stanley's presence, but she behaved herself for the most part. She was condescending but civil to Sandy, mostly because of gratitude that someone was willing to live with and care for Stanley. Stanley and Sandy stayed with us for a weekend and returned to Buffalo thrilled that they had been part of the reunion.

After the photographs were taken, we returned to our respective homes, and I received a phone call from Mommy.

"One of the photographers stole fifty dollars from me. You have to call them and get it back!"

"Mommy if they stole it from you, they're not going to admit they have it. What can we do about it?"

"It was a fifty-dollar bill, and now I don't have it anymore, and you won't do anything about it. You never do anything I ask you to do!"

We were all seriously concerned about Mommy. I hinted to Daddy that she might need medical help with a psychiatrist. Despite the fact that he was the main recipient of her outbursts and would have been the one to benefit the most if something could be done to help Mommy, he simply shook his head and said, "She'll never agree and will be irate that you think she's insane." That was the end of that.

Chapter 43

THE GROWTH OF CAREERS

Despite growing concerns about Mommy, life was rewarding for both David and me in our careers and private lives. The boys were doing well in school and were popular with their classmates. Dina gave us stability in child care while we worked. Having Daddy and Mommy in Livingston was still a big help despite Mommy's increasing eccentricities. Daddy could pick up the boys from school if David and I were unable to do so. (After Daddy passed away, the boys confessed that he had spoiled them with candy and ice cream treats when he picked them up, which was their secret to keep from David and me.)

David's career was progressing well. He impressed his boss, Ernie Daman (figure 125), and in 1972, he was offered a significant promotion. He was asked to be chief engineer for the newly formed Advanced Nuclear Energy Equipment Business for Foster Wheeler. It caused David to carry on an internal debate with himself since the offer would take him out of the ranks of research engineers, which he enjoyed, and into management.

In the end, he realized the offer was too good to refuse and accepted. He did not, however, tell me about the promotion. I found out from one of his engineers, who was astonished that David had not informed me of the good news.

I was embarrassed and hurt that he had not confided in me, and in a fury, I asked him, "Why didn't you tell me?"

He was startled at my anger and said, "Because I know you are sacrificing your career to support mine, and I thought I'd be rubbing it in by telling you of my promotion."

I realized then that being a general's son and being brought up by amahs and soldiers had left David with little clue about what a wife cared about.

I said, "If I am sacrificing my career for yours, don't you think knowing about your successes will make the sacrifice worthwhile? Don't you see that what would make such a sacrifice awful would be for you to waste your opportunities?"

In no uncertain terms, I told him I wanted to hear of good news thereafter from his own lips and not from one of his engineers. He was contrite and promised he would share any news with me, and he kept his promise.

David's reputation rose in the engineering world, and in 1994, he was inducted into the National Academy of Engineering, essentially a hall of fame for engineers. I was enormously proud of him. I am certain that had I tried to develop my own career by doing research, I would not have made as many contributions as David did, for which he was rightfully recognized.

When he retired from Foster Wheeler in 2001, David was the president and CEO of Foster Wheeler Development Corporation, which was involved in the research, development, and commercial demonstration of technology. That was a high position in American industry for an Asian.

My own career at Montclair State evolved into a full-time job after I had held the part-time job for three years. At that time, tenure was awarded after only three years of teaching in the state of New Jersey. When I was in my third year, I was told I qualified for tenure, but the person who had been hired as an adjunct to cover the other half of my teaching load did not. They needed me to take the full load, or they would have to find someone else to fill the full load. I agreed to become a full-time assistant professor.

When I was in graduate school, research was the goal toward which students were pointed. Teaching was something the professors at Einstein did sparingly around their research. Dr. Waelsch and the other professors taught only one class for part of one semester, and they usually grumbled about it.

The teaching load at Montclair State and the other state colleges was heavy: we were to teach three or four courses each semester. We were assigned three courses if one of them involved labs and four courses if there was only lecture involved. The lab courses were usually for four credits, and lecture-only courses were for three credits.

I loved the teaching part of higher education, even though admissions at the college, which were almost open, allowed students to be enrolled whose preparations for college-level courses were woeful. In the beginning, I had to figure out at what level to teach my courses so they would be fair to, I hoped, all the students.

I decided that students taking my courses should be prepared to accept jobs as research assistants, teach in high school, or go on to graduate schools. In short, I would not dumb down my courses because we were a state institution. Our graduates would eventually be competing with the graduates of prestigious private colleges and universities. They needed to be prepared as well as I could teach.

It bothered me greatly that year after year, I had to fail a significant number of students in my required genetics course. I had expanded the course from two credits to four credits, with three lecture hours per week and a three-hour lab. I developed a reputation for being a demanding instructor, but genetics was perhaps the most analytical of all the biology courses. The problems students had to solve to prove their understanding of the concepts and laws of genetics were akin to mathematics, so for me to teach the material adequately, students had to analyze and not just memorize.

One year not long after I had started to teach at Montclair State, I had a student in my genetics class for biology majors whom I thought would be very good. He started the semester by coming to every class and asking good questions. Then he started to miss a class now and then, and when he was in class, he would fall asleep more often than not.

Since he sat in the first row, I could not help but see him struggle to pay attention, and of course, there was no indication he was keeping up with the work. I was getting annoyed, thinking that if he was so disinterested now, why take up a seat in my class that someone more interested could fill? One day, after he had again fallen asleep, he approached me after class and apologized.

"Dr. Pai, I am so sorry that I'm falling asleep," he said. "I have recently been moved to the midnight-to-eight shift at work. I get home for two hours of sleep and then come to class, and sometimes I just can't stay awake."

His apology and explanation certainly diminished my annoyance, and I told him I understood and hoped he could eventually get a better shift. To my regret, the young man had to withdraw from class shortly afterward. His case underscored how difficult life was for many of the students at a state institution. They were there because most could not afford private schools. Some were holding more than one job. If anything, I thought to myself, they deserved the best educators, maybe more so than those from affluent families who did not have to work to support their academic goals.

Because I gave students a complete syllabus from day one and included days on which I would be giving them exams, I rarely allowed students to request extra time for study. There was one exception, however: a student whom I knew was holding three part-time jobs to pay for college and living expenses.

Donna Bennett, an African American woman, had lost both her mother and father and was on her own. She wanted to go to medical school to become a doctor, a goal she'd set at her terminally ill mother's bedside. When time came for the final exam on genetics, she came to my office and said, "This exam is so important to me for med school, and I am exhausted because my jobs keep me going almost without sleep. I know you don't normally give students extra time, but I need it, Dr. Pai. Is there any way you can give me the exam at a later time?"

I looked at her, and my initial reaction was to deny her request. But I looked again, and the fatigue was obvious in the circles under her eyes and her gaunt appearance. She had come to me for help more than once, and I was impressed with her intelligent questions. Her grades were good, and she would have gotten an A for genetics if only the past exam grades had been used, but it was a low A, and a bad performance on the final exam would give her a B for the course.

"You're right," I said. "Normally, I would deny you extra time. But I can see how tired you are, and I know you're a good student. Go get some sleep, and I'll give you an exam next week. If you tell anyone about this, you're in deep trouble!"

She thanked me, and when she took the makeup exam, which had problems and questions different from (and perhaps a bit more challenging than) the ones the rest of the class had faced, she did a superior job and received an A for the course. When she graduated from the New Jersey School of Medicine and Dentistry four years later along with three other classmates from Montclair State, she invited me to be present. I was so proud. Donna and I are still in touch after thirty years, and she is now a practicing ob-gyn in Florida.

Fig 125 David and his boss and mentor, Dr. Ernie Daman

Chapter 44

RECOGNITION FROM SWEET BRIAR COLLEGE

My alma mater, Sweet Briar College, at around that time (1972), decided to recognize me and invited me to give the opening convocation speech at the start of the school year. They asked me to talk about the experiences I had as a working mother. I thought the subject was fitting for the students of a women's college. At that time, women had far fewer opportunities for careers, and 90 percent of my graduating class had been engaged to be married. I'd been part of the 10 percent who were not engaged. I believe my talk represented the problems of young women of that time, many of which still exist today.

As Sweet Briar College was my first real home in the United States and also where I met my husband, I accepted the invitation to talk and worked hard to offer something with substance. Also, I was happy to be able to give back to the institution that had been instrumental in the development of my career. Following are excerpts from the talk I gave:

> This is an enormously exciting and totally unexpected privilege for me to be here as the principal speaker at the opening convocation of my own alma mater. When I received the invitation from Dr. Whiteman, even though it was written on the official letterhead paper of the president's office, my initial reaction was that it must be some sort of joke!
>
> Actually, I didn't really think anyone was playing a joke on me because it was too far-fetched an idea for anyone to dream up! I puzzled over the invitation for some time, because, and I guarantee you this is not false modesty, I do not fit my own stereotype image of who and what the main speaker at such an auspicious event should be: namely, someone who has contributed notably in her field, someone with great wisdom, and someone who is somebody. I am none of these.
>
> Well, then, why was I asked, and perhaps a more appropriate question would be, why am I here? With regard to the first question, I concluded that it must be

for the very fact that I mentioned before: that I do not fit the stereotype image of a speaker, and therefore, as an ordinary person, my experiences may be ones to which you can relate. Because I saw great wisdom in this reason, I accepted Dr. Whiteman's invitation …

Not being a typical speaker, then … I would like to have a heart-to-heart chat with you on subjects in which you and I must have great interest in common … I would like to share with you some thoughts that have served me well as a woman in our complex society.

I am a woman whose family is of paramount importance yet who has found that venturing outside the home with a career has made that family that much dearer and, paradoxical as it may seem, has made that family that much closer.

But before we go on to that, another reason I agreed to speak today is that I have never been able to turn down an invitation to revisit Sweet Briar and my close friends here, and this chance to speak gives me the rare opportunity to publicly state my feelings of commitment and great debt to my professors and my college.

I have been associated with a number of different academic institutions since I left Sweet Briar … If I could turn back time and be given again the joyous opportunity, which you have, of being a student, and if I were given my choice of where to go amongst the undergraduate programs I have seen, I would without hesitation choose this college again.

I won't pretend it is because this college would offer me a better education than any of the others—though it could and did offer me as good an education. It is because this is a small women's college where the student is taught by the professor and not graduate students. And where you are individuals in whom your professors can recognize potential if it exists because they know you, and this more than grades, I found, opens doors to the future.

For example … on recommendations from Miss Belcher and Miss Bennett, I managed to participate in a summer program in research training for college students at the Jackson Laboratory in Bar Harbor, Maine. I was invited back the next summer to be a counselor for the precollegiate research training program there, and on the strength of this, I was accepted to Bryn Mawr as a graduate student. From Bryn Mawr, the recommendation of my professor there led to a doctorate. So you see, one door leads to another, but someone has to make the first door available to you.

It has been many years since I was here as a student, and I don't know if, with the times, the closeness between faculty and students has changed. I hope not.

Learning consists of facts committed to memory, certainly, but facts can always be found in a book.

The true worth of an education is in the acquisition of enthusiasm, a word which I am told comes from Greek words meaning "the fire within." This you do not get out of books alone but from your professors, which is why personal relationships are so important in education. Take advantage of what you have here; enjoy it.

As for after graduation, you have before you the most exciting time that has ever awaited women in this country. As never before, even though the situation is far from perfect, you have the option of countless ways of organizing your lives, from traditional roles of wife and mother to the increasing number of opportunities to combine family and career. Let me say that my own personal feeling about being full-time wife and mother is that if this is what suits you, then it is every bit as worthy a way of life as anything else.

The great interest and attention generated by the courageous pioneers of the women's liberation movement to the real problems that exist in our society for women who desire a different role in life have, I detect, caused a kind of reverse peer-group pressure for those who lean to the traditional role.

The reactions I have encountered, for example, of some women upon discovering that I hold a PhD reflect both this pressure and, I think, the person's feelings about her own life. Suddenly, I find them on the defensive for why they are not working outside the home or taking courses. I don't feel anyone has to apologize to me or anybody else for being a homemaker.

Incidentally, another reaction, which is kind of amusing, is that occasionally, some people, upon coming face-to-face with a female PhD, begin to use big words, as if multisyllables prove their untapped intelligence. I remember when we were looking for a house, one owner, upon asking me what I worked at, began immediately to use big words in a rather lengthy discourse on the intelligence of her six-year-old daughter, adding that "We're very proud of her because she's considered so promiscuous!"

Perhaps because of my heritage, I am firmly convinced that the family unit is the basic unit which holds any society together. Here I disagree with some of the activists in the women's lib movement who feel that to be a wife and mother means automatic oppression, and therefore, one should simply do away with the family structure. To me, this is throwing the baby out with the bath water.

I know of no greater happiness that a woman can encounter than to be a wife and mother. It is a biological role that we can neither change nor compromise. It is to me the very fabric of life itself.

If you aspire to be a working wife and mother, let me say it is not difficult, given a few conditions. You need a husband who encourages you to put to use your training and abilities and therefore is willing to share chores that have been traditionally that of the housewife. In these times, unfortunately, such a man is still somewhat extraordinary, though traditional male attitudes are beginning to change, especially among the young. You must also have conscientious, reliable domestic help, preferably full-time, live-in. Finally, there is the need to have a slight but distinct tendency to schizophrenia!

As for the first condition, nobody can help you find the right husband, obviously, but if you intend to go on to advanced work with an eye to continuing in the future, then it only makes sense to make this aspiration clear to whomever you intend to settle down with … If you cannot reach an understanding about your desire and right to work without putting it down in black and white in a marriage contract, then may I suggest there is something remiss in either your relationship or your powers of reason?

Hiring a good domestic is a big problem in this country. This is not because there aren't good people available. But unless you and/or your husband earn a very good wage, the very high salaries demanded by labor laws for live-in help, for example, which do not take into account the fact that you have the expenses of her room and board, medical insurance, besides helping her pay for social security, and the fact that your earnings push you into a higher tax bracket, renders working for some young mothers a luxury they cannot afford. Day help is, of course, less expensive, but for a divorcée or widow earning a secretary's or educator's wage, the cost of such help is still prohibitive.

Why a corporation is allowed to write off limousines as tax-deductible expenses, while a working mother is not allowed any tax break on the expense of hiring a domestic, which is far more essential to her than a free ride to the golf course is to an executive, has remained beyond my comprehension. It is for the elimination of inequities such as these that women must work together within the political system …

In contrast to what many people might feel about a mother who hires live-in help and goes off to work, my housekeeper, whom I consider my working partner rather than my servant, frees me not to get away from the children; she frees me to be with them. In other words, when I am not teaching or writing, I do not have to worry about the house-cleaning but can devote time to my family.

A great boon and an alternative to domestic help for the working mother would be the establishment of day-care centers, which are few and far between now and, at any rate, are often unavailable to other than welfare mothers. Contrary to those who feel that not having mothers at home would cause children irreparable harm ... may I say with all due respect, I could not disagree more. What I have found since going back to work is that having been away from them part of the day, I am anxious to be with my family and they with me ... A big decision you will have to make when the time comes for you to embark on a career is to choose the type of work that will allow you to maintain the kind of family life you want. For a scientist, there are two major avenues to follow: there is research, and there is teaching. I was trained more for research than teaching; however, following my summer as a postdoc, I realized that full-time research is beyond me for at least the next several years. It simply involved me too much and kept me away from home too much.

As a professor, the workload is no less, but I can bring much of my work home. My boys know when I am working and for the most part are good about leaving me alone. And though I am therefore not actively involved with them while they are playing with friends, I am at home, we are together, and that is what I more than they need ...

It is not possible, of course, for a six- and a seven-year-old to behave as if their mother was not home at all, when they know very well that she is, so there is a good deal of interruption. This is where a tendency for schizophrenia comes in handy because you have to be able to switch from exam papers to paper planes fairly smoothly. Sometimes the hardest part of being a working mother for me is making a decision when there is pressure from both sides as to which is more important at that moment, the papers or the paper planes ...

What type of work outside the home you choose, if any work at all, is, of course, something each of you will decide when the time comes. What is important in making this decision is that you be perfectly honest with yourself and your family. Whatever it may be, it is a decision which must suit your own circumstances, your husband, your family, but above all, must suit you.

There is nothing sadder or more ineffective than a dissatisfied wife and mother. To make a decision that you really feel is right brings the kind of inner peace that sustains and makes any sacrifice a joyful decision ...

I have said enough. What I guess I've tried to say to you is simply that your future someday will be only as great as your willingness to work for your goals and to seize the opportunities offered to you by a sound education. An aspiration for a career can be totally compatible with maintaining a close family life. And perhaps, as in my case, your future may be much greater than your own expectations.

It was said, in one of the speeches at the dedication of the Wailes Center, that a child once wrote to his father serving in Vietnam a wish, which I wish also for you. He wrote, "I hope you live the rest of your life." Be not timid in your aspirations. Who knows? Someday they might lead you to the podium as a speaker at an opening convocation.

At the end of my talk, I was floored by a standing ovation. I must have touched upon things the students wanted to hear. Flustered, I turned to Miss Belcher and asked her to stand and share the ovation with me. I should have asked Miss Bennett to also, but in my excitement, I forgot. Sorry, Miss Bennett!

I have spoken at Sweet Briar a number of other times: I was named Distinguished Alumna in 1998; in 2006, I was inducted as a charter member of the Sweet Briar College Athletic Hall of Fame; and in 2008, I was invited to give the commencement speech at graduation. In none of those events did I feel I deserved the honor, but when my alma mater called, I responded. I am proud of having been elected to Phi Beta Kappa as well as the College Athletic Hall of Fame. I feel the two honors prove that athletes are not always dumb and that scholars are not always dorks!

Chapter 45

BONSAI AND A FAMILY TRIP TO ASIA

In 1974, David had a meeting to attend in Japan. We decided it would be a good opportunity to take our sons to the Far East, something they were old enough to benefit from by being eight and nine years old. The trip was in May, and my classes were over. One of the reasons I chose to enter teaching rather than research was to have the summer free to do things with my family.

At the time, David was the chair of the Pressure Vessels and Piping Division of the American Society of Mechanical Engineers, and an international meeting for engineers was scheduled in Tokyo. While he was attending the meetings, I could take the boys with me to visit sights in Japan. While we were in Tokyo, I wanted to visit the home and nursery of the family of my bonsai master in America, Mr. Yuji Yoshimura (figure 126).

Mr. Yoshimura had encouraged me to visit his family's bonsai nursery, which was located on the outskirts of Tokyo. A friend we knew in New Jersey met us for dinner one night and volunteered to accompany me to the nursery the next day. She had been living in Tokyo, where her husband was establishing a business. When I met her the next morning after breakfast, she had brought a box of chocolates to give to the Yoshimuras. I was impressed with her acumen in Japanese culture, in which one does not visit without bringing a gift.

When we drove to the periphery of Tokyo, I was astonished that there were no street signs. That was typical, my friend said. I'm sure that has changed. How would they be able to use GPS in cars? The taxi driver had a sense of where the nursery was, but the closer we got, the more befuddled he was. Think about going to a place just outside of a city you are not familiar with, and there are no street signs. It was a helpless feeling. Finally, we saw someone riding a bicycle and flagged him down. The driver asked if he knew where the Yoshimura Bonsai Nursery was, and the young man was kind enough to get back on his bike to lead us to the nursery. I have no idea why there were no street signs or if they now have them.

We had a lovely visit to the Yoshimura Nursery and admired the beautiful trees there, some of which were more than a hundred years old. My bonsai master, Yuji Yoshimura, had ignored the tradition that said he, as the oldest son in the family, should take over the family business. Instead, Yuji had decided to take his knowledge of the art to bring it to the United States.

Yuji's father was not there that day, nor were any of his relatives. I was impressed with the art of their bonsais. They also had some old and precious trees they cared for on behalf of owners who needed help to care for their treasures while they were away. We handed the box of candy to the young man at the end of our visit and left in the taxi, which had waited for us. The driver remembered the route back and returned to our hotel with ease.

I would go to Mr. Yoshimura once or twice a year for an all-day lesson. One day I brought a limestone rock to him that I had picked up in Crete; I could not decide how to place it as part of a root-over-rock planting. Mr. Y turned the rock over a couple of times and said firmly, "This way!" And he was right. I was grateful to learn the old art of miniaturizing trees from such a master artist. I have always felt that of all the Japanese bonsai masters in the United States—and there were several by the 1970s—mine was the greatest artist.

My bonsai master died in 1997 of lung cancer. He was a smoker. Upon his passing, he was honored for his role in bringing the art to the United States. There is a conference room at the National Arboretum in Washington, DC, named for Mr. Yoshimura. David and I attended the ceremony when the naming occurred.

The hobby of bonsai was better than a psychiatrist's couch for this working mother with aging parents. When I was working on a young tree, all my frustrations and worries disappeared as I designed how the tree should be trained to best bring out and enhance its natural beauty. I could sit in front of a tree, studying its every branch, for an hour. My family and my housekeeper would tease me by moaning and groaning as I bent the branches and trunk of a tree and wired them into the desired shape.

The styles of bonsai come from nature: upright like the giant redwoods; windswept like trees near the oceans, which have most of their branches turned in the same direction as the wind blows; cascading like trees whose trunks have bent downward; and so on. We mimic the styles by using wire to cause curvatures in the trunk and branches in young trees. Sometimes it takes years to reach the hardening of the limbs and trunks so that they can maintain the desired positions without wire. Bonsaists are naturally optimists since, unlike painters, they must wait so long to reach the point of creating a finished piece of art.

The Japanese struggle with land that is mostly uninhabitable. Ninety percent of the people live on 10 percent of the islands. Still, I was impressed with how the Japanese made their environment so lovely, and much of it was their work with trees. Many of the sidewalk trees were trained like giant bonsais. Every little house in the countryside seemed to have a small garden planted with shrubs and flowers. The landscape was a reflection of their discipline and appreciation of nature.

Our houses in Livingston, on the other hand, provided me plenty of room to work on my trees and keep them safe in the backyard, especially the house we moved to in 1984. That house had a six-foot chain-link fence around the almost acre of land in the backyard. With a southern exposure, it could not have been better for my trees. I studied with Mr. Yoshimura for nearly thirty years. At the height of my addiction to adding to my collection, I had approximately seventy-five trees, of which around thirty were trained. Figure 127 shows me with the first tree I worked on, an Alberta spruce. I had that tree for thirty years, and when we moved to North Carolina, I donated it to the Yama Ki Bonsai Society, which Mr. Yoshimura had organized.

In 1993, Mr. Yoshimura sent a letter to a few of his students, including me, in which he posed the following question: Is bonsai an art, a science, or both? He quoted a number of definitions of *art* and *science*. This was my response:

> Dear Mr. Yoshimura, Thank you for thinking of me in addressing the provocative question of bonsai as art and its relation to science. I hope my thoughts will be somewhat helpful and that they will not be too jumbled! I feel that perhaps the question itself hints at a dichotomy that I'm not sure necessarily exists in many aspects of the fields of human activity, art vs. science. Hence the definition of *art* that includes the sentence "Art is opposed to science" I would agree is only partially valid.
>
> It has always been my feeling that both involve the same two activities or qualities from their practitioners, namely observation and appreciation of nature. As a scientist, I am sometimes frustrated when the word *creativity* is often applied only to the "creative arts," as if science does not need creativity. I define *creativity* here as being able to see something in a way that no one else has before, although many may have been exposed to the same thing and often. Those of us who are scientists recognize that in this sense, what separates the truly great scientists from the rest of us is their creativity in exploring the natural world.
>
> The process can produce much in science that is truly beautiful (e.g., the structure of crystals, the double helix of DNA, the exquisite blend of structure and function of tissues). The application of scientific knowledge also leads to much that is beautiful in art. Although the artists may not know the physics or chemistry of pigment production or metalwork, they are practicing physics and chemistry. The effects of temperature on matter is another factor that impacts on much that is considered art.
>
> What separates science from the creative arts, in my mind, is what those in the different areas do with their observation, appreciation, and expression. In art, there is the license to interpret phenomena in a subjective, personal manner that does not necessarily reflect or represent reality. Science *must* necessarily reflect or represent reality. Hence, our hypotheses or interpretations must change if further investigation yields information that refutes original ideas. In science, these lead to the desire to find explanations for what exists in an objective, testing manner open to change as we come to new knowledge.
>
> If we define *creativity* as producing something that is not there before we create, can science and art be considered to diverge here? I don't think so: even here, new

understanding is created by scientific inquiry. While in science, the new understanding may not be visual, it is therefore still creative.

As to the question of whether bonsai is art, I agree with those who believe it is both the application of science and also art. When I went with you and others to Cornell University that year, and we were addressed by professors of horticulture (and in turn we taught them something of bonsai), I was struck by the fact that bonsaists seemed to offer them more information than they could offer us. This is, I believe, because scientists have to play by the rules of the scientific method, while bonsai artists can accept empirical knowledge, such as the consistency of soil, the amount of water, the types of wire used, etc., without having to explain it—as long as it works!

Yet we are practicing applied scientific knowledge in our care of the trees. We are also imitating reality in the styles of bonsai (e.g., windswept, twin trunk, formal upright, etc.), which comes from observation of natural tree forms resulting from the forces of climate, temperature, etc. In this sense, bonsai does fit the definition of *science* that is "the knowledge to recognize actuality." But we are taking license to shape a plant into a form and size that it would not naturally take unless it were to be exposed to those forces, and even then, it would not achieve the elegance of form that you can produce by your artistic eye and talent.

Carole Gilbert commented, "Some bonsai, particularly yours, are partially an improvement over nature." We produce an image that is, to us, beautiful. Scientific knowledge, as mentioned before, is not always visually beautiful or visual at all. But this may be only due to our limitations in technology that does not allow us to see what is there. I think of recent tunneling electron micrographs of DNA molecules that showed last year it is indeed a double helix, some forty years after its structure was first deduced through modeling by Watson and Crick.

As you have recognized, there is much that overlaps science and art, and much of both categories applies to Bonsai. But even as an art, bonsai is unique because each work is a living organism and continues to develop, whereas painting and sculpture are what they are when done. Perhaps in the long run, we should not try to categorize at all. Art, like beauty, is truly in the eyes of the beholder. For example, I also see art and beauty in athletic endeavors. While not many would categorize a soaring, perfect golf shot as art, I would, and it was the application of science that produced the club and ball (and a perfect swing) that created that perfect shot.

Along these lines, as you wrote, art has become broad in scope and definitions, and it should be. I would agree with you entirely that "art is the result of the human creative impulse for beauty." Its implementation may require the application of scientific knowledge.

This stream-of-consciousness response to your request for a comment on the question of bonsai as art is probably redundant and rambling and very different from other comments you may have received. In the end, is bonsai an art? Absolutely to those of us who find it a creative outlet. I do know that I defy anyone to stand before your creations and feel they are not art!

Always, Anna

I never entered bonsai competitions, as did my fellow Yoshimura students, because I could not afford the extra time it took to prepare trees for competition. But also, I did not need for others to judge my work. If I liked what I did—and even more, if Mr. Yoshimura praised my trees—that was all I needed.

When we moved to a retirement community in North Carolina in 2009, I had to relinquish my collection. A young man who wanted to go into the business of bonsai bought some of my trees, and I donated the others to the Yama Ki Bonsai Society, which Mr. Yoshimura organized in the 1970s. Having trained my oldest tree, an Alberta spruce, for thirty years and others for one or two decades, I could not stop some tears from flowing as my trees were driven off. But I knew they would be in good hands.

Now I will go back to the trip in Japan. One incident that happened in a hotel elevator in Tokyo has been etched in my memory because it was so comical and, at the same time, embarrassing. David, our boys, and I were in the elevator, along with a handful of Japanese men, going to our room.

Not long after the elevator started to rise, Mike, our eight-year-old, turned to me and, in a loud stage whisper, said, "Mom! I'm taller than all these men!"

The polite Japanese, all of whom I'm sure understood English, never moved a muscle. Actually, Mike was right!

We spent about a week in Tokyo. It was the boys' first trip to the Far East and their first meaningful trip out of the United States. We had gone to the World's Fair in Quebec when they were five and six years old. The trip to Japan was their first exposure to populations that were, like us, Asian, and I was curious to see their reactions.

They were cognizant of the environment. Ben said to me one day, "Gee, Mom, they all look like us!" He did not express any joy or concern about that; he simply accepted it as fact. One thing that annoyed him was a consequence of the language barrier. Neither David nor I spoke Japanese. One day I took the boys to a McDonald's fast food restaurant to get them hamburgers for lunch. Ben disliked having pickles and veggies in his hamburger, so I used what words I knew to order just a plain hamburger.

Typically, the young woman taking the order nodded and said, "*Hai*," which is an affirmative response.

When the hamburger was brought out, it had both veggies and pickles in it, and Ben was upset. As he took the offensive things out, he was further upset by the fact that other patrons seemed fascinated by his actions. "What are they looking at?" he muttered angrily.

I realized that the polite Japanese hated to say no or "I don't understand you" and found it easier to say, "Hai," and go about their business as usual. At that time, food for tourists in the hotels and other restaurants was expensive. I was floored that the hamburger cost me nearly ten dollars and a cup of coffee cost five dollars. That was in the 1970s.

One of the places I took the boys on that trip was Kyoto. We took a short cruise on the Sea of Japan to reach Kyoto. I was astonished to hear the guide say that it was a dead sea, having been so fished out they did not think there was any marine life left in the sea. I found it incredible that the people of Japan ate so much seafood. No wonder my brother Solan, who enjoyed deep-sea fishing near Long Island, once said that when boats returned from a day of fishing, Japanese buyers were waiting on the docks to buy tuna and other prized fish with cash. The fish were then quickly flown to Japan.

Kyoto was lovely, with beautiful gardens as only the Japanese could have designed them. One park we were taken to had a beautiful lawn of moss. It was green and lush, and our guide mentioned that when the Americans came in after the end of World War II, they dug the moss lawn all up, not recognizing the beauty of the growth. David joined us as his meetings concluded.

We saw some beautiful gardens and a palace in Kyoto with singing floors. A diagram on the wall showed how the floors had been constructed so that no intruder could enter the palace without alerting the guards, as stepping on the floors produced creaks. It was a castle in the days of samurai warriors. The emperor who stayed in the castle at that time ordered the floors be built so that an intruder could not step anywhere without creating a creaking noise. We saw a diagram that showed complex engineering, and we ourselves could hear the floors creak. The boys thought it was fun that no matter what they did, the creaking would take place.

From Kyoto, we flew to Taipei, the capital of Taiwan, to visit David's two youngest brothers, Albert and Charlie. One impression our young sons got out of the trip to Japan and Taiwan was their surprise to be in an environment where most people they encountered were Asian. I think being somewhere where we were no longer minorities gave them self-confidence.

I also was happy to see that some of our distant relatives had children close to the ages of my sons. I wondered how they would get along since language was a barrier. It turned out that most of the Chinese children we saw knew a few words of English, which was taught in primary schools. Between those few words and sign language, the children got along famously. Friendships were formed easily and quickly. David had a good reunion with his brothers and other relatives.

We did not stay long, but one memorable experience for one of our boys, Ben, occurred when his father took him for a haircut. In a typical Taiwan barbershop, men are given a shampoo and a scalp massage as well as a cut.

Our number-one son was at a stage of life—nine years old—when he disliked being touched, much less massaged. David said he could not help chuckling when the female barber began to wash Ben's hair and massage his scalp. He said Ben kept shriveling down in the chair until he was almost prone. When Ben returned from the traumatic experience, he grumbled that he had a headache. The trip was not long, but it gave our young sons an awareness of their Asian heritage, something that later trips were to reinforce.

At that time, in the 1970s, we could not see my uncle Young Marshal and my aunt, who were incarcerated in a house outside of Taipei. However, after Chiang Kai Shek and his son, Chiang Jin Guo, both had died, we were able to see Uncle after a trip to China in 1988.

Fig 126 Mr. Yoshimura creating a Japanese garden

Fig 127 My first bonsai, an Alberta Spruce

Chapter 46

ACADEMIA POLITICS AND ANOTHER TRIP TO ASIA

Choosing teaching over a career in research was, for me, the right choice to make. I enjoyed working with young people, and while instructors were not paid during the summers, having the three months free to spend with my family was wonderful. The flip side of the coin from enjoyable teaching was academic politics, which both irritated me and caused conflict with some of my colleagues who seemed to enjoy pursuing their own political goals. First, there was the campaign to unionize the faculty of Montclair State.

I voted against the campaign because I felt that intelligent, highly educated people should be able to come to terms on anything—a pretty naive belief. Not so! The potential of belonging to the American Federation of Teachers, or AFT, which would add power to the faculty in negotiating contracts and salaries, was too tempting to refuse, and the AFT was voted in. One percent of every faculty member's salary would be withdrawn from his or her paycheck as the fee for membership.

I did not mind paying to support efforts to improve our salary levels and benefits, but I did not like having no input into how else the union would spend the money. For example, the union contributed to the campaigns of politicians whom I did not necessarily support. Also, strikes were called that I knew would hurt students the most. Lost class time would not be made up in any way, and lost class time was lost knowledge.

The first time the leaders of Montclair State's union called a strike, they invited all departments to make suggestions for alternative ways we could achieve our goals without a strike. The biology department faculty got together and hashed out a way we thought could bring the president and other management people together with faculty that would obviate the need for a strike.

We tapped our six-foot-four electron microscopist, who had a booming voice, to be the one to present our ideas at the next union meeting. To our surprise and resentment, the newly elected president of our local union castigated the department by saying we were trying to undermine the union's strike order.

"But didn't you invite faculty to come up with ideas that would allow us to reach our goals without a strike?" someone asked.

The answer was a nonanswer: "The membership and council have voted to have a strike, and your department is not helping us to be successful."

It was then that I realized the strike was really for the sake of the union and not for getting better salaries or benefits for the faculty. I was disappointed; many in the department were embarrassed and resentful. Further, when the strike was underway, I had to cross our picket lines to feed and water my mouse colony. That was unpleasant. The more belligerent faculty thought I was acting as a scab, someone who on her own was ignoring the strike. They were ready to attack and be intimidating. When I explained why I needed to get to the animal room, they relented and let me through.

As time went on, most of us simply withdrew from doing anything for the union. However, two of our department's faculty, those who seemed to enjoy conflict, chose to become active in the union. I think they were probably just as glad that we were submitting to whatever edict the union put forth.

While I deplored the need for strikes and some of the other activities of a union, I have to give credit to the union for indeed improving our salaries and benefits. Further, the availability of union lawyers provided faculty with legal expertise that would not have been there otherwise. A few years later, I personally benefitted by just the presence of legal help from the union, something I will discuss later in the chapter.

Another aspect of academic politics was in the decisions made about the curriculum of every department. I had noticed in reading statistics about students who did not graduate from Montclair State and transferred out that the students who left were not only students who could not handle college-level courses. A significant number were Montclair State students who had high grade point averages—our better students. They were students we expected to retain until graduation. The university curriculums should have made them interested in staying with us.

I brought the issue to the attention of the president of Montclair State at the time, Donald Walters. After my meeting with Dr. Walters to discuss the need to address the problem, he asked me to chair a committee of faculty members from different departments to come together to confer about the value of such a program for Montclair State students and to develop a College Honors Program. We decided it should be a program that would begin in a student's freshman year and carry through to graduation, with special courses, seminars, and requirements for College Honors students regardless of their majors.

My committee had a mix of veteran and relatively young professors, all of whom were enthused about the idea of a College Honors Program that would be effective at a state institution such as Montclair. We looked at the honors programs of many colleges and adopted some aspects from them. We also realized the program would give various departments in the different schools the opportunity to develop interdisciplinary courses.

In the School of Mathematics and Sciences, for example, I invited a chemistry professor and a physics and astronomy professor to meet with me to talk about an interdisciplinary seminar in the sciences that would be given to all students in the program. We were excited by the prospect of teaching such a course. A number of other departments in other schools also had fun developing an interdisciplinary approach to their subjects.

We eventually wrote up the following seminar description:

> In the first semester, natural and physical phenomena are explored with the goal of exposing students who are not necessarily science majors to methodology and critical analysis of the sciences. Theories on the origin and evolution of the universe, the planets, and life on earth will be covered in that order. Topics such as those that have no final scientific explanations or end points are included so that beyond learning facts and theories, we want students to become acquainted with the process that is science.
>
> In the second semester, armed with knowledge about the natural world covered previously, students are led in an exploration of our planet. Resources, what we have, and how we find and manage them are discussed. The latter part of the semester will introduce new technologies and ethical concerns raised by new technologies, such as genetic engineering.

We also required honors students to do research in their chosen fields once they decided on a major. In their senior year, they were asked to do a research project under the guidance of a major professor and write a thesis on their project. Honors students from all areas would be asked to give presentations of their work at a symposium that would be open to the general student body and faculty.

When we presented the completed College Honors Program (CHP) to Dr. Walters, after reading it, he said, "It knocked my socks off!"

I had to defend the program to the board of trustees, not only because of the expense of the program but also because some felt such a program was too elitist for a public institution with a wide range of student capabilities. One of the trustees brought up that concern.

I countered with this argument: "Nobody minds when our best athletes are given special treatment, even full scholarships. But when our best students are given some special treatment, then it is elitist. To my mind, students in a college honors program are varsity learners." Out of the corner of my eye, I saw Dr. Walters nod and smile.

Further, we included in the program a mechanism by which students who might not have qualified for the program as entering freshmen could, even up to entering their junior year, apply for entry to the College Honors Program if their record at Montclair State showed improvement in their academic performance. Another member of the board said, "You know what colors the students invited into the CHP will be predominantly, don't you?"

I thought, *I would guess that you are saying there will be more white and Asian students than African American students. Perhaps, but again using sports as an analogy, do you object to basketball teams that are mostly black? There is absolutely no discrimination against students for any reason. They simply have to qualify. I submit that placing students whose preparation is not adequate to allow them to assimilate into the CHP right away is a disservice to them. It will make them feel inferior if they stumble and fail to keep up their grades as required.*

Although I did not voice those thoughts, I did wonder if the board members had overlooked the fact that I was a person of color also. Why would I allow discrimination against other people of color?

The CHP was passed unanimously by the board and implemented for the first entering class as soon as participating professors were given time to organize their courses and order lab materials. I was invited to be in charge of the program from its beginning. However, I had been approved earlier for a year's sabbatical and had arranged to spend it at the Roche Institute of Molecular Biology (RIMB) to learn new techniques with Dr. Michael I. Sherman. The RIMB was only ten minutes away from Montclair State. Reluctantly, I had to decline running the CHP. It was gratifying enough for me to know the program was in existence.

One day shortly after the CHP was approved, I was on a committee that was to meet with President Walters. Usually careful to be on time for meetings, Don arrived late. He apologized and sat down at the head of the table. "Sorry, folks!" he said, chewing. "Been really busy this morning."

Then he did something that astonished everyone: he raised his feet up onto the table and, eating a muffin, spilled crumbs over the front of his shirt. That was unlike Don Walters, who was usually immaculately dressed and formal at meetings where he presided. Nothing much was said, and the meeting was quickly terminated by the provost, who was as shaken as the rest of us were at the president's behavior.

The early ending of the meeting did not seem to bother the president. He only said, "Sorry to have brought you here, but that happens sometimes."

After the president left the room, the provost said, "I'm going to find out what's going on, and I will let you all know."

We left in somber silence, knowing that something was terribly wrong. Soon after that, an announcement was made to the college that President Walters had been diagnosed with an inoperable brain tumor. It was aggressive, and he died just a few months later. I was saddened by the sudden turn of events. He had been so supportive of the College Honors Program. I felt he was an ally in my holding firm on standards of education.

His wife invited me to give a eulogy at a ceremony honoring him at the college. I was choked up while giving it, which surprised me since our relationship had been only a working one. I guess I felt that he and I were so much on the same page when it came to academic policies that I was saddened at the loss of a fine administrator and leader. If memory serves me, I believe he did not live to see the CHP initiated at Montclair State.

Later, in the 1980s, when I was invited to serve on the board of directors at Sweet Briar College, at meetings for strategic planning, I initiated talks while chairing the Academic Affairs Committee to develop a College Honors Program for my alma mater. I also insisted that the science curricula and requirements needed to be more rigorous. The degree for science majors was a bachelor of arts. I strongly advocated that a second degree, a bachelor of science degree, be developed with more rigorous requirements for graduation.

Such rigor was not something all faculty at Sweet Briar agreed with. The then chair of the biology department argued vehemently with me against it. "It will scare students from majoring in biology," she said.

I disagreed with her. "You underestimate our students," I said. "If Sweet Briar is to be considered one of the top women's colleges, comparable to Wellesley and Radcliffe, for example, or Barnard, we have to have decent science programs."

I am pleased to say I was right. In some years of the first decade of this millennium, I was told biology had the most majors of any subject at Sweet Briar. The new faculty hired for the sciences after that year of strategic planning instituted summer research programs for students that are popular and productive. Both an honors program and a BS degree were adopted for the college, and now there is even an engineering degree program available.

If I have done nothing else worthwhile in my life, the two honors programs and the increased rigor at Sweet Briar in the science programs for a BS degree are my lasting contributions. (Later, I also endowed a scholarship at Sweet Briar to help young women from Asia attend the historic, small liberal arts and sciences college. I named it the David and Anna Chao Pai Scholarship.)

In the 1980s, a few years after the College Honors Program had its first students at Montclair State, I personally benefitted from the presence of the union on campus. The incident happened when I taught the biology part of the Science Honors Seminar for students of the CHP. One of the students was an older woman who looked to be well into her twenties and perhaps early thirties. She spoke with an accent and dressed every day as if she were going to a cocktail party after school. She sat in a front-row seat and seemed to hang on my every word.

My section was the last section of the seminar, and the exam I gave contained three essay questions. That student—I will call her Marta—disappointed me by answering only two of the three questions. She spent too much time on the other two by incorporating many facts that were irrelevant to the questions. One of my least favorite tactics used by students on exams was putting in all kinds of information covered in class in hopes that somewhere in the hodgepodge was the answer to the question. I gave Marta a C for my part of the seminar, which brought her grade down to a B for the course.

During my office hours one day, I heard a tapping on my door and opened it to find Marta there with a man. "I need to talk to you about my grade in the Science Honors Seminar, Dr. Pai. This is my husband, Grigory. He is a lawyer."

Some warning bells sounded in my head at the information that he was a lawyer. Why would I want to know his occupation? I should have asked him to wait for us elsewhere, but instead, I allowed them both to come into my office.

She tearfully proceeded to plead her case for a better grade. "Dr. Pai, I am afraid that I will not be able to get into law school after I graduate because I have this B on my record. I just ran out of time; I did not skip a question because I didn't know the material. I put in a lot of effort on the first two questions."

"Marta, you had as much time as everybody else in the class," I answered. "You put too much into your answers to the first two questions. Much of it was irrelevant to the questions, and I disregarded what was not relevant. You did not even touch the third question. I really should have given you a D, not a C, on the exam. If this is your only B, I strongly doubt it will block your acceptance to law school."

While she and I were talking, her husband was walking around my office and looking at cartoons I had put up that I either had received from students or had found that commented on education with tongue in cheek. In one, there was a drawing of two people wrestling on the floor. The legend said, "To my students, give up now; I'm always right."

With an oily smile, he asked me, "Is this your teaching philosophy, Dr. Pai?"

"Well, I've never really wrestled with any students, but in science, answers are usually right or wrong," I said.

"What do you think about tenure, Dr. Pai? I think it allows poor teachers to hang on like dead wood," he said with a smirk, with his face close to mine.

Now I am mad! "I don't like tenure and have said so. It may allow some undeserving educators to hold on to their jobs, but I'm pleased to say there is no dead wood in our department. But should you think that someone is defective as an educator, there is a procedure by which people may complain about someone with tenure. I'm not sure what the steps are, as I've never been complained about in twenty years of teaching. You can start by asking the chair of the department."

I opened my office door and pointed to the chair's office. Grigory grabbed Marta's elbow and made a show of going to the chair to complain. Marta had wiped her tears and looked smug that Grigory, she hoped, was putting me on the defensive.

As they walked down the hall, I had a sudden brainstorm and called after them with my arms crossed. "If you seriously plan to complain and request my dismissal, please let me know so that I can get in touch with my union lawyers. Also, give me your address so they may get in touch with you."

At those words, they stopped in their tracks. Marta looked questioningly at Grigory, who half turned to face me. "Oh, union lawyers, eh?" he asked with a smirk. The unctuous man then pushed Marta on the back to start walking again, this time to the exit. I knew I would never hear from them again. Unfortunately, they were not the only ones to use various claims to hopefully convince me to change a grade to a higher one in my twenty-eight years of teaching at MSU. I always understood the gravity of being a grade giver and always tried to give the best grade I could, but I always felt that grade inflation was a professional lie.

I was promoted to associate professor in 1976 and to full professor in 1985. When I retired in 1997, I was given the honorary title of professor emerita. In the twenty-eight years I taught at Montclair State, nobody in the biology department ever had anyone activate the procedure for their dismissal.

Chapter 47

Administration and a Monumental Failure

In the spring of 1978, several colleagues approached me and asked me to submit my name for election to chair of the biology department to begin in fall 1979. Three of our newer faculty were to be applying for tenure that year. They said they felt they had the best chance to get tenure if I were chair. The problem was that if all three received tenure, then the department would have 100 percent tenured faculty, a situation we knew the administration would not allow. We all pretty much knew that at most, only two of the three would be tenured.

I could not refuse my friends' request and became chair during a difficult time for the department. When there was a departmental problem and a case was to be presented for the consideration of administrators, my colleagues often called on me to give arguments on behalf of the department. I always thought it was ironic that an immigrant for whom English was a second language was considered a better speaker than the natives.

The three candidates for tenure were all worthy, in my mind, to be tenured. I even tried to give up my tenure so all three could be retained for the department and for our students. When I asked about the possibility of giving up my tenure, I was told that by law, I could not.

I was particularly worried about one of the candidates, who I thought was one of the two top ones but whom, I had heard, was not liked by the provost. Jim was young, bright, knowledgeable, and direct and might have at some point stepped on the toes of the provost when the provost was the dean of the School of Mathematics and Science, of which the biology department was a large part.

At that time, the administration paraded a new policy called shared governance before the faculty at large, indicating they were open to opinions about policy from us and wanted our participation in governance. While it sounded good to faculty, few believed our opinions would carry equal weight in administrative deliberations. We were right.

I pleaded with our new dean, a member and former chair of the chemistry department, to help me bring Jim's case to the provost and board of trustees. He said he would do everything he could, but I saw little evidence of anyone arguing in favor of retaining all three candidates. The possibility that the decision had already been made was clear to me after a meeting of the board of trustees supposedly before they were to consider tenure for candidates.

I asked a board member I knew from another meeting for help, as she seemed to be sympathetic to faculty concerns about Jim's chances.

She turned to me and, in a low voice, said, "Do you understand that if your department is all tenured, you will not get another tenure line for the next ten years? That's how long we think it will be before one of your senior faculty will retire."

I had no reply. The students also organized a small demonstration to show support for Jim. I knew it would be futile but decided to let them proceed. It would give Jim a small measure of satisfaction in knowing he had support from his colleagues and his students. I knew he would be denied tenure anyway, and he was. I was happy to write Jim a strong letter of recommendation, and he was soon hired by the Environmental Protection Agency at a nearby office.

I felt I'd failed Jim, but I told myself that nobody as chair could have saved him the job that he loved and did well. I thought bitterly about the fact that the administration had decided for the department whom to keep and who should leave. The term *shared governance* made me nauseous. Who should know each professor the best? The answer in anyone's rational mind had to be the department chair. Yet I had no say in the decision.

It was a tough time for me because before I was elected chair, a representative from the publisher Prentice-Hall had asked if I would be interested in writing a textbook on genetics for biology majors. They knew about *Foundations of Genetics*, which I had written for non–science majors, published by McGraw-Hill, which had sold well.

I knew the project would be more time-consuming than *Foundations* because more technical information should be in the textbook than for nonmajors, but my experience with McGraw-Hill had been so smooth and the editors had been so helpful that I assumed the people at Prentice-Hall, a well-known publisher of textbooks, would be equally helpful. The representative assured me that would be the case when I was hesitant about accepting their invitation to publish.

I began writing right away at nights and on weekends, and when I became chair, there was still a lot more to do. To write a textbook, it is necessary often to use illustrations from previous publications. As an author, I had to write for permission to the publisher and to the person whose paper or book contained the illustration I wanted to use in my book. Often, permission was granted gracefully, and others required payment.

A friend in the math department agreed to write the chapter on the use of statistics in genetic studies. I will not go into the gory details, but the production editor we were assigned was less than helpful. She pressured me into agreeing to publish in 1981, when she did not yet have the illustrations ready for me to proofread. However, because my McGraw-Hill editors had been so astute and helpful, I decided to trust the

PH production editor because I was ensconced in the tenure problem and other problems for the biology department. That was a big mistake.

When the book came out in 1981, it looked good. The cover was better than the cover for *Foundations*, so I was pleased. However, when I began using the book, I was horrified to note how many mistakes it had, all but one in the illustrations. I notified Prentice-Hall and my coauthor. Had that situation happened to me alone, I could have handled it better, but knowing that a friend's name was on the book also put me into a deep depression.

That was the worst thing that had ever happened to me in any aspect of my life, but knowing that Helen's reputation was also tarnished was the most painful part. I apologized to her deeply, and she was gracious in her reply since she too knew of the recalcitrance of our production editor. After the first semester of using the book, I wrote the chief editor about all the mistakes, and Prentice-Hall removed the book from sale.

It gave me little relief to know the production editor had been fired. All along, she had delayed doing her job on the manuscript. Then, at times, she'd asked for additions to the book suddenly. For example, one day she'd suddenly asked for an index at the end of the book. An index is a crucial part of any textbook, but for some reason, she'd insisted I prepare it in two days. A good, thorough index for my book would have taken a week to prepare.

What a difference there was between my experience with McGraw-Hill and my experience with Prentice-Hall. Of course, I had been naive in thinking that because the first experience was so good, the second would be too. Even before she demanded an index in two days, I had written to the chief editor at PH to ask for his help in persuading her to work better with us. He'd assured me he would speak with her, but if he had, he'd spoken to someone with deaf ears.

With the confluence of my inability to tenure all three of my colleagues and the failure of the book I had worked on for countless hours at nights and on weekends, I understood why some patients with clinical depression could no longer face life. I'd lost so much face that the pain was almost suffocating. What reputation I had established with my first book was blown out of the water by the second book.

I could not talk to my parents about the matter. First of all, I was not sure they would have understood the depth of the problem, and secondly, I did not want them to have to bear the burden of my problem. The only person in the family I could talk to about the issue was David. He knew how I felt.

Looking back on that episode now, I can equate my reaction to that which Mommy experienced when she failed her English course at the United Nations and her name and grade, along with those of others who'd taken the course, were posted. I can understand now, Mommy.

The car radio was, as usual, tuned to a news talk station as I drove home in a daze after discovering the mistakes in the book. I felt humiliation I had never felt before, and I felt crushed by failure I'd never before experienced. A voice on the radio penetrated my mental fog. It declared that if high achievers experienced devastating failure and survived, they would become stronger.

It was as if someone were talking to me through the radio! I felt goose bumps developing on my arms, and the hair on the back of my neck stood up. I felt a sense of relief that others had fallen as hard as I had and still had continued their lives and been productive.

Was there a force that, in fact, knew who I was and what had been done to me? Was the reporter on the radio addressing my traumatic experience directly? The coincidence was too great and too true to have been coincidence alone. But what else could it have been? I told David about the experience, and he was as questioning about it as I was.

Even remembering the incident makes my goose bumps reappear.

I told my new colleague, who'd been hired to also teach genetics when the number of biology majors rose to six hundred, not to use my textbook, and I explained why. The word no doubt spread throughout the department and also the rest of the school. I decided I would not hide from colleagues. While I had made a terrible mistake, I would try to be better in what I did.

I was the one to request that Prentice-Hall remove my book from sales. They gave the copyrights to the book back to me, though I did not pursue the corrections. I have a copy of the book, and it remains my biggest disappointment in life. Not a single person ever brought the subject of my book up to me. My coauthor and colleague was gracious in her response to my apologies to her. I was deeply grateful. It made recovery possible and easier.

Chapter 48

CORGIS AND GOLF

Another reason my recovery was possible was my decision to mate our young female corgi to her breeder's stud dog. Rusty, our first Pembroke Welsh corgi, had died on the operating table of the vet in Livingston. He'd had a tumor in his abdomen removed, and the vet caring for him at Livingston Veterinary Hospital called and said he had to operate again to check a kidney that might have been infected. At that time, Rusty was eleven years old, and our old friend could not take another operation. The sad part was that there was no kidney infection. I could not help wondering if he could have recovered and lived if the vet had not operated again.

When they carried him from me before the operation, Rusty gave me a look I will never forget. He never had liked to go to a vet, and he didn't like it that day. He looked back at me and gave me a long, pleading look to take him back. I wish I had followed my instincts to say I'd changed my mind about another operation for him. At dinner that night, we were all sad. It was my sons' first encounter with the death of someone they'd cared for. Dina, the boys, and I were all in tears. David finally said, "Okay, I can't stand all these tears. Tomorrow we'll go visit the breeder if she has any puppies available."

He surprised me. David had imposed strict limitations on Rusty. He could enter only certain rooms in the house, mainly the rooms with wood flooring and no carpets, and he was not allowed on any furniture or in any of the bedrooms. Remember that David only reluctantly had given me permission to get a dog, since he never had had dogs in his house in China.

He would pet Rusty occasionally with the back of his hand but would immediately wash his hand if he had to touch Rusty with the palm of his hand. When his sister Patsy came to visit, anyone who touched the dog would be shooed to the bathroom to wash his or her hands right afterward.

David's aversion to touching dogs was also shared by some of our Chinese American friends. One friend, Nancy, whom I mentioned earlier, was a marketing executive with General Foods. When she came to our house to visit, we had to keep Rusty in the kitchen. She was not alone among our Chinese friends. Their upbringing and, of course, personal likes and dislikes were the reasons for their reluctance to touch our dog. One day Nancy told us she had been given a dog food account to market. I laughed and told her it was retribution.

To someone like me, who had grown up with dogs and had dogs sleeping in bed with me, the avoidance of being contaminated with a dog's germs was strange. But I didn't make a fuss about it because I didn't want to push David to saying no dogs at all in the house. Dina and our sons were as fond of Rusty as I was, so we were all happy that David had decided he would accept another corgi in the house.

One day a coworker of David's at Foster Wheeler came to our house for the first time. He had heard about my bonsai trees and wanted to see them. He had read that miniaturization of trees required pruning and, at times, the cutting of roots. He was a man with a great sense of humor, and when he saw Rusty, he exclaimed, "You bonsaied your dog!"

When we first got Rusty, corgis were not common pets in the United States. One day I took him for a walk in a park not far from home. We passed two senior ladies relaxing on a bench who were obviously interested in Rusty.

As we walked away, I heard one of the ladies say, "Well, I know he's half dachshund, but I don't know what the other half is!"

That lady was more correct than she knew. Corgis, dachshunds, and English bulldogs all have a mutation of their legs almost identical to the mutation in humans for chondrodystrophic dwarfism. Scientists have compared the leg bones of human dwarfs with those of the three dog breeds, and the problems are the same. One difference is that dogs can inherit copies of the mutations from both parents and still be born alive. In humans, having two copies of the mutation is a lethal situation. All the living human chondrodystrophic dwarfs have just one copy of the mutation, which is dominant in humans.

I believe the corgi breed has gained in popularity. It is a wonderful breed, as the queen of England knows. As a working dog, it is smart and trainable, a big dog in a small package. I have never had a corgi chew on furniture or shoes, as have other breeds that friends and relatives have had. Except for our current corgi, Pierce, whom I will speak about later, none of my other five corgis ever gave me any trouble in the house. They are loving but not cloying like lap dogs. A few minutes of contact is enough until they are ready for more, and they'll let you know when they are ready. They do not like to be held around the neck but love tummy rubs. I like that their big necks and chests (for small dogs) give them a loud bark. See again figure 124. They sound like large dogs when they bark at a noise they hear outside the house, so they're good watch dogs. A corgi's neck is so thick with hair that a normal collar would slip right over its head, so I chose to use a harness over a choke collar for all my dogs.

When Rusty died, luckily, the breeder had a lovely little female available for sale, but she asked me not to spay her, as she thought there was potential the puppy might develop into a corgi with show qualities. Muffin was one of my best dogs. Muffin was smart, gentle, and loving. In fact, of the six corgis we've had, she was the only one that would chase and retrieve a tennis ball.

The other corgis showed us they were herders, not retrievers. Some of them chased a ball and then just left it; others didn't bother chasing a ball. However, rather than chasing the ball, in dog parks, my corgis all chased the dogs that chased the ball. It was interesting to me that their instincts were clearly those of dogs that chased and herded cattle in Wales by nipping at their heels. Their short legs were of advantage so they could drop to the ground quickly if the cattle kicked back at them. They definitely do not have retriever instincts.

When Muffin did develop into a good-looking corgi, she was mated with one of the breeder's stud dogs, and the deal we struck was that the breeder would get the pick of the litter. I decided to agree because a corgi puppy, even in 1981, cost $700. I thought breeding was a good way to earn some money on the side.

One of my colleagues at Montclair State saw Muffin while at a party in my house and fell in love with her. She said she wanted one of the puppies. At one point during the party, we couldn't find her husband—he was in the basement, holding Muffin and playing with her. He too was entranced by my little dog. As she was a friend, I told Bonnie Lustigman and her husband, Sheldon, that I would sell them a puppy at a greatly discounted price, $250. They were delighted.

We had just returned from a week's vacation, when pregnant Muffin began to behave in an unusual manner. That evening, I noticed she was constantly demanding my attention, more so than usual. She also seemed to want contact with me, which self-reliant corgis normally asked for only briefly and then walked away. When I sat on the floor with her, she crawled onto my lap, and I noticed she was trembling.

It's time, I said to myself, and I took her to the laundry room, where we had made a nesting place for her and the puppies on the floor of the closet. We had spread newspaper on the floor, and she started tearing the papers into strips. I told everyone that I would be spending the night in the laundry room with Muffin.

Shortly before midnight, she began to strain, and the first puppy came out. Instinctively, she began to lick at the amniotic sac that was still around the newborn. It was a red-and-white male—a big one too! I had a table lamp in the room, and I turned it on to keep the puppy warm while Muffin gave birth to more. She was so sweet we frequently called her Muffie as a nickname.

In my research with mice and then with my Muffie, I always was struck by how stoic female animals were when giving birth compared to allegedly superior humans, who tended to yell and moan. I have never heard an animal give voice to her pain while birthing. Maybe we just have more pain sensors than they do.

Through the night, she gave birth to five puppies: three females and two males. I only had to help one breathe. I had read in a book about whelping puppies that if one was not breathing, then it was necessary to intervene right away, first jarring the puppy gently and then swinging it around. Greatly worried, I swung the puppy around. It took in a breath. I returned it to Muffin, and she cleaned it up. It was exciting to me that she did so well, because she was only a little more than a year old.

I took the puppies to the breeder a day later, as their tails had to be cropped to follow the standard for Pembroke Welsh Corgis. Cardigan Welsh Corgis all keep their tails. Their faces are not as cute, to my mind, as the Pembrokes'. To crop the tails, the breeder simply twisted a rubber band around the base of each puppy's tail. I was happy it did not seem to hurt the puppies. In two days, the tails withered and simply fell off. I have no idea who decided that Pembrokes should not have tails and Cardigans should, or why.

As young and inexperienced as she was, Muffin was a perfect mother. She had ample milk for all the puppies and left them only to relieve herself outside and to eat. She ate a lot and then immediately turned her attention to her babies. She cleaned them when they relieved themselves by licking their behinds. The puppies were never dirty, nor was their nest (figure 128). Mother Nature is amazing!

The whole family was enchanted by the puppies as they grew and developed personalities. We laughed as they played with each other and tumbled over their mother. Their legs were only an inch long, their ears flopped, and their heads and feet were round (figure 129). They could not have been cuter.

I registered the puppies to prove their lineage, which would allow me to ask full price for the corgis. There is nothing cuter than a Pembroke Welsh corgi puppy, and I had five to play with for a couple of months. Muffin continued to amaze me by knowing when to start weaning the puppies from her milk. She began to feed them less and less by leaving the box they were in, starting when the puppies were around six weeks old.

When the puppies were around seven weeks old, she also began doing something that caused me concern at first: she began pushing one puppy after another, the males only, to the point where they would fight back. I realized she was teaching them to defend themselves. After a week or so, she then turned to the three females and did the same thing. There was no end to my astonishment and respect for how my young pet knew what her children needed from her.

Then the time I dreaded came, and I put an ad in the local newspaper that I had Pembroke Welsh corgis for sale. It did not take long for prospective buyers to begin ringing my phone with queries. I had decided to keep Muffin's firstborn, a red-and-white male we named Radar after Mike's favorite character on the popular television program *MASH*. He was a happy puppy and greeted us with joy every day. One morning, he splashed through the dogs' water dish, which happened to be in front of him, to get to me as fast as possible.

The breeder decided to take one of the red-and-white females. I had my colleague over to choose which puppy she wanted, and she chose one of the two remaining females. The puppy would have mostly red and white hair but perhaps would have some sable hair (red hair with a tinge of black), which is always attractive. She told me she would call her dog Princess, as befitting the kind of treatment she would receive.

The tricolor male (black, red, and white), whom we called Joe, was bought by a retired airline pilot, who sent me a sweet Mother's Day card and wrote that they were delighted with the puppy. I visited them the next year and found the puppy had developed into a handsome adult. He had been trained to bring the man his slippers every night and not to leave the yard, no matter what he saw. Muffie's little boy would not go beyond the boundaries of his yard, even when he saw deer and other wildlife across the street. A few years later, his owner sent me a sad card saying his beloved corgi had died of leukemia.

The last female puppy, who was red and white and whom we called Bo Bo, was bought by a young man who brought his six-year-old daughter with him to see the puppy. The little girl wore a plain homemade dress and was quiet. They did not look well off, and I was not surprised when the buyer said he could not afford to pay me the entire price. He had $150 as a down payment and would send me fifty dollars every month thereafter, he said.

Clearly a knowledgeable corgi lover, he talked about his experience as a corgi owner. He mentioned a kennel I knew, from which his family had obtained a puppy during his childhood. He had always hoped to have another corgi as a pet for his own children. I could not tell him I would not sell him the puppy, and I agreed to the payment strategy. However, I would not give him Bo Bo's papers until they paid in full. The father and daughter took the puppy with happiness on their faces. The little girl held the puppy with affection.

After they left, I worried about my puppy's well-being. If they were so poor, would they be able to give her the kind of food and care I wanted for her? I decided to buy puppy chow and some Mighty Dog beef to take to them the next day. He had given me his address, and as I drove there, I became increasingly worried about Bo Bo.

The road they lived on was in an area in Livingston I had never gone to because there were no stores and only woods. I hadn't even known people lived on that road. Someone had cleared an area where the buyer's house and one other house had been built. I was disturbed to see the shack they lived in. Nobody was there, nor was the puppy. One of the windows had no glass and was covered with fabric. There was a broken tricycle in the yard, but I saw no other signs of inhabitants.

I decided to go to the other house to ask about the family. The thought occurred to me that if I were to be mugged, no one would know where I had gone. But my concern for my puppy rose with every minute I was there, and it propelled me forward.

I left the food at the front door of the buyer's shack and walked to the neighboring shack. There was a white German shepherd mix tied to a tree and barking as I walked to the front door. When I knocked, the door opened, and a grizzled old man wearing a dirty T-shirt answered.

"Excuse me, sir. The people who live next to you bought my puppy, and I brought some food for it. Do you know where they are?" I asked.

The old man shook his head. "I know they gots a puppy, but they seems to have lef', and I dunno where they went to."

I thanked him and returned quickly to my car, confused and with a heavy heart for Bo Bo. I decided to call the man, who had given me his work phone number. He'd said he worked for the telephone company, but as it was the weekend, I had to wait until Monday to call. When I called, I was told that he no longer worked there and had left, and they didn't know where he was. It was clear that the man had planned all this out.

The money was not that important to me; it was the welfare of my Bo Bo I cared about, and to this day, I wonder about my puppy. I decided he struck me as someone who truly loved corgis, and because he seemed poor, I would not go to the police. If he was poor but still somehow had gotten together $150, he would treat the puppy well. I decided to let the problem go and just hoped Bo Bo would have a good life with her new family.

The Lustigmans were happy to have Princess, and they were the antithesis of my experience with the people who'd bought Bo Bo. I called them the day after they took the puppy home.

"How is Princess doing?" I asked.

"Just fine," Bonnie said. "She's eating breakfast with us and loves bagels and cream cheese!"

I laughed and said, "Don't forget to give her puppy chow and Mighty Dog beef like I told you."

"Oh, we will. Just couldn't resist giving her some of our food too."

When Princess was about a year old, Bonnie took her to obedience training because Princess was so smart. After the course was over, there was a final exam for the students to show how well they had learned. Alas, Princess flunked.

"What happened?" I asked in surprise.

"Well, Princess didn't like the instructor and refused to do anything she asked," Bonnie explained. "But we took her home in abject humiliation and ran her through the graduation exercise again. She did everything perfectly!"

"Corgis do have a reputation for stubbornness!" I said, laughing.

I decided after selling the puppies that my idea about using Muffin to supply me with more puppies to sell was not worth the heartache that Dina and I experienced with each sale. We had become so attached to the dogs that I cried as each one was carried away from me. It was fun to have the puppies. It was not fun to lose them.

In 1986, we moved from Wingate Drive to a house three blocks away. The move was precipitated by increasing health problems for my parents, which made us feel they needed to move in with us. Having smoked for more than seventy years, from the time he was twelve years old in China, Daddy had developed serious emphysema. He had quit smoking only in the early 1980s.

Blue had died in the 1970s, at which point Mommy had insisted she wanted to buy two Doberman pinschers for security reasons. We tried to dissuade her from that breed because they were large dogs, and we were worried they could knock her down. But typically, logic lost, and they bought two young pinschers whose ears had been clipped and taped to plastic cups to train them to stand up. Looking at my tiny mother surrounded by two dogs that were almost as tall as she was and had two cups on their heads, I could only shake my head at the comical sight, finding it funny and worrisome at the same time.

Juno and Nobi, named by my father, were gentle dogs who loved my parents. I was relieved the dogs were not rambunctious and did not throw themselves at my aging parents. Another comical sight was when Mommy sat in her wide, couch-like seat to watch television. There was room for one of the dogs to join her. Because the seat was low to the ground so Mommy could sit comfortably, the dog would have its rump on the seat with Mommy and its front legs on the ground, with the hind legs protruding out.

The dogs lived less than ten years, as large dogs are known to do. Mommy's cats also began to die from old age since some of the ones she'd collected from the streets of Chinatown in New York City were probably already fairly old. When they no longer had dogs or cats to care for, we discussed with them the possibility of moving in with us. That was how we came to move to a large house on West Hobart Gap Road.

I first was attracted to the house because it was the only house with a tennis court I had seen in Livingston. David and I were active tennis players at the time, and having a court of our own would be a treat. When I saw that the house was for sale, I mentioned it to David since the Wingate Drive house did not have a ground-floor bedroom and was too small a house for my parents to move into with us.

The large house for sale had four bedrooms on the second floor but also had a bedroom and full bath on the ground floor, right next to the great room. I felt it would be a perfect place for my parents to join us, a ground-floor apartment where they could have the great room as their living room.

Before we bid for the house, we spoke with Mommy and Daddy and pointed out the advantages for them to move in with us. I pushed to the back of my mind my worries about how well Mommy and David could get along in the same house. I knew my husband would try hard to get along but would suffer anxiety and exasperation with my mother.

Mommy and Daddy agreed. We asked our real estate agent to put in a bid for the house, which had been on sale for more than a year. Our bid was accepted, and we were the owners of a house with five bedrooms, three and a half bathrooms, and twelve rooms overall, with nearly two acres of land. Dina and I put in a raised garden, which I knew Mommy would enjoy since she had put a garden in her backyard, where she'd grown cilantro, scallions, and chives.

At that point, Daddy and Mommy changed their minds and decided they would not move in with us.

Our friends all thought we would have been moving into a smaller house because the boys were both in college. "No," I said, "we're moving to a larger house." When I told them why, they joined us in shaking our heads. But as it turned out, buying the house at that time was a good investment. We lived there until our own aging process dictated that we needed to move to a retirement community in 2009.

Over the years, we have had five generations of corgis to date. Muffin lived to be twelve years old. We had to have her put down because she had developed signs of having a brain tumor and was suffering greatly. We were away on vacation, when Dina called and told us about her condition. To this day, I wish I had flown back to be with her when she died. Instead, I had to tell the vet to euthanize her on the phone because David and the family wanted us to stay and finish our week of vacation. Radar lived for another year after Muffin died, and he died also at twelve years of age, of a heart attack.

Dina pushed us to buy corgis again. She promised to stay with us after we retired to care for the dogs. We then bought two more puppies from two different breeders. We bought Gruffy, who was the son of breeder Lois Zelenski's champion female, the top-ranked corgi female in the country. Lois was willing to give Gruffy up because he had a lazy left ear, which would preclude him from being shown, but in every other way, Gruffy was a great-looking corgi. Because we wanted him as a pet and not a show dog, our buying him from Lois was a win-win situation.

Gruffy proved to be one of the smartest dogs we have had. He seemed to understand our moods, and he was a great companion. He had a look that was nothing short of regal. When I sent a picture of him posing to his breeder, Lois wrote that she wondered if she had made a mistake in not keeping him for show.

When he was around ten, the vet discovered that he had a benign fatty tumor near his front legs. An operation to remove it was only partially successful. Eventually, the tumor formed again, and in his later years, it grew to cover his entire chest. It did not seem to be painful, but Rusty had shown us the stoic nature of Pembroke Welsh corgis, so I can only say it did not cause Gruffy to show signs of pain.

Ginger and Gruffy were good companions for each other (figure 130). They played and slept together. If I'd had the stamina, I would have always had two dogs together (figure 131). They kept each other company (figure 132). Dina's being home all day was to their advantage also. She walked them every morning, despite the fact we were living in a house with a fenced-in backyard nearly an acre in size.

One day Ginger found a part of the fence that was raised slightly. Digging under it, she and Gruffy were able to escape the backyard. When we realized they were gone, Dina and I immediately set about to find them. We didn't have to go anywhere for Gruffy—he was on the front porch, asking to get into the house. When Dina went around the corner of our street, she found Ginger upside down on the sidewalk, having her tummy scratched by a policeman. He had seen the dogs in our yard and knew where they belonged. That was the only time our dogs found freedom from the fenced-in yard.

We had to euthanize Ginger when she was eleven because she developed neuromyopathy, a degenerative disease that gradually caused her to become paralyzed. Gruffy, though, was the longest-living corgi we have had. He lived to be sixteen years old. He moved with us from New Jersey to a wonderful retirement community in Davidson, North Carolina, called the Pines at Davidson.

Before we moved, I spread the ashes of the four dogs we'd lost in and around our backyard so their spirits would be in a familiar place. Losing a pet is like losing a cherished member of the family for all of us. Each one had his or her own personality and left us with different memories. I still miss them all.

When David and I attended a friend's wedding out of town in 2013, Gruffy was boarded at a local veterinary hospital he was familiar with. He was fine when we dropped him off, but his sixteen-year-old heart could not last until we returned home. He died the morning of the wedding. It was ironic that the two dogs that were the best dogs, Muffin and Gruffy, both died while we were away. They were good to us till their last days and saved us the terrible experience of seeing them breathe their last. I still choke up when I think about all the dogs that gave us so much love that have gone from our lives.

Now we have our sixth, and likely last, corgi. Lois Zelenski, whose kennel was named Tallyrand Kennels and who sold us Gruffy, of course knew how old Gruffy was. I emailed her when we moved down to the Pines at Davidson. I wanted to tell her how much we loved Gruffy and let her know he was older than any of our previous pets. She told me Gruffy's mother had lived to be sixteen years old, which was how old Gruffy was when he died.

I wanted a smaller dog and emailed her to ask if she had maybe a runt of a litter that she would not keep for show. In 2012, she told me she had a young corgi male who was good looking but had grown so large that she could not show him and would not breed him since his puppies would also likely be too big. She asked if I would consider buying him. He was loving and loved people and other dogs equally, and he was house-trained.

What persuaded me to say yes were the photos she showed me of baby Pierce, whose show name was Tallyrand's Piercing the Darkness (figure 133), and the fact that he was house-trained.

I also had the knowledge that Gruffy had lived to be sixteen. Perhaps longevity genes were in other dogs of hers also. I needed a dog that was not yappy, which corgis were not, and was friendly to everyone, so I bought Pierce. Lois had moved to Washington state from New Jersey and said she would arrange to have him flown to us. She only flew dogs on direct flights for fear of losing them if they had to be transferred from one plane to another. There were no direct flights from Washington to North Carolina, but there was one from Seattle to Atlanta, so that was the arrangement.

Ben, who lives in Charlotte, which is twenty minutes by car from us in Davidson, drove with me to Atlanta to pick Pierce up. The dogs shipped on that plane were to be picked up in a part of the airport that was specifically for animal passengers. It took almost two hours after the due time of arrival for Pierce to finally be delivered. We took him in his crate to a small gated area the airport had for dogs to relieve themselves after the long flight. We estimated that Pierce had been in his crate for seven straight hours.

When we opened the gate of the crate, Pierce emerged and looked to me to have a snakelike body about 20 to 25 percent longer than any Corgi I'd had or seen. He was understandably frightened and recoiled when we tried to pet him. He wouldn't do anything, despite the fact that he must have felt the need to relieve himself because of the long flight. After a while, we decided to load him into the car and leave for home. We figured he would relieve himself during the five-hour drive back.

We stopped three times and walked him each time for about twenty minutes and were astounded that he would not relieve himself in any way. He was active, so I knew he was okay, but I worried about his refusal to yield to nature. I dropped Ben off at his home. When Susan came out to see Pierce and tried to get him to leave his crate, the young dog immediately lay flat and put his head on the floor of the crate, which made us all laugh. It was a movement typical of corgis to protect themselves from being kicked by cattle they were herding. I decided I'd better get him home.

By the time we got him home, I calculated that he had kept himself unrelieved for twelve hours. *This is a unique dog*, I decided. I took him outside, and he still wouldn't do anything, so I let him go back into his crate and closed the door. About a minute later, I heard him crying. I went to him, put on his leash, and took him out again. Finally, he peed—for about five minutes, it seemed! After that, he was quiet to stay in his crate for the night. A walk the next day gave him the chance to do everything.

Pierce, now six, is unique not only because of his size but also because of his personality compared to our other five dogs. He is without a doubt the most loving corgi we've had. Corgis as herders are loving, but unlike lap dogs, they do not allow us to hug them for long. They will just walk away. Pierce sometimes cannot get enough loving and will roll over onto his back or put my hand in his mouth to urge me to continue to pet him. He wants everyone he sees on our walks to pet him and is visibly disappointed if others walk past without acknowledging him. But at times, he will wait five to ten minutes for others to catch up to us, and then, as they bend to pet him, he turns away. I tell them that's a corgi's hello. He is friendly to all dogs we see.

I must say that as we progressed through the years with dogs to replace those who died, David's attitude toward dogs in the house softened completely. Whereas David petted Rusty only with the back of his hand, he would grab Pierce with both hands and even kiss him. Whereas Rusty was allowed only in the rooms without carpeting, from Muffin on, all dogs had free run of the house. I think gentle Muffie had a great deal to do with the change in David toward our dogs. Poor Rusty must be upset in doggie heaven to see all this!

But as friendly and as beautiful as he is, what has impressed us and our family and friends most about Pierce is his intelligence. There is no question Pierce is the smartest—and most devious—corgi we've owned. Unlike the other five corgis, Pierce has actively looked to steal food but only when we are not home. He ate a box of twelve oatmeal raisin cookies once and nearly poisoned himself to death. It was the only time his theft of food made him sick. He ate two-pound boxes of milk chocolate twice and was fine afterward, though chocolate is supposed to be toxic for dogs. He managed to learn how to open a plastic container of his dry food by watching me open the latch that keeps the container closed. He ate so much that I had to take him to an animal emergency room, where they kept him under observation overnight.

I replaced the first container with a larger one that had a recessed screw top. Again, he must have watched me unscrew the top to access the food. To this day, nobody can figure out how he managed to unscrew the top and get into the food again. He had to turn it in the right direction and know to pull the top off. His teeth marks are all around the edge of the top. He survived that event also, though his stomach was stretched amazingly with all the food he ate. We call him our JD, for "juvenile delinquent." From the side, he looks as if he's fat, but he is not. His abdomen wall has been stretched so many times that it dangles.

Pierce has a beautiful face (figure 134). As long as he is, Lois was right in saying his proportions are exactly what a corgi's proportions should be: four to one, length to height. Almost everyone who sees him exclaims over how handsome he is. We agree. He is good at communicating with us through his expressions and body language. He is the only dog we've had who puts his paw on our knee or pokes us when he wants some affection. He's like the trained dogs one sees in movies, only he's doing what comes naturally. He is funny, and we are in love with him—and he knows it!

In the 1970s, Daddy discovered golf, a development that gave him something athletic to do that took him out of the house. He had always been involved in sports—jai alai in China and tennis in the United States. He decided to experiment with golf in the 1970s and got hooked on the sport. It was something he could do by himself, without needing others to play with him. There was a public course not far from where my parents lived in Livingston that charged reasonable fees.

He was so enamored of the sport that he insisted we take it up also. We did, and while it took time for us to really enjoy the sport because we were both so busy at work, eventually, David and I caught the bug as well. Time was a problem because when a round of golf is played, there is usually no time for anything else. It takes a good five hours to play a round on a public course, where they take on too many golfers, meaning players have to wait after every shot before the group in front can move enough to allow them to hit their balls again.

We played with Daddy as much as we had time for. His favorite outfit for golf was white: white pants, a white shirt, and a white hat. I could tell he thought he looked sharp. When we didn't have time to play with him, he would go by himself, and at the public courses, the starter would put him in with a group who needed one more to make up a foursome.

We would ask him, "How did you play, Daddy? Who did you play with?"

Sometimes he was happy with his game, and sometimes he was not. A couple of times, he answered, "They put me with a couple of old guys who were in their sixties." We would smile and point out that he was older than the "old guys."

The game was good for him. When Ben and Mike were old enough to learn the sport, they would go out sometimes with their grandfather. They told us after Daddy died that he allowed them to drive the cart, though they were not supposed to, according to course rules. It was something else my father did to spoil my sons!

My sons were developing well. Physically, they were average in height and weight, which distressed Ben, as he loved playing basketball and wanted to be tall. Both eventually grew to be around five foot nine just like their father. The numerous games the boys were playing, such as baseball and basketball, began to impact our daily schedules. I enjoyed their growing size and strength, as they were able to help me with chores, such as tending to the raised garden we'd put in the backyard (figure 135).

One day Dina, David, and I received an award from Ben and Mike. I no longer remember what induced them to give it, but Ben wrote a citation to us, and both boys signed it. They must have done something and, in thinking about it, decided they had overreacted to chastisement. The award is one of my favorite souvenirs (figure 136).

The boys did well in school, getting mostly As but also Bs. They were in public school through elementary school. Along with a number of neighbors' children, they attended Burnett Hill School, which was within walking distance from our house. In those days, we had no reason to fear letting children walk without adults when they reached a responsible age and could safely cross streets with light traffic. When Ben reached middle school, he attended Heritage Junior High (grades seven through nine), the school directly behind our house. Livingston had only one high school at the time, and Ben enrolled there when he reached tenth grade.

I was pleased that we stayed in Livingston for so long that it really became the boys' hometown, and they both had their own groups of good friends. Ben's friends tended to be the jocks, and they were on the same teams. Mike's friends tended to be more on the nerdy side. But all the close friends of our sons were good kids; there were no ruffians or problems with drugs that we knew of. However, a first parent-teacher meeting at the high school bothered both David and me.

We were speaking to the man Ben had said was his favorite teacher, an English teacher. The teacher said, "Ben is doing well. He gets Bs," but he thought Ben could do better if he didn't read sports books in class.

As an educator, my immediate but silent reaction was *Why don't you take the book away from him? And why are you satisfied with Bs?*

David was also dissatisfied with the teacher's statement. Our reaction no doubt was due to our Chinese upbringing, wherein it was just expected that children would do their best to excel, and we knew Ben was smart enough to get As, especially in English. Ben had taught himself to read when he was not yet four. When his kindergarten teacher first held up a book and asked her class what they thought the book's cover was about, Ben raised his hand and read the title.

We talked about the issue with Ben and told him we felt that his teachers generally accepted that he was doing well as long as he was getting some As and mostly Bs, and we decided Ben needed a school with smaller classes. We looked into a local private school, Newark Academy, and decided to transfer him to the school, which seemed to offer closer supervision of the students. Ben did not want to leave his buddies at Livingston High and pleaded with us to let him stay with them. We told him we wanted him to try NA for a year, and we would assess the situation then. Fortunately, we saw Ben accepted by his classmates and, of course, teammates since he was among the best athletes at the school. He was happy at the school, and by the end of the year, he knew he wanted to graduate from NA. Later, he said to us that he felt going to NA was what allowed him to be accepted early admission to Duke University, his number-one choice of colleges.

When Mike finished Heritage Junior High the year after Ben first attended classes at NA as a day student, we gave him the choice of going to NA or enrolling in Livingston High, and he too chose the private school because he saw what benefits his brother had gained from it. Although he was not on as many varsity sports teams as Ben, though he did play golf on NA's varsity team, Mike too was able to be accepted early admission to his number-one college, Cornell, where he was also able to play varsity golf.

Only once did my mother join Daddy, Mike, and me to play golf. All I remember is a drive she made on a par three. It was a good hit, on the sweet spot of the club head, but unfortunately, she had teed it up and driven it when the foursome in front were just walking halfway to the green. The ball whistled over their heads, and they stopped and turned to look back. We hadn't seen Mommy tee the ball to hit because we were chatting about something. We cringed when we heard the ball hit and apologized profusely to the irate golfers who almost had gotten hit. Without thinking, we turned to tell her not to hit when the front foursome were so close.

She was embarrassed, and Mommy never played again. In retrospect, I wonder what would have happened if we had been more patient in explaining why she had to wait and if Daddy had taken her under his wing to develop as a golfer. I wonder how good she might have been. Both Solan and I were natural athletes, so we probably got our coordination genes from both parents. Not including Mommy in our golf outings was another aspect of life circumstances that might have denied my mother a chance to enjoy something she might have been able to do well.

In the early 1970s, Mommy decided to take English lessons at the United Nations. She had already signed up by the time I heard about it. I was not thrilled about the decision because I felt that learning a language, even one she heard every day when watching television, would be difficult for someone of her age. Also, she was not familiar with being in a classroom and doing homework. However, I was happy she had decided to take up the challenge, and I hoped Daddy would give her all the help she needed. The attempt, however, ended in a disaster for Mommy.

She failed her final exam and the course, and the grades were posted for students to see. However, instead of posting just a student's number, for example, they posted names. When my mother saw that she had been publicly exposed as having failed a course, she suffered a humiliation and loss of face that sent her into depression and seclusion. She was inconsolable, and her reaction was to scream at Daddy and blame him for her embarrassment.

As an educator, I too was upset that names had been posted next to the grades. I was always careful to use only student numbers if I had to post grades. Those who failed the class did not need the stigma of failing. There was nothing I could do except agree with Mommy that the United Nations had handled the grade posting poorly. The incident caused her to slide deeper into paranoia and increased her irrationality.

She must have felt unimaginable pain. She was the daughter of the Old Marshal and the sister of Chang Hsueh Liang, Young Marshal; she'd failed a course in English at her husband's place of work; and her failure had been told to the world. She had brought shame to her family's name. I hoped Daddy would be humane enough to at least try to console her, but their relationship was so antagonistic by then that I wondered if it would be possible. I hoped he did not rub it in.

With both boys going to expensive private colleges, our incomes would be greatly impacted. At the same time, I had developed a course in genetics for nonmajor students at Montclair State. There were no textbooks I could use, as books for biology majors were too technical, so I decided to write such a textbook, which I based on the lecture notes I handed out almost every session. McGraw-Hill had contacted me, and when I told them what I would like to do, they were encouraging. In 1974, the first edition of *Foundations of Genetics* was published, and because it sold well—and thus helped pay for the boys' college expenses—McGraw-Hill published a second edition in 1985.

Fig 128 Muffin and her very young babies

Fig 129 Muffin's babies circa two months old

Fig 130 Gruffy on top and Ginger below

Fig 131 Looking for squirrels

Fig 132 Radar, left, and Muffin play Tug of War

Fig 133 Pierce at 2 months

Fig 134 A happy Pierce

Fig 135 Ben, Mike, and Rusty with the garden in the background

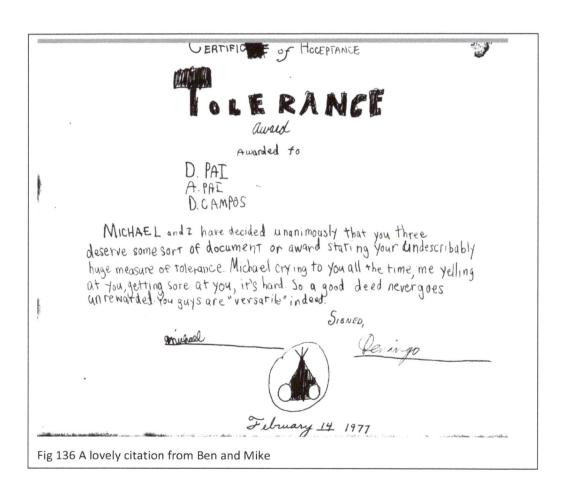

Fig 136 A lovely citation from Ben and Mike

Chapter 49

ISSUES OF HEALTH

After the fun summer of 1982 with the corgi puppies, life became a question mark one fall night after we had gone to bed. As I routinely did every month, I began a self-examination of my breasts, palpating as my gynecologist had taught me. As I expected, I found no problem when I examined my left breast, and I started to examine my right breast with the same expectations. Suddenly, I became alert when I felt something along the periphery of the breast, near my sternum. It felt different from the rest of the breast tissue—it was not soft, but I could move it, so I knew it was not a bone.

My mind began racing. Suppose it was a tumor? But I had just been to my gynecologist two months ago for a checkup, during which the exam always included palpation of my breasts to search for tumors. As usual, he had found nothing wrong. Perhaps it was a piece of dense breast tissue, which often was confused on a mammogram with a tumor. Perhaps it was a cyst and not a solid tumor at all.

I knew I had to see a physician as soon as possible and decided not to tell David or the boys about my concern. It was an important time for Ben because he was a junior in high school, and we had plans to take him to several colleges to see which ones he liked and would apply to. If he knew I had found something strange, it would worry him and perhaps affect the manner in which he interviewed during our visits. I knew I could not let my secret out.

The next day, I called Dr. Todd, my gynecologist, and told him I had found a lump in my right breast. He told me to go see a breast specialist at Columbia Presbyterian Hospital, where my brother Solan was a staff physician. Solan had gone through the medical school program, internship, and residency there. Dr. Todd called the breast specialist to make an appointment and called me back to tell me I should go see him the next day.

In writing my textbook for McGraw-Hill, I had frequently gone to the hospital to use their library. I told David that was the reason I was going to the hospital again. I found the breast specialist to be a wonderful man, caring and gentle. He looked like a middle-aged Huck Finn, with straight gray hair that hung over his forehead. I have forgotten his name, but I will never forget him as a person. He knew Solan and was solicitous with me and tried to assure me that it was probably just a cyst.

"Eighty percent of lumps in the breast are cysts," he said. "I'm going to insert a hypodermic needle into it, and if it is a cyst, we'll see fluid drawing into the needle. Don't worry about pain because breast tissue is so devoid of nerves you won't feel anything except a pinch."

In fact, I hardly felt even a pinch, but I began to worry. Had he drawn fluids, I knew he would have let me know right away. He did not say anything for a couple of minutes.

When he finally spoke, he said, "Hmm, I'm not getting fluid, Anna. I'll send the tissue I've pulled out to the lab and will call you as soon as we know what the situation is."

He did not have to tell me the odds were that what I'd found was a malignant tumor—cancer.

He called me the next morning and gave me the diagnosis: "It is cancer, Anna, but I believe it's so early that the prognosis is very good."

At that moment, when I faced my own mortality for the first time, the first thing I said to the good doctor was "Are you sure the lab saw the sample of my tissue and not someone else's?"

He assured me that it was from my breast. "What you have to do now, Anna, is decide on the course of treatment. Talk to Solan about this, and talk with your husband, of course. You can have a lumpectomy and possibly chemotherapy and radiation, or you can have a mastectomy that will remove the breast. Think about this and let me know what you want to do."

With my head spinning from the news, the weird first thought I had was that I had just bought a new, expensive graphite tennis racquet and a suit with a blue jacket and skirt.

What a waste of money! I thought. Perhaps at that moment, I was ready to face the possibility that I would not survive.

I said nothing to anyone until after we took Ben and Mike to see Duke. The two boys both liked Cornell and Duke. Mike, one year younger than Ben, said that whichever university Ben chose, he'd choose the other.

"I'm tired of getting the same teachers that Ben had the year before and hearing them say to me, 'Ben—I mean Mike.'"

As I mentioned in the previous chapter, Ben decided to apply early admission to Duke and was accepted. Mike applied early admission to Cornell the following year and was also accepted. We were proud of both boys and relieved.

As I had to carry the news of my cancer during Ben's visit to Duke, the trip was good for me, as it took my mind off the decision for treatment. In fact, a former student, Deborah Dawson, was teaching at Duke at the time, having completed her PhD in biostatistics. We were able to visit with her and have lunch with her.

Deborah had come to me in her senior year at Montclair State to request that she be allowed to do some independent research with me. I had just had a student do research with me who had disappointed me in her work, so I was somewhat leery about having someone do research whom I had never had in class with me.

"Can you tell me something about yourself? What is your major, and what is your GPA?" I asked.

"I have a double major, Dr. Pai, in biology and mathematics. My GPA is 3.9."

Goodness, a GPA of 3.9 out of 4.0 and majoring in two rigorous areas! I asked in jest, "What happened to the 0.1?"

"I'm not very good at gym" was her rueful answer.

Needless to say, Deborah did a fine piece of research and received an A for the independent research course. She was one of several of my students who eventually received PhDs, and there she was at Duke. I really felt my age to know that someone I'd taught was now an educator at the college level!

After we returned home, I had to tell David about the cancer. When we were in bed that night, I said to him, "I have something to tell you that you're not going to like hearing."

"What?"

"Remember when I told you I was going to Columbia Presbyterian to use the library last week?"

"Yes?"

"That wasn't true. I went to see a breast specialist about a lump I found in my right breast. Honey, it's cancer."

For the first time since I'd heard the news, I became tearful in thinking about the pain I would cause David and the boys if things did not work out.

David was stunned and alarmed. He asked to feel the tumor, and I put his fingers on it. His voice quavered. "What do we do now?"

"The doctor thinks it's very early, so the prognosis is good," I responded. "The tumor is a small one, and it seems to be encased in a membrane. What we have to do now is decide which line of treatment I want to take. It can be removed with a lumpectomy or mastectomy. I am leaning toward mastectomy. What do you think?"

"Honey, the decision is yours entirely," David answered. "Let's talk to Solan. He's a gynecologist and should have a lot of good advice for us."

Solan came to our house the next day soon after I called him. When I opened the door to let him in, his expression changed when he saw me. It was an expression of concern and angry regret that I would have to go through some kind of treatment.

While we were growing up, Solan and I rarely, if ever, expressed our affection for each other. Nor did my parents encourage us to do so. Again, I attribute that to the manner in which siblings in Chinese families felt the pressure to excel in school. We were perforce competitors as well as siblings. However, I actually idolized my big brother. He was funny and smart, and Mommy and Daddy listened to him. Some of Bill Cosby's facial expressions were similar to how Solan would make everyone laugh, and he was making those faces before there was a Bill Cosby on television.

In that situation, Solan's expression told me he was worried and cared. I shrugged to tell him I was coping and led him into our dining room, where David joined us as we sat around the table. Solan supported my idea about having a mastectomy.

"I think a mastectomy would make me feel better that we would get rid of any other transformed cells in that breast," I said. David said he didn't think it would be off-putting to him, and it was up to me.

"I agree," said Solan.

"Well, then I will ask for that line of treatment and hope the cancer hasn't spread into any of the lymph nodes nearby. The breast specialist said he thought it was a very early cancer, and if so, the chances of recovery were very good."

Solan nodded and agreed. With little else to talk about, he left to go back to work. I called the breast doctor. He said he'd reserve time in the operating room and call me when he had a time available.

Perhaps it is naïveté on my part, but I have always had complete faith in my doctors at Columbia Presbyterian Hospital. I was sure my breast doctor would do everything he needed to do to assure me of no future recurrence—that was, unless he found some metastasis into the lymph nodes. That was information he would not have until after the operation and after they'd had time to study the excised nodes.

In those days, all the lymph nodes in the armpit closest to the affected breast were removed and studied, which affected circulation in the right arm. I still cannot keep my arm close to my side for long periods of time, as fluid builds up, and the edema in the arm becomes uncomfortable. After the operation, the pain was similar to someone pushing a softball bat into the armpit. I need to be able to move my arm and keep it elevated. I try to reserve the aisle seat on airplanes so I can sit with my right arm on the aisle and do not need to share the armrest with another passenger. My family knows that in cars, I need to sit next to the car doors on the right of the car if I am not driving. Today the surgeons only remove a couple of the nodes to check for metastasis, and there is little effect on arm circulation.

A few days after the operation, I heard my Dr. Huck Finn chortling as he rushed down the hall to my room, saying, "The nodes were clean! The nodes were clean!" That was the news we'd wanted to hear. In fact, because the cancer was deemed so early and seemed to be encased in a membrane, neither chemotherapy nor radiation was considered a necessity. To be honest, I was more afraid of the chemo than the cancer itself. My nervous system does poorly whenever I take medication for anything that affects the brain. Painkillers, opioid anesthesia, and even motion medication would cause me to react with nausea and worse, so I greeted the news that I would need neither chemo nor radiation with great relief.

I was never as thrilled as the day when, about six months later, I could rejoin David and our friends the Grubers on the tennis court. Until then, I did not have the arm movement necessary for tennis. I am so right-handed I don't even know I have a left hand! I have heard that mastectomy patients in those days who were not able to or did not care to follow a doctor's instructions to do the proper exercises to bring the arm function back to nearly normal never did achieve normal function with the affected arm. I exercised faithfully.

Four years after my operation, David's health problems began. We went to Florida for a week of sun and golf in December of 1985. When we returned home, my father picked us up at Newark Airport. It was a brutally cold day, with temperatures in the single digits. David told Daddy he would get Daddy's car from the parking lot. We waited for what seemed an inordinate amount of time before we saw him drive up.

He said little as we loaded the bags into the car and drove home. Later, he told me he had had an episode of indigestion when he exited the terminal to get the car. It had been enough to make him sit down on the curb for a few minutes before he felt he could get up and take the bus to the parking lot. I thought little of it, as he had a history of acid indigestion and was rarely without antacid medication.

A couple of weeks later, I had arranged for a surprise fiftieth birthday party for David, whose birthday was January 7. I had reserved a large table for our Tiger friends. After a pleasant dinner with dear friends with whom we had grown old, everyone returned home, and David again told me of experiencing chest pains. This time, we were both concerned, as the problem seemed to be recurring, and antacids were not helping.

David said he didn't think it was his heart because the discomfort did not happen during exercise or when we played indoor tennis. It seemed that if it was his heart and not indigestion, he should have encountered the problem while undergoing physical stress. Solan told him to check with a cardiologist at Columbia Presbyterian Hospital. Dr. Lovejoy gave David some nitro pills and told him to take one the next time he experienced chest pain. David was to immediately call him to describe the effects of the pill.

A few days after seeing Dr. Lovejoy, one early morning in bed, while thinking about work, David told me the pain had recurred. He immediately took one of the nitro pills. In less than five minutes, the pain subsided. As instructed, he called Dr. Lovejoy to report on the experience. David spoke with the doctor and listened to his response. Then he looked at me with some alarm.

"He said he wants you to drive me to the emergency room at the hospital right now!"

I jumped out of bed and got dressed while David threw some underwear and his toiletries into a bag and also got dressed. We drove to Columbia Presbyterian Hospital, and I dropped him off at the emergency room entrance and parked the car. I ran to the ER. David had already been put into a stall and had the EKG wires on his body. Dr. Lovejoy was there and had called his students over to look at the pattern of David's heartbeat. He said that the abnormality in the pattern was classically that of a blockage in the left descending coronary artery, and he wanted the students to see it.

That was the first time we realized David's problem was not just indigestion but a serious heart situation.

Fortunately, they were able to find an operating room that would allow a surgeon to operate on David that day. The surgeon was Dr. Craig Smith. He came into David's room before the operation and spoke about a litany of things that could go wrong and cause death during the operation. As he proceeded, I became angry. I thought to myself that we were concerned enough; we didn't need to be told how many things could go wrong.

I knew he had to say what he said because of doctors' problems with malpractice suits. He was young and one of the rising stars of the department. I suspect that as he matured, he probably was less blunt and had a better bedside manner. In recent years, he rose to be chair of the department, and he was the surgeon to operate on President Clinton.

They first gave David an angiogram to locate the precise place of the blockage. They intended to simply place a stent that would open up the coronary artery, a procedure known as angioplasty. Unfortunately, they found the plaque to be in a fork of the coronary artery, which meant that in installing a stent, they might cause a piece of the plaque to break off and possibly cause more problems in another part of the coronary arteries. Thus, angioplasty was not possible. They needed to do a bypass operation—open-heart surgery.

As the operation progressed, they found more blockages. The procedure, which they had thought would involve simply placing a stent in a blocked coronary artery, turned into a seven-hour open-heart surgery that involved five bypasses. They used the mammary artery and veins from his legs to create the bypasses so that blood could be shunted around the blocked areas.

When I was told I could go in to see him, I was warned that he would not look good. What an understatement! He had many tubes going into his mouth, his nose, and different parts of his chest. Staples had been used to pull his sternum together again, and his legs were bandaged where veins had been excised. My heart went up into my throat when I saw him in his postoperative condition.

He had been put on the heart-lung machine during the operation so they could stop his heart from beating while installing the bypasses and still have the blood circulating through his body. Perhaps because of that and the fact that they'd had to split the sternum to open the chest, he was also shivering from being cold. He looked terrible. I could feel tears rising in my eyes and tried to blink them away. I was glad they'd warned me, but I still had not known he would look quite that bad. *How could anyone recover from this kind of trauma?* I wondered.

I leaned close to whisper to him and tell him of my love for him. With eyes closed, he nodded. I was happy to see that he understood what I said. David spent a full two weeks in the cardiac ICU. During that time, he slowly recovered and was able to breathe on his own and needed progressively less painkiller medication as he continued to heal. Later, we were told they'd had to hurry to put him on the heart-lung machine during the operation because he'd started to have a heart attack. He suffered injury to the heart, and it now was functioning at 50 percent of normal function.

I had been given a sabbatical for the year, so without classes, I could visit him every day in the ICU, and while he did not feel much like talking, I read to him at his request. I don't remember which book I was reading, but I do remember that he had a hard time staying awake because of the pain medication. I had to read the same pages over and over again.

A source of concern for me was the food he was given after he left the cardiac ICU. On the cardiac floor, the food given to patients was totally salt free. As the institutional food was difficult to like anyway, I was afraid David's refusal to eat much of anything would negatively affect his recovery.

I spoke to his attending nurse and asked if I could bring some Chinese food, such as rice porridge, for him. I promised I would go light on the salt. She checked with the doctor and said it would be better than having him sick with malnutrition. They gave me permission to warm food up in the nurses' room, where they had a microwave.

I made the same porridge I would make for Mommy when she was transferred to a nursing home in 2002. It was really a thick rice soup with minced chicken. I made sure it was tasty enough and salty enough for David to taste some salt. He ate it with relish. While I was warming it up in the nurses' room, invariably someone would walk in and say, "What are you cooking? It smells so good!"

After going home, David had to stay in bed to continue his recovery. The process hit a jarring bump when he developed pneumonia and had to return to the hospital for another stay of almost three weeks. Finally, he did recover fully, and we were able to return to a normal life again. That was just the beginning of numerous operations to correct cardiovascular problems for David. In 2000, he had to have a stent placed in another coronary artery. We were told all but one of the bypasses done in 1986 were again blocked, but the mammary artery was still functioning strongly, and there were new coronary arteries forming to help the one bypass that was still functional.

In 1997, David was given a CAT scan for a minor digestive system problem, which revealed an abdominal aortic aneurysm that was close to the danger point in size. Eventually, doctors discovered he had a total of four other aneurysms in iliac blood vessels to the legs and popliteal arteries in the legs.

To our good fortune, Columbia Presbyterian Hospital, which became New York Presbyterian Hospital after a merger with Cornell New York Hospital, had hired a world-class vascular surgeon. In the years 2007 to 2013, Dr. McKenzie performed amazing surgeries to place stents of different kinds or bypasses to prevent the aneurysms from increasing to the point of exploding. Poor David hardly had any more veins that could be used for any more bypasses!

As time went on, we discovered that David's family members were all beset by terrible vascular genes. His father died of a stroke at seventy-two, and his mother died of high blood pressure before she was sixty years old. Of his ten siblings, the two oldest brothers died of strokes; his third brother had a stroke but died of complications from an aneurysm repair. David was son number four. A younger brother, son number six, also had a serious stroke but survived. His oldest sister died suddenly, no doubt of some catastrophic cardiovascular problem. The youngest of his three sisters died of acute hepatitis. The middle sister has had ministrokes.

After David was diagnosed with the abdominal aneurysm, two of his younger brothers, numbers five and seven, were urged to get checkups for aneurysms, and both were also found to have abdominal aortic aneurysms. One of them also had a bypass operation. In 2014, we received a sad phone call informing us that David's youngest brother, Charley, had died suddenly, no doubt from some catastrophic cardiovascular problem. If ever there was a family that exhibited a genetic basis to cardiovascular disease, it was the family of General and Mrs. Pai.

Following all his operations for the aneurysms, David developed atrial flutter, an arrhythmia of heartbeat that can cause the atria to flutter as many times as several hundred beats per minute. His cardiologist said it was due to the trauma of his many vascular operations. Several times, he had to have electrical shocks known as cardioversion to stop the flutter, but it kept coming back. Eventually, cardiac ablation managed to stop the flutter. Cardiac ablation is a procedure in which catheters with electrical tips are inserted into the heart to burn small areas of the heart that cause the abnormal beats.

In spite of all the operations and hospitalizations, we were grateful that modern medicine had found ways to deal with many complex cardiovascular problems. There is no question that the three surviving siblings in David's generation owe their lives to the skill and training of doctors. Skilled doctors gave David and his sister and two brothers the ability to survive and live almost normal lives.

Chapter 50

MY PARENTS AGE; OUR CHILDREN GROW UP

During all that duress between 1986 and 1995, Mommy and Daddy were living quiet lives in their house in Livingston. However, they continued to worry me, as their relationship remained stormy. We visited them often and took them out to eat at our favorite Chinese restaurants, but those were about the only times they were with anyone other than themselves. They seemed always to be arguing. I became convinced that people should try to avoid social isolation as they age.

With the boys away at school, the care and responsibility for my parents fell more to me than ever. Daddy developed emphysema, which was not surprising because he had smoked since he was twelve in China and continued to smoke—in the house and elsewhere—after we immigrated to the United States. In the 1980s and early 1990s, his health deteriorated noticeably. He would have spasms of coughing that lasted perhaps a minute or two, during which time he was essentially incapacitated. That issue made me think about his continuing to drive.

I had known all along that the time when we had to speak to Daddy about not driving anymore would be difficult. Daddy was only driving locally by then. I talked to David, and he agreed that even driving locally was dangerous because Daddy might have a coughing spasm while driving. We decided to bite the bullet one day and brought up the subject to Daddy. We wanted to wait until we saw him suffer a spasm the day we were to talk to him. We did not have to wait long.

After he recovered and could breathe easier, I said, "Daddy, these spasms are getting more frequent, aren't they?" He nodded, and I could see in his eyes that he knew what was coming. "We've been very concerned about them because we worry about you having a spasm while you're driving."

Daddy shook his head dismissively. "I can take care of myself," he said.

"It's not just about you taking care of yourself. If you get a spasm and have an accident, it certainly isn't something you meant to do. Suppose you injure somebody else. Or even worse, suppose you accidentally kill someone," David said.

"You don't really drive anywhere anymore anyway," I added. "You can always tell me what you need, and I can get it for you. I've talked to the owner of our local restaurant, North Sea Village, and he has agreed to deliver food to you. Isn't that great?"

We had gotten to know the owner quite well since he was pleased to see Chinese customers and knew we had spread the news to fellow members of a Chinese social club we had joined, the Livingston West Essex Chinese Association. When we explained to Mr. Chen about my parents' situation, he graciously agreed to deliver their food orders. We promised we would not let it be known that he was doing that favor for us, as he did not want to be in a position to have to deliver food to all his customers. I cannot tell you how much the gesture meant to this working mother. It saved me countless hours.

Another benefit was that it relieved Mommy (as well as me) of the need to cook for them. Daddy never had developed a liking for Western cuisine, and he continued to need Chinese food for his meals. It was one of the prohibitive problems that kept us from considering retirement homes for my parents. The only one we knew of catering to Chinese was all the way in California. Neither Daddy nor Mommy was willing to consider leaving home anyway, which also contributed to the social isolation of my parents in the last decade or so of their lives.

After a couple of discussions about not driving, my father finally agreed to stop driving. I did not have the heart to take his car keys from him, though. To take his keys struck us as disrespectful—as a sign that we did not believe him. He said he would need them to warm up the car every week. For the most part, Daddy kept his promise. Once in a while, though, the druggist whose store was next to North Sea Village would tell me with a smile, "Your dad drove here yesterday." I did not worry too much about Daddy driving once in a while and only two blocks. I would just shake my head and ask her to call me if he showed up several times a week. She never did call.

His problem was not just emphysema, however. In 1987, I was startled when Daddy seemed to have trouble finishing his sentences. I immediately called his general practitioner in Livingston, who suggested I take Daddy to a neurologist. I did so the same day, and the neurologist only asked him two questions before saying he needed to go to the emergency room at the local hospital to have a CAT scan done. The scan showed that Daddy had a subdural hematoma—blood under the skull on top of the brain that was pressing on his brain—which was causing him to have trouble speaking and answering questions.

He was operated on quickly, and the blood was siphoned out. The leak appeared to have stopped. Later, Daddy said he had not fallen, nor did he remember ever hitting his head on something, both of which would have explained the presence of the hematoma. Since he was in his late seventies, fortunately, the natural shrinking of the brain with age had provided a small space between the brain and skull that allowed the presence of the blood without too much pressure on the brain. That saved his life.

When I explained to Mommy what was wrong, she was impressed and exclaimed, "Then he is very lucky that he survived!"

I drove her to the hospital to see Daddy, who was in the ICU under observation. When she saw him, she expressed concern about his well-being.

"Don't worry, Mommy. It's scary to see something on his head, but it's just to drain the blood out."

I was happy to see her reaction, and I think Daddy was too. *Maybe,* I thought, *knowing how lucky it was that the hematoma did not kill Daddy, Mommy realizes how much Daddy really means to her.* Daddy had to stay in the hospital for several days. Each time I brought Mommy to see him, they seemed happy to see each other, and while there was not much talk, it was a pleasant reunion each time. It made me happy.

I was anxious to see Daddy home and hoped there would be no arguments for a while. On the day he was released from the hospital, I drove him home. No more than maybe five minutes after he set foot in the house, they began to argue. *Sigh.*

In 1992, another dangerous accident happened to Daddy. I was in school, giving a lecture to one of my classes. After the class was over, I returned to my office. Normally, because of being busy, I did not check my telephone for messages until shortly before I was ready to leave for home, but that day, for some reason, I decided to see if I had any messages. I did have one, and it was from Daddy.

Calmly, he told me he had fallen down the basement stairs, and I was to call him at home. Anxiously, I dialed his number. Daddy answered and told me he had hurt his hip and had to crawl up the stairs. "Oh my God, where are you now, Daddy? Can you walk?" I asked with bated breath. If he'd pulled himself up the steps, he must have made whatever injury he had worse, I thought.

"I'm in a chair in the living room. I need to go to the hospital. I can't walk," he told me.

"I'll call an ambulance for you, and I'll meet you at the hospital," I said.

"No, I want you to come take me to the hospital," my father answered, sounding as if I were disrespectful for not offering to go to him immediately.

"Daddy, if you can't walk, how do you expect me to carry you to the car and into the hospital?" I asked, wondering when the accident had happened.

"Oh," he said.

I repeated that I'd meet him in the emergency room. I called an ambulance and then called David to tell him what had happened, and I said I would call him when I knew what the injury was.

As I drove from Montclair State toward our hospital, I couldn't believe Daddy had crawled from the basement to the living room and pulled himself into a chair. Maybe he'd just sprained something, I hoped. How painful it must have been for him to get himself eventually into a chair if the injury was a fracture.

Then I felt frustration that he would not call David to help. David could have been there in five minutes because his office was only on the other side of Livingston from their house, and Montclair State was twelve miles away. Daddy had called me instead, and it was only by luck that I'd gotten his message when I had. I had to counsel myself to remember that he was probably in so much pain that he could no longer think clearly.

When I reached the hospital, I asked the ER receptionist about him. He was being x-rayed. When the doctor came to give me the diagnosis, it was what I feared: a displaced fracture of his left hip. I closed my eyes when I thought about him crawling up the stairs. What pain!

I did not realize then and discovered only later that Mommy no longer knew how to use the telephone to call for help. He'd had to crawl upstairs to get to the phone. I did not even want to think about what could have happened if I had not checked my messages when I had. It took him a while to heal, but my father was a tough, wiry man, and again, he survived.

In 1994, yet another sign of Daddy's deteriorating health appeared. Mommy called me and said, "Your father wanted me to call you because he is having trouble breathing."

That day, I was home and not teaching at Montclair State. I rushed over to their house, and Daddy was sitting with his arms up over his head. I could see that he was struggling to breathe. I immediately called 911 and requested an ambulance, which came in a few minutes.

The EMTs came in with a gurney and asked my father to get on the gurney. I told them, "Please help him, as he's having trouble speaking and moving." They then helped him reach the gurney and rolled him out.

Later, Dr. Gillette, my parents' general practitioner, told me, "His trouble breathing is only in part due to lung problems. It's really his heart, which has had to work too hard since his lungs were not working properly."

The doctors were able to help him recover from that bout of illness, and Daddy was happy to be home. He received a phone call from a friend, Mrs. Chu in New York City, and he proclaimed to her, "*Ay Yah, Chu Tai Tai!*" *Ay yah* is a common Chinese exclamation expressing alarm about any number of things, and the latter part means "I almost said goodbye to this life!" I knew then he understood the gravity of his experience. I wondered if Mommy did.

While Daddy was going through various episodes of ill health, Mommy's physical health was good, but mentally, there was deterioration.

One day, after Daddy had recovered well from his broken hip, she said to me when we were visiting them at home, "Someone is sleeping in the front yard."

The statement made my blood run cold. It was winter, and the temperature at night was in the twenties and thirties. Why would anyone in a well-off town, such as Livingston, be sleeping outdoors in their yard? It was a statement that made no sense at all.

"Mommy, it's cold. Too cold for anyone to be sleeping outdoors now. Where in the yard was he sleeping?" I asked.

She pointed to a part of the yard that had always had a depression in it. "You can see where he was sleeping—it's dented down. I saw him in the night," she responded.

I looked at Daddy, and he just shrugged and laughed a scornful laugh. "This is what I have to live with," he said with bitterness in his voice.

"Mommy, what did he look like?" I asked.

"He was half black and half white," she answered.

I could only nod, looking away from her. Mommy had always carried a bias against African Americans. She believed they could not be trusted. Her fear of them had led to my parents' having double locks on their doors to the outside and my mother's asking for Doberman pinschers as pets. I have no idea why she was so prejudiced. Was it because of movies and television? Could she have acquired her feelings in China and simply brought them with her? Whenever I protested against some of her outrageous comments about black and Hispanic people, she would dismiss me by saying I was too dumb to understand.

Each incident, such as the one of her seeing someone sleeping in her yard, convinced me we had a serious problem that was getting worse. She was not having trouble recognizing us, but there was no doubt some dementia was beginning, as well as paranoia. Was it schizophrenia? Still, Daddy would not consider getting a psychiatrist.

But life was not totally consumed by worries. Ben had been accepted to Duke early, and a year later, Mike received early acceptance to Cornell, so our family was spared the anxiety of having to wait for word from multiple institutions. We were more than proud of our sons for working hard enough and doing well enough to be accepted to their first choices for college.

One of the problems for a mother of children who are close in age (recall that Ben and Mike are only fifteen months apart) is that when they are of college age, the nest empties quickly. In Ben's sophomore year at Duke and Mike's freshman year at Cornell, we first drove Ben to Duke, which started a few days earlier than Cornell. Then we drove Mike to Cornell and got him settled in.

When we returned home, the house seemed quiet. The phone rang, and I answered. It was Mike.

"Hi, Mom. Everything's okay. Just wondering if you were home yet."

"Hi, Mike. We are home, and I'm glad everything's okay. Call me to let me know if you need anything from us."

He said he would and hung up, anxious to join his new friends. I sighed, missing them both already.

No more than five minutes later, the phone rang again, and this time, it was Ben, who knew our schedule for taking Mike to Cornell.

"Hi, Mom," he said. "Are you okay?"

I smiled to think of the coincidence of their calls. Their brain waves must have met in midair!

"I'm fine, Ben, just a little lonely." I knew by their phone calls that my boys had grown up, and I felt such love for them.

At least two more times that year, they called almost at the same time. Things like that, for which science has no explanation, fill me with wonder.

Ben not only received an excellent education at Duke University, as we expected, but also met his future wife and life companion there. Susan Leigh Scott (figure 137) was Ben's classmate. Ben fell in love with her and was fortunate that when Susan had to choose between him and another boy who also dated her seriously, she made the right decision (in our opinion, of course) and chose our son.

They were engaged in the fall of 1987, after their graduation from Duke, and married two years later (figure 138). I had some worries about whether there were any concerns on the part of her southern family that she would be marrying a Chinese. Susan told me that when she'd told her mother about the engagement, Sara had indeed said, "You'll do what you want to do." Although she never said it directly to us, Sara did use the term *Chinaman*. (For general information, Chinese consider the terms *Chinaman* and *Chink* insulting. Americans sometimes use them without malice, not knowing the words are objectionable to Chinese. I actually heard a news commentator use the word *Chinaman* on the radio. I wrote to the station about it and never heard the word used again.)

After Sara and Ben came to know each other, there was no question Sara became fond of Ben. Once, when we were chatting about the young couple, Sara said to me with a grin, "If the two ever split up, Anna, you can take Susan, and I'll keep Ben!" She was, of course, joking, because Susan was a wonderful daughter to her. Susan lived at home and spent a year after graduation from Duke getting certified to teach high school science.

It was then I realized happily that my future daughter-in-law had a strong backbone despite her gentle southern demeanor. She simply said anyone who wanted to stay away from the wedding was welcome to. One thing was for sure: their wedding was a model of integration. Ben asked his best buddies from high school to act as ushers. The first usher down the aisle was his best friend, Martin Taylor, an African American (figure 139). Another of the ushers was Paul Chae, a Korean. Mike was his brother's best man. We had a lovely reception in the church basement, and it meant a lot to David and me that Yung and Nancy Wong (see figure 94) and Martin and Ellie Gruber (see figure 121) were there to celebrate with us.

After the wedding, Ben and Susan lived in Madison, New Jersey, not far from Livingston, while Ben was working at Citibank in New York City and going to business school at NYU at night. I was proud that he had the ambition and determination to finish and get his MBA degree despite all the commuting he had to do. I did all I could to make sure they stayed near us for as long as possible, such as cooking Chinese meals once or twice a week for them.

Ben did something else that made me proud. He had always enjoyed playing basketball in high school for the school team as the starting point guard and always had been interested in that sport on many levels. One summer, he decided to seek competitive basketball in New York City. I wrote the following essay about where that interest led him.

There is a subculture in New York City that exists on hardtop surrounded by wire fencing. It is the site of warrior conflict and mano a mano competition. The weapon is a basketball; the site is the West Fourth Street basketball court. My introduction to the subculture was through my older son, Ben, a small-boned, lightweight, light-skinned Chinese whose one consuming obsession in life is hoops. Through his participation in a basketball league for businessmen, Ben joined the Citibank team, and they won the league championship. Carried away with their success, the coach and some of the team members formed a summer team that joined the West Fourth Street League.

Games are played on a smaller-than-regulation court called the Cage by the locals. But there is an electronic scoreboard and certified officials for the league games. Occasionally, players who are good enough to become professionals, such as the New York Knickerbockers' Anthony Mason, have thundered dunks on this court.

It is not unusual for hundreds of spectators to gather for the big games, standing around the fencing that keeps nonplayers out and errant passes in. It is also almost entirely African American in both the players and the spectators. Sheltered, ignorant suburbanite psyches probably prompted the locking of car doors just driving past such a scene.

To a basketball junkie, it was important to test his mettle against the best, and Ben looked forward to playing on the West Fourth Street court. He would stand out because of his ethnicity and size, and his fair southern wife would be no less noticeable as a spectator. Trepidation at how this couple, already interracial and so different from the others, would fare in that environment was muted when they reported that Ben had become a crowd favorite as the summer progressed. Not a starter, his hustle and determination even led the regulars among the crowd to chant his name on occasion, urging the coach to insert him into the lineup.

So one day we met one of his teammates in Greenwich Village, a big white boy whom my colorblind son had recruited, and proceeded to walk to the court. A number of people were milling about, as the official games had not started. Some young and some not-so-young men from the 'hood were playing half-court pickup games at both baskets. Fully conscious that they had an audience, they attempted feats that were perhaps beyond their athleticism but were sure to draw attention.

When team members arrived, greetings were not by words or by smiles but by just a nod of the head, which was returned. This was the cool way to say hello. Cool was the thing to be! When a player in the pickup games made an extraordinary basket, there was exaggerated nonchalance on his part, as if to say, "No big deal. Do it all the time!"

Ben pointed out their opponents for that day, all "brothers," and all looked like they could pick him up with one hand and throw him over the fence. "We can beat them," Ben said, and he was serious. Soon some of his teammates arrived, and they matched the other team brawn for brawn.

The officials were late, and as we waited, there was time to take in the almost family-like atmosphere of the regulars. The players just dropped their duffel bags on the ground in an outside area reserved for family members of the league participants. Ben said he was told that only once did anyone have a wallet stolen. I had the feeling if they ever caught the thief, he would have been tarred and feathered by everyone on behalf of the victim. People at the scorer's table gathered in easy conversation. The league players were mostly silent in nervous anticipation of the contest to come.

There is nothing that matches the feeling before a competition for athletes: it is part elation in doing something you enjoy and are good at; part dread because nothing is more depressing than losing; and part eagerness in anticipation of the challenge of a worthy opponent. Overall, the adrenaline that flows makes you feel alive and blessed with a body that will respond with almost any movement you want to make. Maybe it's endorphins, but it is addictive. And as an athlete ages, the loss of these skills is akin to the pain of withdrawal.

An athletic arena can bring about total camaraderie between races in a way that no other societal venue could approach. Black, white, and yellow are as one in their love of the game. That is the upside of this subculture. The downside is that for those who have little else that is pleasurable in life, hoops can become too important.

What effect did the attention showered on the stars of the West Fourth Street court have on the youngsters that were so intent on proving their worth in the pickup games? What would the dream of being a player in the West Fourth Street League bring them in life, even if they succeeded in reaching their dream? And how many Anthony Masons could there be among them? The excitement of just being there clearly overcomes depressing realities. In the exhilaration of competition, athletes can stop thinking about life.

Oh, the game? Just as they were about to tip off, the skies that had turned leaden opened up, and the game was rained out. It was the last game I could attend, and the next year, Ben changed jobs and no longer played in the West Fourth Street League.

Still, we had an exposure to a subculture that none of us will forget!

In 1993, Ben and Sue gifted us with our first grandchild, a beautiful girl whom they named Leanna, which was a combination of Susan's middle name and my name (figure 140).

We enjoyed having the little one in the family so much. I wondered if Mommy would be pleased since Ben's first child was a girl, but she was just happy to have a great-grandchild. I was overjoyed, since I had two brothers and two sons, to have a granddaughter. With tongue in cheek, I said to my sons when Leanna was born that now I knew someone would care for us when we got old. That comment elicited an irate "Mom!" from both boys—as it was meant to.

After Ben graduated from NYU with an MBA degree, the little family moved to North Carolina to be nearer to Sara, Susan's mother. Ben had worked hard with evening courses after work. We were proud of him. Susan's father had died of a heart attack when Susan was only ten years old, and she wanted to be closer to her mother to care for her in the event of health problems. We could not have been prouder of our daughter-in-law. They moved to Charlotte, North Carolina, when Leanna was four years old. Ben worked for First Union Bank and then for Bank of America, where he is now a senior vice president in the antifraud department.

Four-year-old Leanna made my heart melt the first time I visited them in North Carolina. We had a fun few days together, and Susan and Leanna accompanied me to the Charlotte and Douglas International Airport when it was time for me to return home. In those days, they were able to go with me to the gate. When boarding was announced and I got up to go to the plane, sweet Leanna burst into tears and ran after me, crying, "Nai Nai, don't go!" Several passengers voiced their reactions with "Aww." I stopped, gave my little granddaughter a hug, and promised her I would return soon. I will never forget that moment of bonding. I was sure I had the world's sweetest granddaughter (figure 141).

Not long after they moved to Charlotte, they had a son, whom they named Keith. He was four years younger than Leanna. Again, we saw that the children of Asian American marriages seemed to pick up the best features of the two parents. While Leanna looked like her mother, little Keith looked like his father, with one surprising exception: he had blond hair when he was born (figure 142). Both grandchildren's hair darkened as they grew older, and now both have brown hair (figure 143).

Mike's dream of marrying and having a family was not as quick to happen as he (and we) had hoped. While at Cornell, he had a girlfriend, a classmate, in their freshman year, but for whatever reason, she decided to call off their relationship at the beginning of their sophomore year, which stunned and deeply hurt my younger son. He dated other young women but did not find anyone he felt could be a life companion. We shared his disappointment and could only hope he would eventually be as lucky as Ben.

Mike graduated from Cornell in 1988 with a degree in operations research, the business aspect of engineering. After working at Arthur Anderson and then Price Waterhouse, Mike decided to also get an MBA, this time at Duke. Having played golf on the Cornell team, his goal was to eventually work in the golf industry to promote the sport he loved. We were a Dukie family since Daddy and Ben had studied at Duke, and now Mike was. We hoped he might meet the right girl finally while at Duke.

However, we were again disappointed, as Mike did not find a soul mate while studying at Duke. After graduation with an MBA degree, he progressed through a number of jobs, including marketing. However, his goal continued to be to work in the golf industry. So he then turned his sights to working in some aspect of the golfing market.

Shortly after graduation from Duke, he received a job offer with Hanes, but then came his breakthrough into the golf industry. It came when a classmate of his from Duke recommended him to the Maxfli golf ball company, which she had worked for. She was to be married and would be moving to the north. She knew of Mike's goal, and when Maxfli called Mike and offered him a job marketing their golf balls, Mike accepted immediately. Thus began Mike's odyssey through various golf ball companies.

He enjoyed meeting and working with some of the top golfers to advertise Maxfli balls, such as Tom Watson, Jack Nicklaus, and Greg Norman. He reported to us that he really liked Tom Watson as a person, as Tom was nice to him and everyone he worked with.

From Maxfli in Greensboro, North Carolina, he was offered a job at Callaway Golf in San Diego. Ely Callaway had decided to expand from his golf club business to enter the golf ball business and built facilities specifically for research and manufacture of golf balls. Mike was delighted to be working at and for Callaway.

During the years Mike worked for the various companies, David and I used not only golf balls but also sets of clubs from the company he worked for at the time. In fact, every time Mike changed jobs, we had to change equipment and balls. I loved my Callaway equipment. Unfortunately, though, Ely Callaway was diagnosed with liver cancer only a few years after Mike was hired to help market the balls. It was a virulent cancer, and he died less than a year after the diagnosis.

Ely's plans for the company to enter the golf ball market competitively had generated some discord among the golf club part of Callaway. The golf club people felt they should be in charge of golf balls also, but the boss had decided golf ball production and marketing should be a separate entity from the rest of the company. After his death, the successor to Ely was a club man, and the golf ball company was closed down.

While that was a negative development, Mike's social life was getting a big uplift. He had once complained to me during a phone call, "How come all the girls I date are bimbos?"

I didn't appreciate girls being called bimbos and said only, "I don't know. You're the one asking them out!"

I felt for Mike because he was already past the age of thirty-five, and I knew he yearned for marriage and a family. Then his luck finally turned around, thank goodness. In 2004, he met Katherine Marie Noonan (figure 144), a lovely graduate student finishing her studies for a PhD in neuropsychology. She already had two master's degrees in the field, so she definitely was not a bimbo!

After Callaway disbanded the golf ball people, a Japanese company, Srixon, hired Mike and another Callaway ball executive to market their balls. The first three letters of the brand name were from Sumitomo Rubber Industry of Japan. They hired Mike and his boss because they realized Srixon needed their American expertise in marketing. Mike and Katherine moved together to Duluth, a suburb of Atlanta, Georgia. Katherine found a job at Warm Springs, helping patients rehab from brain injuries.

They married in 2005 (figure 145). I was as happy on their wedding day as I had been when Mike was born. I had worried that he might never marry. I knew he would be a wonderful husband and a terrific father, and he wanted to have those roles for himself. He waited for the right person. In 2007, they presented us with grandson number two, Aidan, who was born with red hair and the fair complexion of his mother (figure 146). Two years later, grandson number three, Nathan, was born, the first and only one of our grandchildren to be born with black hair (figure 147).

History is repeating itself as far as interest in golf is concerned. When Ben and Mike were eleven and ten years old, we bought children's golf clubs for them. Ben, being the older one, was able to learn the golf swing sooner than Mike, for whom the clubs were still a little too big. But when Mike showed real enthusiasm—and talent—for the sport, Ben turned his attention to team sports and became a good baseball and basketball player, starting for Newark Academy's varsity teams. Ben, as I mentioned earlier, was also chosen for a prep school all-star baseball team.

When Mike's sons were seven and five, Mike was able to supply them with small clubs for golf. At first, Aidan was the better swinger of the golf club, and he enjoyed it, but when Nathan showed even more liking of the sport, Aidan started to separate himself from golf. Sibling rivalry is innate between boys close in age. Leanna and Keith were four years apart, and no such rivalry existed, probably also because of their difference in sex.

Fig 137 My daughter-in-law, Susan Leigh Scott

Fig 138 Ben and Susan Pai with me and Sara Scott, Susan's mother, after the wedding

Fig 139 Ben and best buddy in high school, Martin Taylor

Fig 140 Ben, a first-time father, holding his daughter, Leanna

Fig 141 Leanna Pai, age two, in a new outfit

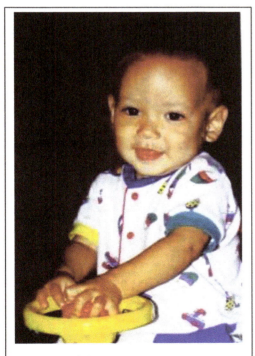

Fig 142 Keith Pai, age 2

Fig 143 Leanna and Keith, ages 8 and 4

Fig 144 Mike and Katherine

Fig 145 Mike and Katherine at the altar

Fig 146 Young Aidan, age nearly two

Fig 147 Baby Nathan

Chapter 51

WE RETURN TO CHINA

In the 1950s, President Dwight Eisenhower became interested in and established an exchange program that would allow people of one nation to visit with people of another nation for the purpose of exchanging culture and expertise between countries. The program came to be known as the People to People Ambassador Program. Participants were experts in many fields as diverse as professional tennis or, in David's case, a particular aspect of engineering. The experts were asked to visit people who wanted to benefit by learning from them. This type of interaction is something that I feel is extremely important. The more we know about other cultures, the more understanding we can be of their behavior, and understanding leads to tolerance and peace.

In 1985, David was asked to lead a group of engineers to China to help Chinese engineers modernize their manufacturing and raise their industry standards in order to qualify their products for an international market. That need had been exacerbated by the decade of the Cultural Revolution (1966–1976). To ensure readers understand the devastation caused by the Red Guards in that decade, it is important for me to discuss briefly those years of Mao's regime.

The Cultural Revolution was a terrible era in Chinese history. It followed Mao's attempt to mobilize people into collectives and to have them increase the production of steel by melting whatever metallic items they had, such as cooking pots, in backyard furnaces. The low-quality steel thus produced was useless for industrial purposes.

When Mao announced the policy in 1958, it was known as the Great Leap Forward, but it failed miserably and caused a famine that resulted in the deaths of untold millions of Chinese people. Thus, Mao's prestige waned considerably in the early 1960s. Because of his loss of prestige, and also possibly because of his fading powers of reasoning, Mao declared that capitalist elements had sneaked into positions of power and needed to be removed.

Some leaders, such as Liu Shaoqi and Deng Xiaoping, the state president and the party general secretary at the time, recognized the disaster and tried to change Mao's economic policies to more realistic goals. The leaders were summarily removed from their posts and denounced. It was the first time one part of the Communist leadership had opposed another part, a step that led to a decade of anarchy.

Nevertheless, Mao began to recover his popularity with the people of China, especially the youth of China, whom he called on to take the lead. He gave them license to attack whomever they wished, including their own parents. The young militants were called the Red Guard. The belief that all cultural ethos of antiquity were bourgeois led to a policy to destroy as much as possible, and the era was called the People's Cultural Revolution.

More millions were persecuted and died. We saw videos of people, some who suffered because they were erudite and some who suffered for no reason at all, humiliated by being paraded through the streets with their hands bound. Boards declaring their alleged crimes were on their backs, and dunce hats were on their heads. People were jailed, tortured, and executed.

When I went to visit a professor at Beijing University, he took me on a walk around the campus. Behind one building was a multistory wall surrounding a part of the campus. When I asked what that area was for, he smiled a wry smile and answered, "That was for holding bad people during the Cultural Revolution—like me."

It was a time of madness. Centuries-old sculptures and other forms of art were destroyed. We saw a wonderful, small, rocky hill in Hangzou that was covered with numerous statues of Buddha and goddesses (figure 148). It became a target for the Red Guards.

Students at Hangzhou University, which was not far from the beloved carvings, heard about the Red Guard's plan to destroy the religious art. The student body gathered around the hill, arm in arm, to prevent the young marauders from getting to the statues. They also implored Zhou En Lai to help them, and Zhou responded by ordering the Red Guard to cease and desist. It was one of several instances in which age-old heirlooms were saved from wanton destruction. Alas, many others fell victim to the Red Guards.

I have spoken with many professors who were summarily ordered to leave their teaching jobs to go to pig farms. In their place, farmers and people with rudimentary education became the instructors and administrators of universities and hospitals. Because of the Cultural Revolution, an entire generation of Chinese students lost their opportunity for meaningful higher education.

In 1985, a cousin of my father came to visit us and told us stories of her experiences during the Cultural Revolution. I wrote a letter to my sons, who were in college then, and here is some of what I related to them:

> Some of the stories she told us about the cruelties of the Cultural Revolution could curl your hair. One of my cousins—whom I remember from my trip back to the PRC in 1950 because he was really good looking, and all the girl cousins had crushes on him—is dead. The Red Guards beat him to death. He was pretty arrogant, and I suspect he wouldn't do what they wanted him to and paid the price.
>
> Another couple that my parents asked about are also dead. They tied themselves together and electrocuted themselves in joint suicide. I can't understand how people

could cause other people so much misery that they would go to such desperate lengths to escape the misery. And to think I wanted to stay in China in 1950! You know I would have been a prime target of the Red Guards because of my Western background. In so many ways, I'm one of the lucky ones.

This same relative said that the government is really taking stern measures to keep to the one-child-per-family policy.

All of that information added fuel to the hatred Mommy felt for the Communist regime. In 1976, when Mao died, his wife and three others (known as the Gang of Four) who were instrumental in promoting the Cultural Revolution were jailed. Some of the persecuted leaders in the People's Republic of China, such as Deng Xiaoping, were restored to power. Deng himself had suffered abuse, and one son was a paraplegic as a result of being thrown out of a third-story window by Red Guards.

After the Cultural Revolution was declared over and professionals were allowed to return to their own careers, there was a need for China to catch up with the progress of sciences—such as engineering and genetics—that the Western world had made during the decade of the Cultural Revolution.

Chinese engineers contacted the People to People Ambassador organization, requesting a meeting with American engineers in the pressure vessel and piping technology field, a key to industrialization. Most of the experts in the field belonged to the American Society of Mechanical Engineers (ASME). The oil, gas, and electricity production industries all use pressure vessels and piping systems extensively.

The fact that David was a Chinese American fluent in the Chinese language, chaired the Pressure Vessel and Piping Division (PVPD) of ASME in the 1970s, and was then the vice president of ASME made him a natural choice to lead the American group. I was proud of my husband for having reached a high level of renown as an engineer.

We were immediately attracted to the invitation. It represented a chance for us to return to China under official auspices after so many years. We gave only fleeting thoughts to the fact that during the civil war in China, General Pai, David's father, had been number three on the list of Nationalists who were declared enemies of the Communist movement. Number one, of course, had been Chiang Kai Shek, the Nationalist president, and number two had been Li Zong Ren, the vice president.

We were sure, however, that there would be no trouble since they'd requested our help. There was also no doubt the Chinese knew that David would be the head of the delegation. In addition, they also knew that my uncle was the Young Marshal, Zhang Xueliang, of Xian Incident fame. My mother was not happy about our trip, especially when she heard it was to help Chinese engineers. However, she understood the honor it bestowed on David to be the leader, and she grudgingly accepted our decision to participate.

David assembled a group of twenty-five engineers (figure 149) who were well known in various aspects of that area of mechanical engineering. Some of the engineers worked for large engineering firms similar to David's company, Foster Wheeler, and others worked in academia as well as national laboratories. The exchange program had been jointly designed with engineers from the Chinese Mechanical Engineering Society.

Eleven wives, including me, joined their husbands on the trip, and I was responsible for the ladies. While my Chinese vocabulary was limited, I could speak Chinese well enough to interpret conversational Chinese. The group overall was compatible. They were willing to help and eager to learn about China and its culture. Knowing in advance about the trip, I applied for and received a sabbatical leave from Montclair State.

We first flew to Seattle, Washington, where we met with officials from the People to People organization. The main speaker was a Texan named Cameron Hightower, who spoke to us about Chinese culture and habits. He gave an excellent briefing to us, stressing Chinese traits and how our hosts were likely to respond to us as their guests. He also warned us that sanitary conditions in public restrooms were anything from inadequate to unbelievable. He advised that if we liked to sing in the shower, we would be better off humming because water in most hotels at that time was not potable. We were to find all his admonishments on target.

He told David and me that we must sit in the front of the buses we would take, so we could exit the bus first before the others. The reason for this was to cater to the traditional Chinese views regarding authority and hierarchy. While the practice was in conflict with our Western views of equality and individual rights, I suspected the stability thus imposed on Chinese society was one factor that had resulted in its longevity.

The next day, we flew from Seattle to Narita Airport in Japan. Sleep was fitful as we flew because of meals, a movie, and the almost unending daylight as we chased the sun halfway around the world for eleven hours. Because there had been terrorist bombings at the airport, security included body searches as well as x-rays before we were allowed to board our plane to Hong Kong. From there, we flew to Beijing, stopping first in Guangzhou, the southernmost province of the People's Republic of China (PRC).

I wrote the following in my diary:

> As we taxied to a stop after landing in Guangzhou, I looked out the window to take in my first glimpse of PRC scenery—and saw an amusement park with a Ferris wheel, roller coaster, the works! Any inclination to get sentimental over this moment vaporized. I wondered why it was built way out by the airport. At any rate, it was an unexpected sight. The park didn't appear to be in operation, though.

Our plane to Beijing was an impeccably clean jet plane. The flight attendants were attractive young women. They were trying to Westernize air travel in China. The box lunch we were served included boiled pork, boiled beef, a thin slice of Chinese ham, toast, pound cake, string beans, bread, and a peanut brittle. It was way too much for me!

When we exited the airport after customs, we saw Dr. Mao, who had come to greet us. He was a professor of engineering at Qing Hua University, the MIT of China, and had spent a year at Foster Wheeler, working with David. We had invited him to our house for dinner in New Jersey on more than one occasion. He introduced us to a Miss Zhang and Miss Chao (no relation), who would accompany us throughout our trip. In the PRC, and we would have local guides as well. Women in China now go by their maiden names even if they are married. Miss Zhang was a Communist Party member and no doubt assigned to oversee our conversations with Miss Chao, a lovely young local guide. In addition in Beijing, our local Beijing guide was a young man, Mr. Wen. I did not photograph any of the guides. It was clear to us that Mr. Wen and Miss Chao were careful in avoiding conversations of a political nature.

David and I were beyond excited to finally set foot on Chinese soil. How the city had changed! There were major streets, with perhaps six lanes in either direction. Multistory buildings and high-rises had replaced the one-story homes I remembered. Not until we reached the countryside did I see the familiar small tiled houses surrounded by high walls that I remembered from my trip in 1950. Mommy and Daddy would indeed have found the place as foreign to them as it was to us.

We were to stay at a fairly new hotel outside of Beijing called Fragrant Hill Hotel, which boasted as its architect the world-renowned Chinese American architect I. M. Pei, whose name is frequently mistaken to be ours but is unrelated. As we neared the hotel, the only fragrance I detected was the putrid odor of night soil, which penetrated the fog of fatigue. How ironic the name of the hotel!

I was astonished when the bus driver occasionally turned off the headlights, as it was past one o'clock in the morning. "It's to save gasoline," the guide who'd joined us on the bus told me. There was no point in arguing in favor of the lights being on during night hours.

At the hotel, chaos ensued. Hotel management made requests of us, which David announced to the group. Then they changed the requests, and David had to reannounce. Some people were given rooms they would have to move out of the next day for reassignment. Some people who asked for singles got suites.

On the surface, the hotel was impressive, but when David and I got to our suite, the walls were dirty and splotchy, with things spilled on them that could have been washed off easily. The mattress was so soft and lumpy that David slept on the sofa. Black caulking around the large mirror in the living room was visible, and light-switch plates that never had been installed correctly were left hanging.

Remember, this was in 1985. By our next trip to China in 1988, the large hotels were run by professional hotel people, some from European countries and the United States, and they taught the Chinese how to maintain hotels and provide the services most Americans are used to. But in 1985, we were in a hotel in a developing country.

We had heard that I. M. Pei, the hotel's architect, was unhappy with the construction of the building. In addition to the problems mentioned above, there were no drawers in the sparse furniture of what was supposed to be the luxurious suite for the delegation leader. There was no way to call out—which might have been intentional. The hotel personnel were often diffident and occasionally rude.

At that time, hotels in Beijing proper were in short supply. Because of the size of our group, we had been bumped out of a hotel in Beijing to Fragrant Hills, about a mile outside the city. Since all meetings were scheduled to take place in town, being a mile away was somewhat inconvenient.

We had arrived at the hotel at one thirty in the morning, so we went to bed right away—and rose at four thirty, three hours later, because of jet lag. Later in the morning, we were greeted by Chinese engineers with a bus that drove us to the Beijing Zoo for a delicious Chinese lunch. Miss Chao was the English-speaking guide who stayed with the women for all our sightseeing and shopping. Everywhere we went, we were greeted by local officials who seemed happy to be in our presence. Figure 150 shows David and me at a meeting that I no longer remember. Our excitement and joy at being in China were obvious.

Lunch was delicious. There were at least eight courses, including one considered a delicacy by Chinese but difficult for Americans to enjoy: sea cucumbers. Sea cucumber has an almost gelatinous, slippery texture and has little taste, so it usually is cooked in some kind of gravy. Nobody, including David and me, cared for it. The first two or three meals included that dish, and afterward, David responded to requests from our group and asked that in future meals, they perhaps substitute a vegetable dish for it. No doubt our hosts were surprised we preferred such plebian dishes to something thought to be an elegant treat.

That day after lunch, we walked to the area where the giant pandas were kept, always a favorite with all tourists. Along the way, I noticed a soldier washing a large Mercedes-Benz limousine. I nudged David and said, "Look at the Benz limo! I guess some animals are still more equal than others, even in a Communist country." I have always believed that total equality among humans is an unattainable ideal, given what I have learned about human nature in my long life, and the limo seemed to support my belief about Communism.

The pandas were sleeping, however. After a few minutes of watching them, we were told to return to the bus waiting for us in the large parking lot. The women were to go sightseeing, while David and I were to join the engineers for a visit to Qing Hua University. As David and I approached, Miss Zhang extended her arm, blocking our way onto the bus. "Delegation Leader Pai and Mrs. Pai, please come with me," she said. "We'll be going in this." She motioned toward a waiting car. It was the Mercedes-Benz, all cleaned and shiny!

We were so surprised that we meekly left our hooting companions and entered the car. On the way to the meeting, we asked firmly that we be allowed to sit on the bus with the engineers for the rest of the trip. Some wag among the engineers gave our limo the name BW, or Bourgeois Wagon. David and I had use of the BW when we alone were invited for an official banquet or when I visited different universities to learn about their biology curricula and research. I told David I wanted the same treatment when we got home.

The special treatment told us in no uncertain terms that they knew exactly who we were and who our families were. Typical of the Chinese culture, David and I were to be treated with unusual respect because of the respect in which Chinese held my uncle the Young Marshal and David's father, General Pai, for his exploits against the Japanese during World War II (see again figure 25). David was also addressed as Delegation Leader Dr. Pai, while I was addressed as simply Mrs. Pai. I was rarely addressed as Dr. Pai, but people rarely did so in the United States either.

I wrote the following in my diary:

> We were greeted by dignitaries of Qing Hua University when we arrived there. The vice president of the university, a woman, ushered us into a large welcoming room. David and I sat on the center sofa with Professor Zhang and other senior staff members, including Professor Mao. The rest of our delegation were asked to sit in armchairs flanking the sofa. We all sat across the room from the lesser staff members of the university, who were seated at a long table against the far wall. So much for equal status!
>
> A faculty member of the engineering department of the university gave us a summary of the program in English and introduced all the staff who were assembled. After David introduced our delegation, I was invited by a biologist to visit the biology department as the men were led off to visit the engineering department.

I had asked some contacts I had met at various universities and meetings if I could visit them to study their biology curricula and research. Because I had not gone to school in China at all, my vocabulary in Chinese was only conversational, and I needed an interpreter so I could ask faculty questions about their science. When the time came for me to visit Qing Hua University (comparable to MIT in their engineering and science curricula), I made sure the ladies had transportation and a guide to sightsee in Beijing. I bade them good day and drove with an interpreter to the vintage institution to meet with a biology faculty member.

Unfortunately, because my interpreter was an engineer, conversation with biology faculty was difficult. The engineer did not know how to translate biological terms in Chinese to English and vice versa. But we all struggled on. The biology department was well stocked with equipment for biochemical and molecular biology research, having received a large grant from the World Bank.

However, the equipment appeared to be sitting unused. They had few faculty trained to use the equipment and not enough reagents and supplies to use in their research. Many young Chinese scientists were sent to laboratories all over the world to receive training. By the end of the decade, Chinese biochemists and molecular biologists were beginning to do research to catch up to the rest of the world.

I asked a professor how many courses he taught every semester. "One," he answered.

Having taught at Montclair State for nearly twenty years by 1985 with a teaching load of three and sometimes four courses a semester, I said, "With such a light teaching load, in the United States, a professor would be expected to do research and publish every year. Do you have such pressure to publish?"

"No," he said. It then occurred to me that the policy or attitude reflected by his comments was something referred to as "iron rice bowls." In a Communist nation, where there was almost always a guarantee of having a job, for professors, life was much more devoid of pressure to excel than what instructors were used to in America.

We arose early the next day, as our destination required a long drive. I wrote in my diary,

> Miss Zhang was constantly involved in trying to ensure enough space for each day's presentation. The demand by students and working engineers to attend the sessions is great. I can't say I blame them. I feel the same way when a well-known biologist is giving a talk in my area at home. Thirst for knowledge can become compulsive …
>
> Another day, I was scheduled to visit the Academia Sinica of Beijing, a research institute. I had met one of the staff members in Los Angeles in an August meeting of the International Societies for Developmental Biology, a Dr. Yan. He had sent me an invitation to visit him when I reached Beijing and had set up the meeting through the Chinese engineers.
>
> We were met by a Dr. Chen, as Dr. Yan was at another meeting. We chatted briefly about the institute in their reception room over some hot tea. There are some two hundred staff members and assistants in all, and in the developmental group, there are at present fifty-five staff members. Again, as at Qing Hua, there have been acquisitions of equipment, but there is need for reagents, supplies, and more training to operate all the sophisticated instrumentation.
>
> We dropped in on Dr. M. C. Niu, a retired professor from Temple University, whom I had met twenty years ago as a graduate student at a meeting in Oak Ridge, Tennessee. I had last seen him at a meeting in California and heard then that he was spending considerable time in the PRC, helping them in molecular techniques.
>
> Later, Dr. Yan joined us and showed me through the institute. Much of their research seemed to involve the transfer of genes into eggs of different species to influence their development. One project was the attempt to transfer bovine growth hormone gene into fish, like carp, to increase their bulk and provide more food. This is applied research, taking established techniques and using them for a practical purpose. They really are not in a position where they can afford the luxury of basic research.

The iron rice bowl (guarantee of income) I encountered in my discussions with academics could be another weakness of the Communist system. We encountered an example when David and I went to a government clothing store. I wanted to buy Mao hats for my sons, as they had requested. The young saleslady was by herself in the store. There were no other customers there.

She sullenly asked what we wanted, and when I told her I wanted Mao hats for men, she turned to the nearest counter, grabbed a hat clearly too small for grown men, and threw it onto the counter. I protested about the size. "Young miss, my sons are grown men; these hats are too small!"

She responded, "All hats are the same size."

Even though larger sizes were on shelves behind her, we decided to leave since we figured she would only be ruder if we decided to pursue the purchase.

In 1985, Deng Xiao Ping had just begun to convert the economic system of the People's Republic of China to free enterprise, and there were a few privately owned stores. When we went into those, the service was immediate and helpful, and the stores stayed open for hours after the government stores closed. I never did buy Mao hats for Ben and Mike, though.

We were treated to visit some of the famous places in Beijing, such as the Great Wall, the Summer Palace, and the Forbidden City. Everywhere, we encountered large crowds, which grew even larger by our presence. In 1985, Americans were still considered subjects of curiosity, as I had been in the 1950s when I attended as an alien various high schools and then Sweet Briar College.

At one gathering in 1985 China, a young man with his toddler son in his arms walked right up to one of our engineers. He probably thought I could not understand Chinese and said to his son after peering closely at the engineer's face, "Their noses really are big!"

I must say that at that time, the Chinese were not bashful to ask questions of us that we would have thought were not polite in the United States, such as "How much money do you make a year?" My answer was usually "Enough." As low as my salary was because I was an academician in the United States, compared to the salaries at that time of Chinese educators, they must have thought we were incredibly rich.

I must mention here that every car ride in the PRC was an adventure. The multitudes of bicyclists and pedestrians on or crossing the streets were crazy when it came to challenging cars to hit them. They cut across traffic, rode in the middle of the road in front of honking cars, and continued without blinking an eye. They had no regard for cars aiming straight at them. After seeing several near misses, I decided to stop looking ahead and looked out the side windows.

As I mentioned earlier, we had Miss Chao as our guide throughout the trip, as well as local guides, but there was also a Communist Party member joining the group: Miss Zhang. Miss Chao was careful about what she said when Miss Zhang was around. David said there was always a party secretary present at various discussion sessions with the engineers. Any sensitive question the Americans posed needed the party person's nod before the technical people dared to answer.

That was to change, as David's subsequent business trips indicated. By the late '80s guides could speak fairly freely, and there were no party members following us around.

After the visit, I was driven back to Fragrant Hill (in the chauffeured Mercedes, of course) to dress for dinner with a high official of the government, someone in charge of overseeing relationships with overseas Chinese.

David was told the individual was a very high-placed person who did not normally receive visitors. I wrote the following in my diary of our trip:

We were led by our guide Miss Zhang to the second floor. There were four or five waitresses in the hall and a few waiters who seemed curious to see who were being brought to see the important man. A man in a business suit led us into a large room. He then turned us over to another man, probably an aide, who then introduced us to Yang Shing Ren.

Mr. Yang was a heavyset man, fairly big for a Chinese, about David's height. Unlike most Chinese, he had a large nose, and we later found out he was indeed from a Muslim background, like David. His ancestors, like David's, were from Persia. This no doubt was another reason he had wanted to meet us directly.

We sat on the main sofa against one wall and exchanged pleasantries. Then Mr. Yang just sat and smoked. With his heavy-lidded eyes, stern appearance, and black Mao suit, I felt as if we were supplicants in the presence of a Mafia don! Actually, none of the other Chinese spoke unless spoken to. Whenever Mr. Yang told a joke, everyone laughed very hard. There was a sassy young waitress who seemed to amuse him. Mr. Yang was clearly a lot "more equal" than others.

The dinner was served, and the food was absolutely superb: the best butterfly shrimp I've ever eaten, the best gung bao chicken, the best Beijing duck, veggies and fish, etc. Everyone ate with gusto. Some of our American friends who had made trips to China claimed the food in the People's Republic of China was no good at that time. This was not our experience. The dinner was excellent, but remember, we were getting special treatment.

Mr. Yang was cordial but very formal. He rarely looked at me. When he asked a question about cancer, he asked David, who in turn asked me. Actually, he probably thought I wouldn't understand his heavily accented Mandarin, which showed he was not a native of northern China, and he would have been right. He actually never did speak directly to me. Not knowing how he would feel about being photographed, I had not even brought a camera. Unlike other dinners with officials, where they insisted on pictures, no one took any photographs with Mr. Yang.

I noticed that Mr. Yang ate little and that he was wearing a sweater under his jacket. No wonder he was sweating—it was still fairly warm outside. People here really overdress. While I am in shirtsleeves, they're in layers of sweaters.

When the last course was done and the ubiquitous ice cream served, Mr. Yang slapped the table and said, "That about does it." We stood, shook hands, and were led out of the room to our own floor. Quite an experience!

The entire trip was an experience. We all learned a lot about life in the PRC in 1985. We received a thorough visit of Beijing. Our schedule took us to all the well-known historical and scenic sights, such as the Great Wall; the Ming Tombs; Tiananmen Square; Mao Ze Dong's crypt; Tian Tan (Temple of Heaven), which gave a wonderful view of the city; and the Summer Palace, which the last empress built for herself with money that was supposed to be used for building ships for a navy. The Forbidden City, home of emperors and finally open to the public after the revolution led by Sun Yat Sen, was our last site to visit.

As we traveled to all those places and were driven to various parts of the city, we remarked on how happy the populace as a whole seemed. Certainly, the children were all well fed and all dolled up. It was as if each couple with a child were determined to dress their child better than any others. Ruth Green, one of the engineers' wives, and I had Polaroid cameras, which we used to give children and their parents instant photos. The photographs delighted them and invariably drew a crowd.

We, the wives on the trip, really had more fun than the engineers. Often, when we were scheduled to tour a site, such as going to Tian Tan, the men had to leave us to visit a factory or have a conference. At that time, we were frequently taken to the Friendship Stores run by the government specifically for overseas tourists. In fact, Chinese citizens were not allowed to use those stores to buy art or anything else. I did not like the fact that some of the best things, such as cloisonné and jade sculptures, were available to foreigners but not to Chinese.

One evening, David and I again left the group because we had been invited to dine at the home of the director of the Committee for Cultural Affairs in Beijing, a woman, Mrs. Chen. We were joined by our guide Miss Chang and Professor and Mrs. Mao. Professor Mao had spent a year as a visiting specialist with David's company, Foster Wheeler, and then was retained for another year as a consultant. Professor Mao was a faculty member at Qing Hua University.

Professor Mao once told us of having worked for two years to translate an important reference book for engineers into Chinese. When he was given a small compensation for his work to be published, he was ordered to split the money with his colleagues in his department at the university due to the Communists' policy for making everyone "equal"—not much stimulus for individuals to do anything progressive or constructive beyond their paid responsibilities!

Mrs. Chen's husband, Chen Sze Yuan, used to work with David's father and with General Li Zong Ren. Mr. Chen had been instrumental in inducing General Li to return to the mainland in the 1960s. For that, Mr. Chen had been rewarded with a high position in the People's Congress and a private house, along with servants.

As for the dinner, I wrote in my diary some impressions of the evening:

> The entrance to her home was difficult to locate, as it was off in a small side alley. There was barely enough room for the taxi we were in to pass through the gate into her yard. There was a car at the entrance that was her car, or one she was assigned. Talk about unequal animals again! A manservant showed us in, and she greeted us in the living room quarters.
>
> The house was as I remembered Beijing houses: one story, tiled roof with red tiles, with a courtyard and fruit trees. She ushered us into a separate house where we were served a delicious meal cooked by her own chef and served by a girl servant. It was another sumptuous meal, very well cooked and extremely tasty. One of the dishes was pork and garlic plant leaves, something I had never eaten before, and it was excellent.
>
> The house was certainly adequate. There was a bathroom with plumbing and a bedroom and living room, the latter to which we repaired after dinner. It was very sparsely furnished, with simple tables, a sofa, and armchairs. There was much clutter about the rooms, as there are no closets, and I saw no armoires for storage. We chatted for a little while, then exchanged gifts, and were driven back to our hotel.

One morning, I was to visit Beijing University. I was accompanied by Mr. Wen, a young engineer who acted as a translator for me on my visits to institutions of higher learning. It was interesting for me to chat with him on the sometimes long drives to the different universities. Like many young people, Mr. Wen had found his education delayed by six years of the Cultural Revolution, during which he worked in coal mines and also as a maintenance worker in a train station.

He said, "The young people after the Cultural Revolution tend to be less involved and interested in party politics."

Interestingly, on one trip, when Miss Chao, our guide, was with us, she debated that point. "Actually, if you are not a party member in college, you are ostracized."

The existence of vocal disagreement was in itself an interesting sign of the times: people were more willing to debate as long as it was not about governmental policies.

At Beijing University, a lovely older gentleman, Professor Wu, greeted me. (I mentioned him earlier regarding the Red Guard's wall behind one of the buildings at Beijing University to hold professors as prisoners.) During the Cultural Revolution, the intelligentsia of China suffered as much as anyone. Everyone we spoke with praised Deng Xiao Ping for his reform efforts. I felt Deng was very smart. However, people hadn't built a cult fascination with him, as had happened with Mao; I did not see one statue or even a picture of him anywhere.

My conversation with Professor Wu brought out an aspect of college-level education in the PRC that differed from ours in the United States: students, regardless of their majors, became specialists in their fields by the time they graduated. However, that happened at the expense of what we call liberal arts education. Professor Wu felt that students were given a much-too-narrow education by the time they received a bachelor's degree at graduation. The biochemistry program at Beijing University was a five-year program, and biology was a four-year program.

I felt much kinship with Professor Wu and was taken by his courtly manners and gentle dignity. I could not imagine a gentle soul like him being roughed up by teenagers in the name of the Cultural Revolution. There was no logic to events associated with that time.

The psychological scars on the people were still apparent. There was constant comparison between conditions in 1985 and during the decade of the Cultural Revolution. More than once, people said they did not believe the craziness of the Cultural Revolution could ever exist again in China, almost as if to reassure themselves that such horror would not be repeated.

There were two incidents during our visit to Beijing that have been etched into my failing memory. One humorous one was when Miss Chao told me one day that she had come across a word in English that she could not find in her dictionary. I asked her to spell it, and she said, "Y-u-p-p-y." Think about that. How would you define *yuppy* to someone brought up in a Communist system in which nobody was supposed to be different from anyone else? She was well educated, so I couched my explanation in terms of free enterprise.

The other incident was an attempt one late afternoon on the part of the wives to be pedestrians in a city of (at that time) nine million people.

In my diary, I wrote,

> We drove to a restaurant to meet the men for dinner. With yet a half hour before dinnertime, we decided to cross the street to see the contents of a department store. This was not a Friendship Store but one serving the people. We had not been in such a store before.
>
> The one problem was to cross the street and get back in one piece, because it was rush hour. In Beijing, rush hour consists of maybe six lanes of bicycles and two lanes of trucks and cars going in one direction and the same going in the other direction. Eight of us decided to brave the tides of bicycles and, arm in arm in a single line across with Miss Chao, stepped into the street.
>
> With squeals and giggles, we managed somehow to cross the first flow, but about five feet from the curb on the other side of the street, we stalled. Once we hesitated, we were lost, because suddenly, we were in the midst of an ocean of bicycles all around us so that no movement was possible!
>
> Fortunately, an army truck was turning right toward us from a nearby side street.

The driver saw our plight, and with his fellow soldiers riding with him laughing and pointing, he pulled his truck across the flow of traffic so that we quickly had clear passage to the sidewalk. With relief, waving and blowing kisses to the soldiers, who waved back, we scrambled the last five feet to the sidewalk. Nobody was more relieved than Miss Chao, who was supposed to see to our safety!

In the store, we encountered something we were to see more than once: a growing cluster of people gathered, as if someone were showing them something of intense interest that required them to crowd closely for a better view. When I maneuvered to get a glimpse of the center of their interest, it turned out the spectacle was only two men arguing.

The two arguing were oblivious of the two dozen or so people pressed in on them so that they were practically pushed together nose to nose. We saw the same kind of scene in a handful of car or bike accidents that caused arguments. In part, I guessed that life was rather devoid of excitement there, and whenever anything happened, people seized upon it. It might also have been that the people were on a rotating six-day work week there, and those were people who had the day off with nothing better to do. It certainly seemed there was no lack of interested spectators, no matter how trivial the incident.

Anyway, some of our group purchased open-air pants—pants for toddlers not yet toilet trained—for their grandchildren and as baby shower gifts (figure 151). Our trip back across the street was much easier for us veteran jaywalkers. A salesperson told us that two blocks down was a street overpass we could use to get to the other side. Even the locals—probably because they were locals—did not attempt to cross the street as we had. Our dinner conversation was filled with our giddy disclosure of the adventure of crossing the street, which left our husbands shaking their heads at the thought.

Dinner was again excellent, with the cold plate appetizer first, as usual, and then the hot dishes. Fish and soup were served last and then dessert. They served an interesting dessert called *bashee*, which was fruit fried in batter and coated in hot, caramelized sugar. One picked up a piece of fruit with chopsticks or a fork, drawing the melted sugar out in thin wisps, and then dunked the piece into ice-cold water quickly to harden the caramel. The result was a crunchy sugar covering over still-hot fruit—yummy! One of our hosts said the same could be done with ice cream instead of fruit. The restaurant did not have that available, however.

We spent our last two days before leaving Beijing touring famous sites, such as the Great Wall and the Ming Tombs. The Great Wall was breathtaking when one thought about the effort made by the people who constructed the wall so long ago without modern machines to convey stones to the wall. Some people have measured the wall to be longer than thirteen thousand miles.

The first emperor to unify China was Qing Shi Huang in 221 BC. He ordered the building of the wall along the northern borders of his empire. Various authors have estimated that hundreds of thousands to possibly a million workers died over the hundreds of years that various sections of the wall were built. There is conjecture that bodies of some who died during the construction are buried in the wall.

After I'd experienced the multitudes of people in Beijing, and even more in Shanghai, how China would be able to sustain life for a billion citizens was a depressing thought for me. How could China maintain itself in the modern world? Yet when I saw structures, such as the Great Wall, that required enormous capacity for tedious and dangerous work, it made me realize this characteristic of its people, willingness to "eat bitterness" "*Cher koo*" was how China had survived its tumultuous history. The phrase refers to a willingness to suffer hardships for the good of the people or country.

I realized that China as a country would probably survive in perpetuity as long as the people were willing to work to the point of sacrifice. Certainly, the people are still doing menial chores that we in the United States would not think of, such as chiseling paint by hand off the outside of a multistory high-rise.

Our next destination was Hefei, the capital of Anhui Province, where the Chinese had headquarters for their pressure vessel and piping technology. The site was in a less well-known part of the country, which had been chosen for the research center because of Mao's fear of having to go to war against the Soviet Union in the 1960s. Many important facilities were moved to the countryside as a means of achieving dispersion. The engineers would spend two days in Hefei, touring the Chinese research facilities and factories and exchanging views with their Chinese counterparts.

The morning we were to leave Beijing was a busy one. We were looking forward to visiting the Forbidden City, a trip scheduled for the morning before our late-afternoon flight. Unfortunately, the night before, we were told by phone that our flight had been moved up to 11:10 a.m. We hurriedly informed our group of the change. Also, as during every trip we subsequently took to the PRC in the fall, I caught a serious cold that began with a sore throat.

One consequence of the change in the flight schedule, we were told, was there would be little time to explore the magnificent halls of the Forbidden City, but we could walk through without any time to stop anywhere. We entered the city by its back entrance and, as obedient visitors, simply marched through without stopping and boarded the buses waiting for us at the front entrance. We were determined that if the future held any more trips to China for us, leaving time to explore the Forbidden City would be a priority.

The sweep and majesty of the great halls of the Forbidden City, overlooking white marble balustrades and terraces, were breathtaking. Each hall was greater than the previous one. The movie *The Last Emperor* has given the world's moviegoers a great visual look at the magnificence of the Forbidden City.

We gave gift pens to the young Chinese engineers who had accompanied us all around Beijing. We bade them goodbye and wished them well. We were glad we had been told during our briefing in Seattle to have gifts available. (We had also been told that American cigarettes were highly coveted by a nation of men who seemingly all smoked; however, we declined to give them something that would eventually make them sick.)

The bus took us to the airport, along with Miss Chang and Miss Chao, who would be with us for the duration of the trip. We arrived at the airport at ten thirty in the morning. Having forsaken a real visit in the Forbidden City because we needed to hurry in order to board our plane out of Beijing, we were dismayed to hear an announcement that our plane was grounded in Shanghai because of bad weather. It would land at four thirty in the afternoon, six hours after we had arrived at the airport. We could have spent several more hours touring, but we accepted the delay as part of the uncertainty of travel in the PRC.

When the plane landed on the ground in the afternoon, we gathered our things and went through a security door that beeped at everything—buckles, buttons, and more. The foil around my cough drops got me stopped! But we were glad the plane had arrived, and without comment, we filed onto the plane as we were directed. We settled down, hoping the wait would not be long before we were to take off. However, our hope was in vain: we waited and waited, and the plane got warmer and warmer, as the temperature outside was probably in the high eighties.

I realized suddenly I had not seen any of the crew on the plane. No one was in the cockpit. Remember, this was 1985, not long after the Cultural Revolution that had set China back in every way. I asked Miss Chao to inquire whether we could have some air-conditioning on. I already had a sore throat, and the stifling air was enough to make me more ill. Miss Chao left the plane and did not return. Miss Chang then left to ask and also disappeared.

Finally, after well over an hour of sitting there with no crew members in sight, I went to the galley door at the rear of the plane, which was open for some ventilation, and looked toward the terminal door. Miss Chao was near the nose of the plane. She shouted that the reason for the delay—incredibly—was because the crew had gone to eat a meal.

I was proud of our group (as I had been throughout the trip) that instead of reacting with anger at something the Chinese had done unexpectedly—such as herding us onto a plane only for the crew to decide to have a meal—there was only disbelief and joking. We all deplaned and milled around the rear of the plane. The Chinese passengers were more vocally unhappy than we were.

A young man dressed in the uniform of a pilot finally appeared and was besieged by the upset Chinese passengers. Miss Chao berated him for thinking only of himself. His retort was that his only responsibility was for the safety of the plane, and if he was hungry, he couldn't fly safely. He claimed it was the ground personnel's fault and, in a huff, boarded the plane and went into the cockpit.

We were still milling about at the back of the plane, when suddenly, we heard the engines turn on. I had a vision of a headline in the *New York Times*: "A Group of American Engineers Roasted by Jet Propulsion in Beijing." We clambered aboard and resumed our seats. Our flight attendants appeared to hoots and clapping. They professed not to know we had been kept in the stifling heat for almost two hours.

Incredibly, instead of the plane taking off, we sat some more. We were told that it was already so late, they'd decided to wait for seven passengers coming in on another plane who wanted to go with us. That was the last straw for one distraught Chinese passenger, who was almost in tears as he told the flight attendant he had waited three days for the plane and that day had missed two meals. He'd had it, and he demanded to get off the ground immediately. The flight attendant tried to soothe him, saying, "You're so late that waiting a little more won't matter."

The planes that flew us from Beijing to Hefei, Anhui Province, to visit manufacturing facilities were not the modern 737 jets we were used to in the States but were old Russian planes that had been used for many years. When we were boarding the plane, I noticed that the tires on the plane were bald.

I turned to the engineer behind me and said, "Look at the tires on this plane!"

He nodded and said to me, "Did you see the duct tape on the wings?" I didn't want to look. To this day, I am not sure he was just joking! Finally, we took off and landed safely in Hefei. The bus ride to the hotel was jovial, and we were loud, giddy with relief from not having to wait anymore and knowing we were down safely. I could not wait to get to bed finally.

The incident did not help my respiratory problems. Miss Chang and Miss Chao were concerned about my health and arranged to have a female Chinese doctor see me. She asked if I wanted my temperature taken, the kind of question that assumed a yes answer. She handed me a huge thermometer that looked to be a foot long and quite wide. It was so big I thought it must have been a rectal thermometer but a large one. The doctor must have seen the confusion on my face because she motioned for me to put it under my armpit.

I received all kinds of Chinese medicines and antihistamines. One was a brew to help sore throats. Another was in the form of tiny black grains. The cough medicine must have had a narcotic in it because it made me drowsy. I had brought acromycin, Anacin, and Dimetapp. I decided to stay with the American medicines and not take the Chinese ones, which I did not know could be taken safely with the American meds.

We did not spend more than two days in Hefei, and I spent most of the time in our hotel room, not wanting to give my cold or flu to others. The children in Hefei were less well clothed and coifed than the ones we had seen in Beijing. There was not much sightseeing for us to do in Anhui, a rather poor province. Our group spent some time in another Friendship Store.

Our next stop was Shanghai, long the most cosmopolitan and Western of China's large cities. The flight to Shanghai was without all the drama we'd experienced in Beijing's airport. It was smooth, with little delay. We stayed in a fancy hotel in Shanghai, Je Jiang Hotel, the same one President Nixon had stayed in when he visited China in 1972. It was in much better shape than Fragrant Hill in Beijing.

Among the sights we saw in Shanghai was a carpet factory where all work was done by hand. One person looped the yarn through the base fabric and cut it roughly. Two other workers tamped the yarn down and trimmed it. It looked like tedious and boring work, but all the workers were bent to their tasks with intensity, as the paint chippers at the hotel had been. One of the wives exclaimed, "This is cruelty!" She did not comprehend that there was pride in those workers in producing a beautiful carpet. Also, the idea of doing a job simply because it must be done is a concept too foreign to American society.

As I mentioned earlier, the ability to *Cher Koo* (eat bitterness), which is so much a part of the Chinese society, will result in China's perseverance. This attitude gives me hope that China will survive despite the myriad problems that having to sustain a billion-and-a-half population engenders.

I wrote in my diary,

> You have to give credit to these people, these Chinese. What industry, patience, and persistence! They are an exasperating people—rude despite their formalities and protocols, crude despite the elegance in their history, bull-headed in their independence despite their dependence on other nations.

Among the more memorable events during our Shanghai tour was a remarkable show of acrobatics that concluded with a trained panda. Pandas are notoriously difficult to train, so the show was an exception. She was roly-poly and as lovable as she could be. There was also much shopping to do in Shanghai, but my favorite was visiting the Shanghai Botanical Garden. To my delight, the gardens were filled with large and medium-sized bonsai (figure 152).

There were rock plantings galore. Some of the bonsais were too freeform for my Japanese-trained taste, but some were magnificent. Like the Chinese nature compared to the Japanese, Chinese bonsai tend to be less formal and less trained than Japanese bonsai, which I think are more elegant. To me, it is similar to the difference between Chinese society and Japanese society. One is more laissez-faire, and the other is more rigid. There are strengths and weaknesses in both.

I always tell American friends who plan trips to both Japan and China to go to China first and then Japan. After seeing the pristine gardens and immaculate streets of Japan, encountering the often messy streets of China would be a negative experience. I have always thought the rigor of Japanese society was in part due to the fact that 90 percent of the population of Japan lives on about 10 percent of its land. The rest is not arable or livable. Without the rigid rules of Japanese society, survival would have been difficult.

In Shanghai, as in Beijing and Hefei, David and I were feted by a high official at a dinner banquet. It was held in a private dining room, and we were served by one of the smoothest and most efficient waitresses I'd ever observed anywhere. She seemed to foresee our needs before we knew we had them. I wondered what she might have been in a country like the United States—probably anything she wanted to be.

We met a Mr. Hung, who had studied at Cambridge and would be escorting us to our next stop, Hangzhou. He spoke English with an elegant British accent. Again, as soon as dinner was over, we were ushered out, just as had occurred at the banquet with Mr. Yang in Beijing. It seemed protocol dictated that nobody sat around to chat after dinner.

We rose at five thirty in the morning to have our bags packed and in the hall by six o'clock in the morning. When we boarded the bus, we were given breakfast boxes containing two boiled eggs, juice, sandwiches, a muffin, and a piece of pound cake. It was way more than most could eat. Before leaving the bus, we gathered all the untouched food and decided to discreetly leave it on the bus. We worried the bus driver might be insulted if we offered the food to him directly.

The plane was on time, and we flew to Hangzhou, a well-known (to Chinese) resort town. Hangzhou is also the site of Zejiang University, where much work is done on pressure vessel and piping technology. (It was also the university where students refused to allow the Red Guards to destroy old religious sculptures carved into a rocky hillside during the Cultural Revolution.) It was one more opportunity for the Chinese engineers to learn from our American engineers.

One of the attractions in Hangzhou is a famous lake called West Lake. West Lake is a large lake ringed by willow trees and by a walk that allows one to walk completely around the lake (figure 153). There are graceful arched bridges and islands with pavilions.

The welcoming banquet for our group was a sight to behold. There was a table laden with Western and Chinese dishes; another table with spring rolls and dumplings; and yet another with desserts, tarts, cakes, and cream puffs. There were approximately twenty Chinese in the welcoming delegation.

A Professor Chu made the welcoming remarks, which were not well translated by a smiling graduate student. Mr. Hung kept pacing, muttering to himself, and shaking his head at the young man's English. When Professor Chu looked as if he were going to introduce every one of the Chinese individually, Mr. Hung stepped up and told him to stop.

Lunch was delicious. Afterward, they presented all of us with sandalwood fans and silk embroidery of West Lake. They were showing us in every way they could that they were pleased with our mission.

The hotel was elegant, jointly financed by Belgians and Chinese and supervised by Singaporeans. It was the best we had stayed in on the trip. We knew that as time went on, more and more hotel professionals from other countries would be asked to manage hotels in the most important cities. David and I were assigned a suite that was a corner room with a balcony affording a view of the entire West Lake. The rooms still had no drawers or chest space, and there was no reason to unpack. We would have been essentially putting the clothes into a pile somewhere else. We did not doubt that if we returned to China in the future, the rooms would be improved.

The men went to work with the Chinese engineers, and the women went shopping. We went to a silk mill, the largest in the PRC, where some 2,400 people worked. There were large groups of silkworms feeding on mulberry leaves. We saw machines that spun the silk threads and fascinating computer-driven weaving machines. The workers fed cards with patterns into the computers. I could not understand how, but the cards made the machines weave the correct threads into silk and silk-brocade fabrics. The fabrics were unbelievably inexpensive; most were less than three dollars per meter.

The following is from my diary:

> We had an early dinner and walked at a brisk pace to the lakefront, where we boarded

excursion boats to go to a West Lake tea party on one of the islands in West Lake. It was rainy and chilly, but we were in high spirits. There in the middle of China, in the middle of West Lake, a group of middle-aged Americans and one Chinese American couple began roaring out "Row, Row, Row Your Boat!" Our Chinese hosts laughed out loud.

Why can't governments get along as well as the people of different countries?

The next day was also a day of excursions for everyone. The following is from my diary:

> We walked to the lake to board an excursion boat. While in the boat taking us to another part of West Lake, one of our escorts, Miss Zhang from Hangzhou, told us the legend of the White Snake of West Lake as we passed a bridge that commemorates the legend.
>
> There were two celestial beings, a White Snake and a Green Snake, who were sent to earth as a beautiful princess and her handmaiden. They saw a handsome young scholar, Xu Shen. They made it rain so as to provide an excuse for the princess to seek shelter under the scholar's umbrella. He fell in love with the princess, and they were married.
>
> One night, he came to bed late and found a white snake in his bed. Alarmed, he fled. A short while later, he crept back and saw no snake but just again his beautiful wife. Troubled by this, he sought the advice of a monk. The monk saw that the scholar's visage was that of a man troubled by problems at home. The scholar told the monk of his experience.
>
> The monk told the scholar to drug his wife and see if she was indeed a white snake. He did so one night while she slept, and to his horror, she turned into a white snake. The scholar and the monk entombed the snake in the bottom of a pagoda.
>
> But the snake, as princess, had given birth to a son. The Green Snake took the boy and escaped to a monastery where, as a handmaiden, she'd been trained as a warrior. When the son grew up, she told him about his mother, the White Snake. Together, they avenged the White Snake by putting to death the scholar and the monk. At their demise, the pagoda collapsed, and all three—the two snakes and the son—rose to heaven.

The pagoda, called the Thunder-Wind Pagoda, is on one of West Lake's islands, and one of the bridges is the site at which the White Snake met the scholar. Miss Zhang said that at the time, there was talk that the pagoda should be restored, but a women's rights group (I hadn't known there was such a group) objected, saying the pagoda was a symbol of women's enslavement by men.

In another part of West Lake, there were three stone structures extending from the water of the lake like little temples, ringed by buoys of some sort. When there was a full moon, one candle was lit in each. The reflection by moonlight threw three candle reflections around each structure.

On another day, we visited one of the largest Buddhist temples I had ever seen, the Lingyen Temple. The walk up to the temple was impressive, with rock formations—cliffs, really—into which were carved countless figures of Buddha. Again, this was the area I mentioned previously that was a target of the Red Guards during the Cultural Revolution.

Our last stop was the tomb of Yueh Fei, who was instrumental in China's defense against the Xiongnu invaders (a Turkic tribe from Asia Minor) in the twelfth century AD. He was betrayed by a traitor of the South Sung Dynasty, and his victories were reported as defeats. He was ordered by the emperor to be beheaded.

When the truth came out, the people were so outraged that they made dough into strips to symbolically represent the traitor and deep-fried them. That was the origin of a salty cruller called *yoh tiao*, the common breakfast of fried dough that my grandmother was eager to eat when we went back to China in 1950.

The tomb is a large grassy mound in which Yueh Fei and all his family, who apparently were all executed, as was the custom, are buried (figure 154). Also entombed in the mound are the remains of the general's closest aides, who committed suicide after Yueh Fei died. Facing the mound some fifty yards away are life-size iron statues of the traitor and his wife, kneeling with their hands bound behind their backs in apology to Yueh Fei forever (figure 155).

The dinner that day was to be our last dinner together as a group. As dinner was served, Mr. Hung stood and made a speech, expressing the deep appreciation the Chinese engineers felt for having learned so much from the American engineers. David then stood to respond, saying how grateful we were for the wonderful trip the Chinese had designed for us and for their unending hospitality.

Then there was an exchange of gifts and awards to Miss Chang, Miss Chao, Mr. Hung, and others who had accompanied us on the various legs of our trip. I then spoke on behalf of the women, who'd been highly entertained with sightseeing and shopping. I mentioned my own gratitude for the trips to the various universities to talk with faculty and tour their labs.

Bob Cloud, a member of our group, then rose and read a poem he'd written complimenting David and me and expressing America's debt to China for the Chinese Americans like us who had contributed to the welfare of the United States. It was warm and heartfelt. We sincerely thanked him for the tribute. We also were relieved to know that the mission had accomplished its goals and that in a small way, we had improved relations between our two countries.

The next morning, we rose early to join everyone for breakfast and go to the airport with the group. David and I were not going home with them, as we had made plans to visit Shanghai again to meet with his sister Diana and her family. From Shanghai, we all were traveling to the Pai family hometown of Guilin in Guangxi Province in southern China. After that visit, we were going to Hong Kong to visit with David's oldest sister, Patsy, and an older brother, Robert, who had both moved to Hong Kong. Finally, we were going to visit my uncle Zhang Xueliang, the Young Marshal, who was still under house arrest in Taiwan. David's two youngest brothers, Charlie and Albert, were also in Taiwan.

At the airport, we saw the group through the security gate and went to stand at a fence by which they had to pass to get to their plane. We waited for an hour for them to be processed. When they emerged, we waved balloons and yelled, "Bon voyage!" They were surprised we were still there and came to us to shake and slap hands. Even after the last ones got on the plane, we could see hands waving in the windows of the plane. Some close friendships had developed during our long and exciting trip.

What a terrific opportunity to experience our homeland again. No matter how American we were, there was a part of us that was undeniably Chinese. We were proud of the progress China had made in recovering from the Cultural Revolution. We were impressed with the willingness of the Chinese to "eat bitterness" and get things done, no matter how difficult or boring. We nonetheless worried, as we felt the great strain that a population of a billion people (now a billion and a half) in the country imposed on its economy and politics. Lastly, we could not have been happier to have participated in something that brought China and the United States closer.

For David and me, there was still much excitement to come on that trip.

Fig 148 Hangzho statues carved into rocky hill.

Fig 149 David (middle front) and the People to People delegation of engineers.

Fig 150 David joking with local officials.

Fig 151 An American with a curious child wearing open air pants.

Fig 152 Shanghai Botanical Garden entrance

Fig 153 View of West Lake

Fig 154 Yueh Fei's Tomb

Fig 155 Traitors who lied about Yueh Fei

Chapter 52

AN EXTENSION OF OUR TRIP: GUILIN, HOMETOWN OF THE PAI FAMILY

After seeing our group off in Hangzhou, David and I returned to the hotel to pack. We were to take a plane later that day to Shanghai, where we were meeting David's sister Diana; her husband, Henry Hsieh; her oldest daughter, Peggy; and Peggy's husband, Scott Macintosh. We had planned an extension of our first trip to China in decades to visit relatives and former homes of the Pai family in Shanghai and Guilin.

We put our packed bags in Miss Chang's room (she was not leaving for another day) and invited her, Miss Chao, and Mr. Hung for lunch to thank them for their help on our trip. We then collected our luggage and returned to the airport, where we boarded a plane for the short trip to Shanghai.

Henry's sister Eva and her husband, Peter, greeted us at the Shanghai airport. They introduced us to another couple, who were Henry's liaison in China and arranged all their trips to China. They had made our reservations at a hotel for the night. The gentleman, Xue Lian Jun, was a cousin of Henry's. His wife's name was Ling Mian. We took the two couples to dinner, after which they returned to the airport to meet Diana and her family coming from the United States.

Later, I was told that Henry's sister actually was guo jee from the family of Mr. Xue, who had several sisters, while Henry's family had no girls. You might recall from the chapter on my grandfather, the Old Marshal, that he was guo jee from his own family to the Zhang family, which had no boys. It was a practice in those days that families moved their offspring to be part of the family of close friends or relatives who needed a child of a sex they did not have. So Eva was actually Mr. Xue's sister, not Henry's, something that all concerned accepted with equanimity.

The next day, Eva invited us to her house for lunch. She was living in a house they previously had owned but which the government had taken over during the civil war. It had been returned to Henry and his sister in the aftermath of the Cultural Revolution. To get their property back, Henry had had to agree to undertake the expense of renovating apartments to which the people who had been living in his house were moved. Once that was done, Eva had been allowed to move back to her family's property.

The house we saw needed to be renovated. A pipe had broken, and there was a river of dirty water in the walk leading to the house. Bricks had been put in the water as stepping stones. I wrote in my diary the following:

> We entered the ground floor and greeted some elderly ladies and Peter, who were preparing the food for lunch. One of the women was Eva's mother. We climbed to the fifth floor on wooden steps, very narrow, narrower certainly than in the US. The paint on walls was peeling and not altogether clean. Later, Peter and Eva told me some of their story regarding life during the Cultural Revolution.
>
> One day some fifty Red Guards entered and took over their house. Peter was away—I'm not sure why—and Eva was alone. She was told to stand in the room into which we were led for lunch. It is a spacious room, now containing a double bed as well as living room furniture. Off this room is a Western-style bathroom with no shower.
>
> Eva was told to stay in this room while the Red Guards ransacked the rest of the house. She was not allowed to move from one in the afternoon to three in the morning, standing the whole time. They did not harm her, she feels, because she had just returned from working on a farm and was shabbily dressed.
>
> All their furniture and belongings were removed. Eva was forced to live with the poorest of peasants in the countryside.
>
> She said, "I slept with rabbits and chickens! What was my crime? Being a member of a wealthy family!"
>
> They eventually moved six families into their house, one family per room, everyone sharing a single bathroom and a single kitchen. This accounts for the unclean aspects of the house, as most of the families had only been moved out shortly before we arrived. One still remained and was to move out in a few days
>
> The Hsiehs were pleased that the government had decided to return some property to their former owners. The government also made some reparations with their money, *ren men bi*, but the money could not be taken out of China and had to be spent there. The payments are on the order of 10 percent of the value of property lost. Henry and Diana were planning to purchase furniture and art that could be taken with them to the United States.
>
> Eva and Peter were able to get exit visas and were planning to go to Hong Kong

first and eventually to immigrate to the United States. They are absolutely determined to face this uncertain future because they fear there may yet be another reversal of policy, and then their seventeen-year-old daughter, Shirley, would receive similar treatment as Eva had endured from the Red Guards.

Henry's family had been rich and powerful. They had owned a large rubber products company and operated a fabrics mill not far from the house. The family lost everything in the civil war.

We were impressed with the lunch they served, truly a banquet. There were around eight cold dishes, followed by eight hot dishes, soup, and lastly topped off with a delicious crab dish. In addition, there were three different desserts! They had spent a lot of time and money to host their American relatives. Perhaps Henry had helped them out by sending them some money beforehand.

Most of the food was made by Eva's mother, Eva, and Peter. They had taken cooking lessons in preparation to immigrate to the United States, and their cooking was truly excellent. I hoped they would be able to succeed in their goals. They deserved it after the suffering they endured during the Cultural Revolution. Peter and Eva escorted us to Guilin, hometown of the Pai family.

The flight to Guilin was uneventful, and when we deplaned and walked to the gate, a noisy and emotional reunion took place between David and two cousins he called Seventh Older Cousin and Eighth Older Cousin. The two older men seemed almost on the verge of tears to see their younger cousin again.

In addition to the cousins, General Pai's secretary and his wife, Mr. and Mrs. Huang, were there to greet us. A few others were in the party to greet us who had been involved in making arrangements for our visit.

We drove to the Rong Hu Hotel, built on the grounds of the old Pai estate. As we drove by a house, David told me it was where his mother and most of his siblings stayed. Because he and Diana had accompanied their father to Chungking before the house was built, he had never lived in it.

After we had bade our party good night, David and I strolled over to see the house, which was unlocked and empty and was being renovated. We looked into a couple of rooms on the ground floor. The rooms are large and have high ceilings. The house is enormous, large enough to accommodate a family of ten children and assorted cousins.

We wondered if the government would ever consider returning the house to us.

When we mentioned this to one of the people assigned to escort us to various places, the answer was very vague and not encouraging. In fact, we were told later they could not return the house because there were plans for the house to become a museum honoring General Pai. We do not know if this has been done.

The next morning, we were asked to rise early so that we could go sightseeing. As we drove through the town and countryside of Guilin, we noticed the people are not as prosperous looking as in other major cities that we've visited. In the countryside, the people in fact looked poor. The houses generally looked run down.

The children wore bright but shabby clothing, and the adults also wore shabby clothes. Many looked rather unkempt and dirty, but nobody looked like they were starving. The children freely urinated or defecated in public. We were to find this habit eliminated as early as our next trip to China in 1988.

The fields looked fertile, though, neat squares of crops, including rice plants, either bright green or yellow (depending on their stage of growth), forming a colorful quilt work of fields. There were other crops we couldn't identify and groves of fruit trees.

Here in the countryside, I saw scenes reminiscent of Chinese paintings. There were barefoot children tending water buffalo or bent over helping in the fields. Men and women carried enormous loads in buckets suspended from a pole carried across the shoulder, their faces brown and wrinkled from the sun and just plain hard work and difficult lives.

Older men and women, often toothless, were squatting on their heels on sidewalks, watching the traffic go by, their main entertainment. I'm certain that the routine nature of their lives is what causes crowds of people to form instantaneously whenever any event outside of the usual occurs, such as an accident or an argument.

The squatting position people take fascinates me because I think my legs would feel cramped very quickly, and I would lose my balance. The Chinese, little and big, squat so stably it almost appears as if nature made the human body to squat. I have seen people perched on a narrow wall in this position. In the absence of furniture, they eat their meals in this position. I have even seen people squatting next to an empty chair. As David commented, they would make natural baseball catchers!

Another image of China is one that was repeated in all the places we visited. Everywhere there are people clutching brooms made of twigs tied together (figure 156). They sweep these over the streets and paths to clean them of leaves and litter. I have been impressed with the cleanliness in the cities we have been to. There is dust, certainly, but very little litter.

We were taken to visit the Reed Flute Caves of Guilin. They were discovered by farmers in the 1930s. When the Japanese invaded, the farmers and their families fled to the caves and were never found by the enemy. Now centers for tourism, the caves are magnificent, with interesting limestone formations that resembled animals and plants for which they were named and lakes (figure 157).

Among the well-known scenic areas of Guilin we were shown was a park with Flower Bridge and Camel Mountain. The latter is one of the limestone karsts of Guilin that happens to look like humps on a camel's back. The karsts are great cones of limestone that rise abruptly from the earth.

I have seen Chinese paintings of mountains that look like the karsts and always thought that the almost abstract paintings were due to artistic license. But the karsts of Guilin really do look like chicken croquettes (figure 158). Limestone karsts of Guilin houses and even multistoried buildings are simply built around them. One can only hope that the extraordinary geology will be preserved as the tourist trade expands.

We were the hosts at the dinner for relatives and local government officials at our hotel. There were several tables full of people. I sat with Peggy, Scott, and Peter at the lowest-status table with the lowest-status men. Communism supports the idea of a classless society, yet there is no doubt a keen sense of position. David and I were never treated as just equals to the rest of our People to People delegation. He was always addressed as the delegation leader.

The meal was rather uncomfortable for us, in part because of the stilted conversation and in part because of the food served: we had masked civet, turtle, pigeon, and frog legs. Thank goodness there was also fried bread, or bing, and dumplings, which us nonnative diners filled up on.

After the meal, we sat in the lobby and chatted a bit. There was a calligrapher practicing his art of writing Chinese with brush pens but in a most unusual manner. He was writing a poem on a blank scroll, but he was doing it with both hands, writing two lines simultaneously. And he was doing it with flair, as his calligraphy was quite beautiful (figure 159). Think about trying to write two lines of any text with both hands in English—and we don't even need to make it artistic!

The next day, we took the fabled cruise up the Li River. Our van had to drive many miles more than normal because the usual starting point of the cruise was at such a low level due to drought that the boats could not be taken out. We drove to the middle part of where the Li River cruise normally reaches.

Even there, the river was so low that we needed a tug to pull us along because we were on the VIP boat, which was a large vessel. Even so, we scraped bottom several times, setting off the warning bell. When the bell rang, the tug would speed up to make sure we could get over the river bottom. I hoped they knew there were no big boulders that could rip open the boat.

The scenery was magnificent, truly one of the amazing sights of the world! The river is lined on both sides with karsts of various shapes, under which are nestled small villages with huts, some thatched. Surrounding the clusters of small houses are the neat patches of farmland, where mostly rice is grown, though there are also leafy vegetables of some kind.

Near each village there are houseboats on the river. Often, lacy fishing nets were hung out on poles. We did not see any fishermen with cormorants, which are well known on Li River. I suspect the river may be too shallow for the birds to dive down to catch fish. The birds have collars around their necks so that they cannot easily swallow the fish they catch. I am told they respond to whistles that are solely the ones used by each owner with his own cormorant.

One of the karsts was called Nine Horse Mountain because there were white strokes, almost like a painting, and supposedly one could count nine horses on one side of the karst. We couldn't really see more than three or so horses. Perhaps when the mountain was first seen there were possibly nine, but no longer.

Toward the end of the cruise, the sharp thrusts of the karsts into the sky softened at one point into hills. The hills were neatly terraced with rice paddies. I wondered if the people who lived among such beauty were aware of their surroundings, or did they take all for granted, like so many of us in the US who ignore the beauty in our land?

When the cruise ended, I saw some boys with cormorants perched in baskets at the ends of long poles. When one saw me pointing my camera at his birds, he covered them up with his big coolie hat. I then realized they were there to pose for money from tourists. I did pay an older man money to take his picture (figure 160) and that of his bird (figure 161). I believe I paid five US dollars for each.

I had hoped to buy some rocks that had the shape of karsts to use in plantings of bonsai when I returned home to the US. However, there was no time, and we were driven back to the hotel. That evening, we were to be hosted by the vice governor of the province of Guangxi and the mayor of Guilin. David's father, General Pai, was one of the heroes of Guilin and all of Guangxi, and David and Diana were to receive due recognition as his children.

As has been the rule in our meetings with high officials, our meeting in the evening began with everyone sitting around the periphery of a large greeting room. David and Diana sat with the vice governor at the head of the room, and people were distributed around with the lesser officials sitting opposite the place of honor. After some formal picture taking, we went to dinner at a huge, round table that seated some twenty persons. The food again was exotic: civet, turtle soup, frog legs, and fried whole birds.

When they brought out the turtle soup, they placed the bowl right in front of Scott. There was a whole box turtle, shell and all, upside down in the soup! Scott looked a bit upset and finally asked, "Could someone please at least turn the turtle right-side up?"

Turtle soup is supposed to have medicinal properties to the Chinese. It is very expensive, costing over the equivalent of a thousand ren men bi dollars in Hong Kong. At that time, the exchange rate was eight ren men bi dollars to one US dollar. The presence of turtle soup in a banquet marks a meal as a very special one indeed.

Because of the menus of the banquets we were given in Guilin, I was reminded of reading somewhere a quotation of a Chinese saying that the Cantonese (who live in the province of Guangdong, just east of Guangxi) eat anything with legs except a table and anything with wings except an airplane. It seemed to apply to Guangxi as well!

I was reminded of a story of an American who was being hosted at a dinner in Guangxi. One of the dishes was a combination of meat and vegetables that the American felt was tasty, and he asked his host what kind of meat it was. "Moose" was the answer.

The American was surprised. "I didn't know you had moose here," he responded. "Are your moose as big as American moose?" he asked, gesturing with his hands many feet apart.

"Oh no," his host replied. "They are only this big." He held his hands about six inches apart.

The new and different cuisine took its toll on my digestive system, and I fell victim to food poisoning. Because of it, I had to stay in the hotel while David and a few relatives visited the village where General Pai had been born and raised. It was just as well that I stayed back in the hotel, because when David returned, he told me the village could only be reached by about an hour's walk on mud and dirt roads.

General Pai rose from poor beginnings, which explained his lifelong interest in making education and better living conditions available to the people of Guangxi Province. He was worthy of the respect and idolization the people of Guangxi held for him.

David and I then traveled to Hong Kong from Guilin for a few days of visiting his oldest sister, Patsy; her husband, David Loo; David's older brother, Robert; and his wife, Kathy. Robert, who worked at Foster Wheeler, had been assigned to Hong Kong to begin forming business associations for his company with Communist China. We stayed in Patsy's apartment up in the hills of Hong Kong. David Loo worked as a general manager in his family's Tai Ping Carpet company, a high-end rug manufacturing and distribution company.

At dinner, we laughed, exchanging stories of problems travelers had had in the People's Republic of China. We told them about the fiasco of flying out of Beijing, when our flight was delayed for hours so the pilot and crew could have dinner.

Robert told of an American who'd requested three fried eggs for breakfast at his hotel in China instead of one, which was usually served. Annoyed, the waiter had brought him four eggs all at once on separate plates. Another American complained that he'd gotten no fresh towels in his hotel room. It had turned out that the people who were cleaning his room were angry that he'd thrown his used towel onto the floor after one use, as was habit in American hotels, so they wouldn't bring him more towels. We Americans are truly spoiled, and the workers in the new hotels of China in 1985 had no idea what travelers from the Western countries expected of them. On our later trips to China, the attitude and service at hotels were much more courteous and understanding of Western habits. I threw out a sock with a hole in the heel one day. Later that day, when I returned to my room, there was the sock—mended, washed, and ironed—on my bed.

I do not have much of interest to say about the first few days we stayed in Hong Kong because I was still suffering from the aftereffects of food poisoning and did little beyond resting in hotel rooms. It seemed to me that the three major activities of residents there were shopping, eating, and making money, not necessarily in that order.

In fact, I was uncomfortable with the money culture of Hong Kong. There seemed to be much emphasis on how rich people were and how to make it known. One day I saw a limousine painted pink. The chauffeur, perhaps to his embarrassment, was dressed in a pink chauffeur uniform. Patsy told me the lady who owned the limo also dyed her poodle pink. I guessed she must have had so much money she didn't know how to spend it all.

I wonder how her life and the lives of others like her were impacted when the PRC government took over Hong Kong again in 1996. It had been ceded as a colony to Great Britain following the first shameful Opium War (1839–1842), which was waged by the British against China and ended in the Treaty of Nanking, in which Hong Kong was ceded to the United Kingdom and China was forced to trade with the Western nations. In addition, Kowloon and an area called the New Territory, both on mainland China across the harbor from Hong Kong, were also ceded to the British. The Second Opium War (1856–1860) was waged by the United Kingdom to legalize the trade of opium to China.

To my mind, the Opium Wars that the British waged in China would be like the drug lords of Mexico and Colombia—who supply hard drugs, such as heroin, to feed the habits of addicts in the United States—waging war against the United States to keep the flow of drugs into our country and, having been successful in such a war, being ceded large areas of territory in the United States. That was what the people of China had to bear following the wars.

Is it not understandable then that when the Communists won the civil war and promised China would no longer be the doormat for Western powers, the Communists created great pride and excitement initially among the people of China? Remember, I was almost deluded into staying in China in 1950.

One of the fun days of our trip in Hong Kong gave us the pleasure and privilege of viewing two different and impressive collections of bonsai. My bonsai master, Yuji Yoshimura, had told me to contact a banker, Mr. Wu Yee Sun, who had a magnificent collection of bonsai. I had written to Mr. Wu before we embarked on our People to People trip and received an invitation to visit his home. Despite recuperating in Macao from a throat problem, Mr. Wu decided to take a hovercraft from Macao to meet with us personally.

He was small in stature and frail, being in his eightieth decade of life (figure 162). His throat problem caused him to speak in a raspy voice. His bonsai collection was indeed mind-boggling. There were landscape plantings so large that they required a mechanical wrench and several men to move them (figure 163). Mr. Wu had three full-time employees who tended to his trees.

Sadly, none of Mr. Wu's family were interested in continuing to maintain his collection. Mr. Wu said he was beginning to send his bonsai to various nurseries and gardens in Canada and the United States. I wrote the following in my diary:

> He told us as we continued to walk and chat that he was the third generation to participate in the art of bonsai in his family and pointed out a few trees started by his grandfather. They had wonderful trunks of many inches in diameter. To keep such trees alive in small amounts of soil requires daily attention as well as knowledge of the needs of different species. I wished I had days to study his trees rather than the two and a half hours we actually had.
>
> The style of Chinese bonsai, as I have mentioned, is much freer than that of the Japanese, which is more elegant but less natural. Chinese do not wire all the needles of a pine to direct upward, for example, and there are what Mr. Yoshimura would call conflicting branches all over the trees. But as I wandered through Mr. Wu's collection, I began to get a better sense of Chinese bonsai …
>
> We were invited into the mansion for a dim sum snack. The house is full of antiques. He has a large collection of antique bonsai pots that must be very valuable. He handed me a small one that he said was about twelve hundred years old. I could hardly move or breathe for fear of dropping it!

We signed his guest book before leaving, and he presented me with a calendar and a copy of his bonsai book. Patsy told Mr. Wu about my family, and he knew of General Pai. He was greatly excited to learn of our families, and I was glad it pleased him to have us as guests, as he had really extended himself to be hospitable to us.

We returned to Robert's apartment, and after lunch, we drove to the New Territory, an area on the mainland of China across the harbor from Hong Kong administered by the British as a result of the Opium War, to a working Taoist temple. Patsy had arranged for us to visit the temple, as it too had a large bonsai collection.

The temple was painted in bright colors, predominantly red and gold. There must have been a retirement community there, as elderly men sat around chatting, and elderly women puttered around, dusting the altars and tables loaded with fruit and other food offerings neatly stacked on plates.

In one room, a monk in embroidered robes was leading a group of a dozen or so lesser monks in saffron robes in prayer. A man was playing a high-pitched reedy instrument at the same time. The smell of incense was in the air.

We waited for the bonsai caretaker to come talk to us. I was disappointed in the appearance of some bonsai that were visible. The trees were not trimmed, and basic shapes were lost by branches growing wild out of the trunk. The caretaker came to join us, a stocky man in his thirties, wearing a Dior tennis shirt, with a swaggering air to him. He led us to a locked back garden housing his best trees. There are some one thousand trees all told at the temple. He and two helpers work on them full-time.

The trees are trained in the natural Lingnan style, he explained, and have not been trimmed of late because of the pending winter. This explains some of the wildness of his trees. Indeed, we did see some magnificent trees, hundreds of years old, with gnarled and great trunks five to six inches in diameter. However, the trees were generally clearly not as well styled as Mr. Wu's.

At the end of our visit, the caretaker gave us calendars, and we contributed to the temple. He waved as we drove off.

In the evening, we joined Patsy's mother-in-law, Robert and Kathy, and some Pai family friends at the Regal Meridian Hotel for an elaborate dinner. Every course was served by a waiter on clean plates. Teacups were warmed first in bowls of hot water before we had our choice of six teas brewed and poured without leaves into the warmed cups. The food, unfortunately, was uneven in quality.

The next day, we visited a group of markets called, at that time, the Stanley Markets, as they were located in an area named Stanley. The place was mobbed, and with the heat and humidity of Hong Kong, it was difficult for people to move about. But the merchandise was unbelievably cheap compared to prices we paid for the same goods in the United States.

Since we were still actively playing tennis at that time, David and I bought several shirts and other articles of clothing for tennis for about one quarter the price at which they were sold in the United States. I wondered how the sellers had come to have the merchandise so that they could afford to sell it so cheaply. I did not ask anyone, however, and just accepted it, as did everyone in Hong Kong, apparently. I wonder if the Stanley Markets are still in existence.

I began to wilt again after shopping, and David showed some annoyance that I was still ill from food poisoning. I guess I was a drag since I chose not to join him for a number of meals, deferring instead to have soup and toast back at the apartment. I returned his annoyance, though, since it was not my choice to be ill. Ah, the nuances of marriage!

Patsy's two sons, Mark and Carl, went to a private high school, Andover, in the United States when Patsy and David Loo relocated back to Hong Kong. During short holidays, the boys would stay with us in Livingston, as we had the room. Both young men were bright and good models for our sons, who were quite a few years younger. While we were in Hong Kong in 1985, we had a chance to meet with Carl's new girlfriend, Frances Wong.

We were invited to dinner one night at the home of Carl's girlfriend. Frances's parents were old friends of Patsy and David Loo. We drove to the New Territory, where Clifford Wong, Frances's father, had had the foresight to buy lots of land when land was cheap. He then had developed it into prosperous suburban-like communities. Needless to say, his investment had turned into a gold mine, and he'd had a mansion built for himself and his family on top of a hill in the New Territory.

The mansion sat inside twenty-foot-high walls and an electric gate. Posh and elegant, the house had huge rooms for entertainment. There was the requisite swimming pool, as well as a game room my sons would have loved. Another room served either as an exercise room or a disco, replete with stereo and flashing floor and ceiling lights. At least three Filipino maids scurried around after us. They had one doorman, who was probably also their chauffeur, and full-time nurses for Clifford, who'd suffered a severe stroke at the age of fifty-two.

Clifford came down to greet us with the help of a cane and the support of one of the nurses. He was a tall man and looked as if he had been a handsome man, but the stroke had distorted his face. His right side was affected, as was his speech, which was slurred. It was sad to see him so afflicted at the height of his success. I thought to myself that I would be surprised if Carl didn't yield to pressure to return to Hong Kong in the future to help with the family enterprise, though David Loo wanted Carl to stay in the United States for more work experience.

We were driven to the country club of their development and had a good dinner that was mostly seafood. The Cantonese who populated Hong Kong were good at cooking seafood Chinese style. Both David and I liked Cantonese cooking the best because of their artistry with steamed fish—a dish that told us if the chef was really talented—and sautéed fresh vegetables, which were much tastier than the boiled veggies that were part of our American cuisine.

After dinner, we returned to the mansion and found Clifford still up and waiting for us to return. We chatted awhile. I was moved when he ended his conversation with Carl with the plea "Please don't hurt my daughter." He was afraid Carl might decide not to marry Frances. He need not have worried: Carl married Frances, and they had four children. Carl did return to Hong Kong and made his home there.

That dinner marked the end of our short but memorable stay in Hong Kong. We packed up and looked forward to our trip to Taiwan. Not only would we see all of David's brothers who lived there, but we would meet my big brother Solan and his wife, Jeannie, there. Together we would visit my uncle Zhang Xueliang, the Young Marshal, who was then eighty-five years old, and Aunt Edith, both still under house arrest at that time.

Fig 156 Street cleaner and tourist exchanging curious looks

Fig 157 Lake in Reed Flute Cave

Fig 158 Limestone Karsts of Guilin

Fig 159 A unique calligrapher

Fig 160 Cormorant Fisherman

Fig 161 A Cormorant

Fig 162 Mr. Wu Yee Sun, David and me

Fig 163 Two large forest landscape bonsai

Chapter 53

A VISIT TO A NATIONAL HERO, THE YOUNG MARSHAL

The flight from Hong Kong to Taiwan was routine. We flew Cathay Pacific, and the service was outstanding in courtesy and promptness. Upon our arrival in Taipei Airport, there were four different lines we had to get through, from picking up baggage to customs inspection. It took a full hour to emerge and greet David's sixth brother, Albert, who was waiting with a car from the travel agency where he worked.

When we arrived at the hotel, Solan and Jeannie were already there. They said the Young Marshal was expecting us that afternoon and was ready to take us sightseeing. Clearly our uncle had much more freedom now that Chiang Kei Shek and also his successor and son, Chiang Jing Kuo, had died. Madame Chiang had moved to Long Island, New York, and then New York City, where she died at the age of 105 in 2003.

I was still not completely over the food poisoning that had beset me all through our stay in Hong Kong and should have opted to skip the sightseeing, but the opportunity to finally meet that storied figure in modern Chinese history and his devoted wife was more than I could resist.

I wrote the following in my diary:

> A car with driver was waiting for the four of us outside the hotel after lunch. We were driven to the outskirts of Taipei, the capital of Taiwan. The way to the Young Marshal's house was a series of twisting country roads. It was almost impossible to remember the way.
>
> The driver did not speak to us at all. As we neared the house, he gave one long beep and two short ones on the car horn. Since this was done each time we visited, it was obviously a signal to the guards that we were there.
>
> Across from the opening to the driveway, a man emerged from the house in response to the horn signal. He looked at us and waved to a man at the driveway opening, who then waved us onto the property. Both men were no doubt guards

who were part of the secret service detail assigned by the Chiang family to guard the Young Marshal. The Chiangs wanted to make sure that this national hero would not defect to the People's Republic of China, which would welcome him with open arms.

As we drove up to the house, Jeannie said, "There he is!"

I turned and saw an elderly man in a loose tunic and slacks, with an open shirt collar and a dark brown beanie on his head. He was undoubtedly the Young Marshal (figure 164). The Zhang nose, almost aquiline for a Chinese; the long Zhang upper lip; and the Zhang slightly underslung jaw were evident. They were Solan's characteristics as well. Solan's and Stanley's features favor the Zhang family, while I look more like my father's.

Uncle's eyes seemed swollen and not focused as we greeted him. We heard later that he was nearly blind from cataracts and retinal degeneration. However, when he heard of our coming, he postponed the already scheduled cataract operation.

His first words to me were, in Chinese, "*Yuh* (a Chinese way of expressing surprise)! You grew to be so tall!" with the Manchurian twang to his Mandarin.

I am only five feet four and a half inches, but compared to women of his generation, I am no doubt considered tall. Actually, I am taller than he is, but he may have shrunk with age. His manners, so folksy and direct, made us feel comfortable right away.

Then our aunt Chao Sze, Aunt Edith (her American name), appeared. We had met her in the United States a year ago when she was allowed to enter the US for medical reasons. The doctor she saw in Taipei thought she had symptoms of lupus, but after examination by doctors at Columbia Presbyterian Hospital, which had been arranged by Solan, the diagnosis was that she did not have lupus.

Now in her seventies, she still shows signs of the beauty and vibrancy that caused the Young Marshal to fall in love and take her on as a lifelong companion in captivity (figure 165). She joined him even though in the first few months after the Xian Incident in 1936, there was still the possibility of execution being their fate. She simply loved him more than she wanted to live without him.

In 1964, when my parents were visiting in Taiwan (their last trip to the Far East), after thirty years of house arrest together, Aunt Edith and Uncle Peter (Christian names they chose for themselves after becoming born-again Christians, in part due to Madam Chiang's influence) called Mommy and Daddy at their hotel and told them to come to their house quickly. Worried about them, my parents hurried to them. When they saw them, Uncle Peter said with a big smile, "We're getting married!" They are now (in 1985) almost in their fiftieth year of house arrest!

We were led into the house for some tea on that first day of our visit. It was a house that was built for them and for which they paid. The sizable fortune that the Young Marshal inherited when his father, my Lao Yeh, was assassinated had no doubt been transferred to the United States with his son and his son's guardian for safety.

Their house is spacious, comfortable, and well designed. There is a sizable living room, an adequate dining room, and a large kitchen. The rooms are comfortably furnished, and there are cabinets filled with vases, stones, and figurines. They were mostly Sung Dynasty pieces.

Uncle quipped, "Sung is not only the tenth-century dynasty; it is also the Chinese word for the verb *present*." He chuckled at his little joke.

Uncle pointed out a large painting of leaves and branches over the fireplace. It was a painting by Madame Chiang. And a framed scroll of calligraphy.

About the scroll, he said, "This was written by Chiang Kai Shek himself when the two of us got drunk together!" Clearly their relationship was one of love and hate!

Throughout our visits, the Young Marshal referred to Chiang and Madame in very respectful terms. He showed us a bouquet that he had bought to commemorate Chiang's ninety-ninth birthday. I wondered if this behavior was by habit to impress his captors or if fifty years of brainwashing had succeeded. Or if indeed he feels some loyalty to Chiang, or perhaps because he feels he wronged Chiang in the Xian Incident. He has always said he deserved whatever punishment Chiang doled out because he had, after all, carried out a coup d'état.

These and others were questions that circumstances made impossible to discuss. We were always mindful of the fact that despite increased freedom, the old couple was still under house arrest. We certainly did not want to cause them trouble. Unless he opens up in the future—which is highly unlikely—we'll never really know what his mind-set was.

After a few minutes, we left the house and entered two cars, with Jeannie, Aunt Edith, and me in the smaller car and Solan, David, and Uncle Peter in the larger car. Each car was chauffeured, with an escort (probably a spy) riding shotgun in the front passenger seat. The same horn signals were given as we drove out of the compound.

The day was overcast, and it rained on and off as we drove to the northeastern part of Taiwan, where the Young Marshal wanted to show us his favorite seaside resort.

I was again not feeling well and was not helped by the long lectures by Aunt Edith about religion that I got along the way.

She had been operated on for lung cancer a few years ago and more recently was buoyed by the information that she did not have lupus. Having been spared twice, she now feels that God's will is to have her spread the Word. Unfortunately, I, her target for that day, wasn't feeling up to being very responsive.

I'm sure she thinks I'm doomed. Not only was I not very receptive to her exhortations, but also, I'm a biologist and a scientist and therefore, in her mind, prone to mess with nature. I don't feel ill of her for trying to save my soul. I just don't accept some of her beliefs. I certainly don't accept the thesis that people who believe in Christ have a monopoly on morality and/or salvation, which is a major point in her evangelist argument.

Aunt Edith and Uncle Peter are born-again Christians, Baptists, and proudly showed us certificates of graduation from an institution in the US where they obtained a long-distance education about Christianity. They attended church services on Sundays with the Chiangs occasionally, even though Madame Chiang was Methodist.

Uncle said that Aunt Edith was inclined to proselytize, while he was more comfortable studying the philosophy of religion. Indeed, my aunt encouraged David and me to study and believe. She gave us a Bible (that I still have), which she had signed in the hopes that we would be converted.

We arrived at the ocean and drove along the shore. There were few buildings anywhere, and one futuristic structure lay unoccupied. Aunt Edith said the builder had gone bankrupt for the lack of buyers. The shoreline looked beautiful. Given the crowded cities of Taiwan, I wondered why there weren't large numbers of dwellings in this region that the residents of the cities could use for vacations. The economy of Taiwan was such that surely there were people rich enough to invest in real estate developments.

We stopped at Uncle Peter's favorite spot. It was lovely, with a harbor formed by rocks jutting into the sea in a semicircle. It required a walk up and down uneven steps to get to the beach. We cautioned Uncle Peter to go slowly. Whether by habit and familiarity with this area or to prove his agility still existed, the eighty-five-year-old man led us down the walk at a brisk pace. We looked around and admired the scenery.

One of the escorts called to us and said rain and fog were moving in off the ocean. Sure enough, as we turned back, drops began to fall. Uncle Peter told us to go on, as he had to obey a call of nature. As we hurried to the cars, Solan laughingly told us that on the way, Uncle Peter had suggested stopping for a potty break because we women were always having to go. Turns out he had to go and didn't want to admit it! By the time we reached the cars, we were pretty wet, and the rain was a downpour.

We did not stay long at their house and drove back to Taipei to Sixth Aunt's home for dinner (figure 166). Sixth Aunt was a half sister to my mother.

Mommy had told me Sixth Aunt was a good cook, and it was true. We had a wonderful meal, and every dish was well prepared. There was a stewed spare ribs dish that David enjoyed, bean sprouts, beef and broccoli, vermicelli salad, beans, dumplings, and a sweet soup for dessert.

I wished I could eat more, but since Kweilin, food intake was almost always followed by nausea. They served a delicious hami melon and watermelon. (You may recall that serving hami melon was the signal for the Young Marshal's aide to execute the two men who were believed to be Japanese sympathizers in the assassination of the Old Marshal (chapter 7). Mercifully, we left fairly early, and I fell into bed at the hotel at once.

Even though I felt awful, I was exhilarated to finally meet the Young Marshal and find him well and with a delightfully sharp sense of humor. He teased Solan constantly about my brother's girth. Clearly my own tendency to tease those about whom I care the most is a family trait shared also by Solan and our uncle.

His appearance and mannerisms when he speaks are very similar to Mommy's and lead to their ability to regale others with stories of the past. The Young Marshal clearly enjoys being on stage and being the star. He is an engaging and charismatic man. It is not difficult to see how he must have been a natural leader—and the renowned womanizer he was reputed to be in his younger days.

Happily, when we visited him in 1985, he was allowed to leave his house again the next day, and we accompanied him to the home of the late, great Chinese artist Zhang Da Qien, who had the same surname as Uncle but was not related. Uncle and the artist were close friends and saw each other frequently. Both were old rascals, and I can imagine their meetings included sharing of alcohol and stories of past happy days.

Uncle took me to Mr. Zhang's house because the artist also enjoyed bonsai and the use of rocks as art objects (figure 167). I still have a viewing rock that my uncle received from his friend, which he then gave to me (figure 168). At my request, he wrote a note stating that the rock was his, and then he gave it to me (figure 169). He also gave me an ornate pot. I have donated the rock and the container to a museum. Uncle himself was not a bonsaist but an orchid aficionado. He claimed to have hundreds of pots of orchids and, with pride, showed us his collection (see again figure 164). He told us his interest was not in the flowers of the orchids but in the many varieties of leaves. I have not heard any other orchid growers claim the leaves were their focus of interest.

That he was still under arrest, however, was underscored by the presence of guards at the entrance to the house in which they lived, although clearly their lives had improved after Chiang died. I was not allowed to photograph the sentries. Also, when they left their home to visit friends, they were driven by government agents, as we all were on the first day of our visit. Chiang was said to be primarily concerned that Uncle might defect to the Communists, who always touted Uncle as a true hero and martyr. He did, after all, save their movement with the Xian Incident, though that was not his intention.

One day, after dinner, we were chatting at the dinner table. We were impressed that Uncle Peter could remember details of battles he'd fought more than fifty years ago, including where they were fought and for how long and the names of the leaders involved. When asked about the Xian Incident, however, he refused to comment. I am sure the rooms were bugged, which might have caused him to avoid discussing his famous action.

He did enjoy telling us about his trysts as a young man, when he was known to be a ladies' man and something of a playboy. He mentioned with a chuckle that he had been with Mussolini's daughter one year when he was in Italy. I glanced over at my aunt, and we made eye contact. She was leaning on her hand, looking a bit bored.

When she saw me look over to her, she shrugged, smiled, and said, "I've heard this story fifty times!" (figure 170).

The next day, we decided to have a dinner with Uncle and Auntie, and he said he would arrange to be driven to the restaurant in the five-star Lai Lai Hotel. We invited Sixth Aunt and David's brothers Danny (his oldest brother) and Charlie (his youngest brother, the seventh), their wives, and Albert (the sixth brother) to dinner. Jeannie invited some of her cousins who also lived in Taiwan. There would be a total of twenty-one of us (figure 171). Solan, the oldest of the siblings, insisted he would host the dinner. The following is from my diary:

> We had been given one of the large private rooms of the hotel restaurant, no doubt because the Young Marshal and Aunt Edith were to be the guests. Also, David's youngest brother, Charlie, seems to have connections, or *guan xi*, for every and any purpose.

Guan xi, or connections, have always played a major role in Chinese culture. One might equate guan xi in part to the saying "You scratch my back, and I'll scratch yours." Or, one might assume, it might be due in part to a central aspect of Chinese culture: reciprocity.

> Before dinner, we all sat on the sofas off to one side, chatted, and had pictures taken. When dinner was to be served, we all were seated at an oversize, round table that

could accommodate all twenty-one of us. It had one of the biggest lazy Susans I have ever seen.

But as the food came out, it became apparent that neither the Young Marshal nor his wife had any hesitation in turning down each dish, as they refused to eat most seafood (not clean) or fried foods (not healthy). Everyone became more anxious as the dinner progressed that we had not ordered the proper dishes.

However, because of the general nature of their dismissal of the dishes, it became apparent that no matter what was ordered, this would have probably happened. Thanks to the large number and variety of dishes, there were enough acceptable dishes for the old couple to eat and be full, and everyone relaxed.

As usual, the Young Marshal held center stage, good-naturedly poking fun at the relatives he knew and, of course, Solan. My brother had visited him more than once in recent years, so they were quite familiar with and fond of each other. Uncle Peter was in obvious good spirits and did not hesitate to respond to toasts to himself and his wife with brandy. David and I could only toast them with water since we're both allergic to alcohol.

Uncle Peter and Charlie (the youngest Pai brother) hit it off very well because both raise orchids, and both love to fish. (Charlie is farthest right in the standing row of figure 171). David always said of him that he was one of the smartest of the brothers. Later, Charlie said he wanted so much to ask the Young Marshal why he hadn't fired one more shot (at Chiang Kai Shek) in his military career. Had he done so, Charlie joked, Uncle would not be raising orchids, and Charlie would not just be fishing (meaning that General Pai would have had more freedom to govern).

I was pleased the Young Marshal impressed the Pais. This is an extraordinary man. And though she stays in the background, perhaps at least as extraordinary is his wife. We took many pictures during our entire visit.

The next day, Charlie picked us up to go to the Pai family cemetery plot. When General Pai had passed away, the sons had gotten together and decided they would all chip in and have a memorial built. Not only would their parents be buried there, but also, there would be plots for the siblings who wished to join them there eventually. David's second-oldest brother, Richard, was given the task of overseeing the construction of the memorial. I wrote in my diary,

> The family plot is large and an elaborate memorial to General Pai and his wife. There are several tiers of gardens and steps and a concrete railing leading to the site of the crypts (see again figure 116). On the pillars nearby the crypts are carved calligraphy writings of a number of people honoring the general and his wife. Behind the crypts,

on marble slabs, are Arabic writings from the Muslim faith. David's third sister, Amy, is buried there too. She died at a young age of acute hepatitis.

Unfortunately, time has taken its toll on the structures, and the maintenance is costly. Charlie and Richard still go and direct the caretaker, a retired soldier who served under the general. What will happen when the old soldier is no longer able to work is hard to say. The Taiwan government may assume some of the cost because of the high regard in which General Pai is held by many Chinese.

There is also a plaque in English from the Trutter family, who once had taken Richard under their wings after he graduated from Indiana Technological University. He had survived a horrible car accident that put him in a coma for weeks. He met Papa Trutter (as we were told to address him) socially while working for an Illinois highway department for several years in Springfield, Illinois. Mr. Trutter also lived in Springfield with his family. We visited the Trutters in Illinois once. They were most gracious and warm, typically American in their readiness to open their hearts and home to us. They virtually adopted Richard as part of their family.

After we returned from the cemetery, we had a quick lunch with Solan across the street from the hotel because the Young Marshal said his car would call for us at one o'clock. He had a full day planned out, including a bonsai and rock exhibition and taking us to buy bonsai pots and then dinner at his house.

The driver came right on time. When we got to Uncle's house, he was waiting, though he looked a little sleepy. Perhaps our arrival had awakened him from a nap. Aunt Edith did not join us for the day's activities because she had a bad leg that had been broken once and could not walk very easily.

Jeannie and I sat with Uncle in the big car, and our two husbands sat in the smaller car. The Young Marshal constantly cautioned the driver to be careful and drive slower. He and his wife show the same kind of self-preservation tendencies that I've seen in my mother.

Our first stop was the grounds of the former home of Chiang Kai Shek. It was not clear to me if it is still used as the presidential palace. Jeannie and Solan had joined Uncle Peter and Aunt Edith as they attended Sunday services there in a chapel that had been used by the generalissimo and madame.

We drove up a long, straight driveway hundreds of yards off the main road. At the entrance to the property, there was a roll of barbed wire. A young sentry stepped out to check our credentials. The escort in the front passenger seat stepped out to talk to him and showed him something in his wallet.

The sentry rolled back the barbed wire, and he and two other guards at the entrance saluted smartly as we drove by. The Young Marshal returned their salute in sort of a half wave.

There was to be a bonsai exhibit the next day that was open to the public, so they were still arranging the trees and judging them. There were some magnificent trees, much more elegant in form than those we saw at the temple in Hong Kong. Indeed, these are much more similar to Japanese bonsai, so that may be why I found them so impressive. Uncle Peter took obvious delight in my interest in the bonsais and rocks and rushed us through so that we would have time to see everything.

It had begun to rain fairly hard. When the rain began as a drizzle, I opened my umbrella and held it over the Young Marshal. He literally ran from under the umbrella, protesting he didn't need it. I guess he is trying to maintain his sense of manliness because he refuses any form of support, no matter where we are walking or how rough the terrain. As it rained harder, though, I noticed that he was walking under the escort's umbrella. I guess that was more appropriate in his mind.

From there, we drove to the home of one of China's greatest modern artists, Zhang Da Qien, who had died recently. His home is now a museum of sorts, open to the public at specified times (see again figure 167). He was a good friend of the Young Marshal. After looking at pictures of him and hearing the Young Marshal describe his eccentricities, I can see why the two were so close: they were two of a kind!

I wish I could have met the artist when he was alive to photograph him. Photos showed that he looked like a real character: bald on top, with long white hair lower on his head, white beard, and always dressed in Chinese robes and a Chinese silk hat. In his photos, he always carried a staff, probably more for effect than use. The two men must have had some wild stories to tell each other, as they both were legendary womanizers when young.

The Young Marshal told us that Zhang Da Qien hurt himself for posterity by being too prolific and too generous in giving away paintings to friends. Uncle had several of his friend's paintings in his house. I'd love to have any of them, as they are truly brilliant. They are a combination of classical brush painting with a modern flair.

Uncle took us on a tour of the house, and we saw a wax figure of the artist painting. He said the wax figure was an exact representation of the artist at work. There are paintings and viewing stones all over the house.

Zhang Da Qien is buried in the yard of his house, and Uncle paused at the grave site to pay his respect. How sad this aspect of aging is, I thought, as your friends also age and leave one by one. But there must be some comfort too in the thought that when it is your turn, you have all sorts of love waiting for you if there is in fact an afterlife.

We then drove to a nursery with which Uncle was familiar for me to buy bonsai containers. I chose ten from the large number and varieties of pots that were there. Uncle appeared to enjoy haggling over the price for me and got a discount that brought the total to less than one hundred dollars, incredibly cheap compared to prices I have had to pay in the United States. Most of the bonsai containers I bought from Mr. Yoshimura were Japanese and of very high quality. They would eventually be delivered to my American home.

We returned to the Young Marshal's house, and I am sure I was more tired than the Young Marshal, who seemed as fresh and vocal as when we started out. We found Aunt Edith waiting for us with presents, a sweater for me and an instamatic camera for David.

For dinner, Aunt Edith had cooked a variety of dishes herself: meatballs, shark's fin soup, vegetables, small meat pies, and stewed pork. Their cook made a few more dishes. A man who looked like a soldier served us dinner. We therefore saw seven men, including the two gate guards, attending to the Young Marshal and his wife.

We decided that the Nationalist government supplies this support for my uncle and aunt to protect and nurture them as much as to keep them in a form of captivity. The couple is too important in modern Chinese history and too revered by Chinese people in general for them to be harmed.

We were joined at dinner by a cousin, Linda, the daughter of Mommy's fifth brother. (Linda and her mother, Fifth Aunt, whose English name was Macy, were very close to Mommy and Daddy while they lived in Manchuria and Beijing, and apparently are even closer to the Young Marshal and his wife).

Throughout the dinner and even well afterward, the Young Marshal recounted memories of past battles and events and girlfriends. He told of serendipitous victories achieved by accident. Once, a leader of one of his armies withdrew quietly from a front at night. When the Young Marshal was informed of the retreat, he sent orders immediately for the army to return to the front.

Chuckling, Uncle said, "The enemy saw the army coming but thought they were reinforcements for the troops they had seen pulling in during the day. They gave up and themselves withdrew, and we won!"

On another occasion, a train loaded with a cannon and troops had broken down. As they waited for a replacement engine, they saw an enemy train coming from the opposite direction. Without thinking, a soldier trained a cannon at the oncoming train and fired. The shell entered the nose of the train and traveled from one end to the other and created such a vacuum that all the enemy troops perished by their bodies literally exploding!

A masterful storyteller, as was my mother, the Young Marshal kept us engrossed for hours. He wanted to set one widely known story straight. There was a popular rumor that at the time of the Japanese invasion of Manchuria in 1931, the Young Marshal was not attending to business but was attending a Chinese opera with a movie star known as Butterfly.

"However," the Young Marshal said, "the person who started the rumor was trying to give me a bad name. There was no Butterfly. I was in the company of nurses because I was being treated for opium addiction."

(Later, Mommy told us that when he decided to join Chiang Kai Shek, Uncle Peter, Uncle's first wife, and Aunt Edith were all ordered by Chiang Kai Shek to quit their opium addiction cold turkey. They did so, and this was at least one reason Uncle was grateful to Chiang Kai Shek—for saving their lives rather than executing them).

Uncle Peter told us of a close call he had in Monte Carlo. He was playing blackjack and sitting next to a beautiful young woman to whom he had given some chips. When she quit and left the table, he followed, thinking that she wanted him to be with her, which was apparently the case. Suddenly, she waved at him behind her back. Curious, he continued to approach her, when he heard an old man saying to her, "Hello, darling. Time to go to bed." She had been warning him of the approach of her husband! Uncle said he veered off, not missing a step, and the husband had no idea of their intentions!

During all this time, Aunt Edith was with him. I wondered if these stories about his cavalier ways as a young man must have stung her. Yet she still loved him enough to give up life and child to stay with him. He was quite a man!

They mentioned the Xian Incident (discussed in chapter 6) only once during our visit. The Young Marshal said that his decision to turn himself in after capturing Chiang and extracting a promise that Chiang would join the Communists to fight the Japanese was a matter of principle. He always believed in being responsible for his actions.

Aunt Edith joined in and said that he had acted to save lives and that there would have been more deaths if he had not acted. She nagged at him to recount for us how they found religion.

He responded that he did not feel that subject was as interesting or as important as the military history he had talked about. But he then did address the subject, saying that Madame Chiang was the driving force of their conversion. Uncle recounted that Madame had said to him, "You should not make a second serious mistake in your life by not accepting Christ." The first serious mistake in her estimation was, of course, the Xian Incident.

Since then, some seventeen years ago, they had studied theology together. Uncle said that his focus on religion and Aunt Edith's focus were different. He is interested in the philosophy of religion, while she is focused on evangelism. They had taken correspondence courses with a Baptist college, and both had received diplomas.

The Young Marshal gave me a lovely viewing stone and an old, ornate plant container with carvings. I asked him to write me some calligraphy explaining the origin of the stone. He bent close to the paper on his desk because of his failing eyesight and wrote a few lines (see again figure 169). He smudged some of the words, and Aunt Edith cleaned them up. They are among my most valued possessions, as is the Bible she gave me.

That was our last visit together while they were still under house arrest. Solan was leaving the next day to return home, and we were to spend a last day with David's relatives before we too were to return home. At about ten o'clock in the evening, we reluctantly decided to end our visit with them, although the Young Marshal maintained he could still go on visiting with us.

"*Wo hai kuh yee tan tan!*" (I can still chat more!), he protested. But we demurred, worried that Uncle needed to rest.

They urged us to return next year. If possible, we said, we will. Solan is serious about collaborating with me in writing a book based on our family's history, with Uncle Peter and Aunt Edith as prominent characters in it. If we are to succeed, he said, we must take advantage of the few years we have left with our uncle, the Young Marshal. I agreed. They walked us out, and as we were driven off, they were waving from the steps of their house.

We spent a day with David's siblings Charlie and Danny and their families. In the evening, after dinner, we made goodbye phone calls to Uncle Peter, Aunt Edith, and Fifth Aunt. Uncle Peter again urged me to return next March because they would commemorate Madame Chiang's birthday with a bonsai exhibit. I told him I would try. Our momentous trip to China in 1985 was over.

The next year, 1986, was the year David had open-heart surgery and five bypasses. Complications from that surgery made it impossible for us to travel. In 1988, Uncle Peter and Aunt Edith were released from house arrest and moved to Honolulu, Hawaii. They were attended to in Hawaii both by nurses and by Fifth Aunt, Fifth Uncle, and Linda, who had also moved to Honolulu. In 1990, Uncle Peter and Aunt Edith came to New York City, as I described earlier, in chapter 6, to celebrate his ninetieth birthday. Figures 172 and 173 show two letters David and I received from her, dated February 9 and August 3, 1990, explaining why she could not come to have Thanksgiving dinner with us.

After they moved to Hawaii, we did have the opportunity to visit with them again, although I do not remember the exact year. It was likely around 1995 or 1996. We found Uncle Peter using a wheelchair, as he was no longer able to walk as well as when we'd seen him in Taiwan, and he was having trouble with his hearing and eyesight. Fifth Aunt, Fifth Uncle, and their daughter Linda were with Uncle Peter and Aunt Edith every day, along with several home health-care people. It was clear the couple were enjoying their freedom (figure 174). It was the last time we saw them alive. Aunt Edith passed away in 1999 from lung cancer; Uncle Peter, the Young Marshal, died in 2001 at the age of 101, as I described in chapter 6. David's failing health also precluded us from making long trips.

Their year of liberation from house arrest, 1988, was also the year Solan was diagnosed with colorectal cancer. He and I never had time to write the book together. This book is my feeble attempt to accomplish what my big brother sincerely wanted to do and probably could have done better.

Fig 164 Uncle Peter, the Young Marshal, and my brother, Dr. Solan Chao

Fig 165 Uncle Peter and Aunt Edith, 1985

Fig 166 Sixth aunt, her grandbaby and Uncle Peter

Fig 167 At the house of the artist, Zhang Da Qien

Fig 168 Viewing Rock, a present from my Uncle Peter

Fig 169 Uncle Peter writing a note about the viewing rock he gave me

Fig 170 Uncle Peter telling stories and amusing Aunt Edith

Fig 171 Our dinner party for Uncle Peter and Aunt Edith

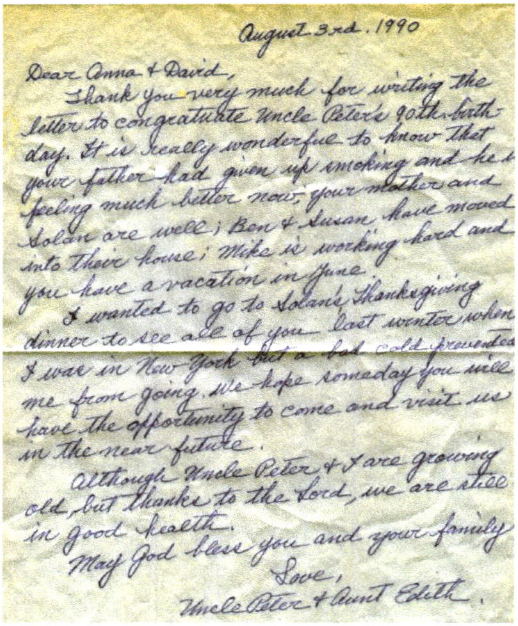

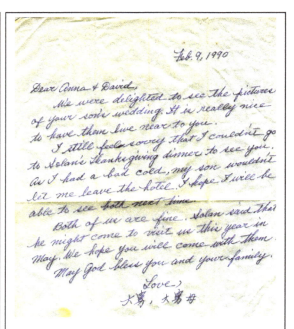

Fig 172 Letter hand written by Aunt Edith

Fig 173 Letter hand written by Aunt Edith

Fig 174 Uncle Peter and Aunt Edith in Hawaii

Chapter 54

WE REVISIT CHINA IN 1988

In 1988, three years after our momentous 1985 visit to China, Hong Kong, and Taiwan, David had another international meeting of pressure vessel and piping engineers in China. The meeting happened to correspond with our son Mike's graduation from Cornell University. Ben and Susan had graduated from Duke University the year before. We decided to bring Mike with us to China as his graduation present. Both Ben and Susan were occupied with graduate studies and could not afford the time for the trip.

We took Mike to some major cities we had visited in 1985. The hotel situation was much improved. Professional people from all over Europe and the United States had taken over the running of major hotels in the major cities. We did not, however, have an opportunity to visit Fragrant Hill Hotel to see what upgrades had been done in the years since we left the PRC in 1985. Some of the hotels we stayed in caused Mike to exclaim one day, "I don't feel like I'm in China. This looks like any American luxury hotel!"

In three years, the country had made giant strides to improve what it had to offer to the increasing numbers of businesspeople from the West. In light of China's population of more than a billion consumers, American businesses were establishing offices in the major cities, such as Shanghai, Beijing, and Guangzhou.

While neither David nor I kept a diary on that trip, Mike remembers the trip well. In response to my request for him to write down some of his memories of his first trip to China, the following, in his own inimitable words, is an account of the trip:

> I did not keep a diary. However, I do have some distinct memories of the trip since it was my first to China. If I recall, our itinerary was this:
>
> We flew from JFK airport on Long Isl and to Beijing. Dad had meetings.
>
> - Despite me being twenty-two at the time, you insisted that I hold your hand to cross the street because of the bicycles, as you were afraid I was going to get run over!
>
> - You and I toured Beijing University with the professor who had been imprisoned by Mao in the Cultural Revolution.

- We met with students openly discussing their displeasure with the Communist Party. Then, many months later, came the Tiananmen Massacre in 1989.

- We went to the Forbidden City and Tiananmen Square. I recall the ticket to the Forbidden City had a Mitsubishi ad on it, at which Dad started cursing.

- We went to two different places to see the Great Wall. One was where most tourists go, and the other was a part of the wall that was less well known at the time. I do remember there was a tiny little shop at the base of the hill that had an actual Coke machine and, to my enormous pleasure, had icy-cold Coca-Cola.

- As we walked around, the kids were fascinated by your camera and the big lenses.

- And yes, there was a translator with us, who was cute. And had it been up to you, you would have arranged our marriage right then and there (and we would never have had Kath (his lovely wife), Aidan, or Nathan (his adorable two young sons) in the family, so it worked out in the end).

I need to insert some comments regarding the above. Yes, I did grab Mike's hand to cross the street in Beijing because of the lasting effects of my traumatic attempt to cross the street during rush hour in 1985, when a group of fellow travelers and I were surrounded by a zillion bicycles. David felt the ad on the ticket should have been about a Chinese product rather than a Japanese product.

The young lady who accompanied us on the Great Wall was clearly attracted to Mike, especially when she found out he was single and did not have a steady girlfriend. She was attractive and intelligent and spoke English well, and Mike had disappointed us by not finding anyone at Cornell to join our family. The young lady was so taken with Mike that after we returned home, she made a phone call to try to reconnect with him. I received her call; Mike was not home. When told of the message, he declined to call her back. *Sigh*.

Furthermore, I received a phone call from someone we met on the trip who was calling on behalf of a friend. With some awkwardness, he said, "Dr. Pai, I have a friend who has an attractive daughter who would like to come to the United States to meet Mike. She is smart and would like to meet your son, who impressed us all."

I was astonished. The man was so desperate to send his daughter out of the country that he was willing to give her up sight unseen to someone he had never even met!

"I'm so sorry," I responded, "but in America, parents have little influence on their children with regard to whom they marry. Please tell your friend we apologize, and we wish good luck to him and his daughter."

Even in the late 1980s, China was still recovering from the effects of the Cultural Revolution. We received many other requests from people we had met on our two trips for help in establishing some help for their youngsters, requests we could not accommodate. Let's go back to Mike's memories.

We flew from Beijing to Xian.

- I recall that there were people on the plane to whom a table and chairs constituted luggage to be stowed in the overhead compartment! Also, since air travel was completely state run at the time, the planes came and went as they pleased with ETAs and ETDs not really applicable. I remember we waited like seven hours for this flight.

- We went to see the Terracotta Warriors. At the time, there was not a big tourist structure, as was there when we went back in 2005. There was really just one building.

- We went to the resort where the Xian Incident took place. And if you remember, as we were touring up in the hills a bit, our guide went and spoke to somebody (like the caretaker) and told them who you were. They then opened up a couple of exhibits that were typically not open to the public. When we looked around inside, a throng of people came and looked through the window (they weren't allowed in) to see who the VIP was!

We flew from Xian to Chongqing.

- This plane was five hours late. I distinctly recall it was a Russian-built two-engine prop. When we walked out onto the tarmac to board, there was a mechanic in bare feet standing on a bamboo ladder, doing something with a wrench in one of the engines. You told me not to look.

- We had the hot pot that had these little red things floating in the soup that were hotter than a volcano erupting. It was one of the tastiest things I can recall having, but I still have scar tissue in my mouth ... Dad reminded me that Chongqing was the capital of Szechuan Province—the home of spicy cuisine!

- We walked around the street and the hillside near where the wartime Pai compound was and ran into an older couple who remembered where the Pai family compound was and had a vague recollection of Dad and Auntie Diana.

- Did I mention that the hot pot was really hot?

Having the hot pot was something I feared when I saw it brought to the table. There was a noticeable layer of chili oil floating on top of the soup. Chinese hot pots were wonderful meals to be served in the wintertime. Traditional hot pots were made so that a tube filled with burning charcoal heated the surrounding water or soup in the pot. Then thinly sliced pieces of different meats—chicken, beef, pork, lamb—as well as pieces of vegetables were available to the diners who would, using small individual sieves with handles, dip the raw meats into the boiling liquid. The meats were then cooked to the diner's individual taste for how well done he or she wanted them, and sauces were available to flavor the meat. It was, in other words, a fondue meal. By the end of the meal, the liquid was a delectable soup that finished a satisfying and healthy meal.

I had contracted the flu while in Xian and had flown to Chongqing with a fever. Normally, I avoid really spicy foods, but I had no choice but to join David and Mike in having hot pot. I struggled but managed to eat some of the food and drink the soup after ladling some of the chili oil floating on top out of my bowl into an empty bowl. I began to perspire heavily because of the spicy heat of the soup and went to bed as soon as I could. The next morning, I awoke fever free. I know it was the hot pot that burned the flu viruses out of me!

Mike continued,

> We got on a boat on the Yangtze River and sailed to Wuhan with a group of Canadians and Germans.
>
> - I just remembered—thank god for the peanut butter and crackers you brought, since the meals for the three or four days on the boat were the same.
>
> - We saw a big dam. I remember Dad mentioning how industrial the views looked and how he was afraid of what the countryside would evolve into.
>
> - The Seoul Olympics were on a small TV in the dining room. I remember we watched the US men's swimming team with Livingston's Chris Jacobs and watched him win a gold in the men's four-by-one-hundred medley relay (he ended up winning two golds and a silver).
>
> - There was a big group of Canadians on board who were ecstatic and a bit obnoxious when Ben Johnson won the men's hundred-meter race. Then they were crushed when we got to Wuhan, because he had just been disqualified because of doping.
>
> - One of the Canadians mistook me for a deckhand and asked me a question in slow, broken English. I think I replied with "Got no idea. I don't live here," much to his surprise.
>
> We ended up in Shanghai at a Sheraton Hotel.
>
> - I remember you and Dad arguing about who was going to go downstairs to meet with some old family friends of Dad's and me making a plea that I couldn't go with you. Rather than listen to you guys bicker, I went straight to the restaurant and got a cheeseburger and strawberry milkshake. Life couldn't get any better at that moment!

- We toured old Shanghai and the areas where the British used to hang signs of "No Dogs or Chinese Allowed."

- I remember thinking that Shanghai didn't look at all like Beijing. And it wasn't as commercial or Western as it is today.

Funny how there are certain things that you can recall so vividly. But it was a really neat trip!

At that point in his life, in 1988, Mike had not yet developed the sophisticated taste buds that he now has. No matter how good the food was, if it was Chinese, to him, it was not as good as a cheeseburger or other fast food. Actually, David and I thought the Chinese food on the boat was quite good. I'm not sure about the other passengers, but perhaps the quality of food served to us was high since we always ate at the captain's table. Now in his midforties, my younger son eats spicy foods and sushi.

The cruise on the Yangtze still gave us a view of the Three Gorges in 1988, a famous scenic spot on the river (figure 175). Once the dam was constructed, the rise of the river water partially obscured the Three Gorges. What a price for progress!

Fig 175 The Three Gorges on the Yangtze River in 1988.

Chapter 55

I LOSE THE WIND BENEATH MY WINGS

As I wrote earlier, I do not recall that my parents encouraged any of their children—Solan, Stanley, and me—to care for each other while we were growing up. We were competitors, more academically than in sports, at least Solan and I were. But no matter how intense the competition was, despite the fact we rarely expressed love for each other, Solan was my hero, the wind beneath my wings.

When I learned how to knit, I decided to make a sweater for Solan. Because I had dragged the knitting everywhere, I decided to wash the sweater before giving it to him. I did not realize that my knitting was rather loose, and parts of the sweater stretched. When I gave it to him, he put it on and laughed. "Do you think I'm a gorilla?" he asked, holding up his arms. The sleeves were about a foot too long! He thanked me and asked if I could fix it. I couldn't, and that was the end of that sweater.

My big brother was a handsome dude (see again figure 53). He was athletic and smart, and he was funny. As I said, the faces he made sometimes were similar to those of Bill Cosby and made me laugh out loud. He inherited a visceral response to injustice and at times railed against Mommy's attitude toward people she had grown up to consider her servants. He had a quick temper and lack of patience with people in general who showed disrespect for China and Chinese.

When we were teenagers, we accompanied our parents to Hong Kong. In the late 1940s, China was still in the throes of the civil war. One of Daddy's perks of being a member of the United Nations Secretariat was a home leave to his native homeland. Since we could not enter mainland China, we were allowed to go to Hong Kong, where Mommy and Daddy still had close friends.

One of those friends, who had the surname Liu, was very rich and invited us to his mansion for a welcoming banquet. I have never since been to a feast the equal of the one Mr. Liu served us. Whereas a normal banquet had one soup, cold appetizers, hot dishes, a noodle dish, and a fried rice, the Liu banquet had everything in multiples: two different soups, many hot dishes, and three different noodle dishes. When the last four courses were brought to the table, the stuffed diners could simply applaud each dish, and they were then removed untouched.

Mommy was also excited to be in Hong Kong, where she could hire a tailor to make Chinese dresses for her and me, something she freely had done while in Manchuria. But in dealing with the man choosing material and specifying what the dresses should look like, Mommy treated the tailor as if he were her servant. Again, she had grown up acting that way as a Manchurian princess, and she slipped into that attitude without thinking twice about it.

Solan, though, became upset that Mommy showed the tailor such disrespect, although the tailor seemed to accept it as a matter of course. When the tailor left after bowing, scraping, and thanking Mommy, Solan angrily chastised Mommy, who was stunned by his anger. She made things worse by laughing at him.

"Mommy, he's a human being just like you! Why are you treating him like he's an animal or your servant? He's not your servant!" Solan cried.

"What is wrong with you?" Mommy asked. "I am giving him my business, and I will pay him for his work. Do you want me to kowtow to him?" Then she got angry. "Don't speak to me in that tone of voice! Leave me alone, and keep quiet!"

Stanley, Daddy, and I only listened to the spat and dared not say anything.

In another incident on that trip, Solan refused to get into a rickshaw because he felt it was inhumane to make a man run while pulling people behind him. It took both parents yelling at him to get him to sit in the rickshaw. Both incidents reflect Solan's compassion and sense of justice for all persons, something he demonstrated time and again as a physician. Those two incidents also could not more clearly expose the generational and cultural gaps between our parents and their children, who grew up in the United States.

Solan once told me he chose obstetrics and gynecology as his field of specialization in medicine because he wanted to do surgery but felt the training for surgery was too long.

"I have to start earning money sooner than I can as a surgeon," he said. "We want children, but I have to be able to support a family first. OB-GYN has a surgical component to it, but it's a shorter training program."

After graduation from medical school in 1961, Solan was accepted as an intern at Columbia Presbyterian Hospital and did a residency there also. He began as a resident in 1963, and since he was finally receiving an income, he and Jeannie presented my parents with their first grandchild in 1963, Carolyn, a beautiful, sweet, loving girl. His two girls bracketed the birth of my two sons. His second child was also a girl. Also beautiful and loving, Patricia Anne was born in 1966. We call Carolyn and Patty Anne by Chinese nicknames: Shrong and Mei, respectively. My two wonderful nieces have been as lovable to me as if they were my own. They are the daughters I longed for.

Solan finished a five-year residency as the chief resident in OB-GYN at Columbia Presbyterian Hospital.

When I was to give birth to my second child, Mike, in 1966, I was in Harkness Pavilion of the hospital. A young resident came into my room and introduced himself to me: "I'm Dr. So-and-So, a first-year resident." I no longer remember his name.

I smiled and thought, *He must be new, and he must know I'm Solan's sister and felt compelled to tell me he was new. Young man*, I thought to myself, *I really don't want to know how inexperienced you are. You should stop telling patients you are a first-year resident!*

Solan worked hard at his chosen career path to become a world-class specialist in his field. Many of Mommy's and Daddy's friends became his patients. It pleased my parents to no end when they were told their son was a wonderful, kind, and caring physician. That was something they could take great pride in. Jeannie told me that more than a handful of his pregnant clients ended up naming their children after him. I laughed to think there were little Solan Smiths running around New York City. Solan's American name was a phonetic translation of how his Chinese name was pronounced.

I found that a side benefit for our family because of Solan's rising reputation in the general New York City Chinese population was that Mommy was more willing to listen to Solan. He was bringing honor to our family, and Mommy reveled in the praise she heard about her son. It made her rightfully proud. I could call Solan if I was having trouble persuading her to do something. He would then talk to her and succeed in bringing her around. It made a difference in dealing with Mommy.

One of his most lasting contributions as physician was to recognize that the people of New York City's Chinatown were woefully underserved in medical care. The culture of Chinatown was such that some people who were born and grew up in Chinatown never learned to speak fluent English. Everything they needed or wanted, except for medical care, was right there, and they did not need to speak English. However, when they needed a doctor, they sometimes could not find one to consult because of the language difficulty.

To provide them with substantial medical care, Solan persuaded young Chinese American doctors—and there were many at Columbia Medical School—to establish a branch of their practice in Chinatown, as he did. To this day, there is still a group of young Chinese American doctors of different specializations providing the care the people need. Dr. Marcus Loo, one of David's nephews, now a world-class urologist, has continued to have a part-time practice in Chinatown. He said the needs of the Chinese there continue to be met by many medical doctors, including himself. Solan has been recognized many times for his service to that community.

Because so many of the people in Chinatown spoke little English and rarely ventured out of their closed community, Solan opened a free clinic there, where he saw patients on Saturdays and Sundays. Jeannie worked in his office to the extent that she could throughout his training. When he began to build up his practice, Jeannie worried about the people's habit of paying for services with cash, which meant they would leave his office at the end of the weekend with substantial amounts of cash. Fortunately, nothing ever happened.

Shortly after his work in Chinatown, Solan turned his attention to another underserved community of New York City: Harlem. He took over the OB-GYN department of Harlem Hospital in the early 1980s to address the problems that affected underserved and poor communities, such as insufficient prenatal care for mothers and overly high perinatal deaths of newborns.

It was a time when the people of Harlem were victim to lawlessness. Solan said he heard gunshots on occasion when rival gangs were having battles on the streets near the hospital. He frequently traveled to Albany to speak about the problems and the needs of the people of Harlem and New York in general to legislators and the governor's staff members. By the end of his five or six years at Harlem Hospital, the prenatal and perinatal care he'd established in the hospital had reduced the number of perinatal deaths in Harlem Hospital to be better than the average numbers at Columbia Presbyterian Hospital.

He also felt the training of residents, especially in gynecological surgery, was inadequate. He purchased a movie camera, and when he operated, the camera was over his shoulder, which allowed him to take movies of his techniques for various operations so the residents could review what he was doing and how. He always spent much time teaching, no matter where he was or what he was doing.

From Harlem Hospital, he moved to Long Island, to North Shore Hospital, where he was the vice director of the OB-GYN department. He worked there for a number of years. His family moved to Oyster Bay, where he purchased a motorboat and enjoyed taking members of the family for outings. Our personal lives could not have been better. But like a bolt from the blue, Solan called me one day in 1988 and told me he had been diagnosed with colorectal cancer.

"Don't tell Mommy and Daddy yet because I'll be undergoing treatment and hope to beat this thing like you beat breast cancer," he told me, trying to act as if he were optimistic about the prognosis. I later learned that it was already in stage four.

"I'll be undergoing an operation," he said, "but I'll tell them it's for hemorrhoids."

My blood froze. I was much more upset at that news than when I'd heard about my own cancer diagnosis.

"What happened? How do you feel? When did you go to the doctor?" I asked.

"I had bleeding but thought it was hemorrhoids, and I went to my proctologist to see if we could do anything about them," he answered. "Dr. Ford said he didn't like the looks of what he saw. An immediate operation was necessary to explore further."

The operation revealed a condition that was our worst fear: it was cancer, and it had already spread to his body wall.

My first reaction was fear of losing Solan, whom I not only loved but also idolized as one of the finest human beings I'd ever known. My second reaction was panic. How could I handle Mommy and Daddy without being able to go to Solan for help that I knew only he could give me? My third reaction was a mixture of anger and regret. He was a physician, but he'd let himself become obese. He loved to cook, but when he cooked for us, the food was all creamy and fattening—and, unfortunately, good. Another part of the problem was due to his overworking and lack of exercise. In short, he did not take care of himself because he took care of so many others.

While I was teaching, I frequently attended workshops to keep abreast of new techniques I thought the department needed. One of the best workshops was on electron microscopy at Northeastern University. It was intense. We worked at least twelve hours every day. We eagerly attended meals as respite from the work we were to complete each day. Similarly, in retrospect, I believe Solan developed his bad eating habits because he worked so hard all the time, and food became the comfort his schedule required.

Solan's eating habits only share the blame for his weight problems, because I know we inherited fat genes. No matter how little I eat and how hard I try, I cannot return to my premenopausal weight. I believe I am not obese, though I feel I am overweight now. Solan was obese, and obesity is known to be a factor in increasing the risk of colon cancer. He himself believed he paid too little attention to his own well-being by working too hard for too long.

As a physician, he should have taken more and better precautions for himself, as I'd had my first experience with breast cancer six years before he was diagnosed with cancer. Statistics show that a history of breast cancer in a family is often linked to colon cancer. Indeed, the genetics of cancer is so complex that any person with a family history of any kind of cancer needs to be more alert to the possibility of developing cancer him- or herself. This is not to say that if you have a relative who has cancer, you will inevitably have it yourself, but you must be alert.

Regular appointments for colonoscopy are a proven way to prevent the onset of colorectal cancers. Further, colon cancer is something that can be detected by bleeding and other symptoms, and if the cancer is detected soon enough and the colon's affected area is resected and removed, as with the removal of breast cancer in my case, the patient can live a normal life span.

Why didn't he go right away to a doctor for help? Why did he wait until it was too late? Do physicians have a feeling of invulnerability? I have tried to forgive my big brother by thinking to myself that it must have been a virulent form of cancer that was impossible to destroy no matter how early the diagnosis.

He fought the cancer for eight years. I was not told about all the treatments he received, but I do know he went to the Mayo Clinic in Minnesota, where they implanted radioactive particles into the affected areas in hopes of burning away the cancer cells.

He called me after the procedure. In tears, I told him, "You'd better get well! I can't handle Mommy and Daddy by myself!"

In a voice loaded with worry for me, he replied, "I know, I know. I'm trying!"

I really wanted to say that I would miss him terribly and loved him a lot, but something in our upbringing had always prevented us from voicing our feelings to each other. (We managed to write our true feelings in letters, however, which will follow at the end of this sad chapter.)

I think we both knew that short of a miracle, his was a losing battle. Before long, he had to tell Mommy and Daddy about the seriousness of his illness. I can only imagine the hurt and sadness our parents felt. As a parent myself, I am terrified I might live too long and have to bury one of my children.

Mommy and Daddy were devastated to hear about their favorite child. Solan told them that while he faced a shortened life, he did not fear the end; he had achieved all the goals he'd had for his career, and he was not unhappy that he would escape the degeneration of old age. Mommy cried and wondered out loud what she had done to deserve the fate of losing her first born son.

With Jeannie and their daughters, Shrong and Mei, to help, Solan managed to have a fairly decent half dozen years. He was still able to return to work and was recruited to become the director (the medical term for a department chair) of OB-GYN at St. Luke's Hospital in New York City. He made it known that he was in the advanced stages of colorectal cancer, but they wanted his expertise anyway.

It was a good move for him, as it brought him closer to us and our parents and to his own doctors. He was stimulated by having the opportunity to manage a program in a well-respected hospital. He and Jeannie lived in a small apartment across from St. Luke's that the hospital provided for Solan when he assumed the directorship, though they retained the house in Oyster Bay on Long Island.

Solan asked if he could use some of the scenic photos I had taken on trips to different parts of the world. He wanted to have them blown up big and used on the walls of his department as decor. I, of course, was happy to do so. I wonder if they are still on the walls at St. Luke's Hospital. It made me feel good that he must have thought I was a good photographer and that he wanted others to see my work.

In 1995, he was obviously struggling with the pain and finally had to resign from St. Luke's after only a couple of years. His family moved to Oyster Bay for his last year of life. Solan wanted no more intervention and asked only to be kept comfortable with painkillers.

I drove Mommy and Daddy to Oyster Bay on weekends to see Solan and to keep them company. Mei, who was married and living in New York City, commuted to Oyster Bay to help care for her father. Shrong had lived in England for a few years, was married, and had become a mother herself. She returned to the United States as often as she could to help and was with him in his last days.

He never asked, "Why me?" during his long illness, and he masked the pain when we were around. He even maintained his sense of humor. When a relative of Jeannie's was there to visit one day, Solan invited their young daughter, who was around six years old, to join him on his bed. He used the controls of the hospital bed to give her a ride, moving the bed up and down, sometimes the head, sometimes the legs, and sometimes head and legs together, as both giggled.

A few days before his death, we drove Mommy to Oyster Bay to have dinner and visit with Solan. He had essentially stopped eating because of his illness, but he made the effort to eat, which pleased Mommy. He even left his bed to eat with us at the dining table.

Not long after that, he was on heavy doses of morphine and in a coma. We went to visit him again, this time to say goodbye. I am not sure he knew we were there, but we spoke to him anyway so that he might feel good about our presence. I saw some movement of his hands. The girls told me he was going through the motions of making stitches. He was working, operating, till his last moment of breath!

When we left the house that last time, Shrong and Mei and I hugged, knowing the end would come at any moment. The next week, the day after a happy reunion we had planned a year before for David's family at our house (a gathering of thirty-eight people for three days), I received a call from Shrong that my big brother had passed away. It was August 13, 1996.

Solan's funeral service, held in New York City, was attended by a large crowd. Besides family members, there were friends, patients, patients' families, and colleagues from all the hospitals at which he'd worked. Columbia Presbyterian Hospital honored Solan by designating a meeting room to be named for him. Mommy and Daddy arrived at the funeral home early to say their goodbyes. Daddy cried, saying to Solan that he was glad Solan was no longer feeling pain. "*Bao bai, ni koh bu tung liao!*" (Dearest son, at last you are no longer in pain!).

Mommy could do no more than cry from unbearable sorrow. She fell against his casket as if she could hold him. To me, Daddy said, "I will not live more than two years." It was to be a self-fulfilling prophesy.

We had arranged to have a driver take my parents home before everyone arrived. Daddy's emphysema was getting worse, and we were concerned that having them there throughout the whole ceremony would be more than they could take. Ben and his family, Mike, and Stanley and Sandy were there also.

Later, when Shrong, Mei, and Jeannie returned to Oyster Bay after the funeral, they told me they were standing outside the house, when they saw a white bird fly toward the house. It circled the house before flying away. They said they felt it was Solan's soul telling them he was okay and saying goodbye.

The three letters below were our goodbyes to each other. I wrote my initial letter to him when we first realized how extensive the cancer had become. His first letter was a response to mine, and he wrote the last letter when he knew that death was imminent. I cannot help but choke up every time I read them. I miss him still terribly.

> Dearest Big Brother,
>
> I just spoke to Jeannie, and she gave me the bad news about the metastasis. It hit me like a ton of bricks, and I realized then that all along I had been harboring the unreasonable hope that there was in fact hope. No matter how strong our training as scientists and the objective mind are, emotions are always stronger. We've always been able to express ourselves better in writing than in speaking, and there's no reason to change that even now.
>
> This letter is to say to you what I cannot say out loud. Something in our upbringing

and/or in our culture renders this so difficult to do with each other and our parents, although we behave differently with anyone else. As we have said in the past, it is most likely due to our upbringing. For a family that has stuck together through thick and thin, we really have been relatively dysfunctional with respect to expressing our feelings. And yet you must know those feelings are there and are strong.

I know there is nothing I can do to ease your physical pain. But if this helps to ease your mental pain, I promise you that Jeannie and the girls will never be in need as long as David and I are around. I have already made up my mind to postpone retirement from my job. First because of the uncertain future as far as Mommy and Daddy are concerned and secondly because some modest success in achieving some goals at work recently has made the tedious aspects more tolerable.

Did I tell you I got my NSF grant last year? Spent my spare time the past year spending $74,000 buying equipment for my research and my department. This is peanuts to you, I know, but it is a big grant for Montclair and our department and me. The longer I work, the bigger the pension. So all this is by way of saying I know you have arranged things so that Jeannie and the girls will be well set up. Don't worry about Mommy and Daddy and Stanley and Sandy; we'll all take care of them. Don't worry about me either. David has managed our affairs very well. We'll be comfortable in our old age.

As far as Mommy and Daddy are concerned, I will let you decide when and how you will tell them about your condition. In the meantime, I will be what I have been, which is vague. I cannot agree with Mommy when she says you have no more cancer, but I do not tell her the whole story either. They continue in denial, which is just as well and easier for you. When the time comes, you'll know what to do, as always.

I hope one thing: that you now know how much Daddy cares and loves you. He has just not been able to tell you and has not known how to be a loving father. I really believe this; I always have. To the point that these egocentric people are capable of loving anyone but themselves, they do love us and are proud of us.

I cannot envision life without you. All along, no matter what troubles existed or what I could foresee, I could draw strength from the knowledge you would be there for me. No matter how we disagreed on various things, ultimately, you would be there for me. That you may (I still hope) not be is to me an incomprehensible turn of events. After my bout with breast cancer, I thought I would be the first to go. In a selfish way, this was a relief that I would not have to endure the loss of those I love. No such luck.

Since you have been sick all these years, I have felt every emotion that one would expect: disbelief, anger, frustration, guilt. I have cried until I can no longer cry. And then I have cried some more. At times like these, I wish I had the faith that others have which would let me believe there was some point to such bad things happening to such a good person. But I don't and can only fight the bitterness.

I know one thing: I love you and am so proud of you, and I know you feel the same about me, and this is a great comfort. I don't know the meaning of life, but without this kind of love and without having striven to be the best we can be, there could not be any meaning to it at all.

If there is anything you want us to do, let me know, and we'll do it. Anna

Dear Anna,

I read your letter after I woke up and you had left. It made me cry, but it was beautiful, and I thank you for it. I know that it is hard for either of us to properly acknowledge the other. It is a dysfunction that was not caused by our generation but one which you and I could not overcome. In some way, the rivalry and the competition that existed between us as children poisoned the atmosphere, and it was too strong to overcome. It is probably impossible now to trace how that developed, and perhaps it is irrelevant now in any event.

I have been able to accumulate enough of an estate that Jeannie and the children should be all right for the rest of their lives if they are prudent, and there will be some for our parents and Stanley as well, so you won't have to go it alone. I only ask that David will help with some advice on planning the estate. I trust his instincts and honesty. I have also asked Bobby and Tung for advice when the time comes. Perhaps they can form a committee.

I approach the end of life with mixed emotions. Professionally, I realize that I have accomplished about all I would have if I lived another decade or two. From a personal standpoint, I have lived fully the part of life worth living. I can dispense with old age. Perhaps these are rationalizations, but they are not far from the truth. One of the things I regret is that you and I could never get beyond this feeling that we could not or should not feel pride or love toward each other. I guess it is enough that at the end of life, we can acknowledge what has always been there.

Like you, I also knew that I would go to the wall for you and yours, but I could never say it until now. I feel we both missed a lot over the years because we could not be closer. Although it is perhaps natural to assess blame, at this point in my life, I no longer feel the anger toward Mommy and Daddy as I once did. They were in many ways terrible parents, but they did the best they could with what they understood. As careful as I have been to structure my activities to be sure my own family was protected, it constantly amazes me that somehow we were able to get by with so little rational planning on the part of our parents.

As for assessing my life so far, I think I can honestly say that I have never knowingly compromised any closely held principles in my life, which is not to say I have lived without fault. But I am fairly at peace with myself because I have done the best I could with what I was given. Whether I have accomplished anything is for others to judge, but I did try. I have received a certain amount of recognition in my life, and I would be lying if I said the notoriety was not pleasing. I have been very, very lucky in many ways, and I am extremely grateful.

I approach the last months of life still unsure how I feel about religion. I know there must be a God because there is too much evidence of intelligence in the universe. What I cannot understand is why there is so much evil allowed, but I'm willing to accept the fact that I may not have the capacity to understand all things. Still, I do not believe that life, which I will describe as awareness, ends with the cessation of the last heartbeat. There must be a conservation of matter energy and organized awareness that will come in the future. At least that is what I hope. We will all see.

If you have any anger or sadness about what is happening to me, I would say to you that the best revenge for both of us is for you to live to be a hundred and enjoy every minute of the way!

We obviously are endowed with lethal oncogenes, so be sure you and the kids get frequent checkups. I am sure that I have a lot to answer for with my own illness. I paid too high a personal price for my success. It has been shown that sleeplessness has a deleterious effect on killer cells, and think of all the hundreds, even thousands, of nights when I didn't rest.

Still, I decided on my own that it was more important to risk it than to fail, and failure is what I feared the most in my life. If I were to do it again, I'd probably do the same. But you need to be vigilant for the children because they also have bad genes for cardiac disease. They must be careful.

Although the fat lady is warming up, she has not yet sung. We still have a little time. I would like to see you all as often as it is convenient for you. See what you can do. Solan

Dear Anna,

Sooner or later, it had to come down to this. Death is inevitable for each of us, and it should not be feared. Really and truly, I am not afraid of death as it approaches. I do regret the end of life because there are a few things I haven't done yet or experienced. I will never see grandchildren, for example. But I do not fear death. For all I know, there is something sublime that awaits us all.

When I think of our common beginnings, yours and mine, I am really full of pride for both of us. We have both achieved a great deal. You have not only had a marvelous teaching career and been an author of successful textbooks but have been a great mother for Mike and Benjie and a great wife for David. You have been greatly responsible for another generation of good people and taught hundreds of aspiring scientists, teachers, and physicians.

I honestly know of no one who has done it better, and one of my regrets is that for some reason I don't clearly understand, I could not let you know it earlier. I have said this to you before, and it is probably better not to delve into it any further.

As you may have noted at dinner Wednesday night, I have asked Jeannie to be sure that she continue our share of the responsibility to take care of our parents and Stanley and Sandy. I do hope you will carefully explore how that help to Stanley will be dispensed … Perhaps a lawyer can help. I too am amazed he has survived so well, but I give a lot of the credit to Sandy.

I hope you will continue to have a great life. You have had a good beginning and terrific midportion. Enjoy life to its fullest. The best thing you can do for me is to live well into the next millennium and enjoy it to the fullest.

As for me, I am satisfied personally with my career and my family. The kids are marvelous. I found out today that she (Shrong) has another offer from a very large promotion firm. If this one also works out, she will be able to buy me that gold-plated Rolls-Royce after all (private joke). Mei and Angus have been pure joy for me, and something soon will evolve—you will see. As for me, the rest is epilogue.

I love you very much. Solan

I wish I could somehow tell him that I'm doing what he wanted; I've lived well into this millennium and have lived well. I wish I could tell him that his three grandchildren—Mei's Cameron and Shrong's Buddy and Reyna—are wonderful, beautiful young people who give us all much happiness (figure 176). Solan saw Leanna and Keith but did not live to see Cameron, Buddy and Reyna, or Mike's two young sons, Aidan and

Nathan. He would have enjoyed our younger generation so much. As Shrong said, if Solan had lived to see his grandchildren, they all would have received ponies—and much more—before they were six!

Rest well, big brother. Rest in peace. Our lives were much fuller because of you. You made me a better person because I saw how you cared about what you did and how you cared for our parents and everyone around you. I love to think your spirit is with me always. I even talk to you in case you can hear me. I love and respect you so much and always have.

Fig 176 Buddy standing, Reyna at Jeannie's right, Cameron on the left

Chapter 56

MORE TRAINING AND EARLY RETIREMENT

The year 1996 was both gratifying to me in my teaching career and agonizing physically and emotionally due to Solan's illness. I persisted in teaching and doing what research I could with mice in order to have students interested in mammalian development join me in learning how to work with mice. I taught them the recording methods I had learned with Dr. Waelsch.

However, I recognized that mammalian systems were impractical to use with students because of the fairly long gestation period of mice, about twenty-one days. By the time I taught them the rudiments of caring for mice as experimental animals, it was difficult to assign projects to interested students that could be easily done in the rest of the time we had in one semester.

I regretted not having learned to do research with Miss Oppenheimer's fish. Their gestation period was shorter, they had more offspring, and working with fish would have also been cheaper than having to buy bedding and food for the mice. I realized I needed to change my focus from mice to fruit flies.

When I qualified for my first sabbatical leave in 1978–1979, I did some research on scientists who were working on mammalian development and found that Dr. Michael I. Sherman (figure 177) was working on developmental mouse mutations at the Roche Institute of Molecular Biology (RIMB), the research arm of Hoffmann-La Roche, which was about ten minutes away from MSU. I wrote to Dr. Sherman and asked if I could spend some time in his laboratory to learn new techniques.

He graciously invited me to join him in his research, and I spent a year in his lab, studying embryonal carcinoma (EC) cells and the T6 developmental mutation in mice. Ironically, EC cells as a model for the study of genetic control of differentiation in mice is directly descended from the pioneering work on teratomas carried out at Jackson Laboratory in Bar Harbor, Maine, by Dr. Leroy Stevens, my supervisor during the summer research training program for college students (see chapter 24).

I felt that my experience at RIMB would bring side benefits for our students and department and for the university as well. Indeed, following my year at RIMB, I was able to get funding from Hoffmann-La Roche that allowed the biology department to hold an annual toxicology symposium for the next eleven years. It was open to the public and also fit in with a new degree program in toxicology offered by our department. I chaired most of the symposiums. They were well attended.

Other important benefits included having eight biology majors hired at different times by staff scientists at RIMB as part-time research assistants, which clearly boosted the students' résumés for getting postgraduate jobs. Also, contacts I made there on occasion were guest lecturers for our students. I benefitted not only by learning new techniques but also by participating in research with Mike and others that resulted in my name being on a research article that was published. Toward the end of my teaching career, the administration at MSU put more pressure on those of us doing research to publish, and I was glad my year with Mike Sherman had resulted in a publication.

At the same time, my mouse colony suffered from the inadequate animal room we had for research animals. For some inexplicable reason, the room had been put on the roof of the biology building, exposed to summer heat and winter cold. Twice, I lost my entire colony when power was lost and the air-conditioning or heating failed without my knowing about it until it was too late to save the animals. For reasons I have already mentioned, I knew it was time to consider a different research focus, and I chose *Drosophila melanogaster*, the fruit fly, a classical important source of information for the study of developmental genes.

I had attended a workshop on microinjection in 1992, learning about a new technology that allowed scientists doing research on fruit fly development to introduce DNA into embryos in an attempt to have the DNA taken up into cells that would develop into its egg or sperm cells. The injected DNA, if it was absorbed into the nucleus of a cell and became part of a chromosome, thereby changed the genetics of the individual that developed from that germ cell.

I felt that technique, which, at the time, was among cutting-edge research approaches to understanding development in fruit flies, was something I could bring to Montclair State to teach to some of my students. Accordingly, in the spring semester of 1993, I was given a sabbatical leave to be a visiting scientist in the laboratory of Dr. Christine Rushlow at the Roche Institute of Molecular Biology (figure 178).

There, under the tutelage of that brilliant young scientist, I learned of the advantages of studying *Drosophila* as models of development. Fruit flies were cheap to buy and maintain and developed quickly enough for students to carry out simple experiments in one semester. For many years following my sabbatical with Chris Rushlow, I had all my students carry out research projects by doing genetic crosses with inbred strains and then writing their analyses as if they were submitting papers for publication. The practice became a part of their laboratory experience in my genetics course.

In 1994, I applied for and received a $74,000 grant from the Instrumentation and Laboratory Improvement Program of the National Science Foundation for the purpose of buying research equipment for students who signed up for independent research projects with me. Ever since my summer experiences at the Jackson Laboratory, I had been convinced of the need to stimulate students with research, especially in their undergraduate years. Obtaining the grant meant I could collaborate with Dr. Rushlow in her research, with select students involved as my research assistants. Unfortunately, we never found mutations that were important to her studies on the development of dorsal structures, but a number of students were able to carry out real research.

The one negative in the change of experimental focus was that it was not possible for all students to master the techniques of handling fruit flies without letting some go loose. At certain times in the academic semester, my colleagues occasionally complained of fruit flies finding fruit brought in brown bags as part of their lunches. I could only apologize and cross my fingers that there would be a minimal number of escapees per semester. However, my students all were exposed to a modicum of real research, and because of that, I received the NSF grant.

I was named Sokol faculty fellow in the spring semester of 1996, an honor established by an alumnus of Montclair State for a faculty member of the School of Mathematics and Sciences. The award carried with it a monetary prize to help faculty with their teaching and research. From the point of view of my career, I was being rewarded and recognized for my science and my teaching.

As gratifying as those developments were for my career, Solan's illness and its consequences on the family increasingly took a toll on me physically, or so I thought. I began to suffer from diarrhea and, at one point, daily spikes of fever for about a week in late winter. I thought the issues were a result of stress from watching my brother's struggles. I did once ask our general practitioner about possibly getting tested for Lyme disease. He did not think that was my problem, as, at the time, I did not have some of the expected symptoms, such as the target rash.

However, I decided to see a gastroenterologist, Dr. Jonathan LaPook of Columbia Presbyterian Hospital in New York City. When he looked at the routine blood test I had taken for him, he noted that my liver enzymes were quite elevated. He then decided to send some of my blood to a laboratory that specialized in the diagnosis of Lyme disease. The diagnosis came back positive: my liver enzymes had been elevated to ten times the normal level, and I indeed had Lyme disease (LD).

No sooner had I been told I had LD than a small, square patch of red skin I had noticed near my left collarbone began to expand, became circular, and eventually formed the target rash that most people read about. When I returned to see Dr. LaPook, I asked if the rash indicated I had been bitten by the tick at that spot. He responded that the target rash did not indicate where the tick had bitten and that I had two more of the rashes on my back. I had not even thought of looking at my back for signs of an infection.

I knew Lyme disease was transmitted by deer ticks, but I never saw a tick on me or felt anything like a tick bite. I could have picked up the tick anywhere, as I had seen deer in our backyard and on the golf course. I was put on a regimen of strong antibiotics and was fortunate not to sustain long-lasting effects from LD, such as crippling joint pain.

At that time, in early summer 1996, I arrived at the conclusion that I had to do something to make life easier—or even possible. I felt I was working full-time in support of my family and full-time at my teaching job. Since there was only one thing I could eliminate from my life—teaching—I came to the reluctant decision that I had to resign from Montclair State University, where I had taught for twenty-eight years. I wrote a letter of resignation to the Montclair State University administration, the dean of the School of Mathematics and Sciences, and Bonnie Lustigman, then chair of the biology department, effective the end of the academic year 1996–1997.

In higher education, it is always necessary to give departments a full academic year to search for and replace a faculty member with tenure. Genetics, being a required course for students in several majors, would need someone well qualified to teach such an important core course.

I was not entirely comfortable with the thought of leaving the university at that point. I had spent a year researching and ordering microinjection equipment for the department. I was the only person in the department who knew how to use the equipment. I hoped the department could find someone to hire who was interested in the equipment for his or her courses, or perhaps a molecular biologist could use the equipment for his or her courses or research.

Also, I had just been named a Sokol fellow. Both the grant and the Sokol's cash award carried with them the understanding that they would help me with my research and teaching, yet I had no choice but to leave MSU. Being a full-time caretaker of my parents was incompatible with also being a full-time faculty member from the point of view of doing everything well. Contracting LD was the determining factor in my decision. Remember too that David was continuously fighting his family's terrible cardiovascular genes. His health problems were becoming more and more serious. I could not take the chance of ignoring a disease that could cause crippling effects on me if not taken care of properly, which would impact all the members of my family.

As soon as I wrote the letter of resignation, a huge weight was lifted from my shoulders. I knew it was the right thing to do. I knew I could not afford to get sicker in light of Solan's illness and Daddy's and Mommy's frailties. I hoped the administration would understand that I'd reached my decision only after the diagnosis of LD.

Dick Lynch, our former dean and the provost of Montclair State University at the time, replied with a gracious and understanding letter. The department began the search for my replacement as soon as the school year 1996–1997 began. In the spring of 1997, they gave me a farewell dinner at a local restaurant, at which faculty and students, especially those who had done research with me, were present. I choked up in my farewell speech to them but hoped they all took to heart my declaration that we faculty were involved in the most important profession for civilization—education—and that they should be proud of it (figure 179). I am flanked in the photograph in figure 179 by Drs. Lee Lee and Bonnie Lustigman, who became friends as well as being colleagues. Lee Lee was hired during my years as chair of the biology department, and Bonnie Lustigman was the chair of the department during my last year at Montclair State University. Other members of the faculty and some of my students (figure 180) were at other tables. Greg Prelich was a slightly older student who returned to study genetics with me and eventually went on to get his PhD in molecular biology, working with yeast. Ironically, after he finished his graduate degree, he obtained a position in the genetics department at the Albert Einstein College of Medicine, where I had gotten my PhD with Salome Waelsch.

Graduation in May 1997 was a bittersweet event for me. For twenty-eight years, I had enjoyed the raucous, joyous event, as many of our graduates were the first in their families to have a college degree. I knew I would miss those moments as well as the teaching of young minds. There is no other profession that offers the kind of gratification an educator gets when a student who has been struggling suddenly sees the light of understanding or experiences the real excitement of a young mind that has found amazement, as when I myself saw the tubular heart of an eighteen-hour chick embryo start to pulsate, and feels a strong need to learn how a phenomenon happens.

As faculty marched out in the recessional after the graduation ceremony was over and passed the biology graduates, I removed my cap, waved at them, and blew them kisses, which they returned. Figure 181 shows me after graduation with four of my graduate students.

I reminded myself that retirement was not all sad: there would be no more politics or fretting over students and colleagues whom I felt were dogging their efforts. I had worked hard for my students and could leave them with a clear conscience that no matter how inadequate I felt because I could not reach all of them, I had done the best I could. I hoped they knew that my affection for them was real. They were my academic children, and I cared very much for them and their futures.

As the summer progressed, however, I still was bothered by my intestinal problems. Then Dr. LaPook said he had only one more thing to try, as he could not detect any symptoms that explained my continuing problems. He told me to take a probiotic, a medicine that was essentially cultures of benign bacteria found naturally in the intestines. After three days of my taking the probiotic, my problems ceased. Apparently, the treatment for Lyme disease had taken a toll on the good bacteria as well as the bad bacteria. The probiotic restored the good bacteria to my system. I was relieved and elated.

I felt so much better that when some of my Tiger friends asked me to join them on a bike trip to Italy's Po Valley, I agreed, never having gone on a bike tour before and believing that such a tour would give us a good idea of how people lived in that region and give me great photography opportunities. David was not in favor of such a trip and declined to go, although he said I should go if I practiced riding before the trip.

It had been decades since I'd ridden a bike, so I had to buy one, and I practiced by riding around our neighborhood. As a child, I had ridden a bike everywhere, but I'd never had one with different gears. It took a while to learn how to use the gears and the hand brakes. Still, I found it was not difficult to recover the feeling of bike riding, and I felt comfortable enough to join the Tigers in Po Valley (figure 182).

The trip was only a week long, and it was a memorable experience. There was a group of about sixteen of us, both Tigers and Tiger friends and family. We visited some local landmarks, such as the home of the great Italian composer Puccini. Because the Po Valley is mostly agricultural, we saw few cities, mostly villages and many farms. The people we encountered in the countryside were friendly and invited us to visit their homes, which we didn't have time to do.

One thing I didn't like about the trip was that the real biking enthusiasts in the group would not stop to take photos and were more focused on riding a certain route within a certain amount of time. This old photographer would lose sight of the group when I stopped to do some shooting and then would have to pedal as fast as I could to catch up with the rest. One time, I stopped to shoot an interesting farmhouse. While I was walking to get different angles, a large man came out the front door, not smiling, and walked toward me. I had my bike close by and decided I'd better try to catch up with my group. It occurred to me that nobody would have known where I was if I disappeared.

I loved being with my friends but missed David and was glad the trip was only a week long. As always when in Italy, I thoroughly enjoyed the food we were served. It seemed that even if the food was a side dish of spaghetti and tomato sauce, it was delicious. I also felt the strenuous exercise was good for my arthritis, which had gotten worse because of the Lyme disease. After the trip, I signed up with personal trainers to continue to rehabilitate my joints.

Another memorable experience on the trip was turning the TV on one morning to CNN and seeing Princess Diana's portrait framed in black after a fatal car wreck took her life in France. We were all stunned by her death.

Another experience led to my first attempt at creative writing. One day on our bike trip, we visited a small town and walked through it with a local guide. At one point, she pointed at the town's cathedral and proudly claimed the church possessed two vials of the blood of Jesus Christ. Now, throughout the whole trip, a physician friend of some of the Tigers had picked my brain about genetic engineering, in which he had a deep interest. When the local guide informed us about the vials of the blood of Jesus Christ, I poked the good doctor and said, "What do you think about taking the DNA out of those vials and transforming egg cells with the DNA to clone Jesus?" We chuckled about the outrageous thought, but it stuck in my mind and would not leave. I eventually wrote a science-fiction novel about cloning Jesus Christ, called *Choices*, and put it in the context of a female Chinese scientist doing genetic engineering research in a higher-education setting.

Because I was writing about my experiences at Montclair State University and people still there, I decided to use a pseudonym, A. C. White, which was a pseudo-pseudonym. A. C. are the initials of my maiden name, Anna Chao, and my married name, Pai, means "White" in Chinese. I had no knowledge about getting a novel published and wrote to a number of literary agents, who on the main were not interested in an unknown fiction writer, and the same was true of publishers to whom I wrote.

When I sent my manuscript to the copyright office in Washington, DC, I received a letter from Dorrance Publishing Company, who asked if I might be interested in having the manuscript published. I replied in the positive to the question and entered into agreement with a publisher different from those that had published my textbooks. With Dorrance, I paid for the publication of my book. They did send out publicity about it and said the success of a book they published depended primarily on the author's arranging book signings and giving talks.

I hoped that what publicity Dorrance put out and the listing of *Choices* on Amazon would be sufficient. It was not, and I have myself to blame because I put little effort into selling it. I did have one book signing at the Montclair Golf Club, where David and I were members, arranged by a friend, and several dozen copies of my novel were bought by friends. But that was all. Some friends who tried to buy it from Amazon said they were unable to get a copy.

I was too busy with family problems to be able to devote time to finding what the problem was, as my first experience as a novelist was decidedly disappointing from the point of view of earnings. The experience taught me that to be a noted novelist requires as much work after the book is written as it requires during the effort to write it. I was nonetheless gratified that I could produce a story people enjoyed, as those who have read it have told me. Having been trained in scientific writing, which requires no subjective thoughts and clear, concise presentation of facts, I worried my writing would not be compelling in telling a story. It was a satisfactory first effort.

Fig 177 Dr. Michael I. Sherman, photo courtesy of Dr. Sherman

Fig 178 Dr. Christine Rushlow, photo courtesy of Dr. Rushlow

Fig 179 With colleagues from the School of Mathematics and Sciences

Fig 180 A table of students who worked and studied with me

Fig 181 Graduation with four students who received their MA degrees at my last graduation ceremony

Fig 182 The Tigers and others on a bike tour of Italy's Po Valley

Chapter 57

A SELF-FULFILLING PROPHECY

The effort of writing my novel took my mind off Solan's death. I found that time never passed as quickly as it did while I was writing. I still had my parents to care for, and that was always a priority for me. Both Mommy and Daddy had reached the mideighties in age. I remember Mommy complaining once that when she reached the age of eighty, she felt a noticeable decrease in her ability to walk fast and do physical work. Fortunately, she no longer needed to care for any cats, and her only dog was a small pug, Bo Bo.

Daddy's emphysema became more severe, and Dr. Gillette put him on oxygen at home. I made sure Mommy understood the fire hazard that having a tank of oxygen in the house represented. She seemed to regress in her ability to carry a logical conversation, though if the subject of their life in China arose, she was fully able to participate in that conversation.

Her unusual behavior manifested itself in different ways. One day I went into her bathroom and was startled to find all manner of things—clothing, pocketbooks, and more—piled up in her shower. I asked Mommy, "Why did you move so many things into your shower?"

She said, "It is for security. If they are in the shower, they are safer." That did not make much sense to me, as the shower was glass enclosed, and everything was visible, but by that time, I knew it was useless to point out facts, so I said nothing about that.

Since there was no bathtub in her bathroom, I asked, "Where do you take a bath then?"

"I take a sponge bath every day," she responded. There was nothing I could say about the curious setup. Indeed, she never looked dirty or seemed to be dirty.

In their lives after losing their beloved Solan, Mommy rarely brought up Solan's name. Daddy never repeated his statement about how long he would live beyond his son. I wondered why he had chosen two years, why not three or five? He had had a bout in the mid-1990s with a life-threatening health problem, when I had to call for emergency medical technicians to take Daddy to our local hospital, where Dr. Gillette told me Daddy was suffering from congestive heart failure due to emphysema and prescribed oxygen for Daddy to use at home.

On another occasion a year or so later, Mommy called me to say Daddy was complaining about shortness of breath again. I had to call again for an ambulance to take him to our local hospital. His heart stopped beating in the emergency room on that occasion, and he lost consciousness. The doctors and nurses in the ER had to intubate him and restore his heartbeat. We were worried when the doctor on call did not come to talk to us for a long while.

On that occasion, the intubation was difficult, and they injured his vocal cords. Thereafter, he spoke with a raspy voice and could not speak loudly, which created another problem between him and Mommy when he returned from the hospital. Mommy had become hard of hearing. She refused to wear a hearing aid initially because it made all noises too acute for her, she said. However, she could not hear Daddy well because of his injured vocal cords. The two would get frustrated and exasperated and argue.

Because he had lost consciousness, the doctors kept him in the hospital for several days for observation. On the day after he was intubated, I drove Mommy to the hospital to visit with him. He made an almost comical statement about the nurse we had hired to stay with him through the night: "She slept with me on the bed, but we didn't do anything!" He spoke with an attitude that was almost boastful and challenging to Mommy.

I couldn't believe my ears. Was he still under the influence of anesthesia, or had he been dreaming and thought it was real? Why would a nurse want to sleep with an eighty-six-year-old patient with congestive heart failure, and why would the patient tell his wife about that irregular behavior? I looked at Mommy, fearing she would explode and make a scene, but she looked back at me, almost chuckling, and said, "He's talking nonsense!" Daddy seemed not to hear her comment, and I quickly changed the topic of conversation. That is the only time I can remember when Daddy spoke nonsense and Mommy made sense!

Daddy recovered from that incident. He was well aware of how close he was to dying, because Dr. Gillette had talked with him. With the pain of having to bury Solan, he must have thought about his own mortality. I had always worried about the possibility of Daddy contracting lung cancer. He had smoked in China, he said, from the time he was twelve until he was in his seventies. Who knew what kind of cigarettes they had smoked in China?

He did finally crack the habit of smoking in his seventies and never contracted lung cancer. Looking back on my own history of breast cancer and Solan's history of colorectal cancer, I have to wonder how much secondhand smoke we ingested while young. I remember Daddy smoking both cigarettes and pipes in the house.

Given his emphysema, Mommy often berated Daddy for not listening to her and stopping his habit. She showed him little sympathy when he developed chronic bronchitis and tracheitis and coughed uncontrollably at times.

"If you had listened to me when we were in China and stopped smoking then, you wouldn't have had all these problems!" she'd say.

He would retort, "I am already eighty-six years old. I think I've lived a very long life! What more do you want?"

In early August of 1998, Daddy again experienced difficulties in breathing. This time, I contacted Stanley and Sandy and Solan's two daughters, Mei (whom I asked to convey the news to Jeannie) and Shrong, who was still living in London. I informed them that I was worried about Daddy and said they should come visit with him as soon as they could. Several did manage to join us.

My older niece, Shrong, had a baby boy and said she would try hard to join us. She flew in with her first child, a son they called Buddy, who had the biggest cheeks I had ever seen in a child—until I saw his sister a few years later, who I believe had even bigger cheeks proportionally. I sent Stanley and Sandy bus tickets to come to New Jersey from their home in Buffalo, New York. Mike was working at Callaway Golf in California at the time and immediately made plans to fly to New Jersey.

I received a phone call from Mommy a few days later that made me once again call for an ambulance. It was late morning. I told my parents I would meet them at the emergency room. David and I drove to the hospital, parked the car, and waited for the ambulance to arrive.

Daddy was on the gurney with an oxygen tube in his nose. They had him propped up a little, and we made eye contact. He looked tired and a little frightened as they rushed him into the ER. I did not have time to say anything to him. While I was worried, I expected we would see him at home again, weakened but still mentally alert. I called the children, and they all rushed to the ER waiting room.

We waited, as usual. As time dragged by, we became increasingly worried and fearful. The doctors did not appear for what seemed like forever. We expected them to tell us, as they had on previous occasions, they had finished treating him and give us the room in which he was resting. Finally, Dr. Gillette came to us. He looked grim. My heart sank.

"I'm sorry you had to wait for so long," he said. "Mr. Chao was being intubated, when he went into cardiac arrest." I closed my eyes for a moment. "We had to work on him for a while and finally restored a heartbeat, but he is in a coma. Anna, I don't think he can survive this."

I fought hard to keep the tears from flowing and asked Dr. Gillette, "How much time does he have?"

"It's hard to tell."

Could it be this is the end for Daddy? I thought to myself. *Surely he will wake up soon and be able to return to his home.* "Can we see him?" I asked. The doctor said yes and told us to wait about half an hour, by which time they would have moved him into a room. The question on all our minds was how long he had been without a heartbeat, but none of us asked the question because we all feared knowing the answer. It clearly had been too long because it had left him in a coma. What condition would he be in when—if—he woke up?

When we went to his room, he was unconscious and hooked up to machines that monitored his vital signs. He had a tube in his mouth that was helping him breathe. He looked small in the hospital bed. I held his limp hand. As I touched him, I noticed a momentary change in something on the monitor, which, to me, indicated he sensed my presence.

I said in Chinese to him, "Daddy, we're all here. The doctors are helping you. You have to fight really hard to wake up."

In turn, each member of the family came to his side and murmured greetings. When Shrong reached his side, she said to him, "Yeh Yeh, it's Shrong. I'm here with my baby." Again, the monitor flickered. While he might have been in a coma, Daddy was reacting to our voices. Stanley and Sandy stood together and prayed for Daddy.

After we had a few minutes each with Daddy, we all sat and chatted. Even under such sad circumstances, just being together was a comfort and numbed the sadness. Sandy, Stanley's wife, had worked for many years as a home health-care person. When I brought up a question about staying with Daddy through the day and night, she said she had known of people in comas who hung on for days. When the time came for dinner, she said we could stay, but there was no telling how long Daddy could hang on.

So we left, and I have regretted it ever since. At around eleven o'clock at night, Dr. Gillette called. "He was a terrific fella," Dr. Gillette said, "and I'm so sorry to have to tell you, but he passed away just now." Everyone was still at our house, and I passed the word on.

I thought about my father and how he'd been able to provide for us in a foreign country. I thought about how he'd joked with us, with me especially. On one of our yearly moves when we were young, he'd stopped in front of a ramshackle old house that looked as if it would collapse any moment and, in a cheerful voice, said to us in the car, "Well, here we are—what do you all think about our new mansion?"

I remembered how he'd played tennis with Solan and met Solan's power with guile and spin shots that exasperated my teenage brother no end because Daddy would win.

He terrified us when we were young because he would chastise us and yell loudly. He had two red streaks on the back of his neck that would get bright when he lost his temper. As youngsters, we could not rationalize that his bad temper (and Mommy's too) might have resulted from inexperience in parenting. All we felt was guilt that we had angered our parents.

But we knew he cared for us too, especially his grandsons. I could always count on him to attend to them if I was tied up at work. I knew that despite Mommy's irrationality, he had promised his assassinated father-in-law, the Old Marshal, that he would care for Mommy all his life, and he did, no matter how miserable she'd made him in the last two decades of his life.

I cried. We all did. It was August 11, 1998, three days short of two years after Solan had died.

I had told Mommy that night over the phone that Daddy was holding his own. I hadn't gone to her because I hadn't wanted her to see how worried I was. While Mommy was not always logical, she could still possibly sense whether we were telling her only a partial truth. I decided we would wait until the next morning to go see her and give her the bad news. I dreaded doing so.

The next day, David and I, with heavy hearts, drove the seven minutes it took to reach their house on the other side of Livingston. She was sitting at their dining table when we entered the house. I did not have an extensive enough vocabulary to be more consoling about Daddy; I simply said to Mommy, "Daddy is gone."

Her eyes widened, and she lay her head on her arms on the table and wept. "He's gone? He's thrown me aside and left me?" she wailed. "How could he do this to me?" We could only pat her on the back. As acrimonious as their marriage had been for some twenty years, I knew a deep feeling had existed between them. They'd been together for seventy years.

I told her we would make all the arrangements for the service and the cremation. We already had a crypt ready for my parents at Ferncliff Cemetery in New York. Years before, Jeannie had bought a crypt for Solan and herself. David and I had bought one for us, and Ferncliff was where Solan's ashes had been interred. At the time, Mommy had said she did not want to be cremated because she was afraid the fire would hurt too much, so we'd bought a plot at Ferncliff where Mommy would be buried. Many Chinese were interred at Ferncliff, including one of the Tigers, Frankie Tang, who also was afflicted with colorectal cancer and died in 1991.

Daddy, on the other hand, had requested that he be cremated and that part of his ashes be taken back to China to be spread on a sacred mountain, Tai Shan in Shandong Province, where he was born. Mommy then said that when she passed on, she wanted the rest of his ashes to be put in her casket and buried with her.

I decided I had better sleep at Mommy's house that night in case she needed help. I must confess to being nervous because I wasn't sure of Mommy's reaction to Daddy's death. Indeed, I was not sure of my mother's sanity. I did not sleep well or much because Mommy's days and nights had been turned upside down, so for much of the early hours of the morning, I could hear her shuffling steps going about the house in the dead of night.

Daddy used to close the door to his bedroom and lock it to get some peace and sleep. I would have liked to do that, but if I did, I knew I might not hear Mommy if she needed help, so I could only lie there and wonder what she was doing. To be honest, I was a bit afraid. I no longer trusted Mommy to do anything rationally, and with so much sadness, I wondered if she would hurt herself. When morning came and she was sleeping, I breathed a sigh of relief.

We made arrangements for a memorial service in New York City, where most of my parents' friends were. Stanley requested that he be allowed to speak at the service. I felt that his evangelical nature and the chasm that still existed between him and Mommy would create an uncomfortable situation for Mommy. I apologized to Stanley and Sandy, and without bringing Mommy into it, I said that Daddy was not religious and had said he did not want prayer at his services. That seemed to appease my brother and his wife, though they were not happy about it.

I wrote the following tribute on behalf of my brothers and myself, which David read at the service:

> With the loss of a loved one, we are always left with our memories as well as our tears. Following are some of the attributes that come to mind as we remember our father:
>
> ### Courage
>
> This was a man who was ripped from a life of privilege and comfort by war and found the strength to support a young family in a foreign land. While he always felt his support was inadequate because he did not provide the privilege and comfort into which he was born, what his children became—a prominent physician, an evangelist, and a college professor—attests to the fact that his support was more than enough.
>
> ### Enthusiasm
>
> His and his wife's passion for the high art of Beijing opera, in which they had been trained by luminaries in China, led to the formation of the Yeh Yu Chinese Opera Association. We watched with amazement as they and their friends were able to recall from memory alone the entire libretto, music, orchestration, and staging of numerous operas. The joy of seeing a beloved aspect of Chinese culture on the faces of the Chinese people attending the performances was remarkable and moving.
>
> A natural athlete, his last sport passion was golf. We remember one round when he hit a perfect shot out of the rough. Engrossed in the flight of the ball, he walked smack into a palm tree. Somewhere in Florida, a dented palm tree stands as a monument to his enthusiasm!
>
> ### Integrity
>
> He led by example in always trying to do what he thought was the right thing, the honorable thing. As a fallible human being—like all of us—what he thought was right did not always turn out to be, but more often than not, it was right.
>
> ### Love and Loyalty
>
> His love for our mother was unquestionable and unwavering. He had vowed on his knees before her assassinated father's casket he would care for her to his dying day. That vow was fulfilled this week.
>
> ### Simplicity
>
> He was a simple man. His values were straightforward and his likes and dislikes clear. In keeping with this attribute, we end this tribute by saying, simply, we loved him.

The four grandchildren spoke in sequence of their ages: Shrong first as the oldest grandchild, then Ben, then Mike, and, finally, Mei. I found them to be much more eloquent in their descriptions of their love for him.

Shrong's eulogy was as follows:

> Two days ago, Ben, Mike, Mei, and I got together to discuss what it was we wanted to say about Yeh Yeh today. It took us all of thirty seconds to decide that although we had different experiences and memories of him, the thing that stuck out in each of our minds was the undeniable sense of unconditional love that we all felt from him.
>
> At every gathering, he was affectionate; at every meeting, he was nothing but enthusiastic and joyful to be with us. He never spoke to us in anger or disappointment. And although he came from an environment in China, which was more than a world away from our American upbringing in New Jersey, he accepted our Westerness and never judged us. He simply loved us.
>
> It has taken all my life to appreciate him and see him for the truly exceptional person he was.

Ben's eulogy was as follows:

> Just the other day, I realized that I never got mad at my grandfather. Think about the important people in your life—your parents, spouse, children, friends, relatives, bosses. I have gotten angry at just about everyone but never at my grandfather. That is both extraordinary on one hand yet understandable on the other. Because everyone who knew him loved him, from the barber who cut our hair forever to people he had just met. He was impossible not to like.
>
> I thought about him often recently, and in my ruminations, three things stood out:
>
> First, he was the ideal grandfather. By any measure, he was really the perfect grandfather.
>
> He loved his grandkids unconditionally. As Shrong mentioned, he loved us without bound and without judgment. When I was younger, I lacked self-esteem, but Lo Yeh always made it very clear he thought I could do anything. That confidence helped me immeasurably as a child and still carries me today.
>
> He had an endless supply of wisdom. As with other perfect grandfathers, Lo Yeh drew on a seemingly endless well of wisdom to tutor his grandkids. He never hesitated to share his wisdom yet at the same time never forced his beliefs on us, nor did he ever judge us. There is something about the wisdom of a grandfather. It sinks in more effectively than wisdom gleaned from any other source.

He would do anything for his grandchildren. Everyone had to eat. If he had his way, I would eat eight meals a day. I would have dessert twelve times a day. My kids would eat even more. Lo Yeh saved many a day by simply being there for us. If school let out early due to inclement weather, he would be the one to pick us up. If nobody was available to take us somewhere, he would chauffeur us around. All visits with him were special occasions, even when we lived nearby and saw him often.

He indulged his grandchildren. I remember trips to Paramus Park, a huge shopping mall in New Jersey. It would be the three of us: Lo Yeh, my brother, and me. It was a dangerous combination: an indulgent grandfather with disposable income and two greedy grandsons to help him spend it. We developed a vicious cycle of sorts. He would take us to the mall and buy us toys. We would bring them home, play with them, and, as boys would, break them. This, of course, necessitated return trips for replacements.

He had this change purse, a leather contraption with various compartments, all filled with silver—nickels, dimes, quarters. It was magical. Every time we passed a gumball machine, he broke out the change purse. Knowing that gumball machine visits were taboo, he always admonished us not to tell our parents where the loot came from. Lo Yeh, we never told!

The second thing that stands out was his impatience. His impatience was legendary. It was so extreme that it was endearing. He's in the room with us now, and he is looking at his watch, hoping I'll be done. In my wedding video, his impatience got captured for eternity. We were married in a church ceremony, and after the bride and groom walked up the aisle, the guests filed out row by row, starting with the front of the church and moving backwards. Lo Yeh was in the second row. You can see him in the video, trying to sneak out with the first-row guests.

His impatience brings me to my third point. For someone so impatient, he was in no great hurry to leave this earth.

In the past five years, I have told three different bosses at two different employers that at any time, I might have to take some days off because my grandfather was ill and could go at any time.

Not until this week did I have to actually use those days off. About five years ago, shortly after my daughter was born, he had his first serious episode. During my visits to see him in the hospital, I would ask him to please, please stick around awhile longer. Get to know your great-granddaughter, I pleaded. He obliged. On top of that, he got to see my son and Shrong's son Buddy as well. He got to see three of his seven great-grandchildren, which makes me very happy. That might have been the greatest gift he ever gave us.

The other day, we had lunch together, and my grandfather remarked that he loved my kids so much it made his heart "itch." As I look at my children, I see traces of Lo Yeh in both of them. Keith has a birthmark on the back of his head just like Lo Yeh. And Leanna, when she is ready to go somewhere, will buckle herself into the car whether we are ready to go or not. When I see that, when I see Lo Yeh through my kids, I understand what he was talking about. And my heart itches too.

Mike's eulogy was as follows:

I want to celebrate my Lo Yeh by telling a few stories about the passion for golf we both shared. This is how I will remember him best.

As a wide-eyed young teenager, my Lo Yeh gave me one of the greatest gifts I have received in my life. He taught me about his love of golf. I witnessed the passion he had for the game. And I saw his joy when he realized his passion was becoming mine also. It is on the golf course where my fondest memories of him were formed.

The vivid memories I have of my early years in golf are of my first regular foursome: Mom and Dad in one golf cart, my Lo Yeh and I in the other. This was actually the first time I had ever witnessed anyone defying my parents. When Mom and Dad would plead with Lo Yeh to drive carefully, he couldn't resist me egging him on to go faster and faster down the hill. Or in earlier times, when I was too young to drive, he would let me drive the cart while Mom and Dad weren't looking and of course made me promise I wouldn't tell!

I learned what perseverance was whenever he would play the fourth hole at the old Florham Park CC. This hole had a large pond in front of the green. You could be safe and hit to the grass beside the pond—but not my Lo Yeh. He would aim directly over the water in an attempt to conquer the hole. As often as not, his balls would find a watery grave. Yet he would keep hitting balls until one finally made it onto the green. I can still see the triumphant look in his eyes when he had finally made it over the water.

I also saw the gadget side of him—and those of you who knew him well know exactly what I'm talking about. There is a tool called a ball retriever, which is quite simply a long pole with a small basket on the end that can hold a golf ball. You use this device to retrieve balls that are hard to reach (in the water, for example). But my Lo Yeh didn't have just any ball retriever. No, sir! He had this telescoping contraption that, as I recall, was easily a mile long if it was a foot. No ball out of reach for my Lo Yeh.

There were times when he and I would go and play on a public course and be paired up with other players he would call "old geezers" under his breath. He was afraid that these "old guys" would slow us down. Of course, Lo Yeh was in his seventies, and they were in their sixties!

As an immature young golfer, there were times when my temper would get the best of me on the golf course, and each time, Mom and Dad would scold me for my behavior. Knowing I felt guilty about misbehaving, Lo Yeh was always there with a kind word and a reassurance that everything would be all right. He never passed judgment on me, understanding that it was a result of the impetuous nature of youth. During these times, he stressed to me that golf was a privilege and a game to be enjoyed.

In his last years, as his age robbed him of his ability to play the game he loved, I knew he still lived the game through us. He was always interested in our latest rounds and always wanted to talk about the most recent tournament he had watched on TV.

While his health failed him, his passion never dimmed. So too his love for his grandchildren is eternal and unwavering and to be forever cherished.

Mei's eulogy was as follows:

By now, I think it's evident how fortunate and privileged the four of us feel to have had Yeh Yeh as our grandfather. Despite the sadness this week, we shared a lot of joy and laughter remembering all the good times we had with him. I have chosen two readings for today in Yeh Yeh's memory. To me, the greatest testament of his success is all the love we share in our family, which he has fostered for three generations. This first reading represents his unconditional love for us all. The lines below are just a portion of the poems.

Do Not Be Afraid

Do not be afraid, for I have redeemed you.

I have called you by your name;

You are mine.

When you walk through the waters, I'll be with you;

You will never sink beneath the waves.

> When the fire is burning all around you,
>
> You will never be consumed by the flames …
>
> You are mine, O my child; I am your Father.

This second poem reflects how I think Yeh Yeh would want us to feel about his passing. Rather than mourn his loss, I believe he would want us to celebrate his life. He lives on in all of us and in his great-grandchildren.

> Do not stand at my grave and weep.
>
> I am not there, I do not sleep.
>
> I am a thousand winds that blow.
>
> I am diamond glints on snow.
>
> I am the sunlight on ripened grain.
>
> I am the gentle autumn rain …
>
> Do not stand at my grave and cry,
>
> I am not there; I did not die.

After the service, we invited everyone to join us for dinner at Peking Park, a large Chinese restaurant on Park Avenue in the city. I kept a close eye out for Mommy and was pleased and relieved that she was being sociable and participated in conversations in a normal way. She even laughed occasionally when someone brought up a funny memory.

The next day, just family picked up the two containers we had chosen for Daddy's ashes and stored one in the niche that Solan had bought for Daddy's ashes at Ferncliff Cemetery. I retained one container to bring back with us on a trip to China that we had planned with the family.

Chapter 58

PHOTOGRAPHY AND AFRICA

While I was in college, someone gave me *The Family of Man*, a book of photographs by some of the world's best artists, collected by the great Edward Steichen. Since then, I have thought that art, photography, was one of the most powerful tools one can use to reflect and comment on life and our natural world. In 1990, Al Stein, a colleague and serious amateur photographer, showed me a print of one of his scenic color photographs. He had captured a lightning strike among the canyons of Capital Reef National Park. The print was astonishing.

I said to Al after complimenting him on the print, "When I retire from teaching, I plan to go into photography seriously."

"Why wait until you retire?" Al asked.

"Well, other than being a working mother and caring for aging parents, writing textbooks, cooking for my family, and working on my bonsai, I guess there are no reasons to wait," I said with tongue in cheek.

Al persisted. "It sounds to me like you *need* to add photography, which, believe me, can give you not just fun but excitement when you see that you captured an image like this one. A lot of times, the true quality of an image isn't apparent until the film's been developed and printed out. Do you have a good camera?" he asked.

"No, I don't have a camera period," I answered.

"Tell you what," Al said. "I go into New York City every week to two photography stores, and I can introduce you to a couple of the salesmen who've become my friends. They can help you get started."

"What brand of camera do you use?" I asked.

"Canon. I like that you can get different interchangeable lenses that will fit all the cameras I have. Most of the better brands, like Nikon, also have this flexibility, but I just started with Canon."

The more we talked, the more excited I got about photography. Al did indeed take me to a store that catered to serious amateurs and professionals, the name of which I have forgotten. The other store was B&H, a gigantic store owned and operated by Hasidic Jews in New York City, which has ever since served as my source of photographic equipment. The storefront now occupies an entire block in the city. I started out with film cameras, using slide film. By using slide film, I did not have to pay for prints of shots I didn't like. One could scan the slides and just pick out those that were good enough to make prints.

One of the best decisions I made was to join the Livingston Camera Club in 1991. There I found experienced photographers, such as my friend John Murray, who were willing to give advice and help out novices like me. LCC members met twice a month for nine months of the year, and we would have guest speakers as well as monthly intraclub competitions judged by professional photographers from other clubs. The comments of the professional judges as they critiqued our photographs, whether they liked them or not, were educational. Shortly after I began taking photos, I was seriously hooked on photography.

In 1995, my work was exhibited at a small gallery in Livingston. I wrote the following essay in introducing myself and my work:

> In 1988, I saw and was inspired by some Cibachrome color prints of a colleague at Montclair State and serious amateur photographer, Al Stein. I made the comment to him that photography has always been one of my favorite forms of art and that when I retired from teaching, I would take it up seriously. He asked me a simple question: "Why wait?" and promised to help me get started.
>
> He accompanied me on trips to purchase camera equipment, and then, as I practiced and became addicted, he introduced me to printing. He allowed me full use of his darkroom at his home. We began to plan for the future when both of us would retire from our positions as biology professors at Montclair State University. I am so glad that I acquiesced to his enthusiasm, as I shared his love for the art for far too few years. More than four years ago, as we were planning to join the Livingston Camera Club, Al was diagnosed with esophageal cancer and passed away in less than a year.
>
> His dear wife, Ruth, said that since I was the only friend he had that showed any interest in printing, she wanted me to take all his darkroom equipment, as she herself was not interested in it. So I was privileged to receive his equipment and had one of Al's friends from the camera store estimate what the value of the used equipment was. I persuaded Ruth to accept my payment. What I achieve in photography I dedicate to Al's memory.
>
> I have been a member of the Livingston Camera Club (LCC) for four years and was elected president last year. I have been fortunate to have won several Print of the Month awards and two Print of the Year awards from the club. I also won a medal prize in a Federation of Camera Clubs of New Jersey interclub competition for my shot of the American flag at Pearl Harbor (figure 183).
>
> My photographs have been displayed at Montclair State University, the Pepsi

Cola campus, the New York Botanical Garden in conjunction with the Yama Ki Bonsai Club exhibition of bonsai trees, the Livingston Town Hall, and the Livingston Library.

I credit much of my improvement as a photographer to participation in the Livingston Camera Club. Critique during competitions and the generous willingness of fellow members to share their expertise have been of inestimable help. I learned of and have studied in photography workshops with David Vestal, Brian Lav, and Tim White. I look forward to the day when I can devote more time to improving my techniques and skills as a photographer. Until then, I cherish the opportunities that I have had.

In addition, I have been privileged to study for twenty-five years the art of bonsai with Yuji Yoshimura, who I believe is the greatest bonsai artist in the United States. I find bonsai and photography have a logical confluence of interests. Common to an interest in biology, photography, and bonsai is a love of nature and an awareness—even awe—of the beauty of the natural world.

As an evolutionist, I do not give the existence of humans on our planet an exalted position over any other species that has evolved. However, to my limited human knowledge, I do believe we are unique in two aspects (which are admirable): the ability to imagine and the need to create. There is no other living organism I know of that can see a wildflower and feel the urge to present it as a photographic image, incorporate it into a tray landscape, describe it in poetry, or represent it in music—or find a way to understand it scientifically.

Each activity—bonsai, photography, and the science of biology—studies nature in a different way, but they are not without overlap. A fundamental essence of all three is harmony. In living systems, there is harmony of metabolism and structure. We call it homeostasis, without which life is not possible. In bonsai, we look for harmony of form, in the absence of which there is conflict and loss of beauty. In photography, we speak of composition, which to me is harmony of elements in an image.

From all three, the harmony I see and feel brings a quiet joy and peace that is of the purist form. It offers me not only respite from chaos that I know is part of nature and life but also hope and renewal.

One of my great privileges in life was to become friendly with Gordon Parks, whose photography I first encountered in *Life Magazine*. I had the good fortune of being friends with Gordon's last wife, Genevieve Young, and through her came to learn about a truly Renaissance man in Gordon (figure 184). A charming, athletic, talented man in many ways, he survived a difficult childhood and adolescence. Despite his beginnings, Gordon Roger Alexander Buchanan Parks became a world-class photographer, composer, author, and musician, with a long list of being the "first black man to achieve such and such." For example, he was the first black photographer to work with *Vogue* and *Life* and the first black man to direct a full-length movie, *Shaft*. His unbelievable life has been described in published autobiographies and biographies that I urge you to look up and read. All of his achievements came straight out of his genes; he was never formally trained in any of his various talents.

After we'd become good friends, I ventured to ask Gordon one day to give me some advice on how to become a good photographer. He puffed on his pipe for a second and then turned to me and said, "Just go out and do it, baby!" It was simple but sage advice. Afterward, I was somewhat embarrassed I had asked such a dumb question, thinking about how he had become prominent in so many areas without help from anyone else. I have aspired to do what he said. Gordon died in 2006 in New York City. Every ethnicity was present in the hundreds of mourners at his funeral service.

One of the judges at the LCC competitions, whose work I also admired greatly because he was a world-class nature and wildlife photographer, was a Cuban immigrant, Gil Lopez Espina (figure 185).

Gil not only served as a judge but also accepted our invitation to give multimedia slide shows as a guest speaker. He specialized in African wildlife photography. An art teacher at Belleville High School, he spent his summer vacations camping in the African bush.

The call of Africa proved too strong, and one year—I believe it was 1996—he resigned his teaching position to organize his own travel and safari company, which he named Fototreks. He took small groups of serious amateurs or professionals, no more than six photographers, on the three trips I took with him. The trips were two weeks long. He promised each photographer would have an entire bench of whatever vehicle we used, so we would have the freedom to move from one side of the vehicle to the other to shoot, depending on where the wildlife we encountered might be.

Knowing Gil and knowing how meticulous he was in his presentations and how familiar he was with Africa and the wildlife he photographed so much and so brilliantly, I found going to Africa with him a great temptation. I had retired from teaching at Montclair State and was still in mourning for my big brother and wanted to be preoccupied with something else, something I had never done before—going on a photo safari.

I talked to David about my idea to go on a safari with Gil, and he was very much in favor of it, but since the trips were all scheduled for summer months, he preferred to stay home and play golf at our club. Also, as he was a night owl, the daily schedule of getting up at five o'clock in the morning was not conducive to his accompanying me to Africa!

My first photo safari with Gil in 1998 was to two private game parks in South Africa: Phinda and Londolozi. There were six of us on the tour with Gil, and I knew all but two of the others through the Livingston Camera Club. I looked forward to that adventure with friends who felt the same way about photographing nature and wildlife as I did. For me, traveling with friends with the same interests always adds to the enjoyment.

The flight was long. We took off from JFK Airport on Long Island on a direct flight and ended in Johannesburg, South Africa, fourteen hours later. Twice later, for other photo safaris, we flew to European countries to connect to flights to Jo'burg. Those were even longer trips because of the layovers. My final trip with Gil was in 2004, when the flight from Jo'burg home took a total of thirty-six hours. I must say, it exhausted me!

When we first flew to Africa, Gil told us that the reality of life there was such that when we got our luggage and cleared customs, we should not pause but walk quickly to a van that would be waiting just for us. That precaution was necessary in 1998. We did as he ordered. Gil also explained that sometimes we could not take the shortest route to our destinations because of troubles that frequented those roads. I am happy to say that on three photo safari tours with Gil, we never encountered any such problems.

My experiences in Africa during the three photo-safari tours with Gil occurred almost two decades ago. The conditions we found then in the game parks in which we stayed no doubt have changed over the years, so in my narrations of some wonderful and exciting trips I took, do remember that time has passed. To learn about the resorts where we stayed, go online to see what they now offer in the way of buildings, food, and game drives.

Knowing Gil as the perfectionist that he was, I expected Phinda and Londolozi to be superb resorts, and they were. Our accommodations were luxurious by South African standards at that time. We stayed in small cottages that had electricity, running water, heat, and air-conditioning, with two of us in each cottage. Everywhere we went, there was netting over the beds to keep mosquitoes away. At the time, malaria was still a large problem in Africa. Among the more interesting lodges we stayed in was the tree house in Tarangire Game Park in Tanzania. A huge limb of the tree protruded into the tree house (figure 186). Some of the resorts were beautifully landscaped, such as the Serena Lodge in Kenya (figure 187).

At times, as we moved from one game park to another, the most primitive accommodations (figure 188) involved permanent tents with floors but no electricity or running water. All permanent tents were made of thick, sturdy plastic, and heavy zippers kept the "doors" of the tents securely closed. I was told a terrible story at the camp we visited in Botswana. An American family had a ten-year-old boy who wanted to sleep separately in a small tent they themselves had brought. When the locals told them it was too dangerous because the tent was not of the same quality as the permanent ones, they insisted it was; they had bought an expensive one supposedly safe from wildlife. Sadly, they were wrong, and the boy was killed by a family of hyenas that night. It is the greatest of follies to consider ourselves more knowledgeable than locals, who are intimately aware of the behavior of indigenous wildlife.

Interestingly, when I took my granddaughter Leanna with me to Tanzania, she said of all our accommodations, she enjoyed the primitive tents the best. In some, there were solar lamps with limited illumination that we could use after sunset. Water for showering was brought to us at times that we could specify. The warm water was poured into a bucket that was high outside the tent and attached to a pipe that ran into the tent. At the end of the pipe was a showerhead with a valve by which we could turn the water on and off. There was adequate water for washing off the soap, but we knew long showers were impossible.

Because we had such early and quick starts to our days on safari, we took most showers at night. In the tents, it was important to dry oneself as quickly as possible after washing and don pajamas just as quickly. With no heating, the nighttime temperatures could dip close to freezing. We would jump under the layers of comforters and blankets on our beds and lie there soaking in the sounds of Africa at night: an occasional roar from a lion, the *ding-ding* of fruit bats, and the repetitive snorting of hippopotamuses.

Although nighttime temperatures could be as low as in the thirties, every day the temperatures rose to the eighties. Thus, we had to wear clothing in layers. I usually wore a long-sleeved shirt, a vest, a sweater, and a jacket over everything. As the morning and afternoon wore on, I usually ended without the sweater and jacket. As it was best not to wear shorts or short-sleeved shirts because of the fear of mosquito bites and sunburn, everyone wore long pants. Beds in our tents or rooms were surrounded by thin curtains called bed nets to protect from mosquitoes at night.

It was important that tourists take antimalaria medicine to prevent the disease, which is transmitted by mosquitoes. However, the threat of malaria is much diminished in their winter. In four trips to sub-Saharan Africa, I saw perhaps a total of five mosquitoes and was bitten by none. Yet in their nonwinter months, malaria is still a scourge, killing hundreds of thousands every year, 90 percent of them in sub-Saharan Africa.

The first night in Phinda, a guard came to escort us to the dining room for dinner. We were warned never to walk outside our cottages without an escort because the resort had no barriers to keep the wildlife out. Our guards never carried guns, only large flashlights. We were told that once, an elderly couple either forgot the warning or did not take it seriously. They decided to visit friends in a nearby cottage. The buildings were maybe only forty feet apart. Tragically, some lions in the vicinity were hunting and killed the couple.

During the day, movement was free, without need for guards, although I encountered a huge bull elephant one day when I left the gift store in Phinda. He was about thirty yards away on the sidewalk, and I was able to duck quickly behind some trees and return to the shop until he left.

That first night, as we stepped out of the cottage and began walking to dinner, I happened to look up and stopped in my tracks. The sky was an inky black, and the stars were brilliant. I had never seen so many stars in my life. The Milky Way was a swath of so many stars it looked like a lit pathway in the sky, cutting through the darkness. The stars' visibility, of course, was due to the absence of light and air pollution, which we live with in the United States. My reverie was interrupted by the guide, who gently said, "We must go now, madam."

That first evening, after dinner, we went to a patio with a clear view of a man-made water hole for animals to drink. We sat around a blazing fire pit because it was winter, and at night, it was very chilly. After a short time, an adult elephant sauntered to the water hole to quench its thirst. A few minutes later, a second adult came into view. (The water hole was illuminated by a light.)

The first elephant wheeled around, and the second hesitated and then ran toward the first. For a second, I thought they were going to fight, and I was angry not to have my camera. However, they apparently were friends, because they met, and each trunk wound around the other in what I guessed was their version of a handshake or a hug. Elephants are the most social of animals. They are the most intelligent, the biggest, and the only one that caused me any concern on my photo safaris.

To be able to sit around a fire with friends and watch wildlife carrying on was wonderful. Gil pointed out a cluster of stars low on the horizon. "See the Southern Cross?" he asked. Sure enough, a small group of stars were aligned in a cross.

We arose from bed at five o'clock in the morning. The sky was still dark, but we wanted to be ready to shoot with the light of the rising sun. We had a cup of tea and a cookie or two and climbed into our Range Rover after being introduced to our driver and tracker.

At Phinda, every ranger had a permanent partner as his tracker. They always drove together and seemed to be the best of friends. The majority of rangers were white, probably of Boer heritage, and the trackers were mostly natives who lived close to Phinda. Each man was assigned a rifle that he kept at all times, something that was to be the cause of a terrible tragedy a year later.

I asked one of our rangers about the training for being a ranger. He told me there was some studying to be done, as they were expected to be able to identify not only wildlife but also the flora of the park. Then they were trained to use their rifles and instructed on what to do if the wildlife seemed to be angry and agitated. In the final test, they were given just three bullets and were to walk on foot into the bush and take down with one of the bullets an impala, which they were to then carry back to camp. The meat was usually given to neighboring villagers.

As both Phinda and Londolozi were private game parks, we were allowed to drive into the bush to follow game during our game drives. The public and state parks required all vehicles to remain on the roads only. Gil also told the rangers and trackers that the group were all professional photographers. He instructed them to maneuver our open Range Rovers, if possible, so that the sun was behind us to shine on the subjects we wanted to shoot with our cameras.

Those particular game parks also had a rule that no more than three tourist vehicles were to surround animals at the same time. We were to remain as quiet as possible. Those restrictions were to keep the animals' environment as natural as possible. The rangers who drove and their tracker partners, who sat on a seat in the front of the truck while we were tracking wildlife, were also to remain as quiet as possible. They were not to upset and chase animals that might already be frightened. Once we were close to the wildlife, the tracker left his seat attached to the front of the vehicle and sat in the last row of benches for protection.

One day our ranger drove us to a part of the game park where he had been told there was a breeding group of elephants. We stood still, waiting to see a group of females and young ones, usually led by a matriarch. The bulls usually walked some distance behind the breeding group. We saw a vehicle loaded with tourists following a breeding group that seemed to be running from the vehicle.

Our ranger said, "That vehicle is too close, and the tourists are too loud."

The group of elephants was led by the matriarch, usually the largest female, who was dominant over the other females. The matriarch led the group into a dense cluster of bush and trees that was perhaps thirty yards from where we were. After a minute or two, the matriarch burst from the bush and turned toward us, seemingly mistaking us for the truck that had been chasing her group.

She was clearly angry, because her ears were flipping up and down, and she was moving her trunk back and forth (figure 189). She took a few steps toward us and then turned to join her group. Our ranger started to turn our vehicle to move away, when she emerged again. After taking a few more steps than she had the first time, threatening to charge again, she again spun around to go to her charges.

Our ranger that day, one of two rangers at Phinda who was a native, exclaimed, "We have to leave—and quick! Hang on. If she comes out again, she will really charge us!" He wheeled our Range Rover around and gunned the engine. Elephants were known to be capable of destroying a vehicle with their tusks and their enormous strength. We did not object to the ranger's desire to leave quickly!

True to his word, Gil gave every one of the six tourist photographers in our group a whole bench in the open Range Rovers to him- or herself so that we could slide from one side to another. There were no more than three photographers in each Range Rover, which had three separate benches. We all had our cameras on tripods with quick-release mounts. We securely fastened the tripod to the bar on the back of the seat in front of our own seat. That arrangement allowed us to shoot with maximum stability and still have time to remove the camera from the tripod instantly if we needed to shoot at subjects that were moving around.

All our cameras were single-lens reflex cameras that had interchangeable lenses. I used several different lenses with my Canon cameras. On my first trip to Africa, I had two camera backs and at least five lenses, all in a carry-on-sized bag. At that time, I still was using a film camera. I brought 120 rolls of thirty-six-exposure film, some for good light conditions and some for low-light conditions.

A couple in our group of six photographers developed their own film, whereas the rest of us sent our film in to Kodak. They also intended to stay in Africa when our tour was over for a total of a month. They had brought a whopping nine hundred rolls of film, which they carried in a laundry bag. I have since thought of them and wondered what they would have had to do in the days following the plane hijackings of 9/11 and the resulting complex security regulations. Thank goodness for digital photography!

Digital cameras were just beginning to come into their own, and as soon as I could afford to, I switched to a digital Canon camera that could still use the lenses I used on my film cameras. As age began to catch up with me over the next years, out of necessity, I needed to carry less equipment and a smaller bag. Now I am down to a wide-angle 18- to 250-millimeter zoom lens; a 400-millimeter telephoto lens; and a small camera bag to carry all but the telephoto lens, which has its own carrier.

Digital cameras are a boon to wildlife photographers. With film cameras, there is the need to bring many rolls of film. The need to change film frequently could cause the photographer to lose images that he or she could rue forever. Even those rolls with thirty-six shots seemed to be quickly used up, necessitating a pause in the shooting. With memory cards, there are a limitless number of shots. Should it be necessary to change memory cards, there is plenty of time to do so when tracking an animal that might take more than an hour to find.

Bringing memory cards for a digital camera is much easier than bringing film. Another advantage is that I had both camera backs loaded with film—one carrying relatively fast film and one carrying slow film. I would have to switch from one camera to another, depending on the changing light conditions. Digital cameras have settings that can be quickly changed, so only one camera is needed.

Software, such as the powerful Photoshop program, allows one to correct many aspects of the image before printing. I took a photography workshop shortly after I bought my first digital camera. I set the camera to Program, which uses the settings the camera decides on automatically. Then I used a formula I learned in the workshop to set a camera manually for exposure and speed. The settings were identical. Since then, I have not strayed from the Program setting, except for on special circumstances. I am sure one can find the same thing is true for all the known brands of cameras.

We drove around the large acreage for our game drives, sometimes just hoping for good luck to run across wildlife to photograph. We did not stay together on our game drives since usually there were three vehicles assigned to our group. Because sighting animals was a question of luck, sometimes one group would elicit some envy from the others if they happened upon a scene that was particularly photogenic. For example, those in one vehicle one day saw and shot a fish eagle with a fish in its beak. It took me a fourth trip to Africa to see and finally succeed in getting a good shot of a fish eagle, which looks like the bald eagle.

Some of the birds were dramatic looking, to say the least, such as the African secretary bird (figure 190), which is a large bird standing three to four feet tall. It is a ground hunter. If we saw one seemingly dancing on the ground, we were told it probably was stomping on a snake, one of its prey. Our guides were not sure of the origins of the name *secretary bird*, but possibly its large head feathers, which stood out, looked to some like ancient quill pens that secretaries might have used.

On one game drive during my first trip with Gil, we had an exceptional tracker. His name was Ehrens, and he and his ranger were close buddies. Ehrens was the subject of a *National Geographic* article on game parks and trackers in South Africa. He was effervescent in his love of the wildlife and proud of the *National Geographic* article, and he made sure I knew the issue it was in. If I remember right, it was in one of the 1986 issues.

One afternoon, we were having little luck in finding wildlife in the form of a big cat. Ehrens saw something—a spoor (the track or trail of an animal). It was not distinct, but Ehrens was determined to follow it. He felt it was a challenge to his ability to find animals for his photographers. It took about two hours, but eventually, he found a leopard for us. The native trackers were so familiar with animal behavior and the tracks they left in the dust and had such keen eyesight that they invariably saw the animals before we did.

After we took our shots, I turned to Ehrens, who was sporting a big grin, and said, "Ehrens, that was terrific!"

He smiled wider and said, "That was super terrific!" I stood corrected.

Ehrens was so good I asked his ranger partner, "How difficult is it for someone like Ehrens to be trained as a ranger? He seems to be very bright."

The ranger answered, "He was already offered a position as ranger, but even though we're paid two or three times what a tracker is paid, he declined. He loves tracking too much to change."

I managed to speak with Ehrens about his family. He showed me a photograph of his wife, who was attractive, and spoke of his two young sons. Clearly, the tracker was a happy man who loved his job and was close with his partner and with a family he enjoyed. I was happy for the impressive young man, who was full of self-confidence but not annoyingly so. I came to like Ehrens a lot in the few days we knew him.

The experience of my first trip to South Africa in 1988 was enjoyable. We had good food prepared by chefs who had been sent to Europe to train. They were proud of their expertise, and we were served paella and steak along with all kinds of vegetables and fruit. One evening, there were splendid appetizers: kebabs of impala and barbecued wild boar meat. The impala meat was sweet, though I was not comfortable eating it, having just shot some photos of those beautiful creatures (figure 191). The wild boar meat tasted like pork, as one might imagine.

Two experiences at Phinda were especially noteworthy. One day we spotted something moving in a tree. When we drove closer, we saw a lion cub about four months old. A closer look revealed four cubs, all about the same age. Two were using the tree as a lookout for their mothers, who had gone out to hunt (figure 192). Pregnant lionesses usually leave their prides when birthing time nears. Frequently, more than one pregnant female in the pride will leave together. Some nurse their young until the cubs are old enough to care for themselves before returning to the pride.

Unfortunately, as in the family we found, the mothers leave the young to hunt for their own food, having taught them to hide if they sense danger near. Not having any protection from predators, such as adult big cats or hyenas, they themselves are delicacies as prey. Our ranger that day told us the cubs belonged to two mothers who'd started out with seven cubs total and now had only four left.

The ranger said that when lions mate, the female only has 25 percent chance of conceiving. Because of the lack of protection when the mothers go hunting, each offspring has only a 25 percent chance of surviving to be one year old. In light of those statistics, together with the loss of habitat, it is no wonder the lion population has dwindled to alarmingly small numbers in Africa. In 1960, there were two hundred thousand lions in Africa. The present census is that there are now fewer than twenty-five thousand. They are magnificent animals. I can only hope that conservation efforts will be successful in saving them from extinction.

We were told that rangers at Phinda had orders to shoot to kill any poachers they found. The governments in several African countries were trying to teach poachers they managed to capture the need for them to use their knowledge of wildlife to protect the animals. It was a difficult situation because the offer of big payoffs for body parts of animals, such as the ivory tusks of elephants and horns of the rhinoceros, which brought thousands of dollars, was more than impoverished natives could refuse.

One ranger at Phinda was a converted poacher. I spoke with him a few times. He was still bitter about life in South Africa, even though he was now salaried and could live better than when he'd been poaching. Dire problems apparently still existed.

I asked him, "But aren't you able to make a better life for your family than you could before?"

He answered somberly, "Oh sure, but if I buy my family anything, like a TV, my neighbor could come in with a gun and take it from me."

"What happens when you tell the police?" I asked.

"They won't do anything. In fact, they might be in on it, so why is my life that much better?" I had no answer.

To return to our discovery of the four lion cubs, we knew the mothers would return to the spot where they had told their offspring to stay and wait for them. Sure enough, after about fifteen or twenty minutes, we saw the cubs in the tree become agitated. Looking in the same direction they were looking, we saw the two lionesses side by side, making their way to the cubs. They stopped when they were close and gave a low *humph* sound (figure 193).

The two cubs in the tree scrambled down to join the other two, who were already running toward their mothers. There was such rejoicing and excitement from the cubs (figure 194)! The mothers, tired from the hunt and having eaten well, as their bulging stomachs indicated, were ready to take a nap. They lay down to sleep and feed their young. Soon the babies, having eaten to fullness, lay down and also slept (figure 195). Since we were on a photo safari, we had no set activities or agendas other than mealtimes and schedules of game drives. Because of our flexibility of schedule, we just stayed near them and waited for the lions' siesta to end.

In about an hour, one cub awoke, and his first activity was to try to wake up his mother. He jumped on top of her but could not rouse her (figure 196). Then he walked to her head and chewed on her ear (figure 197). Still, she gave no response. Finally, he crawled under her head and lifted it up, and that succeeded in waking his mother up (figure 198). The sequence was a photographer's dream; our cameras clicked nonstop.

Soon all were awake and greeting each other. The cubs began to romp with each other like big kittens (figure 199). No doubt the play fighting was important to establish a hierarchy of dominance. It was the way we saw other young animals establish a hierarchy of dominance, such as young cape buffalo.

After a while, the mothers suddenly stood up and faced the same direction, having heard some noise that worried them. The cubs responded immediately and were as still as statues (figure 200). Ernest Hemingway, who loved to hunt in Africa, once wrote, "There is nothing as still as a wild animal on alert." It was true; even the young were trained to react. It was, after all, a matter of survival.

The anxiety of the mothers relaxed as soon as they saw a giraffe approaching, and the cubs began to play again. With great reluctance, we left the small family because we needed to return to camp, but we had many photos and memories to remind us of the wonderful experience. We returned to camp happy with our game drive that day and with fervent hope that all four cubs would survive.

One other experience at Phinda that I recall vividly reflects the amazing intelligence and power of communication of elephants. One of the group and I decided one afternoon to forego the afternoon game drive and go to a Zulu village that had been created for tourists. We knew it would be more or less a tourist trap, but we still wanted to go. In spite of the inroads of modern life into native traditions, we hoped to learn some fragments of actual Zulu culture. A ranger in training and his veteran partner tracker drove us to the village.

In the village, there were grass thatched huts we could look into to see how whole families slept and lived in such a small space. We watched bare-breasted women weaving baskets with dried grasses. The young man who apparently was the chief of that group of natives led them in a warriors' dance. The authenticity of the dance was somewhat demoted in my mind because the handsome, athletic young chief signaled his men with a store-bought whistle.

The presentation lasted for about an hour, perhaps a little more. We then headed back to camp. Remember that our ranger that day was a ranger in training. His tracker was Rokomons, who was helping his inexperienced partner. Gary, the ranger, was solicitous and wanted us not to miss a game drive entirely. It was fairly late in the afternoon, and Gary said he had received word over his cell phone that there was a group of elephants not far from where we were.

"I think I can get you there in time for you to have some light for photos," he said.

"That sounds good to me," my friend replied, and Gary stepped on the gas.

About twenty minutes later, he had driven to a part of the park where the narrow dirt road was lined on both sides by heavy bush. He slowed to a halt.

"They said the eles were around here, so let's wait and see if we can hear them."

We sat there for about five minutes, when I heard a crack that sounded as if an elephant had stepped on and broken a sizable limb. I turned to the side behind us where I thought the sound had come from and indeed saw a pair of big tusks coming out of a clump of trees. Two other bull elephants followed the lead elephant. The elephants had not made any sound we could hear before emerging after the crack I'd heard. I wonder if the leader had stepped on a branch on purpose to tell us they were near.

One thing we had learned was that as big as elephants were, if they wanted to be quiet, you could not hear them. One day a bull elephant made me jump. We were at a pond, watching and shooting some elephants across the pond. All of a sudden, about ten feet from me, an elephant ripped a big leaf off a plant to eat.

The people I was sharing a Range Rover with and I had had no idea there was a huge animal that close to us. He was hidden by the plants, which had large leaves, and he had made no noise at all until he intentionally pulled the leaf off, announcing his presence. He wasn't interested in us and made no move toward us. We left as quietly as we could.

The pair of tusks emerging from the trees the evening after we visited the Zulu village was impressive. Equally so were the total of three bull elephants rushing through a flat area beyond the thick bushes on the right side of our vehicle. They did not seem to take any notice of us, and I assumed they were hurrying to keep up with the breeding herd that must have been in front of them. Suddenly, all three veered left through a small opening of the bushes about forty yards down the road and stood facing us, shoulder to shoulder, blocking the road entirely.

I quickly half turned to my camera bag, needing a wide-angle lens. I had put my longest telephoto lens on my camera, thinking I would need it for a far shot of the breeding herd, but the three bull elephants were too close for me to shoot all three in one image. But before I could change lenses, I looked behind us. About forty yards down the road, three more bull elephants had entered the road and filled it, standing shoulder to shoulder like the ones in front. We had been ambushed! Where we were standing, the bush on either side of us was thick, and even if we'd needed to, we could not have turned to drive away.

"Don't move," the ranger in training said in a whisper.

Rokomons said nothing but quietly and slowly reached behind his seat, where there was a big bowie knife, and he held the knife behind his back. The thought crossed my mind that somehow the six bulls had conferred and planned the ambush, yet none of us had heard any sounds before the crack of the limb announced their presence.

Scientists have studied the different ways elephants communicate, and one intriguing finding is that they can transmit messages by stamping their feet on the ground. We had not even heard that happening. However they'd done it, the ambush had been well organized. Each elephant knew where to stand.

I turned my attention to the three in front of us. The one in the middle was larger than the others, and he proved to be the alpha bull as he began slowly moving toward us. The other two stayed behind. His ears were flapping, but there was only a small movement of the trunk from side to side, not like the whipping motion of the female matriarch I described before, who was clearly agitated. He was not trumpeting, thank goodness. He continued to stare at us and walk toward us. Then he stopped about twenty yards from us.

Dear reader, regarding what I'm about to describe to you, I cross my heart that I'm telling the truth. The huge elephant stopped and then shook his head and shrugged the way humans do when we realize something or someone is not a threat or a danger. At his dismissive movement, he and the other two elephants in front of us retraced their steps through the bushes. The three behind us also returned to the clear area through the bushes, rushed past us, and followed the others.

Because the ranger had ordered us to be still, I did not have the correct lens on my camera. The only photograph I have of the encounter is a fuzzy shot (because by that time, it was almost dark) of one of them passing us and looking straight into my camera as if to say, "Scared you, huh?" (figure 201).

In my four trips to photograph wildlife in Africa, I built up enormous respect for elephants. These behemoths are capable of strategizing and building strong family ties as we do. They love and care for their kin as we do. Because they are as capable of deep love as we are, perhaps with even more altruism, their intelligence is mind-boggling. We are naive and arrogant to believe we have much more intelligence than animals, when the main difference is they do not have our form of speech. Nor do we have theirs.

Rokomons turned to the rest of us and said calmly, "I knew he was not going to attack. He was just curious why we were here, and probably we are between them and their breeding herd." Then he added, "I did not pick up the knife to hurt him. I would have used it to bang on the car to scare them off."

His ranger partner apologized to us and said he was at fault for having put us in a potentially dangerous position. I was just annoyed I'd been unable to take the shots I'd wanted to. What an opportunity to show through images how controlled and organized the elephants were to put us at their mercy.

Because of my four trips to Africa and my time observing their natural behavior in the wild, I respect the intelligence of most species, especially the elephants, and find myself unable any longer to enjoy visiting zoos. No matter how well they are cared for and how well their enclosures are made to simulate their natural habitats, the wildlife know they are captives surrounded by humans and cannot behave the way they would in freedom.

Circuses are another form of entertainment I have long eschewed, even before I had the privilege of seeing wildlife in their natural environment. I've always found it demeaning to make magnificent animals, such as lions and elephants, behave in clownish ways while dressed in costumes, forcing them into unnatural movements. Then the big cats go back to cages, while the elephants are chained. Is it any wonder circus animals occasionally lose control and attack people?

I will describe two other experiences involving elephants, which occurred on my trip with Gil to Botswana in 2000. My friend Dr. Chris Rushlow (see again figure 178), who had invited me to spend a semester in her laboratory in 1995 on while I was on sabbatical leave from Montclair State, joined me on that trip. After hearing about my previous trip to Botswana, she decided to go along.

We began the trip to Botswana by staying in Moremi, a picturesque game park in the Okavango Delta region right next to the Chobe River. The two of us were so excited about being in Botswana that we found it hard to go to sleep. Our accommodations at Moremi were permanent tents with no electricity or running water.

After sunset, solar lamps provided a little bit of light, and we had bottled water to drink and brush our teeth with. Chinese usually bathe at night, and I asked for some hot water for a shower at nine o'clock. The shower was located in a small closet-like area attached to the tent that one entered by a door between the tent and the shower. It was, however, an open-air shower that had no roof.

The shower was made ready right at nine o'clock, and the warm water felt great. However, leaving the shower and stepping into the cold night air of the tent was like leaving a sauna to jump into a snowbank! Remember, it was winter, and the night temperatures could be as low as in the mid to high thirties. I'd never dried myself or dressed in my pajamas and dived into bed so fast! When we both were finally in our beds, under heavy blankets and quilts, we were still excited and chattered away.

The musical *ding-ding* sound of fruit bats, the *hmph-hmph* sound of hippos in the Chobe River nearby, and an occasional lion's roar were too magical to ignore. Finally, I said, "We need to sleep; we have to wake up at five o'clock." At that point, it was perhaps one o'clock in the morning. We both decided to take a sleeping pill, and that did the trick. Unfortunately, it did the trick too well! The next thing I knew, Gil was shaking me by the shoulder. It was already five thirty, and everyone else was ready to leave. When I turned over, I heard him say, "Oh my God, I'm so relieved!" He was understandably annoyed we had overslept.

I looked at him with bleary eyes, and he said, "I called you two loudly while standing outside the tent and got no response. Then I decided to come into the tent and called loudly and still got no response. I thought you might have died! But then I thought, what are the odds you both died on the same night?" Now he was chuckling. "I was happy to see no blood, so I knew you weren't attacked by hyenas or something. Come on, you two! Get dressed, have a biscuit and a bit of tea, and let's get rolling. I'll wait for you two, and the others can go on first." He left the tent, still shaking his head.

Thoroughly embarrassed, Chris and I quickly dressed, grabbed our camera equipment, and ran to the dining room, where the rest of our group—four photographers, two guides, Gil, and a friend of his, Colin Meade, a South African who was a local guide—had finished a prebreakfast biscuit and a cup of tea. After a gulp or two of the tea that first morning, Chris and I each took a biscuit and announced we were ready for our drive. We were to have our real breakfast much later, around nine thirty, in the bush as a break from the wildlife drive.

Just as in South Africa, we were given baskets containing cereals, hard-boiled eggs, breakfast rolls, milk, coffee, tea, and fruit. They were placed inside our Toyota four-by-fours, which were closed vehicles, unlike the open Range Rovers in South Africa, where the baskets had been strapped onto the end of the Range Rovers.

One morning, a young lion about a year old tried to pull off the breakfast basket and was frightened away by our tracker. We did not have any such problem in Botswana.

Since there were three vehicles assigned to us and only two guides, every day two photographers would be on their own. I didn't like that arrangement because I didn't consider myself a well-trained photo-safari person and because Chris was on her first trip to Africa. I also did not like the fact that we were not allowed to keep our cell phones with us. We had to hand them over to a member of the Botswana army for safekeeping. I was glad we would have Gil with us that first morning.

I did not understand why we were not to have cell phones and felt more insecure without them, because if we had car troubles or another issue, there was no way to contact Gil or Colin. But we were in a national park and had no choice in the matter but to go off regardless of whether we had Gil, Colin, or neither. Fortunately, Chris was familiar with manual-drive vehicles, which I was not, and she did all the driving when we were without our two guides, while I sat in the back seat.

One late afternoon, when she and I were by ourselves, we saw a magnificent sunset developing and decided to delay going back to camp to photograph the scene. We were the only car in sight by the bank of the Chobe River. Chris parked the car at an angle to the river with the nose of the car pointing more toward the river than parallel to it so that we both could shoot the sunset. I must say, the sunsets in Botswana were consistently gorgeous, the most spectacular I had ever seen, night after night (figure 202).

We were happily shooting away, when Chris turned to one side to change film and, looking up and toward the back of the Toyota four-by-four, said, "There's an elephant on top of us!"

I turned toward the back of the car and saw nothing but elephant hide. Although we were the only car at the long bank of the Chobe River, a mature elephant had decided to come right up to our car to intimidate us. Neither of us had heard her coming. At the last second before colliding with us, she veered to go down the bank of the river at the same time I turned to look. She was followed by two youngsters and then another older one, probably a juvenile offspring.

When the juvie, as the natives call the older elephant offspring, turned to go down the same part of the sandy bank as the mother had to reach the river for a drink, that part of the bank gave way and sent the juvie sliding down to the shore of the river. It was not much of a fall, about four or five feet, but I could hear the grunt the elephant made when it fell onto the firmer ground.

Immediately, the mother turned from drinking and ran back to the juvie. When the juvie stood up from the fall, the two stood side by side, glaring at us as if we had caused the fall. They were no more than about ten feet from us, though down below the bank. I wanted badly to use my flash to take a picture of them facing us, but I decided it was best not to annoy them any further. I had a feeling they were not particularly belligerent, more embarrassed than anything else, and probably would have trouble climbing up the bank of loose sand.

Just in case, I whispered, "Chris, get your hand on the car keys in case they start to come after us."

At that point, they both turned away and joined the two little ones, who were drinking at the river. Chris immediately started the car and backed away from the river so we could drive off before they changed their minds. We were relieved and had learned an important lesson: we should always park the car so that a quick getaway would be possible. The incident had also taught us that the elephant had been sending us a message: we should be wary because she was not afraid of us. She was probably also teaching her children how to intimidate.

Another experience with an elephant taught me that wild animals have their own thoughts about humans, as we have about them—and they are probably more insightful than we are. We were on a small boat on the Chobe River, and we were stopped near the bank while our guide expounded on the wildlife. A lone mature elephant sauntered toward us.

When she reached the bank by the river shore where we had stopped, she sat down on her rump with her hind legs parallel on the ground and front legs straight, propping her body up, a position I had rarely seen an elephant take. She was sitting parallel to the river. I got up from my seat to photograph her when she started to flip her trunk back and forth while staring at us (figure 203). Suddenly, she stood up, looked ahead, moved her head back a bit, forcefully dug her tusks into the sand, and flopped over onto her side (figure 204).

"Colin!" I cried. "I think there's something wrong with this elephant! It looks like it's sick. Is it dying?"

Colin, watching the elephant, shook his head. "No, it's just cavorting!"

I looked back at the elephant, and sure enough, she raised her head and then clambered to her feet and leisurely walked away. For some reason, nobody else had taken photos of her during her cavorting. When I had the film developed and slides made, I was stunned to see that she was looking straight into my camera in every frame—except when she plunged her tusks into the ground and flopped down. As she was getting up, she was looking straight at me as if to say, "Did you get all that?" (figure 205). She was, as Colin knew, just cavorting. No, it was more: she was performing for me!

I realized then that while we go to places, such as Moremi, to observe the wildlife, the wildlife is at the same time observing us. The elephant knew what I wanted and gave it to me. I would never in the world know what an elephant might want! In many ways, my trips to shoot wildlife in Africa taught me there are no dumb animals. Some, such as the elephants, are smarter than others. Certainly, we can no longer assume that just because they cannot speak and write, as we do, they are inferior.

After Botswana, I went with Gil to Kenya in 2004, along with some of the same friends from the South Africa trip. By then, I had a digital camera, which made shots taken in very low light possible. Two experiences in Kenya captured in my photographs were especially exhilarating. One occurred when I was alone with a ranger in our vehicle. My roommate, who was to have been the second photographer in the car, had stayed in our room at the resort to rest. One of my favorite targets to photograph on all our trips was the lilac-breasted roller.

It is a small bird not much bigger than a canary and looks as if a painter dipped different parts of it in different colors of paint. It has pastel lilac, pastel blue, white, and brown on its body and electric dark navy-blue feathers on its wings. It is an amazing-looking little bird (figure 206). The difficulty in getting good photographs of any roller is that the bird tends to flit around quickly. But that day, we found a roller perched on a termite mound. It appeared to be eating termite larvae.

There was an abundance of that source of food throughout Africa, and because of the low temperature at the time, the roller had puffed up so that it was insulated against the cold. The larvae and the cold caused the roller to be still on the mound for many minutes, and it was facing our car directly. I must have taken two dozen shots of it. It too stared straight into my camera, and I was thrilled.

The second memory occurred when I was again alone with the same ranger. He had heard there was a lioness near where I was shooting a scene that covered a wide expanse and contained numerous species of wildlife. We abandoned the array of wildebeests, elephants, zebras, and giraffes to join other tourists gathered where they had seen the lioness. The tourists told us the cat had left, so the gathering broke up, and the cars moved away.

We lingered there for a bit after they left, as I wanted to photograph a cluster of trees above a ditch. Suddenly, the lioness appeared. She was a large one and had been hiding in the ditch. At that point, ours was the only car there, so she must have felt it safe to reappear. She came to the side of our car and peered around the front. Then I realized what she was looking at: not far away, a small group of perhaps four zebras walked leisurely past the front of our car with their heads bobbing up and down, as they walk when they are relaxed. She was using our car to hide herself from the zebras.

When the zebras had proceeded about thirty yards away, they walked behind a huge dead termite mound, one big enough to hide them all so they would not see the lioness. She sprinted toward the mound; climbed onto it; and, as the zebras reappeared past the mound, jumped on the last one. The zebras scattered, running as fast as they could. The ranger was ecstatic. "I've never seen a lion kill from beginning to the end! Wait until I tell my friends!" he said excitedly, and he turned our car to follow the chase.

The chase did not last long. The poor terrified zebra was quickly caught and pulled down. Once it was on the ground, the lioness grabbed its throat. She was lying beside the zebra in a position to keep her prey on the ground and also avoid the thrashing legs of her victim. That is how lions usually kill their prey: by suffocation. Before long, the thrashing diminished, and in about ten minutes, the zebra stretched a foreleg out straight. When the leg slowly lowered to the ground, I could see its abdomen cave in, and I knew it was dead.

By that time, a number of tourist cars had gathered around the scene. We were in a national game park, Maasai Mara, and there was no restriction on the numbers of cars that could gather at a scene of wildlife. The hunt and kill were the first I had witnessed also, and the experience was exhilarating but upsetting too. I shook for most of that day. I noticed there were several young children in some of the cars. I wondered what kind of impact the scene would have on those youngsters.

I was grateful for my digital camera because I did not need to change film during the unusual opportunity I had to record a lion kill from beginning to end. I must have taken at least 100 to 150 shots as the hunt proceeded. The lioness dragged the dead zebra down into another ditch nearby to eat. Most of the tourist cars departed, but we stayed until she had eaten and emerged from the ditch, no doubt to find her pride or cubs and lead them to her treasure.

My ranger was beside himself with excitement that he had seen the hunt and successful outcome. I understand that hunting is necessary for the predator to live, but it was still difficult to watch. I immediately thought about humans killing humans in wars. Now I understand better why post-traumatic stress disorder is commonly found among military veterans of wars. If watching a lion kill a zebra could upset me as much as it did, then not only watching humans kill humans but also, even worse, being the hunter looking for humans to kill must be intolerable.

When my granddaughter Leanna was eight years old, she asked if I would bring her to Africa. Happy she was interested, I told her I would when she turned fourteen. In 2006, she reminded me of my promise. Gil Lopez had by that time met and married a Brazilian woman who had persuaded him to move to Brazil, so Gil had sold Fototreks, his photo-safari business. I did not feel that a photo safari was the ideal thing for a teenager anyway, so I searched for a more family-friendly trip. In 2007, Leanna and I joined a family safari tour to Tanzania.

The Thomson Family Adventures company paired us with an Italian American family with three children: a boy of thirteen, Alessandro, or Alex; another son, Freddy, who was ten; and a six-year-old girl, Beatrice, who immediately decided to follow Leanna like a shadow. Leanna had always attracted young children. All four children got along famously, and I was glad I'd decided on a different kind of tour of Africa for Leanna and not a photo safari.

One of the highlights of the tour was a visit to a school, Ayelabet, in a village called Karatu. Before we'd left the United States on the trip, the tour company had given each child a pen pal who was a student at Ayelabet. The pen pals were of the same gender and age, and they'd exchanged letters introducing themselves. A staff member of the company had translated the letters into language the recipient could read. Our trip to Ayelabet was for the pen pals to meet each other and for our American children to see the schools that African children of that village attend.

When we arrived at the school, the female principal and two teachers, one a woman and the other a young man, were waiting with a group of some twenty-five children dressed in their school uniforms. They greeted us and sang what I assume was a welcoming song. Then each of the children in our group was introduced to his or her pen pal. Leanna met hers, Lohi, and the two seemed comfortable with each other (figure 207).

Alex, who was tall for a thirteen-year-old, was introduced to his pen pal, who had the stature of about an eight-year-old. Alex towered over him. The principal told them to stand together and laughed at the difference in height. I thought she was insensitive to laugh at the boy, who looked embarrassed. I asked the lady teacher if he had come from a pygmy tribe. She shook her head and just said no. The boy might have been starved while he was young. Who knew if he would ever grow to a normal size?

I was happy for that experience, as our children had a chance to see what kind of school children in a third-world country had. Compared to American schools, Ayelabet was primitive. There was no electricity, so modern technology, such as computers or even overhead projectors, was not available. Teachers had nothing more than books and a blackboard to use. There were no lights in the classrooms (figure 208).

Leanna's mother had prepared a present for her pen pal, Lohi, who was a sweet-looking girl about Leanna's height: a tote with supplies for school, including notebooks, pencils, and pens. The girls around the same age as Lohi crowded around to see what she had gotten. Shyly, she thanked Leanna. All the girls had the same haircut as the boys: very short. We were told that was for sanitation purposes, as lice was a problem in the school. I saw several girls around Leanna's age surround her and Lohi, and they walked off chatting. Leanna told me later about their conversation.

Leanna was wearing a bandanna over her hair. Her long, soft, straight brown hair hung down her back. One of the girls touched her hair and asked, "What is this?"

Leanna answered, "My hair." The girl asked if they could touch it. Leanna took off her bandanna, and they all touched her hair. Apparently, none of them had ever seen soft, straight hair before.

I noticed that some of the boys seemed to be older than I expected in a grade school. I said to the teachers, "How many years do these children attend this school? I see some who seem to be older than most of the rest."

The man answered, "It is difficult to say how many years a student will be with us. The problem is that some of the children live quite far from here, and they walk to school. We have no food here for them, so they have to walk home for lunch. Sometimes they have to help with something at home and cannot come back. That delays them from finishing school."

A depressing thought crossed my mind. The four children in our group from America all had been exposed to computers, probably since they were toddlers. Once, when I was babysitting Leanna, who was perhaps a little more than two years old, my son Ben, her father, gave me a disk and said, "She likes to play this game for little ones. Just help her sit in front of the computer if she gets fussy."

I put the disk in the computer and propped Leanna on the desk in front of it. She had her thumb in her mouth. Never having played the game on the computer, I wasn't sure what to do. Leanna realized that and pointed to keys I should hit so she could play the game. Often, in conversation with friends my age, someone will exclaim about how comfortable today's children are with computers, just as we were comfortable with manual typewriters long ago.

The depressing thought that crossed my mind at Ayelabet was how long it would take the Botswanan children to lift themselves out of poverty if they had to compete in the world markets against American children already comfortable with computer technology by the time they went to grade school. I hoped

Leanna and the other children were affected enough by their visit to realize just how privileged they were compared to their pen pals at Ayelabet.

Our visit to the school ended with some soccer and basketball that the children jointly played. It was a good visit, and all the children enjoyed it. We bade goodbye to the newfound friends and promised we would send some money to support the school. Thomson Safaris had set up a way to do so. The Italian father mused that he'd like to send them a computer, but the uncertainty of when the school could get electricity was daunting. I believe they decided at the end to send the school books.

The Italian parents and I were deeply moved by the needs of the children of Karatu. How much our children and grandchild were moved was a moot point. That evening, when we returned to camp for dinner, Freddy said he wished he could have a hamburger. The waiter heard his request and said their cook could give them hamburgers. The news excited all four children—and disappointed them greatly when, instead of hamburgers, they got meatballs.

There was a great deal of grumbling. I was a little disappointed by the complaints, as we had just visited a school where children had to walk long distances to go home for lunch. Those children would have been overjoyed, I was sure, if they ever got meatballs for a meal. But it was not fair to judge our children, I said to myself. Their American lives had led them to expect everyone in the world had similarly comfortable lives. Travels are terrifically educational for children, as few countries have citizens with lifestyles equal to those of common people of the United States of America.

Leanna and I enjoyed the animal drives, although there were few cheetahs to be seen. I was especially disappointed that we saw no black rhinoceros in the Ngorongoro Crater of Tanzania. They are close to extinction, and we had heard there were some fifty black rhinos in the crater. The day we drove to the crater, however, was chilly. The guide said the black rhinos and others were probably hiding from the cold.

That was the only trip to Africa on which I experienced any kind of disappointment. We saw many species of wildlife and birds. Perhaps one day I will be lucky enough to publish more of my photographs from numerous animal drives. I have always recognized how fortunate I was that my family indulged my absence from home to go on those trips and that I had access to the trips. I was fortunate that my husband did well enough in his career to allow me to be able to pay for those and trips elsewhere, including to the Galapagos; South America, including Patagonia and Machu Picchu; China; and Europe. Some of those were family trips.

This chapter tells of only a few experiences during the four trips I took to sub-Saharan Africa. When we were in Botswana, Colin Meade, our local guide, told us of a saying: "When the ancient dust of Africa settles in your bones, it will never leave." The dust has indeed settled in my bones, and it is propelling me to return yet again.

***

When David and I knew we were going to move from Livingston to Davidson, North Carolina, I told my friends of the Livingston Camera Club, which I had belonged to for nearly twenty years, of the move and my regrets at having to resign from the club. I had not been able to attend meetings of the club in any consistent way from 2006 to 2008 because of the breast cancer I'd discovered in 2006 and David's increasingly complicated illnesses.

As I still had some time before the move, I volunteered to help prepare the schedule for the last time I would be a member. To my astonishment, I found that one of the meetings in the spring before we were to leave was dedicated to me. It brought tears to my eyes. The plan was that I would show some of my favorite photos as a farewell favor to my fellow members. I did not know that all the members had put one of their own prints into a loose-leaf notebook for me, a surprise they presented at my last meeting.

I started the last meeting I would attend at LCC with an expression of thanks to all:

> I was stunned to see that this meeting had been scheduled when I first printed out the LCC's schedule for this year! I honestly feel I have done only what a member of any organization should do: to be active and do what I can to make the club strong and to further our interest in the art of photography.
>
> It seems only a few years ago that I came to an LCC meeting in 1991 with a colleague from Montclair State who was a talented, serious amateur and urged me to do photography. We were both impressed with the club and the high quality of the photography by members and made plans to join. Alas, my friend was soon diagnosed afterward with cancer and passed away, leaving me to join the club alone.
>
> I attribute much of my progress as a photographer to this decision to join, to learn from my more experienced and talented friends in the club, and to hearing the critiques of the various judges at our competition. For you newer members of the club whom I have not met because the past two years kept me away due to health problems of my own and my husband's, I urge you to take advantage of all these sources of knowledge about the art of photography.
>
> While I agreed with the judges maybe 50 percent of the time, still, when I did agree, I learned something new. If you take this point of view, then the competitions will be less of a tense experience. And do remember that even if a judge trashes a shot that you like, photography is an art, a subjective activity, and ignore him or her!
>
> As for learning from other members, John Murray was the first one to take time to show me techniques. I believe it was how to mask slides. I was so ignorant when I first joined that I did not know what a photo essay was. Remember, I showed slides

I had taken at the famous Fourth Street basketball court in New York City and then read an essay about my reaction to the experience. And nobody laughed!

Remember too that photography is often a matter of being in the right place at the right time. You need opportunities, and I have been one of the most fortunate people along these lines, having had four trips to Africa and one to the Galapagos and other destinations to feed my interest in wildlife and nature photography.

I just brought some of my shots that the veteran members will recognize. They were all well received. I didn't bring those that were not well received because we'd be here another month! These represent to me something special that I experienced through the years as a member of LCC. I will miss you all, and thank you again for being here today and for being my friends.

Fig 183 The American Flag at the Arizona Memorial, Pearl Harbor

Fig 184 Gordon Parks

Fig 185 Gil Lopez Espina

Fig 186 Our Tree House in Tanzania

Fig 187 Serena Lodge in Amboseli, Kenya

Fig 188 Leanna in Wildlife Game Park, Tanzania

Fig 189 An Angry Matriarch

Fig 190 African Secretary Bird in nest on Acacia tree

Fig 191 Impala at dawn

Fig 192 Lion cubs up a tree

Fig 193 Returning from the hunt

Fig 194 Mama's back, baby's hungry!

Fig 195 A sleeping cub with a full belly

Fig 196 Wake up, Mommy!

Fig 197 Maybe if I chew on her ear?

Fig 198 Do I have to wake up?

Fig 199 Lion cubs at play

Fig 200 Lion cubs on alert

Fig 201 Elephant rushing past me

202 Sunset on the Chobe River, Botswana

Fig 203 Clowning around

Fig 204 Still clowning around

Fig 205 Finishing her performance

Fig 206 African Lilac Breasted Roller

Fig 207 Pen Pal Lohi and Leanna

Fig 208 Ayelabet School room

Chapter 59

MOMMY ALONE

The trips to Africa were exciting and wonderful. I was more than grateful for them because they took my mind off the losses of my brother Solan in 1996, my bonsai master in 1997 to lung cancer (he had been a smoker), and my father in 1998 to emphysema (he had smoked since he was twelve years old in China) and my mother's aging and increasing dementia. She was eighty-eight when Daddy passed away in 1998. She and Daddy had been together for seventy-two years.

The days following the service for Daddy were busy as we handled the legal documents and informed various agencies of his death. During that time, I realized with some disbelief that my mother no longer knew how to use the phone. We had programmed the phone so that she had speed dial for numbers she would probably call frequently. The first number, one, was to the police; the second was to David's and my home.

One day Mommy locked herself out of the house. She went across the street to a neighbor's house and asked him to call me.

"Of course," he said. "What is her number?"

She answered, "Two."

Fortunately, he was able to look us up in the phone directory and called me. I hurried to Mommy and asked if she wanted my whole number. She shook her head and said, "Your father always called for me. I don't want to use the phone like that."

After the first night of Daddy's passing, Mommy told me I did not need to sleep there anymore. I was grateful to obey. David and I approached Mommy again about moving in with us. I hoped she would not agree, and she did not. I think she realized she would not be happy with us because of personality differences. With David's health problems and his family's history of cardiovascular disease, I feared the effect that having to tolerate Mommy's unstable behavior would have on David's blood pressure.

Still, I despaired about Mommy living alone in her house. If she'd been concerned about her security while Daddy was alive and even when they had large dogs with them, I knew she would feel even more insecure about living by herself with only a pug. All her cats had died of old age years before. I had bought Mommy a pug puppy after the two Dobermans died. She called the puppy Bo Bo, meaning "Little Treasure" in Chinese. Bo Bo was now her only company.

Bo Bo was a true lap dog. Having only had corgis, which were independent herders who loved us deeply but had limited tolerance for much hugging, I realized the personality of a pug was clearly different. Bo Bo could not get enough human touch. He would sit on the floor and lean against someone's legs if he was not being petted. Mommy used to give him a seat next to her at mealtimes, and she would of course share what she ate with him. Figure 209 shows Bo Bo sitting behind Mommy one day while she was eating a meal.

In two years, Mommy had lost the two men who meant the most to her in her life: Daddy and Solan. The question of where she should live remained. Mr. Chen of the North Sea Village restaurant a block away from their house continued to deliver food, so meals were not a problem. The problems were her loneliness and vulnerability. If she remained in her house, someone would have to see her every day. Since I had retired in 1997, it was not a problem for me to visit every day. However, I could not stay and supervise her every minute, as Daddy had done.

The most vexing problem was, of course, her mental and emotional instability. She needed to live in an environment where there would be supervision 24-7. She had made it clear to us that she did not want to move in with us. I now wonder if her refusal was because she still harbored some dislike of our Salvadorian housekeeper, Dina. Or, not having received from me the kind of total obedience and filial piety she expected, perhaps she didn't care much for me either. She had always expressed jealousy to me that Daddy would listen to me and not to her.

While we knew of assisted-living facilities, having looked at some with the idea of moving Mommy and Daddy both into one, we also knew there would be problems of language comprehension for Mommy alone. Would she be able to follow instructions about fire drills, for example? Would she be able to communicate health problems that might arise?

We had decided not to find a place for both Daddy and Mommy while Daddy was still alive and mobile. The factor blocking their acceptance of life in assisted living had been Daddy's insistence on Chinese food at meals. Had there been a facility in Chinatown, New York City, there would have been no problem about food. But I'd also wondered how they would feel about living with people they might not have thought were of their same class.

Western food was not a problem for Mommy, however. Recall that in her childhood living in Shenyang in Manchuria, her family had had two kitchens: one for Chinese food and one for Western foods. Since Western cuisine was considered something special, Mommy had always enjoyed anything Western. However, in thinking about the future, I could not see a solution to the language problem. Then there was the question of finding a place where she could keep Bo Bo.

One day in late summer 1998, a possible solution to the dilemma appeared out of the blue. Some first cousins in Maryland told me their mother, my fifth aunt, was now living in an assisted-living facility called

Sunrise in Rockville, Maryland. She had been widowed earlier in the year, which, strangely, we had not been aware of. She was the younger full sister of my mother's. I'd always loved my fifth aunt. She was beautiful and, unlike Mommy, modest and self-effacing (figure 210). Mommy had begun to use a wig of black hair that made her look ten years younger.

As a young woman, my fifth aunt had left home and studied in England for a year. In those days, women were given tutors who taught them to read and write, but that was all that was expected of them. For my fifth aunt to go to England was unusual and to me represented someone who had courage to get some further education. I dared not ask Mommy about why she did not also go to England. It was disrespectful to even think of such a question.

My fifth aunt and Mommy had gone through a difficult few years in the early 1940s after we all immigrated to the United States. One of my parents' best friends—I'll call him Mr. Cho—had met and been smitten with my fifth aunt. My parents were delighted with his interest, and Mommy did all she could to help Mr. Cho succeed in wooing Fifth Aunt. Mr. Cho was smart, and Mommy said he told Fifth Aunt he would get as many PhD degrees as she wanted him to have if she would marry him.

Fifth Aunt, however, rejected Mr. Cho. She had fallen in love with a handsome young man who was tall in stature for a Chinese man, whereas Mr. Cho was rather short. Fifth Aunt simply would not obey Mommy about marrying Mr. Cho and instead married her handsome beau. Fifth Uncle, Mommy argued, was attractive but had no college degrees and no training in a field that would lead him to lucrative careers.

I believe Mommy meant well and believed Mr. Cho would be able to better support Fifth Aunt and give her a comfortable life. When her younger sister would not listen to her, Mommy felt insulted. She should have been heeded because she was the older sister. When Fifth Aunt and Uncle fell into hard times with their finances because Fifth Uncle indeed had little in the way of skills and could not find jobs that paid well, Mommy was not sympathetic.

She was not above pointing out to Fifth Aunt that Mr. Cho had succeeded in his studies, had gotten a PhD, and was making a good living. After Fifth Aunt rejected him, Mr. Cho eventually met and married a nice woman whom I liked. I did not fully understand why Mommy was almost gratified that Fifth Aunt and Fifth Uncle were struggling, but it was clear she was annoyed that her younger sister had refused to listen to her.

After a few hard years, Fifth Aunt and her husband both were able to get jobs as government civil servants. They had worked on their English and were fluent enough to be hired. I thought that might have bothered Mommy, as she was still struggling to even be conversational in English, much less proficient enough to find outside employment.

Dr. and Mrs. Cho, whom I called Uncle and Auntie Cho, had a happy marriage. I digress here to tell about a strange experience my family had with them in a New York City Japanese restaurant. The Chos were in the city for a business meeting for Uncle Cho. They came to visit us in the apartment on West 104th Street that my parents rented after the United Nations Building was built in 1952. It was summertime, and I was home from college.

When it was time to go out for dinner, Uncle Cho said to Daddy, "I have this strong urge for tempura. Are there any Japanese restaurants around here?"

Daddy made a face at him and answered, "Are you really going to make me go to a Japanese restaurant? You know I hate anything Japanese!"

"Yes, but where else can you get good tempura except at a Japanese restaurant?" Uncle Cho said. "Come on. It won't kill you, and I won't ask you another time."

Finally, Daddy relented. "Only for you, old friend. Only for you. There's a Japanese place near Columbia University. This will be my first time in a Japanese restaurant."

We were to meet another couple at the restaurant. Grumbling all the way, Daddy drove us to the restaurant. Uncle Cho explained that his friends would be coming from a nearby afternoon wedding. They arrived at the restaurant almost at the same time, all dressed up.

When a hostess approached us for seating, we could hardly understand her because of a heavy accent. Indeed, she could not speak English well at all, which made Daddy even unhappier. She looked at one lady dressed in satin and asked, "Wedding?" The lady nodded. "Ah, wait, please," the hostess said, not pronouncing *please* well.

She left us and talked to someone, who nodded vigorously, and when she returned, she motioned for us to follow her. She took us to an elevator, and we all went to the third floor, which I thought was kind of strange since there were empty tables in the restaurant. When the elevator door opened, we stepped into a hallway with rooms on both sides. A couple of waiters went into a room with diners sitting on the floor, Japanese style. The hostess opened the door to a room, bowed, and motioned us inside. It was a room with a low table, and we had to remove our shoes and sit on the floor. It looked like a special room for a special meal.

Two Japanese women dressed in beautiful Japanese clothing followed us. They looked like photos I had seen of geishas in Japan. They were bringing little plates and bowls of what looked like appetizers. Even Daddy was impressed with the service. Another lady then came in and asked, "Who the host?" and Daddy raised his hand. She walked to him and asked, "How much you want to spend each person?"

Daddy, still unhappy, joked, "A quarter?"

She laughed and said, "What kind of meal you want?"

Daddy told her, "We're here for tempura and noodles."

"Oh, okay," she answered with a smile. "Please wait." She left.

We resumed our chatting with the Chos and their friends and found out they too were Chinese opera fans. They talked with Mommy and Daddy about wishing there was a place that put on such performances. Beijing opera was, of course, something my parents were well trained in. The discussion reminded them of their previous life in Beijing, and the conversation became excited. Uncle Cho was also trained in Chinese opera and had acted on stage in China as an amateur, as my parents had.

After about twenty minutes, we were hungry and wondered when a waiter would come to take our orders. Then we noticed the appetizers were all gone. While we'd been engrossed in chatting about Chinese opera, the waiter had quietly removed them. We waited another five minutes, and Daddy said to Uncle Cho, "Sorry, but I'm not waiting any longer for tempura. Let's go!"

We put on our shoes and retraced our steps to the elevator. We saw no one in the hall. We laughed, albeit a little nervously, talking about maybe getting a message that we weren't welcome. When we reached the ground-floor restaurant and left the elevator, we looked for someone to talk to and ask what was going on. There wasn't a waiter or a hostess in the dining room.

We ended up eating in a nearby Chinese restaurant and tried to figure out what had just happened. Uncle Cho, who had been to Japanese restaurants, analyzed our unique experience of having been kicked out of the restaurant by not being served.

"I think that when my friend nodded when the hostess asked about a wedding, the hostess thought we were a wedding party and there to celebrate. She didn't speak English very well. Then, when another hostess asked how much you wanted to spend per person and realized we were there for tempura and noodles, they wanted us out of the formal dining room and, really, out of the restaurant." Uncle Cho laughed. "And the Japanese, being Japanese and so polite, decided the best way to get rid of us was to disappear! They must have had someone on the third floor call down when we left the room!"

We all thought that was a perfectly plausible explanation and laughed at the memory of it. Even Daddy had to chuckle a little, but we never went to another Japanese restaurant.

The Chos, as I mentioned, had a happy and loving marriage, but it came to a tragic end in the 1970s, when Uncle Cho was diagnosed with a brain cancer. Daddy received a phone call one day that shocked and saddened us all. We later found out that Uncle Cho's cancer had been declared inoperable. He and Auntie Cho checked into a motel near where they lived and committed suicide. They each took an overdose of sleeping and pain medication. A maid discovered their bodies in bed side by side. I cried when I heard the news. Life is certainly not fair.

Because of Fifth Aunt's financial hardship, I was reminded of Mommy's words to me as a child to study hard enough to be independent and not dependent on a man. As their financial situation improved, Fifth Aunt and Uncle had become active in buying houses, renovating them, and selling them for decent profit. We did not see much of them or their two daughters for many years, but when my cousins married, we were invited to their weddings, and a reunion of sorts took place between the two sisters. Mommy never gave Fifth Uncle much credit—or respect—for being able to succeed in supporting his wife and family.

Hearing of Fifth Uncle's passing and Fifth Aunt's decision to live in an assisted-living establishment was possibly a great solution to give Mommy a place to live that she would enjoy. Not only would she be cared for without having to put up with David and me, but she would also be living where her sister could explain things to her in Chinese. It was a win-win situation. I was elated. I called Jeannie, my sister-in-law, to tell her the good news, and we made plans to go visit Sunrise and Fifth Aunt with Mommy.

However, deep in the back of my mind was a nagging worry. The two sisters would see each other every day. As smart and as good as I thought my aunt was, would she be able to coexist with my mother? Would Mommy try again to be the dominant sibling? I knew the answer to that question but tried to push the thoughts out of my mind. I could not think of an alternative plan for Mommy. I rationalized that they would have their own rooms, so that would give Fifth Aunt some respite. Still, I worried.

When I told Mommy about Sunrise and said that Fifth Aunt was already living there, Mommy looked happy and even excited at the thought of being there with her sister. She clearly was uncomfortable with living alone. I made an appointment at Sunrise for us to speak to someone there and tour the facility. It was about a four-hour drive to Rockville, Maryland. David was still working, so I drove Mommy and Jeannie to our appointment there.

Mommy sat in the back seat. Jeannie sat up front to keep me company and help me navigate. At one point, I suddenly heard the back door open. Fortunately, we were off the highway, and I was somewhere where I could pull over immediately to the side of the road. Oh good Lord—was she trying to leave the car while it was still running? Jeannie and I were taken by surprise.

I put on the emergency light and said to Mommy, "What are you doing, Mommy? You know you shouldn't play with the door while the car is moving—that's so dangerous!"

She chuckled. "I thought this handle was for the window," she answered like a child who had just been mischievous. Jeannie and I decided Jeannie should sit in the back with Mommy to keep an eye on her. Life with Mommy promised to be full of surprises—and not necessarily pleasant ones.

Fig 209 Mommy eating lunch with a companion

Fig 210 Mommy and Fifth Aunt at Sunrise

Chapter 60

THE END OF ORDINARY

The visit at Sunrise went well. We met with the young lady in charge. Mrs. Brown looked to be in her forties and was a friendly person with a ready smile. As we walked, she greeted residents we encountered by their first names as she led us to see the library, lounges, dining room, and individual rooms. After a tour of the facility, she led us to Fifth Aunt's room.

I could not have been happier to see Fifth Aunt and to see how well kept and clean the residents and the rooms were. Indeed, even after Mommy moved to Sunrise, if I drove down without notice for a visit, I found the residents being treated well and lovingly by the attendants in charge. One further advantage for Mommy was that residents were allowed to have small pets, so she could keep BoBo for some companionship.

The onerous task of cleaning up Mommy's house to prepare it for sale was the next step. Of greatest concern for Mommy was what to do with things she had brought to the United States when we immigrated. She had some twelve metal trunks, foot lockers she had dragged with her wherever we moved. They obviously could not go with her to Sunrise, where there was no room for such things.

She unlocked them and opened them to show us beautiful handmade embroidery. They had been part of her dowry when she was married. She also had piles of Chinese dresses, both hers and mine (which no longer fit), and dozens of pairs of shoes that no longer fit her lifestyle. There was jewelry, including a diamond necklace, some small diamond rings, a court necklace, and various other items of unknown value.

After several discussions during which we assured Mommy we would care for her things and had no interest in usurping them, we decided to keep all the foot lockers except one in a large storage area under the great room of our house in Livingston. One trunk would be used to store her jewelry and other precious belongings we would take to Sunrise. We used one that could lock with a key Mommy had. We put a piece of cloth over the trunk so that it served as a small table for her. Best of all, she could rest knowing how safe it all was. Or so we thought.

Mommy's paranoia and increasing mental instability were manifest when, during the cleanup of her house, Ben and Shrong, my older niece, volunteered to help us go through the rooms to pack away things she wanted or would need in Sunrise. After they left, Mommy called me at home and exclaimed that she could not find her pocketbook, where she kept some money. She said, "Ben or Shrong must have stolen it!" I couldn't believe my ears. When I hurried to her, I looked at her, and she belligerently and defiantly looked back at me, her head shaking from the senile Parkinson's disease.

Her accusation angered me more than anything she could have said about me. How could she think so ill of her own grandchildren, especially after they'd volunteered to help her pack and discard unusable things for hours? I felt it was a slap in the face of my child and Solan's daughter, whom I loved as my own.

After a short search, I found her pocketbook with all the money in it. I don't remember where she had hidden it. I do remember being so angry at her for accusing her own grandchildren of thievery that I could not keep myself from yelling at her while handing the pocketbook to her.

"Mommy, how could you accuse your own grandchildren of stealing from you? Can't you for once blame yourself for something?"

For a change, she too realized how wrong she was, and she called herself a bad Chinese insult: "I am a turtle's egg." I was so startled by her reaction—by hearing a parent be self-degrading—that it shut me up completely. I wonder if my mouth dropped open. I'd grown up hearing that Chinese parents could never say anything wrong under the sun. A turtle's egg? Did Mommy really think that of herself? Did she really believe that what she'd accused her grandchildren of was as bad as she said? I'll never know.

Two things we found in cleaning up the house were disturbing and indicated she should not be living alone. One was a bathrobe with one sleeve burned. Like most Chinese who cooked, Mommy had wanted a gas stove. She had obviously had a near accident in which her sleeve had caught on fire. Now I understood why the retirement places we had looked at online never had kitchens with gas stoves.

The second thing we found showed us how fearful she was to live alone. She had stored between her bed and the wall several things to use as weapons if an intruder entered her house. The weapons included an ax and a kitchen knife. Seeing that and becoming aware of how sadly uncomfortable she was tugged at my heart. No matter how much she made me angry or hurt, she was still my mother, and I felt guilty that I was not caring for her better than I was.

We made the move on a weekend so David could help us. I was relieved that Mommy seemed excited and pleased by the move. We all were. I wondered about Fifth Aunt's reaction, though, but had to close my mind to the possibility she might not have only positive thoughts about it. I didn't know what to do even if my aunt were not happy, though she did not express any such doubts when I told her of our plans. She sweetly invited me to sleep on the sofa bed in her unit when I drove down without David to visit. See figure 210 again, which shows Mommy and her sister, both still beautiful in my eyes, shortly after Mommy moved to Sunrise.

One of my greatest concerns with the move was the tendency Mommy had developed of hiding her valuables in ridiculous places, such as her shower. I took great pains to show Mommy that her metal trunk was the safest place as long as she had her key. There were actually two keys, and I kept one because I was sure she would forget where she hid hers.

I showed her the jewels I had taken out of her safe-deposit box at the bank in Livingston, so she would not accuse us of keeping any. She seemed to accept the security of the trunk, so we left with a false sense that all was well with the move. We bade Mommy goodbye with a kiss, and she seemed happy as we were leaving and satisfied with her new life.

We also stopped to say goodbye to Fifth Aunt. I was happy I would see her frequently now, as I intended to visit Mommy every weekend. I gave my phone numbers to the administrators and asked them to please call if Mommy needed translators if Fifth Aunt was not available for her. They seemed genuinely caring, and I could not have been more relieved.

As the first months passed, Mommy seemed to become accustomed to the daily programs for meals. I noticed with some alarm, though, that Bo Bo was getting rotund (figure 211). Before long, I realized that Mommy was overfeeding the little dog, who was rapidly getting to be a grossly overweight dog. Mommy would forget she had fed him at times and would feed him again. She kept rolls and breads from her meals in her pocket to give to Bo Bo. She had him sit either near her or on her while she ate, and she was liberal with her handouts.

I told Mommy she had to cut down on his food. "But he always acts hungry and eats everything I give him!" she said. Then, one day, she did something that made me take the dog away from her. There was a small area of grass where dog owners could walk their dogs. I walked out with Mommy one day when she was walking Bo Bo. To my consternation, I saw her kick the dog when he did not walk as fast as she wanted.

I realized that perhaps having a dog at her advanced age was more than she could handle, and perhaps Bo Bo was suffering the consequences. He was now an obese dog but still one of the sweetest, most loving dogs I had known. I told Mommy that perhaps she needed us to take Bo Bo for a little while to give her a break. She did not protest, so I believe she was relieved not to have to walk him no matter the weather.

She had always had dogs, including some large ones, but even Mommy had limitations as an octogenarian. She once commented to me, "When I turned eighty, I could feel myself slowing down. I just can't move as fast as I used to."

When we got home with Bo Bo, I took him to see our veterinarian. All the staff exclaimed that Bo Bo was the biggest (fattest) pug they had ever seen. The poor boy weighed in at forty pounds, which was twice the heaviest weight of most normal pugs. I explained about Mommy forgetting about feeding him and feeding him several times a day.

I found Bo Bo to be a wonderful companion dog. I wished Mommy could have handled him. But I had never been eighty, and I wondered how I would feel about having a dog when I was that age. His endearing personality was different from that of my corgis. He wanted human touch as much as possible. His corkscrew tail was always wagging; he was always happy no matter what. The corgis I had at the time, Ginger and Gruffy, accepted him, and he loved them as well. They all slept together on their bed.

We put Bo Bo on a diet, and he lost about twelve pounds over a year. He was still well overweight, however, and eventually died of congestive heart failure. One day he showed signs that he was unable to breathe well and was walking with difficulty. He still managed to crawl up the two steps that separated the dogs' room from the kitchen to eat that morning.

He greeted me with a wagging tail, as always, and ate his food, as always, but he was clearly suffering. I took him to the vet immediately, and when I handed Bo Bo over to have him treated for what appeared to be heart problems, he looked at me and wagged his tail. To the end, he was loving. A few hours later, the vet called and said Bo Bo had died. They couldn't revive him. I cried.

I never told Mommy he had died, and she never asked about him. One day, when I was visiting her, I asked if she missed having a cat, thinking that if she wanted one, I could get a kitten for her to play with. Also, cats were easier to care for and usually did not overeat. Her response threw me for a loop.

She said, "I don't like cats!"

"What? But you had more than a dozen cats in the garage, including some that you picked up as strays. If you didn't like cats, why did you pick up so many?"

"Because in Buddhism, they say if you're good to animals, you'll go to heaven when you die."

It was the first time I realized the Buddhist religion meant something to her. All the toil resulting from having so many cats and dogs had been because Mommy believed they would provide her entrance to heaven and not because she loved them. I do not believe she did not also care for them, at least for the dogs. She used to talk to them and hug them.

She and Lo Lo, her mother, were rarities in China for keeping pets in the house, as people do in America. David, for example, had dogs in China that were kept outside and used only for hunting purposes. I thought about Lo Lo feeding ants and a squirrel in Durham, North Carolina, when Daddy was studying for his master's degree. Had she also done that to be sure of entering heaven? Had she taught that to Mommy? I did not pursue that train of thought with my mother because at that point, it was difficult to know if anything Mommy said was true or simply her imagination.

One weekend, when David drove with me to Sunrise to see Mommy, we were startled to see that she was upset when we entered her apartment. "What's the matter, Mommy?" I asked.

"A cleaning lady stole two of my diamond rings!" she cried.

They should have been in the locked trunk that served as a table for Mommy. Had she unlocked the trunk and forgotten to lock it up again?

I asked her, "Where were they? Where did she steal them from?"

She said, "I wanted to just look at them but decided not to put them back and hid them under my armchair. Then, when I looked at the little bag that I had them in, the bag was there but not the rings. Can we get them back?"

My reaction was a mixture of anger at her childish thought that under her chair was a safe hiding place and pity because of how miserable she looked and no doubt felt. It was like something a child would have done, and my reaction was like that of a parent. We had indeed switched places in our relationship.

"Mommy, that's why we told you to keep your jewelry in the locked trunk to be safe, because you have the only key," I said. "How can we even prove your maid took those rings? Who would we point to as the thief?"

She realized then that the rings were probably lost forever. I wondered if she had actually hidden two rings as she said, although she held out a little leather bag as the one she had put the rings in.

Her eyes filled with tears, and she said with trembling lips, "I'm so stupid! I would kill myself, except I'm afraid of pain!"

We tried to calm her down and told her that it was a small mistake as long as she had kept most of her jewelry in the trunk. She asked me to take her jewelry back north with us to put it into a safe-deposit box at a bank. We told her we would and retrieved the jewelry boxes and bags and brought them home with us to New Jersey.

As soon as I could, I put them into our safe-deposit box in a Livingston bank, something I had proposed to Mommy before the move while knowing she would prefer to have them herself. After the incident with her rings, Mommy was relieved not to have her jewelry with her anymore. I checked to see what items were there, particularly a diamond necklace strung together like pearls and what looked like a very old court necklace, which Mommy said dated back to the dynasty era.

I knew that giving up her jewelry must have been a wrenching experience for Mommy because the jewelry was all she had left to remind herself of a previous life of herself as a Manchurian princess known for her beauty and as the daughter of the Old Marshal. She had been married to the handsome only son of the former viceroy of Manchuria, and the world had been theirs to enjoy.

Then the assassination and the aggression of the Japanese had started the decay of their lives. Now she was a widow, and she no longer had her beloved doctor son. I grieved for her, especially because there was nothing I could do to make her happier, and I was spiriting her beloved possessions away. Everything I was doing for her only seemed to make her more and more unhappy. But the worst was yet to come.

After Mommy had been at Sunrise for more than a year, I received a call from Fifth Aunt's daughter, my cousin. She said Fifth Aunt and her daughters had decided to move Fifth Aunt out of Sunrise because their rates had gone up, and they could no longer afford Sunrise. As Fifth Aunt and Fifth Uncle both had worked in clerical positions for the government, my cousin said she qualified for a retirement home for civil servants that was good and much cheaper than Sunrise.

While Daddy's pension from the United Nations, plus some supplementary funds from us, was enough to pay for Mommy's stay at Sunrise, we could not afford to help Fifth Aunt also. Had we been able to chip in to pay for her to stay at Sunrise, I wondered if she would have chosen to stay. Always in the back of my mind was the question of whether Fifth Aunt could tolerate her older sister's presence and wanted to move.

Who knows what the two sisters spoke about at meals? I know they always were seated at the same table. I could only desperately hope Mommy would be clear enough and understanding enough not to offend Fifth Aunt about Fifth Uncle, their finances, or anything else. I never saw my aunt again, as she died not long after she moved out of Sunrise. I will always doubt that Fifth Aunt's decision to move out of Sunrise was simply a financial matter.

I spoke to the administrators of Sunrise when I heard Fifth Aunt was leaving. They assured me that Mommy was fine living there without Fifth Aunt. She had become used to the routines and was not nervous to be without her sister as a translator. However, our trials and tribulations with my mother at Sunrise had not ended with her familiarity with routine. One day I received an email from the chief administrator, along with a photo of a stack of dishes on the closet floor of Mommy's room.

The administrator, whom I will call Alice, wrote that the chef at Sunrise had come to her with a request to purchase more dishes. Alice was surprised there was such a need, as she remembered having recently ordered sets of dinnerware. She and the chef then searched the rooms of residents in case some had used dishes and forgotten to return them. None of the residents had more than one or two, and most had none—except for Mommy. The attached photo they had taken of Mommy's closet floor showed a significant stash of dishes and bowls.

On our next weekend visit to Mommy, I asked her why and how she had taken so much dinnerware and stashed it in her closet.

"Mommy, Alice said she found a lot of dishes and bowls in your closet. How did you get them, and why did you take them?"

Instead of appearing ashamed, Mommy lifted her shoulders and pursed her lips, a habit she had when she knew she had done something wrong but didn't care. "I went to the kitchen at night and brought them up. I took them in case I needed dishes in the future."

"Mommy, they will always bring you what you really need. You don't need to hoard anything here at Sunrise." I then had another thought. "Have you taken anything else?"

Again, her shoulders lifted, and she chuckled. "I did bring up a small end table from downstairs that I like."

"A table! How did you manage to pull it up a flight of stairs?" I asked incredulously.

"It was no trouble at all," she said, proud of how strong she still was.

Clearly, Mommy had been turning night into day again, and worse, she was not only taking dishes and a small piece of furniture but also going into the garbage cans. Later, we had a meeting with Alice. "If we cannot convince her, with your help, to stop roaming around at night," she said, "we will need to consider what must be done to keep her safe. We found items from the garbage cans in the kitchen in her room also. As you can imagine, that is dangerous because there could be toxic cleaners in the garbage cans that she doesn't recognize or even broken glass."

David and I were in agreement and a little embarrassed that Mommy was clearly no longer able to recognize right from wrong and was acting like a small child. "What can be done?" I asked.

"Well, the first thing is for Mrs. Chao to be seen by a psychiatrist. We have a physician who comes to treat various residents here. We just need your permission for Dr. Martin to see her and to prescribe medication if necessary," Alice answered. She produced some documents for me to sign, and I was happy to do so because finally, there was an opportunity to have Mommy see a doctor and get help if it was possible.

Daddy and Fifth Aunt, who might have raised traditional Chinese objections about psychoanalysis, were gone. Mommy, though, would probably not understand that she was undergoing psychoanalysis in her present state of mind, so I told Alice I would sign the papers allowing someone to see her. I asked Alice to let me know what day she would be examined so I could make sure they could call me if I needed to translate something for Mommy. As it turned out, they never called while she was being interviewed.

When we asked for the results of the interview, Alice told us the doctor said there was dementia, and she would be given some medication to calm her down. When we visited her, we were told she was taking a mild dosage of tranquilizer. Indeed, she seemed less dissatisfied and critical of Sunrise. I immediately regretted listening to Daddy in the past when he'd said she would never agree to see a psychiatrist, one of those doctors who treated "crazy" people.

Had Mommy gotten help through medication, Daddy would have had a much better life with her, but cultural differences in the attitude toward psychiatry had prevented us from giving her the help she needed. Culture was also what had kept David and me from ignoring Daddy's wishes and doing what we thought would be helpful.

The situation got worse, as Mommy continued to roam at night. The administrators at Sunset called me and said she could not continue to live in the assisted-living apartments. They were, of course, concerned about liabilities if she were to hurt herself or worse in her wanderings. However, the Alzheimer's unit, where she would have to move, on the top floor of the building, worried me greatly.

I had been taken there when we were checking out the facilities of Sunrise. The people there included ones who were deeply affected. They wandered aimlessly, and a couple had approached me, saying something that was not understandable. I would not have wanted to live up there, as it would have made me uncomfortable, and I feared for Mommy. She might have had dementia and probably mild schizophrenia, but she was still able to recognize us and carry on a conversation. I felt she would be frightened to death to be locked on that floor.

The only immediate alternative to having her suffer what I knew would be a traumatic experience in the Alzheimer's unit was to bring her home. I thought of possible consequences of having Mommy live with us and realized we would be risking not only her safety but also ours. She was obviously out of control, unable to recognize the danger of wandering at night with the liberty to do what she wanted regardless of the dangers involved.

We would have to move Dina out of her room on the ground floor to what had been Mike's bedroom upstairs with us. But Mommy would then be alone downstairs. Would she continue to dig into garbage? How could David, Dina, and I stay up all night to monitor her actions? David's health would not allow him to lose so much rest. In fact, that was true for Dina and me also. I needed my strength to tend to David with all his vascular problems. Dina would probably leave us if we asked her to keep the same bizarre schedule Mommy kept. Also, Mommy would never listen to Dina, who, in Mommy's mind, was a lowly servant to be treated as she'd treated her countless servants in Manchuria.

Then a thought froze my mind with its potential danger: she would be free to try to use my large restaurant-style gas range, which had large burners to give me the level of heat I needed for cooking Chinese. Her intent could be an innocent one, perhaps to make a cup of tea, yet she could set herself on fire, as she had once done in her own house. That thought alone was enough to convince me that as painful as I knew Mommy's life would be in the Alzheimer's unit at Sunrise, I had no other choice to make. Temporarily, she would have to suffer the move upstairs with the more afflicted residents, but at least she would be safe.

I decided the only long-term solution would be to take her out of Sunrise and bring her up to some kind of facility in New Jersey, preferably near us so we could see her more often than just every weekend. In the meantime, until I could find a place to move her to, she would have to put up with the Alzheimer's unit. I told Alice that if they felt they needed to move her in a hurry to do what they could, and I would call Mommy to explain what was to happen.

When I got Mommy on the phone, I had to break the news to her that she had to move from her apartment to the upstairs unit. I couldn't remember for sure, but I thought she had never seen the Alzheimer's unit.

"Mommy, Alice called me and said you continue to walk about at night. You know you're not supposed to," I said.

"I haven't taken anything, so I don't know why they care," she answered.

"Suppose you fall and hurt yourself," I said. "They are afraid we would sue them."

She laughed. "I wouldn't fall. I never have."

"But they're afraid you might. They're going to move you upstairs to another apartment." I hesitated, wondering if I should warn her about the move. I decided not to mention it. I knew that an explosion would come when she saw those she would be living among, and I wouldn't blame her. I said, "I will come in a few days to help."

She seemed to accept the news with remarkable composure. I was sure then that she had never been upstairs before or did not remember that it was for residents with severe dementia and Alzheimer's. *Good luck*, I said to myself. *I wonder what's going to happen once she gets up to that floor.*

I immediately looked online for retirement places in and near Livingston that we could afford, and I called each one. When David could join me, we visited a number of places, and we found one not far from Livingston, maybe just fifteen minutes away. It was just for people with Alzheimer's and dementia; there were no residents for assisted living.

We found there were far fewer people wandering around mumbling than there were upstairs at Sunrise. The place was clean and bright, and residents had access to the whole building because there was just one floor. All the doors were locked, of course, and could only be opened by a code pressed onto an electronic gadget on the wall next to every exit door. We signed Mommy up at Arden Court, and we made plans to move her out of Sunrise as soon as possible.

She called, as I'd known she would, when she had been moved. She was crying, and she screamed at me over the phone, so irate she could barely speak.

"What are you doing to me? These people are crazy! They walk around mumbling and even walk into each other's rooms. I stay in my room as long as I can, and I lock my door so they can't come in, or they would! Your brother would have never done these things to me, and he wouldn't have let you do them either!"

I was on the verge of tears too and felt terrible that I had put my mother through such terror and misery. I apologized to her. "Mommy, *dui bu chi*. I'm sorry! These people will not hurt you. I know it's scary, and I wish there was something I could do, but Alice said they had to move you because you continue to roam around at night." I swallowed hard. "We've found a place up here in New Jersey that looks very nice. I am getting the paperwork done to bring you up here. It's very close to where we live, and we and the children will be able to come see you more often."

"Do it quickly, or I'll die up here!" she cried.

"I promise," I said, on the verge of crying myself.

I felt terrible that she was so frightened and upset. I couldn't blame her. I knew she'd meant it when she accused me of being the cause of her discomfort. It would not have occurred to her that she had caused the move by disobeying the administrators at Sunrise. I was miserable at the thought that whatever Mommy had thought of me as her daughter before, she probably hated me now.

As soon as we could, we drove down, packed her things up, and put them in the back of our station wagon. The only pieces of furniture she had in her room that belonged to her were her steamer trunk and a small table and two chairs I had bought because I knew she'd liked to read her Chinese newspapers at her dining table at home.

Ben borrowed a large van from Foster Wheeler to help us drive Mommy and her belongings. Her clothing all fit in a large suitcase. She was still angry with not just me but also David and said little to either of us on the way back to New Jersey.

Whether she decided to forgive me or, more likely, forgot about her traumatic stay at Sunrise, it did not take long for her to act normally toward us once she settled down at Arden Court. Visits from her granddaughters, Shrong and Mei, also helped greatly. Shrong and Mei lived in northern New Jersey, so they were able to visit with Mommy frequently.

I learned something new about my mother at her new home: her English name. I had not known she had one. As far as I know, Daddy did not, or at least he never told us he had a name in English. On one visit shortly after we had moved Mommy from Sunrise to Arden Court, we saw she had a name plate on her door like everyone else's, just the first name. Hers was Bertha. I expressed surprise and asked her, "How did you get this name?" She chuckled and said she couldn't remember. I have not yet met another person with the name Bertha—a unique name for a unique person.

Mommy was much concerned about the fact that Mike had reached the age of thirty in 1996 but had still not found someone he would marry. Almost every time I went to visit Mommy, she would ask the same question: "Does Michael have a girlfriend yet?" I would tell her not yet, and she would sigh.

She was much calmer at her new home and seemed satisfied there, if not happy. Occasionally, her actions reminded us that she still needed constant supervision. One such time occurred when we signed her out of Arden Court. We took her to eat a meal at a nearby restaurant. She enjoyed the cheese muffins and the noodles there and always ordered chocolate ice cream for dessert.

That day, the restaurant was using some small pottery dishes for bread plates. They were new and colorful. Mommy liked them—and wanted to put a few in her pocketbook. "They have so many," she said. "They won't miss one or two." She looked at me for some sign of approval.

Once again, I had to play the bad guy. "No, Mommy. They don't belong to you. We can't take the restaurant's dishes. If you need some, I'll buy some and bring them to you." Mommy shrugged with a bit of a smirk.

The new millennium began. David's health was deteriorating. In 1986, as I mentioned, he had had open-heart surgery and five bypasses for blocked coronary arteries. It was the first sign of the Pai family curse due to genetically weakened vascular systems. Four of the bypasses installed in 1986 were now themselves blocked. In 2000, he had to have angioplasty done, the insertion of a stent due to blockage of the bypasses. I was grateful Mommy was nearby, so visiting her was not a problem, and I could still keep an eye on David. The angioplasty he had then and many subsequent operations at Columbia Presbyterian Hospital, where Solan had long ago introduced us to the best vascular surgeons, were done successfully.

In 2001, David decided it was time for him to retire from Foster Wheeler, a company he had worked for diligently since we were living in the Bronx in the 1960s. He had been promoted several times and eventually named the president and CEO of Foster Wheeler Development Corporation, the research subsidiary company. I was proud of him. When he told me once that he understood I had sacrificed my career in research for his career, I told him I doubted I ever could have reached the level of success he had, and I meant it.

I was concerned about the angioplasty he needed and decided to throw him a retirement party. We invited all the Tiger friends, the Grubers, and his closest friends and coworkers from Foster Wheeler. We had moved to a large house by that time, and we had a dinner catered and served in the great room, which had plenty of room for everyone. As a retirement present, I gave David a print of himself on which I Photoshopped a full head of hair. He had lost most of his hair by the time he was in his forties. The angioplasty David had was successful.

We continued to visit with Mommy and realized she was not walking well anymore. Her back seemed to suddenly be twisted, and she needed a cane to help her move about. One day, when we took her to a nearby diner she liked, I was startled when I touched her shoulder and felt only bones. She had lost a lot of weight. The people at Arden Court said she was not eating well. She in turn complained that they were trying to force food down her throat, and she hated the thickened water she had to drink.

David and I learned through the final years of my parents' lives that stability of their health persisted on a plateau for a few years but then was interrupted by a period of relatively rapid deterioration. That pattern would then repeat itself. I was worried Mommy was on the brink of another such period of deterioration. When she declined having chocolate ice cream for dessert, I knew something was seriously wrong.

Her mental capacity also seemed to continue to diminish. One day she complained to me, "My false teeth are uncomfortable. They move too much."

I looked in her bathroom and found a tube of material to glue false teeth to the palate securely. "Mommy, don't you use this?" I asked, holding the tube out to her.

"What's that?" she asked. She had forgotten how to secure her false teeth. Both Daddy and Mommy had almost all false teeth. Dental hygiene was not a strong point in their lives. It was not something they understood to practice in China. Hence, they lost most of their teeth. I learned how to brush my teeth in health class in school, not from my parents. Flossing was not a known technique in those days.

Despite Mommy's frequent mention of her own bravery during the tumultuous days following the Japanese invasion of China, when our family had to find safety in Beijing first and then had to retreat to Hong Kong before immigrating to the United States, I knew she feared pain. Visits to the dentist were accompanied by great anxiety. She confessed to me one day with a little embarrassment that once, she'd been so afraid and tense that she had bitten her dentist.

Life for Mommy became more and more difficult, until, in a fairly short time, she was confined to a wheelchair, having lost the ability and perhaps the strength to walk. As much as I despaired over her deterioration, I knew there was nothing to be done about aging. She was ninety-two.

One of the necessary changes as she continued to deteriorate was that she had to wear incontinence pads, as she was no longer able to walk to the bathroom or clean herself afterward. She pleaded with Dina, Shrong, and me one day when we were visiting to help her to the bathroom. She didn't want the indignity of having her incontinence pad changed again.

"I hate my diaper," she groused.

I could understand her refusal to have her diaper changed. I thought of her days as a Manchurian princess and contrasted them to her present life in the United States. Oh, the disrespect she must have felt to have some stranger change her diaper! The three of us acceded to her request. It took all three of us to get her out of her wheelchair and onto the toilet. As I said earlier, even moving an eighty- or ninety-pound person totally incapable of helping was extremely difficult. After that experience, Mommy must have realized she had to live with diapers. Thereafter, she never again asked our help to move her to a bathroom.

As her physical abilities declined, her ability to speak also became more and more limited. She never failed to ask about her grandchildren, though, especially about Mike, who was the only one of that generation still unmarried.

"Does Michael have a girlfriend yet?" she would ask almost as soon as I sat down to visit. I would have to shake my head, and she would shake hers in disappointment.

We did not have much to talk about other than the family. She was happy to see photographs of her great-grandchildren. Leanna was born in 1993 and Keith in 1997 to Ben and Susan. Shrong gave birth to Buddy Fox in 1998 and Reyna Fox in 1999. Mei's Cameron was born in 2000 (figure 212) and completed the youngest generation.

While she had fretted that she had no grandchildren for several years after Solan and I married our respective spouses, in the course of four years, from 1964 to 1968, Mommy was gifted with four grandchildren (two from me and two from Solan and Jeannie), and over seven years, from 1993 to 2000, she had five great-grandchildren. Mike and his wife, Katherine, married late and had their children after Mommy had passed away. Aidan was born in 2007, and Nathan was born in 2009 (see again figures 146 and 147).

I wish I could have told her about Mike's wife, who has a PhD and two master's degrees. She would have been impressed and happy, and I wish she could have seen Mike's two sons. She would have admired the kind of women both sons married. I badly wanted Mommy to focus on the positive things in her life, but she could not or did not want to. As she aged, it seemed the only memories she kept were those of her days in Manchuria and Beijing, which, of course, was understandable. But I wanted her to think about Daddy in a positive way and to consider how well her children had developed and how well they'd married, especially in Stanley's case.

It seemed that in remembering life as a Manchurian princess, she could only look at her life in the United States as a misfortune. She'd had to leave her home and her country to come to America, a country she felt was only a temporary refuge from war. Then losing all her belongings and homes to the Japanese in World War II and the Communists in the civil war must have been traumatic for her. After she watched the Nixon trip to Beijing on TV in 1972, the knowledge that her world had disappeared and would not exist even if she were to return to China must have been heartbreaking.

We, her children, could not empathize with her because our lives were those of ordinary people; we knew no other life, as our mother did. We could be grateful Daddy had found his job with the United Nations Secretariat. All grown-ups in the United States held jobs, didn't they? Why couldn't Mommy be happy and satisfied? Now, with the wisdom of age, I do understand, Mommy, and I am sorry I could not before. I would have been much more sympathetic and patient, and you surely would have been happier with an understanding daughter.

Assisted-living facilities usually require that their residents are capable of walking. In 2002, when Mommy could no longer walk even with a walker, the administrators of Arden Court recommended a nursing facility only fifteen minutes from our home in Livingston. Mommy was assigned a room with three other ladies with various problems. One lady was especially nice to Mommy and to David and me when we visited. That was to be Mommy's last residence. That was where I brought her some shee fan, a thick rice porridge with some minced chicken, which I fed her with a teaspoon. Figure 213 is the last photo we took of Mommy at the nursing facility.

Just about two months after she was moved to that facility, I received the call I'd dreaded for years: "Your mother was found nonresponsive today."

I had filled out papers for Mommy regarding the time when she would reach the end and had checked "DNR" (Do not resuscitate). But when I got the telephone call, I panicked at the thought of losing her and told the nurse, "Call an ambulance, and take her to the hospital to see if they can help her!"

"But you ordered DNR for her," she responded. I knew I was going against my initial order, but when I was faced with losing her, I was not ready. I had not known I would not be.

"I know, but I changed my mind. Please send her to the hospital, and I'll get there as soon as I can!" I pleaded with the nurse, and she relented.

I called David and told him to come home, and I called Ben and Mike to ask them to fly up. I called Jeannie and Mei. Shrong was flying in from London that day. I called and gave directions to Mei on how to drive to the hospital, and I told Dina about Mommy and said we would be away probably all day. Mommy was already at the ER when we arrived at the hospital. She was comatose, and there was a tube running into her mouth to help her breathe. My beautiful mother was a wizened old woman; her hair was disheveled, and her mouth was open.

"Mommy." I bent close to her ear. "I'm here at the hospital. The doctors will help you feel better. Be strong," I said. There was no sign that she heard me.

A nurse came in shortly and tried to obtain blood from a vein in her arm. I saw a small amount enter the needle, but then it stopped. "Can't get blood anymore," she muttered. I knew then that my mother's heart had failed and no longer was pumping blood. I left the room in tears and went to a public phone to contact Shrong. I had only begun to give Shrong directions, when David came to me and said, "She's gone." I told Shrong to take her time and not rush, as it was too late. We returned to Mommy's bedside and wept.

We held a memorial service for her at a funeral home in Livingston. Not as many of her friends attended as had attended Daddy's service, mainly because they were all too old to make the effort to attend, or they themselves had passed on. I wrote the following eulogy:

> In a life that spanned eight years short of a century, our mother, born in Shenyang, was the beautiful and adored daughter of the Tiger of Manchuria, Marshal Chang Tso Lin. In her early life, she would know not only luxury but the power of her father, and flip side of the coin, she and her family knew revolution and war. Her experiences included the assassination of her father and a wrenching migration to the safety of a totally new and different world of the United States.
>
> Not only did she have the strength to shepherd a young family to safety from a war-torn China, on one occasion having to cross enemy lines in disguise, she had to adjust to a life of self-sufficiency in the new world. Coming from a background of wealth and privilege impossible for us to comprehend, she had never seen the inside of a kitchen, for example, yet became a superb cook. Our parents were never to return to China, recognizing with great sorrow that their world had disappeared.
>
> Perhaps her favorite accomplishment was to establish with our father the Yeh Yu Chinese Opera Association, through which they brought to the Chinese community of New York City a beloved part of their culture. She also performed, playing male roles into her sixth decade.
>
> Her kindness to animals was legend. She rescued stray cats (including pregnant ones) from the streets of Chinatown, and she confessed later when they had all passed on from old age that she didn't even like cats!
>
> One of our favorite comical memories of Mommy was how she would watch TV in a low armchair when she had two huge Doberman pinscher dogs. There would

always be one of them sitting next to her in the same chair, his front legs on the floor, his hind legs sticking straight out, his behind on the chair, dwarfing her. Another was of her beloved Pug, Bo Bo, always seated next to her at the dining table for meals. It was not a surprise that Bo Bo eventually expanded into the biggest Pug anyone had ever seen!

In an arranged marriage with the only child of the Manchurian viceroy, Chao Er Shun, she came to love her husband fiercely, the deceased Chao Shih Hui, and tended to him through a long and difficult life. While we children were often frustrated by her distancing from the American way of life, we knew it was due to not only a generational but also a cultural gap. She never let us forget our heritage, and this is something I am trying to do for my children and grandchildren. And we knew she loved us and did the best she knew how.

She constantly exhorted us to aspire to academic success and not be satisfied with mediocrity. It was definitely in part due to her influence that one son, Solan, became a world-class physician; another son, Stanley, an evangelist; and a daughter, Anna, a PhD professor. She was enormously proud of her grandchildren, Carolyn, Ben, Mike, and Patty Ann, and their spouses. Her great-grandchildren, Leanna, Keith, Buddy, Cameron, and Reyna, were her pride and joy.

Her passing leaves an empty space in our hearts. We can only hope that she is now joyously reunited with her parents; her husband, our father; our brother Solan; and countless cats and dogs in heaven!

Writing this book has shown me the major mistake I and others in my family made, including Daddy while he was alive: none of us realized she could not help herself. She was unable—probably long before that point—to know right from wrong. She seemed to return to her life as a daughter of a powerful warlord, when anything she wished to do was right. She was incapable of being anything else as she aged, and we did not understand that—just as she could not understand it of Stanley. I apologize humbly, Mommy and Daddy. You did not need to suffer as much as you did.

Life probably could have been much easier and better for both parents. I am so sorry! Had we realized that, we could have found help for her earlier in the way of a psychologist or a psychiatrist. However, we would have had to overcome Chinese culture to convince Daddy it was necessary. Such assistance would have necessitated finding a Chinese physician. But would that have been possible? We will never know.

Following Mommy's wishes, she was buried at Ferncliff Cemetery, where we all have bought niches for our ashes after cremation and where Solan's ashes are interred, as well as those of our Tiger friend Frankie Tang. Mommy was not cremated, as she feared the pain of being burned, and an urn bearing half of Daddy's ashes was placed next to her in her casket. The family was at the burial, and we each placed a rose on her casket and said our own goodbyes.

I was relieved for her, as she was finally at peace and no longer anxious, lonely, and afraid. It was a strange feeling for me to know that David and I were now the oldest in our family, with the exception of Stanley. I continue to think often of my parents and Solan. I still talk to Solan more than my parents. It's just the result of habit. My thoughts turn to my parents usually when I encounter something I think would have pleased them.

As I mentioned, we followed Mommy's wishes. I felt some relief for her. No more did she have to endure wearing a diaper or having to choke down food. She had no more need to grieve over Solan and Daddy and no more need to fear life.

And finally, no more ordinary.

Fig 211 A rotund BoBo

Fig 212 Photo taken around 2010; Front row left to right: Leanna holding Nathan, Reyna Fox Buddy Fox, Keith Pai, Cameron Chao, Aidan Pai; second row, me, Susan, Mei Chao, Katherine Pai, Mike Pai; third row, Mike Fox, Shrong Fox, Ben, Jeannie, Sheila Noonan (Katherine's mom), David

Fig 213 David, myself, and Dina visiting Mommy confined to a wheel chair

Chapter 61

A *ROOTS* TRIP TO CHINA

In 2005, David and I decided our two grandchildren at that time were old enough to benefit from a trip to China. Ben and Susan's daughter, Leanna, was twelve years old, and Keith was eight years old. Ever since Keith was a toddler, we had fixed his eighth birthday as the earliest time we should take the trip. At that age, we felt he could handle the long and wearing trip to the Far East and would be old enough to understand the significance of such a trip.

We were anxious to bring them to China while we were in good enough shape to do so. It was important to us that our grandchildren be exposed to China and our families' contributions to modern Chinese history. We intended to take them to Beijing, Kweilin, Xian, and Shenyang (Manchuria) at least. With David's continuing struggles with his cardiovascular problems at the time, we worried that waiting too long would be a mistake.

Our direct family totaled nine people: Ben and his family; Mike and Katherine; Katherine's mother, Sheila; and David and me. David's brother-in-law, Henry Hsieh, had taken his family just a short while ago to China on a trip arranged by a cousin in Shanghai, Lien Jun Hsieh. Having decided to go, we asked Henry to contact Lien Jun to see if he would be able to also arrange a trip for us through the China Youth Travel Agency of Shanghai.

When Lien Jun told us that if we could have ten or more people on the trip, there could be significant discounts on airfare and lodging, I emailed some close friends, telling them of our desire to visit sites of historically important events involving both David's and my families. Among those who jumped at the chance to take the trip were a dear friend and classmate from Sweet Briar, Virginia "Gina" Marks Paget, and Gina's close friend Chris Carlson. Two of our Tiger friends, Ann Yu Rigby and her husband, Jim Rigby; Ann's sister, Lucina; Lucina's husband, Bob Green; and Ann's daughter, Audrey Yu, made up our group of sixteen.

Besides taking our two grandchildren to soak in some knowledge about their Chinese heritage, the trip had an additional mission for David and me. In 1998, my father had succumbed to emphysema, having smoked cigarettes for some sixty years. Before he died, he had requested that I spread half his ashes on a sacred mountain in his home province of Shandong. Daddy was born in the seaside city of Tsingdao, which is now known to Americans for their beer. At the same time, Mommy had said she wanted some of his ashes to be buried with her, as she feared cremation and wanted to be buried in the ground.

We requested that the crematorium put half of Daddy's ashes in one container and half in another so we could satisfy both requests. In 2005, David and I decided to leave for the trip a few days earlier than the others to carry out our mission to spread Daddy's ashes on the sacred mountain, Tai Shan, in the town of Tai An. In Chinese, *tai* means "grand"; *shan* means "mountain." I was to discover on a different part of the trip that *shan* also means "mountain range." I once asked why Tai Shan was considered sacred and was told it was the highest mountain in the region and, therefore, the closest to heaven.

When our plane arrived at Jinan Airport, a local guide and two officials of the Shandong Provincial Overseas Affairs Office greeted us. They gave us a banquet for lunch and drove us to the shore of the infamous Yellow River, just outside of Jinan. David said the Chinese compare fish in the Yellow River to prisoners because the river is turbulent, muddy, and prone to flooding.

At dinner, an official of Tai An and some of his assistants gave us another banquet. We brought up the subject of spreading Daddy's ashes and asked if there was any protocol for us to follow. The official sucked in his breath, thought for a moment, and then replied, "That is difficult to say. It could be something easy to do, or it could be hard. If you bring it to the attention of officials, it may take a while to get a response."

We immediately recognized that the answer was perfect bureaucratic doublespeak, as David called it later. In other words, without actually saying so, he was advising us not to go by official pathways but to just go ahead and do so without considering regulations. One of the assistants talked to our local guide, Mr. Zhen Jijun, about a location he thought was appropriate.

The next day, Mr. Zhen took us to Tai Shan, and we ascended the mountain by a tram. There are seven thousand steps from the base of the mountain to the top. The tram took us to the last landing, and then we walked the final steps to the top (figure 214). The view at the top was impressive.

Tai Shan is five thousand feet high and is the highest mountain in the eastern coastal plains. It is considered sacred simply because it is the closest to heaven on the east coast of China. Taoist monks have lived there for centuries, and as a sacred mountain, it has been visited over the years by emperors, poets, scholars, and famous military men. Many wrote poetry and essays about it. They also had their calligraphy carved into the sides of the mountain (figure 215).

We were led to a scenic spot that was designated with a plaque: "The Number One Mountain under Heaven" (figure 216). There were no shops or tourists there. It was peaceful and had a wonderful view of the descending back side of Tai Shan and the valley below. I was happy with the spot and emptied the bag holding half of Daddy's ashes (figure 217). A breeze came and took much of the ash into the air. Through tears, we said goodbye again. It was a sad but poignant moment, and I knew Daddy would be happy we had been able to fulfill his wish. He was home again, where, as a child, he was adored.

We backtracked to return to the tram for the descent. Along the way, Mr. Zhen asked if we would take a picture with him. Knowing of our families' histories, the young man felt honored that he had been able to guide David and me to carry out our mission and wanted a keepsake photo. We stopped at a booth that advertised having a digital camera and printer that would allow photos to be printed in little time. The owner took our photograph with Mr. Zhen and turned to a computer to process a print for us.

A man who'd been chatting with the owner came over while we were waiting for the prints. He startled us by asking, "When will America attack China?"

His question demonstrated how a closed society can mislead its citizens. David assured the man we had never heard about the United States attacking China.

"China and the United States are big trading partners, and there is no animosity toward China from the American side," David answered. Then he added, "If, however, China decides to take Taiwan by force, I'm not sure President Bush would stay neutral."

The answer seemed to placate the gentleman, though I wasn't sure he was convinced. During the Bosnian War, the United States had mistakenly bombed the Chinese embassy in Bosnia in 1999, for which President Clinton apologized. The Chinese government, however, had been outraged because there were fatalities as a result of the bombing. The Chinese Communists no doubt had told the people of China the bombing was an intentional act by the United States.

The photographer then interrupted the discussion by showing us the photograph he had printed out. Mr. Zhen seemed to be genuinely excited to have a photo of him with General Pai Chung Xi's son and the Young Marshal's niece.

We returned to our hotel for lunch, and after lunch, a guide picked us up and drove us to Qu Fu, the birthplace of Confucius, which was about a hundred kilometers south of Tai An. The day was hot, and David was happy he had brought shorts to wear. The Chinese people follow designated dates religiously. In the People's Republic of China (PRC), shorts season starts on June 11 (May 5 on the lunar calendar). As it was not yet May on their calendar, we did not see a single Chinese wearing shorts, even though the temperature easily must have been in the eighties.

May 5 also is the celebration of Dragon Boat Festival, during which dumplings made with sticky rice wrapped in lotus leaves are commonly eaten. The occasion is to commemorate the suicide by drowning of a famous scholar and statesman, Chu Yuan, who lived in the third century BC. He committed suicide by drowning in Dong Ting Lake in Hunan Province rather than retracting his writings that were critical of the emperor at that time.

Chu Yuan was so beloved by the people that they decided to throw sticky-rice dumplings into Dong Ting Lake on the date that he died, so the fish would eat the dumplings rather than Chu's body. Every year since, on May 5, dragon boats have raced to see which first reaches the place where he drowned. This tradition has engendered dragon boat races all over China and in many parts of the world where there are Chinese communities.

The next day, we returned to Jinan and were again treated to a sumptuous lunch by the officials of the Jinan Foreign Affairs Office. We thanked them and flew from Jinan to Shanghai, where the rest of our group were scheduled to land that afternoon. As always, I was eager to see our sons, their families, and our friends. Mike and Katherine had only been married for a year and would not have their first child until late the following year.

We were met in Shanghai by Mr. Lien Jun Hsieh—a cousin of David's brother-in-law, Henry—and Lien Jun's wife, Ling Mian. The couple were the ones who'd contacted the Chinese travel agency to book our reservations for the trip. We checked into the Ramada Plaza Hotel. Right behind the hotel was a pedestrian road with stores and restaurants in abundance.

At night, the entire mall was lit with neon lights, probably brighter than Times Square in New York City. No cars and trucks were allowed to drive on the road; however, one had to be careful when near the crossroads, as people drove their bicycles, motorcycles, and cars at normal speeds when crossing the pedestrian mall.

We were happy to see a McDonald's, a Kentucky Fried Chicken, and a Pizza Hut close to the hotel. We'd been apprehensive about whether young Keith would be able to adapt to Chinese food beyond his favorite, pot stickers (fried dumplings).

In fact, we were to find on the trip that because our entire group was included in the frequent banquets by various foreign affairs officials wherever we visited, it was difficult to impossible to order something as plebian as pot stickers. Since we had warned our friends and family that only David and I had been invited to some banquets during our previous visits to China, our fellow travelers on the trip were thrilled to be included in all the banquets we were given.

The next day, Lien Jun and Ling Mian escorted our group to visit two of the former residences of General Pai following the defeat of the Japanese in World War II. The houses were taken over from the Japanese. In 1946, General Pai was appointed minister of defense, and as he was the highest-ranking military person in China, he and his family were given the houses to use as government issues.

The general's office was in Nanjing, about 150 miles west of Shanghai. General Pai's unwavering search for the best possible schools for his children led him and his wife to decide to keep all the children and some nieces and nephews to stay in Shanghai. David and his youngest brother, Charley, however, stayed with the general to keep him company for a year.

In 1947, David and Charley returned to Shanghai to join the rest of the family. We toured that house in 2005. It was an elegant mansion. As David's father, General Pai, was at the height of his career at the end of World War II, we know he must have been given high priority in the government requisition system. David's memory of his stay in that house is a good one. With so many young people, there was no lack of camaraderie and noise. He wrote the following in his journal of the trip:

> Mealtimes involved two big, round tables. Meals were served by servants and quickly eaten so that those who finished first could play Ping-Pong in the recreation room next to the dining room. (Since Chinese serve food in family-sized servings and not individually, having nine siblings and cousins at the same table also required eating fast to get one's share. David always ate faster than most people I knew.)
>
> The house was of a French design, with a large living room, large enough to have a dancing party with live bands. We would occasionally throw such parties and invite our schoolmates and friends. It was the best of times—until the Reds came in 1949.

The Communists had taken that house after they won the civil war and made it into a naval outpatient clinic. I imagine the large rooms with beams in the ceilings would have been ideal for a large family to use. The neighborhood of the house has now been named Literary District because many literary celebrities, such as Lu Shun, an early twentieth-century writer whose criticisms of life in China at the time, among others, led to the beginning of the Communist movement, had lived there.

We visited a second house that General Pai was given. It too was a Western-style house, with a spiral staircase and high ceilings. In fact, outside, it looked as if it had been built to resemble the White House in Washington, DC, with pillars at the front door. David remembered it had a large backyard with ornate statues, and in many ways, it was a more glamorous house than the one they'd lived in that became a clinic. Actually, there was a third house the Pais owned in Shanghai at that time. David wrote,

> It was a lovely German house located on Hong Qiao Road, and it was used to house Kenneth (his famous modern Chinese writer brother), who contracted tuberculosis during the Second World War and had to be segregated from the rest of us. The property had a lovely front yard and a long driveway leading to a small two-story house with large windows and modern appliances. Kenneth spent four lonely years there.
>
> We were allowed to visit him occasionally … It was always a treat for me to visit Kenneth because his chef was expert at Western-style dishes. To this day, I have not tasted mayonnaise as tasty as the way he made it. His potato salad and oxtail ragout was without peer! Kenneth was a voracious reader. His isolation had a lot to do with his love of literature, which was the foundation to his success as a writer, in addition to his talent, of course.
>
> I have not returned to see this house. I understand that it was commandeered by the proletariat, and at one time, several families lived in it. The house and the surrounding grounds are now in disrepair. People must have thought my father was a

very rich man to own all those fancy houses. In reality, all of them were government issues taken over from the Japanese by the Chinese government.

There is no doubt the houses were not originally owned by Chinese but by Europeans. The nineteenth and early twentieth centuries were a time when Chinese in their own country could not enter or move freely in the various concessions of the European countries. It would have been akin to a foreign country buying New York City's Central Park and placing a sign there that said, "Americans and Dogs Not Allowed." Such a sign, "Chinese and Dogs Not Allowed," was placed outside the gate to a park in Shanghai. It is not difficult to understand the enthusiasm generated by the Communist movement that promised that foreigners would no longer be able to humiliate Chinese in their own country.

From Shanghai, we flew to Guilin, David's hometown in Guangxi Province in the south of China, where General Pai grew up and was respected for his progressive administration during the reconstruction of Guanxi in the early 1930s. His military accomplishments against the Japanese added to the general's prestige, even though he was also responsible for Nationalist victories during the civil war against the Communists.

I might add here that had Chiang Kai Shek listened to General Pai, he never would have lost the civil war to the Communists. However, because General Pai was so widely respected and popular, Chiang worried he might want to usurp power (which was never the case). He essentially isolated the general from policy making and even fabricated a pretext of Guangxi rebellion and issued arrest orders for the general and other high-ranking officers. Eventually, General Pai was reinstated by Chiang but too late to help the Nationalist cause.

Instead of having the wisdom of a proven military strategist, Chiang surrounded himself with yes-men. Despite their having a huge advantage over the Communists in weapons, armaments, and soldiers, bad decisions and mistakes led to the defeat of the Nationalists.

We left Shanghai in late afternoon and arrived in Guilin in the evening, in time to be treated to a big banquet by Guilin officials and Mr. Ding Ting Mo, the retired head of the Guangxi Provincial Assembly. Our local guide turned out to be Pai Chong Ping, whose name indicated she was a relative in the Pai family, and she had the same generation name as David's father, although she was obviously decades younger.

Because of David's family history, we were allowed to stay in the Yung Hu Hotel, which was usually reserved for VIPs visiting Guilin. By Western standards, the hotel did not seem that luxurious at that time. It was situated on Pai family property, on land that had been the backyard and riding stable when the Pai family lived there. The knowledge that we were staying somewhere where most people could not stay was adventure enough for us (figure 218).

The next morning, we toured the main house, which was empty, and the grounds of the property (figure 219). We decided to ask with tongue in cheek if there was any possibility for the government to return the house to us. We were told politely that would not be possible because they were planning to use the house as a museum to honor General Pai and his battles against the Japanese. Figure 220 shows another house that was given to General Pai which is now used as a hospital.

Guilin had undergone much improvement since our visit in 1985. Once again, we visited famous tourist sites, such as the Seven Star Park and the impressive Reed Flute Cavern, with its underground pools and calcium carbonate rock formations (see again figure 157). All were lit with different-colored lights, and taped music occasionally added to the ambience of a unique place.

The banquet that evening was hosted by Mr. Ding Ting Mo, the retired head of the Guangxi Provincial Assembly. Professor Mao had requested that he oversee our visit to Guilin. Professor Mao, you might remember, had interned at David's company, Foster Wheeler Development and Research, for two years and had become a good friend. Professor Mao and Mr. Ding had been classmates in college and were also good friends. The banquet consisted of some unusual local favorites served individually, Western style. It was not food to an eight-year-old's liking, but we were proud of our grandson Keith because he did not make a fuss. My guess is that there was a trip to Mickey D's sometime later in the evening!

David was especially pleased to eat the rice noodles. He had spoken to me about the rice noodles he remembered fondly, but he'd been greatly disappointed when we had some during our 1985 trip to China. At that time, they were poorly prepared and tasteless. In 2005, twenty years later, the chefs had regained their touch, and the rice noodles were tasty again.

The next day, we took the famed Li River cruise from Guilin to Yansuo (figure 221). It remains a highlight of scenic tours to Guilin (figure 222). With limestone karsts rising out of the land everywhere; waterfalls, as in figure 222; and the huge size of bamboo on the shores of the river, the Li River cruise presents a unique landscape.

We had to be towed in some places because of a drought that had caused the river to be unusually shallow. That probably was the reason we saw no fishermen fishing on the Li River with their cormorants, a scene that has been painted and photographed over and over. The birds have metal rings on their long necks to prevent them from swallowing the fish they find and catch. Each bird responds to its owner's unique whistle, brings the fish to him, and is rewarded for its catch.

The only person who did not seem impressed by the cruise was my eight-year-old grandson. I asked him, "What do you think of this scenery, Keith?"

His answer was "All I see is a lot of mountains!" *Sigh*.

When we returned to Guilin, we were treated to yet another banquet. Whereas the day before, officials of Guangxi Province had been our hosts, that night was a banquet by the City of Guilin, hosted by the deputy mayor of Guilin, Mr. Chen Jian Jun. David had written a biography of his father, and after dinner, he gave copies to officials of Guilin and Mr. Liu Hong Wei, deputy manager of the Guilin Cultural Preservation Bureau.

In addition, David gave them a commemorative volume published after his father's funeral that contains a short biography as well as a collection of the general's decorations and pictures, along with poems and essays written by notable persons at his funeral in Taiwan. For all of us but especially David, it was a memorable evening and a delightful visit to his hometown.

Our next stop on the trip was Xian and a visit to the Terracotta Army and the resort Hua Ching Tze, the site of the Xian Incident involving my uncle the Young Marshal, Zhang Xue Liang. I discussed the Xian Incident in detail in chapter 6 and will not repeat that information here. I will only mention that my uncle's headquarters is now a museum to commemorate the Xian Incident. As David wrote, "It was good to see the reverence with which the Young Marshal is held by the people."

Qing Shi Huang Di (260–210 BCE) is considered to be the first emperor of China, as he was the first to bring the disparate Chinese states into one united country. (*Di*, in Chinese, means "emperor.") Qing Shi Huang was also responsible for the initial construction of the Great Wall. The construction of terra-cotta soldiers began in the late third century BCE. The Terracotta Army, and other artefacts believed buried with him, were to provide him protection and comfort in the afterlife.

The Chinese continue to work to increase the numbers of restored terra-cotta soldiers and other figures in the "army" (figure 223). The sheer number of the soldiers is mind-boggling.

According to *Wikipedia*, it has been estimated that there were some 8,000 soldiers, each one with a unique face; 130 chariots with 520 horses; and 150 cavalry horses. Soldiers with different roles are dressed in different uniforms. The higher officers are taller than the others. A historian of the time has estimated that perhaps seven hundred thousand men participated in the construction of the army. It is a sight not to be missed by anyone who is visiting China (figure 224).

We also drove west a mile to the site of the tomb mound where Qing Shi Huang Di is buried at Mount Li. Although the burial site is known, the tomb has not been opened because samples of air from the tomb have shown a high level of mercury. It is believed he ordered the construction of a facsimile of all of China that he united, and the rivers were simulated by large quantities of liquid mercury (figure 225).

There is a theory that Qing Shi Huang Di died of mercury poisoning. In seeking some way to live forever, the emperor consumed mercury given to him by the court physician, who did not know any better. Now that we know of the toxic nature of mercury, it appears the first emperor of China sealed his tomb for eternity. While he did unite China in 221 BC, the first emperor's reputation is marred by the numbers of people who died obeying his demand for incredibly difficult construction, such as the Great Wall (figure 226) and the Terracotta Army. It is also believed that the soldiers who carried his body into the tomb were sealed in the tomb with him.

While we were in Xian, David and I had dinner with his cousin Eric Pai, who had come from Taiyuan, about 150 miles northeast of Xian, to visit with David. Eric was one of the Pai relatives who'd lived with General Pai's family in the big house in Shanghai that is now an outpatient clinic. He had various jobs during the Cultural Revolution to survive, such as coaching basketball and driving a truck. As David wrote,

He was sent down to the countryside to farm and for reeducation because one time, when he was asked by a student which country had the best basketball team, he made the mistake of telling the student that Americans were the best basketball players. This was, of course, against party doctrine. However, while in reeducation, he met his wife, who was his supervisor! It was good to see Eric, even though it was brief.

We left Xian to travel to Beijing by train. Although it was early June, we found the temperature to be quite high. It felt like summertime, with temperatures in the ninety-degree range. The abrupt change caused some of us to opt for air-conditioning in our hotel rather than some of the trips to famous sites in and around the capital of China.

We did go to Tiananmen Square, a huge paved area around which are important government buildings and the tomb of Mao. Sponsored events, such as national holiday parades, are held there (figure 227). It is also where, in June 1989, students demanding more democracy led a rebellion that was met with force from the government, which resulted in many fatalities.

I wanted to know how the common people of Beijing looked at the events of that time, and I asked our guide, a bright young man who spoke good English, "What do people think now about what happened in 1989?"

He looked at me and said, "The government says that nothing happened, and nobody got hurt." Then he abruptly turned and walked away, clearly not wanting to discuss the event.

I had been invited to teach genetics at Beijing University in the fall semester of 1989. The June rebellion made it impossible for me to accept the invitation. I was horrified at the violence perpetrated against the students, though I have read that the young people might have made a tragic mistake. In a meeting with high government officials, the students were said to be disrespectful as well as passionate. That behavior, which was contrary to the Chinese culture of respect for elders and authorities, if it happened, might have prompted the forceful response.

At any rate, regardless of how I felt, Mommy was further enraged at the Communists for the fatalities incurred among the young rebels. I am sure that had I decided to honor my invitation to teach at Beijing University, I would have been exposed to the same hysteria and anger that had caused Daddy to retire early from his job at the United Nations. Both to avoid that discord and to appease Mommy, I wrote to my contacts at Beijing University and canceled my plans to teach there.

Later that year, David and I attended a performance of *Les Misérables* on Broadway. In addition to the wonderful music and the moving story based on the classic novel, there was a scene of students at a barricade, rebelling against the government, and their demise when government forces, with overwhelming numbers, broke down the barrier. It created such a strong feeling of déjà vu given the Tiananmen disaster in June that I could not stop tears from forming and keep from feeling a sense of melancholy. *Les Mis* remains one of my favorite musicals, perhaps my favorite.

Right next to Tiananmen Square is the site where emperors lived, which was not open to the public in any way. Thus, the many buildings that held the emperors' thrones, staff of eunuchs, and army were designated the Forbidden City. I include a photograph that shows the scene one comes upon now that the entire Forbidden City is a museum and open to the public (figure 228).

We ended our visit to Beijing with a dinner that David and I hosted for Professor Mao and Gary Nedelka, the CEO of Foster Wheeler China, whose office was in Beijing. Professor Mao remained a consultant to Foster Wheeler for twenty years. He was another intellectual who'd been sent down to a farm for reeducation during the Cultural Revolution. During that time, however, he'd become a group leader and taught science and mathematics to younger trainees. His wife had been a professor of history at Tsinghua and was also retired. We were pleased to hear that in their retirement, they lived in a lovely new apartment in the northern suburb of Beijing.

We joined our tour group after dinner to see a wonderfully choreographed play called *The Legend of Kung Fu*. There were many scenes with kung fu fighting, which fascinated Keith, as well as unbelievable demonstrations of athleticism and strength of mind and body.

One example was a scene in which a man lay on top of a board that had a bed of nails pointed upward. He then had a slate board placed on top of his stomach, and another man used a sledge hammer to break the slate. The man on top of the nails simply rose up without a trace of anything penetrating his skin. Amazing! When we returned to the United States, Keith was trained in kung fu for a few years. In quite an achievement, he reached the lowest level of the highest (indicating advanced ability) color, a black belt, before he stopped his lessons.

In our movement about Beijing in 2005, we saw construction everywhere. The city was preparing for the 2008 Olympic Games. Although few of the buildings that would house the various competitions were completed, we saw so much activity that our guide wryly said the national bird of China was the (construction) crane. The Sixth Ring Road was being built around the city to bypass the city traffic, which already created heavy traffic jams at intersections.

We all wondered how the air pollution in and around Beijing would affect the Olympic athletes. The burning of coal as the main source of heating and the increasing numbers of automobiles, trucks, and buses had made the smog almost unbearable for walking, much less for competing in athletic endeavors. We later read that the Chinese were also concerned and tried to address the problem by shutting down factories or moving them to distant countryside sites and banning most cars from the city during the games.

Even though Beijing is always interesting, I was more than anxious to reach our next stop, Shenyang, the capital of Manchuria and my mother's hometown. Unfortunately, Mike and Katherine could not go with us, as both had to return to the United States because of their jobs. Hopefully I can make the trip in the near future with them and their children.

Shenyang was where Mommy's father, the Old Marshal, had had his home and from where he'd ruled

Manchuria in the early 1920s. The Old Marshal had expanded his rule to territories south of Manchuria, including Beijing; however, when the Sun Yat Sen–led revolution successfully overturned the Qing Dynasty in 1911 and the Revolutionary Army of the Nationalists began their Northern Expedition in 1926, Grandfather withdrew his forces to return to Manchuria.

Interestingly, David's father, General Pai Chung Xi, was the chief of staff of the Revolutionary Army at the time. After the Old Marshal was assassinated by the Japanese in 1928, General Pai sent the Young Marshal a telegram urging him to join the Nationalist cause. General Pai and the Young Marshal never met. As David wrote,

> It is interesting to note that my father … communicated with the Young Marshal by telegram to urge him to come over to the Nationalist cause and avoid further bloodshed. The two never met in person, however, because shortly afterwards Chiang decided to get rid of the Guangxi faction in the Revolutionary Army …
>
> On a fabricated pretext, Chiang accused the Guangxi forces of rebellion in Hunan. Overnight Chiang issued arrest orders for Father along with General Li Tsung Jen and other ranking officers of the Guangxi Army. Father and General Li had to escape to Vietnam to avoid harm. This was one of Chiang's many missteps which eventually handed China to Mao Tse Tung and the Communists.

When we visited my uncle the Young Marshal in Taiwan in 1985, he told us he responded to General Pai and asked him to spare the Manchurian troops and people during the Northern Expedition, one of the goals of which was to disempower the northern warlords.

During the Northern Expedition, Uncle decided to join the Nationalists because he felt Chiang was the only one who could unite China. Later, when the Second Sino-Japanese War started in 1937, Chiang recanted, knowing he needed General Pai and his Guangxi Army to help in the war against Japan. General Pai was restored to high office and became a key contributor in the war of resistance. However, he was often ignored during the civil war and afterward. Chiang frequently omitted the general from military strategy meetings, which was the beginning of the downfall of the Nationalist cause in the civil war.

David, our friends, and I often commented that it must have been karma that led David and me to colleges in Virginia, where David and I met when my roommate organized a mixer for foreign students while I was a junior at Sweet Briar College. It is something to wonder about when one considers that my uncle and David's father could have been in battle against each other but instead became allies.

Both were to suffer from Chiang Kai Shek's ineptitude and paranoia. My uncle was placed under house arrest for fifty years for his role in the Xian Incident, and General Pai and his family were spied upon under Chiang's orders for many years in Taiwan.

When we arrived in Shenyang, we were greeted by a local guide and two officials of the Foreign Affairs

Office of Shenyang: Mr. Yang Jiangjun and Mr. Wang Peng. The latter told us he was a graduate of China's Northeastern University, a school founded by the Young Marshal. They were excited we were there and looked forward to hosting us at a banquet as well as on a visit to the Zhang estate and compound, which had become a museum that was open to the public. Figure 229 is a map of the Zhang family compound. It is mounted on the wall of the museum to show where various houses are.

When we visited the estate, we were awed by the buildings. Recall that the Old Marshal had six wives. My grandmother was the fourth wife. Each wife and her children lived in separate houses but within the Zhang compound. The Young Marshal's house was the most grandiose and built after he assumed power. It was more modern in architecture and resembled a palace (figure 230). Mr. Zhang Li, the head of the museum, gave us a personally guided tour. The main house was palatial in size, and the decorations and furnishings were elegant, made of the finest materials (figure 231).

Somehow, as we wandered around, word spread to other tourists that we were there, and they began to follow our group. When they clamored for an opportunity to take pictures of and with me, Mr. Li had his assistants act as a shield so we would not be overly imposed on or inconvenienced. The scene was again evidence of the Chinese emphasis on family: because I was a direct descendant of the Old Marshal, I was an instant celebrity.

Having lived almost all my life in America, where being a relative of someone famous did not give one such instant celebrity, I was not comfortable with the attention and was grateful for the assistants who shooed the tourists away. However, I was proud that my grandfather and uncle were still held in such high regard by the common people. That was again evident when Uncle died in Honolulu in 2001, as many people, young and old alike, gathered to attend his funeral service.

When we entered the main house, I had an experience that made my hair stand on end: the first thing I saw was a wax figure of my grandfather sitting at a desk, writing (figure 232). I never had met the Old Marshal, as he had died well before I was born. It was a strange feeling for me to see the wax figure and know that was what my ancestor had looked like. I wondered what Mommy would have said about the figure. I would have loved to have known him.

During the whole visit, I thought of my mother. Had we been able to take the trip while she was still physically able, would she have agreed to join us? Would she have seen changes that had occurred since she lived there? Would she have been pleased by how her home was converted into a museum? I bet she would have been pleased by the attention she would have received from the people visiting her home.

It was enormously interesting for David and me to see in person what Mommy had often spoken of—the elegance of her home and some of the historically important rooms. We saw one room in the Young Marshal's house with two stuffed tigers, which I assumed my uncle had hunted and had preserved. That room, the guide told us, was where Uncle had served *hamigua* (a sweet melon) to the traitors believed to have been involved with the Japanese in the assassination of the Old Marshal. Uncle's aide had then shot the traitors (see again figure 32).

We saw the house of the Old Marshal's fifth wife, to which he was carried after the bombing and where he succumbed to his injuries (see again figure 18). As David said, there was much history, both of the family and of the country, hidden in those buildings. They are the subject of many books and movies.

The next day, in a driving rain, we visited the Old Marshal's domed mausoleum in Fu Shun, about 150 kilometers northwest of Shenyang. Although the storm made walking about the premises difficult, we could see that the site of the mausoleum was excellent. It had been built facing a large lake that had become a reservoir. The view across the lake included a dragon-shaped mountain. The guide told us Grandfather had chosen the site himself. It was also near a battlefield where the Ming Dynasty had lost to armies of the Qing Dynasty. Grandfather no doubt had felt the site had good feng shui, or harmony with the environment.

Inside the mausoleum was a large, circular room painted with yellow stars against a royal-blue background all around on the ceiling and walls. In the center of the room was a platform on which grandfather's remains were to have been placed in a casket. However, his remains were not there. When the Japanese invaded Manchuria in 1931, the Old Marshal's remains were moved and buried near the town of Jing Zhou to prevent the Japanese from destroying them. They have not yet been returned to Fu Shun.

That night, upon our return to Shenyang, Mr. Han Ming Yao, vice director of Foreign Affairs of Shenyang, gave us a banquet. Mr. Zhang Li, the head of the museum at the family compound, was also present. I had made copies of some old historical photographs of both the Old Marshal and the Young Marshal and other members of my family. When I formally presented them to Mr. Zhang, he was delighted to have the photographs since he was also a historian.

The banquet was held in a wonderful garden restaurant located on a large organic farm. All the vegetables served that night had been produced by the farm. The food was excellent, and while it could not have been a cheap place to eat, the restaurant was fully packed with diners. Our group was impressed by not only the food but also the natural settings of the seating areas. Leanna and Keith were awed by a tree that seemed to be growing in the middle of the restaurant (figure 233).

The visit brought more meaning to stories Mommy used to tell about the grandeur of her life and the power of her father. She'd said more than once that he had the power to order someone to be executed, which was done immediately at his command. As the American that I am, I did not find that an admirable thing. To my mother, though, it was simply a proud memory of the power and control her father had had over Manchuria and its people.

The trip to Shenyang was to impress on our two older grandchildren, Leanna and Keith, their Chinese heritage. David and I hoped that one day we would be able to go to Manchuria again when our two younger grandsons, who are ten and eight at the time of this writing, were old enough to understand the importance of their Chinese grandmother's and grandfather's families in twentieth-century Chinese history. Perhaps they will use this book as a source of family information.

I was happy we had the opportunity to visit my mother's home. I wish she could have been there to revisit her childhood.

We returned to Shanghai to stay for two days of touring that most cosmopolitan and Western of all Chinese cities. We were guided by Lien Jun and his wife, who, as I said, had worked with the Chinese travel agency to plan our entire trip. One of the highlights was a short ride on the magnetic levitation, or maglev, train (figure 234). David wrote,

> Magnetic levitation as a means of moving vehicles has been researched by a number of countries, including Germany, Japan, and the US, among others. China became the first country to install a commercial version, although it is with German technology and supplies. The ride, which peaked at over four hundred kilometers per hour, was indeed impressive. The maglev train served a short stretch in Pudong, territory on the other side of the Wanpo River from Shanghai, in which its destination was the airport.
>
> The ride was very impressive. The seats were comfortable and spaced well. The trip to the airport takes at least forty minutes by car. The maglev made the trip in ten minutes (our top speed was approximately 269 miles per hour). Whether the capital cost of such installations will be low enough soon for general application remains to be seen.

On the way to the airport, we happened to pass a second maglev train returning to Shanghai. The two trains passing created a terrifically loud clap of air that sounded like a huge lightning strike. I could not help but think about the roads with impossible numbers of cars in the United States, such as the Long Island Expressway, which runs the length of Long Island in New York. There were times when David and I wanted to visit Solan in Oyster Bay on the east end of the island, but the traffic was at a standstill on the Long Island Expressway, and we had to turn around and go home. What a major improvement in the lives of residents there (and their visitors) if they had access to a maglev train, which could transport them to their destinations quicker by a factor of four.

Another highlight of the tour of Shanghai was a visit to a tall tower on Pudong called the Pearl of China, which dominated the Shanghai landscape. We ascended by elevator to an observation deck that allowed tourists to view the Shanghai landscape. It was difficult to see through the hazy air. One of our guides tried to be positive about the air in Shanghai, saying that conditions were improving and that there were now days when one could see that the sky was blue. Rather than making me feel encouraged about the future, though, the comment was sad, I thought.

The next morning, we departed Shanghai by bus to visit Hangzhou again. The resort city was still lovely, including West Lake and the Buddhist temple, which I mentioned in the chapter on our trip to China in 1985.

The city had grown tremendously in twenty years. As in Beijing and Shanghai, with growth, the traffic on the road around West Lake had become heavy with automobile traffic jams. Again, what a price for progress! Still, it was important that our older son and his family as well as our friends who had never been to Hangzhou could see one of the most popular resort places in China.

When we returned to Shanghai, David received a pleasant surprise: he had a telephone message from a grade school classmate, Dr. Huan Sze Qing. They had parted after they finished sixth grade in Nanjing in 1947. Dr. Huan had recently seen David's writer brother, Kenneth, on one of Kenneth's trips to the PRC. They made plans for lunch the next day with another classmate in Shanghai, Tan Peng Fei (figure 235).

They greeted each other warmly, even though it had been fifty-eight years since they last had seen each other. I was impressed they still remembered each other, because I could not remember any of the myriad classmates I'd had as my family wandered the East Coast of the United States in the 1940s. Dr. Huan was yet another victim of the Cultural Revolution. After graduating from medical school in 1959, he was denied his license to practice medicine because his father had gone to Bao Ding Military Academy (which General Pai also had attended) and served in the Nationalist Army. Like many others, he was sent to the country to farm for so-called reeducation. Such inane madness!

He was finally rehabilitated in 1979 after Deng Xiao Ping took over. He was allowed to practice medicine and, with further training, became an internist. Tan Peng Fei had an easier time. He became a movie producer of some note in China, specializing in classical movies. He never underwent reeducation. His wife, unfortunately, had been a stroke victim. David wrote, "It was a bonus to see these two old classmates. Seeing them and learning of their life stories made me appreciate my own karma ever more."

Fig 214 Tai Shan, view from the tram

Fig 215 Calligraphy carved into Tai Shan

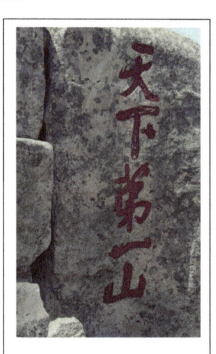
Fig 216 A plaque marking the place we were to spread Daddy's ashes

Fig 217 A second goodbye to my father

Fig 218 Sheila, Mike, Katherine and Ben walking from the Yung Hu Hotel

Fig 219 Former house of Pai family

Fig 220 Pai Mansion

Fig 221 Li River cruise boats

Fig 222 Waterfalls by the Li River

Fig 223 Area of continued excavation

Fig 224 The Terra Cotta Army

Fig 225 The actual tomb of Qing Shi Huang Di

Fig 226 Part of the Great Wall with a steep grade outside Beijing

Fig 227 Our group at Tien An Men Square

Fig 228 The Forbidden City

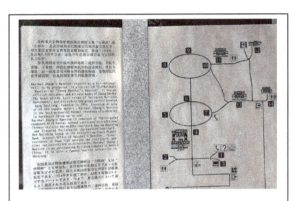

Fig 229 The Zhang Family Compound

Fig 230 The Young Marshal's Mansion

Fig 231 Elegant furnishings

Fig 232 Wax figure of my Lo Yeh working at his desk

Fig 233 Leanna and Keith in the garden restaurant in Shen Yang

Fig 234 Model of Magnetic Levitation Train

Fig 235 Dr. Huan on the left, and Mr. Tan on the right

Chapter 62

HUANG SHAN

David and I had decided to use the end of the trip to experience one of the most famous scenic tourist areas in all of China: Huang Shan. The name means "Yellow Mountain" in Chinese, but remember that when *shan* (mountain) is used in a name, it refers not to one peak, as it does in English, but to a mountain range. We had no idea what our visit would entail in the way of hiking, or we probably would not have met the challenge and would have declined to participate. The entrance to the park was imposing (figure 236).

The rest of our group, Ben's family and our friends, could not spare the time to join us, so we bade them goodbye and a good trip home and headed to the airport to fly to Huang Shan. Friends and relatives who had visited Huang Shan before had warned us that it would be an arduous climb. We heeded their advice and bought crude walking sticks for less than a dollar each, and they turned out to be a great help indeed (figure 237).

We had brought a small carry-on wheelie to take with us, as we would have to stay overnight at a hotel on Huang Shan, but the staff at the hotel we stayed in the night before the climb told us even that was too much to carry. The next morning, a guide came to take us and a number of other people at the hotel to a tram that would carry us partway up the initial mountain peak. We left most of our belongings at the Huang Shan hotel and took only a plastic bag containing a change of underwear and our toothbrushes and toothpaste. Even that small collection proved to be enough of a burden that we handed the bag over to the porters who helped us traverse some of the hardest parts of the range.

I had my camera equipment in a small backpack that I would not abandon, as the scenery of Huang Shan was celebrated, and it promised to produce exceptional images. I had to bite my tongue, though, as I saw the porters reach for the plastic bag David was carrying. Instead of the light plastic bag, I was carrying a camera bag with batteries, memory cards, and an extra lens and camera back that together must have weighed ten pounds. Not one of the porters offered to carry my camera bag.

Truth be told, I would have refused had they offered because I did not trust them with my equipment, but still, I was miffed they never offered. Was it because I was a woman? I guess they knew who would be giving them their tip.

David wrote,

> We finished the initial tram ride at 11:00 a.m. Between climbing and sightseeing, it took until 7:30 p.m. to reach our hotel at the top. The climb after taking the tram was still excessive, even brutal. When we reached our hotel, the guide told us we walked seven miles, mostly climbing. The views of Huang Shan were spectacular, straight out of classical Chinese paintings.
>
> There was another old folk in our group, a seventy-seven-year-old ex-Communist guerrilla from my home province of Guangxi. He joined the Communist movement when he was twenty, while still in college. He became an administrator of Ching Zhou, a large metropolis in southern Guangxi. When he and his son-in-law found out about my family background (the automatic question people ask when they find out that I'm from Guilin and my family name is Bai is whether I'm related to Bai Chongxi), the conversation became more interesting.
>
> The son-in-law is an executive in a defense industry establishment and is very familiar with Father and the recent history of Guangxi. He was very complimentary of Father. The old guerrilla, on the other hand, remains in the old-cadre mode. He even said that if Chiang Kai Shek had gone over to the Communists, Chairman Mao would have been willing to give Chiang a cushy job! How naive!

Huang Shan exceeded my expectations for scenery. Figure 238 shows the beginning of the long path, all paved in concrete, that would lead to our hotel. One definitely should visit Huang Shan when one is young(er)! Figure 239 shows another part of the path we had to reach. I must confess it was sometimes disheartening to hear our guide point out parts of the path—like the one in this figure, which seemed to be about a week's hike away—that we were to reach that afternoon.

But the beauty of Huang Shan made our effort worthwhile. Also, we were lucky with the weather. We had sunshine the entire day—Huang Shan had only 150 days of sun a year. We spent part of the next morning seeing more sights. Huang Shan's scenery seemed to be endless. Figure 240 shows another view of the scenery that made the mountain range so beloved and famous in China.

The hotel at the top of the last peak, where we were to spend the night, was another disappointment when we finally reached it. It was supposed to also be a four-star hotel. Along the way, some of our group stopped at lesser hotels, which were cheaper. The cheapest hotel was available but had no running water. There was a slightly more expensive hotel, which had running water but no hot water.

Our so-called four-star hotel did have hot running water and electricity but was obviously a state-run enterprise with the expected bad attitude toward service. As we arrived late enough to have missed the serving of dinner, the people of the dining room let us know they were not happy they had to prepare dinner for us. We didn't care as long as we had something to eat quickly so we could fall into bed!

We descended the last peak down the back side of the mountain on a tram. After lunch, we were taken first to a tea factory and then to a snake farm. The tea factory was not of the same quality as the one in Hangzhou. The snake farm was interesting. It turned out that Huang Shan was famous for its five-step snakes. Legend had it that if you were bitten by such a snake, you'd die before you could walk five steps!

They were ugly-looking creatures with sharply triangular heads and black and gray spots. Their venom was reputed to have high medicinal value. The place was noted for the snake oils (venom in an oil solution). The stuff was supposed to be good for massage and to drink. Anna and I declined to try either, although a number of our group tried both.

The only other American in our group was a younger woman, May Sun, who had brought her ten-year-old daughter, Alice, on the tour. May agreed to a massage of her legs with the snake venom oil. I asked her how the massage felt. Did the snake oil seem to help her sore leg muscles (which we all had from the climb)? May Sun just shrugged and said she felt nothing at all. I was just happy the snake oil did not hurt them!

David wrote,

> We had a late plane to catch from Huang Shan to return to Shanghai. We decided to go to dinner with May and Alice, and the guide recommended a restaurant where we experienced an impressive high-tech operation. The restaurant was a two-story structure. The inside half of the bottom floor was the kitchen, with numerous display counters for dishes of the day.
>
> We were quickly ushered upstairs to table number 42 and given a bamboo slab with the number 42 on it. We were told then to go downstairs to look over the food and place our order. Since Anna was still laden with her camera equipment, she volunteered to hold the table while I went down with May and Alice to order.
>
> There were no less than fifty varieties of dishes on display, all fresh and appetizing. Each time we stopped in front of a dish, a girl with a handheld device like a BlackBerry would help us with the order by punching in the order and our table number. There were at least three girls working the ordering counters in like fashion. In all, we ordered fourteen items ranging from small appetizer dishes, noodles, and wonton to full-course dishes.
>
> By the time we returned to our table upstairs, half of the dishes we ordered were already there, to Anna's surprise. The rest came very shortly thereafter. The bill came to ninety-seven renminbi, or less than twelve dollars, for the four of us. It was one of the better meals we had in China. This restaurant was a demonstration of Chinese ingenuity unlocked by free enterprise!

Our flight back to Shanghai arrived at midnight. The next day, David invited Tan Peng Fei to lunch. His other classmate, Dr. Huang, had returned to his home in Nanjing. Lien Jun and his wife had decided to stay with us on the last day until we left. They had planned a wonderful tour for us and at an unbelievably low price. The entire trip cost each member of the group less than $4,000—a price that reflected government subsidization. For a real treat, they took us to a Yang Zhou restaurant. Yang Zhou was a nearby city noted for its cuisine. The food was so tasty David said it was a good thing we did not live there, or he would have gained fifty pounds. Lastly, he wrote,

> China has come a long way at great speed. The unchained Chinese is a formidable force, as is evident in the country's enterprising spirit and its material achievements. Major problems remain, however. The foremost two problems, in my mind, are the unequal distribution of wealth and the environment. It looks like China is developing at great speed in the coastal cities from Guangdong Province to Fujian, continuing all the way to Manchuria. These coastal enclaves are experiencing hyperactivity, drawing large migration from the countryside to feed the labor requirements.
>
> It must be remembered that all the coastal enclaves consist of no more than four hundred million people. The remaining eight hundred–plus million are still left in the hinterland, where their lot has not improved much. The gap between the haves and the have-nots is getting wider, whereas in the old days, everyone was poor. This is a recipe for instability. Until China can solve this problem, the future is in the balance. As for the environment, there is a clear recognition of the problem. What is needed is the will to solve it. Let's hope the next generation of leaders is up to the tasks.
>
> This was an excellent trip from beginning to end … We set out with two missions, and I am happy that we accomplished them both. We are proud of Leanna and Keith, at twelve and eight years old, for hanging in there throughout the trip.

For me, the highlight of the trip was our visit to the Zhang family compound. After seeing the luxury and experiencing the intense interest other tourists had in our presence, I can understand better my mother's obsession with her early life and her father's power. I can also understand better why she always expected a certain amount of adulation from any Chinese she met because of who she was. She grew up with that adulation; she was surrounded by it, and she loved it, which is not difficult to understand. Then circumstances beyond her imagination and beyond her power to control took all of it away.

They lost so much. Her life was reduced to being an ordinary housewife and having to clean house, wash clothes, cook food for her family, and be a mother to her young children—activities that she had taken for granted would be done by servants. The radical change resulted in a form of social isolation for most of her life because of language difficulties and cultural ignorance.

I am now convinced that the most important aspect of adapting to a new country and culture is language. The sooner an immigrant can speak and understand the language, the sooner he or she will be able to adjust.

For that reason, David and I agreed that immigrant children should attend schools that did not teach in their original language. It is, of course, easier for immigrants to learn in their own language in the beginning, but it retards the development of their new language and therefore retards their progress to be assimilated into their new country. To be sure, there should also be classes to teach both languages.

My mother was a victim of immigration. Yet she survived and brought up three children who can be considered good human beings capable of love and productive citizens of their country, the United States. Could I or anyone else have done as well?

I am now over eighty years old. I have had many more great times than I or anyone should deserve. There are many things I have not touched on, including many places I had the privilege to visit: Machu Picchu, the Galapagos Islands, Italy multiple times, many countries of Europe, the Canadian Rockies, and many others. The United States, my country, is a beautiful country with unforgettable national parks. To have seen them is not unimportant in my life, but to write about them all would make this autobiography intolerably long. There are books written about them all.

My life indeed has been fuller and richer than I could ever have hoped. If my days on earth are limited, I have no problem with that. My sons, Ben and Mike, have grown into fine men whom I respect greatly. They are married to marvelous women whom they—and I—love deeply, Susan and Katherine, respectively. I have proudly watched my grandchildren, Leanna, Keith, Aidan, and Nathan, grow and have been impressed by them. Shrong and Mei, Solan's daughters, are women I would be proud to have as my own daughters. They too have terrific children: Buddy, Reyna, and Cameron. I adore them all.

In the end, I still do not know what meaning there is to life, but I believe that if there is no love, there cannot be any meaning to life at all. I have been loved by my husband, my family, and many friends. I believe my parents and brothers loved me too. What more could I ask for? If the end came today, I would not regret it. To want more than I have been given would be unabashed and unforgivable rapacity. I know of no person who has been more fortunate than I.

What would I wish for those I love after I am no longer with them? This is my wish for all those I love: I hope you can live—truly live—your whole lives.

Fig 236 At the entrance to Huang Shan

Fig 237 David at the beginning of our enormous trek

Fig 238 The beginning of our hike

Fig 239 Another part of the path to reach!

Fig 240 More Huang Shan

EPILOGUE

At 9:56 a.m. on July 23, 2016, a struggle that began thirty years ago claimed the life of one of the most courageous, determined human beings ever to have walked this earth, someone with the most integrity a human being could possibly have. My husband of almost fifty-seven years (our anniversary was August 29), David H. C. Pai (figure 241), succumbed to decades of fighting his family's cardiovascular genes and, at the end, congestive heart failure.

Thirty years ago, he needed a five-bypass open-heart operation at the age of fifty, during which he suffered two heart attacks that reduced the injured heart to 50 percent of its capacity to pump blood to the rest of his body. In spite of that, my only love refused to be incapacitated and lived an amazingly active life. Even as age added its negatives to his body, he maintained his willingness to work and play at high speed.

He immigrated to this country with some older siblings at the age of sixteen and attended high school at La Salle Military Academy on Long Island. The strict monks who taught at the academy took away his English-to-Chinese dictionary as soon as they found him using it and gave him a regular English dictionary, whose definitions he could not fully understand. Nonetheless, through tenacious hard works which was his modus operandi in life, he improved his grasp of English and graduated with his classmates. He entered Virginia Military Institute's class of 1958. It was karma that led him to a college only thirty-plus miles from Sweet Briar College, my Virginia alma mater.

As I described in the chapter titled "Warm, Dry Hands," we met in 1955 and began dating seriously in my senior year, 1956–1957. We were engaged in 1958 and married in 1959. We both decided to go on to graduate studies, and in our first year of marriage, we lived in Bethlehem, Pennsylvania, where David was finishing his MS degree in engineering at Lehigh University. I had finished my master's degree in embryology at Bryn Mawr. We then moved to an apartment in the Bronx, New York, where David studied for his doctorate in engineering at New York University and worked full-time at Foster Wheeler Corporation. I enrolled for my doctorate in genetics at the Sue Golding Graduate School of Albert Einstein College of Medicine. I finished my degree in 1964, and he finished in 1965. We then moved first to Metuchen, New Jersey, to be closer to David's job, which was then in Carteret, New Jersey. When Foster Wheeler moved to Livingston, New Jersey, we moved to Livingston to raise our family of two boys, Ben and Mike.

Through both his brilliance as an engineer and his tenacious hard work, David's career progressed. Foster Wheeler Corporation, where he was to work for his entire forty-two-plus-year career, was an international Fortune 500 company. He eventually was chosen to be the CEO and president of a subsidiary company of Foster Wheeler, the Foster Wheeler Development and Research Company. It was great success for an immigrant from China. He was eventually elected into a branch of the National Academy of Sciences, the

National Academy of Engineering, in 1994. Membership in the NAE is one of the highest honors conferred on engineers. NAE is essentially a hall of fame for engineers.

Despite his many achievements, what people loved most about my husband were his humility and sense of humor. He was never too proud to laugh at himself. I will share one of my favorite examples. One summer, we visited my college buddy Gina Marks Paget and her husband, Jim, at their summer home near a Florida lake. As our boys knew, because of his lack of patience as well as technique, David was not a competent fisherman, but one day he accepted Jim Paget's invitation to fish in the nearby lake.

To our surprise, he was the first to catch a fish. When he pulled it out of the water, we all fell down laughing. I took a photo of it before I started laughing so hard I could not see through my camera. See figure 242 for the reason. This photo of my color-coordinated husband and his catch became a favorite of David's as well as the entire family's for all time. Google tells me the name of the fish is sheepshead, or *Archosargus probatocephalus*.

During the past thirty years, he struggled through multiple health crises, including eczema over every part of his body. Determined to live and live well, he underwent at least seventeen procedures for blocked coronary arteries, five aneurysms, atrial flutter and atrial fibrillation, anemia due to myelodysplasia, and congestive heart failure, both while we lived in Livingston, New Jersey, and afterward at the Pines of Davidson, our retirement community in Davidson, North Carolina.

Thanks to his own determination, modern medicine, and superb doctors at New York Presbyterian Hospital (formerly Columbia Presbyterian Hospital), Lake Norman Regional Medical Center Hospital, and Charlotte Medical Center, David was the first of seven brothers in his family (he was the fourth son) to reach the age of eighty in 2016.

As his physical strength diminished over the years, David's favorite pastime activity changed from playing tennis and golf to playing duplicate bridge both socially at the Pines and seriously at a local ACBL-sanctioned bridge center in nearby Cornelius when we moved to Davidson. Most people at the Pines considered him among the best players, if not the best, and he was an enthusiastic tutor to beginners. He was the only partner I ever had in accredited bridge play, and we were a good team. Once, in Cornelius, we managed, with luck, to generate a rare 80 percent game.

At the Pines, we won four of five annual marathon bridge tournaments and came in second once when we played with each other as partners against fourteen other pairs. With a dear friend, Cary Johnston, as another partner, he was again a winner once and second once. In sum, of seven marathon tournaments he played at the Pines, David won five and came in second twice.

Through multiple physical problems, he never asked, "Why me?" With his usual focus, he did what he could to make the best of his situation. In 2016, I had to drive him at least three times to the emergency room of the Lake Norman Regional Medical Center. Each time, he would stay for a few days in the hospital. When our daughter-in-law Susan proposed early in 2016 that we organize a family reunion in late July, we all agreed it would be a good idea. We fully expected David to recover once more from his ailments by the middle of the year and knew he would enjoy seeing friends and family whom we missed after our move down south.

As the months passed, however, he did not improve. We had to write to those who had said they would join us in our reunion to say that David would not be able to join us in activities, although he was excited and anxious to see everyone. We told the ones who were coming that we would understand if they wished to change their plans to come to Davidson. Everyone answered that he or she would come anyway. David was happy to know of their loyalty to him.

By mid-July, he was a patient in the Pines' health-care center because due to his congestive heart failure, fluid had built up in his lungs. That had happened several times before, and it once again made his breathing difficult. I became concerned because David was also losing a lot of weight. I cooked Chinese dishes I knew he liked, brought them to him, and fed him by hand. He had lost his appetite, but with coaxing from our sons, he would eat, though he ate small amounts compared to his normal robust appetite. But each mouthful encouraged us that he would once more overcome and recover. We were in denial.

In order to give him some diversion, we arranged permission to bring Pierce, our corgi, whom David loved and spoiled, to a door to the outside that was near his room in the health-care unit. Pets were not allowed in the health-care building, but the administrators said that if David wanted to spend a few minutes with Pierce, they would unlock the door and let the two reunite for a few precious moments. They did, and Pierce was beyond excited to see Daddy again after many days. Later, as we passed that door on our daily walks, Pierce would sometimes look at the door, and I knew he was thinking of David.

However, as with the previous times, when his breathing became more labored, David was transferred to the Lake Norman Regional Hospital for a level of oxygen that he could not get in the health-care center, which also could not give him IV treatments of strong diuretic medicines, as the hospital could, to clear his lungs of excess water. My tough husband never lost his mental clarity. Our sons and I continued to expect David to recover from the episode of decline.

The doctors at the hospital, however, could see the signs of impending terminal illness. One, a cardiologist David had met several times in the emergency room at the hospital and whom David respected and liked, tried to prepare us by telling us of the expected continued decline of David's weakened heart. It was a long talk. In retrospect, I now realize he was preparing us for the end. When he finished and left the room, I looked at David and asked, "What do you think?"

David looked at me and said calmly with no sign of fear, "It is what it is." I looked away and could not speak, as I was trying hard not to cry.

After two days of hospitalization, the doctor said to us, out of earshot for David, that it was time to consider sending David to a hospice house. The doctors recommended the Levine Dickson Hospice House in Huntersville, a place I had heard of from several friends whose spouses had been moved there. It was a beautiful place, they said, with large rooms, and we could even bring pets into the room.

My sons and I were counseled by staff members from the hospice, who tried to convince us that hospice did not necessarily mean inevitable death, something we hungered to hear. They said hospice's function was to provide patients with more comfortable conditions than hospitals could provide. They could give David the high level of oxygen he needed, which, as I said, the Pines' health-care facility could not provide. We agreed to have David transferred to the Levine Dickson Hospice House and asked the hospital to make the arrangements for the transfer.

The day of the transfer, he seemed to perk up, though I thought I heard a doctor say to another, "A matter of hours," at the hospital. However, I assumed he was speaking about another patient. Our granddaughter Leanna had flown from Boston, where she was enrolled in a graduate program for art therapy. She and David chatted easily when she arrived at the hospice house. He even ate food that day, something he had not been able to enjoy for some time. After an arduous day, he said he was tired and wanted to go to sleep. Since it was his first day at a new place, I decided to sleep in his room that night in case he needed help. We gave each other a kiss good night and said, "I love you," before turning in. I'm glad we did because he never woke me up that night, and he never woke up from that night.

A nurse woke me up early in the morning when she ran into the room with an oxygen mask for David because his breathing had become so labored. I hurried to his bedside and saw that he was no longer breathing normally but was gasping and unresponsive. I had seen the same struggle when Mommy was dying. In a panic, I called my sons and Ben's wife, Susan, and told them they had better come to the hospice as soon as possible. They arrived quickly and realized with me that this was probably the end. Although he had been ill so much in thirty years, we were stunned that we were actually losing him. Is it possible to not be in denial?

We took turns holding his hands and whispered to him without getting any reaction. We all told him that we were there and that we loved him dearly. The boys and I also, more than once that morning, told him we didn't want him to leave us but said that if the struggle was too much, he should let go if he needed to. At one point, I lifted his right eyelid to see if there would be any change in the shape of his pupil, and to my surprise, a tear that was in the eye rolled down his face; however, his eye was unseeing, and the pupil did not change shape.

I wiped the tear with my shaking hand. I thought about our lives together and recognized how unbelievably lucky we had been. That is not to say we had no moments of conflict. We argued, sometimes loudly, though not a lot. We always were able to forgive and forget. We gave each other a good life. David always said he did not believe couples who claimed they never argued. Fifty-seven years sounds like a long time, but it passed so quickly.

Shortly before ten, my unbelievably resilient David made a different gasping sound. Mike asked with concern, "Was that him?" I nodded and realized he was suddenly quiet, no longer gasping.

The nurse placed her stethoscope on his chest, listened for a few moments, lifted her eyes to me, and solemnly shook her head. She said, "Time of death 9:56." I felt as if a dagger had been thrust into my heart.

From Manchurian Princess to the American Dream

I couldn't breathe. I felt my sons put their arms around me, and they sobbed along with me. Their father, my husband of fifty-seven years, was gone. Through our enormous depth of sorrow and our tears, we told each other that after thirty years of pain and anxiety, he was finally at peace and pain free. But I could not feel relief—just unbelievable anguish.

In the next few days, with my children's help, I organized a visitation at the Pines after the cremation to give our myriad friends an opportunity to say goodbye. We placed photographs around the living room that represented important events in his life and in our lives, including the color-coded fish. We set a formal photograph portrait of David next to the urn bearing his ashes. The urn had a silhouette of a golfer swinging a golf club. David would have liked the urn. Mike's wife, Katherine, flew in from Oregon with our two youngest grandchildren, Aidan (nine) and Nathan (seven). We greeted each other with hugs and tears.

Longtime residents of the Pines told us they had never seen so many people attend a visitation. Some 250 people signed the attendance book. Considering there are only four hundred residents at the Pines, including those immovable in assisted living, health care, and the Purcell wing for dementia and Alzheimer's patients, and many residents were away to escape the heat and humidity of North Carolina's summer, the number of people who attended was astonishing. Some were friends from outside our community. A week later, in New Jersey, at the Montclair Golf Club in West Orange, where we were members and near where we'd lived for forty-two years, the visitation there also was fully attended. My modest, without-ego husband would have been floored at the expressions of love by so many.

In the days afterward, Mike continued to stay with me to keep me company. We would occasionally cry together. Mike flew to New Jersey while I rode with Ben and Susan and David's ashes to New Jersey, where we would stay a few days for the visitation at the golf club. We decided to drive because taking ashes onto a plane required more complications, such as having to open the urn for inspection. Mike and his family stayed with his brother-in-law in Long Island, and Ben, Susan, and I stayed with Ed and Rosalie Chambers, dear tennis and golf friends of decades ago. Ed is also a retiree from Foster Wheeler.

David's nephew Eric Pai made arrangements with Montclair Golf Club in West Orange, where David and I were members for more than a decade and where Eric too was a member, to have another visitation for all our family—including Eric's mother, Kathy; a sister-in-law of David's; and a widow of David's third brother—and many friends up north. The room was a good size, and it was an excellent venue to reconnect with people we had left behind when we moved to North Carolina. The club had set up rows of chairs for those delivering eulogies. Following are the eulogies from our granddaughter Leanna and our two sons, Ben and Mike. Two of our best friends spoke a few words, and two of David's colleagues from Foster Wheeler also expressed their feelings. I include them here.

Leanna said the following:

> It helps me to give a disclaimer before I start so I am not so frustrated with the inadequacy of mere words. There is no way I could explain to you my relationship

with my Yeh Yeh or what he meant to me. There is no way to reduce a life so full of love, encouragement, and celebration to words on a page. But of course, we're human, and we try. If I have learned anything in the past few weeks, it is that there is very much a time and place for grief in this life. I see how it honors the ways we impact one another. To put it simply, if a man dies and there is no one there to grieve, we know that something must have gone wrong in his life. So how appropriate it is that so many of us are gathered here to celebrate the many things that have gone right for Yeh Yeh.

For those who don't know, I'm Leanna, David's oldest grandchild and the only girl. I have always enjoyed that role, the first and the only. It has always made me feel a little more puffed up than it probably should. It's really more luck than anything that I showed up and found myself part of the most loving and supportive family that I've ever witnessed. God was looking out for me when he gave me you all. And when he gave me my Yeh Yeh. I have never known a man who was so accomplished who also loved and was loved by his family so well. I knew Yeh Yeh was accomplished, but he never told me himself. I'm almost frustrated with him about it. I knew he had a PhD and was an engineer, but I didn't even know what kind of engineering he did (which I now know was mechanical engineering).

When I found out he was CEO of Foster Wheeler Development Corporation, which he also did not tell me, I asked him about it, and he told me that back then, they made everybody a CEO. "All I had to do was show up," he said. And that's all he ever said about that. Did you know he has four patents? I didn't. I found out last week. This was a man who couldn't work the VCR. I mean, you think you know a person. I would say a good half of the details of his accomplishments listed in his obituary I didn't know about. And although it was frustrating that I suddenly have all this extra stuff to brag about how my Yeh Yeh is the best that I could have been using this whole time, I'm really thankful. Because it allowed me to see him for who he really was. He never let his accomplishments get in the way of us having a relationship.

Growing up, even though we lived four states away, I knew my Yeh Yeh. I knew he played golf as if he could never get enough, and he and Nai Nai always had corgis, only corgis. Well, there was one pug. He was adopted. I knew Yeh Yeh kept up with the Yankees and the Knicks, even if it was just to complain about them, and he was a huge Blue Devils fan only to be trumped by my father. I knew he played bridge, although when I was younger, I wasn't totally sure how you can play with a bridge (I thought maybe under it), and I knew every night he ate oranges.

As I got older, the things I knew about my Yeh Yeh became a little deeper. He and Nai Nai (Anna) moved to Davidson, and I'm so thankful I've come to know them as an adult—well, as an older me at least. I've still got my training wheels on. I began deciding what career path to take, and I knew my Yeh Yeh would support me no matter what. I have always felt that I could do whatever I wanted to do, and I could be whoever I wanted to be. Now that I'm older, I realize that confidence is no small feat, especially for a girl these days. And Yeh Yeh really proved that support when I decided to be a starving artist, of all things.

I'm sure becoming an artist and now going for a master's degree in art therapy left Yeh Yeh with a few questions. The field is so new sometimes I don't think I even know what art therapy is. But he never said that I couldn't do it. He was always proud of me. He and Nai Nai are a large part of the reasons I decided to pursue my master's. They encouraged me to continue my education and to go after my master's with their total support. Having such unconditional love and support from my family in this endeavor is not something that many people in my field can say they have. My strongest memories of Yeh Yeh and the things he said the most often to me were "Good job, *bao* (treasure or sweet)," "Congratulations!" and "Atta girl!" And the way he would always say, "Hey!" as if seeing me was the best surprise he got all day, even if he was expecting me. Every little victory was worth a celebration.

It's almost hard. Because his love was so constant and so fierce but so incredibly humble that you could almost miss the enormous depth of it all. In the end, I am empty because, of course, there is a new space in my life. But I am also so full. Full of Yeh Yeh's love for me, full of the gifts he left behind, like my education, all of the lessons he's taught me, all of the support that he's given me. These things give me the confidence to be who I am today. When I think of my Yeh Yeh, I really can't be anything but thankful. Thankful for the life he's given me, for the ways he allowed me to truly know him, for the ways he was so generous with his time and his love. I am proud that I know I speak for many when I say these things. The longer I think about him and his life, I discover more ways that he loved me and provided for me. And I really couldn't ask for anything more.

I am thankful to have been spoiled rotten in the best way by such a wonderful Yeh Yeh for a full twenty-three years.

Ben said the following:

> The human heart is an amazing organ. A typical heart beats about a hundred thousand times a day; thirty-five million times a year; and, over a lifetime, more than two billion times. The heart gets no days off, no vacation time, no holidays. You can't take it down for system maintenance then put it back up. As long as its owner is alive, it never stops.
>
> Because it's such a remarkable thing, the word *heart* is also associated with qualities that we admire in people: compassion, courage, toughness, competitiveness, determination, will, perseverance.
>
> So when I think about Dad, the first word that comes to mind is, of course, *heart*. Because he embodied all of the qualities I just mentioned. And also because of his history of heart ailments. It is a bitter irony that a man who showed so much heart all of his life was undone by a congenitally weak heart. Yet at the same time, that heart of a lion also allowed him to become the first of his brothers to reach the age of eighty. He never should have lived that long.
>
> Most of you are well aware of Dad's health history. Thirty years ago, Dad survived quintuple-bypass heart surgery that saved his life. That set off three decades of declining health and one surgical procedure after another. We lost count after sixteen surgeries and countless hospitalizations, not only for his heart but for his circulatory system (he had five aneurysms) and bad back. The phrase "Dad's in the hospital again" became a way of life over the past three decades.
>
> He bounced back from every procedure and hospitalization with incredible determination. It was amazing. I thought he would live forever. He kept fighting; he was by far the toughest guy I have ever known.
>
> You almost have to think of Dad's life in two parts: the first fifty years and the last thirty. His story starts in 1936 in Guilin, China. He was born the son of General Pai Chung Xi, whom he idolized, the chief of staff in the Revolutionary Army that overthrew the last dynasty. My grandfather was later named minister of national defense for Chiang Kai Shek. David was the seventh of ten children, and he had six brothers and three sisters.
>
> The military was a strong influence in his life and shaped much of his personality. He immigrated to the United States in 1952 and graduated from La Salle Military Academy in New York. He attended Virginia Military Academy in Virginia, where he met a gorgeous spitfire from nearby Sweet Briar College named Anna Chao. Dad graduated VMI in 1958, and he and Mom were married the following year.

In 1960, Dad earned his master's degree from Lehigh University and also began working at Foster Wheeler, a large engineering company, where he would spend his entire forty-one-year career. In 1965, the year I was born, Dad received his doctorate in civil engineering from New York University. One of my favorite pictures is one of Dad in his graduation cap and gown, cradling a football-sized me in his arms (see figure 117).

Dad was a mechanical engineer by trade and built an impressive record at Foster Wheeler. He authored or coauthored more than fifty papers, edited two books, and holds four patents. He became active in the American Society of Mechanical Engineers, eventually becoming a fellow and vice president of that organization. He was eventually named president and CEO of Foster Wheeler Development Corp., the R&D arm of the company.

In 1994, Dad was elected to the National Academy of Engineering. The NAE works hand in hand with the National Academy of Sciences to advise the government on matters pertaining to energy and the environment. You cannot apply for membership; you are elected by your peers. It is basically the Hall of Fame for engineers. I flew down to Washington, DC, with Mom and Dad for the induction ceremony, which took place over a weekend. It was a big deal—to everyone except Dad.

See, he never talked about his honors or titles. Those patents—you want to know what they are for? So do I. I have no idea. Dad never mentioned any patents. Dad never bragged about anything he did.

He was more interested in talking about other things. His interests were varied. He loved modern Chinese history and current events. He was a self-educated and successful investor. He was a big sports fan, both he and my mom. He avidly followed the New York football Giants and the New York Knicks, which planted the seeds for my lifelong love of those teams. When I went to college at Duke University, he became a diehard Blue Devil basketball fan. He also taught me how to properly yell at the TV when our teams didn't perform up to our standards.

He was a good golfer, with a hole in one to his credit, and also a good tennis player. Both of these were activities he could do with my mom. They would golf with other couples, and they played a mean mixed doubles tennis game. It enriched their marriage because they were able to play together. They had a spectacular marriage, fifty-seven years. Mom was every bit Dad's equal in terms of education and accomplishments. They made each other better. They became role models for me and my brother on how to combine work, play, and family.

Some other things you should know about my dad:

Despite his brilliance as an engineer, he was comically bad at using technology. He did not know how to program the family VCR. He typed with one finger, his index finger. Many of you no doubt remember receiving his emails ... written entirely in caps. He could not be bothered using the Shift key only at the beginning of sentences or for proper nouns. He was one of the last converts from flip phone to smartphone. We used to schedule sessions to show Dad how to use his new iPhone. I consider it a massive victory that he actually returned about five of my texts.

He picked up every restaurant check. He insisted on it. Dad was an amazing bridge player. The highest rank one can attain in the bridge world is life master. There are a few of them living at the Pines. I have been told by multiple people that both Dad and Mom could have been life masters. They just never bothered to go through the certification process. It was fun for Dad to just play and to teach the game to others. The Pines holds an annual bridge marathon tournament. My dad lived there for seven years. Five times, he won the tournament (four of them with Mom and one with a friend, Cary Johnston). The other two years, he finished runner-up, one with Mom and one with Cary Johnston.

I can't list all of the life lessons I learned from Dad, but I can share a few:

1. *Be present. Show up every day. Be involved.* Dad kept his commitments. He was married to Mom for fifty-seven years. He worked his entire forty-one-year career at the same company. He could have gone elsewhere, probably made more money, but he stayed and tried to make things better. He worked a lot of hours but made sure he was home for dinner every night. It was important to Mom and Dad that we all be together as a family every night, so that's what we did. If Mike or I had a game, Dad was there. I could always hear him, even in the middle of a basketball game. He was always shouting encouragement. He never yelled at umpires or referees, never yelled at coaches or players or other parents. Just positive things to me and my teammates.

2. *Do the right thing.* Pops was not perfect; nobody is. I hope this comes out the way I mean it, but he never did anything wrong. I don't mean he never made mistakes, but he always did the right thing. He was always honest and forthright. He never acted out of anger, pride, or fear. He had no ego. To our chagrin and his everlasting delight, Dad never even got a traffic ticket, although he was the most aggressive driver in the family. There's a song by the band Three Doors Down called "If I Could Be Like That." The chorus goes like this:

If I could be like that

I would give anything

Just to live one day in those shoes.

If I could be like that

What would I do?

One day around eighteen to twenty years ago, I was driving down Harris Boulevard in Charlotte. It was in the midst of another one of Dad's health scares, and I was worried even back then that we might lose him. That song came on the radio, and the next thing I knew, tears didn't just well up; they streamed down my face. The chorus just reminded me of Dad. He became my moral center. Whenever I have found myself straying from what I want to be, I remember that song and ask, "What would Dad do here?" That usually gets me back to where I need to be.

3. *Network. Get to know people. Build relationships.* When I first started my professional career after college, Dad was always telling me about the importance of networking. I had graduated in 1987, and it was a popular word back then. I thought I knew what it meant, but it wasn't really until my thirties that I really got it. But I watched Dad enough to finally realize how important it was. I learned to build my own personal networks at work, both within and outside my departments. For the past decade or more at my current employer, I have found roles based purely on personal relationships.

4. *Be there for your family.* Nothing was more important than family; that was drilled into us at an early age. When I was a child growing up, I had a hard time understanding that sometimes families have strife, and sometimes couples break up. My parents were so good together that I was spoiled; I just thought everyone's parents were perfect like mine. Dad became something of a go-to person within our family. I have older cousins who are extremely successful, but they'd occasionally ask my dad for professional, career, or investment advice. Dad also quietly supported family members financially without talking about it. In terms of his parenting style towards me, he gave me a great blueprint for life in short sound bites: work hard—arrive at work before your boss and leave after he does; you can tell a lot about a man by the way he sweeps the floor; always say please and thank you; life is not fair—you will be discriminated against, and you have to deal with it. He generally let

me make my own mistakes and learn for myself. But if he had to prevent disaster, he would step in.

I hope Dad realized the impact he had on people and what a great legacy he leaves behind. When Dad was ill and no longer able to go to the dining room at their retirement community, Mom couldn't walk ten feet in the room without people telling her they were praying for Dad. After Dad passed, Mom was walking her dog one day, and some Pines maintenance men stopped the golf cart they were riding in to give Mom a consoling hug. We went to eat at a Chinese restaurant last week where we frequently have dined. The manager asked where Dad was, and when Mom told her he was gone, she was visibly shaken. Even though we didn't order it, she brought Mom a bowl of the hot-and-sour soup that Dad always loved.

I look around the room and think of his legacy and how he touched all of us.

Mom, I know he drove you crazy sometimes. He couldn't hear well towards the end, and sometimes he didn't listen. But he adored you. You had a model marriage that, whether you know it or not, serves as a blueprint for many of us. You made each other complete. Without you, his success would not have been possible.

Mike, I'm glad you were good at golf. So many of Dad's happiest times were playing golf, a game that I could not play. I'm glad you were able to share so many good times with Dad playing the game you both loved. He also loved getting all those free clubs, balls, and bags.

Susan, Kath, Shrong, and Mei, you were the daughters he never had. He loved you and was proud of you.

Leanna, Keith, Aidan, and Nathan, your grandfather had many honors and titles in his life, but there was none that meant more to him than Yeh Yeh. He loved being your grandfather. He never lit up as much as he did when he was with you. I'm glad he fought so hard to live a long life, so he could get to know you all.

To my relatives, you weren't just cousins, nieces, or nephews. He viewed you as brothers, sisters, or his own kids. He always thought of you all as part of our nuclear family.

Marty and Ellie, you were his Jewish brother and sister. I like to say Chinese and Jewish people are the same, only different.

To the Tiger Group, you all shared the times of your lives together for fifty years. You traveled the world together. You played tennis, rode camels, danced, and dined all over the world together. You shared your joys and also your sorrows together. You created memories that will last forever. You showed us what friendship means.

To the people of The Pines of Davidson, thank you for embracing my parents from day one. It was not an easy decision for my dad to move down to North Carolina. I moved my family down twenty years ago and immediately tried to get my folks to move down with me. Mom was open to it; Dad wasn't. Not at first. He was still finishing out the final five years of his career. He had friends and family up here. He had his Chinese food, his doctors, and he had his beloved Montclair Golf Club. But eventually, in 2009, he agreed to move down. And from day one, the residents treated my parents as if they were their own relatives. Mom and Dad have told me that moving down was one of the best decisions they have made.

So I thought he would live forever. When I was younger, I dismissed the idea that the body dies but the spirit lives on. I wasn't having that. I wanted my loved ones to be with me all the time. But as I have reflected on his life and thought about his legacy, I realize that he will live on, in all of us.

Mike said the following:

I know we are here to honor and celebrate my dad. I will try to do that by sharing some words that come to mind when I think of him and the lessons both parents taught us all through the years.

Decent and Unpretentious

My dad was quite simply the most decent person you could meet. They say the true measure of someone's character is in how they treat those who can do nothing for them. Dad was the living embodiment of that statement. Didn't matter your station in life. Your occupation was irrelevant. In Dave Pai's eyes, you were all the same and should be treated with respect, as he would have you treat him. Though he was a CEO and cleared to fly first class on business trips, he never flew in other than in coach (no doubt much to the dismay, I think, of his people). His real message to us was never ever get too full of yourself—one of Dad's and Mom's favorite sayings was to be nice to the people on your way up in life, because they may be the same ones you might see on your way down.

In his passing, I have come to see just how profoundly he touched everyone he came across. I have been amazed at the tributes that came pouring in, from people we grew up with, who said they always felt welcome in his presence, to people he didn't know well.

Brilliant

My earliest recollections of my dad are those of him being the smartest man in the world and somebody who could seemingly fix anything that broke: a toy, a faucet, an appliance. As an engineer, CEO, and member of the National Academy of Engineers, clearly others thought the same thing as well. I majored in engineering because I wanted to be like him, even though I may not have totally loved the discipline. While I didn't pursue it as a vocation, he was still proud that Ben and I opted to pursue advanced degrees. Though when I went to work marketing pantyhose for my first job out of graduate school, I was half expecting him to ask for a refund for my college tuition. Of course, he was a bit of a contradiction too in that as brilliant an engineer as he was, he was utterly incapable of dealing with simple home electronics. Couldn't program a VCR, struggled surfing the internet with AOL, was a posterchild for bad online passwords, and had a six-month hate-hate relationship with his iPhone. I had to keep reminding him that pressing harder on the touch screen didn't make it work any faster!

Hardworking

Dad and Mom always said you get what you get in life by how hard you work—you are not entitled to anything. Ben and I had it so easy compared to Dad and Mom. My admiration for what they've achieved and the life they provided for Ben and me is endless. They were immigrants who spent their formative years in a racially divided America and faced hostility. But that shaped this attitude that they tried very hard to instill in both of us: an honest day's work for an honest day's wages. He was always frugal: despite the fact that they had a supply of golf balls because of my work, Dad and Mom still owned and made liberal use of a ball retriever. "Leave it as a seed ball," I would say, reminding them that if someone found the ball and played with it, they may become a full-time player of the ball. "Why?" Dad would say. "It's a perfectly good golf ball."

Determined

Dad was one of the most determined people you would ever meet. He fought his genes valiantly for thirty years. Never complaining, always looking for ways to improve his situation. Having grown up playing a ton of golf with him, I learned that his determination always came out on the golf course. We played in the father-son tournament here at Montclair Golf Club, and after three consecutive years, once, when Dad hit a nine-iron shot into the creek on the fourth hole of course three, he told me, "I'm not hitting a nine-iron into the creek again this year. So you hit eight-iron off the tee so I can hit a five-wood!"

Loving

And finally, my dad was an incredibly loving, generous, and kind husband, father, grandfather. He had his quirks and could drive all of us, Mom especially, nuts. But don't we all have quirks? He reveled in seeing Ben and me succeed. Beamed with pride that we both married way above our stations. And was happiest during holiday and family gatherings when all of his beloved grandchildren came to hang out. This was a man who despised baseball and often didn't make it through one inning before dozing off, yet he took us to as many Yankee and Met games as we wanted to go. This was also a man who had no patience for fishing but was always game to throw a line in with us and see how fast he could reel a fish in once hooked—we called it fly-fishing. And this was a father who sat calmly and listened as I tried to play a scale on my clarinet then as Ben did the same on his violin. I think his need for hearing aids was likely a result of these family recitals.

In recent years, he got the greatest pleasure out of his four grandchildren. When I used to take the boys to day care in the mornings, our favorite activity was to call Yeh Yeh and Nai Nai on the way to and from "school" every day. It became our routine. And no matter how often we called or how lousy he felt as his health began to fail him, you could hear the excitement in his voice when the boys yelled, "Hellooo, Yeh Yeh!"

So as heartbroken and sad as I am, these are lessons, stories, and memories that I will take with me forever. And remember this: when you hear a bell, it might mean an angel got his wings, but in my book, it means Dave Pai just made another birdie in heaven.

Yung Wong, a Tiger friend, said the following:

My name is Yung Wong. It is nice to be back here at Montclair Golf Club. Over the years, David and Anna invited us here many times for golf and dinner. My wife, Nancy, and I have been friends with David and Anna for over fifty years. We have watched each other's children grow up and now grandchildren. We have had countless gatherings—hundreds—for tennis, golf, bridge, mah-jongg, and, very important to David, good Chinese food. Along with other friends, we have taken trips together to Egypt, Italy, Mexico, Spain, Portugal, Hawaii, as well as other parts of the United States.

David was among the first of the generations of Chinese students sent by parents to the US after Communists took over mainland China to seek a better life. He was a successful engineer and businessman and became the CEO of a Foster Wheeler subsidiary. He won many awards and recognitions for contributions to his fields of expertise, including election to the National Academy of Engineering. He exemplified the immigrant who achieved the American dream.

What was most important to David was his family: a loving partnership with Anna; his two boys, of whom he was really proud; the two daughters-in-law whom he adored; and, of course, his four grandchildren, who were his pearls.

I can't begin to tell you about all the memorable events and experiences we and the Pais shared. I would just like to relate two events. Really about both David and Anna.

David and Anna moved to Davidson seven years ago to a retirement community called the Pines of Davidson, close to the campus of Davidson College in North Carolina. They were immersed in various activities and programs that the Pines offered, gave talks, exhibited Anna's photography, won bridge tournaments, and became one of the most popular couples. A week ago, the family held a visitation at the Pines to memorialize David. Of four hundred total residents at the Pines, 230 came to express condolences to the family. Many of their Pines friends commented to me that David and Anna were the best thing that happened to the Pines because of their energy and friendliness, their wealth of knowledge, and the contributions they have made to the community.

Three years ago, David and Anna visited with us for a few days in Florida. The second morning, at about eleven o'clock, a call came from Aidan and Nathan, the two boys of Michael, their second son, who live in Oregon. The boys were on their way to school (it was eight o'clock in Oregon) and wished their grandparents a good morning. At around eight o'clock that evening, another call came from Aidan and Nathan to report to their grandparents how their day went. We thought that was very nice. The next morning, another call came in. Guess what happened at eight o'clock that evening. When we asked what's going on, whether there was a problem in Oregon, David and Anna explained matter-of-factly the boys called twice a day. Every day! Every week! This is the bond between David and Anna and their grandchildren and their whole family.

These two incidents reflect who David and Anna are. My wife, Nancy, and I feel blessed that we have been their friends for over five decades.

Dr. Martin Gruber, a close friend, said the following:

I met Dave in 1963. I was a PhD student at Columbia University, and as part of the degree requirements, I had to pass a French exam. Because my undergraduate degree was in engineering, my only exposure to foreign languages was one year of Latin in high school. To alleviate this deficiency, I enrolled in a three-week program to prepare

PhD students in order to pass a test involving translating French to English. The first night of the class, the teacher (who I thought was very old but was probably twenty years younger than I am now) asked each student to read a paragraph in French. When she called on me, I tried to explain that I had no idea how to pronounce French, but she insisted I had to read it anyway. When I did, she was angry and claimed I had purposely murdered the French language! She finally moved on to the next student. Soon she came to Dave, and he said, "If you think that other guy was bad, you should hear me."

Well, for the next three weeks of class, Dave and I huddled together in the back of the room, living in mortal fear of this gray-haired ogre. In fact, the only other time I saw this same expression of fear in David's face was at my son Jon's bar mitzvah. Dave was sitting next to me, and when he saw me get up to read a passage in Hebrew, he must have flashed back to our days in French class. I can still hear him say, "Good job, Gruber," when I sat down.

Something good came out of the bad three weeks: a friendship began to grow between me; my wife, Ellie; and Dave and Anna, a friendship that has lasted over time. In those three weeks, we discovered that all four of us played tennis and bridge. We later discovered that we shared the same values with respect to our families and to life.

Our two oldest children, Jon and Stacey, are almost the same ages as Ben and Mike. We spent a lot of time together as couples and with our children. We had so many laughs together and shared sad times also, as good friends do. While we were never able to beat them in tennis and only occasionally at bridge, our relationship flourished. I cannot think of another two people we respect and love as much as Dave and Anna. Dave's intellect and moral values and humility set an example to our family. I know Dave's spirit will live on in his children, grandchildren, friends, and relatives. We will miss him.

We also received kind words from Ernest Daman, David's former boss and mentor at Foster Wheeler. In response to my email announcement of David's passing, Ernie sent the following:

What can I say? You really said it so well. When I talked to Dave in April, he sounded ready to tackle his next medical challenge with the same courage you described so well. Dave was one of the smartest colleagues I ever had; his contributions to engineering were significant! With sincere condolence, Ernie

One thing that touched everyone at the visitation in New Jersey was the eulogy given by Ken, the former CEO of Foster Wheeler, who became a good friend as he sponsored our membership in the Montclair Golf

Club in the late 1980s. He struggled valiantly to speak to the crowd of friends and relatives at the visitation, as he was suffering from terminal cancer. He spoke of his respect for David, who, he said, contributed greatly to Foster Wheeler. It was poignant to see Ken, who, in good health, was active and strong into his ninth decade. He was known to walk the golf course with a caddie and with friends of the same age, all well into their eighties. His wife, Helen, to whom Ken had been married for more than sixty years, was one of the most fun people to be with. Ken passed away only a few days after we saw him at the visitation. David would have been deeply touched and honored that Ken insisted on being there and speaking despite the pain and fatigue he must have experienced. Thank you, Ken and Helen, for everything!

Ben and Susan had me stay with them in their Charlotte home for a couple of days after we came home. Mike and his family left New Jersey after the visitation and flew home to Oregon. The emptiness of our cottage that I now live in alone seemed suffocating when I first slept in it without David. My sweet artist granddaughter made me a beautiful small arrangement with white silk roses. I have it on my kitchen table, where I eat breakfast and lunch. I've placed it across the table, right where David sat, so I will not be looking at an empty chair.

My brain has not functioned properly since the trauma of his death. Friends who have also lost their life partners have told me that time will bring back the functioning. It has been two whole months since that morning at the hospice house, and I am still befuddled. In paying bills, I got one of my envelopes back for insufficient address. I looked at the envelope, and instead of writing, "Newark, NJ," next to *Newark*, I'd written, "Just outside." I have no idea what caused me to be distracted to the point where I wrote, "Just outside," instead of "NJ"! It has never happened before. Even more, when I looked inside the sealed and stamped envelope, the bill was there but no check to pay the bill.

I cannot express adequately my pride and joy in my family. Mike has visited, and he, Ben, and Susan have kept me going in innumerable ways. My children have gently led and assisted me through days of working with lawyers and the people at TIAA, who handle my finances now. I believe I could not have survived the first two months without their support. Katherine has done her part by caring for the younger grandchildren in Oregon when Mike is here helping me.

Leanna is now in graduate school, studying for a master's degree in art therapy, and Keith is a sophomore at Belmont University and becoming known for his guitar talent as a music major. How he became a performing musician is a short story about karma. When he was a freshman in high school and his sister was a freshman at Meredith College in Raleigh, the family decided to go visit Leanna one weekend. It happened that a state fair was open in Raleigh, close to the college.

Keith went to one of the booths, where he threw balls at bottles. He succeeded in knocking over enough to win a prize. The booth was nearly out of prizes since it was close to the end of the fair. There was a stuffed animal and a used guitar. Keith chose the guitar. He cleaned it and had it repaired and decided to take some lessons on it. In two years, he was so good he was performing. Now he is going to be a professional musician. He applied to Belmont University's noted music program in Nashville, Tennessee, where candidates for admission must audition. Keith did well at his audition and was accepted. One wonders what he would have done if he hadn't gone to that booth or thrown the balls so well! I'm glad David lived to know of the discovery of Keith's talents.

I cannot believe how terrific my family members have proven themselves to be. They and my extended family, the Tigers, and my friends at the Pines and elsewhere have made the onset of my transition to a new life much easier and less painful. I cannot thank them all enough.

Pierce misses David also. My sweet corgi has a new habit now when there is thunder. He goes to David's room and stays there until the storm leaves. He never did that when David was home. Pierce has been a wonderful companion. He warns me at the slightest sound of anyone approaching the cottage, and his hearing is amazing. He sleeps by my bed at night. He greets me with uncontainable love and joy every morning when the alarm rings and when I return home after leaving the cottage. I have a small sign in my kitchen that says, "Dogs are the only true love that money can buy." There is no question this is so!

I cannot yet express fully the enormous loss I feel. It seems that every atom of my life is different. Tears are not far away ever. I continue to feel David is still with me. Often, I feel the need to tell him something immediately that I've heard or read that I know he would enjoy, and I am taken aback for the umpteenth time as I realize I cannot. I need to be able to ask him questions about Chinese history, which he loved so much, and have him read some Chinese writing that I cannot read. I hear his laughter and see his loving face. He really did live his whole life, and I know I must continue to live mine, as he would want me to. It is difficult to believe and accept that I must live the rest of my life without him. My existence has a huge, dark, empty hole.

He wanted so much to see this book published, and I could not fulfill his wish—in part because, ironically, his illnesses required so much of my time. But he made this book possible because he made my life possible. Thank you, love, for so much (figure 243).

Fig 241 David Hsien Chung Pai

Fig 242 Color coordinated catch

Fig 243 Yesterday, when we were young

CPSIA information can be obtained
at www.ICGtesting.com
Printed in the USA
BVHW022355200619
551603BV00003B/5/P